# THE RACIAL HISTORY OF MAN

# THE
# RACIAL HISTORY OF MAN

BY

## ROLAND B. DIXON
PROFESSOR OF ANTHROPOLOGY AT HARVARD UNIVERSITY

ILLUSTRATED

CHARLES SCRIBNER'S SONS
NEW YORK · LONDON
1923

# PREFACE

THIS book is in large measure an experiment. In the first place, it is an experiment in method, a method devised and tried out several years ago upon the data relating to the peoples of the Oceanic area, in an attempt to bring some sort of order out of the anthropological chaos which seemed there to prevail. The results were to me so encouraging that I was led to apply the method to the data for all the rest of the world, with what success the following pages will show. The book is also something of an experiment in that I have attempted to approach the whole racial problem *de novo;* have concerned myself primarily, therefore, only with the actual data, the raw facts of physical measurements, and have intentionally paid little or no heed to the conclusions of previous students. Not that I do not regard these with great respect, but that I wished to be wholly unprejudiced, to have no thesis to prove, to take nothing for granted, to be able to apply to the whole body of data on man's physical characteristics one single method of analysis, and to follow the evidence fearlessly to whatever conclusions it might logically lead. The book is thus wholly uncontroversial, and is primarily an exposition of the results of the application to the existing body of data, of a somewhat novel method of analysis of racial types.

I have attempted to utilize all the published data, yet in so wide a field and so extensive a literature it is inevitable that some material has been overlooked. Some titles, also, I have been unable to find in libraries in this country, and attempts to secure them, particularly the Slavic ones, have in most cases unfortunately proved fruitless. The bibliography given in the

Appendix is a selected one, and represents but a fraction of the materials consulted. It is, moreover, almost wholly a list of sources for actual data, primarily those giving individual measurements of crania or living persons, and contains few, if any, titles of a theoretical, descriptive, or controversial character. Even with this restriction the limits of available space required the elimination of many of the less important titles. For Europe, in many cases, only papers published subsequently to the bibliography appended to Ripley's "Races of Europe," or not found therein, have been given.

For unpublished data of great value, which have with fine generosity been placed at my disposal, I am indebted first of all to Doctor Franz Boas, of Columbia University, without whose great store of materials, placed freely in my hands, the chapter on North America could hardly have been written; and also to Doctor Ales Hrdlicka, of the United States National Museum; to Doctor Clark Wissler, of the American Museum of Natural History, New York; to Professor A. L. Kroeber, of the Department of Anthropology of the University of California; to my colleague, Professor E. A. Hooton, of Harvard University; to Doctor Edward Sapir, of the Victoria Memorial Museum, Ottawa; to Sir Francis H. S. Knowles, of Oxford, England; to Miss M. Wilman, of the Alexander Macgregor Memorial Museum, Kimberley, South Africa; to Mr. Chi Li, of the Graduate School of Harvard University; and to Doctor Nenozo Utsurikawa, of Keio University, Tokio, who has also very kindly collected and sent to me much material published in Japan.

I also wish to make special acknowledgment to the following publishers and authors for permission to reproduce illustrations: The Bureau of Census, Department of Commerce, Washington, for Fig. 2, Plate XXXV. The U. S. Geological Survey for Figs. 1 and 2, Plate XXXVI; and Fig. 3, Plate XXXVII. The Bureau of American Ethnology for Fig. 4, Plate XXXV. The American Museum of Natural History for Fig. 3, Plate XXXV, from the *Bulletin of the American Museum of Natural History;* and Fig. 3, Plate XXXVI, and Fig. 3, Plate XXI, from *Memoirs of the Jesup North Pacific Expedition.* The American Anthropological Association for Fig. 2, Plate XLIII. The University of Pennsylvania Anthropological Publications for Fig. 3, Plate XLIV. Dodd, Mead & Company and H. H. Johnston, for Fig. 4, Plate XIII, from *Liberia,* and Fig. 4, Plate XII, from *Uganda Protectorate.* D. Appleton & Company and W. Z. Ripley for Fig. 2, Plate III, and Fig. 4, Plate II, from *Races of Europe.* D. Appleton & Company and H. N. Hutchinson for Fig. 1, Plate XVIII, Fig. 2, Plate XVIII, Fig. 2, Plate XX, from *Living Races of Mankind.* John Murray, London, and A. F. R. Wollaston for Fig. 1, Plate XXVII, from *Pygmies and Papuans.* Frederick Starr for Fig. 1, Plate XIII, and Fig. 2, Plate XIII, from *Congo Natives.* Hutchinson & Company, London, and Sir Harry Johnston for Fig. 1, Plate XII, and Fig. 4, Plate XVIII. The *Journal of the Royal Anthropological Institute of Great Britain and Ireland* and Professor Felix von Luschan for Fig. 1, Plate XXI, and Fig. 2, Plate XXI. The *Journal of the Royal Anthropological Institute* and Doctor C. S. Myers for Fig. 3, Plate XIII. Doctor Randall-Maciver for Fig. 3, Plate XI, from *Libyan Notes.* E. Chantre, for Fig. 1, Plate XI, and Fig. 2, Plate XI, from *Recherches Anthropologiques en Egypte.* The *Skrifter Videnskabsselskabet Christiania* for Fig. 3, Plate II. The Government Press, Madras, and E. Thurston for Fig. 3, Plate XVIII. And to the following authors for permission to reproduce various illustrations: Doctor Clark Wissler, of the American Museum of Natural History; Mr. C. C. Willoughby, of the Peabody Museum, Harvard University; Doctor H. E. Gregory, of the Bernice Pauahi Bishop Museum, Honolulu; and Doctor Gudmund Hatt; and to acknowledge my indebtedness also in this respect to the works of Hyades, Aranzadi, Cardoso, Ehrenreich, Hagen, Koch-Grüneberg, Lehmann-Nitsche, Martin, and Neuhaus, to the *Revista del Museo de La Plata,* the *Archiv für Anthropologie,* and the *Zhurnal* and *Izviestia* of the Society of Friends of Natural History, Anthropology, and Ethnology at Moscow. And last, but not least, to thank most cordially Messrs. Charles Scribner's Sons for the great pains which they have taken to secure the best possible reproduction of all these illustrations.

ROLAND B. DIXON.

HARVARD UNIVERSITY,
September, 1922.

# CONTENTS

ix

# CONTENTS

# ILLUSTRATIONS AND MAPS

# THE RACIAL HISTORY OF MAN

# THE RACIAL HISTORY OF MAN

## INTRODUCTION

THE term "race" is one which has unfortunately acquired a somewhat varied meaning in our every-day speech. We refer to the Negro or the Mongolian "race" and in so doing have in mind primarily certain general physical characteristics of color, hair, and features, while linguistic, cultural, historical, and political factors play but a comparatively subordinate part in our conception. We also speak, however, of the Latin, the Anglo-Saxon, or the Celtic "race," but here, although physical characteristics are in some measure concerned, it is more on language and culture, and in considerable degree on historical and political unity that our mental picture rests. From the standpoint of the anthropologist this latter use of the word "race" is inadmissible, for to him a race is a biological group, based on community of physical characters. For groups characterized on the one hand by linguistic, or on the other hand by cultural, historical, or political unity, he employs the terms "stock" and "nation."

A race, then, is a group defined and characterized by certain physical characteristics, and the problem before us is to determine how many such groups are to be recognized in mankind; how they are distributed and by what routes they have spread over the surface of the earth; how they have interacted upon each other; and what and where and when was their probable origin.

At the very outset we must recognize that the problem is one of great complexity. Whatever be our conclusions as to the number and character of the fundamental races, we can hardly expect to find these widely spread in their original form to-day. Man has existed, as we know, for tens of thousands of years,

3

and during this time by migration and conquest the original racial factors, whatever they were, have been so interwoven and blended that the vast majority of all living men must have a complex racial ancestry, and such a thing as a pure race can hardly be expected to exist. However distinct, therefore, races may once have been, the peoples of the world to-day are complex mixtures of these original types, in which we must seek to discover, if we can, the constituent elements.

Since our conception of race is based on purely physical grounds, we may first inquire what are the criteria upon which such a characterization must rest. The criteria of race may be divided into two groups: (1) external or superficial, and (2) internal, structural, or skeletal. The former includes such factors as pigmentation (skin, eye, and hair color), the character of the hair (straight, curly, frizzly, woolly), the character of the nose (aquiline, depressed, etc.) and eye, etc., and are obtained primarily as the result of observation. The latter involves the form and size of different parts of the bony skeleton, and is derived in the main from direct measurement. Criteria of the first class are simple and obvious, and were thus the first to be used in differentiating and classifying peoples. They are open, however, to serious objections. In the first place, they can be used only in connection with living men, and are useless for the study of the skeletal remains of ancient peoples. In the second place, although it is easy enough to distinguish a black skin from a white one, or a light eye from a dark one, or straight hair from woolly, or an aquiline from a snub nose, in practice it has been found extremely difficult to determine with real accuracy the great number of intermediate shades or forms. Thus, while these purely observational or external criteria are of great value in distinguishing between different groups of men, their use is surrounded by many practical difficulties, and is restricted by serious limitations.

Criteria depending on measurements either of the skeleton or the living subject are obvious enough in some instances, as, for example, in the case of stature. But the large majority are not obvious and have been devised intentionally in the search for some series of measurements or ratios between measurements, which should prove to be valid in distinguishing one group of people or one race from another. Out of the very large number of measurements and ratios which have been tried and advocated at one time or another, a relatively small number have come to be accepted as undoubtedly of real significance in the determination and classification of races. Apart from stature, these are mainly confined to the skull or head. The most widely used, and commonly regarded as most important single criterion of this sort, is the cranial or cephalic index, which expresses the ratio of the breadth to the length of the skull or head. Other indices regarded as of undoubted value are the altitudinal or length-height index, and the breadth-height index of the skull, which express the ratios of height to length and height to breadth respectively. The facial, nasal, orbital, and palatal indices are also of proved importance, and show the ratios between the breadth and length of the face, the nose, the eye-sockets, and the palate. To these may be added the capacity or volume of the brain-cavity, and a number of others.

Now criteria of this sort, based on measurements, have the advantage that some at least of them may be made on the skeleton and the living subject as well, so that modern peoples may be compared with those of the past. Being purely metrical in character, they are less subject to the uncertainties which beset observational criteria, although differences in technic on the part of different investigators may lead to slight variations in the results.

The earlier as well as many of the later attempts at a classification of mankind into races were based primarily upon external or observational criteria, the color of the skin and the character of the hair being the two factors most generally employed. Such a classification, for instance, is the familiar one into five races—the black, the brown, the red, the yellow, and the white. It was early found, however, that no single criterion was adequate, for the conditions were too complex. Some combination of criteria was therefore necessary in order to devise a valid scheme. In these, structural or metrical criteria were often used, but generally only to form subdivisions of primary races based upon pigmentation or hair form.

The different investigators who have concerned themselves with the question have reached widely varying results. Some, seeking to simplify the problem, have divided mankind into a small number of races marked by few and broad similarities, and have ignored the great variations in other details which prevail within their groups. Others have been more impressed by this variety, have felt the differences to be of real significance, and have thus been led to construct schemes involving twenty or thirty or even more distinct races and sub-races. In spite, however, of all the labor and ingenuity expended upon the question, anthropologists are not yet in complete accord on many fundamental points. Thus, some regard all the aboriginal peoples of America as forming but a single race, and consider the wide variety which undoubtedly exists as due to variation around a normal type. Others believe the New World peoples to belong to two or more distinct racial groups. For some the population of Europe is made up of the representatives of three races only—the Nordic, the Alpine, and the Mediterranean; for others a larger number of racial types are present.

Moreover, apart from these wide divergencies in their results, there is, I believe, an unsatisfactory feature in all these schemes, in that great reliance is placed upon the use of averages and the data are therefore not treated on the basis of the actual combination in the individual of the several criteria upon which the classification is based. For instance, a series of skulls is measured and the average or mean or mode of the cranial index, the facial, nasal, orbital, and palatal indices, etc., calculated, and the people represented by the crania are then said to present the characters of these averages—they are, we will say, mesocephalic (medium-skulled), euryprosopic (wide or low-faced), mesorrhine (medium-nosed), etc., etc. Now it may well be that if the actual combinations of head, face, nose, orbit, and palate forms in the individual skulls are examined, hardly a single skull will show the association of characters stated on the basis of averages to be typical of the group. A large proportion of the whole series may consist of individuals who are brachycephalic (round-headed), euryprosopic (wide-faced), platyrrhine (broad-nosed), etc., etc., while an almost equally large number may be dolichocephalic (long-headed), mesoprosopic (medium-faced), leptorrhine (narrow-nosed), etc., etc., with minorities showing other combinations of the several characters. All such contrasts are blurred or concealed when the measurements are averaged, and so the series of crania may in reality be in no sense uniform, but made up of several clear-cut and radically different groups, each marked by its own specific combination of characters. Only, I believe, by thus taking into account the actual combinations of characters in the individual, can we reach a correct understanding of the true nature and relationships of any people.

It is extremely probable that the real criteria of race are rather complex, and that various external features of pigmentation, hair-form, etc., together with many structural and metrical factors, are involved. But we are still in this matter groping more or less in the dark, since we do not yet know with certainty whether there is any real correlation between the various criteria employed. We are not certain, for example, how far the form of the skull is necessarily associated with the form of the nose, or the stature or the skin color. It seems logical to assume that a broad or round skull and a broad face should go together, and that the breadth of one should vary concomitantly with that of the other. Yet in view of the fact that disharmonic forms are far from uncommon, in which a broad head is associated with a narrow face, or a narrow head with a broad face, it is possible that after all there is no necessary correlation between these two criteria, and that they, as well as all the others, may vary quite independently. In other words, we cannot point to any group of criteria and say that these are inherently connected and form a true racial standard.

The present status of the whole question of race is, therefore, somewhat confused and uncertain. For not only is there wide divergence of opinion between different investigators in regard to the number, distribution, and origin of races, owing to the varying criteria which each adopts, but a certain hesitancy to face the larger problems boldly and without prejudice is apparent. The horizon has often been limited to a particular geographic field, and the student has been loath to view the local problem as a part of a much larger whole. The use of a multitude of criteria has in many ways complicated the question, and we are in danger of failing to see the forest for the trees.

There is need thus, I believe, of some radical simplification of criteria and of some method of approach which promises more definite results. Our whole attitude toward the problem ought, moreover, to include a frank acceptance of demonstrable relationships wherever they may be found, and a greater willingness to follow the evidence to whatever conclusions it may lead. Finally, the historical aspect of the question must be given greater weight, for no matter what the ultimate decision may be as to the number and characteristics of the different races, we can hardly suppose these to have all originated at once. Some races must be older, some more recent, and the spread of mankind over the world must have been by waves of varying racial composition, the later overlying the earlier, in part amalgamating with them and in part, as is the case in the rest of the animal world, driving their remnants into marginal or refuge areas.

In this belief, therefore, the present attempt at a new analysis of the peoples of the world into their constituent racial elements has been made. Since, as we have pointed out, we have as yet no absolute standards of race, against which we may measure peoples to determine their true racial character and affiliations, we can only set up arbitrary standards, and, using these as our measure, determine the character and relationships of people *in terms of our arbitrarily selected units*. We have no *a priori* right, to be sure, to call these units "races," but we may by this method divide mankind into a series of groups or types which possess the great advantage of definiteness, and by direct comparison between these we may discover relationships which otherwise would remain obscure. And if, in the selection of criteria for our standards, we employ only those which on the basis of existing knowledge give promise of being really significant of race, we may hope that the results may give us at least an approximation to the truth.

What criteria shall we select? They must, in order to be applicable to both living individuals and skeletal material, be internal or structural. There are, however, but very few measurements ordinarily made on the latter that can be exactly duplicated on the former, so that in the main we are limited to criteria based on analogous and comparable measurements. Further restrictions are imposed by practicable availability, since certain measurements now recognized as of much value are not given by investigators of a generation or two ago, upon whose data we must in many cases depend. After much trial and experiment, three criteria have been selected as being, all things considered, the best—the cranial or cephalic index, the altitudinal or length-height index, and the nasal index. The use of more than three factors seemed unwise, as the number of possible combinations of the type to be noted presently would be so large as to be unwieldy when applied to the ordinarily available series of measurements, which rarely include as many as a hundred crania or individuals.

The three indices selected vary in their applicability. The first can be satisfactorily used both for crania and living persons. The nasal indices on the living and on the skull, although not exactly correlated, are nevertheless analogous and probably comparable, at least in their extremes, i. e., a broad or narrow nose on the living is probably equivalent to a broad or narrow nose on the skull, although a medium form cannot be thus correlated. The cranial length-height index cannot be directly compared with that taken on the living, since the height is measured on the skull from a point at its base which is not accessible in the living, for whom the height is the so-called auricular height, measured from the ear orifice. As in the case of the nasal index, however, it is probable that at least in their extremes the indices on the living and on the skull are comparable.[1]

The indices, as already stated, express ratios, and are given in the form of percentages, so that a cephalic or cranial index, let us say of 74, means that the breadth of this particular head or skull is 74 per cent of its length; a nasal index of 47 means that the width of the nose is 47 per cent of its length, etc., etc. For convenience each of these indices is customarily subdivided into three divisions. In the case of the cranial index all skulls with indices lying below 75 are classed as Dolichocephalic or long-headed; those whose indices lie between 75 and 80 are called Mesocephalic or medium-headed; while those for which the index is 80 or over are classed as Brachycephalic or round-headed. For the altitudinal index we have three similar sub-divisions: Chamæcephalic, or low-skulled, when the index is below 70; Orthocephalic when it falls between 70 and 75; and Hypsicephalic, or high-skulled, if the index is above the latter figure. For the nose the three groups are: Leptorrhine, or narrow-nosed, for indices below 47, Mesorrhine for those between 47 and 51, and Platyrrhine, or broad-nosed, including all above the latter figure.[2]

Now the cranial, altitudinal, and nasal indices of any skull must lie in one or the other of the three subdivisions into which each index is divided; thus it may be Brachycephalic, Ortho-cephalic, and Platyrrhine, or Dolichocephalic, Hypsicephalic, and Leptorrhine, or Mesocephalic, Chamæcephalic, and Mesorrhine, etc., etc. The total number of different combinations of these factors is 3 × 3 × 3, or 27, and into some one or other of these twenty-seven groups every skull or head must fall.

On this basis, then, we may analyze any series of living or cranial measurements, and discover its composition so far as

[1] The auricular height can of course be measured on the skull, and a more certainly comparable index thus obtained. Unfortunately this measurement is not given in many of the older publications.

[2] For the indices derived from measurements on the living somewhat different divisions are made in all these cases.

these groups or units are concerned. Thus, in a given series of crania there may be a certain number which are all Brachycephalic, Hypsicephalic, and Leptorrhine; others which are Mesocephalic, Orthocephalic, and Platyrrhine; others again which are Dolichocephalic, Chamæcephalic, and Mesorrhine, etc., etc. One series may show great uniformity, in that the large majority will fall into one or two of the twenty-seven possible groups; another series, on the other hand, may show a striking diversity of composition, in that ten or fifteen or more of the groups may be represented. Concrete examples will make this plain. A series of crania from Northwest Greenland proves on analysis to be made up as follows:

| | | |
|---|---|---|
| Dolichocephalic, Orthocephalic, Leptorrhine........ | 23 = | 60.5% |
| Dolichocephalic, Hypsicephalic, Leptorrhine........ | 7 = | 18.6% |
| Dolichocephalic, Chamæcephalic, Leptorrhine...... | 3 = | 7.9% |
| Dolichocephalic, Orthocephalic, Mesorrhine........ | 2 = | 5.2% |
| Mesocephalic, Orthocephalic, Leptorrhine.......... | 2 = | 5.2% |
| Dolichocephalic, Hypsicephalic, Mesorrhine........ | 1 = | 2.6% |
| | 38 | 100.0% |

Here over 60 per cent of all the crania fall into one group, with nearly 20 per cent in another, so that these two groups together account for practically 80 per cent of the total. The series is thus strikingly uniform.

Contrast with this a series of 100 from Northern Italy:

| | |
|---|---|
| Brachycephalic, Orthocephalic, Leptorrhine................. | 25 |
| Brachycephalic, Orthocephalic, Mesorrhine................. | 11 |
| Brachycephalic, Hypsicephalic, Leptorrhine................. | 10 |
| Brachycephalic, Orthocephalic, Platyrrhine................. | 7 |
| Brachycephalic, Hypsicephalic, Mesorrhine................. | 6 |
| Brachycephalic, Hypsicephalic, Platyrrhine................. | 5 |
| Mesocephalic, Orthocephalic, Mesorrhine................. | 5 |
| Brachycephalic, Chamæcephalic, Leptorrhine.............. | 4 |
| Mesocephalic, Orthocephalic, Leptorrhine................. | 4 |
| Mesocephalic, Orthocephalic, Platyrrhine................. | 4 |
| Dolichocephalic, Orthocephalic, Leptorrhine.............. | 4 |
| Mesocephalic, Hypsicephalic, Mesorrhine................. | 3 |
| Mesocephalic, Chamæcephalic, Leptorrhine................. | 3 |
| Mesocephalic, Hypsicephalic, Leptorrhine................. | 3 |

Mesocephalic, Chamæcephalic, Platyrrhine.................. 2
Brachycephalic, Chamæcephalic, Mesorrhine............... 1
Brachycephalic, Chamæcephalic, Platyrrhine............... 1
Dolichocephalic, Chamæcephalic, Platyrrhine............... 1
Dolichocephalic, Chamæcephalic, Leptorrhine.............. 1
                                                        ———
                                                        100

In this case more than three times as many groups are found, the majority of which comprise less than 10 per cent of the total number of crania. Such a series is obviously extremely mixed. An analysis of this sort thus enables us to determine not only the actual composition of the series in terms of our units, but also to form an opinion as to the uniformity or variability of it.

Comparison on this basis, furthermore, quite obviously enables us to determine the degree of similarity between two series. Thus the two just given have almost nothing in common, since the groups which make up the bulk of the Eskimo series form only 8 per cent of the Italian. If, however, we compare with the Eskimo series one from the Alikaluf, living about the western end of the Straits of Magellan, we find a different result. The Alikaluf series is as follows:[1]

Dolichocephalic, Hypsicephalic, Leptorrhine............ 42.8%
Mesocephalic, Hypsicephalic, Leptorrhine............... 35.7%
Dolichocephalic, Hypsicephalic, Mesorrhine............ 7.1%
Dolichocephalic, Orthocephalic, Mesorrhine............ 7.1%
Mesocephalic, Orthocephalic, Mesorrhine.............. 7.1%

In this case a strong relationship between the two is apparent in that almost 60 per cent of the Alikaluf series is made up of crania having the same combinations of indices selected as criteria, as are found in the case of the Eskimo.

In dealing with measurements on the living the procedure is the same, only as the measurement of the auricular height is often omitted by the observer because of its difficulty and uncertainty, we are frequently reduced to the two criteria of the

---

[1] The percentages given in this and the following tables are only approximate, being carried only to the first decimal place.

cephalic and nasal indices only, giving us nine instead of twenty-seven groups. It follows that in comparing living series we cannot be as certain of real similarities, since, although two series may each be marked by a large proportion of individuals belonging, let us say, to the Brachycephalic-Leptorrhine group, we cannot be sure but what those in one series may have predominantly high skulls, while those in the other may be low, and the two Brachycephalic-Leptorrhine groups thus not be really comparable. Conclusions based, therefore, upon measurements of the living only, must be regarded as tentative in comparison with those based on crania, but as sufficing, nevertheless, in the absence of cranial material to indicate the broader outlines of the problem.

Reference should be made at this point to two difficulties which inevitably beset almost any comprehensive investigation of the physical characteristics of different peoples: the insufficiency of the existing data and the fact that even those which we possess are not in all cases strictly comparable. The lack of data is of two sorts, absolute and relative. For many of the peoples of the world, and for most peoples in their early history, we have no accurate or satisfactory measurements whatever. Of others our knowledge is extremely meagre, in that the total number of crania or individuals measured may amount perhaps only to a half a dozen. So small a number of cases is quite inadequate to serve as a reliable sample on any scheme of classification. The minimum number which can be regarded as satisfactory is fifty, and conclusions based on less than a hundred must always be accepted with reserve. Yet it is but rarely that such extensive series are available, and we are forced to depend upon what is to be had. As we go back to the earlier periods of human history, this inadequacy of our data is very pronounced, so that when we come to the Palæolithic period the number of reasonably complete crania available is extremely small. Precious beyond words as these remains of very early man are, we must not forget that conclusions drawn from such very meagre data are necessarily only tentative.

The second difficulty which tends to make the results of comparisons, on this or any other method, to some extent uncertain, is due to the differences in technic on the part of different observers. Slightly different methods of making almost every measurement have been employed in different countries and at different times, with the result that measurements made, let us say, by a French anthropologist fifty years ago are not exactly comparable with those made by a British or German investigator of to-day. In recent years a practical uniformity of method has been attained, although something yet remains to be done in this direction, and modern data are therefore, as a rule, exactly comparable. Since, however, we are obliged, in the case of many peoples, to rely on data gathered and published a generation or two ago, such materials can be compared with more recent data only with care, and conclusions held subject to reservation.

A third difficulty, of much less importance however, may also be referred to, *i. e.*, the uncertainty of the identification of crania according to sex. Male and female crania from the same people usually present considerable differences in absolute measurements, those of the female being generally the smaller. There are also often notable differences in proportions, the cranial index, for example, being commonly higher in the female than in the male, although not always so. While identification of the sex of a skull is in most cases easy, there are always some which are more or less doubtful, and in the case of some peoples the identification is very difficult. A slight uncertainty thus may be involved, owing to the inclusion of what are in reality female crania with a male series. In the present study, unless otherwise expressly stated, conclusions are based on crania classed as male.

It will be well before we go farther to sum up at this point the general argument. It has been shown that the usual criteria for the determination of racial types are, so far as they relate to *external* factors, unsatisfactory, in that they are inapplicable to skeletal data; and that for any comprehensive study of racial problems which must involve historical considerations we must rely upon *skeletal*, primarily cranial characteristics. From the relatively small number of such criteria generally recognized as probably of racial significance, which are also analogous for crania and for living persons, and which are furthermore generally available, three were selected. These three indices being divided, according to general usage, into three subdivisions each, we obtain a total of twenty-seven possible combinations of these, which then may be used as a basis for the analysis of any people. This analysis enables us to determine the composition of the people, *in terms of our twenty-seven factors*, and their uniformity or diversity and relationship to other peoples, *on this same basis*.

But what are these factors or groups, characterized each by a different combination of the subdivisions of our three criteria, and whose relative proportions among different peoples we are enabled to determine? Have we any right on *a priori* grounds to regard these arbitrary combinations as "races"? Certainly not! Although since current conceptions and classifications of races make large use of these three criteria and their subdivisions, we might anticipate that *some* of the groups might coincide with recognized racial types. Investigation along these lines at once reveals the fact that one particular kind of group does thus approximately correspond to certain generally accepted races. Thus the Negro race is usually characterized as being Dolichocephalic, Hypsi- or Orthocephalic, and Platyrrhine; the Australoid is Dolichocephalic, Chamæ- or Orthocephalic, and Platyrrhine; the Alpine is, on the average, Brachycephalic, Hypsicephalic, and Leptorrhine; the purer examples of the Mediterranean are Dolichocephalic, Chamæ- or Orthocephalic, and Leptorrhine. Stated in general terms this would seem to imply that many of the generally accepted races, as now understood, tend to be characterized by such combinations of our three selected indices as exhibit these in their extreme forms, *i. e.*, they are groups which do not comprise any of the medial factors (Mesocephalic, Orthocephalic, Mesorrhine). This suggests the possibility that groups without medial factors may be regarded as definite types, now rarely found in their pure state, and that all the groups comprising one or more medial factors are the result of the blending and fusion of these. In how far there is any justification for thinking that these types actually constitute "races," we may leave for discussion in our final chapter; we are here concerned with them only as somewhat arbitrarily selected factors, which, in some cases at least, seem to have a distinct racial significance.

If we are willing to accept as a working hypothesis that the eight groups of this sort are fundamental types, from which all the others have been derived by blending, we have placed in our hands a key which will unlock many a door and open far-reaching vistas into the problems of the classification and distribution of peoples. For we may thus resolve our primary analyses already described, into their ultimate and fundamental factors, greatly simplifying comparisons and enabling us to bring out hitherto unsuspected relationships and to outline a coherent theory of the origin and spread of the many varieties of mankind.

But, before any such theory can be accepted even as a tentative working hypothesis, one immediately obvious difficulty must be confronted. In assuming that intermediate forms have arisen from the blending of two extreme forms, the whole complex question of heredity is at once raised. If the relative proportions of the skull and nose are subject to the laws of Mendelian inheritance, then the origin of medial forms cannot well be accounted for on the basis of mixture, since according to these laws the offspring of contrasted forms reproduce the parental types. For certain external criteria, such as pigmentation and hair-form, strong cases have been made out for the operation of Mendelian laws in man; but for most of the other criteria and specifically for head-form little conclusive evidence proving such inheritance has yet been presented. The very recent extensive investigations of Frets[1] are largely invalidated by his indiscriminate inclusion of children with adults in his calculations. If, however, we extract from his tables those cases in which the two

[1] Frets, 1921.

parents are of sharply contrasted types (Dolichocephalic and Brachycephalic) and consider only the adult children, the evidence is distinctly in favor of the development of mesocephalic or medial forms. So far, then, as our present knowledge goes, we are probably justified in regarding head-form, and, by analogy, nose-form, as not directly subject to Mendelian inheritance, and in regarding the origin of medial forms as due to blending.

Accepting, then, as valid the method proposed for the ultimate analysis of any people for whom adequate data are available, it will be necessary to make clear a few details in regard to its practical application. To facilitate reference to the eight fundamental "types" and the nineteen "blends" which together make up the twenty-seven possible groups into which the three indices selected may be divided, they may be represented by abbreviated formulæ, letting

| | | |
|---|---|---|
| D = Dolichocephalic. | H = Hypsicephalic. | L = Leptorrhine. |
| M = Mesocephalic. | O = Orthocephalic. | M = Mesorrhine. |
| B = Brachycephalic. | C = Chamæcephalic. | P = Platyrrhine. |

Then D–H–L = Dolichocephalic, Hypsicephalic, Leptorrhine; M–C–P = Mesocephalic, Chamæcephalic, Platyrrhine; B–O–M = Brachycephalic, Orthocephalic, Mesorrhine; etc., etc. The eight primary or fundamental types will then be:

$$\text{D–H–L, D–C–L, D–H–P, D–C–P}$$
$$\text{B–H–L, B–C–L, B–H–P, B–C–P}$$

The nineteen forms derived by the blending of any two of these will then fall into three classes:

| | | | |
|---|---|---|---|
| *A.* | B–H–M | M–H–L | D–H–M |
| | B–O–L | M–H–P | D–O–L |
| | B–O–P | M–C–L | D–O–P |
| | B–C–M | M–C–P | D–C–M |
| *B.* | B–O–M | M–O–P | |
| | M–H–M | M–C–M | |
| | M–O–L | D–O–M | |
| *C.* | M–O–M | | |

The "blends" in the first class can each arise only from a single pair of fundamental types; thus, B–H–M can only be derived from the fusion of B–H–L and B–H–P; M–H–P can be formed only by the mixture of D–H–P and B–H–P; D–O–L from D–H–L and D–C–L, there being but one medial factor involved. The blends of the second class, on the other hand, with two medial factors, may be derived from either of two pairs of fundamental types, thus B–O–M = B–H–L + B–C–P, or B–C–L + B–H–P. The single blend constituting the third class, having all three factors medial, may be derived from any one of four possible pairs, since M–O–M = B–H–P + D–C–L or B–C–P + D–H–L or B–H–L + D–C–P or B–C–L + D–H–P. Blends of the second and third classes may, of course, also arise through the fusion of other blends, thus B–O–M = B–O–P + B–O–L, but these in their turn resolve into the same fundamental factors as given above, so that for the sake of simplicity we may usually resolve the blends directly into their ultimate "types."

Where now the preliminary analysis of a series of crania yields only fundamental types and blends of the first class, the ultimate analysis is simple, and there can be but one result. If, on the other hand, the preliminary analysis shows many blends in the second or third classes, the final analysis presents uncertainties, since the result will depend on which pairs of fundamental types are regarded as responsible for the blends. If some fundamental types are present in strength they serve as indicators; in their absence the final result must be regarded as more or less uncertain. In resolving the blends into their respective types, the purely arbitrary assumption has had to be made that the two constituents shared equally in the result, and that thus half the percentage represented by the blend should be assigned to each "type." Doubtless this is far from always being the case, so that for this and other reasons the actual figures obtained for the several types are not to be regarded as in any sense mathematically exact; they are merely rough indications of relative values only.

A concrete example will aid in making the application of the method and the character of the results clear. Turning to the Eskimo series given on page 11 we have:

$$
\begin{aligned}
\text{D--O--L} &= 60.5\% = \text{D--H--L} + \text{D--C--L} \\
\text{D--H--L} &= 18.6\% = \text{D--H--L} \\
\text{D--C--L} &= 7.9\% = \text{D--C--L} \\
\text{D--O--M} &= 5.2\% = \text{D--H--L} + \text{D--C--P} \ (\text{or D--C--L} + \text{D--H--P}) \\
\text{M--O--L} &= 5.2\% = \text{D--H--L} + \text{B--C--L} \ (\text{or D--C--L} + \text{B--H--L}) \\
\text{D--H--M} &= 2.6\% = \text{D--H--L} + \text{D--H--P}
\end{aligned}
$$

Here the fourth and fifth groups are each capable of two interpretations; in view, however, of the fact that the D–H–L type is so much more strongly represented than the D–C–L it is probable that it is the former rather than the latter type which is concerned, and that we may reject the resolution given in parentheses. On this basis, then, the fundamental types are present approximately in the following proportions:

$$
\begin{aligned}
\text{D--H--L} &= 55.3\% \\
\text{D--C--L} &= 38.1\% \\
\text{D--C--P} &= 2.6\% \\
\text{B--C--L} &= 2.6\% \\
\text{D--H--P} &= 1.3\%
\end{aligned}
$$

This may be interpreted as meaning that the Eskimo of northwestern Greenland are in the main the result of the fusion of two fundamental types, the D–H–L and the D–C–L, in which the former evidently plays the leading part, and that the influence of any of the other types is practically negligible.

Treating the Alikaluf series in the same fashion, we have:

$$
\begin{aligned}
\text{D--H--L} &= 42.8\% = \text{D--H--L} \\
\text{M--H--L} &= 35.7\% = \text{D--H--L} + \text{B--H--L} \\
\text{D--H--M} &= 7.1\% = \text{D--H--L} + \text{D--H--P} \\
\text{D--O--M} &= 7.1\% = \text{D--H--L} + \text{D--C--P} \ (\text{or D--C--L} + \text{D--H--P}) \\
\text{M--O--M} &= 7.1\% = \text{D--H--L} + \text{B--C--P} \ (\text{or D--C--L} + \text{B--H--P, or B--H--L} \\
&\qquad\qquad\qquad + \text{D--C--P, etc.})
\end{aligned}
$$

The last two factors are here capable of more than one analysis, but, on the same basis as in the previous case, the preponderant strength of the D–H–L type makes the decision between the alternatives clear. The final result is thus roughly:

$$D-H-L = 71.2\%$$
$$B-H-L = 17.8\%$$
$$D-H-P = 3.5\%$$
$$D-C-P = 3.5\%$$
$$B-C-P = 3.5\%$$

The Alikaluf thus are to a much greater extent than the Eskimo derived from a single fundamental type, and this is the same which is in the majority among the Eskimo. Here, however, we find a considerable B–H–L factor which was absent among the latter.

It cannot be too emphatically stated that at this stage of our inquiry there is no implication that these "types" so isolated are "races." In the final chapter the question of their possible racial significance will be discussed; for the present, however, the use of these types in the attempt to analyze and compare the various peoples of the world is merely the employment of a standard of reference, of a common measure which can be universally applied to determine their character and relations on the basis of this arbitrary standard.

Here, however, a doubt may arise as to whether these standards possess any real uniformity. The whole scheme of the eight "types" and nineteen "blends" arises from the division of the three indices into three subdivisions, upper, medial, and lower; but since these subdivisions are purely arbitrary, what reason have we for regarding the groups based upon them as real? We form a group, for example, of those crania which fall into the classes respectively called Dolichocephalic, Hypsicephalic, and Platyrrhine, but is there any reason for believing that these crania are actually long, for example, and that their indices do not in the majority of cases lie so close to the arbitrary dividing line between Dolichocephalic and Mesocephalic that the crania are more truly to be thought of as members of a group which is actually between these divisions and having no necessary relation to either? And, further, have we any justification for thinking that crania of the D–H–P type found among one people are really similar to those belonging to the same type among another?

The answer to both these questions may, I believe, be given in the affirmative.  If we take a number of crania belonging to any one of the eight fundamental types and calculate the average cranial, altitudinal, and nasal indices, it appears that this is in practically every case clearly typical of its class.  Thus, in the case of a group of the D–H–P type from West Africa we find the cranial index to be 73, unequivocally Dolichocephalic; the altitudinal index 77, clearly Hypsicephalic; the nasal index 55, pronouncedly Platyrrhine.  The D–H–P type here is thus a clear-cut one, possessed of definitely long, high skulls and broad noses. The same results are obtained in the case of other types.  For the "blends" the definiteness is not so clearly marked.

When, now, the indices for such a type among one people are compared with those for the same type among another people, it is found that they are usually very nearly alike, and, further, that the averages of the absolute measurements, for example, of length, breadth, and height of the skull on which measurements the indices are based, are also closely similar.  When it is considered that (1) the data have been gathered by different observers, in some cases using slightly different methods, (2) that the number of crania available in such groups is usually small, and (3) that incorrect sex identification may disturb the results, the closeness of agreement in absolute measurements is quite surprising.  The closeness of these correspondences is shown in the examples[1] on page 22.

For convenience of reference and to avoid the continual use of unfamiliar and forbidding formulæ, names have been given to the eight fundamental types as follows:

| | | | |
|---|---|---|---|
| D–H–L | Caspian | B–H–L | Alpine |
| D–C–L | Mediterranean | B–C–L | Ural |
| D–H–P | Proto-Negroid | B–H–P | Palæ-Alpine |
| D–C–P | Proto-Australoid | B–C–P | Mongoloid |

[1] Absolute measurements in millimetres.

| Locality or Tribe | Length | Breadth | Height | C. Ind. | Al. Ind. | Nas. Ind. |
|---|---|---|---|---|---|---|
| Caspian—D–H–L | | | | | | |
| Russian Kurgans (7) | 186.1 | 134.3 | 142.0 | 72.0 | 76.2 | 43.8 |
| N. W. Greenland Eskimo (15) | 188.2 | 134.4 | 140.1 | 71.4 | 76.6 | 43.0 |
| Mediterranean—D–C–L | | | | | | |
| Ancient Egypt (16) | 188.0 | 134.0 | 128.0 | 71.3 | 68.1 | 43.9 |
| London seventeenth century (16) | 191.6 | 138.9 | 128.8 | 72.5 | 67.2 | 44.0 |
| California (5) | 189.4 | 134.4 | 128.0 | 70.8 | 67.5 | 44.0 |
| Proto-Negroid—D–H–P | | | | | | |
| W. Africa, Gaboon (9) | 181.7 | 133.2 | 140.0 | 73.3 | 77.0 | 55.3 |
| Ancient Egypt (28) | 180.7 | 130.1 | 137.0 | 71.9 | 75.9 | 54.8 |
| Iroquois (4) | 185.7 | 134.2 | 140.7 | 72.0 | 75.6 | 57.0 |
| Proto-Australoid—D–C–P | | | | | | |
| Australia (Victoria) (28) | 183.0 | 129.6 | 124.1 | 68.2 | 64.2 | 56.0 |
| Ancient Egypt (38) | 186.4 | 133.7 | 128.8 | 71.4 | 68.8 | 54.4 |
| California (6) | 190.0 | 136.1 | 128.8 | 71.6 | 67.7 | 53.3 |
| Alpine—B–H–L | | | | | | |
| Switzerland (Valais) (28) | 176.5 | 150.6 | 136.0 | 85.1 | 77.5 | 43.2 |
| Hawaii (9) | 176.4 | 147.6 | 141.0 | 83.7 | 79.9 | 44.7 |
| China (8) | 173.3 | 144.2 | 137.3 | 83.3 | 78.6 | 44.8 |
| Ural—B–C–L | | | | | | |
| Switzerland (Valais) (9) | 184.7 | 154.0 | 124.8 | 83.1 | 67.4 | 43.7 |
| Kalmuck (3) | 185.6 | 153.3 | 126.6 | 82.6 | 68.2 | 42.8 |
| Palæ-Alpine—B–H–P | | | | | | |
| Negrito (Philippines) (22) | 172.0 | 145.0 | 138.0 | 84.0 | 80.0 | 55.0 |
| Switzerland (Valais) (20) | 175.6 | 145.0 | 141.0 | 82.0 | 80.0 | 56.0 |
| Mongoloid—B–C–P | | | | | | |
| Kalmuck (9) | 180.1 | 149.0 | 122.0 | 82.7 | 67.6 | 52.6 |
| Switzerland (Valais) (8) | 183.5 | 152.5 | 125.7 | 83.2 | 68.5 | 53.0 |

It is of the utmost importance, however, to bear in mind that these terms are used with a very definite and very restricted meaning. They designate in each case a particular combination of the three selected criteria and *nothing more*. Thus the Proto-Negroid type designates a form of skull which is Dolichocephalic, Hypsicephalic, and Platyrrhine, and carries with it no necessary implication whatever that any other features which we may be accustomed to think of as occurring in Negro crania are also present; and the statement that among a given people the Proto-

Negroid type is strongly represented does not imply that they have or had a black skin or woolly hair. How far any other characteristics may be associated with the eight fundamental types will, with other questions, be discussed in the concluding chapter. I wish, however, to call attention here at the outset to the possibility that such other characters as may be associated with a "type" in one part of the world may be greatly weakened or even partially absent and replaced by others in another region in which the type has been subject to totally different environmental conditions and been in contact with other types for very long periods of time. The older the type, the further it has wandered, the greater the vicissitudes of its history, the more variable in these respects we may expect it to be.

The method and point of view adopted in the present study have now been outlined, and we may therefore proceed to the task before us. For each continent a general résumé will first be given, in which the broad outlines of its history in terms of our chosen types will be sketched, followed by a more detailed consideration of the various natural or political subdivisions. The conclusions to which we are led will in many cases be novel; in some they will at first sight appear revolutionary or even absurd. Yet if judgment be but suspended until all the evidence is in and available for general synthesis and discussion in the concluding chapter, I believe that their reasonableness will be admitted, and the picture which they give us of the distribution, history, and proximate origin of the different varieties of mankind, will be accepted as a logical answer to the problem with which we started, and one which, in view of the incompleteness of the record, may be a fair approximation to the truth.

*BOOK I*

EUROPE

# INTRODUCTION

THE continent of Europe may be divided geographically into three very unequal parts. The first and by far the largest is that of the great plain which occupies the east and north, comprising all of Russia, Poland, and the Baltic lands, and which sends a long arm westward through northern Germany, the Netherlands, Belgium, and northern France to the British Isles. Forested in the north, grassland and steppe in the south, it is but an extension of the great lowland of northern Asia, with which it is essentially continuous, the low chain of the Urals forming in no sense a barrier. Along its Atlantic margin in Norway and the northwestern part of the British Isles it is limited by a strip of rugged and mountainous country, with rocky and deeply indented shores. South of this great unbroken plain, and extending from the Ægean and the western end of the Black Sea through the Balkan peninsula, Austria-Hungary, and Switzerland to France, lies a relatively narrow belt of highlands and mountain ranges. Broken in its eastern and wider portion by the plain of Hungary and the valley of the Danube, it is narrowed and its elevation intensified in Switzerland, is cut across by the Rhone valley, and beyond the Massif Central of France dies away in the rocky peninsula of Brittany. Just as the plain is but a continuation of the great lowland of northern Asia, so the European Highlands are but the dwindling western termination of the vast belt of plateau and mountain which sweeps across Asia from northeastern Siberia, through Mongolia, Tibet, and the Iranian Plateau to the uplands of Asia Minor. Lastly, as mere appendages to the European continent we have the third subdivision, comprising the Iberian and Italian peninsulas, with the islands of Corsica, Sardinia, and Sicily; appendages which may be regarded primarily as bridges, now broken but once continuous, connecting the European continent with Africa.

These three areas—the plains, the highlands, and the land

bridges—have in large measure shaped and determined the racial history of Europe. And just as Europe is, after all, but a great peninsula of Asia, so its racial history has to a great extent been largely dependent on that of the greater continent. With Africa its ethnic and its geographic connections have been, on the whole, less important.

Almost all the remains of what are historically the most ancient types of mankind have been discovered in Europe. We have reason to believe that equally ancient, perhaps even more ancient remains will be found in other parts of the Old World, when these have been searched with the same care and minuteness that have been exercised in Europe during the last half century. For the present, however, the bulk of our knowledge of early man is derived from the European continent, and it is therefore fitting that any study of the characteristics, distribution, and sequence of races should begin here.

In the early Palæolithic period, which we may place perhaps some fifty thousand years ago, we find in Spain, in France, in Belgium, in southeastern England and in the Rhine valley one single variety of man, generally called the Neanderthal Race. It is characterized, among other features, by a long, low skull and a broad nose, a combination of factors which marks these very early men as examples of our Proto-Australoid type. Yet even at this earliest period there are indications that the population was not wholly uniform, for everywhere except in Germany there is a suggestion of mixture with a brachycephalic type, that to which we have given the name of Mongoloid. That either of these types originated in Europe we have no evidence, and if we are to seek a source for them we are led, in the case at least of the dominant Proto-Australoid type, across the land bridges to Africa. For the Mongoloid factor the evidence is so meagre that nothing certain can be said.

The later part of the Palæolithic period saw a radical change in the population at least of western and central Europe, whence most of our data come. In France, in southern Germany, and in Bohemia the forerunners of the Mediterranean type appear, coming perhaps from the eastward or from the Mediterranean shores of Africa. A second new dolichocephalic type also appears, the Caspian, which has so far been found in Palæolithic times mainly in France. From its distribution in Neolithic times, when it was of great importance, it seems clear that it must have entered Europe from the east, by way of the plains. A third type, known as yet from a single locality only (the Grimaldi caves on the Riviera) is the Proto-Negroid.

During the ensuing or Neolithic period we can trace with greater certainty several wide-spread racial movements. The Mediterranean type, which had begun to penetrate the west at the end of Palæolithic times, had now made itself master of the Iberian peninsula, all of France (except the basin of the Seine), Ireland, and western Scotland, and was fighting with the Palæ-Alpine type for the control of England. In the south it held Italy, Sicily, and Sardinia. In western Switzerland and the Seine basin it was contending with the vigorous Palæ-Alpine type for leadership, and for a time fought apparently a losing battle. Yet its advance-guards found their way across the Rhine into Germany, as far as the Baltic and into Bohemia, where the type is found at this time as a minor factor.

This great thrust of the Mediterranean type from the southward into the heart of Europe shattered and largely destroyed the people of the older Proto-Australoid and Mongoloid types; yet not completely, for fragments still survived. In Spain and France the invading Mediterraneans made a pretty clean sweep, yet even here enough of the ancient population remained to leave its traces in the remote mountain valleys of Portugal and in Brittany to-day. In western Switzerland, England, and Belgium the Proto-Australoid type appears in small proportions in the Neolithic crania, its chief areas of survival lying in two widely separated regions, Sardinia (and probably also Corsica) and the shores of the Baltic and North Seas. The advance of the Mediterraneans northward seems thus to have driven a considerable mass of the older Proto-Australoid and Mongoloid types before them.

While thus the Mediterranean type was spreading northward through western Europe, a new type, the Palæ-Alpine,
made its appearance from the east, entering the continent in part
by way of the Balkan peninsula, but in the main, probably,
around the northern side of the Black Sea, and spreading along
the northern edge of the European Highlands. It is found as
the dominant factor among the Neolithic lake-dwelling population of Switzerland, and is of equal importance with the Mediterranean type in the crania of Chamblandes, near Lake Geneva. From here it may be traced as a strong element in the
Neolithic population of the Jura and basin of the Seine, the uplands of the Ardennes and across into England, where it disputes
for precedence with the Mediterranean type in the Long Barrow
graves. It would appear to have passed northward to Denmark, where it was the strongest single element in Neolithic
times, and to be represented as a minor factor in southern Sweden and also in Silesia. Toward the very end of the Neolithic
period it is dominant on the east coast of Scotland.

It will be remembered that in France the appearance of the
Caspian type was already noted at the end of the Palæolithic
period. In Neolithic times this type becomes of great importance in Europe and seems to have penetrated westward through
the Russian plains to the Baltic, and up the valley of the Danube to central Europe. It appears in Neolithic times as the
dominant racial type in Hungary and Bohemia, whence it probably passed along the northern margin of the Highlands westward into France and down the Rhine to Belgium and Britain.
It is also the leading factor in Neolithic times in Sweden and
appears as a minor element in Denmark. How it reached the
Baltic lands is an interesting question. From Bohemia it might
have passed down the valley of the Elbe, and so by way of the
Danish peninsula to Sweden, coming early in the Neolithic
period prior to the arrival of the Palæ-Alpine type, and perhaps
forced out of Denmark by it. On the other hand, it may have
reached Sweden by way of the eastern Baltic, since the crania
from this region in the period immediately following show a very

large factor of the Caspian type. It is tempting to accept this suggestion and believe that from these eastern Baltic longheads the Goths were derived, who would then in the first century A. D., in their movement southward toward the Black Sea, have been retracing the earlier route by which their Neolithic ancestors came to the Baltic shores.

On the basis of the theory here advanced the population of Europe in Neolithic times is assumed to have comprised factors belonging to three types: (1) the Mediterranean, which probably passed northward from Africa by the land bridges, moving in general north and northeast; (2) the Palæ-Alpine, entering Europe from the southeast and moving west and northwest through the Highlands to the North Sea; and (3) the Caspian, spreading from the steppes of southeastern Russia westward up the Danube valley. In addition there were the remnants of the older Palæolithic peoples, the Proto-Australoid surviving in out-of-the-way corners in the Iberian peninsula, Brittany, and the western portion of the British Isles, and in part driven into the Baltic Lands; and the Mongoloid, the survivors of which lingered mainly in the region of the Alps, or had been driven northward into the Scandinavian peninsula. Yet the picture, complex as it is, is not complete, for still another important type makes its appearance in Neolithic times, one whose method of distribution differed from all the rest, and which in later ages was to play an ever greater and greater part—the Alpine type.

This name, however well it may fit with the distribution of the type in the Europe of to-day, ill accords with its rôle when we meet it for the first time, for in the Neolithic period the Alpine type seems to have been largely confined to the coasts of Europe, and its diffusion seems almost certainly to have begun by sea. If we except the late Neolithic or more probably early Bronze sites in southeastern Spain, the Alpine type was nowhere a dominant factor in the population, although everywhere present where it could have come by sea. In Sicily, Sardinia, and southern Italy, in southern and western France, and perhaps in Ireland it is a not unimportant element, and increases in importance in the basin of the Seine, in Belgium, Denmark, and southern Sweden, while traces of it may be found in the supposedly Neolithic crania of the eastern Baltic. In the interior of Europe, however, in Switzerland, Bohemia, Hungary, Silesia, etc., the Alpine type is either wholly absent or present in small proportions. We can hardly escape the belief, therefore, that its spread was primarily by sea.

But whence? Are we to see in these Neolithic brachycephals, the forerunners, as it were, of the Phœnicians, and regard them as coming from Asia Minor along the Mediterranean shores, and then out through the Straits of Gibraltar and so northward; or were they rather the advance-guards of those daring sea-rovers and raiders from Scandinavia and the Baltic, who in the years to come were to harry the Atlantic and Mediterranean coasts not only of Europe but of northern Africa as well? The relatively greater importance of the type in the western Baltic and shores of the North Sea might seem to favor the latter view, but if the developments of the succeeding Bronze and Iron Ages are borne in mind, it is evident that such a northern origin is practically impossible, and we are forced to adopt the first hypothesis, and regard the Alpines as spreading in the main from the eastern Mediterranean.

Still the picture of Neolithic Europe is incomplete, for yet another type, one quite unexpected, reveals itself in the record—the Proto-Negroid! Traces of its presence in later Palæolithic times have already been noted. With the Proto-Australoid it appears to have been driven out and absorbed, yet like this other, although it survived in out-of-the-way corners in the Iberian peninsula and in France, the major remnants were forced northward to the Baltic, so that in Neolithic time it is an important factor in Mecklenburg, Denmark, and southern Sweden. Its influence may also be traced in Silesia and in Bohemia. To assert the presence in this northern region of a Proto-Negroid element appears at first sight extremely hazardous, for nothing could well be more unlike the fair "Nordic" race associated with this area. Yet the evidence of the crania seems inescapable, and we must apparently accept the fact that a minority of this type has entered into the complex commonly spoken of as the "Nordic race."

The period of the Bronze Age is one of great difficulty for the student of racial history in Europe, owing to the wide-spread custom of cremation, which has destroyed most of the opportunities for determining the character of the population during this period, or has left remains which may give a wholly incorrect picture of the facts. In the western Baltic region little change seems to have occurred, although in the east the brachycephalic types present in earlier times give way almost wholly to dolichocephalic, among which the Caspian assumes first place, with the older Proto-Australoid a close second. The British Isles show at least for southern and central England the replacement of the older Palæ-Alpine by the Alpine type, which is easily the dominant element in the Round Barrows. As the Yorkshire barrows show little of the Alpine element and much of the Palæ-Alpine, there seems to have been a withdrawal of the older type before the invading Alpines.

During the Bronze Age the Alpine type also increases largely in France, Belgium, and southwestern Germany. To some extent, perhaps, it still came by way of the seacoasts, but in contrast to the earlier period it was distributed in larger measure by land along the Highlands. It was probably from this source that the Alpine immigration into Italy took place, first into the valley of the Po, and then later crossing the Apennines and spreading southward along the Tyrrhenian coast to enter into the make-up of the Latins.

The period from the end of the Bronze Age to the beginning of the Christian era seems to have been one of comparative quiet and readjustment, during which no great movements can be traced, but in which extensive and far-reaching assimilation of the various types took place. The Baltic area became increasingly dolichocephalic, the older Palæ-Alpine and Alpine elements being largely absorbed. The Caspian type was increasingly dominant, being strengthened apparently by continual increments from the Russian plains, and from it and the Mediterranean type with minor influences of the earlier long-headed types was developed, during this long period of ten or fifteen centuries, the complex racial blend to which the name of "Nordic" has been applied. For these blond, dolichocephalic people were not a pure race, and wherever we find them show very clearly on analysis their composite origin. The problem of how and why their distinctive blondness arose cannot be discussed here, but will be treated in the final chapter.

In the British Isles during this long period a somewhat similar process of assimilation went on. The great infusion of the Alpine type which had taken place in the Bronze Age was largely absorbed, save perhaps in northeastern Scotland and along the southern coast. The Caspian type had, however, never come into the British Isles in force, so here the factors available for blending were primarily the Mediterranean together with remnants of the older Proto-Australoid and the Neolithic Palæ-Alpines.

Into the Netherlands and northern France there flowed, from the northeast apparently, an intermittent but not unimportant current of Baltic longheads, which does not seem, however, to have penetrated beyond the Seine basin. The rest of France received continual increments of Alpine and the older Palæ-Alpine types, coming in from the Highlands, which had now become wholly occupied by them. As in France so in Italy, the Alpine type steadily and irresistibly filtered in. Yet this was not the only type which made its way thither, for the Iron Age was marked by the appearance in Italy for the first time in any strength, of the Caspian type. This southward drive of what was for Europe mainly a northern type, was in a sense the forerunner of the invasions of the Lombards and other "Nordic" descendants of the Caspian type, which were to occur a thousand years or more later, and seems to have had as little permanent influence on the racial make-up of the people. It seems to have come to the Adriatic shores by way of the Danube valley and around the head of the Adriatic. The brachycephalization of Italy as a result of the southward expansion of the Alpine type was, however, only temporarily stayed. For, although in the sixth and seventh centuries B. C. the populations of the valleys of the Tiber and the Arno were still at least half composed of Mediterranean and other dolichocephalic elements, by the beginning of the Christian era the Alpine and Palæ-Alpine factors had become overwhelmingly dominant.

One other racial modification of moment occurred during this period between the end of the Bronze Age and the beginning of the Christian era. Vague and hazy as is our knowledge of the conditions existing in the Balkan peninsula during prehistoric times, it seems possible to detect a difference between its northern portion, which lies in direct contact with western Asia, and its southern tip, which we know as Greece. Whereas the former seems from the earliest times to have been the highroad by which successive waves of brachycephalic peoples passed into central Europe, Greece appears to have had a more mixed population, which comprised factors of both the Proto-Australoid and Proto-Negroid types. Yet as early as the Iron Age the Alpine type seems to have been in the preponderance as far south as Athens. That the Dorian Invasion brought into Greece a people primarily of this type seems very probable, although perhaps under leaders who were largely of Caspian type. In the centuries following the Dorian Invasion the influcnce of the Caspian type became stronger and stronger. There is reason to believe that this intrusion of Caspian types did not extend in force into the Peloponnesus, where the dolichocephalic elements are mainly of the older types. On this hypothesis the opposition of Athens and Sparta and the rise of Macedonia take on a deeper meaning.

The millennium prior to the beginning of the Christian era, had been one, in general, of comparative quiescence; except for the thrust of Caspian peoples in the vicinity of the Danube and into Greece it had been more a period of amalgamation and preparation. About the beginning of the Christian era, however, conditions underwent a rapid change. The "Nordic" peoples developed in the Baltic lands began to press southward and westward with ever-increasing force, until at last they burst through the wall which the Romans had erected against them, and spread in a mighty flood over western and southern Europe. From the Vistula and the eastern Baltic the Goths, Gepidæ, and Herulæ moved southward to the shores of the Black Sea, and then streamed westward up the Danube to the Balkans and around the head of the Adriatic into Italy, France, and Spain. From the western Baltic, Saxon and Angle, Frank, Dane, and Lombard swarmed into England, France, and Italy; while from the more central parts of the Baltic regions Alemani, Suevi, Vandal, and Burgundian beat against the wall of the Alps, part being deflected westward through France to Spain and beyond, and part winning through to fall upon the north of Italy. For some 600 years the northern lands continued to send forth swarm after swarm of these "Nordic" raiders, conquerors, and colonists, and the question arises how far this great outpouring of primarily dolichocephalic peoples affected the racial character of the rest of Europe. Before answering that question, two other great movements of peoples must be considered.

Beginning somewhat later than the Baltic drift, a movement began among the Slavs, a people living then, it seems, in the plains north and northeast of the Carpathians and speaking a language closely allied to the Teutonic speech of the Baltic tribes. Possibly the migration of the Slavs may have been initiated by the southward movement of the Goths, but be that as it may, about the sixth century the Slavic peoples began to move northward and westward into northern and central Germany and Bohemia, whence they passed on southward into the Balkan peninsula, penetrating as far as Greece. A little later they spread also toward the northeast, reaching as far as the lake region of northwestern Russia, and in Novgorod and Moscow they had established strong states by the eighth or ninth century. The problem of the physical type of these early Slavic-speaking peoples is extremely puzzling, and one to which a final answer cannot as yet be given. All things considered, however, the most plausible theory would seem to be that they were a primarily dolichocephalic folk, of Caspian and Proto-Negroid types. The area of western Russia into which they came was occupied by Finnish peoples, whose physical characteristics are also greatly in doubt. On the whole it is probable that they were predominantly brachycephalic and primarily Alpine, although with perhaps a considerable admixture of the Ural type.

The third immigrant stream came from the eastern and southeastern portion of the Russian plains, and comprised the Alani, Bolgari, etc. Of mixed Caspian and Alpine types, they moved westward, part settling in the lower Danube valley, part passing north of the Carpathians into southern Germany, where they joined with some of the "Nordic" tribes, such as the Vandals. From this same direction, also, came the Avars, Huns, and Magyars, some of whom swept like a flame across Europe, while others settled within the great curve of the Carpathians. Like their successors from the inner Asiatic steppes in later times, these tribes were certainly of mixed origin, but probably in the main of Alpine type.

In sum, then, the period of the Völkerwanderung influenced the racial history of Europe in three main ways: (1) It brought into all of western, central, and southern Europe a flood of mixed dolichocephalic peoples from the Baltic lands, in the main a blend of Caspian and Mediterranean types; (2) it spread through eastern Germany, western Russia, as well as Hungary and the Balkan peninsula a mass of Slavic-speaking dolichocephalic peoples; and (3) it brought peoples of mixed Caspian and Alpine types into the Carpathians. Central, western, and southwestern Europe thus tended to become dolichocephalized, while the east and southeast were brachycephalized. The penetration of western Europe by the Palæ-Alpine and Alpine types, so marked during Neolithic and Bronze times, was thus checked for a season, while the southeast was invaded by ever-increasing hordes of Palæ-Alpines and Alpines, in part derived from Asia.

Behind these, again, came still others, the Pecheneg, the Kuman, and the somewhat mysterious Khazar, all of whom likewise seem to have been primarily of Alpine and Palæ-Alpine type. They settled in or held large areas in the southeast of Russia, and the Khazar being converted to Judaism in the eighth century, thereafter seem to have spread far and wide to the west and northwest, their modern descendants probably forming the preponderant element among the east European Jews.

The results of these several movements were strikingly different, as we see when we compare the conditions in the twelfth century with those existing in the sixteenth or seventeenth. Of the great influx of "Nordic" peoples into western, central, and southern Europe, little trace remained. Southern and southwestern Germany, where the Reihengräber of the Völkerwanderung period show Baltic dolichocephals present in equal number with Palæ-Alpine and Alpine types, has now become almost wholly brachycephalic, with the Alpine type strongly dominant. Northward through the Rhine valley to Belgium and the Netherlands these two brachycephalic types also prevail. In France the evidence of the Frankish dolichocephals is seen only in the basin of the Seine; and although in Brittany and along the western margin of the Massif Central, traces of the old Palæolithic longheads still survived, everywhere else the Palæ-Alpines and Alpines were the dominating elements. Only in the British Isles were the roundheads in minority, for the seventeenth century crania from eastern England, at least, show a population almost unchanged in its composition from Neolithic times, except that the Mediterranean type is even more securely in the lead. Only at Hythe, in Kent, do we find brachycephals dominant. Northeastern Scotland and the northern islands also show strong survival of Alpine types. Switzerland by the seventeenth century had become a purely brachycephalic region, the Palæ-Alpine type being dominant in the southwest, while the Alpine is preponderant in the northeast and east. The whole of the Po valley is overwhelmingly Alpine, and of the long-headed northern invaders and settlers there is hardly a trace. The effect thus upon the racial character of western and central Europe of the

great outpouring of "Nordic" peoples during the Völkerwanderung had been of the slightest. As raiders, conquerors, and rulers
their political and cultural influence was often great and endur-
ing; only rarely, however, did any factor of their racial features
survive.

But what of the Baltic lands and western Russia, into which
had poured the dolichocephalic Slavic-speaking peoples? The
story here is essentially the same, for the dolichocephalic immigrants rapidly disappeared. By the seventeenth century Bohemia, the eastern Baltic region, and western Russia were completely brachycephalized, and the long-headed factors survived
only as a minority in a population in the main of Alpine type.

The last of the great racial movements is that of the Mongol-
Tatar invasions in the thirteenth century. The hordes which
swept so irresistibly across the Russian plains to the gates of
central Europe were in the main brachycephalic, yet except in
the south of Russia it may be doubted if their coming exerted
any appreciable effect so far as racial questions are concerned.
Although they ravaged and pillaged the heart of Russia and
held the Russian princes tributary for two centuries, there seems
to have been no real occupation of the country except in the
south. There, however, the influence of these Asiatic brachycephals can be clearly traced, and there and in the region east of
the Volga large bodies of Tatars are still to be found.

What is the outcome to-day of the fifty or more thousand
years of migrations and minglings which we have tried to sketch?
What is the picture which modern Europe presents to the student? The outstanding racial characteristic of the Europe of
to-day is the dominance of the Alpine and Palæ-Alpine types.
Except for portions of southern Scandinavia, the western Baltic
lands and shores of the North Sea, the British Isles, the Iberian
peninsula, Corsica, Sardinia, Sicily, and southern Italy, together
with small areas in west-central France and southeastern Russia,
the whole continent is dominated by brachycephalic types, which
are thus central, whereas the dolichocephalic types are mainly
marginal. If we compare this present situation with the con-

ditions in Neolithic times and in the period between the sixth and twelfth centuries, the vast expansion of the brachycephalic peoples, mainly Palæ-Alpine and Alpine, becomes apparent. The narrow wedge thrust in earliest times along the Highlands from Asia Minor to the North Sea has expanded until its base extends from the Arctic to the Caucasus, while in the west it has broadened in every direction toward the sea. Of primarily dolichocephalic peoples hardly a trace is left; the brachycephalization of Europe is nearly complete. From the racial standpoint the history of the continent during the last 10,000 or 15,000 years may be summed up as a contest between the older longheads and the later roundheads, and in the contest it has been the latter who have won!

What has been the fate of the vanquished? The Proto-Australoids survive only as remnants in a few isolated marginal areas. In Tras os Montes and Beira Alta in northern Portugal, in the province of Teruel on the Levantine Coast of Spain, in the Dordogne and the western edge of the Massif Central in France, in western Wales and perhaps in Ireland, in Sardinia and in the "toe" of Italy occasional individuals or even small groups, such as in the Plynlymmon district in Wales, may be found which still exhibit the characteristic features of this type. The Proto-Negroid type has shared the fate of the Proto-Australoids, and its only recognizable remnants are found in marginal areas, usually in company with the latter. Its survival has recently been noted by Giuffrida Ruggeri, who calls it Proto-Ethiopian. The Caspian type survives apparently in little greater numbers than these older forms, and for the most part has melted into the complex of the "Nordic" peoples. Here and there, however, strong elements survive, as in northern Portugal, where they may be the descendants of the Vandal and Suevi, in southeastern Scotland and northeastern England, and in Scandinavia. The strongest representation of this type to-day is probably to be found in Russia, among both the Russian and Finnic population west of the middle Volga.

The Mediterranean type is the only one of dolichocephalic

character still existing in Europe in any considerable numbers. It seems still to form the underlying stratum of the population of the Iberian peninsula, being especially strong in central and southern Portugal, and in Catalonia and Aragon; in France it forms a minority in the coastal population of Languedoc and possibly, also, in the Dordogne and Limousine. In the British Isles it probably forms the major element in Ireland, southeastern England, and southwestern Scotland, and is perhaps represented in some measure in the more dolichocephalic portions of the brunet population of Denmark and western Norway. In Sardinia (Corsica?) and Sicily and in the southern third of the Italian peninsula it is present in large proportion.

Turning to the victors, we find the Alpine type to be not only the dominant one in modern Europe, but to be found in greater purity than any other in the continent. In France, except in the Haut Morvan and probably in the more rugged and isolated portions of Brittany and the Massif Central, it is the dominant factor. The same is true apparently for almost the whole of the Central European Highland, only the Canton of Vaud, the Pusterthal, and the marginal area in the north showing a parity between this type and the Palæ-Alpine. It dominates overwhelmingly the whole basin of the Po and extends southward beyond Umbria, but attains its greatest purity and preponderance apparently in the northern Balkans. Northward it stretches through Baden and Wurtemberg and the Rhine valley to the North Sea, while toward the northeast it seems, on the basis of very meagre data, to sweep over the larger part of Russia and Finland. There is, however, a notable difference in pigmentation between the Alpine peoples of the Balkans, Switzerland, and France, on the one hand, and those of the North Sea and Baltic regions, together with western and central Russia, in that whereas the former are normally brunet in color of eyes and hair at least, the latter are increasingly blond, until in Finland the percentage of blonds equals or surpasses that among the dolichocephalic, Baltic "Nordics." Detailed discussion of this striking difference must be deferred to the final chapter, but the conclusions there reached may be anticipated by saying that it is believed to be due in part to the special and peculiar effect which the Baltic environment has had upon all peoples who have come for long under its influence, and in part to the influence of the Caspian type.

The distribution of the Palæ-Alpine type in Europe to-day is significant and in keeping with the outline of the racial history of the continent here proposed. This type, which historically preceded the Alpine type in its entrance into Europe, although still strongly represented throughout the core of the great brachycephalic wedge, is nevertheless dominated and outnumbered by the Alpine. Toward the margins of much of the brachycephalic area, however, the proportions are reversed. In Istria on the south, in the region of the lower Inn and the Canton of Vaud on the north, and in the Haut Morvan in France, the chief brachycephalic factor is of the Palæ-Alpine type. Throughout much of western Europe the Palæ-Alpine gives the impression of a partially submerged type, and if we had sufficiently abundant and detailed data for the whole of Switzerland, it is probable that islands of this type would be found lingering in the more isolated and unfavorable regions.

The part played by the Mongoloid type in the European continent has, on the whole, been small. Traceable apparently in earliest Palæolithic times in Spain, France, and Belgium, it is found in the Neolithic period feebly represented in Switzerland and Italy. In the early Middle Ages it seems to be somewhat more widely spread, since we find evidence of it on the North Sea coasts and along the Baltic as well as in southwestern Russia. In modern times it appears to contribute a moderately important factor to the populations of Switzerland, eastern France, and northern Italy; it does not, however, extend into the Balkan region. It was present in the fifteenth century in Norway, and is found at present in the Sogne and Trondhjem districts. Finally, it is a considerable element in the Bashkir of eastern Russia, is probably to be found among the Finns, and is the dominant factor among the Norwegian Lapps, although much less important among those in Sweden and northern Russia. The data are too meagre for more than a guess at the history of this type in Europe, but suggest that it may have been the forerunner of the Palæ-Alpine type, and have also come in large part with it, from its clearly defined centre on the northern border of the Asiatic plateaus. It is tempting to regard it as reaching the Scandinavian peninsula very early, and as being the vaguely discernible brachycephalic type driven northward by the later predominantly dolichocephalic population.

The last of the eight types, and one which, like the preceding, has played a somewhat uncertain and minor part, is the Ural. Its origin and affiliations are the most obscure of all. Until the Middle Ages it does not appear anywhere, except as a faint trace, and that mainly in Switzerland and the North Sea and western Baltic areas. In the seventh century it is of some importance in Volhynia in western Russia, and in the later Middle Ages increases in strength in the regions where its presence was noted above. In modern times it is chiefly to be found in northern Italy, among the Germans of Upper Austria, in the Morvan and Aveyron districts in France, in eastern Scotland, in the Jaederen district of southeastern Norway, and especially among the Voguls and Samoyeds of the northeast of Russia. Its late appearance, together with its absence in the whole Balkan region, and concentration along the Asiatic frontier, suggest that its coming into western and central Europe may in some way be connected with the drifts of Asiatic peoples beginning at the time of the Völkerwanderung.

The fact of the increasing and now all but complete dominance in Europe of the brachycephalic types has been noted; it remains to consider the process by which this has been accomplished. During the prehistoric period and up to the end of the Middle Ages the penetration of the Palæ-Alpine and Alpine types into Europe and their spread therein may in large part be accounted for on the basis of migration on a large scale. But the spread of the roundheads at the expense of the longheads did not cease with the close of the period of migration, and has continued apparently without abatement to the present time. In some cases, as in eastern Europe, the expansion of brachycephalic populations has, although slow, been nevertheless a visible and recorded movement. In central and western Europe, however, no such perceptible colonization has occurred, and the spread of the Palæ-Alpine and Alpine types must be explained in some other way. Several influences seem to be responsible. During the period of religious persecution at the time of the Reformation large numbers of people, predominantly of brachycephalic types, fled or were driven from their homes to areas which were in general still strongly dolichocephalic. As examples of such movements, those from Bohemia and Moravia to Germany, that of the Flemish weavers to England, and the dispersal of the Huguenots may be mentioned.

Yet such movements alone would not suffice to account for the great extent of the change, the larger part of which must probably be ascribed to slow and unrecorded drifts, due primarily to economic and political causes. The influence of the former has, it need hardly be said, been greatly intensified during the last half century, owing to the industrial transformation. In France, for example, Paris has long been a magnet drawing population from the provinces to an area in which the dolichocephalic elements had been relatively strong; and the industrial development of the north of France has, in the last two generations, attracted laborers from other portions of the country. The unification of Germany and the growth of Berlin as a great capital have brought an influx of brachycephalic population from the south and east into one of the strongholds of the "Nordic" blends; and the great industrial development of the Ruhr and Rhine valley as a whole has brought thousands of Slavs from Poland and the east within the last generation. This increase in the brachycephalic factors in areas formerly more or less strongly dolichocephalic, is independent of the fact that with the rapid growth of great cities there seems to be a tendency toward a differentiation between the urban and the rural population, such that there is a relative concentration in the former of dolichocephalic factors. In the final chapter still other possible causes for this progressive brachycephalization will be discussed.

Slowly, and in recent times insensibly, the Palæ-Alpines and Alpines have thus pressed into the lands still held by their Caspian and Mediterranean predecessors, until the heritage of these older European peoples has shrunk to but a fraction of its former size. And not in Europe alone has this dominance of the roundheads been increasing, for we shall find it to be a well-nigh universal phenomenon. The spheres of the "Nordic" blend and of the Mediterranean type alike have been steadily decreasing; is there any reason to doubt but that the process will continue? The Great War, with its legacies of hatred, its intensification of nationality, and its multiplication and strengthening of frontiers, may retard the change, but the process begun so many thousands of years ago can hardly have reached its end.

# CHAPTER I

## FRANCE AND THE LOW COUNTRIES

### I. FRANCE

THE geographical features whose influence may be clearly traced as affecting and in considerable measure determining the racial history of France, are such as may be easily and briefly described. France comprises three fertile lowland areas and one central and four marginal highland or mountainous areas. As lowlands are to be reckoned the basins of Paris (drained mainly by the Seine) and of Aquitaine (drained by the Garonne) and the deep north-and-south depression formed by the valleys of the Saône and Rhone. The central highland or Massif Central rises in the midst of these lowlands as a rugged, volcanic, and rather infertile region, presenting its steeper slopes toward the south and east. South of the basin of Aquitaine and extending east and west from the Mediterranean to the Atlantic lies the great wall of the Pyrenees; east of the Saône-Rhone depression, the French Alps and the Jura mark the edges of the mountain highland of Central Europe, whose lower northwestern extensions in the Vosges and the Ardennes limit in some measure the Paris basin toward the north and east. Lastly, in Brittany we have a moderately rugged highland, and one which by its peninsular character is to some extent isolated from the rest of France.

The numerous discoveries of early human remains made in France during the last fifty years place us in a position to discuss with some certainty the characteristics of the ancient population of the Dordogne and the Mediterranean shore as far back as Mousterian times. At this period, which marks the end of the early Palæolithic age, the climate of France was cold, and the tropical or semi-tropical fauna and flora of the previous period had retreated into Africa (with which continent land con-

46

nection by way of Spain and Italy still existed), their places being taken by arctic species.

In the caves and rock-shelters of Le Moustier, La Chapelle-aux-Saintes, and of La Quina in Dordogne and Périgord, three skeletons have been discovered which reveal this earliest known population to have been one of short stature (ca. 160 cm.), with a low, dolichocephalic skull and a broad nose, representing thus on the basis of the scheme and terminology here adopted the Proto-Australoid type. The Chapelle-aux-Saintes cranium lies just on the border line of mesocephaly, and suggests that already a faint brachycephalic influence, apparently of the Mongoloid type, had begun to make itself felt.

In the following, or Aurignacian period, although the animal life continues without much modification, the human types underwent an important change. We possess remains of this period from two sites, Cro Magnon and Combe Capelle in the Dordogne and Périgord, and also from the Grimaldi caves at Mentone. The type shown by these is clearly the Mediterranean, with, in the case of Combe Capelle, some admixture with the Caspian type, which only appears in purity in the later Magdalenian period. From the wide distribution of the typical industry of the Aurignacian period along the shores of the Mediterranean it seems most probable that this new type of man came into France from the south.

The close of the Palæolithic age saw the appearance of the third dolichocephalic type, the Caspian already referred to above. The single example so far known comes from Chancelade, again in the Dordogne, where, however, the Mediterranean type was still strongly represented as shown by the finds at Laugerie Basse. In contrast to the Mediterranean, the Caspian type probably came into France through Germany, where its presence at the close of the Palæolithic period is well established.

The advent of the Neolithic period reveals a far-reaching change in the human types present in France, changes which are associated with a striking development of culture, and undoubtedly with a large increase of population. The Palæolithic

types were almost exclusively dolichocephalic; the succeeding
period shows these still in the majority, but to a considerable
extent blended with brachycephalic forms, which for the first
time appear clearly as such.  The scanty remains of the Palæolithic population have so far been found only along the western
margin of the Massif Central and on the Mediterranean shore;
the much more abundant remains of the Neolithic age are more
widely scattered.  Many hundreds of crania have been excavated from these sites, but for the most part their measurements
have been published only as averages, so that it is impossible to
analyze the material on the plan adopted in the present study.
We can therefore only consider the distribution of the average
cranial index, and then endeavor to supplement this with such
additional information as can be secured from the relatively
small number of crania whose measurements have been published in full.

Of the nearly 700 Neolithic crania whose indices have been
compiled by Salmon,[1] in round numbers about 60 per cent are
dolichocephalic and 20 per cent mesocephalic and brachycephalic respectively.  Although for France as a whole the dolichocephalic types are in considerable majority, striking differences
in the proportions are apparent as soon as we divide the material
on a geographic basis, grouping together the crania from (1) the
Paris basin, (2) Brittany, and (3) the Massif Central.  In round
numbers the relative percentages of the three divisions of the
cranial index are found to be as follows:

|  | Dolichocephalic | Mesocephalic | Brachycephalic |
|---|---|---|---|
| Paris Basin............... | 32% | 43% | 25% |
| Brittany................. | 53% | 27% | 20% |
| Massif Central........... | 64% | 29% | 7% |

From this table it is clear that while in the Massif Central
and Brittany dolichocephalic types are in the majority, in the
Paris basin this is by no means the case, brachycephalic types

[1] Salmon, 1895.

being almost as frequent. From this it would seem that we were entitled to draw the conclusion that in the Massif Central the dolichocephalic types which had characterized the Dordogne throughout the Palæolithic period had persisted, but that a large element of brachycephalic peoples had come into the Paris basin. Brittany also had received a considerable share of the newcomers, but had not been modified so largely as the adjacent lowland toward the east.

That in large part these round-headed immigrants must have come from the eastward seems to be shown by the following facts: The Neolithic sites in the region of the so-called "Saddle of Poitiers," between the basins of Aquitaine and Paris, show 60 per cent of dolichocephalic crania and no brachycephalic at all; the sites in the department of Saône-et-Loire, which lies largely in the northern end of the Saône-Rhone depression, show, on the other hand, an even higher percentage of round-headed crania than the Paris basin; lastly, the crania from the departments of Isére, Drome, and Vaucluse, along the eastward side of the Rhone valley and including portions of the French Alps, show a proportion of brachycephaly more than double that of any other part of France. The same results appear if we consider the Paris basin by itself in detail, for here the central departments of Oise and Seine-et-Oise show approximately 27 per cent of brachycephalic crania, while Marne, farther east, has 35 per cent, and Meuse, still farther eastward, rises to 42 per cent.

When an attempt is made to determine the types represented by these round and long-headed crania, the task is made almost hopeless by the scantiness of the available data, most of which, furthermore, comes only from the Paris basin. On the basis of this material, however, it would appear that in the central and eastern portion of the Paris basin three dolichocephalic types are found. The most important in numbers is the Mediterranean, that of minor consequence the Caspian, while at one single site, that of the Grotte de Cougy, these types are almost absent, and in their stead we find a large Proto-Negroid element, with a trace of the Proto-Australoid, *i. e.*, the older rather than the later Palæolithic forms. The brachycephalic types present throughout are the Alpine and Palæ-Alpine, of which the former is in the majority. In the south, in Aveyron and Lozère, on the southern borders of the Massif Central, the conditions seem to have been very much like those prevailing in the whole Paris basin, with the Mediterranean type in the majority, and the Alpine the most strongly represented of the brachycephalic forms. That here, also, the ancient Palæolithic types were not by any means extinct, seems to be indicated by the crania from Sargels on the plateau of Larzac.

Generalizing from these facts, the racial history of France during Neolithic times may be assumed to have been something as follows. The latter part of the Palæolithic period saw the appearance of two new types, the Mediterranean and the Caspian. With the beginning of the Neolithic period a flood of the former types swept over western France from the south, passing along the western borders of the Massif Central and by the "Saddle of Poitiers" into the Paris basin. It is probable that a second stream followed up the coast from Spain. In the central area these Mediterranean immigrants met and largely absorbed what survived of the older Proto-Australoid and Proto-Negroid types, although a considerable body of these were apparently driven before the advancing southerners, toward the North Sea and the Baltic. Somewhat later, perhaps, a wave of Caspian peoples streamed across the Rhine valley, and entered France from the northeast, contending with the Mediterranean immigrants for the control of the Paris basin. These northern dolichocephalic peoples, who were the forerunners of the later Teutonic invaders, may possibly be one with the so-called Magelmoos peoples, whose cultural remains are known from Denmark and the Baltic shores, who are thought to be contemporaneous there with the very end of the Palæolithic period in southern France, and whom Breuil[1] believes to be of Central Asiatic origin. Coincidently with these movements of the two dolicho-

[1] Breuil, 1912, p. 235 *sq.*

cephalic groups, we may postulate a westward drift of the brachycephalic Palæ-Alpine and Alpine types, which, passing by way
of the Central European Highlands, poured into the Paris basin around the northern end of the Vosges, and into the Saône-
Rhone depression by way of the Gap of Belfort, between the
Vosges and the Jura, as well as down the upper Rhone valley
from Lake Geneva and the broad lowlands lying between the
Jura and the Alps. Of the two brachycephalic types, the Palæ-
Alpine seems to have been the earlier, and its presence at this
period in the Ardennes plateau and in Britain will be noted elsewhere. The Alpine type, which was in the majority at least in
the Paris basin, seems not to have reached either Belgium or
Britain in any numbers until the close of the Neolithic period.
The brachycephalic elements in Brittany may be ascribed in
part to a sea-borne branch of Alpines, whose importance was
greater, perhaps, in other portions of Europe.

For the long period lying between the end of the Neolithic
period (which may be put for France roughly at about 2000
B. C.) and the coming of the Teutonic migrations in the fifth
century A. D. we have little in the way of adequate data which
enable us to follow the racial changes in this area. Culturally
the materials are abundant, and we can trace the beginnings of
the metal industry and follow the long development of the
Bronze Age and of the introduction of the use of iron. But of
skeletal remains we possess a surprisingly small supply. This is
in considerable part due to the prevalence of the custom of cremation.

Leaning, as we must, then, largely on archæological and later
historical data, we may attempt to bridge the long gap somewhat as follows. The drift of brachycephalic Palæ-Alpine and
Alpine peoples into France, which began to be important as early
at least as the middle of the Neolithic period, continued to gain
in strength, and about the beginning of the second millennium
B. C. new waves of these peoples brought with them the knowledge and use of bronze, which spread in the course of the next
four or five centuries over the whole of France. We are forced

to assume, I believe, that the spread of the bronze culture involved also a considerable and continued influx of Alpine peoples, and that the older, largely dolichocephalic population was
everywhere gradually conquered and assimilated, except in the
heart of the Massif Central, by the newcomers.

The problem of the connection between the origin and spread
of bronze culture in France and the influx of new racial elements
is difficult and still very obscure. The Bronze Age in France is
subdivided by Déchelette[1] into four periods. The sites belonging to the first are very few, and are, with hardly an exception,
confined to the Atlantic coast of southern Brittany. The second
period is developed mainly in Brittany, and it is not until the
third that the sites become even moderately numerous in eastern France, where they become abundant in the northeastern
portion of the Paris basin, and also cluster in the region of the
Jura and the areas adjacent to the upper Rhone valley. In the
fourth period Brittany again assumes predominance, nearly 60
per cent of the known sites being confined to the peninsula.
Bronze *culture* was thus primarily littoral in its distribution, and
the Gironde and especially Brittany were the main *foci* whence
its influence spread. The eastern area unquestionably, however, received a strong influence from central Europe by way of
the Rhone valley, due, we may believe, to a continuation of the
Neolithic drift of Alpine peoples, who served as bringers of the
culture. Are we, however, entitled to ascribe its spread along
the Atlantic and Channel coasts to a wave of immigrants spreading northward from Spain? All things considered, it would
seem that we are, but that this drift, while of great significance
in the spread of bronze culture, was of rather less importance as
influencing the racial characters of the population.

Toward the end of the Bronze period, perhaps largely as a
result of the trade in amber which had developed with Denmark and the Baltic region, a conquering wave of hardy Baltic
peoples came into northeastern and central France, repeating the
much earlier movement of the same sort which, it is suggested,

[1] Déchelette, 1910.

occurred at the close of the Palæolithic age. Since the Bronze Age population of Denmark, at least, was in large measure brachycephalic, we are justified in believing that this Baltic invasion of France at this time was not wholly made up of dolichocephalic types, so that no very great change would have resulted among the French population.

In the early centuries of the first millennium B. C. bronze was superseded by iron. The knowledge and use of the metal spread from the east over the whole of France. How far we are entitled to associate with the introduction of this new culture a further immigration is not wholly clear, but from the analogy of the invasions which follow in the later Iron Age, it is probable that considerable increments of central European peoples came in the beginning with iron into France.

Of the physical characters of these bringers of iron we know little; it seems probable, however, that they were far from uniform. In Franche-Comté and parts of Burgundy the graves of this period reveal a brachycephalic population of short stature, whereas farther north, in the Vosges and Lorraine, there is an equally strong preponderance of tall, dolichocephalic types. These conditions would appear to indicate that the westward drift of brachycephalic types which, from early Neolithic times at least, had been coming into France through Belfort and the upper Rhone valley, continued throughout the Iron Age; and that tall, dolichocephalic types from Germany were beginning to swarm across the Rhine as the advance guard of the great Frankish and Burgundian conquests which were to break through the frontiers some ten centuries later.

The second, or La Tene, period of the Iron Age, which in France is thought to have begun about the sixth century B. C., was coincident with the last clearly defined wave of brachycephalic peoples, that of the great expansion of the Gauls and other Celtic tribes. Spreading apparently from southern Germany and the northern borders of the Central European Highlands, they overran in the next two or three hundred years not only France and Spain, but also northern Italy and the Danube valley as far as the Black Sea and beyond. While predominantly composed of a mixture of the Palæ-Alpine and Alpine types, this wave of Celtic peoples undoubtedly included some of the tall "Nordic" blends, who already were pushing south and west from their breeding-grounds along the Baltic.

If this interpretation of the archæologic record is correct, we must regard the long period extending from the end of Neolithic times to the beginning of the Christian era as one during which the racial characteristics of France underwent a complete change. We leave it in Neolithic times with a predominantly dolichocephalic population, primarily of Mediterranean type, into which brachycephalic influences of Palæ-Alpine and Alpine types had begun to penetrate in the north and east; we find it in Roman times apparently strongly brachycephalic, with the older types surviving in any considerable degree probably only in the south and perhaps in parts of the western Massif Central. It may be objected to this view of the brachycephalization of France during the Bronze and Iron Ages that the skeletal data are quite inadequate to prove it; that the cultural revolution by no means necessarily implies the coming of large numbers of immigrants; and that the brachycephalic Bronze Age invaders of Britain did not succeed in permanently altering the physical type in the British Isles. All this may be granted, but in view of the history of events in central and southern Europe during this time, of the subsequent history of France itself, and of the present-day composition of its population, the foregoing hypothesis seems the only one which fits the facts.

In the second century B. C., during the early period of Roman rule, a southward movement of "Nordic" tribes began. For the time being it was checked by the Romans, and, except as it had some influence in the Paris basin, seems to have had no further effect. The Roman occupation itself, although it lasted for several centuries, would seem to have had, so far as racial factors are concerned, effects quite incommensurate with those produced upon the culture and language of France. Culturally the population was revolutionized, its Celtic language practically disappeared and was replaced by Latin forms; but racially Roman influence was seemingly slight, for, as will be shown later, the Romans of the Empire were, as a whole, not much different in their primary characteristics from the Alpine invaders which had been pouring into France from the Central European Highlands for 2,000 years.

By the third century A. D. the pressure of the Teutonic-speaking Baltic tribes grew stronger, and the Franks broke through the frontier guards and penetrated into France. By the fifth century they and other tribes, like the Goths and Burgundians, had overrun the Paris basin and the northern portion of the Saône-Rhone depression and extended far into Aquitaine; and by the beginning of the sixth century they had put an end to Roman rule. A large number of graves of the early Frankish and the Merovingian period which follows have been excavated, but unfortunately the detailed measurements of the crania have not been published. So far as can be judged, however, from the data as given,[1] these Teutonic invaders were of tall stature, and a mixture primarily of Mediterranean and Caspian types. The Burgundians and perhaps the Goths may have had a considerable Alpine factor.

During the Carlovingian period, which lasted until the tenth century, the dolichocephalic element in Normandy was probably somewhat further increased by the Scandinavian raids and settlements. The net result of these several centuries of immigration was to bring, thus, a considerable "Nordic" factor into most of northern France, while the south was relatively little affected. That the Huns in the fifth century or the Saracens in the eighth left any lasting mark is very doubtful. More may be said, probably, for the Celtic-speaking Bretons, who, fleeing from the Saxons in southern Britain, crossed the Channel to Brittany, where their descendants still live.

During the period of approximately a thousand years extending from the Carlovingian period to the present day, we are able to sample the population of France only very imperfectly,

---

[1] Hamy, 1893; Hovelacque, 1876; Verneau, 1898.

since the data on the crania have been published only as averages.   Hovelacque and Hervé[1] have, however, given us excellent material for the region of the Morvan (in the northeast corner of the Massif Central) in a series of crania dating from the
seventeenth to the nineteenth centuries.   Analysis shows that
the population of this district had by this time become overwhelmingly brachycephalic, the dolichocephalic factors present
in the Haut Morvan amounting to only about 10 per cent.   The
types present are primarily the Palæ-Alpine and Alpine, with a
minority of the Ural type.   From Dauphiny[2] a smaller series of
crania shows an equal dominance of brachycephalic factors, with
here a minority of the Mongoloid type.

If we turn to Provence, whence we have a small series of
crania dating from the thirteenth to the nineteenth centuries,
we find in general the same conditions, yet here, owing to the
fact that the sex of the skulls has been given (the Morvan series
being unsexed) analysis shows a further significant fact.   For
while both sexes show a very strong predominance of brachycephalic forms, the males are mainly Alpine, while the females
are as strongly Palæ-Alpine; indicating, apparently, that the latter represent the older Neolithic brachycephals, while the males
are to be affiliated more with the later Celtic stream.

The complete dominance of brachycephalic types found east
of the Rhone did not extend to Languedoc on the west, for here
Lapouge[3] has shown that in the crania of the seventeenth to the
eighteenth century from Montpelier, dolichocephalic forms are
present in considerable numbers.   A difference, moreover, is
apparent between the peasantry and the nobility, for while the
former were predominantly brachycephalic, the latter were even
more strongly dolichocephalic, the Mediterranean type seeming
to be that most strongly represented.

For the rest of France no detailed analysis is possible.   All
that can be said is that in Auvergne and Brittany the brachycephalic factors are in the great majority, although the Bas Bretons show something of a dolichocephalic minority.   How far

---

[1] Hovelacque, 1894.            [2] Prudent, 1892.            [3] Lapouge, 1891.

this may be regarded as due to the survival here of a remnant of the ancient dolichocephalic peoples, or how far it is the result of "Nordic" colonists, it is with our present data impossible to say.

We have now traced in some, perhaps in too great, detail, the racial history of France (in so far as that is evidenced by our "types") from Palæolithic times down to modern days, as revealed by the skeletal material. There remains to consider the living population, the product of the many complex blendings of these many thousand years.

The head-form of the living French people has been studied chiefly by Collignon. It is clear from the map (Plate I), based upon his data and showing the average cephalic index for each department, that the present population is very largely brachycephalic, no department yielding an average which can properly be called dolichocephalic. The distribution of the higher indices, marking probably an almost purely brachycephalic population, is significant. It will be seen that the departments having an average index of 83 or over are distributed in a wedge-shaped area cutting from northeast to southwest across the country below its centre. The broad base of the wedge covers practically the whole eastern frontier, and is continuous with the great region of prevalent brachycephaly which covers all of central Europe. From this base, the wedge runs westward through the southern half of the Massif Central, and approaches the Atlantic north of the Pyrenees. It will also be noted that from the centre of the northern side of the wedge an irregular arm extends northwest into Brittany. The wedge itself and this arm serve to define three areas characterized by mesocephaly, and, therefore, with a larger dolichocephalic element, *i. e.*, the Paris basin, the basin of Aquitaine, and the Mediterranean shore.

The first and probably the second of these areas owe their greater proportion of long-headed elements to the Teutonic immigrations, except that the sharply defined region of low indices in Dordogne and Haute Vienne may be regarded as including the last remnants of the Neolithic and late Palæolithic types. The Mediterranean littoral also probably owes its dolichocephalic factors in the main to the Neolithic Mediterranean type, with possibly some survivals of still older Proto-Negroid and Proto-Australoid types.

The distribution of stature corresponds in general with what might be expected from the probable distribution of the several types. The Palæ-Alpine and Alpine types which are dominant over so large a portion of France are in general short, as is also the Mediterranean. Only in the northeast, in the Paris basin, where the "Nordic" influence was strongest, do we find taller statures. The only exception to this is in Burgundy, Savoy, and Dauphiny, where it may perhaps be attributed to the Burgundian influence, as these people were notably tall. The shortest statures are found in two separate areas, (1) the departments of Corrèze, Haute Vienne, and Dordogne, and (2) the northwestern tip of Brittany. Since there is reason to believe that in these two regions the old Palæolithic, short-statured population survives in greatest strength, the decrease in stature may reasonably be attributed to this influence.

The distribution of pigmentation also follows in general that of the several types. Speaking broadly, the blond factor is strongest in the northeast, the brunet in the southwest and south. The Mediterranean, as well as the Palæ-Alpine and Alpine types, are characteristically brunet, while the "Nordic" blend of Caspian, Mediterranean, and Proto-Negroid is primarily blond, as is perhaps (?) the Ural type.

The major features of the living population of France thus find their legitimate explanation in the history whose course we have here followed from early prehistoric times. In brief, that history shows an original people primarily of Proto-Australoid type, which gave place in Neolithic times to one still dolichocephalic, but mainly Mediterranean. This was then slowly but surely replaced and largely superseded by an influx of Palæ-Alpine and Alpine types from central Europe. After the metamorphosis was practically complete, a new wave of long-headed

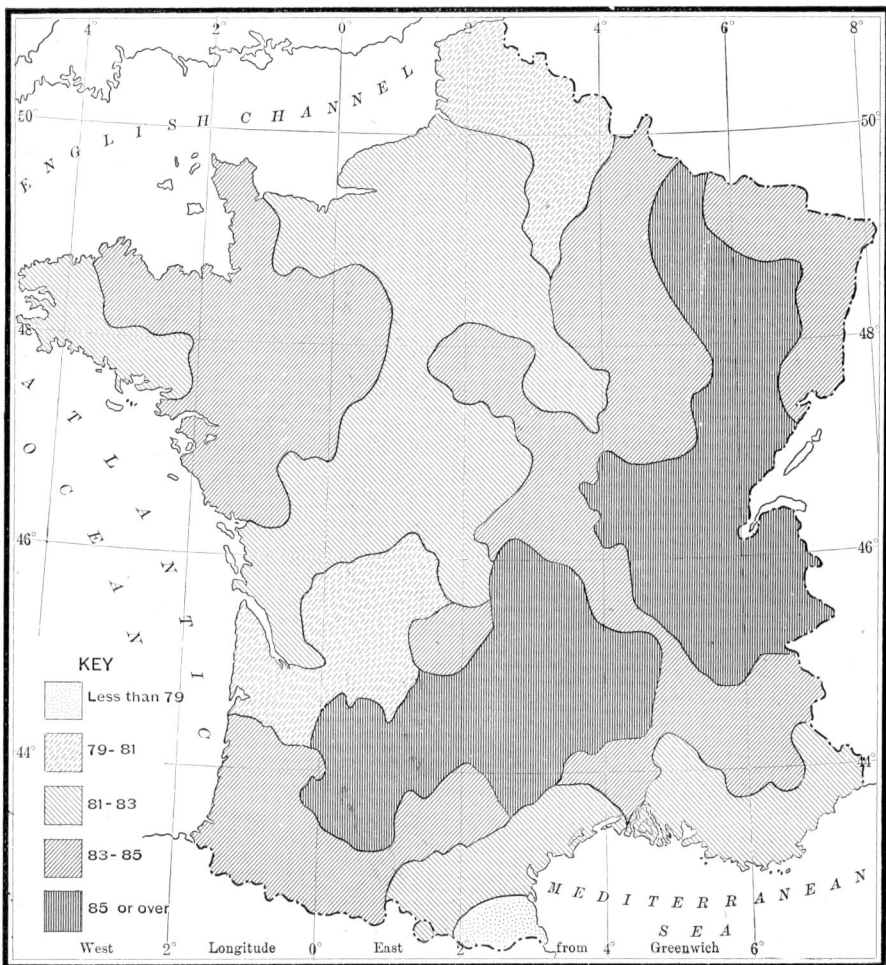

PLATE I.  FRANCE.
Distribution of the Cephalic Index (after Collignon).

folk, the blond Baltic, Teutonic-speaking tribes poured over the north and northeast of France at the same time that it swept victoriously over parts of the British Isles. In Britain this led to a far-reaching change of language, and profoundly influenced the physical type; in southern Germany and Austria the Teutonic invasions led also to a change in speech, but produced no lasting effect on the physical character of the people; in France the invading Franks lost their own language, although they gave their name to the country; and although they and their kindred tribes had a more lasting effect upon the racial character of the conquered people than was the case in Germany or Austria, yet France to-day, in spite of them, forms essentially a western extension of the great central European domain of the Alpine and Palæ-Alpine peoples. In Plate II, Fig. 1, we have an example of the dominant Alpine type as it appears in France to-day.

## II. The Low Countries

The region comprised within the limits of the present countries of Belgium and Holland is divisible geographically into two quite different areas. The northern portion, including all of Holland and northern Belgium, forms part of the belt of low coastal plains which fringe the shores of the North Sea and the Baltic. The southern half of Belgium, on the other hand, is part of the plateau of the Ardennes, which may be regarded as a northwestern extension of the Central European Highlands. This topographic contrast is paralleled by a linguistic difference no less clear, in that throughout the northern lowlands the languages spoken, Frisian, Dutch, and Flemish, belong to the Teutonic group, whereas the Walloon of the southern upland is closely allied to French.

In seeking to discover the character of the earliest population of the Low Countries, we are confined to the southern plateau, for only here have remains of Palæolithic and Neolithic man as yet been found. The crania of Spy and Engis in the valley of the Meuse show that in Mousterian times the occupants of this region were a short-statured, dolichocephalic people, in whom the Proto-Australoid and Proto-Negroid types were blended, although the mesocephalic character of Spy No. 2 indicates that some admixture with a brachycephalic type, apparently the Mongoloid, had already occurred. To all intents and purposes, thus, the population here was similar to that in central France at this same time.

The Neolithic data[1] are more abundant, but again come almost wholly from the same valley of the Meuse. In place of the preponderant dolichocephalic factors of Palæolithic times, we find a large majority of brachycephalic elements, the Mongoloid and Ural types being most important. The Ardennes plateau thus presents a striking contrast with the adjacent regions of France and the British Isles, where the Neolithic population was predominantly of Mediterranean type, and such brachycephalic factors as were present were in the main Palæ-Alpine. The explanation of this difference is not yet clear, but the presence of a very large factor of the Mongoloid type among the female crania found at Ofnet in Bavaria, and dating from the very close of the Palæolithic period, suggests that this element at least may have come by way of the northern border of the Central European Highlands in late Palæolithic times.

What changes occurred in the population of this whole region in the millennia between the Neolithic period and the era of the great tribal migrations of the sixth century and after, we can only surmise, since satisfactory material is almost wholly lacking. Judging from the history of the adjacent region, however, we must infer a large influx of Palæ-Alpines and Alpines, and that the upland at least, and probably much of the lowland, except possibly the northern coast, remained for most of the period almost exclusively brachycephalic. By the sixth or seventh century A. D., however, when the movement of the Baltic peoples was well under way, we find the Frankish crania[2] from southern Belgium indicating a people prevailingly dolichocephalic and characterized by that blend of Caspian and Mediterranean types

[1] Fraipont, 1897; Houzé, 1904b.          [2] Houzé, 1891 and 1904a.

which is commonly called "Nordic." It is at this period that we get our first data from Holland. A considerable series of crania of this period have been found in Friesland and Groeningen, the males of which are quite comparable with the Frankish crania of Belgium, except that in addition to the Mediterranean and Caspian factors there is here present quite a noticeable element of the Proto-Australoid, whose presence in the Baltic region in Neolithic times we shall have occasion to note later. The female crania, on the other hand, show a considerable Palæ-Alpine and Alpine factor. It is tempting to regard this as evidence that the presumed dominance of these types in the Belgian uplands, at least in Bronze and early Iron times, had extended north over all of Holland, as witness their extension to Denmark. The Friesland data, then, of the sixth and eighth centuries would indicate an intrusion from the eastward of conquering Teutonic tribes allied to the Franks, Anglo-Saxons, and others. This conclusion is strengthened by the even more complete submergence of the earlier brachycephalic population of Denmark by the Teutonic "Nordics" in the Iron Age, which would but little antedate the period of the Friesland crania.

These considerations are perhaps further substantiated by the scanty mediæval data which we possess. Crania dating from the period between the fourteenth and sixteenth centuries from the islands in the Zuyder Zee, Amsterdam, and the islands of Beveland and Walcheren in the Scheldt-Rhine delta, show a very large majority of Alpine and Ural types, as though the older brachycephalic population had survived in relative purity in the more isolated portion of the country, where the influence of the Teutonic invasions had not made itself felt.

The characteristics of the modern population[1] of the Low Countries seem admirably to bear out the preceding hypothesis. In the Ardennes plateau of southern Belgium the people are to-day just under medium stature, predominantly brachycephalic and brunet. The same type, but with greatly exaggerated brachycephaly, occupies the coastal provinces of Zeeland

[1] Barge, 1914; Bolk, 1908.

and Zuid and Noord Holland.  On the other hand, the plains of
Flanders and all the rest of Holland present a taller people, in
creasing in stature northward to Friesland; in head-form mesocephalic, with a rising proportion of true dolichocephalic individuals as one goes northward; and a general blondness, which becomes more pronounced as one progresses in the same direction.
That even in Friesland, however, a considerable brachycephalic
element still exists is shown by a series of nineteenth century
crania, in which these factors are actually in the majority, the
Ural type being present in large amount, as it is on the neighboring coasts of Scotland and southern Norway.  This type was
already noticeable in the Ardennes plateau, it will be remembered, as early as Neolithic times, and its long persistence in
this region is a striking fact.

A further contrast between the northern and southern portions of the Low Countries may be pointed out.  In the south,
in the Ardennes plateau, the Teutonic invaders of the sixth and
seventh centuries, although producing a powerful temporary influence on the physical types, had little lasting effect, and the
population to-day has seemingly reverted to the dominantly
brachycephalic types which characterized it before the Frankish
invasions, and the influence of these on the speech of the people
was as ephemeral as on their physical type.  In the open lowlands, however, the result of the Teutonic surge has been different.  There a considerable modification in physical type has
occurred, and throughout the area a Teutonic language now
prevails.

# CHAPTER II

## THE BRITISH ISLES AND SCANDINAVIA

### I. THE BRITISH ISLES

FOR the clearer understanding of the racial history of the British Isles a brief consideration of their topographical features is helpful. The factor of greatest importance lies in the contrast afforded by the eastern and western sides of the islands. The eastern, central, and southeastern portions of England may be described as a gently rolling plain, whereas the western coast and the larger portion of Scotland are more or less rugged. Although the contrast is less marked in Ireland, we may recognize a difference between the central section and the more rugged region to the north, west, and south. The richer and more desirable lands thus lie nearest the European continent, and immigrant peoples would, in occupying these first, drive the earlier occupants westward and northward into the rougher areas. Although in historic times separated from the mainland by the Channel, England was perhaps as late as the beginning of Neolithic times, still joined to France and the Netherlands by a broad belt of lowland, since sunk below the sea.

Linguistically the British Isles are divisible into two very unequal parts. The great majority of the population is English-speaking, but remnants of the formerly much more widely spread Celtic languages still survive in parts of the Scottish Highlands, Wales, and western Ireland, *i. e.*, in the more rugged western marginal region just referred to.

The Piltdown skull found in Sussex gives us our earliest indications in regard to the population of the British Isles. It dates from the earliest portion of the Palæolithic period, and although too incomplete to enable us to place it in our series with absolute certainty, it seems probable that with its high, mesocephalic cranial index, low vault, and almost certainly broad nose, it represents, as does the Gibraltar skull, a blend of the Proto-Australoid and Mongoloid types.

A number of crania, probably of late Palæolithic age, have also been found in England, but are in general less well preserved than those in France, so that definite determination of types is not possible. Of the eight crania, however, which have some claim to be regarded as late Palæolithic, five are clearly dolichocephalic, two are mesocephalic, and one is possibly brachycephalic. As to the other characteristics, we can tell little, and can only surmise, on the basis of contemporary data from France, that the Proto-Australoid type was probably most strongly represented. In stature all these Palæolithic people appear to have been short.

With the advent of Neolithic times our data greatly improve. The people of this period are associated with the megalithic remains and also with the burial mounds, known from their shape as the Long Barrows. The larger part of our data are derived from these latter sites, which are abundant in west central England and in Yorkshire, but we have in addition the so-called "river-bed" crania, found chiefly in the Thames valley. Like their predecessors, the Long Barrow people were primarily dolichocephalic, but were in the main of the Mediterranean type.[1] The Proto-Australoid type, however, which the newcomers supplanted, still played a considerable part, and a third dolichocephalic factor, the Caspian, also appears as a minority, just as it does even earlier on the continent. Roughly, a third of the elements which went to make up the Long Barrow population, however, belonged to the brachycephalic, Palæ-Alpine type. The river-bed crania are, in general, imperfect, but so far as can be determined, are substantially similar to the Long Barrow remains.

For Scotland the scanty data suggest a population primarily of Mediterranean type, especially along the western coast; for Ireland the few Neolithic crania known indicate the prevalence

[1] Schuster, 1905–06.

of this same type, but blended with a brachycephalic factor, which is here the Alpine, and not the Palæ-Alpine, as in England. The former is practically absent from England at this time, and its presence in Ireland suggests the possibility that it came by sea.

The routes by which the Neolithic immigrants reached and spread over the British Isles are as yet not certain. Land connection with the continent perhaps persisted until the middle of the period, and would have afforded direct communication, but it seems probable, as Fleure and James have shown,[1] that the larger part of the Mediterranean peoples came from Brittany across by sea to the southern coast, in the vicinity of the Isle of Wight, and thence spread along the coasts, and across the Irish Sea. With them doubtless came some elements of the Palæ-Alpine type, already numerous in France, although there is reason to believe that some of these latter came very early, entering England from the northeast by land, before the connection with the continent was severed. By this route, also, it seems certain that the Caspian factor reached the British Isles, since at this time it was penetrating from the north into France.

The end of the Neolithic period marks the beginning of a further change. Hitherto the brachycephalic peoples had been a minor although important element in the make-up of the population; during the succeeding, or Bronze period, they played, as in the rest of Europe, a larger part. As the Long Barrows supplied most of the data for the Neolithic period, so the Round Barrows yield the bulk of the material for the succeeding age. While the Long Barrows were mainly confined to the west central parts of England, the Round Barrows are more widely distributed. The new immigrants who poured into Britain seem to have come at first without the knowledge of bronze, but bringing new types of pottery. The use of bronze, however, soon became known, and the possession of weapons of metal must have given the newcomers a signal advantage over the earlier population, who had only stone implements. They may

[1] Fleure, 1916.

well have established themselves as a conquering and ruling class, and largely relegated such of the older occupants whom they did not drive out, to the position of slaves or serfs.

The skeletal remains from the mounds and cists of this period[1] reveal a people of tall stature and prevailingly brachycephalic, the Alpine type being largely in the predominance. The older Palæ-Alpines are, however, not wanting, and in the north, indeed, in Yorkshire and Aberdeen, actually outnumber the Alpines. A third brachycephalic type also makes its appearance, the Ural, present in Belgium already in Neolithic times and characteristic of southern Norway and of Friesland at a later date.

The wave of Alpine and Ural types which thus spread over England and eastern and northern Scotland seems to have reached Ireland only in minor degree; at least, little evidence of brachycephalic crania of this period has been reported. Yet it seems doubtful if the large brachycephalic element apparent in the modern population can be wholly accounted for by later immigration. After half a century at least of discussion, the Celtic question cannot yet be said to be finally settled, but it would seem that we may with reasonable certainty aver that it was with the immigrants who came in the Bronze period, from the Netherlands, Belgium, and France, that Celtic speech was brought to the British Isles. Yet, although probably the majority of the Bronze Age immigrants came thus from the nearer shores of the continent, it is almost certain that in the earlier part of the period considerable invasions came from the Scandinavian and Baltic regions to northern and eastern Scotland, and perhaps to northern Ireland as well.

We have little or no material from the period of three or four centuries intervening between the end of the Bronze period and the beginning of Roman rule. To what extent the Roman occupation had any lasting influence on the British population it is hard to say. Neither the Romans themselves nor any of the peoples who might have been among their legions would have

[1] Schuster, 1905–06.

brought any new factors to the complex, and whatever influence they might have had would have been to intensify the Alpine factors present. The period of Roman occupation, then, is not to be considered as one during which any notable changes took place, but rather as one in which the existing more or less discrete elements underwent a partial fusion and assimilation.

The fall of the Roman power, however, ushered in a new era, which was to continue, with some interruptions, for nearly a thousand years. Already, during the period of Roman rule, sea raiders from Denmark and northwestern Germany began to harry the Scotch and English coasts, but it was not until the power of Rome had been weakened and well-nigh destroyed in Britain, that the new invaders came in force. From the fifth century onward for some time, a stream of Anglo-Saxon conquerors and colonists poured into the south and east of Britain, and spread over the land except in the extreme north and west. The crania from the Saxon graves[1] of the south of England and of the Angles[2] from further to the northeast show that these immigrants were, like the invaders of Neolithic times, primarily dolichocephalic. They resembled these early predecessors in having a large factor of the Mediterranean type, but differed in that a considerable Caspian element was also present. They were, moreover, of tall stature, and had fair hair and light-colored eyes, whereas the Neolithic immigrants were under medium stature and almost certainly brunet.

A comparison of the materials available for the West Saxons, the South Saxons, and the Angles reveals some interesting differences. The South Saxons appear to be the more purely dolichocephalic of the three, and show the largest element of Mediterranean type. The Angles, although but little behind the South Saxons in the strength of their dolichocephaly, have an unexpectedly large element of the Proto-Australoid type, which does not appear at all in the other group. It seems possible, however, to account for this element by the fact that it was prominent in Mecklenburg in Neolithic times, so that its pres-

[1] Horton-Smith, 1896–97; Peake, 1915.          [2] Horton-Smith, *op. cit.*

ence in the Angles, who are supposed to have come from the adjacent Baltic shore of Schleswig, would be quite natural. The West Saxons present quite a different picture. They formed, as it were, the point of the wedge which the newcomers were driving into the older population, and might thus be expected to show, more clearly than the others, the effects of intermixture with the ancient British population. This seems to be the case, for among the West Saxons the dolichocephalic factors presumed to be characteristic of the immigrants are actually in the minority, whereas Palæ-Alpine and Alpine elements come to the fore. These brachycephalic factors might, to be sure, have been brought by the West Saxons from the continent, since both types were common in Denmark at least, yet, all things considered, the former suggestion seems more probable.

While England was thus receiving large increments of population from northwest Germany and southern Denmark, northern and western Scotland was being raided and to some extent colonized by Norwegians and Danes. That these were by no means all of dolichocephalic types is shown conclusively by the crania from the Shetland and Orkney Islands, which show a large Alpine element. For Ireland during this period we have but scanty data, and the crania from the Round Towers in Ulster[1] only enable us to say that the population was very much mixed. We know, indeed, that this northern part of Ireland received, as did Scotland, a considerable number of Scandinavian immigrants, and we must assume that here, as there, this meant a substantial increase in Alpine and probably Ural types. The differentiation between the people of northern and southern Ireland was thus already beginning.

The next glimpse we are able to secure of the racial melting-pot in the British Isles is afforded by the several series of crania which have been secured from old crypts or "charnels" of the fourteenth and seventeenth centuries. Series of this sort have been obtained from Hythe (Kent),[2] London,[3] Rothwell (North-

[1] Grattan, 1858.  [2] Parsons, 1908.
[3] Macdowell, 1903 and 1906-07.

amptonshire)[1], and from Micheldean and Gloucester (Gloucestershire).[2] Unfortunately only the London series have been
published as yet in full. The Kentish crania show an interesting but rather puzzling state of affairs. The seat during the
Anglo-Saxon period of important Jutish settlements, one might
expect to find the influence of these people, allied to the Angles
and Saxons, shown in a strengthening of the dolichocephalic elements in the population. Instead, the exact opposite occurs,
the Hythe crania being in large majority brachycephalic. Several explanations suggest themselves for this phenomenon. We
may assume that the Jutes brought with them a large factor of
the Alpine type, prominent in Denmark in Bronze times; or
we may believe that the Jutish settlers were originally dolichocephalic, like the Saxons, but that they ultimately became absorbed, and that there was a resurgence of the earlier Bronze
Age types, in the manner so strikingly suggested by Fleure and
James[3] for the modern population of the southern Midlands.
Possibly a simpler explanation may lie in the influence exerted
by Walloon colonies of later years, similar to the Flemish ones
to be mentioned in connection with the Bristol crania.

The two London series (Whitechapel and Bishopsgate) afford
our best material. They represent in all probability the lower
classes of the people of London in the seventeenth century, and
show them to have been predominantly dolichocephalic, with the
Mediterranean type present in large majority, and a considerable element also of the old Proto-Australoid factor. The female
crania show a surprisingly large element of the Mongoloid type,
but otherwise agree closely with the male series. The influence
of the Bronze Age immigration of brachycephalic peoples seems
to have left little effect on the later population of this area, and
since the Anglo-Saxon conquest is supposed to have had but
slight consequences in London, it would seem that the dominance of the Mediterranean type could best be explained as due
to the survival of the old Neolithic British type.

[1] Parsons, 1910.                [2] Beddoe, 1878–79 and 1881 a and b.
[3] Fleure, 1916.

The Rothwell crania from Northamptonshire tell a somewhat similar story. Like the London series they show a preponderance of dolichocephalic factors, but, since no nasal measurements have been published, we can only assume that these
prevailingly low skulls are in the main of Mediterranean type.
The two small series from farther west in Gloucestershire present, however, an interesting contrast. That from Micheldean
is even more preponderantly dolichocephalic than the London
and Rothwell series, but the Bristol[1] crania approximate the
Kentish crania in being prevailingly brachycephalic. Two explanations for this brachycephalic element may be suggested. It
is possible that we have here the influence of the Bronze Age
Alpine peoples, who were forced out of the more southern and
eastern districts by the Anglo-Saxon conquerors and settlers, or
that the brachycephalic factors were brought in much later by
Flemish immigrants.

The data on the living population of the British Isles are less
complete than for many other parts of Europe. For stature and
pigmentation they are fairly adequate, but head-form and other
metrical data are sadly deficient. For the larger portion of the
British Isles we have nothing but county averages, based on
small numbers of individuals. These would indicate the head-
form to be rather uniform, the average indices ranging from 76
in the Scotch Highlands to over 80 in western Ireland. Although the county averages are thus everywhere within the
limits of mesocephaly, the recent splendid work of Fleure and
James[2] and Fleming[3] in Wales shows that this appearance of
uniformity is wholly misleading. They have demonstrated that
there is, in fact, a wide variation locally, and have been able to
show that several quite distinct types may be recognized, distributed with reference to geographic features, and attributable
with the help of archæological evidence to several distinct strata
of population. Some are attributable to the Anglo-Saxon and
Scandinavian immigrants, some to earlier Bronze Age peoples,
others represent clearly the Neolithic Mediterranean type, and

---

[1] Beddoe, 1878–79.          [2] Fleure, 1916.          [3] Fleming, 1922.

they even suggest small survivals in extremely isolated regions of the Palæolithic Proto-Australoid and Proto-Negroid factors. Their work has demonstrated the absolute necessity of the study of individual types rather than the use of averages, and shown the real complexity of the population and the persistence of ancient strata. Only when similar methods are applied on a large scale to living populations, not only in the whole of Europe but everywhere, can we hope to unravel the story of the racial history of the world's peoples.

That similar striking variations exist in other parts of the British Isles is shown by Turner's data on modern Scottish crania.[1] His material makes it clear that whereas in Fifeshire, on the eastern coast, brachycephalic forms are in the preponderance, with the Ural type very strongly represented, on the west coast, in Renfrew and Argyle, dolichocephalic factors are overwhelmingly dominant, the Neolithic Mediterranean type being in large majority.

In regard to stature, the general averages show the population of the British Isles to be notably tall, the Scotch having the highest average (174 cm.), followed by the Irish, with 172 cm. and the English, with 171 cm., while the Welsh are the shortest of all, 169 cm. The shortest statures are found on both sides of the Bristol Channel and in a strip running from Sussex through Middlesex to Hertfordshire. The tallest are in southwestern Scotland. In Ireland the west and north are taller than the rest of the country.

In pigmentation[2] the distribution is such that the extreme north of Scotland (including the Hebrides, Orkneys, and Shetlands) and its east coast, together with the eastern and southern coast of England as far west as Dorsetshire, show the largest proportion of blond types. The brunet population is concentrated, on the other hand, on the west coast, attaining its greatest frequency in Argyle, Wales, and Cornwall. Parallel conditions in general exist in Ireland, where Leinster and the adjacent parts of Munster have the lightest, the west coast the darkest population.

[1] Turner, 1903.     [2] Beddoe, 1908; Gray, 1907; Tocher, 1908-09.

Correlating the data as far as possible, it may be said that we can recognize in Great Britain to-day the following types: First, a dolichocephalic, brunet type (Plate II, Fig. 2), with a stature which, while absolutely above the medium, is yet relatively the shortest in the region. This Mediterranean type is present in greatest abundance, probably, in Wales, Cornwall, and Devonshire, where Celtic speech has lingered longest, and may be regarded as representing the old Neolithic population, to whom the Alpine, Celtic-speaking immigrants of the Bronze Age gave their speech, and who have, under the pressure of succeeding waves of invaders, retreated westward to their present seats. It is probable that other bodies of the same type will be found in the economically less favored portions of England, especially in the uplands of the south. There is some evidence in favor of this type being everywhere strongly represented among the laboring classes, and it is probably still, as in the seventeenth century, dominant in the poorer urban population.

Modified by the possession of a taller stature and a larger proportion of gray and blue eyes, as a result of mixture with tall, blond Scandinavian and Teutonic immigrants, we find these descendants of the Neolithic British peoples spread widely along the west coast of Scotland, and throughout much of Ireland, especially in its western and southern parts.

The second main type to-day is mesocephalic or frankly brachycephalic, generally of tall stature and blond or light brunet in coloring. In its distribution this type seems to be more scattered, although it may be expected that a detailed investigation would show considerable areas occupied by them in the central parts of England, and probably also along the eastern coasts of both England and Scotland. They represent, it is believed, the brachycephalic Bronze Age immigrants, mainly Alpine in type, but with a considerable Ural factor. As a type it is said to be particularly common among the squires and landed gentry. In Ireland, this type is probably most in evidence in the centre and south.

Here and there, perhaps in the Old Black Breed of the Shet-

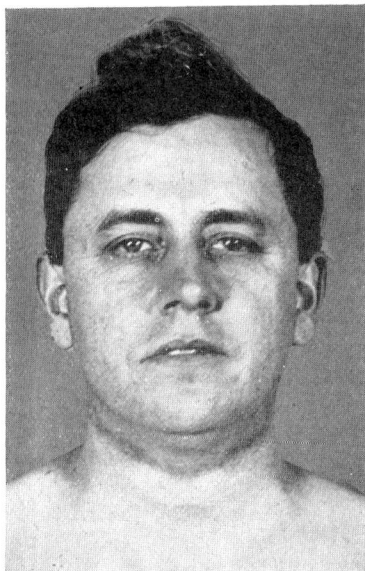

FIG. 1. FRENCH.　　　　　　　FIG. 2. ENGLISH.

FIG. 3. NORWEGIAN.　　　　FIG. 4. NORWEGIAN. (JAEDEREN.)

PLATE II.

lands, the Orkneys, and the north of Scotland, in parts of Wales and probably in some other isolated spots, there are traces of a brachycephalic, brunet type of shorter stature, that seems to represent the last survivors of the Neolithic Palæ-Alpines.

Lastly, we may recognize a tall, blond, dolichocephalic type representing the Teutonic and Scandinavian immigrants of post-Roman times. Like its relative in the Baltic lands it is an ancient blend of Mediterranean, Caspian, and Proto-Negroid types, and is most characteristic of the eastern and southern parts of England and the eastern coast of Scotland. In Ireland its influence may be seen in Ulster.

That occasionally, in remote districts, traces of the Palæolithic Proto-Australoids and Proto-Negroids may still be recognized, seems to be shown by the work of Fleure and James, but we cannot expect that these ancient types should appear except as sporadic and very rare cases.

In one respect the British Isles are in striking contrast to the neighboring portions of the European continent. They have largely escaped the general brachycephalization to which the larger part of the mainland has been subjected. The considerable influx of Palæ-Alpine and Alpine types which came into the islands in Neolithic and later times, seems to have been in large part absorbed, and further increments of brachycephalic peoples on a large scale have not occurred. Yet there is some indication that in recent times the increase of brachycephalic types which has been so striking in the rest of Europe has also occurred in Britain. Measurements of recruits for the army appear to show that the average cephalic index has been rising in recent years. Whether this is to be ascribed to an influx of central European immigrants, or to a resurgence of old brachycephalic elements in the population, or to some other cause, is not yet clear.

## II. Scandinavia: Denmark, Sweden, and Norway

Geographically the Scandinavian area falls into two well-contrasted portions, a low plains region, comprising Denmark and the southern and eastern parts of Sweden, and a rugged mountainous section, including practically the whole of Norway, together with parts of western Sweden. The first of these portions is virtually a part of the north German and Russian plains. Except in the northern part of the Scandinavian peninsula, the modern inhabitants of this region speak closely related languages, belonging to the Scandinavian branch of the Teutonic group. In the north the Lapp and Finnish population speak languages totally unlike the Scandinavian, and belonging to the Finno-Ugrian branch of the Ural-Altaic stock.

There is reason to believe that no part of this whole area was occupied by man in the Palæolithic period, and that the earliest settlement occurred at the very end of the Palæolithic and the beginning of Neolithic times. Although objects of Neolithic age have been found fairly widely distributed in Denmark and Sweden, practically all the crania of this period thus far described are derived from the Danish islands of Seeland and Funen,[1] and the adjacent portions of southern Sweden.[2] The Danish and Swedish series present a curious contrast, and both come from megalithic graves. The former, although showing a slight majority of dolichocephalic factors, has as its most important single element the Palæ-Alpine type, with the Caspian type next in order of frequency. The Swedish crania, on the other hand, are in large majority dolichocephalic, and show three nearly balanced factors of Caspian, Alpine, and Mediterranean types. To put the matter in a slightly different form, the Danish and Swedish Neolithic crania differ mainly in the presence in the former of a large Palæ-Alpine element, and in the latter of a considerable Mediterranean factor. If now these two series be compared with the crania from Mecklenburg in northern Germany of the same period, it appears that this series is even more strongly dolicho-

[1] Nielsen, 1906, 1911.　　　　　　　[2] Furst, 1912; Retzius, G., 1900.

cephalic than that from Sweden, and differs, moreover, from both the Danish and Swedish series in being composed primarily of Proto-Australoid and Proto-Negroid factors.

Three groups of Neolithic crania thus, from an area within a radius of only about one hundred miles, show widely different characteristics. The strong Palæ-Alpine element in Denmark may be pretty confidently regarded as due to the current of peoples of this type which, from western Switzerland, passed into France, Belgium, and the British Isles during this period, and which probably followed the North Sea coasts as far as Denmark, but for some reason failed to pass in any considerable numbers into Sweden. The presence of large factors of Mediterranean and Alpine types in Sweden, and their relative absence from the Danish Islands, offers an interesting puzzle. Both the Alpine and Mediterranean types are much stronger in the Westergotland district than in Skåne farther south, where the Palæ-Alpine and Caspian types are more in evidence, as in the adjacent Danish islands. This suggests that the Alpine and Mediterranean factors in Sweden may have been derived from a sea-borne stream of immigrants, coming across the North Sea from the British Isles. The absence in the Danish islands and southern Sweden of the Proto-Negroid and Proto-Australoid types so strongly represented in Mecklenburg is hard to explain, unless we accept the latter as a peculiar and isolated small group, not really indicating the true character of the Neolithic population of the southern shore of the Baltic at this time.

As in so much of Europe, there is little material to tell us of the physical characteristics of the population during the Bronze Age. All that can be said is that scanty data from Denmark seem to indicate an increase of the Alpine type. For the Iron Age our information is much more abundant, and in comparison with the Neolithic period the changes are significant. In Denmark[1] the strong Palæ-Alpine element has nearly disappeared, and there has been a large increase in the proportions of Caspian and Mediterranean types, with the result that the population in

[1] Nielsen, 1906.

the Iron Age is, in contrast to that of Neolithic times, primarily dolichocephalic. This would seem to argue a westward and northward drift of the "Nordic" peoples of the North German Plain.

In eastern Sweden[1] (Gottland) the former strong factors of Mediterranean and Alpine types have largely decreased, and been replaced by Proto-Negroid and Proto-Australoid elements, which previously had had but slight representation in Sweden. These factors, however, are precisely those whose presence in Mecklenburg in Neolithic times was so striking and peculiar, and it is tempting to see in these facts the evidence of the expulsion of the peoples of the Mecklenburg region by the westward advance of the "Nordic" tribes, and the settlement of the refugees in Sweden. The very meagre data for eastern Norway, which are the earliest we have as yet for this country, indicate that these same Proto-Australoid and Proto-Negroid elements were also in the majority there.

For the period from the Iron Age until late mediæval times, we have no data for either Denmark or Sweden, and this period, which included the great outpourings of Baltic peoples southward into central, western, and southern Europe, is in its anthropological history a blank. For Norway, however, we possess material of much interest. There is much evidence to lead to the conclusion that Norway only received its first population in late Neolithic times, the earliest settlers being Scandinavian-speaking tribes coming in from Sweden, and also northward from Jutland in Denmark. Traditional and linguistic evidence, however, suggests that the Norwegian area, as well perhaps as northern Sweden, had a slightly earlier rude hunting population of Finno-Ugrian speech, allied to the modern Lapp and Finn. These aboriginal peoples were, it is believed, in part enslaved and in part driven back into the mountains and to the northward by the Scandinavian immigrants. As yet, however, we possess no early crania which would enable us to determine the truth of this hypothesis, although certain features of the Norwegian population of to-day seem to corroborate it.

[1] Retzius, G., 1900.

Four series of mediæval crania are available from Norway: one each from Oslo and Tönsberg near Christiania, one from the Jaederen district of the extreme southwest, and one from Trondhjem on the middle western coast. The Oslo crania,[1] from the coast of the Christiania Fjord, are in large measure dolichocephalic, the Proto-Australoid, Mediterranean, and Caspian types being present in this order of importance. At Tönsberg,[2] somewhat farther inland, the dolichocephalic and brachycephalic factors are, on the other hand, almost evenly balanced; the Proto-Australoid type is still the most important single element, although the Mediterranean and Caspian types have practically disappeared. The brachycephalic factors are in the main Alpine, with considerable representation of the Palæ-Alpine and Mongoloid. The presence of this latter type is significant in connection with the hypothesis of a pre-Scandinavian, Lapp-like population, since the Lapp are primarily distinguished by the very large Mongoloid factor which they possess. Taken in connection with the Oslo crania, these from Tönsberg would seem to represent a mixture of the former people with a Lapp-like population in the interior.

The Trondhjem crania[3] are like those from Oslo in being dolichocephalic in very large majority, but the most important factor is here not the Proto-Australoid, but the Mediterranean. Of the brachycephalic elements, the Alpine and Mongoloid are of equal importance. This suggests again the presence of a certain amount of Lapp admixture, and the Trondhjem series, taken into consideration with all other data, would indicate that the population here was derived from the old Neolithic peoples of western Sweden, who had pressed through the Osterdal and Gudbrandsdal to the Atlantic coast. The Oslo and Tönsberg crania would then represent a later wave of peoples from Sweden, bringing the Proto-Australoid factors which were largely absent in the earlier immigrants.

The crania from the Jaederen[4] district are, most unfortunately,

[1] Barth, 1896.              [2] Barth, *op. cit.*
[3] Larsen, 1903.            [4] Larsen, 1901.

a selected series, and do not give a fair picture of the facts, since they were chosen to prove the presence here of a special brachycephalic type. They reveal the presence of the Alpine and Ural types, of which it is the latter which is really significant, for it is this factor which is so characteristic of the mediæval crania from Friesland, Bremen, and the North Sea coasts of Scotland, and which is absent or of very minor importance in other parts of the Scandinavian peninsula. It seems probable, therefore, that the localization of this Ural type on the southwest coast of Norway indicates that it came into Scandinavia from the southward, perhaps from Jutland.

For the living population of the Scandinavian region we possess relatively abundant material,[1] although only averages are given, so that determination of types is possible only in a very general way. We may recognize a large, centrally located area in which dolichocephalic factors reach their maximum. This includes the central and eastern parts of Norway and the adjacent central and western parts of Sweden. In Norway the dolichocephalic types are most strongly represented in the great valleys radiating from the vicinity of Christiania, while in Sweden they are to be found in the area west and northwest of Stockholm. In southern Sweden and especially in the district of Skåne, and also in the whole of the north, the long and round headed elements in the population are almost evenly balanced, and only in Lapland do the latter actually show a majority. The Jaederen and Stavanger districts of southwestern Norway show a majority of brachycephalic factors in contrast to the strongly dolichocephalic character of the population farther east, and these continue to be dominant northward along almost the whole of the western coast. The Lapps in the extreme north are almost purely brachycephalic.[2] For Denmark we have only partial and incomplete data, but these seem to indicate that the population as a whole is closely comparable to that in Skåne in south-

---

[1] Retzius, G., 1902; Hansen, 1907–11 a and b; Larsen, 1905; Arbo, for titles see Ripley, Bibliography.

[2] For discussion of the Lapps, see p. 133.

ern Sweden, *i. e.*, about evenly divided between round and long headed types.

The distribution of stature roughly parallels that of head-form in that a broad belt of very tall statures averaging 171–173 cm. extends in a general east-and-west direction through the heart of the area of maximum dolichocephaly. Although elsewhere in the Scandinavian peninsula the statures are shorter, the population is everywhere to be classed as tall, and the average falls below 170 cm. in Sweden only in Lapland in the north, and in Norway in the adjacent northern region and in the extreme southwest. In Denmark the stature averages in general lower than in Sweden, the shortest being found in the islands of Seeland and Lolland, while Jutland appears to have the tallest population.

Pigmentation finally shows again a striking agreement with both head-form and stature. Blondness, which is a feature always associated in our minds with Scandinavian countries, reaches its maximum frequency in the region extending from Lakes Vennern and Vettern in Sweden, northwest through eastern and central Norway, exactly the area in which the tallest statures and the greatest frequency of dolichocephalic types occur. In Sweden the brunet types become more frequent from this central area toward the north, east, and south, in a few cases rising to equal importance with the blonds. In Norway the south and particularly the west coast as far north as Trondhjem, show the largest proportion of brunets. North of Trondhjem, however, the brunet types are more common in the interior. Denmark shows in general a prevalence of blond types, which are more especially frequent in the south, brunet types being commonest in Jutland and in the islands nearest the Swedish coast.

In the absence of any study of modern crania, or of any individual measurements on the living, it is impossible to correlate these facts with the earlier material. We can only guess that the tall, blond, dolichocephalic group, the typical "Nordic" stratum, is here as in northern Germany, a blend primarily between the Mediterranean and the Caspian types. This form is illustrated on Plate II, Fig. 3. We may also surmise that the brachyce-phalic elements are derived from several different sources. In Skåne and the adjacent Danish islands it is probably in the main Alpine; in western Jutland and southwestern Norway to this Alpine factor is added a strong tinge of the Ural type; while here and there in the interior of Norway, and increasingly as one goes north in both Norway and Sweden, a third element, the Mongoloid, is added, which we may tentatively regard as derived from an aboriginal or very early Lapp-like population. An example of the mixed Alpine and Ural types from Jaede-ren is given on Plate II, Fig. 4.

# CHAPTER III

## THE CENTRAL EUROPEAN HIGHLANDS AND THE BALKAN PENINSULA

### I. THE CENTRAL EUROPEAN HIGHLANDS

THE Central European Highlands may be taken to include the mountainous area comprised within the limits of Switzerland, the Austrian districts of the Tyrol, Salzburg, Carinthia, and Styria, and in the west, Savoy and the mountainous parts of Dauphiny. The topography of this region presents one feature which has probably been of much significance in its racial history, *i. e.*, the deep penetration of the whole mountain area afforded by the valleys of the Rhine, the Inn, and the Drave. To any people approaching the Highland from the north or east these valleys are so many highways leading easily into its very heart, whence other valleys, such as those of the Adige and the Rhone lead freely to the south and west.

It is probable that throughout the whole of the Palæolithic period, the Central European Highlands were quite uninhabited. At least, no traces of occupation during this time have been found except along the northern and eastern margin. With the opening of the Neolithic period, however, we find clear evidence of men living along the northern borders, and beginning to penetrate into the interior along the great river valleys. Thus far most of the skeletal remains have been discovered in and about the shores of the lakes which lie between the Alps and the Jura. For beginning in this period and extending through the Bronze and into the Iron Ages this region was characterized by the peculiar and interesting culture of the Lake-Dwellers.

The crania upon which conclusions as to the racial type of this early population must be based, may be divided into two groups, those from graves and caves, and those from the Lake-

Dwelling sites.[1] The former are predominantly dolichocephalic, and if we consider the sexes separately it appears that the females exhibit this feature much more strongly than the males. It further seems to be true that the earlier sites show a larger proportion of dolichocephalic crania than the later. The Lake-Dweller crania, on the other hand, are predominantly brachycephalic with little difference between the sexes. If we compare those of the early with those of the later part of the Neolithic period, a striking contrast is, however, shown in that the earlier are characterized by a very large majority of brachycephalic types, whereas the later show almost as notable a predominance of dolichocephalic forms.

Analysis of the grave crania shows that the main factor present is the Mediterranean type, with the Proto-Australoid in second place, while the brachycephalic element of most importance is the Palæ-Alpine. The Lake-Dweller crania are much less perfectly preserved, but as far as can be determined, show the same three factors with the addition of a small minority of the Alpine type. In stature all of the types are below the medium.

These facts would seem to find their best explanation by the following hypothesis. The early Neolithic population in the region between the Jura and the Alps was primarily of the Mediterranean type, which at this same time was dominant in France and which had incorporated a minority of the older Palæolithic Proto-Australoids. Into this predominantly dolichocephalic population came as invaders a wave of brachycephalic Palæ-Alpine peoples from the east of Europe, moving either along the northern margin of the Highlands or coming through them by way of the valley highways. Being few in numbers at first, the newcomers sought to protect themselves from the attacks of the older residents by the device of building their villages on piles in the lakes. Here at first they preserved to some degree their independence, but in course of time amalgamated with the land-dwellers, so that by the end of the Neolithic period these had

[1] Schenck, 1903, 1905, 1907-10; Studer and Bannwarth, 1894.

to some extent lost their earlier long-headedness, while the Lake-Dwellers themselves became transformed from a primarily brachycephalic people to one in whom the dolichocephalic Mediterranean types were actually in the majority.

Whatever the causes or explanations of the facts, it would seem undeniable that the end of the Neolithic period saw the population of the northwest border in large measure dolichocephalic. For the Bronze period we have, as for the earlier, two series of crania, a very small one from graves and a larger one from Lake-Dweller sites. The former series is overwhelmingly dolichocephalic, but cannot be further analyzed on account of the imperfect nature of the crania. The Lake-Dwellers, if we take the series as a whole, also show a decided majority of dolichocephalic factors, but are also too imperfect to admit of detailed analysis. If the earlier are, however, contrasted with the later Bronze sites, a change is clearly indicated, such that although the dolichocephalic types are more numerous at the beginning of the period, the brachycephalic forms take first place at the end.

If these various conclusions are justified, we should have the northwestern border of the Highlands, possessing throughout Neolithic and Bronze times a population consistently more dolichocephalic (primarily Mediterranean) than was the case at the same time over much of France, and we should have to assume that the stream of brachycephalic peoples who throughout this whole time were passing into France, must have done so either to the south, by way of the Rhone valley or to the north along the Rhine. Only toward the end of the Bronze Age seemingly, was the lake region overrun.

For the period between the end of the Bronze Age and the close of the period of the Völkerwanderung in the fifth or sixth century A. D. little material is available from which we may judge of the types present. Such data as there are, come still from the northern and northwestern border region in the main, and indicate a much mixed population. A Gallic cemetery of the Hallstadt or Early Iron Age in the canton of Berne shows the male population more strongly dolichocephalic than the female, and apparently comprising a considerable element of the Caspian or mixed Caspian-Mediterranean types, together with an admixture of the Alpine. The female crania, on the other hand, suggest the dominance of the Palæ-Alpines with something of the older Palæolithic Proto-Australoids. Crania supposed to represent the Helvetii from the following or La Tene period of the Iron Age, show a much larger proportion of brachycephalic forms. When we come, however, to the Teutonic Alemani[1] from sites in the Aargau dating from the period of the Völkerwanderung, we find evidence of a strong penetration of "Nordic" forms, of mixed Caspian, Mediterranean, and Proto-Negroid types. This element increases so that in the tenth-century graves the dolichocephalic factors are twice as strong as in those four or five centuries earlier. The Burgundians, who held the upper valley of the Rhone and the area about Lakes Geneva and Neuchatel were in general similar to the Alemani.

In view of these facts, and of the evidence from northern Italy, of the steady influx during the Iron Age of brachycephalic peoples from the north into Italy, and the similar evidence from France, we may regard the period as one in which the Central European Highlands were being flooded by continued immigrations of Alpine and Palæ-Alpine peoples from the eastward, such that the whole region, except its northwestern border, became overwhelmingly brachycephalic. In the following, or Völkerwanderung period, the north and northwest were penetrated and strongly influenced by the "Nordic" dolichocephals, such as the Alemani and Burgundians.

For the period from the twelfth to the sixteenth or seventeenth centuries we are fortunate in having a large mass of data on which conclusions may be based. In the smaller towns it was the custom when the small graveyards became full, to exhume the old burials and stack the bones and skulls in the crypts under the churches, in so-called "ossuaries." The number of crania from these ossuaries whose measurements have been pub-

[1] Schwerz, 1916.

lished [1] runs into the thousands, and conclusions founded upon such abundant data may be considered in the highest degree dependable.

The picture presented is surprisingly uniform. From Lake Geneva in the west to the upper valley of the Drave in the east, from the lower Inn valley in the north to that of the Adige and its tributaries in the south, everywhere the population is revealed as overwhelmingly brachycephalic. In many sections, such as the Rhone valley, the brachycephalic crania amount to nearly 90 per cent of the whole number, the dolichocephalic forms dropping to less than 2 per cent. If the various series of crania are analyzed, it appears that this great brachycephalic majority is composed primarily of the Alpine and Palæ-Alpine types; the former being in general almost twice as common as the latter. There are, however, sharp local differences. Thus in the Zillerthal, a side valley of the lower Inn, the Alpine type is nearly three times as abundant as the Palæ-Alpine, yet in the lower Inn valley itself, the latter factor outnumbers the former in the proportion of three to two! In general, the Alpine type is in the largest proportion in the west (Rhone valley) and south (Adige basin), whereas the Palæ-Alpine is most frequent in the north (Lower Inn) and east (Pusterthal). In this northern and eastern section, also, we find the Ural type quite strongly represented. Only in one small area, that of the Zillerthal, do dolichocephalic factors appear in any strength. Here, however, they amount to nearly 30 per cent of the total, and are chiefly of the Mediterranean and Proto-Australoid types.

With insignificant exceptions the female crania repeat the characteristics of the male, so that by the fifteenth century, or perhaps as early as the twelfth, the population of the whole of the Central European Highlands had become almost purely brachycephalic; of the older dolichocephalic types which had prevailed at least in the northwest, well down into the Bronze Age, and of the great waves of Baltic dolichocephals which came

[1] Holl, 1884–87, 1888; Moschen, 1897; Pittard, 1909; Tedeschi, 1904; Wacker, 1912.

during the period of the Völkerwanderung, practically no trace remained.

The problem of the presence in the region also of a substantial factor of the Mongoloid type deserves brief consideration. In the early Neolithic Lake-Dweller crania, a trace or possible trace of this type may be found, but there is no certain evidence of its presence until the period between the twelfth and the seventeenth centuries. In the crania from the ossuaries of this time the Mongoloid type is unmistakably present—in small numbers in the Rhone valley in the west, in much more considerable proportions in the Tyrol in the east, where indeed it is but little inferior to the Palæ-Alpine. It is possible that the Mongoloid type came very early into western Europe, and was driven back into the Highlands by the later immigrants. It seems, however, more likely that it was a rather late arrival, coming with the flood of Alpine peoples during the Bronze or even later times.

Studies of modern crania from the Highlands are few and confined mainly to the northern and northeastern margin, near Salzburg and in the upper valley of the Mur. The picture presented is in the main similar to that just outlined for the period of the ossuaries. It is interesting to observe, however, that there is a notable decrease in the proportion of the Alpine type from the Mur valley north to Gmunden, with an increase of the Palæ-Alpine, recalling a somewhat similar variation in the rest of the Highlands in the earlier period.

The modern population of the Highlands is divided linguistically into three unequal portions: the extreme west is French, the south and southeast speaks Italian or the related Romansch, while the remainder and larger part is German. Data on the head-form of the living population are extremely scanty, although observations on stature and pigmentation are quite complete.[1] From these it appears that throughout almost the whole of Switzerland the stature is below the medium, the lowest averages lying just north and west of the upper valleys of the Rhone and Rhine. In the canton of Vaud, in the extreme west, the average

[1] Schwerz, 1915.

stature attains the medium.  The eastern portion of the Highland in the Tyrol and adjacent districts, shows a considerable
increase in height, the stature tending to approximate the tall
type of the northern Balkan region.

In pigmentation, the open country lying between the Alps
and the Jura, which received large increments of Baltic peoples
during the period of the Völkerwanderung, is noticeably contrasted with the remainder of the area.  In the former region,
which comprises in general the whole of the drainage of the Aar,
there is a relatively large blond factor everywhere present; whereas in most of the rest of the Highlands a more brunet population is found.

## II.  Hungary and the Balkan Peninsula

Although for some reasons the great plain of Hungary together with the chain of the Carpathians which encloses it on
the north and east, might well be considered in connection with
the region of the Russian plains, its relation to the Balkan peninsula is such that it is on the whole more convenient to treat the
area formerly included within the limits of Hungary, and also
Rumania, in connection with the puzzling and important Balkan region.

The region formerly included in Hungary comprises two very
unlike parts: a central and western, which is primarily plain, and
an eastern and northern made up of the Siebenbürgen district
and the whole of the Carpathians, which is mountainous.  The
whole area is tributary to the Danube, which enters and leaves
through gateways in the surrounding mountain chain, and serves
to connect the whole area on the one hand with the southwestern
corner of the great Russian plain, and on the other with southern
Germany, while its western tributaries such as the Drave and
Sara rise well within the mass of the Central European Highlands.

Of the Palæolithic occupants of this region we know little or
nothing, and even Neolithic remains are very scarce.  From the

western and southwestern portions of the plains area, however,
a few crania of Neolithic age are known[1] which indicate that
the population at this time was primarily of the Caspian type.
The male and female crania differ strongly, however, the latter
being clearly Alpine.  This suggests that the males may have
been an immigrant group coming into a region formerly held
by Alpines.  Although the increase of the brachycephalic factors
in the Central European Highlands, France, Italy, etc., during
Neolithic and Bronze times, seems hard to explain otherwise
than by assuming an influx from the east and southeast, very
little evidence of their presence, at least in the Danube valley,
has yet come to light.  For the whole period lying between Neolithic and Roman times the data for Hungary are very scanty,
but seem to indicate a much mixed population in which the dolichocephalic and brachycephalic factors were about equally involved, the former continuing to be present in strength at least
as late as the second or third century A. D.  This persistence of
Caspian elements in the Hungarian plains would not necessarily
invalidate the theory that the mountainous area to the southwest was occupied, intermittently perhaps, by peoples of Palæ-
Alpine and Alpine types, moving westward into the Central
European Highlands.  We have no early data whatever on the
Siebenbürgen and Carpathian mountain area, and these, too,
might conceivably have had a dominantly brachycephalic population.  That there was a reinforcement of the Caspian factors
in the Hungarian plains during the Hallstadt or Early Iron Age
seems probable, since it was at this time that peoples of this type
appear in strength on the northern Adriatic shore of Italy, and
made their influence felt on the eastern side of that sea as far
south at least as Glasinac in Bosnia.

The great migrations of the period between the third and
seventh centuries brought about extensive changes, and present
us with a number of very puzzling problems.  Three different
groups of peoples poured into or through the southeast of Europe
at this time.  One group comprised the Goths, Gepidæ, Lom-

---

[1] Virchow, 1877, 1890 a.

bards, and other Teutonic-speaking peoples from the Baltic region, who both ravaged and to some extent settled in the area; another was made up of the Slavic tribes, who, like the Teutons, both raided and settled in the land; the third included the Huns, Avars, and others, nomads rather than agriculturalists, who for the most part merely swept through the country, leaving, it is supposed, few permanent settlements and having little influence on the racial characters of the people.

That the Teutonic tribes contributed a considerable dolicho-cephalic factor, comprising Caspian, Mediterranean, and Proto-Negroid types, must be assumed; but so far crania identified as Gothic, Lombard, etc., have not been reported from this region. In regard to the racial factors brought in by the Slavic immigration, a very troublesome problem arises. Although we have no crania of the Slavic period from the Hungarian plain, Toldt[1] has studied those from Slavic cemeteries in Styria and Carinthia along its western border, and dating from the seventh to the ninth centuries or possibly somewhat later. The data are not wholly comparable with other materials, but we can at least be sure that dolichocephalic factors are in the large majority in the case of the males, no brachycephalic crania at all being found, and that the female crania show a largely decreased dolicho-cephalic factor and a considerable number of actual brachy-cephals. It seems to be the case, also, that in both series the Proto-Australoid type is quite strongly represented.

Now this dominant dolichocephaly of these early mediæval Slavic crania is in the sharpest possible contrast to the character of the modern Slavic-speaking population, since this is over-whelmingly brachycephalic (Alpine). Since mediæval times there have been no great migratory movements which might account for the complete transformation. We may account for the phenomenon by assuming that the Slavs were in their phys-ical characteristics closely allied to the various Baltic tribes, and that settling here in a region occupied by peoples primarily of Palæ-Alpine and Alpine types (as we have supposed to be

[1] Toldt, 1914.

the case in the Central European Highlands), they have in the course of time been wholly absorbed racially, although their Slavic speech has survived. On the other hand, if we believe that the original Slavic populations were quite unlike the Baltic tribes, and were primarily brachycephalic in head-form, then we must assume these mediæval crania to be those of some neighboring "Nordic" tribe, which had been thoroughly slavicized. As we shall meet this problem of the character of the early Slav again in a more aggravated form in Germany, and still more so in Russia, we may leave the further discussion of this very controversial question till the section devoted to Russia.

The physical type of the Huns and other Ural-Altaic nomads who formed the third group of invaders seems almost certainly to have been primarily Alpine, with some Ural and Mongoloid factors probably present. That they contributed largely, however, to the slowly developing racial complex in this region seems improbable.

In the tenth century a new invasion and conquest of the Hungarian region took place, that of the Magyars, a semi-nomadic folk of Finno-Ugrian speech coming from the eastern borders of the great Russian steppes. They displaced the older Slavs from the region of the Hungarian plains, which their descendants have continued to dominate until to-day. There is, however, just as in the case of the Slavs, some uncertainty in regard to the original physical characteristics of the Magyar. As in the case of the neighboring Slavs, the modern Magyar is typically brachycephalic. We have no early data, but we know that the ancient Bolgari or Bulgars, a related people formerly living along the Volga River in the vicinity of the early home of the Magyar, were in large majority of dolichocephalic Caspian and Proto-Australoid types.[1] On the basis, then, of their linguistic affiliation with the Bolgari, we might be led to regard the original Magyar as having also been in the main a dolichocephalic people. If so, however, we should have to suppose here again, as in the case of the Slavic crania just discussed, the complete absorption of

[1] Bogdanov, 1879.

the immigrants during the last thousand years. No satisfactory solution of the problem can be expected, however, until we possess some ancient Magyar crania. The modern crania appear to be in very large majority Alpine, like the present Slav.

In stature the present-day Magyar shows wide variation. In the north and west the height is about medium, but in the south and particularly the east the average rises, and the Szeklars, with a stature just under 170 cm., may be considered tall. In pigmentation the Magyars are in general brunet, although a considerable proportion of blonds occurs. The tendency toward blondness is particularly marked in eye-color, blue eyes being unusually common for a region in the south of Europe.

The Rumanians present still another of the many curious puzzles of southeastern Europe. They are sharply differentiated from their Magyar and Slavic neighbors in that they speak a language derived from Latin, although this has been much modified by the inclusion of Slavic words. They claim to be the descendants of the Roman colonists in Dacia. Their present distribution is one at variance with geographic features, in that they occupy both the plains between the lower Danube and the Carpathians, and the Siebenbürgen or Transylvanian mountain country in what was formerly the eastern part of Hungary. Into the much-disputed question of the early history of the Rumanians we cannot enter here, merely noting that it seems now pretty well established that during the period of the great invasions, from that of the Goths onward, they were swept out of the Danubian plains, and mainly concentrated south of the Danube, and that in historic times their movement has been in general northward.

Of early data on the physical characteristics of the Rumanians there seems to be little available, and the material on the living population of the present day is scanty. It appears, however, from the investigations of Pittard [1] and others, that the present Rumanian people are prevailingly brachycephalic, but in varying degree, and that this factor is most pronounced

[1] Pittard, 1920 (with bibliography), Weisbach, 1868.

in Moldavia, less so in the mountainous Transylvania region, and still less in Wallachia. No series of individual measurements having been published, it is impossible to determine the actual types present, but it would seem that the dominant element is the Alpine, with the dolichocephalic factors comprising both the Proto-Australoid and Mediterranean, of which the latter may represent the actual Roman contribution to the complex. In stature the Rumanian is just over the medium (166 cm.) and in pigmentation prevailingly brunet.

### THE BALKAN PENINSULA

For our purposes the Balkan peninsula may be defined as including the region lying south of a line running from the western end of the Black Sea along the chain of the Balkans and thence northwest to the head of the Adriatic. Except for the wedge of lowland occupied in part by the Maritza valley and lying between the Balkan and Rhodope ranges, practically the whole of the peninsula is a rugged mountainous land. Two geographical features have been of importance in the racial history of the region. Of these the first is the closeness of its contact with Asia Minor, the second its relative openness to invasion from the plains and steppes of the north. The Balkan peninsula is united in a double way with Asia Minor, on the one hand by its close approach at the Dardanelles and the Bosphorus, and on the other by way of the multitude of islands scattered through the Ægean which have served as stepping-stones between the continents. The peninsulas of Spain and Italy are both separated from the rest of Europe to the north by high and continuous mountain chains. The Balkan peninsula has no such barrier, but, margined as it is by the valleys of the Danube and the Save, is relatively open to invasion or conquest.

For the Palæolithic period, the only materials we have from this region are the fragmentary crania found at Krapina, in Croatia in the extreme northwest.[1] There has been much discussion

---

[1] Gorjanovič-Kramberger, 1906.

as to the accuracy of the reconstruction of these fragments, and therefore all that it seems safe to say is that they prove the presence of man on this northern frontier of the Balkan peninsula in early Palæolithic times, and that his physical characteristics suggest a blend between the Proto-Australoid and Mongoloid types.

Dating from Neolithic times are a few crania from the region between the Save and Drave, still thus on the extreme northern borders of the peninsula, and these like those of the same period from the neighboring Hungarian plain, are predominantly dolichocephalic.  For the Bronze Age we have no data, but in the Hallstadt or Early Iron Age cemeteries at Glasinac in Bosnia, valuable material has been found.[1]  Unfortunately the measurements of these crania have not been published in full, so that determination of the types present is impossible.  All that can be said is that the crania reveal a greatly mixed population, one site showing a strongly dolichocephalic, an adjoining one a strongly brachycephalic people.  Much farther to the south, in Greece, our oldest data are somewhat later, and comprise a small series of pre-Dorian crania from Leukas[2] and the Dipylon crania found at Athens[3] dating roughly to the eighth century B. C.  Those from Leukas, one of the Ionian Islands on the western coast, show dolichocephalic factors in the majority, while the few Dipylon crania are prevailingly brachycephalic, the Alpine and Ural types predominating.

On such slender data it is impossible to base conclusions of real value, and not until we possess information in regard to the early occupants of the central and eastern portions of the peninsula can we attain any certainty in regard to the racial history of the Balkan peninsula.  We are well-nigh forced by the evidence afforded by western Europe to believe that the transformation of its population, which began in Neolithic times, was due to long-continued immigration of brachycephalic peoples, who came from Asia Minor by way of the Balkan peninsula. Yet of their presence or passage we have as yet no clear indica-

---

[1] Weisbach, 1897.          [2] Velde, 1912.          [3] Virchow, 1893 b.

tion in the Balkan region. Only in the case of the Dorian invasion, coming at the beginning of the historical period, and specifically applying only to a small part of the peninsula, have we a probable example of such a brachycephalic drift.

The evidence for the Alpine character of the mass of the Dorians is twofold and derived from data on the living population. Almost the only adequate material on the present-day Greek population is that on the people of Mani,[1] the central one of the three peninsulas of southern Peloponnesus. Here are what are supposed to be the purest descendants of the Dorians, and their measurements show that the dominant factor is of the Alpine type, with which is combined a minority of dolichocephalic elements, in part apparently Proto-Australoid and in part Mediterranean (?) The other evidence is derived from Crete.[2] Here the Sphakiots and other residents of the western portion of the island are regarded as direct descendants of Dorian settlers. It is precisely in this section that we find, on the basis of von Luschan's measurements, the largest proportion of Alpine types. It is true that in stature these western Cretans are extraordinarily tall, and that they show a considerable proportion of blonds, features which differentiate them from the shorter, brunet people of the rest of the island. Yet von Luschan has shown that the tall stature at least may be reasonably explained by local and historical causes, and the evidence on the whole may be taken as reinforcing that from Mani, to the effect that the Dorians were in large part of the Alpine type, although quite probably under the leadership of a dolichocephalic aristocracy quite probably in the main of Caspian type.

If we may judge at all from what seems to have been occurring during the Iron Age in Hungary and in Italy, there must have been a considerable influx of dolichocephalic elements in the Balkan peninsula at this time; and in Greece at least as late as the period between the fifth and first centuries B. C. dolichocephalic factors, mainly Caspian and Mediterranean, were in slight preponderance.[3] Perhaps we may suppose that during

---

[1] Schiff, 1914 b.    [2] von Luschan, 1913; Schiff, 1914 a.    [3] Virchow, 1893 b.

this period, which includes that of the highest development of Hellenic civilization, the aristocracy was composed primarily of these dolichocephalic types, while the mass of the peasant population was predominantly Alpine. Until, however, the classical archæologist can be made to realize that crania are at least as important as fragmentary inscriptions and therefore worthy of preservation and study, and until the cranial collections long stored in Athens are made available to students, further discussion of the racial history of Greece is almost futile.

The early centuries of the Christian era saw the beginning of the Slavic migrations, which by the end of the sixth century had overrun most of the Balkan peninsula. Data for this most important period are lacking, but from Slavonia, in the extreme northwest, a series of skulls dating, to be sure, from the eleventh century,[1] show the population to have been strongly dolichocephalic. These supposedly Slavic crania raise the same question as in the case of those from Styria and Carinthia discussed in the previous section, for three centuries later we find this border region strongly brachycephalic.

How far the Turkish conquest of the fourteenth and fifteenth centuries affected the racial constituents in the peninsula, it is hard to say. The Turks would have brought, in the main, brachycephalic factors, primarily Alpine, but that their influence was of large importance seems doubtful.

The living population of the Balkan peninsula is extraordinarily diverse from the linguistic point of view. In the north are the Slavic-speaking Yugo-Slavs and Bulgarians; in the west are the Albanians, survivors of the ancient Illyrian, pre-Slavic peoples; in the south are the Greeks; while in Macedonia and eastward toward Constantinople are considerable numbers of Turks.

The study of this modern population[2] is rendered difficult from our point of view by the almost total lack of individual measurements. It may be said, however, that the whole region along the Adriatic, from Istria and Dalmatia south to Greece,

[1] Giuffrida-Ruggeri, 1908 a.    [2] Pittard, 1920.

shows an overwhelming predominance of brachycephalic factors, the Alpine type being apparently more numerous in the south, the Palæ-Alpine in the north. The Albanians[1] show an interesting contrast to the Slavic-speaking population in that they are evidently much more mixed and have a large element of either Mediterranean or Caspian type; in the absence of sufficient cranial material it is impossible to say which. An example of the brachycephalic type of Albanian is given on Plate III, Fig. 1. This raises extremely interesting questions, suggesting in connection with the dolichocephalic Neolithic crania from the Ionian Island of Leukas that the underlying stratum, in the southern portion of the peninsula at least, was comparable to that in southern Italy, and that this part did not, in early times, feel the full force of the hypothetical brachycephalic immigration.

Serbia and Bulgaria in general show a less purely brachycephalic population than that farther west, the proportion of dolichocephalic factors being largest in southeastern Serbia and southwestern Bulgaria. For Macedonia and Thrace there are practically no materials, while for southern and eastern Greece all that can be said is that this area is less purely brachycephalic than the west.[2]

The variations in stature in the Balkan peninsula are considerable. A centre of very tall statures exists in the northwest, in Bosnia, Herzegovina, and Dalmatia, and its influence seems to extend eastward across the upper Maritza valley into Bulgaria. Toward the south the statures decrease, so that we pass from an average of about 173 cm., in Bosnia, to one of 165 cm. in Greece. In pigmentation the people of the whole peninsula are predominantly brunet, the proportion of brunet types increasing from north to south. The blond type of the Homeric heroes has apparently long since been almost wholly absorbed.

Reference may best be made here to the island of Crete,[3] whose importance in the early history of civilization in the Ægean area was so great. Although large collections of crania have

[1] Haberlandt, 1919; Pittard, 1920.
[2] For references, see Ripley, 1899, Bibliography.    [3] von Luschan, 1913.

been excavated in the last few decades, their measurements have not as yet been published in full, so that analysis of the data by the method here adopted is impossible. From the averages, however, it seems clear that the Middle Minoan population was prevailingly Mediterranean in type, and that during the Late Minoan period, the proportion of Mediterranean types rapidly decreased, whereas that of the Alpine increased until at the end of the period the latter was in the majority. The modern population shows considerable variation, such that in the west and north the Alpine type is dominant, while on the southern coast the older Mediterranean is still strong, and in parts of the centre actually in the majority.

# CHAPTER IV

## CENTRAL AND EASTERN EUROPE

### I. GERMANY, CZECHO-SLOVAKIA, AND AUSTRIA

THE area occupied by Germany, the new state of Czecho-Slovakia and Austria, includes two quite different kinds of country. Fringing the shores of the Baltic and extending inland for a distance of a hundred and fifty miles in the west and double that in the east, is the North German plain, continuous to the west with the lowlands of Holland and northern Belgium, and on the east with the vast plains of Poland and Russia. South of this and extending to the northern borders of the Central European Highlands, is a region of greater relief, upland like Bavaria, hill and mountain country as in western Germany and Czecho-Slovakia and Austria. The majority of the rivers drain northward to the Baltic or the North Sea, but the Danube, rising in the far southwest, makes its way eastward through the plain of Hungary to the Black Sea, and opens a wide gateway for the passage of cultures and of peoples coming from the eastward. While the geographical divisions thus run in a general way east and west, the language divisions run at right angles to them; since, while the whole central and western portions of the region are occupied by Teutonic-speaking peoples, a large area in the east comprising most of Czecho-Slovakia and the northeastern borders of Germany is prevailingly or largely of Slavic speech.

In studying the racial history of this whole region we are able to begin our investigation in early Palæolithic times. In the Neanderthal, near Düsseldorf in the Rhine valley, was found in 1856 the incomplete skull which has become the type for one of the oldest forms of man yet known. The Neanderthal skull is dolichocephalic and low, and although the facial parts are wanting, on the analogy of other crania regarded as of the same human variety, it is safe to assume that the nose is broad, so that the skull would, on the basis of the scheme of classification here adopted, belong to the Proto-Australoid type. It is thus similar to the crania of the same period already noted in France.

From the southeastern corner of the area, in Bohemia, two crania of Aurignacian age, at the beginning of the late Palæolithic period, are known. These, the Brunn II and the Brux skulls, show the same low, dolichocephalic forms, but are again without the facial parts. The face of the Brunn skull was probably narrow, suggesting that the nose was narrow also, and if this is true, then we should have here the Mediterranean rather than the Proto-Australoid type, indicating the same change of type in Aurignacian times as already noted for France. Quite recently two crania of the later Magdalenian period have been described[1] from Obercassel near Bonn. These, fortunately, have the facial parts well preserved and afford evidence which seems to corroborate the suggestion just put forward, for the male skull is clearly a blend between the Mediterranean and Caspian types. The female skull, on the other hand, is a blend between the Proto-Australoid and Proto-Negroid, and may be regarded as representing the older Palæolithic stratum.

Of great importance for the study of the racial origins not only of this area but for the whole of Europe, are the crania from Offnet[2] in Bavaria, dating from the very close of the Palæolithic age; the Azilian-Tardenoisian period so called. From this site we have not merely a single skull but a series of fourteen adults, together with a number of children. Two facts of great importance are at once apparent on a study of these remains. In the first place we have not only dolichocephalic forms but also brachycephalic, and of each more than one type is present. In the second place it is clear that, as at Obercassel, the men and women of the community were by no means of the same type. Thus, the males from Offnet show predominantly dolichocephalic factors, while the females have a majority of brachycephalic elements. The types represented are further quite contrasted, for

[1] Verworn, 1919.          [2] Schmidt, R. R., 1912.

the Mediterranean type is the dominant and most important dolichocephalic factor in the case of the males, whereas it is the Proto-Negroid which is most strongly represented among the dolichocephalic minority in the females. Again, in the females the primary factor is the Mongoloid, while the only brachycephalic factor found in the males seems to be the Ural type.

What conclusions may be drawn from these facts? Taking into consideration the data from other parts of Europe, I believe we may say that in the early Palæolithic period the southern portion of the area under discussion was occupied by people belonging primarily to the Proto-Australoid Type; that later, in Aurignacian times, the Mediterranean type appeared here as it did coincidently in France; still later, in Magdalenian times, the influence of the Caspian type came in from the eastward; while at the very end of the Palæolithic period we find evidence of a strong element of Mongoloid type, which in the Neolithic period was to be so strongly represented in the Ardennes plateau somewhat farther west. In connection with these Mongoloids at Offnet, it may be pointed out that the Krapina crania from Croatia were possibly also of this type, but of much earlier date, as if we could trace in this way the gradual penetration of central and western Europe by brachycephalic peoples coming from the east. Yet the possible evidence of this same Mongoloid type in southern France and at Gibraltar in early Palæolithic times would suggest perhaps a dual origin.

The influence of these very late Palæolithic brachycephals is not shown at all clearly in the available record for Neolithic times, for so far as our data go the whole of the region under discussion was dominantly dolichocephalic throughout this period. From the Baltic coast in Mecklenburg and Pommern to the upper Rhine valley and Bohemia, from Hesse in the west to Silesia in the east, the great majority of all the crania published are dolichocephalic; of well-marked brachycephalic crania there are practically none. The contrast thus with France and the Low Countries during the Neolithic period is striking, since there strong infusions of brachycephalic Palæ-Alpines and Alpines took place. But, although the prevalent character of the Neolithic population of the German area was dolichocephalic, the same types were not everywhere predominant. In Mecklenburg in the northwest and in Silesia in the southeast, it was the Proto-Negroid type which was in the majority, with a minority of Proto-Australoid along the Baltic shores. In Bohemia, on the other hand, the Caspian type was dominant, the Proto-Negroid and Mediterranean taking second place.

Now if the generally accepted conclusion is correct, that cord-marked pottery is historically later than the band-decorated variety, we have at once a means, through the studies of Schliz[1] and Reche,[2] of determining the relative age of these several dolichocephalic types. From an analysis of the data it appears that the older "Bandkeramik" is found mainly associated with crania of Proto-Australoid and Proto-Negroid types, whereas the later cord-marked variety occurs with Caspian and Mediterranean types. Since the Caspian type appears relatively weak in northern Germany at this time, but is, on the contrary, the dominant factor in Bohemia and Hungary, it seems probable that it came into this whole region by way of the Danube valley.

A further feature to be noted is the curious contrast afforded by the German area with the neighboring region of Scandinavia. For whereas the whole southern shore of the Baltic east of Denmark was occupied by a nearly pure dolichocephalic population, Sweden and the Danish islands show a large proportion of brachycephalic factors, which reached the Scandinavian region probably along the North Sea coasts.

With the coming in of metal, changes of considerable magnitude occurred in some parts of the area. The North German plain, Czecho-Slovakia, and Austria appear to have retained the predominant dolichocephaly by which they were characterized throughout Neolithic times, but an increase in the proportions of the Mediterranean type is to be noted in the southeast. The southwest of Germany, however, shows a striking change, in that here we find a strong infusion of Alpine and Palæ-Alpine types,

[1] Schliz, 1909 and 1913 a.                    [2] Reche, 1908.

especially along the Rhine valley where they can be traced as far as Worms[1] or beyond. They are also strong in Bavaria, but are somewhat less marked in Wurtemberg. It will be remembered that at this same time all of western Europe was receiving large accessions of these types and particularly of the Alpines.

During the Hallstadt or Early Iron period no notable changes are evident, unless for a slight increase of dolichocephalic types in the southwest. In general, so far as Germany is concerned, this period would seem to have been one of quiescence, in which the new cultural acquisition spread, but unaccompanied by large-scale popular movements. During the La Tene or Later Iron period, however, a new thrust of brachycephalic types took place. Austria, Bavaria, and Wurtemberg became almost purely Alpine and Palæ-Alpine, while Czecho-Slovakia shows a large increase in these two factors. It is to be noted furthermore, that a considerable minority factor of the Ural type is present. Data from the northern part of Germany are scanty for this period, but apparently little or no modification of the previous conditions took place. Thus the North German plain remained an area predominantly dolichocephalic throughout the whole of the Bronze and Iron Ages.

Into this region along the Baltic had come in early Neolithic times remnants of the Palæolithic Proto-Australoids and Proto-Negroids of France and southern Germany, displaced by the incoming Mediterranean and Caspian peoples from the south and east. Later these newer types, and particularly the latter, themselves made their way into these northern lands in force, and there in relative isolation and little disturbed by the streams of Palæ-Alpine and Alpine immigrants who revolutionized conditions in central and western Europe, these dolichocephalic factors amalgamated to produce that blend, in the main of Caspian and Mediterranean types, which has come to be called the "Nordic race." How far this tall, blond, dolichocephalic variety of man is entitled to be regarded as a pure race; how and whence it acquired its characteristic blondness, together with

[1] Bartels, 1904.

other related questions, will be discussed at some length in the final section of this book. For the present it will be enough to point out that from the point of view adopted in the present study, the "Nordic race" is primarily a blend of two radically different types, which it is believed developed locally in the Baltic lands during the Neolithic and early metal ages.

At the beginning of the historic period, then—roughly about the beginning of the Christian era—the peoples of Germany, Czecho-Slovakia, and Austria seem to have been divided into two clearly marked groups. In the south, *i. e.*, in the uplands and hilly country bordering the Central European Highlands, the majority of the population were of the Alpine or Palæ-Alpine types, and the predominance of these brachycephalic forms appears to have become greater the nearer one approached the Highlands either southward toward Switzerland or westward toward the Jura and the uplands of northern France and Belgium. In the North German plain, on the other hand, the dolichocephalic factors, which marked the whole of the area in Neolithic times, still survived, these Baltic peoples being primarily a blend of the Caspian, Mediterranean, and Proto-Australoid types.

During the Bronze Age, and to some extent during the Iron Age, the Alpine and Palæ-Alpine peoples of the Central European Highlands had exerted a continuous pressure along the southern borders of the region under discussion. Pressing northward, they, or fresh increments of the same peoples from the eastward, had spread almost to the edge of the North German plain, submerging or perhaps driving out the older dolichocephalic population. With the coming of the historic period this movement was reversed, and the great southward and southwestward migrations of the Teutonic and Slavic tribes began.

This movement seems to have started at least as early as the third century A. D., but we do not begin to get abundant data on physical types until the period between the sixth and ninth centuries, when the Völkerwanderung was virtually complete. In the so-called Reihengräber or "row-graves" of this period, which are found in large numbers throughout the whole south, we have represented what is presumably the earlier stages of the blending of this new immigrant wave with the older population. In Rhein-Hesse, Baden, and Wurtemberg these cemeteries reveal a population of medium stature and overwhelmingly dolichocephalic. Unfortunately the measurements of these crania are incomplete, and it is impossible to tell with certainty what are the types present. It would seem, however, that the Proto-Australoid and Caspian types, both characteristic of the old Neolithic population, were of greatest importance. In Bavaria the dominance of dolichocephalic forms is by no means so great, although they still outnumber the brachycephalic factors in the proportion of two to one. In the extreme south, however, the latter elements increase in importance. In all of these cases the graves are regarded as those of Teutonic immigrants; farther east, however, in Lower Austria and Czecho-Slovakia[1] the Reihengräber contain the remains of Slavic peoples and are distinguished by objects of typical Slavic character. Yet the types represented in these Slavic crania from Bohemia, Moravia, and Austria are in large part the same as those found in the Teutonic graves farther west! A difference of some significance, however, docs appear in that brachycephalic factors are more numerous and indicate a contrast between the male and female portions of the population. In Wurtemberg, Baden, and Hesse both sexes show a predominance of dolichocephalic factors; in the Slavic Reihengräber, although this is true of the males (in whom the Proto-Australoid, Caspian, and Proto-Negroid types appear), the females have a majority of the opposite factors and are in the main of Alpine and Palæ-Alpine types.

These facts raise questions of great importance, for they not only bring up once more the problem as to what the original Slavic type really was, but also whether there was any fundamental difference between the Teuton and the Slav. The difference between the male and female crania might be explained by regarding the Slavs as an essentially dolichocephalic group, who

---

[1] Matiega, 1891; Niederle, 1892.

had come as conquerors and taken as wives the women of the older, rather strongly brachycephalic population. On this hypothesis the Slav would thus have been essentially similar to the Teuton. Some light is thrown on the question by the Slavic crania of approximately the same period from the Baltic coast in Pommerania, which show both sexes to have been equally and strongly dolichocephalic. This would seem to confirm the belief in the long-headedness of the Slav. Yet other explanations might be found. Thus the mass of the Slavic immigrants might have been prevailingly of brachycephalic types, but under the leadership of a dolichocephalic aristocracy, to which latter class in the main the crania may by chance belong. This seems, however, rather improbable. On the other hand, it might be supposed that the immigrants were, after all, only pseudo-Slavs, and were really tribes who were, in physical type, similar to the Teutonic-speaking peoples farther west, but Slavicized in language and culture through association with the true Slavs farther east. We shall return to this problem again later.

In the period from the ninth to the fourteenth centuries the south of Germany, i. e., Bavaria and Wurtemberg, still retained a strong majority of "Nordic" dolichocephals, at least among the males. In Bavaria, however, the females are sharply contrasted, in that they have a preponderance of Palæ-Alpine and Alpine types. In Bohemia, farther to the east, the change has already affected the males, who now are like the females, overwhelmingly brachycephalic in character. In comparison with the period from the sixth to the ninth centuries thus, a progressive change has occurred, in that what had been an area marked by prevailing dolichocephaly, due to the great immigration of Baltic tribes, has become more or less brachycephalized, this process being most complete in the east and least noticeable in Wurtemberg in the west.

In the previous period there was virtually no material by which to judge of the physical characteristics of the population of central and northern Germany. This is forthcoming in the period between the ninth and the fourteenth centuries, but presents a somewhat puzzling situation. In Westphalia, along the border of the Low Countries, the population seems to have been almost purely dolichocephalic, with the Mediterranean type strongly dominant. In Thuringia, farther eastward, Palæ-Alpine factors attain considerable importance, although dolichocephalic types are still in the majority. In Bremen[1] and in Mecklenburg,[2] in the ancient North Sea and Baltic stronghold of long-headed types, the unexpected occurs, for here brachycephalic types have almost attained predominance, and these are, in the main, of Alpine type, in contrast to the Palæ-Alpines, who make up the larger part of the brachycephalic element in Thuringia and Bohemia. And, also, whereas the Bremen crania are regarded as unquestionably Teutonic, those from Mecklenburg are Slavic, i. e., Wend.

If now we contrast the Teutonic and Slavic peoples of the ninth to the twelfth centuries, here in the north along the Baltic shores, with the same two peoples in the south in the period just preceding, a curious result ensues. In the south, as in the north, we find pairs of peoples, differing in language yet similar in their general physical characters. The northern and the southern Teutonic groups are alike at least in their brachycephalic factors, in that each shows this to be mainly of Alpine type. They differ, on the other hand, in their dolichocephalic elements, the northern or Baltic group being composed mainly of Mediterranean and Caspian factors, whereas the southern group has a large representation of the Proto-Australoid type. The northern group has, moreover, a larger brachycephalic factor than the southern. The northern and southern Slavic groups, on the other hand, differ more from each other than do the Teutonic. For the southern group shows a large factor of the Palæ-Alpine type which the northern does not possess, while the latter has a considerable Mediterranean element which is lacking in the south. As in the case of the Teutonic groups, however, the north has the larger proportion of brachycephals.

In the south the Teutonic and Slavic groups alike were in-

---

[1] Gildermeister, 1879.                          [2] Asmus, 1900.

trusive peoples, and apparently prevailingly dolichocephalic in
an area which had previously been occupied by a brachycephalic
population.   In the north, on the contrary, only the Slavic tribes
were immigrants, since the North German plain was the homeland of the Teutonic tribes.   It would naturally be supposed
that both Teuton and Slav in the north would be at least as
strongly dolichocephalic as their respective southern offshoots,
yet in fact each is *less* so, and both northern groups, Teuton as
well as Slav, show an unexpected strength of brachycephalic factors in a region previously characterized by long-headedness.
How is this paradox to be explained?   The Pommeranian Slavs
show but a fraction of the Alpine factors present in the Wendish
crania from Mecklenburg (which region, in Neolithic times, it
will be remembered, was almost purely dolichocephalic), so that
the Slavs cannot be regarded as responsible for this brachycephalic element; a belief confirmed by the fact that the Slavic
crania from still farther eastward, in Posen and Prussia, reveal
even a smaller round-headed element than is found in Pommerania.   In Westphalia and Friesland on the west, in Denmark
and Sweden on the north, the population of this period was prevailingly dolichocephalic, so that the source of this strong Alpine factor in both Teuton and Slav in northwestern Germany
is extremely puzzling.

Taking everything into consideration, so closely do the early
Slavic crania resemble the Teutonic that it is difficult to avoid
the conclusion that physically the two peoples must, at the period
of the Völkerwanderung, have been extremely similar.   We shall
have to face this whole problem again in more imperative form
in dealing with the population of Russia, Poland, and Finland,
and to the section treating of these countries the final discussion of the question may be postponed.

Let us return again to the consideration of Bavaria and the
southern portion of the whole region.   We have seen that in the
mediæval period, between the sixth and the fourteenth centuries,
the population of Bavaria had changed from one which was in
majority dolichocephalic and Mediterranean in type, to one in

which these factors were barely in excess of Alpine elements, some six or seven centuries later. In Bohemia the change had been more rapid, and by the twelfth century the people here were primarily brachycephalic, the Palæ-Alpine type being markedly in predominance. When next we are able to study the people of this area, the brachycephalization had proceeded much farther. Ranke[1] and Ried,[2] in their studies of the great series of seventeenth and eighteenth century crania from Bavaria, have supplied material which is absolutely conclusive, and this is corroborated by the work of Ammon[3] and Lapouge[4] on the nineteenth-century population of Baden. Where in Bavaria, in the fourteenth century, the proportion of dolichocephalic factors was still slightly in excess of the brachycephalic, four hundred years later the actual dolichocephalic crania have dropped to less than 1 per cent, while the pure brachycephalic crania make up more than 80 per cent of the total; a proportion which is equalled, if not exceeded, in Baden and Austria and among the Slavic population of Czecho-Slovakia. With few exceptions it is the Alpine type which is everywhere clearly the dominant factor, although among the Slavic group the women show a large majority of the Palæ-Alpine type.

There has been, thus, in southern Germany, Austria, and Czecho-Slovakia, since early mediæval times, a radical change in the character of the population. From a prevailingly long-headed people they have become an almost purely round-headed one; yet in the intervening period of roughly a thousand years we know of no extensive migrations or movements which would account for the change. Before attempting to discuss the cause of this modification we must first consider the modern population of the North German plain, and note the results obtained from the study of the living people.

No investigations comparable with those in the south have been made in northern Germany, apparently in large part for reasons which will be alluded to in treating of the data on the

---

[1] Ranke, 1880.　　　　　　　　　[2] Ried, 1911.
[3] Ammon, 1899.　　　　　　　　　[4] Lapouge, 1893.

living population. We have available a series of modern crania from Prussia,[1] but as no nasal measurements are published the determination of types is not possible. So far, however, as the relative proportions of brachycephalic and dolichocephalic factors are concerned, the modern Prussians differ hardly at all from the northern Bavarians of the seventeenth and eighteenth centuries. So that in this region where all the evidence of early mediæval age showed a dominantly dolichocephalic population, we now have one in which the brachycephalic factors are as completely in the majority as in the south. The claim thus of the domineering Prussian to represent the dolichocephalic "Nordic race" is totally false.

With one or two exceptions the anthropological study of the living German people has been limited. In Baden, Ammon[2] has made an extensive and valuable investigation, but this was limited to the small area of the Grand Duchy, and the only important study of the whole country has been that of the great eye-and-hair color census of school-children, carried out under Virchow's direction nearly forty years ago.[3] Further study of the German population has been discouraged or prevented, directly or indirectly, as a result apparently of the abnormal national pride characteristic of the people for the last two generations. As a result of the materials published it had begun to be evident that the Germans were not all of one type, the tall, fair, long-headed race of heroes which had been set up as an ideal and idol. It was obvious that a large proportion were almost indistinguishable, on the one hand, from the populations of Switzerland, Belgium, and northern France, and on the other from the despised Slav. The illusion of the unity and supremacy of the German must be preserved, so further investigations could not be permitted. This seems the only possible explanation at least, of the utter absence of any modern or general anthropological study of the German people, when the great activity of German anthropologists in studying *other* peoples is kept in mind.

[1] *Anthropologische Sammlungen Deutschlands*, IV., Königsberg.
[2] Ammon, 1899.                     [3] Virchow, 1886.

This lack of data in regard to the physical characteristics of the living population, which has been absolute so far as regards all northern Germany, has recently been remedied to a slight degree by the publication of measurements taken in England on German prisoners of war.[1]  The numbers measured were, however, too small to make the results more than tentative.  The data on stature obtained in this way are of very uncertain value. Supplemented by other sources, however, we may obtain the following results.  The tallest statures are to be found in the northwest, in Mecklenburg and Schleswig-Holstein, where the average lies about 173 cm., and where also the percentage of tall statures (*i. e.*, those of 170 cm., or over) is highest.  The shortest statures, on the other hand (166–167 cm.), are found in the south and east, in Bavaria, Silesia, Posen, and Prussia.  The Austrian and Bohemian populations appear to be intermediate between these two extremes, and continue the area of statures above the medium which characterized most of the eastern portion of the Central European Highlands.

The material on head-form secured by Parsons in his measurements on war prisoners is very significant.  Taking this and such other data as are available it appears that there is no portion of the whole area of Germany, Austria, or Czecho-Slovakia in which the present population shows an average cephalic index which is dolichocephalic.  The nearest approach to it occurs in Westphalia and Oldenburg, in the northwestern part of Germany, where the average index is just over 80, *i. e.*, almost at the lower limit of brachycephaly.  Hannover, Schleswig, and the Rhineland lie still nearer the limit, and all other areas are frankly brachycephalic.  Averages are, however, as has already been pointed out, of little real significance, yet we can be sure from the high figure of the average index in the whole south of Germany, in Austria, and Czecho-Slovakia that there can be but a small dolichocephalic element in the population.  In the northwest, however, the lower average makes it certain that there must still be in this region a considerable dolichocephalic factor.  Here,

[1] Parsons, 1919.

therefore, and here alone, do we find any considerable survival of the old Neolithic blend of dolichocephalic types, which is commonly spoken of as the "Nordic race."

For eye and hair color we have, besides the investigations on school-children made in Germany and Austria, the observations obtained by Parsons on German prisoners of war. The material derived from the study of the school-children is of great value on account of the very large numbers of individuals observed, that in Germany alone amounting to nearly 6,000,000. On the other hand, the results are rendered somewhat uncertain on account of the fact that the color of both hair and eyes changes somewhat in later life, so that statistics for children are not really indicative of the adult population, which is likely to be somewhat more brunet, since eye and hair color tend to darken with age. The data obtained on the German prisoners of war are exempt from this difficulty, but lack trustworthiness because of the small number of individuals on which the averages for the different portions of the area are based. A comparison with the other series, however, shows a general agreement, the proportion of brunets running about 5 per cent higher than in the case of the children.

On the basis of the two sets of observations, the facts are very clear. The whole of the North German plain shows a majority of blond types, and this is continued southward in the west through the Rhine province and Hesse. The highest percentage of blonds is found in Westphalia and Hannover. On the other hand, the whole of the south shows a large brunet element, which, however, in no case attains an actual majority. Pigmentation and head-form are thus by no means interdependent.

Summarizing the data on the living population it appears that there is a clear contrast between the people living in the North German plain and those of the southern upland. The former are tall, strongly blond, and, although probably the brachycephalic Alpine and Palæ-Alpine factors are in the majority, the dolichocephalic elements of the "Nordic" blend are

present in very considerable, although variable proportion. The
tall stature, blondness, and long-headedness all seem to reach
the extreme in the northwest, in Hannover and Westphalia. All
of the south, on the other hand, from Baden in the west to Austria and Czecho-Slovakia in the east, has a population which,
although above medium stature, is yet shorter than that in the
north, is much more commonly brunet, and in head-form is
overwhelmingly Alpine and Palæ-Alpine. This southern German type is illustrated in Plate III, Fig. 2.

It is obvious, therefore, that racially the people of this whole
area, and the Germans in particular, are in no sense a unit. In
the north and especially the northwest, much of the traditional
German has survived; in all the rest of Germany the "German"
is hardly to be distinguished from his Slavic-speaking neighbors
on the east, the Swiss in the south, or the Belgians and French
in the west. The belief in the racial purity and uniqueness of
the German so ardently upheld and energetically fostered in
Germany for the last two generations, is thus nothing but a myth,
and the domineering Prussian is less true to the old Germanic
type than the Hannoverian or Westphalian.

Those Germans who, like Ranke, endeavored thirty or forty
years ago to account for the disturbing differences between the
people of southern and northern Germany, explained them away
by appealing to environmental influences. The Bavarian was,
it was true, brachycephalic and in large measure brunet, but
this was the result of a change brought about in the original
"Nordic" type by altitude, differences in food and economic
conditions, etc., etc. These explanations will not, however, account for the changes in the North German plain, and the whole
phenomenon can more rationally be laid to the submergence
and absorption of the original Germanic type by older or later-
coming brachycephalic peoples. The phenomenon is not an
isolated one and we shall meet it again both in Italy and in
eastern Europe.

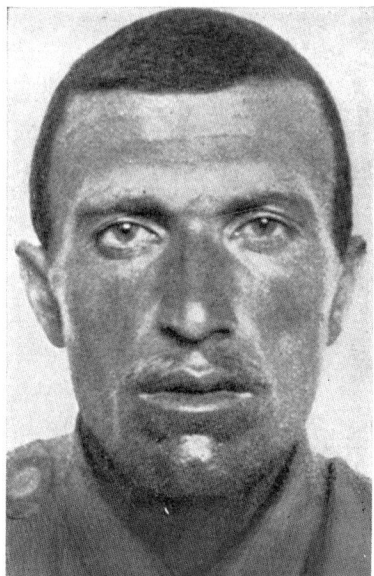

FIG. 1. ALBANIAN.

FIG. 2. SOUTH GERMAN.

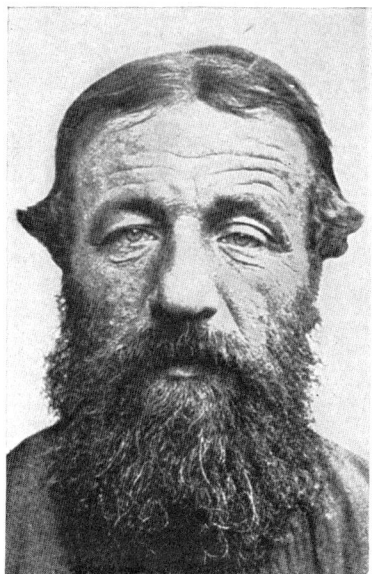

FIG. 3. GREAT RUSSIAN.

FIG. 4. FINN.

PLATE III.

## II. Russia, Poland, and Finland

Eastern Europe holds some of the most important keys to the problems of the racial history of the continent, for it has been both a breeding place whence streams of immigrants have spread westward into the rest of Europe, and also a broad gateway through which have passed great floods of Asiatic peoples. In its physical features the whole area of Russia, Poland, and Finland is one vast plain: forested and sown with lakes in the north, with its streams flowing into the Baltic or the Arctic; grassland and steppe in the south giving place, toward the southeast, to the desert regions along the shore of the Caspian into which Russia's greatest river, the Volga, empties, and to semi-arid lands along the Black Sea into which the other streams flow. Except for the interruption of the Ural chain, which in its southern portions is low and almost negligable, this great plain of eastern Europe is continuous with the steppe and desert regions of Siberia and inner Asia.

The whole of eastern Europe is to-day occupied by peoples speaking languages belonging to two quite different linguistic stocks, the Indo-European and the Ural-Altaic. The first group, which occupies as a single continuous area the larger part of the territory, comprises the Russians, Poles, Ruthenians, and other Slavic-speaking peoples, together with the Lithuanians and Letts, whose languages form a separate branch of the Indo-European stock. To this Lithuanian branch belonged also the ancient Prussians, whose speech became extinct in the seventeenth century. The Ural-Altaic peoples live mainly around the periphery of the first group and are divisible into two sections. The first, whose languages have been grouped under the name of Finno-Ugric, comprise the Livs and Esths in Esthonia on the eastern shores of the Baltic; the Finns in Finland; the Lapps in northern Finland and the north of the Scandinavian peninsula; the Samoyede along the Arctic coast; the Votiaks, Zyrians, and Permiaks south of these along the Urals; and the Cheremiss and Mordvins in Kazan and along the middle Volga. The second group, speaking

Turko-Tatar languages, are found in Kazan and parts of the Volga region; in Orenburg and along the shores of the Caspian to the Caucasus; and in the Crimea. They are known generally as Tatars, although some, such as the Bashkir in the Orenburg region, the Chuvash along the Volga, and the Kirgiz on the Caspian have individual names. Allied to these Turko-Tatar tribes, but speaking a Mongol language, is the small body of Kalmucks, who are neighbors of the Kirgiz on the shores of the Caspian.

Of the physical type of the occupants of this whole vast area during the earlier prehistoric periods we know next to nothing. No finds of Palæolithic crania have been reported as yet, and of Neolithic crania we have but very few. The majority of those for which data are available come mainly from northwestern Russia, in the vicinity of Lake Ladoga and from the government of Yaroslav.[1] Of crania from here, two-thirds are dolichocephalic and the remainder mesocephalic, indicating a population with relatively slight brachycephalic factors. Just what the types represented are it is impossible to say on account of the fragmentary character of the skulls, but apparently the dolichocephalic factors are mainly Proto-Australoid and Caspian. From farther south and west in Poland and in the governments of Kiev and Poltava, a few crania of somewhat uncertain Neolithic Age have been reported, which again show a large majority of dolichocephalic elements, in the main apparently of the Caspian and Mediterranean types. Lastly, we have the crania from Rinnekalm in Livland.[2] Those from the upper layers at this site are of Bronze and Iron Age or later date, but the crania from the lowest stratum, which are believed to be Neolithic in age, are unlike those of similar age in the other parts of Russia, being primarily brachycephalic. The types cannot be determined. The Bronze and Iron Age crania are in sharp contrast with these older skulls, being dominantly dolichocephalic, with the Proto-Australoid and Caspian types of primary importance.

If all these scattered facts be taken into consideration, the conclusion seems to follow that, at the earliest time to which we

---

[1] Bogdanov, 1886.                    [2] Virchow, 1877.

can go back, the eastern Baltic shores were occupied by a brachycephalic folk, whereas the interior of western Russia and Poland
was held by dolichocephalic peoples, in the north mainly Proto-
Australoid and Caspian, in the south Caspian and Mediterranean.
For the larger part of Russia, Finland, and Poland there are as
yet no early data, and our study of the population can begin
only in proto-historic times.

From southern Russia, in the government of Cherson, we
have two series of crania of early historic or proto-historic date.[1]
One is dated between the sixth and first centuries B. C., the other
between the first century B. C. and the end of the first century
A. D.   The earlier site reveals the presence of a primarily dolichocephalic people, much mixed in type, but with the Mediterranean and Proto-Australoid dominant, with a minority of
the brachycephalic Alpines.   This is for the male crania only,
however.   If we turn to the female, we find the proportions just
reversed, the Alpine being in the majority, with the two dolichocephalic factors above mentioned in the minority.   According to Schliz the males represent a colony of Ionian Greeks, the
females, their wives, taken from the native population; definite
proof of this, however, is lacking.   The later series shows a male
population still dominantly long-headed, but of quite different
character, since they are clearly a blend between the Proto-
Negroid and Caspian types; the female crania are also predominantly dolichocephalic, but replace the Proto-Negroid by the
Mediterranean type.   The unexpected appearance of the strong
Proto-Negroid factor in the male crania is puzzling, for in the
rest of Europe at this time it was nowhere found in any such
abundance, at least so far as our records go.   It had been characteristic of the Neolithic peoples of Mecklenburg, Denmark,
and southern Sweden, and Schliz's suggestion that these crania
from the north shore of the Black Sea represent an early Gothic
migration, antedating their known southward movement, has
thus some plausibility.

The archæological investigations of Bogdanov and others in

[1] Schliz, 1913, a and b.

the kurgans or burial-mounds of central and western Russia, afford a large and very valuable mass of data in regard to the physical character of the peoples of this region in the period from about the sixth to the thirteenth centuries. Unfortunately, however, the various sites differ widely in date, and the identification of their makers is far from certain. Some are believed to be pre-Slavic and either Finnish or "Scythian" or Sarmatian; others are held to be Slavic, but there is little agreement between different authorities on these points. Their exact age is also often in doubt, but we can apparently be quite sure that they are not Neolithic, as stated by Ripley.

The kurgan data[1] may best be considered in two geographical groups, of somewhat different age. The northern comprises those in the governments of Vitebsk, Smolensk, Moscow, Riazan, Tver, Yaroslav, Nishegorod, and Kazan, a region which forms the heart of the area now occupied by the so-called Great Russians. Here, in the period between the ninth and the twelfth centuries, the population seems to have been primarily dolichocephalic, the Proto-Negroid type most unexpectedly being most important as a rule, with the Caspian and Mediterranean as secondary factors. The brachycephalic element present as a minority was mainly the Palæ-Alpine. In the two more northerly governments of Novgorod and Kostroma,[2] the conditions were just the opposite. Here the crania show the Palæ-Alpine type to be dominant, with the dolichocephalic factors in the minority; and this predominance of brachycephalic elements appears furthermore to go back, in Novgorod at least, to the Early Iron Age.

The southern area, in which lies the heart of the Ukraine, includes the governments of Chernigov, Kursk, Poltava, Kiev, and Volhynia. In all of this region except Kiev, the kurgan crania (which date back as far as the sixth century) show, like those of the first group, a predominance of dolichocephalic factors, but here, instead of the Proto-Negroid, it is the Caspian and Mediterranean types which are of greatest importance. In

---

[1] For sources see under Bogdanov, in Ripley, 1899, Bibliography.
[2] Konstantinov-Shchipunin, 1897.

Kiev, on the other hand, brachycephalic elements are in the lead, the Alpine and Palæ-Alpine being about equally important, while the dolichocephalic factors are Proto-Australoid and Proto-Negroid.

It thus appears that the larger part of central Russia was, in the period between the seventh and the twelfth centuries, occupied by a preponderantly dolichocephalic people, who had upon their northern and southwestern borders populations which were, on the contrary, brachycephalic. In the north the Proto-Negroid and Proto-Australoid types were in largest proportions, in the south the Caspian and Mediterranean. In the north the population comprised peoples belonging to both the Indo-European and the Finno-Ugric groups, the larger part of Yaroslav, Kostroma, and Nishegorod, together with portions of Kazan, being occupied by the latter, whereas the more western governments were held by Slavic peoples. The south, on the other hand, was occupied in the main by a Slavic-speaking population, although into it and through it, for a thousand years, migratory hordes from farther eastward had intermittently passed.

For most of western Russia and Poland little material is available for this period. A small series of crania from kurgans in the governments of Plock and Kielce in Poland,[1] dating to about the eleventh century, are, however, known. The published accounts being incomplete, all that can be said is that the crania are almost purely dolichocephalic, agreeing in this respect with those from eastern Germany at this same time.

In discussing the racial history of central Europe it has been shown (p. 104) that the Slavic-speaking immigrants into southeastern and eastern Germany and Bohemia in the sixth and seventh centuries were predominantly dolichocephalic, those in the latter country, at least, being notable for the large proportions of Proto-Negroid and Proto-Australoid factors in their make-up. Except for this Proto-Negroid element and a somewhat larger brachycephalic factor, there was little to distinguish these Slavs from the Teutonic tribes of the Reihengräber of southern Ger-

_____
[1] Rutkovski, 1901.

many or the population of the North German plain. Physically, Slav and Teuton seemed closely allied, but final conclusions in regard to the real type of the Slav were deferred until the data from the much larger area occupied by them in Poland and Russia should have been examined. This has now been done, and we are in a position therefore to discuss the evidence as a whole.

The problem of the racial history of eastern Europe is indeed an extremely difficult one. In Neolithic times the population of all of eastern Germany, Bohemia, Hungary, Poland, and southern, western, and northwestern Russia, was predominantly dolichocephalic, the Proto-Australoid type being everywhere apparently fundamental, mixed in the north with Proto-Negroid and Caspian, in the south mainly with Mediterranean, types. Only in Livland, on the eastern Baltic shore, were brachycephalic factors in the majority. From this time on until the time of the Slavic expansion in the sixth to the twelfth centuries we have no material, but when, in the early mediæval period we are once more able to study the population, the main outlines of the picture remain very much the same. Slavic hordes had, meanwhile, from their ancient home northeast of the Carpathians poured over all of Germany as far as the Elbe, over Bohemia, much of Hungary, and large parts of the Balkan peninsula, and to the north, northeast, and east they had spread through the heart of Great Russia and the Ukraine. Yet everywhere except in Kiev in the south, and in Novgorod in the north, the crania show a dominantly dolichocephalic population; the north on the whole true to its earlier Neolithic types, although now with a larger Proto-Negroid element, the south still mainly characterized by the strength of its Caspian and Mediterranean elements. In Kiev we have crania from what are regarded as Slavic as well as from non-Slavic sites, and the crania from both are alike in being primarily of Palæ-Alpine and Alpine types. In the north the same thing occurs, in that the series of Slavic crania from Novgorod is almost the exact counterpart of the supposedly Finnish series from Kostroma. Yet farther to the southeastward the Finno-Ugrian Bolgari in Kazan, and the related tribes in the

governments of Viatka and Perm, were, like the main body of
the Slavs, predominantly dolichocephalic, with apparently large
factors of both Proto-Australoid and Proto-Negroid types.  In
the north, thus, Slav and non-Slav are alike brachycephalic;
in the centre and east both are primarily dolichocephalic; while
in the south, in Kiev, they are again both brachycephalic.  The
division into Slav and non-Slav thus ceases to be significant.

The same holds true, in general, also in the west, for just as
Slav and Finnish-speaking peoples were alike in the east, so
were Slav and Teuton on the opposite frontier.  The Slavs of
eastern Germany, of Pommern, Posen, and West Prussia, of
Bohemia and of Moscow, Tver and Yaroslav were in particular
allied to the Germanic tribes, in that they showed a large element of the broad-nosed dolichocephalic types, although among
the central and western Teutons this was in larger part Proto-
Australoid, whereas in the eastern, such as the Goths and among
the Slavs, the Proto-Negroid was in the majority.

Two to four centuries later, however, by the twelfth and
thirteenth centuries in the south and the fifteenth and sixteenth
in the north, almost the whole of the vast Slavic area, instead of
being one marked by prevailing dolichocephaly, had become one
in which the brachycephalic types were in large majority.  The
cemeteries of Kiev and Chernigov in the south and of Moscow in
the north, however, differed, in that in the former, as in Bohemia,
the dominant element was the Palæ-Alpine, whereas in the latter
it was the Alpine.

How could this complete transformation have been brought
about?  How derive an almost purely brachycephalic population
from one in large majority dolichocephalic within the space of
200 to 400 years?  Our answer to the question must depend in
large part on whether the majority of the Russian kurgans, or
burial-mounds, are accepted as Slavic or not.  If the crania found
in these graves, which date, it is believed, from the period of the
Slavic migrations, are to be attributed to the Slavic conquerors
and settlers, then we have no choice apparently but to regard
the Slav as essentially dolichocephalic, and the almost complete

brachycephalization must be due either to a rapid absorption of the Slavic immigrants by a pre-Slavic, purely brachycephalic population, or to a similar wholesale assimilation by the Slav of some later body of immigrants, also almost exclusively round-headed. If, on the other hand, the kurgan crania are declared to be non-Slavic, and to represent the pre-Slavic population, and the Bohemian and Hungarian crania are held to be the remains of Slavicized Teutonic peoples, then the Slav proper may have been almost purely brachycephalic, and in the course of a few centuries have completely assimilated their dolichocephalic predecessors in Russia, whereas the Slavicized Teutons in Bohemia, Austria, and Hungary were themselves assimilated by the older brachycephalic peoples among whom they had come.

If we accept the Russian kurgan crania as mainly Slavic, and seek for evidence of a pre-Slavic, brachycephalic people who could have absorbed these Slavic immigrants as the dolichocephalic Teutons were absorbed by the older populations of Bavaria and Baden among whom they came, we must turn to the Finno-Ugric tribes, whom we know the Slavs displaced, at least in the whole north of Russia. At once we are involved in another maze of contradictions, for these tribes show the most diverse characteristics. The supposedly Finnic kurgan crania from Kostroma are, as we have seen, predominantly brachycephalic, although only barely so; yet the Bolgari from Kazan, which is the adjoining government to the southeast, show as much of a majority of dolichocephalic factors as the Slavic kurgans in Nishegorod, Riazan, and Tver. The Finns themselves are, to-day at least, in large majority brachycephalic, as are the Esths and Livs of the eastern Baltic coast, yet the crania from the upper strata at Rinnekalm in Livland which are of mediæval age, are predominantly dolichocephalic! The more eastern Finno-Ugric tribes present similar wide divergences, so that it is quite evident that we cannot, without further consideration, solve our problem by declaring that the Finnic tribes were brachycephalic and, while accepting the language and culture of their Slavic conquerors, nevertheless absorbed them racially. Before doing so we must determine, if possible, what was the original Finnish type, and this, as will be seen later, is as much of a puzzle as that of the Slav!

There was, however, another alternative to account for the brachycephalization of the originally dolichocephalic Slav, namely that they themselves, after settling in central and northern Russia, were overlaid by a later group of brachycephals, who completely transformed the older Slavic type, although exerting little influence on the language or culture. The only possibility here lies in the Tatar conquest of the twelfth and thirteenth centuries, which ravaged Russia and held the country to tribute for two hundred years. But, although the Mongols and Tatars who accomplished this were almost purely brachycephalic peoples, the historians are unanimous to the effect that, apart from one or two great raids, they had little or no actual contact with the Slavic population of central and northern Russia. Moreover, the Mongoloid and Ural types, which are strongly characteristic of Mongol and Tatar peoples, would, if the hypothesis of a Tatarization were true, be found to be important elements in the transformed Slavic population. As a matter of fact, however, they hardly appear at all; so for the northern and central Slavs, at least, the hypothesis of a Tatarization seems untenable.

If we turn to southern Russia, the hypothesis of an originally dolichocephalic Slav meets somewhat different conditions. We have no evidence which would lead us to believe that the Ukraine was ever occupied by Finno-Ugric peoples, so that they, whatever may have been their physical type, cannot be appealed to as pre-Slavic brachycephals. It may be remembered, however, that in the government of Cherson, which adjoins that of Kiev on the south, the female crania of the period between the sixth and first centuries B. C. were primarily Alpine in type, and that it was suggested as a possibility that they represented the older, aboriginal population, whereas the dolichocephalic males were to be regarded as immigrant conquerors. This is rather weak evidence, however, for assuming a predominantly brachycephalic population in the Ukraine a thousand years or more later, and particularly when it is remembered that the crania from this same region of Cherson in the first century A. D. were, both male and female, predominantly dolichocephalic. Furthermore, the Ukraine was the region through which swarm after swarm of invaders swept from the east and north for centuries prior to the period of Slavic expansion, and some at least of these, like the Goths, were probably in the main dolichocephalic. It seems difficult, therefore, to find sufficient evidence of a uniformly brachycephalic population in the Ukraine in the period immediately anterior to the Slavic migrations.

The alternative possibility of a later wave of brachycephalic peoples coming after the Slavic settlement, which for central and northern Russia was found to be impossible, here appears, however, in a more favorable light. For not only did this region undergo a long contact with the Tatar peoples in the twelfth and thirteenth centuries and later, but it was swept, time after time, before their advent and during and after the Slavic colonization by other Asiatic hordes, who were primarily brachycephalic. Contemporary data in regard to these Asiatic invaders are not abundant, but crania from Tatar graves of the thirteenth century in Cherson[1] and in the Crimea[2] show them to have been in very large majority of the Palæ-Alpine type, with a notable minority of the Mongoloid. Now it is precisely these two factors which are most prominent in the crania from Kiev and Chernigov, so that it is difficult to avoid the conclusion that a considerable part, probably a large part, of the brachycephalization of the Slavic population of the Ukraine is to be attributed to the influence of the Tatar and other Asiatic immigrants. This seems the more probable, since in the Kiev crania of the sixth century, which alone at that time showed a predominance of brachycephalic factors, the Palæ-Alpine and Mongoloid elements were *not* important; they only became so after the Tatar and other contact. Moreover, the Mongoloid element which is so reasonably to be attributed to the Mongol-Tatar peoples, is *not* found among the Slavs of Bohemia or western Hungary and Austria, so that among

[1] Bogdanov, 1886-87.                    [2] Obolensky, 1892.

the Slavs of the Ukraine, and among them only, is this typically inner Asiatic factor present.  It is true that Slavic writers deny very emphatically that any intermixture with the Tatars took place, but in view of the facts just outlined it would seem that the denial cannot stand.

For southern Russia, therefore, the hypothesis of the dolichocephalic Slav seems on the whole to meet the facts; if we can find good reason for believing that some at least of the Finnic tribes were brachycephalic, it will also meet the facts fairly well in the north; and, as we shall see when considering the Finnic problem later on, there is much reason for this belief.  We have already seen, in discussing the Slavic question in Bohemia and Austria, that the assumption that the Slavs were originally dolichocephalic and very similar to the Teuton was after all the most satisfactory.

The alternative hypothesis that the Russian kurgan crania were not those of Slavs, and that the original Slavic type was brachycephalic as it is to-day, may be disposed of briefly.  If kurgan crania in the north are not Slavic, they must be Finnic. The only contemporary Finno-Ugrian crania are those from the Bolgari in Kazan and from Kostroma, and only the former agree with the crania from Nishegorod, Riazan, Moscow, Tver, and Yaroslav in being predominantly dolichocephalic.  But, although they are comparable in this very general respect, the actual types present show striking differences.  The significant feature of the other kurgan crania is the surprisingly large Proto-Negroid factor which is present, and this is practically absent in the Bolgari series; the other crania have as their main brachycephalic element the Palæ-Alpine type, whereas in the Bolgari this is replaced by the Alpine.  The supposedly pre-Slavic and, therefore, Finnic crania can thus hardly be regarded as allied to the eastern Finnic group.  The probability is very strong that the people displaced by the incoming Slavs in northern and central Russia were in large part the ancestors of the present Finns who moved north and settled in Finland about the ninth century or before.  We must therefore regard the crania under discussion as probably

Finnish. Now, while the question of the original type of the Finns is an extremely difficult one to settle with the data at present available, it seems on the whole most probable that they were primarily brachycephalic. If this is true, then the crania from the kurgans, being dolichocephalic, cannot be Finnish, and the whole theory, so far as it relates to the northern portion of Russia, at least, falls to the ground.

In the south, the problem presents a different aspect. We do not know exactly who were the predecessors of the Slavic peoples in the Ukraine. The terms Scythian and Sarmatian apply to what were certainly much mixed peoples, or to peoples of quite different types. It seems probable, however, that at least a part of the Scythians were allied racially as well as linguistically, to the early Iranians, and were in the main a blend of Caspian and Mediterranean types. The Cherson crania of the first century were, it may be remembered, primarily dolichocephalic, so that we have grounds for believing that the population of the Ukraine, although doubtless greatly mixed as a result of the various invasions which it had suffered from very early times, nevertheless contained a large dolichocephalic factor prior to the spread of the Slavs. A non-Slavic or pre-Slavic origin for the dolichocephalic kurgan crania here is thus entirely possible, and so far the hypothesis of the brachycephalic character of the original Slav meets the facts. It faces, however, a serious obstacle in the kurgan crania of the seventh century from the government of Volhynia.[1] In this region, lying to the north and east of the Carpathians, most authorities locate the homeland of the Slav, and here, in the heart of the area whence they spread, the brachycephalic character of the crania ought to be very clearly marked. Yet in fact they are in large majority dolichocephalic. Unless, therefore, it can be shown conclusively that the crania are non-Slavic, possibly Gothic, the belief in an originally round-headed Slav becomes very difficult to sustain. Unfortunately the archæological identification of the site is uncertain.

[1] Olechnowicz, 1903.

Assuming, however, that this objection is overcome and that, as seems generally admitted, the region north and east of the Carpathians was a great reservoir whence the supposed brachycephalic Slavs poured out, they could have done so only toward the northeast and east, for the early Slavic graves in Bohemia, Styria, Carinthia, and all of eastern Germany reveal a primarily dolichocephalic people, and these cannot be eliminated and explained away as pre-Slavic, for the typically Slavic nature of the objects found in these graves is apparently without serious question. The hypothesis of an originally brachycephalic Slav thus forces us to assume that side by side with the true Slav, who was brachycephalic, were other peoples, Slavic in speech and culture but dolichocephalic and primarily "Nordic" in physical type, and that it was these Slavicized Teutons who spread westward, while the true Slavs moved only toward the north and east!

Such a phenomenon is possible, but the alternative hypothesis that the Slavic peoples were originally dolichocephalic, seems simpler and rather more probable. The crucial point which would decide between the two rival theories seems to be this: How, if the Slav were originally dolichocephalic and in general "Nordic," can we account for the fact that the whole of Poland and the Slavic part of eastern Germany became by the fifteenth and sixteenth centuries as completely brachycephalic as Russia? There is little trace here in prehistoric times of any brachycephalic population comparable to that of the Finns of central and northern Russia; no centuries of penetration and domination by central Asiatic hordes as in the Ukraine. We might try to explain the fact by saying that the earlier immigrants were the Slavicized Teutonic tribes, and that they were followed later by a flood of true, brachycephalic Slavs who thus, spreading over the older layer, accomplished its complete transformation. Yet the historical evidence seems to point in precisely the opposite direction, at least until comparatively modern times, since we know that beginning in the twelfth century a stream of Teutonic settlers spread over Prussia, Posen, and Silesia. In recent times, to be sure, the current seems to have been reversed, at least in Posen and Prussia, leading to the desperate attempts at German colonization, the wholesale expropriation of Polish lands and the cruel repression of the Poles carried out by the German Government during the last forty or fifty years. A definite solution of this aspect of the puzzle seems thus hard to suggest.

The entire problem of the Slav rests in the balance; plausible arguments may be advanced for each of the two contrary views, and until a much larger body of cranial material from all parts of the Slavic area is available, and its identification and dating can be made more accurate, it seems impossible to reach a definite conclusion. To my mind, however, the present evidence tends to favor the belief that the Slav was originally dolichocephalic. Some apologies should perhaps be made for treating this whole question at so great a length, but the importance, complexity, and far-reaching implications of the problem seemed an adequate excuse.

Turning to the study of the living peoples of our area we may first consider the Slavic-speaking population and then those of other speech. Complete and systematic investigation of the head-form of the Russian and Polish peoples has not yet been made, although data based on small numbers are available for the larger part of the area.[1] The population may be grouped in two divisions, one comprising the majority, being characterized by varying degrees of brachycephaly, the other being mesocephalic. In no portion of the whole area are dolichocephalic types present in anything but a negligible minority except where mixture with non-Slavic peoples is probable.

The area marked by predominance of brachycephalic types includes all of the Ukraine and the western and northern part of the region occupied by the Great Russians, i. e., extending from the government of Kursk northward through Smolensk and Pskov to Petrograd and Novgorod, and eastward through Mos-

---

[1] For sources see Ripley, 1899, Bibliography, and also Galai, 1905, Krasnov, 1900, Piontkovski, 1905, Prochorov, 1903 and 1907, Rojdestvenski, 1902, Spiridov, 1907, Tschepourkovsky, 1911, Vorobiev, 1899, Zdroevski, 1905.

cow and Yaroslav to Kostroma and Nishegorod. An example of the Great Russian type is given on Plate III, Fig. 3. Although the average cephalic index varies little throughout this whole area, the relative proportions of brachycephalic and dolichocephalic individuals are by no means everywhere the same, the percentage of the former being greater among the Great Russians than in the Ukraine. The Great Russians of the southeast, in the area between the Volga and the Don, are, on the other hand, on the average mesocephalic, and show a considerable reduction of the brachycephalic factors and a corresponding increase of the dolichocephalic, due apparently to admixture between the Slavic and Finnic populations such as the Cheremiss, Mordvins, etc. A second region marked by similar mesocephaly comprises all of western Russia, extending from Volhynia north to Grodno and Vitebsk, and occupied in the main by the so-called White Russians. The northern and northwestern parts of Poland, including the districts of Lomza, Plock, and Kalicz also form part of this area. The proportion of brachycephalic individuals, however, is here about as great as in the Ukraine. It is interesting and significant, in connection with the problem of the original type of the Slavic peoples, to find that Volhynia to-day has the lowest average cephalic index and the highest proportion of dolichocephalic individuals of any portion of the Russian and Polish area for which data have been published. While the population of northern Poland is, as just stated, closely similar in average cephalic index to the White Russians (and incidentally to the Teutonic population of Prussia), the southern Poles in Poland, Silesia, and in Galicia, together with the Ruthenians, are in their pronounced brachycephaly more like the people of the Ukraine.

On the basis of stature we find the population of the whole area divided into several groups. The taller statures are found in the northwestern portions of the Great Russian area, *i. e.*, in Pskov, Petrograd, and Novgorod, and in the Ukraine and the territories of the Don and Kuban Cossacks. Statures below the medium are found, on the other hand, in the northern part of the Great Russian area, *i. e.*, in eastern Novgorod, Yaroslav,

and Kostroma, and in a broad belt running east and west from
Smolensk through Orel and Grodno to and including all of Poland, where the average stature drops in some cases as low as
162 cm.   The extremely low figures here are probably in considerable part due to the inclusion of Jews, who here, as will be
shown in the chapter devoted to them, are extremely short.   As
in head-form, so in stature, Volhynia stands out from all its
neighbors in that the average stature is greater.   In Poland
in general, striking differences are found between the nobility
and the peasants, the former being well above, the latter well
under, medium height.   The difference is undoubtedly in considerable part due to economic conditions, but may also have a
racial factor.

The study of the distribution of the color of hair and eyes
gives results of importance.   In eye color, light tints everywhere
prevail over dark, the dominance of light types being strongest
in the northwest toward the Baltic.   In hair color, the reverse
is true, in that dark shades are everywhere in the majority, and
increasingly so toward the south.   In Poland, however, the largest
proportion of dark hair seems to be found, curiously enough, in
the north.   Combining the data on eye and hair color, it appears
that blond types in general prevail over brunet, this tendency
reaching its highest development in the northwest, the area of
strongly marked blondness thus adjoining that characteristic of
the north of Germany.   Only in the Carpathians and in Podolia
does the brunet type outnumber the blond.

Comparison of the data on the living with that derived from
the early crania is for the most part impossible, since, as a rule,
no nasal measurements are given.   Only for the government of
Tver, in the heart of the Great Russian territory, are such materials available.[1]   This valuable series shows that brachycephalic factors make up nearly 90 per cent of the population,
the Alpine type (with perhaps some representation of the Ural)
being in very large majority.

We may now turn to the non-Slavic peoples, and may begin

[1] Galai, 1905.

with the Lithuanians and Letts, who occupy in the main the former governments of Kurland, Kovno, Vilna, and Grodno, together with the district of Suwalki in northern Poland. In the mediæval period these peoples extended over a somewhat larger territory, especially toward the west, where they reached almost to the Vistula. To-day the Lithuanians are, like their Slavic neighbors, a predominantly brachycephalic people, of little over medium stature and strikingly blond; the Letts, living farther to the north about the Gulf of Riga, are evidently a much more mixed folk, and have a notably larger dolichocephalic element; they are, like the Lithuanians, strongly blond, but exceed them considerably in stature. The sources of this strong dolichocephalic factor are not clear, but it is to be remembered that on the basis of the finds at Rinnekalm in Livland just to the north of the modern Lettish territory, we have evidence of the dominance of long-headed types from the Bronze period down to late mediæval times.

All the other non-Slavic peoples of Russia (except the German colonies established in relatively recent times) speak languages belonging to the Ural-Altaic stock, and may be divided into three subdivisions: the Finno-Ugrians, the Turko-Tatars, and the Mongols. The Finno-Ugric branch may itself be divided into two sections, the Finnic and the Ugric, the Samoyede forming a somewhat uncertain third. No Ugrian peoples probably are to be found to-day within the limits of European Russia, those that were formerly there having migrated east of the Urals some centuries ago. Their former territory included, however, considerable parts of the governments of Viatka, Vologda, and Perm, and probably extended even farther south. The physical characteristics of these tribes will be discussed in some detail in connection with other peoples of western Siberia (see p. 337 *seq.*), but it may be noted in passing that both Vogul and Ostiak show a large predominance of dolichocephalic factors, the Proto-Australoid and Mediterranean being of greatest importance.

The Finnic section may for convenience be divided into two groups, a western and an eastern. The first comprises the Esths and Livs along the Baltic, the Chuds (Vepses, Votes, etc.), in Novgorod, the Finns and Karels, and the Lapps. The Esths are a tall people (the average stature being slightly above 170 cm.), extremely blond, and with a large majority of brachycephalic factors. The Alpine and Palæ-Alpine types are of greatest importance, but an appreciable Mongoloid element is also present; the dolichocephalic factors are of the Proto-Australoid and Proto-Negroid types, both strongly represented in the early Slavic population surrounding them. For the Chuds, no material of value is available.

The Finns to-day occupy, besides Finland, a considerable part of the northern portion of the government of Olonetz (where they are known as in eastern Finland as Karels) and parts of the Kola peninsula, and extend west through the northern portions of Sweden into the Tromsö district of Norway. It is probable that the Finns came into Finland from the region south of Lakes Ladoga and Onega, about the eighth or ninth century A. D., having been driven northward by the advance of the Slavs. Although much archæological work has been done in recent years in Finland, no measurements of prehistoric crania have, so far as I know, been published, except a brief reference to those found on the southern coast and believed to date from the Bronze or Iron Age. These are, like those of the same period at Rinnekalm in Livland, primarily dolichocephalic, and are by some believed to be the remains of Goths. It is assumed, on archæological grounds, that there was a pre-Finnish population, but as to its characteristics we have no actual evidence.

The present population of Finland[1] comprises a small proportion of Swedish-speaking people, living in two narrow strips on the southern and western coasts, who appear to have been settled here at least since mediæval times. The Finns themselves may be divided into four groups: the western Finns; the Tavast, occupying the central and larger part of the country; the Savolax, toward the north; and the Karels, in the east. In head-

---

[1] Westerlund, 1902, 1904, 1913. For the Russian Finns, see Eliseiev, 1887, and Kolmogorov, 1904.

form these groups show a regular gradation in respect to the proportion of brachycephalic individuals, from the western Finns, who closely resemble the Swedish-speaking population of the coast in having a relatively small proportion, through the Tavasts and the Savolax to the Karels, who have the largest percentage of brachycephalic individuals. Even among the Karels, however, there is a not inconsiderable dolichocephalic factor, although they are certainly in the majority brachycephalic. The determination of the types present is difficult, owing to the fact that no adequate data on Finnish crania have been published. From Retzius's[1] incomplete measurements, however, it is clear that the large majority must be of Alpine or Palæ-Alpine type, yet a respectable proportion of Mongoloid or Ural types may accompany them. In stature the Finn is in general somewhat above the medium, although the average for the Karel is placed at or slightly below 165 cm. In pigmentation the large majority are blond, the proportion of blond types decreasing from the western Finns and Swedish-speaking population where it is as large as in much of Sweden, through the Tavasts to the Karels, among whom the brunet types are in slight majority. An example of the Finnish type is given on Plate III, Fig. 4.

For the Finn, as for the Slav, there is much divergence of opinion in regard to the original type, which some hold to have been dolichocephalic and "Nordic," while others believe the early Finn to have been brachycephalic, as he is in general to-day. In the complete absence of early cranial material, any conclusion must rest on indirect evidence, and the problem is complicated by the fact that it is inextricably bound up with that of the character of the early Slav and the identification of the crania obtained from the Russian kurgans. On the one hand, it may be observed that all the other neighboring and many of the more remote Finnic tribes are to-day, at least, primarily brachycephalic, and the Cheremiss and Votiak, who must have been the nearest neighbors of the Finns before the latter moved into Finland, were so as far back as the eleventh century.[2] To

---

[1] Retzius, M. G., 1878.        [2] Konstantinov-Shchipunin, 1897.

this extent, therefore, we seem justified in regarding the Finn as probably also brachycephalic. It might be contended, however, that the Finn could have been dolichocephalic, and then, if the pre-Finnish population of Finland had been primarily brachycephalic, the absorption of this earlier people might have the same result in brachycephalizing the immigrant Finn, as has been suggested in the parallel case of the Slav. Yet, if this had been the case, it would be logical to expect that the earlier Finnish immigrants who first and most intensively came into contact with the assumed aboriginal brachycephalic population, would show the maximum amount of influence, whereas the rear-guard, who came into a country already partly swept of its earlier occupants, should preserve the original dolichocephalic type in greatest measure. As the Finns entered Finland from the southeast, we ought, therefore, to find the extreme of brachycephaly in the north and northwest, and a large dolichocephalic factor surviving in the southeast. Now it is true that the largest proportion of brachycephaly is found among the so-called Kvanes in the north, but in the east and southeast among the Karels the proportion is only 1 or 2 per cent less, and the strong dolichocephalic factor which one should find here if the Finn were originally dolichocephalic, is conspicuous by its absence.

The facts of the case are far better met, I believe, by assuming that the Finn was originally of a predominantly brachycephalic type, and the presence of a dolichocephalic factor in the population to-day is to be accounted for as follows. It has been pointed out that the proportion of long-headed individuals increases with great regularity from east to west and from north to south, the largest proportion of dolichocephaly being found among the Swedish-speaking population on the western and southern coasts. Historically we know that Scandinavian influence has been important in these sections since early mediæval times, archæologically the presence of peoples strikingly similar to the contemporaneous population of eastern Sweden is established at least as far back as the Iron Age and perhaps earlier. Since, therefore, the character of the dolichocephalic element in the Finnish people is similar to that among the Scandinavian population of the adjacent shores of Sweden; since the intensity of the dolichocephalic factor decreases in almost exact proportion as we recede from this area; and since we know that Swedish-speaking folk have been established on the coasts of Finland as far back as our historical knowledge extends, we are justified in believing that the long-headed element among the Finns is not original but secondary, and derived from long association and mixture with Scandinavian immigrants and conquerors.

The Lapps afford still another of the puzzling problems which this portion of Europe presents. They are a fishing and hunting folk, and are found in the Kola peninsula, northern Finland, in Vesterbotten and Norbotten in Sweden, and Tromsö and Finnmarken in Norway. Within historic times they extended much farther south, both in the Scandinavian peninsula and Finland, and may in prehistoric times have occupied the whole of the latter and the larger part of the former regions. Cranial material from the Lapps is meagre and from those in Scandinavia only; it is, however, very significant. The series[1] is almost purely brachycephalic, the dominant type being the Mongoloid, with the Alpine a strong second. That the Lapps are by no means a uniform people is shown, however, by the data on the living. Although everywhere short, the Scandinavian Lapps[2] attain the extreme in this particular, with an average stature of only 150–153 cm. The Russian Lapps[3] are somewhat taller, with an average of 155–156 cm. In head-form there is an even greater difference, in that, whereas the Scandinavian Lapps are almost purely brachycephalic with very high indices, the Russian Lapp is sometimes actually mesocephalic, and shows a very considerable admixture thus of dolichocephalic factors. A similar contrast exists in the matter of pigmentation, for the western Lapp is distinctly more brunet than the eastern. An example of the Norwegian Lapps is given on Plate IV, Fig. 1.

The conclusion which seems to follow from these facts is that

[1] Mantegazza, 1880.       [2] Bonaparte, 1885–86.
[3] Kelsiev, 1886; Kharuzin, 1890 b.

the western or Scandinavian Lapp is the purer group, the Russian portion of the people being mixed with some foreign dolichocephalic element. To what source must this long-headed factor be attributed? If the Lapps were, as seems most probable, the pre-Finnish population of Finland, and the Finns were, as suggested, in the main brachycephalic, the dolichocephalic factor cannot have been supplied by them. We might attribute it to a pre-Finnish Scandinavian influence for which Kharuzin finds evidence in archaic Scandinavian words adopted by the Lapps, yet, if so, one would expect the Lapps of Sweden and Norway to show the dolichocephalic influence in largest measure, whereas, in fact, they show it least, these elements being found most prominent in the eastern group. It can hardly have been contributed by the Russians, since, although there has been considerable intermixture, the Slavic occupation of the Kola peninsula and northern Olonetz did not occur until after they had settled Novgorod, and the Slavs there were already brachycephalic as early as the twelfth century. I believe the best explanation of the mystery is as follows. In late Neolithic or perhaps early Bronze times, the whole of Finland and the northern half, at least, of the Scandinavian peninsula were occupied by a very short, brunet, almost purely Mongoloid people. In southern Finland they were slightly influenced by Scandinavian contact, leading to increased stature, greater proportion of blondness, and some dolichocephalic intermixture; and it was these modified Lapps which were displaced by the Finns at the time of their immigration in the eighth or ninth century. The Lapps of the Scandinavian peninsula, on the other hand, were in the extreme north but little affected by the Scandinavian occupation of the coast, and preserved their original character largely unchanged. When, then, in the twelfth and thirteenth centuries, the Finns began to press more strongly on the Lapps in northern Finland, these took refuge in the Kola peninsula region, rather than force their way into the relatively limited area in northern Norway already occupied by their relatives. This relatively late Lapp pressure and, perhaps, slight penetration in northern

Fig. 1. Lapp.

Fig. 2. South Italian.

Fig. 3. Portuguese.

Fig. 4. Basque.

PLATE IV.

Norway would account for the statements in regard to the late entrance of the Lapps into Tromsö and Finnmarken, which would thus refer only to this partial overlaying of the earlier Scandinavian Lapps by those from Finland.

The great prominence of the Mongoloid type among the Scandinavian Lapps raises interesting questions. Nowhere else in Europe, indeed nowhere else in the world, is this type found in so large a proportion, not even among the Mongols themselves, and the question arises how to account for the concentration of this type, relatively rare in the rest of Europe, in this remote corner of the continent? Two explanations suggest themselves. On the one hand, we may suppose the Lapps to have come from the inner Asiatic region westward across northern Russia in late Neolithic or even early Bronze times, and so passed into Finland and Scandinavia. Our only Neolithic crania, however, show no trace of this type. On the other hand, it has been pointed out in dealing with the racial history of France and the Central European Highlands that there seems to be evidence of the presence of the Mongoloid type in western Europe in early Palæolithic times; it was present in Belgium in the Neolithic period, and it would not be impossible to suppose that this ancient stratum had retreated northward before the advancing newer types and finally been driven into the most remote northern corner of the continent. Yet if this were so, it is hard to understand how, during so long a period and exposed to so many vicissitudes, the type could have retained its purity to so considerable a degree. For the present the solution of the puzzle seems difficult, but we shall return to it in a later chapter when dealing with the world history of the several types.

The eastern Finnish peoples present somewhat of a contrast to those just considered. They may be divided into a northern and a southern group, the former made up of the Zyrians, Permiaks, Votiaks, etc., the latter of the Cheremiss, Mordvins, and Chuvash. The former group are in the governments of Archangel, Vologda, Perm, and Viatka; the latter live on both sides of the Volga from Kazan south to Tambov. The Chuvash are classed with the southern group because, although they now speak a Turko-Tatar language, there is much evidence to lead us to believe that they are really a Finnish people who have lost their original speech.

The northern or Permian tribes[1] are predominantly brachycephalic, although a small minority of long-headed individuals is present, are under medium stature, and prevailingly brunet; the southern group are somewhat taller, equally brunet, and in head-form rather variable; the Cheremiss and Chuvash being less, the Mordvin[2] more, brachycephalic than the northern group. Only for the Chuvash have we any cranial material, and this indicates that the Proto-Australoid and Palæ-Alpine types are of greatest importance, with the Alpine and Mediterranean coming next. While the northern groups thus, in general, resemble the western Finnish peoples, the southern has obviously been influenced by mixture with some dolichocephalic folk. If the theory that the Slav was originally dolichocephalic be accepted, the long-headed element may have been derived from them; otherwise we should need to call in either the older Ugrian peoples, who had a considerable dolichocephalic factor, or the "Scythians."

The Samoyedes, a nomad hunting and fishing people of the Arctic coast, extend beyond the limits of Europe for some distance eastward along the Siberian shore. Strongly brachycephalic and brunet, they are marked by an extremely short stature (154 cm.) and show in face and eyes strong resemblances to various Mongol and east-Asiatic peoples. Analysis of the cranial data[3] shows that the two primary factors are the Palæ-Alpine and Ural types, so that the Samoyede differs rather strongly from the Lapp, in whom the Mongoloid type was so strongly represented.

The Turko-Tatar peoples of Russia differ from the Finno-Ugric in that, whereas the latter seem clearly to have antedated the Slavs, and to be in some sense aboriginal, the Turko-Tatars

---

[1] Sevastianov, 1912.                    [2] Mainov, 1891.
[3] Sommier, 1887.

are for the most part of more recent arrival, and are the descendants of the Mongol and Tatar invasions and conquests of the twelfth century and after. The Turko–Tatar peoples of Russia to-day are divided into several sections: the Kazan Tatars, the Bashkir in the governments of Ufa and Orenburg, the Kirgiz and Nogai near the Caspian, and the Tatars of the Crimea and the Taurida on the Black Sea. For all of these folk we have, as in the case of most of the Russian area, only average measurements. The Kazan Tatars[1] are in head-form about on the line between brachycephaly and mesocephaly, those which are least mixed being most clearly brachycephalic. Their stature averages a little below the medium, and in pigmentation they are prevailingly brunet. The Crimean Tatars[2] of the steppe and the Nogai[3] of Stavropol are somewhat more predominantly brachycephalic and taller. The so-called Tatars of the southern Crimea, on the other hand, are a much mixed people, comprising remnants of Goths, Greeks, etc., and show wide variations. The Gurzoof Tatars of the southern coast are in large majority brachycephalic, whereas the Mountain Tatars and those in the vicinity of Simferopol have a considerable dolichocephalic factor and are notably taller. The Bashkir[4] are very similar to the Kazan Tatars, except that as a rule they are somewhat taller, and in the northwest portion of their range show a large dolichocephalic element of uncertain origin. The Kirgiz will be considered in a later chapter in connection with the main body of this people, who are in western Siberia.

Cranial material for these Turko-Tatar tribes is available only from the Bashkir and Nogai. An analysis of the data shows that the two groups differ in considerable degree, for while both are in the main of Alpine type, the Bashkir have a large element of the Mongoloid type, whereas the Nogai have an equally strong representation of the Ural factor. The presence of the Mongoloid element among the Bashkir is perhaps significant in relation to the problem of its strength among the Lapps, for there is

[1] Talko-Hryncewicz, 1904.    [2] Lijin, 1891.
[3] Pashkin, 1912.    [4] Weissenberg, 1892; Abramov, 1907.

some reason apparently to believe that the Bashkir were once, like the Chuvash, a Finnish-speaking people, who have subsequently been Tatarized.

The Kalmuck Mongols of Astrachan are quite recent immigrants and may best be considered in connection with the main mass of the Mongols in a later chapter. It may be said, however, in passing, that they are an almost purely brachycephalic folk, with a large factor of the Mongoloid type.

The Caucasus region which forms the boundary between Europe and Asia in the south might be considered here, but its relations are on the whole more close with the Asia Minor region, and the discussion of its complex population, together with the many problems which it presents, may be fittingly deferred to a special chapter in the section devoted to the Asiatic continent.

# CHAPTER V

## THE ITALIAN AND SPANISH PENINSULAS

### I. ITALY

NEXT to the Iberian peninsula, Italy would seem of all the parts of the European continent to be geographically the most isolated. Cut off on the north by the Alps, and surrounded on three sides by the sea, this long, narrow peninsula might be expected to have had a somewhat more simple racial history than much of the rest of Europe. Yet the record tells quite another story.

The racial history of Italy does not begin with any certainty until Neolithic times. In France and other portions of western Europe we have what are, after all, not inconsiderable remains from the Palæolithic period, but, although the climatic and other environmental factors in the Italian peninsula, then joined to northern Africa by way of Sicily, would seem to have been at least as favorable for human occupation as in southern France, almost no skeletal remains of unquestioned Palæolithic age have as yet been found. The much-discussed Olmo skull, discovered near Arezzo in Tuscany, if it be really of Palæolithic age, would establish the presence in Italy at that time of a people characterized by the possession of a low, dolichocephalic skull. Whether this represents the Proto-Australoid or the Mediterranean type is uncertain, owing to the absence of nasal bones. In either case, however, this would be in accord with conditions existing in early or late Palæolithic times in France.

Even with the coming of the Neolithic period, the data are much less abundant than is the case in western Europe in general; and that which we possess comes mainly from the very end of this period and the beginning of metal culture, the Eneolithic period, to use the term employed by the Italians, when copper but not bronze was known. The crania of this period, whether from such sites as Remedello[1] in Lombardy, from Lucca[2] in Tuscany, or from Latium[3] still farther south, show that the population of northern Italy at least was already much mixed. If it is legitimate to base conclusions on such very scanty data, it would seem that there was a distinct tendency toward a pre-dominance of dolichocephalic forms north of the Apennines in the valley of the Po and of brachycephalic ones south of the range. It will be remembered that dolichocephalic factors were at this same time also in the preponderance in the region northwest of the Alps. For the south of Italy the material is too meagre to enable us to say more than that the population here also was clearly mixed. Detailed analysis of the Italian Eneolithic crania is practically impossible, owing to their very imperfect preservation. Judging from the very few complete crania, however, it appears that two dolichocephalic types are present, the Mediterranean and the Proto-Negroid, the latter at least of very short stature. The Proto-Negroid type was, it may be remembered, found in Palæolithic times in the Grimaldi caves near the French-Italian border, so that its persistence in northern Italy is not surprising. The brachycephalic factors were also two, the Alpine and the Mongoloid.

Some light is thrown on the conditions in Italy by the some-what more abundant data of this period from Sicily[4] and Sardinia.[5] In the former island the extensive excavations in the vicinity of Syracuse which have revealed so much of interest to the archæologist, have brought to light a number of crania of Eneolithic date. These indicate that although the population of the eastern portion of Sicily was predominantly dolichoce-phalic, there was also a small element of brachycephalic type. If the two sexes are separated, a rather striking difference be-tween them at once appears, for whereas the males show a strong predominance of dolichocephalic factors, the females have no actual dolichocephals at all and instead a large majority of brachy-

---

[1] Zampa, 1890.  [2] Puccioni, 1914.  [3] Giuffrida-Ruggeri, 1906 b.
[4] Sergi, 1895 b, 1898; Giuffrida-Ruggeri, 1907.  [5] Sergi, 1907 a.

cephalic factors. Analysis of the measurements indicate that the long-headed elements among the males are in the first place the Mediterranean, followed by the Proto-Australoid. The former type is important also in the female series, but is there dominated by the Palæ-Alpine and closely followed by the Alpine. In Sardinia the situation was about the same, although the contrast between the sexes was somewhat less sharp.

From all these facts it seems reasonably safe to conclude that at the end of the Neolithic period the fundamental stratum of the population in the Italian peninsula and the islands was composed primarily of the Mediterranean type, with some survival of the older Proto-Australoid and Proto-Negroid types presumably present in Palæolithic times. Into this predominantly dolichocephalic population came, as into most of Europe at this time, an infiltration of brachycephalic peoples which profoundly influenced the situation not only on the mainland but in the islands as well. In part we may assume this immigrant element to have come into Italy from the north, by way perhaps of the Adige valley and around the head of the Adriatic. Yet it is probable that a goodly portion of the Alpine and Palæ-Alpine settlers or conquerors came by another route. For the islands at least, and especially for Sicily, it is likely that perhaps the larger part came by sea from the eastern Mediterranean, as is suggested by the similarities between Sicilian pottery and that of Crete and the Ægean area at this period. There is much archæological evidence which leads us to believe that these brachycephalic immigrants to the islands (and perhaps to southern Italy) were merely a part of the stream which, touching the southern shores of Spain, passed through the Straits of Gibraltar and on up the Atlantic coast to Brittany, the British Isles, and the North Sea shores.

For the succeeding Bronze Age, data are, because of the wide prevalence of cremation, almost wholly lacking. Archæological evidences, however, lead us to believe that during this period a considerable immigration took place from the northward into the Po valley, and also from the Danube valley around the head

of the Adriatic. The former stream would have brought large
increments of brachycephalic, primarily Alpine, peoples; the
latter probably a mixed group. The result, at any rate, was that
by the end of the Bronze period the population of the Po valley
and Venezia was much more strongly brachycephalic than before. Emigrants from here crossed the Apennines and settled
in Tuscany, while others continued farther south to the Tiber,
where they became in part the ancestors of the Latins.

The evidence afforded by the Iron Age graves is interesting,
for, although the data are scanty, the crania from the famous
cemeteries of Villanova and Novilara[1] (on the northern Adriatic
coast) indicate the appearance in considerable numbers of a type
hitherto almost unknown in the Italian peninsula. This is the
Caspian, which long before this had become a factor of large
importance in most of the rest of Europe, but which now for the
first time, apparently, penetrated south of the Alps. The strength
of its representation along the coast of the Adriatic leads to the
suggestion that these immigrants may have come, like the earlier
brachycephals, by sea. The supposition is far from impossible,
but the presence of strong elements of this type in the Danube
valley at this period, renders an alternative route by land across
the northern portion of the Balkan region worth consideration.

With the beginning of the historic period we are on firmer
ground, and the first of the problems that calls for discussion is
the much debated one of the racial character and affiliations of
the Etruscans, whose civilization in the valley of the Po and in
Tuscany antedated that of Rome. Analysis of the series of about
a hundred crania which are available,[2] shows at once that they
form a very much mixed group. On the whole the dolichocephalic factors prevail, but there is a difference between the sexes
such that the males have a clear excess of long-headed elements,
the females an excess of round-headed types. In both sexes the
Mediterranean type is the most important single factor, followed
by the Palæ-Alpine and Alpine types. These three types had,

---

[1] Sergi, 1907 b.
[2] Cantacuzène, 1909; Frasetto, 1906; Mosso, 1905–06; Sergi, 1915.

however, been present in northern Italy at least ever since Eneolithic times, and we seem to get no definite indication of any clear-
cut differences between the Etruscan and the older population.
If Mosso is correct, however, in his dating of the crania, it would
seem to be undeniable that the early Etruscans were very notably
more dolichocephalic than the later, and belonged, moreover,
primarily to the Caspian and Proto-Negroid types rather than
to the Mediterranean, which was dominant in Italy in earlier
times.   The early Etruscans therefore were to a considerable extent "un-Italian," and their traditional foreign origin is thus corroborated, although but little light is thrown on the vexed question of their provenience.   Since they seem however to have been
in large part dolichocephalic, any close relationship such as has
been suggested to the highly brachycephalic population of Asia
Minor seems impossible.

If the Etruscans were a mixed people, what can be said of
their neighbors to the south in Latium, that Latin people who
were destined to conquer the Etruscans and build up the great
power of Rome?   The series[1] of Roman crania of the sixth century B. C. is the earliest data we possess, and shows that the
Romans of the period prior to the establishment of the Republic
were almost as mixed a people as the Etruscans.   As in their
case, the males are much more strongly dolichocephalic than the
females, and while for both sexes the proportion of Mediterranean
factors is about the same, the males have in addition a considerable representation of both Proto-Australoid and Caspian types,
which are practically lacking in the females.   These latter, on
the other hand, show a large Palæ-Alpine factor which is virtually absent in the males.   The interpretation of these facts is
not altogether easy.   The striking dolichocephaly of the men in
comparison with the women suggests, in view of the large Caspian element present, that possibly an infusion of the Iron Age
Novilara peoples from the Adriatic coast may have crossed the
Apennines into Umbria and Latium, thus greatly strengthening
the dolichocephalic factors in the valley of the Tiber.   Some

[1] Sergi, 1900.

contributory evidence in favor of this view will be pointed out later.

If this hypothesis is correct, it will be seen at once that its implications are important. These may be outlined briefly as follows: By the end of the Bronze period the population of the northern half of Italy at least had become very much mixed. The old Neolithic dolichocephalic peoples, mainly of Mediterranean and Proto-Australoid types, had been overlaid by and largely blended with Palæ-Alpine and Alpine peoples who had come into the Po valley from the north and also (bringing with them the Terramare culture) around the head of the Adriatic from the Balkan region. These brachycephalic immigrants by land had also been supplemented, perhaps, by others who came by sea. The Iron Age is marked by an apparent recrudescence of dolichocephalic types. These appear first along the Adriatic coast at Novilara near Pesaro, at Villanova near Bologna, at Macerata, and perhaps farther south. Where, as at Novilara, the crania are sufficiently well preserved to enable us to determine their type, the striking feature is the great predominance of a type largely new to Italy, i. e., the Caspian. The following centuries saw the spread of these immigrants across the Apennines into Etruria and Umbria, and as far south at least as northern Campagna. By the sixth century B. C. they had become the kernel of the people known as the Etruscans, and as the Sabines they entered into the fusion which resulted in the founding of Rome, where, as the Patrician class, they formed the aristocracy of the Roman people. There was thus a racial factor in common between the early Romans and the Etruscans, which helps to explain some features of the obscure early history of Rome. The Umbrian crania of the third and second centuries B. C. seem to add something by way of corroboration to this theory, since here several centuries later, the Caspian factor still remains one of importance in the population.

The Roman population of the sixth century B. C. was, as we have seen, predominantly dolichocephalic, so far at least as the males were concerned. When we are able to study them again, in the series of crania dating from the period between the second century B. C. to the second century A. D.,[1] we find them to have undergone a complete change.   The male crania now show a large majority of brachycephalic factors, mainly of the Alpine type, the dolichocephalic elements surviving being the Mediterranean and the Proto-Australoid.   The females, however, retain a notable Caspian factor, which four or five centuries before had been so characteristic of the males.   The completeness of the transformation is shown still more clearly by the Pompeian crania,[2] dating from the first century A. D.   Here the dolichocephalic factors have almost totally disappeared, and the Alpine type dominates both sexes in large degree.

The Roman of the Empire was thus something quite different from the Roman of the earlier period.   To what was this change due?   The final answer to this question must await the securing of data for the intervening period in northern Italy, yet the major outlines of the process by which the revolution was brought about seem fairly clear.   In a word, the change must have been due to absorption.   The five or six hundred years between the time of Servius Tullius and the second century of the Empire had been a time of enormous expansion.   Rome had grown to be a great city, and the increase in population had been primarily in the non-patrician class.   We have already seen that by the end of the Bronze period the people of northern Italy at least had, as the result of the immigration of Alpine and Palæ-Alpine peoples, lost its earlier majority of dolichocephalic types.   The Caspian invaders of the Iron Age were, after all, but a minority, and had been absorbed into the mass of the previous population, while the ranks of the brachycephals were constantly augmented by new intrusions and infiltrations from the north and northeast. During the fifth century the Gallic invasion had poured across the Alps into the Po valley, and not until the third century did Cis-Alpine Gaul come under Roman rule.   Meanwhile the whole region had probably become in large majority brachycephalic. Upon all of this northern area, as well as upon the south, Rome

[1] Sergi, 1900.                    [2] Schmidt, E., 1884.

drew for its increasing population, with the result that the rising
tide of round-headed peoples drowned out the older long-heads.
That the transformation was progressive from north to south is
suggested by the fact that the later Etruscans were already predominantly brachycephalic.

For the long period between the second century and the
eighteenth there are virtually no data from which to obtain concrete evidence in regard to the changes which may have taken
place in the Italian population. We can only infer from historical sources what was happening during this period of 1,500 years.
It seems certain that large increments of new blood came into
Italy, particularly in the north, during the first part of this time.
The sources were twofold, (1) the appearance in Italy of legions
made up of foreign soldiers recruited in Spain, in Gaul, Illyria,
and the Danubian region, and (2) the barbarian invasions of the
fifth and sixth centuries. The legionaries from outside Italy
brought varied racial factors to the developing complex of the
Italic people. Some, such as the Gauls, brought largely brachycephalic factors of Alpine and Palæ-Alpine type; others, such as
the Iberians, reinforced the dolichocephalic elements. But while
the influence from the side of the legions was probably by no
means negligible, that of the invasions of the Goths in the fifth
and of the Lombards in the sixth centuries was of far greater
magnitude. Both of these immigrants, although almost certainly much mixed, contributed in the main to the dolichocephalic elements in the population, bringing more specifically that
blend of the Caspian, Mediterranean, and Proto-Negroid types
which is commonly known as "Nordic," with its strong tendency toward blondness and tall stature. It would therefore
seem probable that in the seventh or eighth century the valley
of the Po must have had a considerable dolichocephalic element,
and that this probably extended southward in diminishing
strength, at least as far as Rome. That this is true seems to be
shown by a small series of crania from Aquilæa in Venezia,[1] dating from the period between the eighth and twelfth centuries.

[1] Vram, 1899.

The series indicates that even at this still later time dolicho-cephalic factors amounted to nearly 40 per cent. The influence of this great dolichocephalic invasion seems, however, to have faded rapidly after this, for in a similar series dating from the fourteenth century the long-headed factors have decreased to about 15 per cent, which proportion they have preserved rela-tively unchanged down to the present day.

For the modern population of Italy we possess cranial data from Venezia,[1] Umbria,[2] and Tuscany.[3] Analysis of the material shows that the population in all three areas is very similar; in each the brachycephalic factors are in great majority, ranging from 75 to 85 per cent, and in each the Alpine type is clearly dominant. Certain interesting differences may, however, be de-tected between the region north and that south of the Apen-nines. In the former, and especially in Bologna, the factor of secondary importance is the Ural type, whereas in the region south of the Apennines it is the Palæ-Alpine. The latter was characteristic of the immigrants into Italy in the Bronze Age; the Ural type, on the other hand, was little if at all known in Italy until mediæval times, when it was an important factor in the Swiss population.

For southern Italy, from the earliest period down to modern times, practically no cranial material is available; even from the region about Rome we have nothing of any real value since the second century. About all that the few scattered individual crania from the whole south enable us to say of its racial his-tory is that its population has at all times apparently been somewhat mixed; nevertheless the dolichocephalic factors have been more clearly and continuously dominant here than in the north. The only exception to the general absence of data from the south is the small series of modern crania from Manfredonia[4] in Apulia. The contrast with the region, say, of Umbria in the north is striking. Here dolichocephalic factors are in the ma-jority, although brachycephalic elements amount to almost a

[1] Tedeschi, 1897.                    [2] Moschen, 1896.
[3] Moschen, 1898; Zanolli, 1908.      [4] Frassetto, 1904.

third of the total. The Mediterranean type is of much the greatest importance, and is followed by the Proto-Negroid, both perhaps survivals of the Neolithic fundamental stratum which in the whole north has been replaced by Palæ-Alpine and Alpine types, that in the south have penetrated only as minorities.

Before turning to the living population, a few words must be said in regard to the changes which have occurred in Sicily and Sardinia since Eneolithic times. For Sicily we have series of modern crania from Messina[1] and also from Palermo,[2] and analysis shows that the two series are substantially similar in character, and that so far as relative proportions of dolichocephalic and brachycephalic factors are concerned, the modern population is almost identical with that of Eneolithic times. Yet the types involved have changed. The round-headed elements are the same in character and proportions, but the long-headed factors have been strongly modified. For whereas in prehistoric times the Mediterranean type was in very large majority, to-day while still the largest single factor, it has associated with it a considerable proportion of both the Proto-Negroid and Caspian types. From the Eneolithic period down well into modern times, Sicily has received large increments of population from without—Carthaginian and Greek, Goth and Vandal, Saracen, Norman, and Lombard. With this welter of immigrants it is extraordinary that the general character of the population has remained, after all, so stable. To which of these immigrant groups the new dolichocephalic elements are to be ascribed, is difficult to say with any certainty. The Caspian factor may be due to almost any, except probably the Carthaginian, to which we may perhaps look for part, at least, of the Proto-Negroid element. That this is somewhat more common in Palermo than in Messina would seem to be in accordance with this suggestion.

Sardinia[3] presents a rather different picture. Comparison of the modern crania with those of prehistoric times shows that the present population contains a much smaller proportion of brachy-

[1] Mondio, 1897.                                    [2] Moschen, 1893.
[3] Duckworth, 1910–11; Onnis, 1898.

cephalic elements than the ancient.   As in Sicily, however, the dolichocephalic types have changed.   Whereas formerly the Proto-Negroid type was in large majority, it is the Proto-Austra-loid and Mediterranean types which are most prominent to-day. As compared with Sicily, Sardinia suffered less in the way of con-quest and invasion by outsiders, and the changes observed can-not well be explained in the same way as there.   Perhaps the de-crease in the Proto-Negroid type may be accounted for by the extensive depletion of the wilder tribes, which were captured and sent in thousands as slaves to Rome; no suggestion offers itself, however, in regard to the increase in the Mediterranean and Proto-Australoid types, unless some increase in the former may be attributed to the Jewish and Egyptian settlers sent to the island by Tiberius.

Our knowledge of the living population of Italy we owe mainly to the great series of measurements taken by Livi[1] on military conscripts from all portions of the country.   From his data the following conclusions may be drawn: In head-form the present population exhibits a very significant distribution of the dolichocephalic and brachycephalic factors.   The map given in Plate V, Fig. 1, shows the percentage of dolichocephalic types for the whole of Italy, Sicily, and Sardinia by provinces.   It will be noted that these reach a proportion of as much as 25 or 35 per cent only in the "toe" and "heel" of the peninsula.   In all of Italy north of the Apennines the proportion of dolichocephals is only 5 per cent or less; whereas in all the area to the south (ex-cept in the "toe" and "heel") the proportion ranges in general between 5 per cent and 15 per cent, except in Umbria and part of Tuscany, where it falls to a figure more characteristic of the north, and in the Serchio and Magra valleys near Lucca, where there is a small area of greater prevalence of dolichocephaly.   Of the islands, Sicily shows in general less than 25 per cent of dolicho-cephals, rising above this only in the northeast corner, where the island approaches closest to the mainland.   An example of the dolichocephalic type of mixed Mediterranean and Caspian origin

[1] For titles, see Ripley, 1899, Bibliography.

is given on Plate IV, Fig. 2.    Sardinia, on the other hand,
shows in its southern half probably the largest proportion of
long-headed individuals in all southern Europe outside parts of
the Iberian peninsula.

In Plate V, Fig. 2, is given the complement to the former
map, in this case showing the percentage of brachycephalic
individuals in each district.    Although somewhat less uniform
than the other map, its significance is even more clear.    Here
again the Po valley stands out sharply, with its 80 per cent or
more of brachycephalic individuals, and the striking character
of the northern Apennines as a racial frontier is again shown.
The extent, however, to which the brachycephalic factors have
penetrated southward in the peninsula is especially strikingly
shown, in that it appears that they form 50 per cent or more
of the population as far south as the Campagna and the northern
part of Abruzzi, and only in the district of Cosenza in Calabria
do they fall below 20 per cent.    Sicily is, in general, similar to
the adjacent tip of Calabria, while Sardinia, as might be expected,
shows throughout the minimum proportions.

In stature we may distinguish three main regions.    The first
includes Sicily and Sardinia, together with all of the peninsula
south of a line running from Rome to Ancona.    Here the stature
is short, the average ranging from 159–162 cm.    The second
comprises all the rest of Italy, except the province of Venezia,
and is marked by a somewhat taller stature, although still under
the medium (av. 163–165).    The third is formed by Venezia,
where the stature increases again slightly, averaging 166 cm.,
this rise being in the region which adjoins the area of tall statures
in the Tyrol and the northern Balkan lands.

While all of Italy may with justice be said to be primarily
brunet in coloring, there are, however, distinct grades of bru-
netness observable.    The extremes are found, on the one hand,
in Sardinia and Calabria, where blond or even mixed types are
practically absent, and, on the other, along the northern margin
of the Po valley, where considerable blond factors appear.

The character and distribution of the living population seem

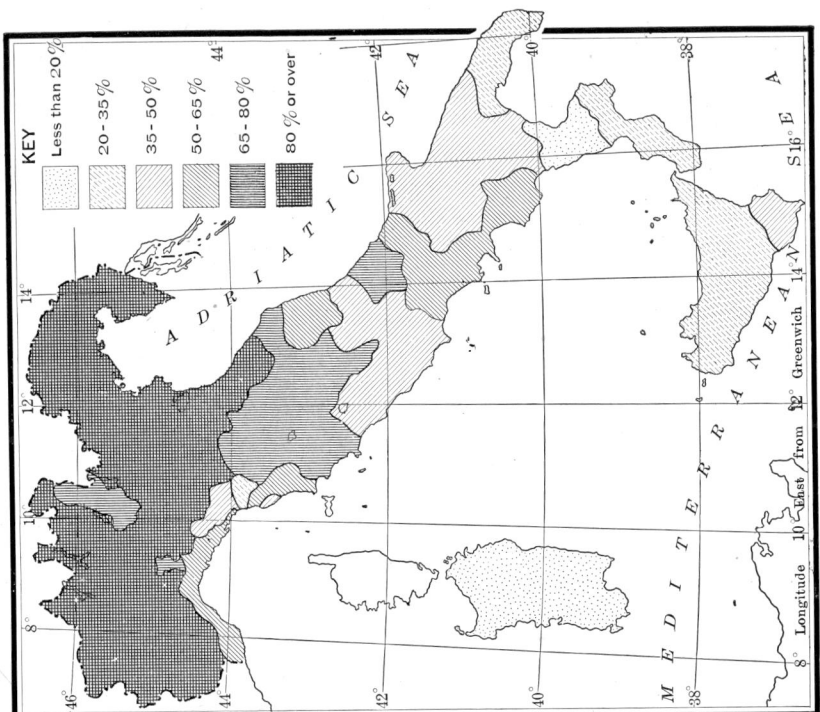

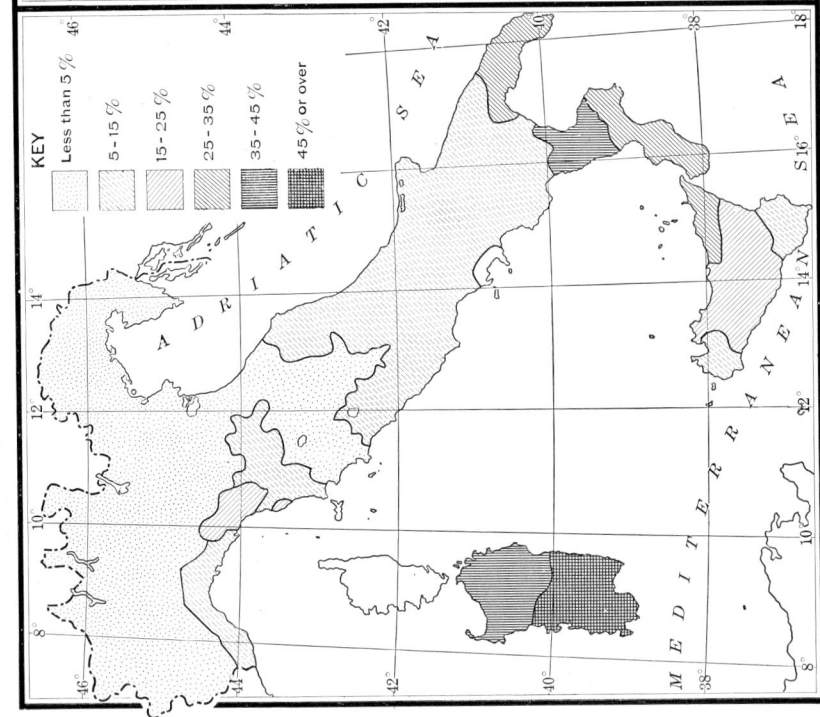

PLATE V. ITALY.

FIGURE 1. Percentage of Dolichocephals (based on data given by Livi).

FIGURE 2. Percentage of Brachycephals (based on data given by Livi).

thus to bear out very well the conclusions drawn from the study of the older materials.  Of the original early Neolithic population, short in stature, probably brunet in color, and mainly made up of the Mediterranean and Proto-Australoid types, with some admixture of the taller Proto-Negroid, there remains outside Sardinia but a dwindling minority.  Only in Calabria and the tip of Apulia do any of these survive in considerable proportion, and here probably it is the Mediterranean type which forms the bulk of the present dolichocephalic population.  Throughout most of the rest of the peninsula the brachycephalic types which since late Neolithic times have poured into Italy across the Alps or around the head of the Adriatic, now dominate, as they seem to have done as early as the first century of our era. Now as then, the most important factor in this brachycephalic population is the short, brunet Alpine type, although in the Po valley to-day there is a not inconsiderable factor of the Ural type, which seems to show a tendency toward blond coloration. Of the influence of the immigrant Goths and Lombards, Baltic peoples of tall stature and predominantly dolichocephalic type, there is little trace, except so far as it may be seen in a tendency toward taller stature and a greater proportion of blonds, in those portions of the Po valley in which they settled most abundantly.

## II.  The Iberian Peninsula

Like Italy, the peninsula now politically divided between Spain and Portugal is cut off from the rest of Europe by a mountain wall, and in comparison with the Alps the Pyrenees have been, on the whole, a more effective barrier.  The relative isolation thus afforded and the close approach of the peninsula to the African coast (with which in Palæolithic times it was still actually connected) have been the chief geographic features whose influence may be traced in its racial history.  The surface features of the peninsula have also been of some importance in this respect, several fairly distinct areas being discernible.  The larger portion of the area is occupied by the central plateau, which lies at an elevation of between two and three thousand feet above the sea.  Bordering this on the north are the Cantabrian Mountains and on the south the Sierra Nevada, although these are in large part separated from the plateau proper by the lowland of the Guadalquivir basin, as the Pyrenees in the north are by the even broader basin of the Ebro.

The modern population of the Iberian peninsula is divided into three main groups by differences in language.  The western portion, including Portugal and the Spanish province of Galicia, speaks Portuguese; the people of the opposite eastern coast in Valencia and Catalonia have for their language Catalan, which is related to the Provençal or Langue d'Oc of southern France; Spanish is the tongue of all the remainder of the population, with the exception of a small area at the western end of the Pyrenees, where both in Spain and France we find the Basques.  In their speech this interesting people are an anomaly, for it is a polysynthetic-agglutinative one, wholly unrelated to the Indo-European or any other existing form of speech, although grammatically it has analogies with the Ural-Altaic and some of the American Indian languages.

In comparison with France, the Iberian peninsula is as yet very poor in any cranial remains dating to the Palæolithic period. Only a single skull, the now famous but long neglected Gibraltar skull, has yet been found within the area.  In type this skull, which dates from early Palæolithic times, appears to be a blend between the Proto-Australoid and Mongoloid types.  The former was that dominant in France at this period; the latter, although it appears later in other parts of Europe, is in the southern part of the continent extremely rare.  It was present, however, in historic and prehistoric times on the Mediterranean shores of Africa, and was an important element in the population of some of the Canary Islands, so that we may perhaps regard its apparent presence at the tip of the peninsula as evidence of African influence.  A single skull of mixed type found at the extremity of the peninsula is slender evidence on which to base conclusions in regard to the Palæolithic population, but if we take into consideration the conditions in France we may hazard the statement that the Proto-Australoid type was also in Spain the dominant factor.

For Neolithic times the data are somewhat more numerous, but unfortunately the crania are so incomplete, or, as in the case of the important series from the shell-heaps of Mugem in Portugal, the published measurements are so incomplete, that the determination of the types present is somewhat precarious. It is clear, at any rate, that dolichocephalic factors were everywhere in the majority, and generally in large majority. As in France, the Mediterranean type seems to have been the most important, although there is evidence of the considerable strength of the Proto-Negroid factor, which, as will be seen, still survives in remote districts among the living population. The brachycephalic elements cannot be determined, but seem to have been relatively much less abundant than in France, and the peninsula appears to have retained its predominantly dolichocephalic character until the end of Neolithic times.

The excavations of Siret[1] on the coast of Granada have brought to light crania dating from the Eneolithic or early Bronze Age, which reveal the population of this southeastern corner of the peninsula as very mixed. Although dolichocephalic factors are in the majority, the predominance of the Mediterranean type has disappeared and is replaced by the Caspian, the hypothetically Palæolithic Proto-Australoid occupying second place. Of the brachycephalic elements, the Ural and Palæ-Alpine types are almost the only ones represented. The conclusions to be drawn from these finds, although tentative in the absence of other comparable material, seem important. The weakness of the Mediterranean and the strength of the Caspian type would appear to imply a rather radical change, which may be accounted for in several ways. Since the latter type was not, so far as we can tell, present in the peninsula in any force in Neolithic times, it must have come in either from France in the north or from Africa in the south, unless, as seems rather unlikely, it came by sea.

[1] Siret, 1887.

Whether peoples of Caspian type had penetrated to southern and southwestern France at this time we do not know, since Neolithic crania from this portion of the country are as yet practically unknown; and if they had, to have reached the extreme southern coast in such considerable strength would almost have necessitated a complete modification of the population of the whole of the rest of the peninsula, of which we have no evidence. There is, however, much greater probability in the suggestion of an African source. As will be shown in a later chapter devoted to northern Africa, the Caspian type was almost certainly strongly represented in the region north of the Sahara at this time, and its presence on the coast of Granada would thus be the result of a spread from Morocco along the peninsula's southern shore. It is a theory strongly championed that the Mediterranean type spread into Spain from Africa; a much later historical movement in the same direction was that of the Arabs and Saracens, so that there would seem to be justification for some such Proto-Berber drift.

The presence at the very beginning of the metal ages of a considerable factor of the Ural type, here on the extreme southeastern coast of Spain, is puzzling. We cannot look to Africa, for there is no trace of it there; there seems little justification in regarding it as sea-borne from the eastern portions of the Mediterranean, for neither in Sicily nor Sardinia, where, if this were the case we might also expect to find traces of it, is there any evidence of its presence. We are left with an origin from the north, from France, and for this we have some little evidence, since it has been shown that in Belgium at least the type was abundant in Neolithic times, and our scanty data show that it was present also in the Paris basin. As before, the absence of all data for southwestern France makes the demonstration of any connection with Spain impossible. We have, however, the point that will be elaborated somewhat later in discussing the problem of the Basque, namely, that among this ancient and isolated people of the western Pyrenees, this same Ural type is still to-day of large importance. Until further evidence disproves the theory, I would suggest that these brachycephals represent the earliest immigration into the peninsula from the northward of which we have any trace.

For the Bronze and Early Iron Ages there are little or no available data, but we may probably assume that, in common with France and other parts of western Europe at the former period, a considerable infusion of brachycephalic factors took place. That some, at least, of the Palæ-Alpine and Alpine immigrants came lured by the mineral wealth of the peninsula, and came by sea from the eastern Mediterranean, seems extremely probable. Galicia and Asturia in the northwest and Sevilla in the southwest were in particular regions so influenced from the sea, and the remains of these early brachycephalic miners have been found, for example, at the copper-mines of Huelva. Somewhat later more numerous floods of Alpine peoples poured in from France around the western end of the Pyrenees and across the Cantabrian Mountains into Old Castile and Leon. Such, for example, was the Celtic immigration of the fourth century B. C.

How far the Roman occupation of the peninsula affected the racial history is here, as elsewhere, a matter of uncertainty. It is undoubtedly true that there was a very considerable infusion of Roman blood in parts of the country, which would have contributed both brachycephalic and dolichocephalic elements similar in the main to those already present. The importance of any such influence is, however, far overshadowed by the period of invasion, which, beginning in the fifth century A. D., brought into the peninsula, as also to France, a flood of peoples from the Baltic Lands, whose racial characteristics were largely those of the "Nordic" blend. Vandals, Suevi, Alans, and Goths contributed beyond doubt, a considerable factor to the racial complex, especially in the north and northwest of the peninsula. The south, on the other hand, would seem to have been relatively little affected; its turn came with the Mohammedan conquests of the eighth century and the several centuries of Saracen rule. During this period we have the coming of Arabs, Berbers, and other north African peoples in considerable numbers, with the result that further increments of long-headed types were added to the population. These were probably in the main Mediterranean and Caspian, with something of the Proto-Negroid type.

The results of the study of the living population have, as in so many cases, been published only in such form as to make analysis of the data impossible, and only general statements in regard to head-form can be made. Basing conclusions on the average cephalic index of the different provinces and districts, the Iberian peninsula has a somewhat more uniform population than France, and one which is much more strongly dolichocephalic. Whereas in France no department shows at present an average cephalic index which falls within the dolichocephalic group, in the peninsula, as may be seen from the map given in Plate VI, the whole basin of the Douro in the north and west, together with a smaller area in Murcia in the southeast, are more or less strongly dolichocephalic, while the Ebro and Guadalquivir basins are only just over the line in the mesocephalic group. In France the average cephalic index of most of the departments is clearly brachycephalic; in the peninsula brachycephalic averages occur only in two areas, one being in the vicinity of Huelva on the Gulf of Cadiz, where strong infusions of round-headed folk took place in the Bronze Age; the other being in the Cantabrian region, along the northern coast from Corunna eastward to Bilbao. From Hoyos Sainz's[1] study of modern Spanish crania it would appear that the dolichocephalic element in the upper Douro basin, in Leon, and Old Castile, was primarily Mediterranean in type. In northern Portugal,[2] however, in the provinces of Beira Alta and Tras os Montes, there is a strong factor of the Caspian type, which yields in the more rugged and mountainous sections to the Proto-Negroid and Proto-Australoid types. Both of these seem also to be of notable importance in the mountainous parts along the Levantine coast, where, in the province of Teruel for example, they are especially clearly marked among the female portion of the population. The brachyce-

[1] Hoyos Sainz, 1913.                    [2] Mendes Correa, 1916–17.

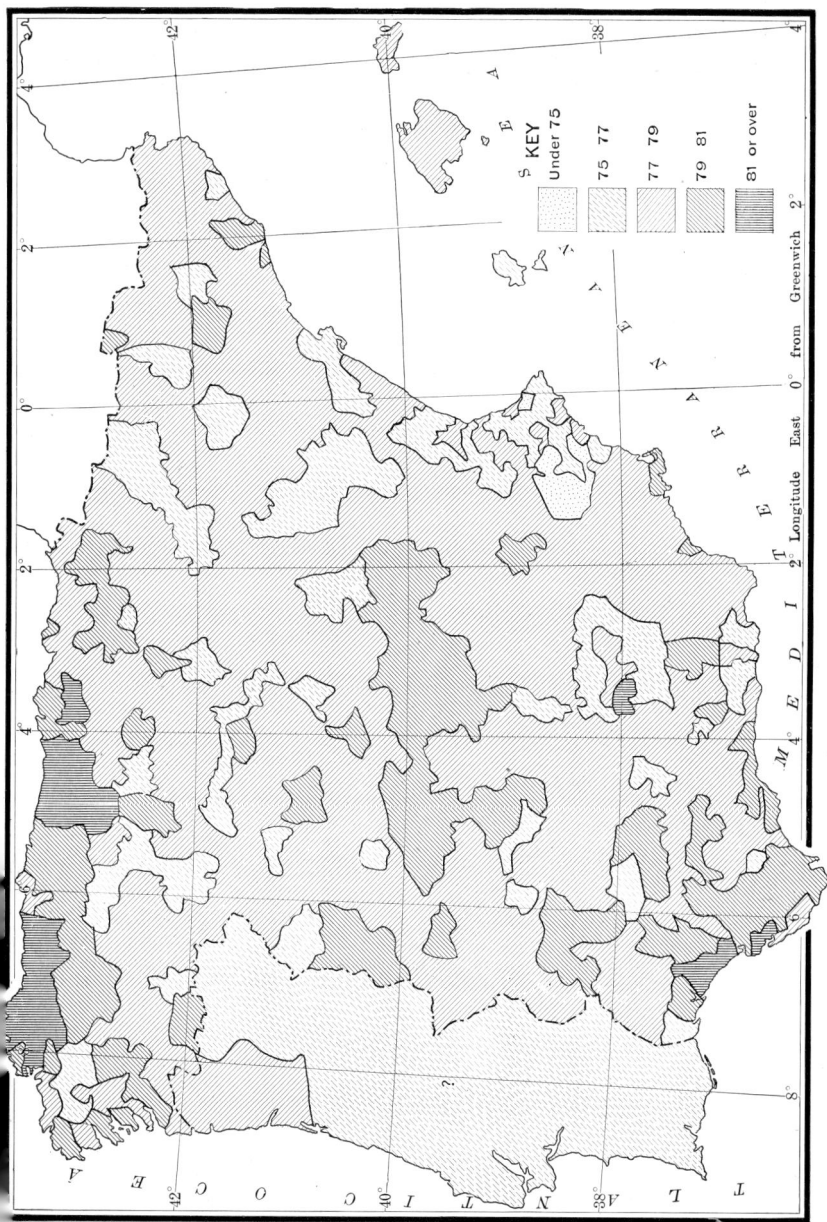

KEY

Under 75

75–77

77–79

79–81

81 or over

PLATE VI. SPAIN AND PORTUGAL.

Distribution of the Cephalic Index (Spain, based on data given by Oloriz; Portugal, rough estimate based on Da Costa Ferreira).

phalic factors throughout seem to be in the main of Alpine type.

The stature of the present-day population varies about as widely as that in France, and the geographic distribution of the taller and shorter types is rather significant, in that the latter are confined almost exclusively to the plateau and the mountain areas of the north and northwest, whereas the taller types cluster along the eastern and southern coasts. To some extent the relative shortness of the plateau population, whose average stature ranges from 160 cm. to 164 cm., is doubtless due to the economic poverty of the region as contrasted with the southern and eastern coasts, but may also be attributed in part to the influence of the short, brachycephalic Celts, who settled mainly in the plateau. The taller statures of the south and east do not exceed an average of 167 cm.

In pigmentation the peoples of the Iberian peninsula are prevailingly, and as a rule strongly, brunet. Blond types seem to occur in noticeable porportion chiefly in the northwest. Here, especially in the shore population, a considerable number of tall, blond or blondish individuals occur, the proportion rising in the case of the fishing population of the northern coast of the Portuguese province of Minho,[1] to as high as 70 per cent.

The results of the study of the living population may be tentatively correlated with the archæological data somewhat as follows: The old Mediterranean type, of medium or under medium stature and brunet character, dominant in Neolithic times apparently throughout most of the peninsula, still forms the underlying stratum of the people, except in the Cantabrian region, the northern Portuguese coast, and in the extreme south. In the upper basin of the Douro, perhaps in southern and central Portugal and in the basin of the Ebro, it is probably fairly pure, but in the region of the plateau has been considerably blended with the Alpine factors brought in by the Celtic and other immigrants from the north, during the Bronze and later periods. These, however, appear to have settled in largest numbers on the slopes of the Cantabrian range. The Proto-Negroid and Proto-

---

[1] Cardoso, 1905–08.

Australoid factors, which were strong in Neolithic times and earlier, have apparently been driven back into the more isolated mountain districts of northeastern Portugal, of Murcia and Valencia, and of the Pyrenees. An example of this type is shown on Plate IV, Fig. 3. The later "Nordic" factors coming in in historic times survive mainly along the northwestern coast. In comparison with France, the Iberian peninsula has received far greater influences from Africa; while the barrier of the Pyrenees has in considerable measure protected it from the floods of Palæ-Alpine and Alpine peoples which from Neolithic times onward have poured into France.

In tracing the early history of the region mention has been made of the Basques, that small group of peculiar people at the western end of the Pyrenees, who in the sixth century or thereabouts spread across the mountains into the edge of southwestern France, so that at present they are found on both sides of the political frontier. The peculiar character of their language early attracted attention, and their origins and affiliations have been the subject of voluminous discussions. Some, like Collignon,[1] have declared the Basque to constitute a definite "race," others, such as Aranzadi,[2] himself a Basque, regard them as a mixed type. In view of the importance which the Basque question has assumed, it will be necessary to treat the problem briefly here.

The first point to be noted is that one feature seems to distinguish the Basque throughout the area of his distribution, *i. e.*, his peculiar type of face. This is one which is wide in the forehead and upper portion, but narrows to a pointed chin below, producing a curious triangular form, well shown in the illustration given on Plate IV, Fig. 4. The second is that analysis of the data on the living shows that the French and Spanish Basques differ considerably in most other respects. As compared to the Spanish, the French Basques are taller and have more strongly brachycephalic and higher skulls; in other words, are, so far as cranial characters are concerned, more clearly Alpine

---

[1] Collignon, 1895.          [2] Aranzadi, 1889.

in type and thus similar to the dominant factors in southwestern France. On the other hand, the Spanish Basques appear to be a blend between this and the Mediterranean type which forms the substratum in the Iberian area.

Fortunately we possess detailed measurements of two series of crania of Spanish Basques,[1] which enable us to judge their characteristics, at least, with greater certainty. The Guipuzcoa series, which may be supposed to represent the purer Basque type, is primarily dolichocephalic, the Mediterranean type being clearly predominant. The brachycephalic factor is almost equally divided between the Alpine and the Ural types. The female crania show significant differences. Although dolichocephalic by a narrow margin, the relative proportions of the different types are completely changed. The Ural is here the most numerous element, followed by the Proto-Australoid, the Mediterranean dropping to third place. The other series from Zaraus, on the coast just west of San Sebastian, differs from the first in that the males show a greatly reduced proportion of the Mediterranean and Ural types and an increase in the Alpine, together with the presence of small factors of the Caspian and Proto-Negroid, which were not represented before. The females, on the other hand, have the Mediterranean as the chief factor, and the Ural type, although only in the minority, is nevertheless three times as important as in the male crania.

The probable interpretation of these facts would seem to be that, in the first place, the Basques of the coast are mixed with a considerable Alpine element attributable to the Celtic and earlier immigrants, whose presence on the northern side of the Cantabrian range has already been referred to. It may be expected that when detailed data for the French Basques are available, they will be found to resemble these. In the second place, we may infer that the distinctive character of the purer Basques of Guipuzcoa lies in the presence of a large factor of the Ural type. As there are available for comparison, unfortunately, no other cranial series for any portion of Spain or southwestern

[1] Aranzadi, 1914.

France, it is quite impossible to prove that the Ural type is present among the Basques to a larger degree than in the rest of the population, although this will, I believe, be found ultimately to be the case. If this is true, we should have to regard the modern Basques as the result of the mixture of a people predominantly of the Ural type with one in whom the Mediterranean element was of primary importance. The latter requirement is met, it would seem, by the fundamental stratum of the Spanish population. As there is as yet no evidence to lead us to believe that the Ural type was present in the peninsula before the coming of the Mediterranean, we must accept it as a later immigrant. That a substantial factor was present on the Granada coast in Eneolithic times has already been noted; it is found as an important element in the Neolithic population of Belgium and, in all probability, also of France, although this is, from the character of the data, as yet incapable of direct proof. Yet the belief in its presence in France is confirmed by the fact that it still survives in strength in two areas at least. In Aveyron, in the southern Cevennes, the small series of modern crania which we have shows it to be the predominant type, while the larger series from the Haut Morvan,[1] on the northern edge of the Massif Central, reveals it as second only to the Palæ-Alpine; that it is also to be found in Auvergne and in Brittany seems probable.

Discussion of the wider distribution of the Ural type in Europe must be left for consideration in the final chapter; enough has been said, however, to show that this factor, which appeared to differentiate the Basques from their neighbors, is one which was in early times, as well as to-day, of equal importance in the adjacent parts of Europe. What, then, is there left to mark the Basques as racially different from the surrounding Spanish and French-speaking population? The answer seems to be nothing! Yet all authorities agree that the Basque does differ from his neighbors in having a peculiar type of face. As has been pointed out, there is evidently no *single* factor to which any peculiarity in the Basque can be reasonably ascribed; there, is, however, a unique *combination* of factors to which perhaps their character-

[1] Hovelacque, 1894.

istics may be traced. In France, in Switzerland, in northern Italy, etc., wherever the Ural type is found as an important element in the European population of to-day, the types with which it is associated and blended are in great majority other brachycephalic forms. In the Basque, however, it is blended with the dolichocephalic Mediterranean, and it is to this peculiar combination of types, which occurs, so far as I am aware, nowhere else, that the characteristic features of the Basques, I believe, are due. The theory that the Basques were a mixed folk and owed their triangular type of face to their being a blend between a brachycephalic and a dolichocephalic people is far from new. The theory was, however, obviously unsatisfactory, since there were many other peoples in Europe who, although also the result of a similar mixture, showed no trace of the peculiarity which such a blending was supposed to have produced in the case of the Basques. The present suggestion, in that it traces the origin of a unique form of facial features to a combination of physical types which is also unique, stands, I believe, on much more stable foundations. If we add the interesting suggestion made by Ripley of an intensification of this peculiarity through conscious selection, the puzzle of the "Basque type" seems in a fair way of being solved.

There remains, however, the question of the language. Are we to regard it as a survival by some freak of circumstance of the speech of those late Neolithic or early Bronze Age immigrants, who presumably penetrated into Spain from the north, or shall we accept it as the last surviving remnant of the ancient Iberian speech, possessed by the older population of Mediterranean type? If we accept the first alternative, we must believe that a language which, if we are to judge from the general distribution of the Ural type, must once have been widely spread over much of western and central Europe, has everywhere else disappeared. This is possible, perhaps, but the other view seems to be somewhat more probable, since there is some concrete evidence of the wide distribution of Basque place-names, etc., in other parts of the peninsula.

# CHAPTER VI

## THE JEWS AND THE GIPSIES

BOTH Jew and Gipsy are men without a country, but, although cosmopolitan in their distribution, they are most numerous in Europe, and so may best be treated in connection with European peoples.

## I. THE JEWS

The questions of the racial origin and unity of the Jews have for long been fertile themes for discussion. The traditional view has always been that they were a true Semitic people, and, indeed, the term Semite has popularly come to be practically synonymous with Jew. They were regarded as a people whose purity of blood had, in spite of wide dispersion, been jealously preserved throughout the centuries. As soon, however, as detailed investigations in regard to Jewish physical types began to be available, it appeared that it was extremely doubtful whether either of these assumptions was true, for the Jews proved to be by no means uniform in their physical characteristics, and the great majority appeared to be of a different type from that found among other Semitic-speaking peoples. In recent years the data bearing upon the whole question have been greatly augmented, and it seems possible to-day to arrive at conclusions which are reasonably certain. These may best be made clear by reversing our usual order of treatment, considering in the first place the physical characters of the modern Jew and then seeking from archæological and historical sources an explanation of the facts.

Europe is the homeland of the great majority of modern Jews, the larger proportion being to-day (or having formerly been) residents of western Russia, Poland, and Germany. These

East European Jews constitute the so-called Ashkenazim branch of the people and include probably more than nine-tenths of the total of the world's Jewish population. The smaller branch, the Sephardim, are the survivors of the Spanish and Portuguese Jews expelled from Spain at the close of the fifteenth century, and to be found now mainly in the Balkan peninsula, in Smyrna, Palestine, and parts of northern Africa, while smaller colonies exist in London and Amsterdam. The Sephardim generally regard themselves as a sort of aristocracy, holding more or less aloof from the other Jews, and claiming to represent the purest survivors of the original Hebrews. We may therefore well begin our study of Jewish physical types with them.

For the Sephardim, as for practically all other Jews, the only data available are measurements on the living, since Jewish crania are well-nigh impossible to secure. For the English group we have only the rather unreliable data of Jacobs, which appear to indicate an average mesocephaly, substantially similar to the figure for the London Ashkenazim. A small group in northern Italy are in the average brachycephalic, although less so than the surrounding Italian population. The Spanioli in Bosnia, who came thither from Constantinople and Salonika in the seventeenth century, hover in average about the lower border of brachycephaly, and seem to comprise about 75 per cent of leptorrhine, brachycephalic factors (presumably in the main of Alpine type), and about 20 per cent of leptorrhine, dolichocephalic types. Our best and most abundant material, however, is that obtained from the Spanioli of Constantinople and Jerusalem.[1] This shows both these groups to be by small majority dolichocephalic, and to consist of a mixture of narrow-nosed dolichocephalic and brachycephalic types. A small series of crania from Constantinople shows a marked predominance of the former factors. It is only, therefore, in Constantinople and Jerusalem that the Sephardim show a majority of the leptorrhine, dolichocephalic types characteristic of the Semitic-speaking Arabs, whereas in Bosnia and London, and especially in Italy,

---

[1] Weissenberg, 1909_b.

the brachycephalic probably Alpine type, is clearly or even strongly predominant.

One of the main causes which has been suggested as responsible for the variation in the physical type of the Jews is that of intermarriage with the Gentile population among which they live, and it has frequently been pointed out that the Jew thus generally approximates the character of the surrounding peoples, whatever this may be. That such intermarriage does indeed occur and has occurred throughout the past, can be demonstrated, although the extent of the practice is very hard to determine. The belief that the Jew merely reflects the physical type of the Gentile population among which he lives we shall find to be borne out in general by the facts. In the case of the Sephardim, however, although it holds for the English, Italian, Bosnian, and Jerusalem Jews, it fails in the case of those in Constantinople, for the surrounding population is here probably in the main brachycephalic.

It will be shown later that the North African Jews, from whom in large measure the Spanish Jews were derived, are predominantly dolichocephalic, so that it would appear that this original character had been best preserved by the Constantinople and Jerusalem Sephardim. As a group, therefore, we may consider the Sephardim to be a people once in the majority of Mediterranean and Caspian types, who have, except in the two cases noted, been largely Alpinized, in part perhaps in Spain, but in the main since their dispersal, as a result of intermarriage with the surrounding peoples among whom they took refuge. In stature the Sephardim Jew differs little from the average of all other European Jews, being slightly below the medium. Although predominantly brunet in coloring, they nevertheless show a small proportion of blond types. The peculiar form of nose which is commonly denominated "Jewish" or "Semitic" and characterized by an unusual degree of "nostrility," is strongly marked among the Sephardim, being present generally in about one-third of all the individuals examined.

The vast majority of European Jews and of those who have

migrated thence to America and elsewhere belong to the Ash-kenazim. Without exception, apparently, they are predomi-nantly and, in general, overwhelmingly brachycephalic, the pro-portion of these factors varying from about 80 per cent in west-ern Germany and Poland to 90 or 95 per cent in southern Ger-many and Russia. The nose is everywhere clearly leptorrhine. Analysis of the data is possible only in the case of the Polish Jews, since for the others no individual data are given. The series given by Elkind[1] shows that the leptorrhine, brachyce-phalic factors are those in the main concerned, and, although there are no crania to confirm it, it seems almost certain that these factors are primarily Alpine in type. The dolichocephalic ele-ment is also narrow-nosed and Mediterranean or Caspian, as among the Sephardim. In stature the Ashkenazim are a little shorter than the Sephardim, this low stature being especially notable in Poland, where the average stature of some groups falls almost to 160 cm. There seems little doubt that this phe-nomenon is due in large part to a stunting caused by the very unfavorable economic and industrial conditions under which these Polish Jews live. In pigmentation the Ashkenazim is less predominantly brunet than the Sephardim, the proportion of blond types being rarely less than 10 per cent, and rising in some cases, as in Galicia, considerably higher. The "Jewish," or "Semitic," nose is of somewhat greater frequency among the east European Jews than among the Sephardim.

Special mention may be made here of the Karaite Jews[2] of the Crimea. They are members of a small Jewish sect, origi-nating in Syria in the eighth century, and which, except for the group in the Crimea and a few in northwestern Russia and in Egypt, is to-day practically extinct. In head-form the Crimean Karaite Jews are practically identical with the Ashkenazim, showing, if anything, a greater proportion of brachycephalic fac-tors than the neighboring orthodox Jews of the Ukraine. They are, however, somewhat taller, and show a much smaller pro-portion of blond types and of "Semitic" noses.

[1] Elkind, 1903.     [2] Weissenberg, 1904.

With the Ashkenazim proper and the Russian Karaite Jews we may class those of the Caucasus, Central Asia, northern Persia and Syria. The Jews of the Caucasus[1] are divided into two groups, the Gruzinian living in the southwest near the Black Sea, and the Mountain Jews, so called, of Daghestan and Baku, at the Caspian end of the range. The latter group, at least, are very ancient residents of the Caucasus, being traceable at least as far back as the beginning of the Christian era, and with only little less certainty for several centuries more. The Gruzinian Jews show an overwhelming proportion of brachycephalic, leptorrhine factors, only 4 or 5 per cent of dolichocephalic elements being present. In stature they are just under medium, and in pigmentation show but a very small proportion of blond types, Chantre[2] alone of several observers reporting a figure comparable or even exceeding the average for the Ashkenazim. The "Semitic" nose is of about the same frequency as among these neighboring Jews. The Mountain Jews are even more purely brachycephalic than the Gruzinian, but in other respects are closely similar. One point, however, may be of some significance, i. e., that they appear to have unusually broad, low faces, which would suggest the probability that the crania may in some cases be comparably low, thus indicating the presence of an element of the Ural type. This suspicion seems to be corroborated by Kurdov's statement that he could very clearly recognize a Kirgiz-like type among them, for a considerable Ural factor is present among this originally inner Asiatic people.

The central Asiatic Jews[3] have long been residents of Samarcand and Bokhara, but, although perhaps almost as old residents as those of the eastern end of the Caucasus, they are known to be racially somewhat mixed. In head-form they show a notably smaller proportion of brachycephalic factors than that found in the Caucasus, although in respect to stature and absence of blond types they are one with the Caucasian Jew. The "Semitic" nose is, however, less common here. The Jews of Meshed[4]

<hr/>

[1] Kurdov, 1905 b, 1912 a; Weissenberg, 1912 b; Djavakov, 1913.
[2] Chantre, 1885–87.     [3] Weissenberg, 1913–14.     [4] Weissenberg, 1913.

in northern Persia are in most respects identical with those of Samarcand and Bokhara, although in stature they are quite noticeably shorter. In Urumia,[1] in the northwest of Persia, the same type of Jew is found, although here there is observable a considerable rise in the proportion of the Mediterranean-Caspian types. The Syrian Jews of Aleppo and Damascus,[2] lastly, seem to form a unit with those which have just been described. There are, however, significant differences between the two Syrian groups. The Aleppo Jew is almost as extreme in his brachycephaly as his brethren in the Caucasus; in Damascus, farther to the south, the proportion of dolichocephalic factors greatly increases, as does the frequency of the so-called "Semitic" nose.

Summing up these results, it appears that the Ashkenazim proper, together with the Jews of the Caucasus, central and western Asia, are in head-form primarily brachycephalic, and in all probability predominantly Alpine in type. In Germany the brachycephalic factors increase from north to south, from Cologne and Frankfurt to Baden; in Russia they attain their maximum in the Mountain Jews of the Caucasus, while the same figure is reached again on the southern side of the Anatolian plateau among the Jews of Aleppo. Such small minorities of dolichocephalic factors as occur are universally of the same Mediterranean or Caspian types which were found in much larger proportions among the eastern Sephardim. The Ashkenazim proper, however, differ from the Caucasian and Asiatic Jews in their slight but definite tendency toward blondness, in which they quite clearly exceed the Sephardim group, as they do in many instances in the proportion of "Semitic" noses.

The similarity in head-form between the Ashkenazim and western Asiatic Jews and the surrounding peoples is very striking. Apparently there is no exception to this rule. In Germany the lower proportion of brachycephalic factors noted in Cologne and Frankfurt, as compared with Baden, is paralleled among the Gentile German population. The larger proportion of dolichocephalic elements appearing in the Jews of Urumia, as compared

[1] Ibid.                                                    [2] Weissenberg, 1911.

with those of Meshed, is probably also to be found among the
Persian populations of the two areas, if we may judge from very
meagre and imperfect data; while the similar increase in these
factors, in passing from the Jews of Aleppo to those of Damascus, is in accord with the greater frequency of dolichocephalic
elements among the Syrian population of the south, as compared
with that of the northern border.

The other groups of Jews for which we have data, those
namely of southern Persia, Mesopotamia, Arabia and North
Africa, form a group quite different from the Ashkenazim, or the
majority of the Sephardim. Measurements of Jews from Shiraz,[1]
in southern Persia, reveal them as strikingly different in head-
form from their brethren farther north. In the south Persian
Jew the dolichocephalic, leptorrhine elements equal the brachycephalic, Alpine ones, and the same holds true in the case of those
in Mesopotamia. In this latter region, moreover, the proportion
of "Semitic" noses rises to something over 60 per cent, a figure
almost twice as high as the average for the Sephardim Jews, and
much higher than is usually the case among the Ashkenazim.

In Yemen,[2] in southwestern Arabia, the Jews have been an
element in the population since the sixth century at least, and
probably earlier. They have formed, more than in the case of
almost any other Jewish group, a closed and isolated community,
having little interrelation either with other Jews or with the
Arabs among whom they live. Their physical characteristics are
therefore of great interest, as they may be presumed to represent
the Jewish population of Palestine as it existed in the early centuries of the Christian era. They show a very large majority of
dolichocephalic, leptorrhine factors, amounting, indeed, to over
80 per cent, the remainder being brachycephalic and probably
Alpine. The surrounding Arab population presents a striking
contrast, since they are in large majority Alpine. We have here
thus repeated the phenomenon noted in the case of the Sephardim
in Constantinople, in that the Jews are radically different in type
from the people among whom they live. In stature these Yemen-

---

[1] Weissenberg, 1913.                     [2] Weissenberg, 1909 a.

ite Jews are very short, averaging less than 160 cm.; they show no trace of any blond element, and only a small proportion of "Semitic" noses.

The North African Jews[1] may be divided into three groups: those of Egypt; those of Algeria, Tunis, and Morocco; and the Karaite Jews of Cairo. There have been Jews in Egypt since very early times, but with the foundation of Alexandria they flocked thither in large numbers, and are said to have formed a fifth of the population of this great city at the beginning of the Christian era. Considerable groups of these Jews survive still in Alexandria and Cairo, and measurements of them show that in physical type they closely approximate the Sephardim of Jerusalem, since the leptorrhine, dolichocephalic, i. e., Mediterranean and Caspian types, are in slight majority over the brachycephalic Alpines. For Jews they are tall, averaging 169 cm., and show no trace of any blond factor. Like the Yemenite Jews, they have a very small proportion of "Semitic" noses, ranking in this respect below all the European Jews, except the Crimean Karaites. The Karaite Jews of Cairo are, as regards their head-form, very like the Yemenite group, having a large majority of the Mediterranean-Caspian types. In stature, absence of blondness, and small proportion of "Semitic" noses, the Karaites agree with the orthodox Cairene Jews. The contrast which they present, however, with their Crimean brethren is radical, at least in head-form, for whereas the Cairene Karaite is dominantly and strongly dolichocephalic, the Crimean group is equally strongly brachycephalic.

The Jews of the North African coast, from Tunis to Morocco, although not as ancient residents as those in Egypt, have nevertheless been settled in the country at least since the second century A. D. By the fifth century they were numerous, and had converted to Judaism several Berber tribes, who offered vigorous opposition to the advance of the Moslem conquerors a century or two later. In the eighth century, after the establishment of Moorish rule in Spain, large numbers migrated thither and

[1] Weissenberg, 1912 a; Fishberg, 1905.

formed the basis of the Spanish Jews.  In physical type these
North African Jews show, apparently, some local variation, for,
although probably all have a majority of the dolichocephalic,
Mediterranean-Caspian types, this factor is somewhat less
marked in Morocco than elsewhere.  Further, although the
brachycephalic factors are primarily Alpine, a small platyrrhine
element appears, whose significance will be apparent in a moment.  The North African Jews show no trace of blondness, and
have a somewhat larger proportion of "Semitic" noses than the
Jews of Egypt, approximating in this respect the Sephardim
group in Europe.

If we compare the North African Jews with their non-Jewish
neighbors, we find in most respects a striking accord.  Throughout the whole region the population is predominantly dolichocephalic, and in the main of Mediterranean and Caspian types,
these elements being somewhat more strongly marked in Egypt
than in the west, just as among the Jews.  If, as the evidence
seems to indicate, the early Jewish immigrants into Egypt were
predominantly dolichocephalic, intermarriage with the Gentile
would not lead to any observable results, since Jew and Gentile
alike were of similar types.  In the region farther west, however,
the conditions are slightly different, i. e., the known conversion
of large numbers of Berbers to Judaism in the early centuries of
the Christian era.  Now, as will be pointed out in the chapter
dealing with northern Africa, the ancient population of the
coast region, although primarily dolichocephalic, included nevertheless a considerable brachycephalic element, and, especially, a
small but persistent factor of the Mongoloid type.  As pointed
out above, the Jews of this region to-day show a small, broad-
nosed, round-headed factor, which does not appear among any
other Jewish group in the world, so far as known.  The inference
is, therefore, that this is probably derived from the early Berber
converts, whose descendants must thus to-day form an appreciable element in the total Jewish population.  This suggestion
meets with a difficulty, however, in that, although the Berbers
have, as is well known, a small but often striking blond element,

no trace of this is reported among the Jews. It may, nevertheless, be regarded as certain that the North African Jew was originally pretty strongly long-headed, and since the Spanish Jews were in large part of North African origin, the source of the Mediterranean-Caspian element among the Sephardim group seems to be explained.

Summarizing the general results of this tedious survey of the modern Jews, it is clear that they fall into two rather sharply contrasted groups. The smaller comprises the North African and Yemenite Jews, the Sephardim of Constantinople and Jerusalem, and perhaps the Mesopotamian and south Persian groups, all of which show a varying predominance of the Mediterranean-Caspian types, with a brachycephalic minority, in the main probably Alpine. The larger division includes all the European Jews, together with those of the Caucasus, Central Asia, and the northern parts of Persia and Syria, all of these being primarily and in some cases overwhelmingly brachycephalic and Alpine, with a small minority of the same long-headed types which were dominant in the other group. The characteristic features of the first group appear in greatest strength among the Jews of Yemen, while the Caucasian and north Syrian Jews exemplify those of the second group in their most extreme form. The supposedly characteristic "Semitic" nose is in general present in somewhat larger proportions among the Ashkenazim than among the Sephardim; it is apparently least common among the Karaites, both of the Crimea and of Egypt and (curiously) the North Persian Jews, while it reaches its greatest frequency among the Jews of Mesopotamia and Damascus.

Which of these two groups, the dolichocephalic or the brachycephalic, represents the original Jew? And whichever we regard as the true Jews, how are we to account for the existence of the other? The answer to these questions must be sought in part in a comparison of the Jew with his neighbors, in part from the history of the Jewish dispersion, and in part in what we know or can surmise in regard to the character of the ancient population of Palestine. The modern Fellahin of Palestine as well as the

Samaritans, are, according to Weissenberg's[1] results, predominantly dolichocephalic peoples, considerably above medium stature, the Samaritans exhibiting both of these characters more strongly than the Palestinian peasant. In proportion of "Semitic" noses, the several groups differ widely, the Fellahin of Jaffa, on the coast, showing this feature in only 16 per cent of the cases, whereas among those of Safed farther north, and in the interior, the figure rises to 37 per cent, and in the case of the Samaritans it reaches 70 per cent! The question of head-form is, however, complicated by the fact that Huxley[2] found the upland interior population, at least of Samaria, to be strongly brachycephalic! His series of crania, however, from Nablus[3] indicates a considerable dolichocephalic majority, the Mediterranean and Caspian types being predominant. In view of the wide divergence of the results obtained by the two observers, we must regard the population as probably very much mixed. One outcome is nevertheless clear, i. e., that the proportion of so-called "Semitic" noses is very much greater among the non-Jewish population than it is among the Jews themselves, either here or anywhere else in the world, a fact that would seem to suggest that this feature is, after all, not a specifically Jewish characteristic!

In a later chapter, dealing with the racial types of Syria, Palestine, Mesopotamia, and Arabia, it is pointed out that we are probably justified in believing the people of Palestine and the adjacent country to have been, in the second or third millennium B. C., primarily of the Mediterranean and Caspian types. Brachycephalic, Alpine peoples, such as the Hittites and related groups, had, however, probably very early worked their way southward from the Anatolian plateau along the Syrian uplands as far, at least, as the northern border of Palestine. These northerners were, as we know, furthermore characterized by the possession of the same "Semitic" nose which has come to be popularly regarded as so typically Jewish. This peculiar form of nose was not only then marked in the population of the Asia

---

[1] Weissenberg, 1910.          [2] Huxley, 1905.          [3] A. M. N. H.

Minor region, but is still very common among the remnants of the old pre-Turkish peoples, such, for example, as the Takhtadjy of Lycia and the Armenians.

The brachycephalic, "nosy" immigrants from the north had doubtless mixed to some extent with the earliest Canaanite Semitic settlers, and the later Hebrews, coming into Palestine in the second millennium B. C., must have absorbed not a little of this element, either by intermarriage with the Canaanites or with pure remnants of the Anatolian group, or by conversion. This result probably occurred irregularly, although the mixtures were probably more common in the north than in the south, where the mass of the Hebrews probably retained substantially unchanged the physical characteristics with which they came into Palestine. That these were predominantly dolichocephalic seems probable, yet the possibility that some round-headed factors may have been brought from southern Arabia must not be forgotten. The population of Palestine and western Syria was thus probably much mixed at the beginning of the first millennium, although not so much so as it is to-day. That some portion, at least, of the Jewish people at this period were already marked by the same peculiar type of nose which was also found among the Hittites, is shown by the representations of the Jewish prisoners on the famous Black Obelisk of Shalmaneser II, dating from the ninth century B. C.

With the dispersion, the conditions under which different groups of the refugees or settlers lived were very different. Those who spread westward and southward came among peoples who were physically more or less closely allied to the original Hebrew group, having a considerable majority of Mediterranean and Caspian factors. Those whose fate it was to settle, voluntarily or as forced colonists, in Anatolia, Armenia, northern Persia, Central Asia, and the Caucasus were in quite a different position. Here they were in the midst of peoples primarily brachycephalic, and, in part at least, characterized by the possession of the miscalled "Semitic" nose. To some extent by intermarriage, in larger part probably by conversion, these features

became more and more prevalent among the Jewish population
of the northern borders of Asia Minor and the Caucasus region.
The most important single factor, however, in the differentiation
of these Jews of the Asiatic borderlands, from whom in very large
part the Ashkenazim of Europe were derived, was the conversion
to Judaism in the eighth century of the Khazars. This people,
whose early history is still obscure, were perhaps a branch of the
inner Asiatic Turkish-speaking folk, who by the opening of the
Christian era were beginning to penetrate into eastern Europe;
perhaps in part derived from some of the ancient population of
the Caucasus. They had for five or six centuries held much of
the region north of the Caucasus and between the Caspian and
the Black Seas. A city-building, strongly commercial people,
with well-organized government, they built up a powerful empire whose influence spread far into the heart of Russia, into
which the Slav had as yet hardly come. Great numbers of Jews
are known to have settled among the Khazars, and their conversion to Judaism followed. In the tenth century, however, the
Khazars were crushed by the rising power of the Slavs and scattered far and wide. In these widely dispersed, strongly commercial people converted to the Jewish faith, and in the great numbers of Jews from the Caucasus and the northern borders of Asia
Minor, who had there been brachycephalized through centuries
of contact with the surrounding population, we may in all probability see the origin of the great mass of the east European Jews
of to-day. We have, it is true, no direct evidence as to the physical type of the Khazars, but there is much indirect evidence to
the effect that they were, like the later immigrant groups from
inner Asia and all the original peoples of the Caucasus, primarily
of Alpine type. How far the Jew, like all the rest of the population of Europe, has been further brachycephalized within the last
four or five hundred years, it is, in the absence of adequate cranial
material, impossible to say. Our only evidence is the small
series of thirteenth or fourteenth century skulls from Basel, in
Switzerland, described by Kollmann,[1] which show approximately

[1] Kollmann, 1885 b.

the same high proportion of brachycephalic elements as do the modern Jews of Baden, who are the nearest group with which comparison can be made.  To how great an extent, further, the perpetuation and even intensification of the peculiar type of nose (popularly considered as distinctively "Jewish," but which we have seen to have been in all probability derived from a wholly different source) may be traced to conscious selection, in that a certain type of features became in a way a popular Jewish ideal, it is quite impossible to say.  Instances of this sort of conscious selection are known or suspected in the case of several other peoples in the world, and it may be that it has played some part among the Jews.

In conclusion, if, as is probable, the northern Arabs or Bedouin of to-day are to be regarded as the best modern representatives, from the racial point of view, of the very early Semitic-speaking peoples of whom the original Hebrews were a part, then the great majority of all the Jews to-day are "Semites" only in speech, and their true ancestry goes back not so much to Palestine and Arabia as to the uplands of Anatolia and Armenia, the Caucasus and the steppes of Central Asia, and their nearest relatives are still to be found in those areas to-day.

## II.  The Gipsies

The Gipsies, like the Jews, are a people without a country, and are widely scattered throughout the world, although the majority are to be found in Europe, mainly in the Balkan region. Coming probably from some part of northwestern India, they appear to have migrated westward through Persia and Armenia, reaching the eastern part of the Balkan peninsula somewhere about the eleventh century, but not beginning to spread in large numbers thence over the rest of Europe until the beginning of the fifteenth century.

Although there is a voluminous literature relating to the Gipsies, data on their physical characteristics are scanty and confined mainly to the Balkan groups.  Pittard[1] has collected a

[1] Pittard, 1920.

very large number of measurements here, but has not yet published them in full.  From the summary of his results and from
other sources it appears that within the Balkan region the
Gipsies are quite variable.  Pittard, on nearly 800 mainly from
the Dobrudja, found them to be a people just below medium
stature, strongly brunet, and with a large majority of leptorrhine, dolichocephalic factors, the remainder being of brachycephalic, leptorrhine types.  Weisbach[1] in Hungary found the
stature substantially the same, but the head-form predominantly
Alpine, a type which in the Dobrudja is only in the minority.

Cranial material is both meagre and incomplete, so that pre-
cise determination of types is impossible, yet it seems to be practically certain that the fundamental stratum among the Gipsies
is a mixture of the Caspian and a small proportion of Mediterranean types, the Alpine factor forming the minority.  It seems
probable that if of northwest Indian origin, they may, before
leaving there, have had some Alpine mixture derived from the
peoples across the border.  This factor was, however, somewhat
increased in the course of their passage westward.  Only after
their further migrations in the fifteenth century did the Alpine
element become dominant, among such as mixed with the
strongly brachycephalic populations of the northern and western parts of the Balkan peninsula and of central Europe.

There are some reasons for believing that the Egyptian and
North African Gipsies are in large majority dolichocephalic.  If
this is true, we have a most interesting parallel between this
people and the Jews, in that both of them, originally primarily
of Caspian-Mediterranean type, have among the primarily Alpine
and Palæ-Alpine populations of Europe diverged widely from
their original type, and approximate that of the surrounding
folk; whereas in North Africa, where the mass of the population
is largely of Caspian-Mediterranean origin, they have retained
in far larger measure their original characteristics.

[1] Weisbach, 1889.

*BOOK II*

AFRICA

# INTRODUCTION

THE geographical and environmental features of the African continent, which have been of major importance in its racial history, can be very briefly pointed out. Extending from the Abyssinian highlands and the "Horn" of Africa southward along the eastern side of the continent to the Cape, and occupying also nearly the whole of the continent south of the fifteenth degree of south latitude, is an upland plateau from three to five thousand feet in elevation. Throughout its northern and part of its southern portion it is mainly grassland and open woodland, but in the south and west is largely desert. Along the northern coast, from the Atlantic shores of Morocco to Tunis, there stretches a second, much narrower plateau and mountain belt, rising to considerable heights in the Atlas range. Lying between this and the great eastern and southern uplands, is the mass of the African continent, which may be divided into three broad belts, running east and west: (1) A desert belt in the north extending with scattered oases from the Atlantic to the Red Sea, and including the Sahara, together with the Libyan and Egyptian deserts; (2) a grassland belt fringing the desert on the south, and stretching from the mouth of the Senegal through the French and British Sudans to the upper Nile, where it meets the eastern grasslands; and (3) a belt of tropical forest bordering the whole northern side of the Gulf of Guinea, and including practically the whole of the Congo Basin. Lastly, and of great significance in the history of the racial development of Africa, in the northeastern part of the continent, the Nile, rising near the angle where the northern and eastern grasslands join, flows north, stretching a narrow ribbon of marvellous fertility across the eastern edge of the desert to the Mediterranean.

There is probably but little doubt that a large part, perhaps the larger part, of Africa was already occupied by man in the

early Palæolithic period.  While clear stratigraphic proof of this
is as yet lacking, the evidence of the Gibraltar skull, of the
Egyptian palæoliths, and of the Boskop and more recent Broken
Hill crania found in the Transvaal and Rhodesia, render the conclusion at least extremely probable.  It is, I believe, possible
from the data now at hand to determine the character of this
Palæolithic population, and the hypothesis may be hazarded that
it comprised four main racial elements, the Proto-Australoid,
Proto-Negroid, the Mongoloid, and the Palæ-Alpine, the latter in
what is probably a special variety.

   In the absence of stratigraphic data it is difficult to say what
was the exact order of appearance of these types, but there is
much in the distribution of these four forms to-day to suggest
that the Mongoloid and Proto-Australoid represent the oldest
strata.  In zoology it is a pretty generally accepted theory
that in any land area of considerable size the marginal types
represent the older fauna, which has been displaced and driven
into outlying districts or into refuge areas by the newer immigrants.  If we apply this same principle to our physical types,
the result, so far at least as the Mongoloid is concerned, is
striking.  For this is found as an important factor in the African
population only in two widely separated regions, the Canary
Islands and the extreme southern tip of the continent.  In
neither area does the type appear unmodified.  The Canary
Islands and the region at the Cape of Good Hope are the two
most extreme marginal points in the continent; it can hardly be
accident that precisely there this type is at its maximum.  It
may be noted, further, that in two other regions it appears as a
minor factor.  One of these lies in the more remote central portions of the Abyssinian highlands, which, rising like a fortress
above the lower lands, would serve as a refuge into which the
last remnants of earlier types in the eastern part of the continent might be swept.  The type is also found in the eastern
Atlas, which for the north of the continent forms something of
a refuge region.  In this latter region the type appears to be
fading out, since it is a more important factor in the crania

from the Carthaginian cemeteries (especially among the women, who may be taken as having represented more truly the pre-Phœnician population) than it is to-day.

It may lastly be noted that faint traces of this type are to be found among the Pre-Dynastic population of Egypt, but that with the beginning of the historic period it disappears. This would seem to show that some five or six thousand years B. C. the Mongoloid type was still faintly discernible, but as a rapidly disappearing remnant, in the Nile valley. That it was vastly older than this in Africa, however, seems to be indicated by the Gibraltar skull, which represents a blend between the Mongoloid and Proto-Australoid types. In connection with the statement that strong Mongoloid factors are found among the modern Bushmen and so-called "Strandloopers" of the southern tip of the continent, it may be pointed out that certain Mongoloid affinities of these people and the Hottentots have been noted by various writers, such, for example, as the peculiarly yellowish skin color and the frequency of a pseudo-Mongoloid fold in the eye.

Wherever this ancient Mongoloid type makes itself felt it has almost always been blended with the Proto-Australoid, which therefore seems by this, as well as other evidence, to be of equal (or possibly even greater age) in Africa. Although this type is much more widely spread than the previous one, yet the tendency toward marginal distribution is fairly observable, if not quite so strikingly as in the former case. Among the present population it is most strongly represented among the Turu, Burangi, and Sanduwi tribes north of Lake Nyassa, the Hottentot, Bushmen, and Kaffir, i. e., in the southeast of the continent. It also appears as a not inconsiderable element in the Abyssinian plateau and among the Ashanti of West Africa. In the Canaries, although not forming as large a factor as in the southeast, it was a very important element in the islands of Hierro and Grand Canary, especially among the female portion of the population. If we turn to archæological data, it appears that the Proto-Australoid type was by a small margin dominant in Egypt in Pre-Dynastic times and decreased largely later, except for a temporary rise in the fifth dynasty and again in Ptolemaic times. The almost total lack of satisfactory cranial data for the rest of northern Africa, renders any conclusions as to early racial types there little more than guesswork, but from the fact that the type was strongly represented in the Palæolithic crania of southern France, and still remained an important element at the beginning of the metal ages in southern Spain, it is perhaps legitimate to suppose that in the adjacent coast of Africa the type was well represented at the same early date.

In the early Palæolithic period, then, we may, I believe, think of the African population as primarily composed of the Mongoloid and Proto-Australoid types and their mixtures. Perhaps somewhat sparsely settled, they probably held most of the north, including large areas in the Sahara, which at this period was certainly more humid and suitable for human occupation that it is to-day. Southward they probably extended to the edge of the forest zone, and, sweeping around it on the east, followed down the grassland plateaus toward the southern portion of the continent. The Congo basin and perhaps the Guinea coast were apparently not occupied.

Perhaps almost as early as either of the two types just discussed was the Proto-Negroid, which to-day has a very wide distribution throughout the continent. The present available cranial data indicate that this type is most prominent in two widely separated regions: first, the east and southeast, among the Jagga of Kilimandjaro, the southern Bantu tribes, the Hottentot, and the Bushmen, and, second, in the region of the Gulf of Guinea, from Cameroons westward to Liberia. The presence, moreover, of admittedly Negroid crania among the oldest of those known from the northwestern portions of the continent; the discovery of Neolithic crania of Proto-Negroid type in the region east of Lake Chad;[1] the presence to-day of a strong Proto-Negroid element in the Teda or Tibbu, who have for long been settled in the Tibesti Mountains in the very heart of the Sahara; and the similar considerable factor in the population of Maure-

[1] Gaden, 1920.

tania and Morocco all give strong grounds for believing that the
Proto-Negroid type spread very widely at a very early period
throughout the whole northern part of the continent, and that
blends between this type and the somewhat older Proto-Australoid made up a large part of the population during late Palæolithic times.   This conclusion is strengthened by the large Proto-
Negroid factor in the Pre-Dynastic population of Egypt, which
in this respect would seem to have been on a par with the modern Galla or Somali, or the Beni-Amer and Kababish of Nubia.

The last of what are apparently the older types is the Palæ-
Alpine, presenting in many ways the most puzzling problems of
all.   It is in its distribution to-day concentrated in the region
of the great forest belt, comprising the Congo basin and the
Guinea coast, with possible outliers eastward of the Great Rift
Valley.   Outside of this "refuge area" of the equatorial forest
this type is, and seems always to have been, but weakly represented.   It was, to be sure, present in Egypt in early Pre-Dynastic times as a mere trace, and increased slightly in importance
up to the period of the Middle Kingdom, thereafter declining
again until it disappeared.   At no time, however, did it ever
form an appreciable factor in the population of the Nile valley.
In the northern coast region the situation is obscure owing to
the absence of cranial material, but there appears to be no certain evidence of the early presence of the type.   The peculiar
small group of short, brachycephalic peoples existing to-day on
the island of Gerba and the adjacent shores of the Gulf of Gabes
may represent a survival of this type, or may, on the other hand,
be related to the old Mongoloid type, whose presence in the
Carthaginian cemeteries has been noted.   As there is no cranial
material, it is impossible to decide between these two alternatives.   A further point must be borne in mind, viz., that the
Palæ-Alpine type in Egypt and Libya is distinctly less platyrrhine
than it is in the heart of Africa, where it is in general associated
with a very short, true pigmy stature, strongly marked prognathism, woolly hair, and all the usual Negroid characteristics.
The people whose crania fall into the Palæ-Alpine type in the

north of Africa had, so far as we know, none of these features, so
that the question at once arises whether we have any right whatever to associate with them the Central African Pigmy peoples,
simply on account of the cranial similarities in the three single
points which we have selected for our criteria? The problem of
the relation of the Negrito peoples to the Palæ-Alpine type will
be discussed at some length in the final chapter, and I shall only
state here that, despite the great superficial differences between
them, there are reasons for believing that both have been derived
from a common source.

In spite of faint traces of this brachycephalic, platyrrhine type
to be found north of the forest zone, there seems no reason to believe that it spread as widely over the continent as the types already discussed. The great tropical forest area is in many ways
a refuge region, and seems to have been penetrated and colonized
only relatively recently by the Negro peoples, who in their spread
over the continent seem first to have flowed around the forest
region before they attempted to penetrate it. Thus, here in
seclusion the Pigmy peoples were able to preserve their very
simple culture as pure hunters, ignorant alike of cattle-raising
and agriculture, of the use of metals or the manufacture of pottery, and in small remnants here and there to keep for us of the
present day something of a picture of the life of the Palæolithic
period. And, although the numbers of the Pigmies still surviving in a relatively pure state seem to be small, the greater part
of the population of the Congo basin to-day is very largely mixed
with their blood.

Into an Africa which must thus have been in the main Negroid around a core of pigmy Negritos, with, in the northwest
and especially the southeast, considerable remnants of the fusion
of the older Mongoloid and Proto-Australoid types, there came
in early Neolithic times a new factor, destined to be of enormous
importance in the future development of the peoples of the continent. This was the first invasion of the Caspian type—tall,
light-skinned, with a tendency under favorable conditions toward
blondness. This new type came into Africa from the northeast

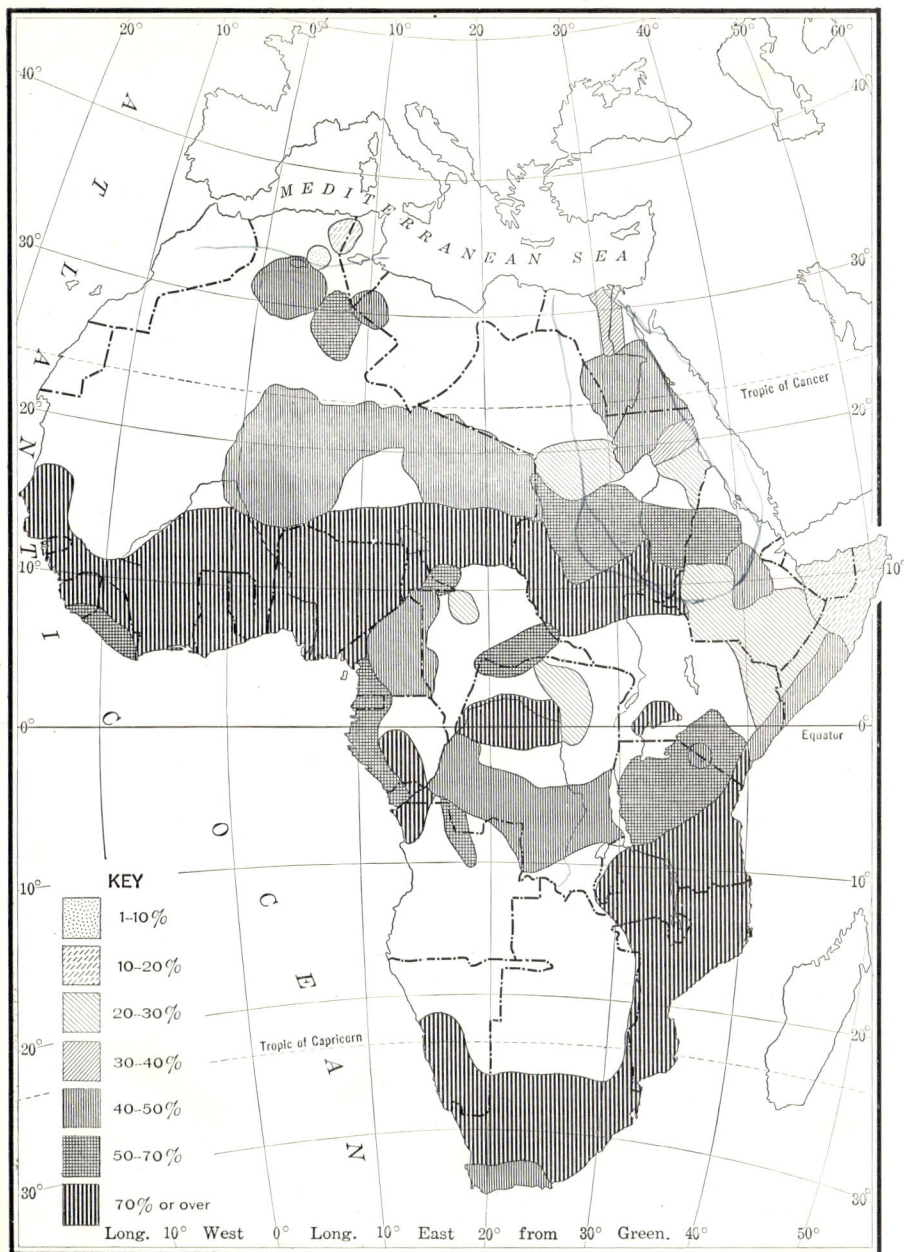

PLATE VII.  AFRICA.

Percentage distribution of Proto-Australoid and Proto-Negroid Types (slightly generalized).

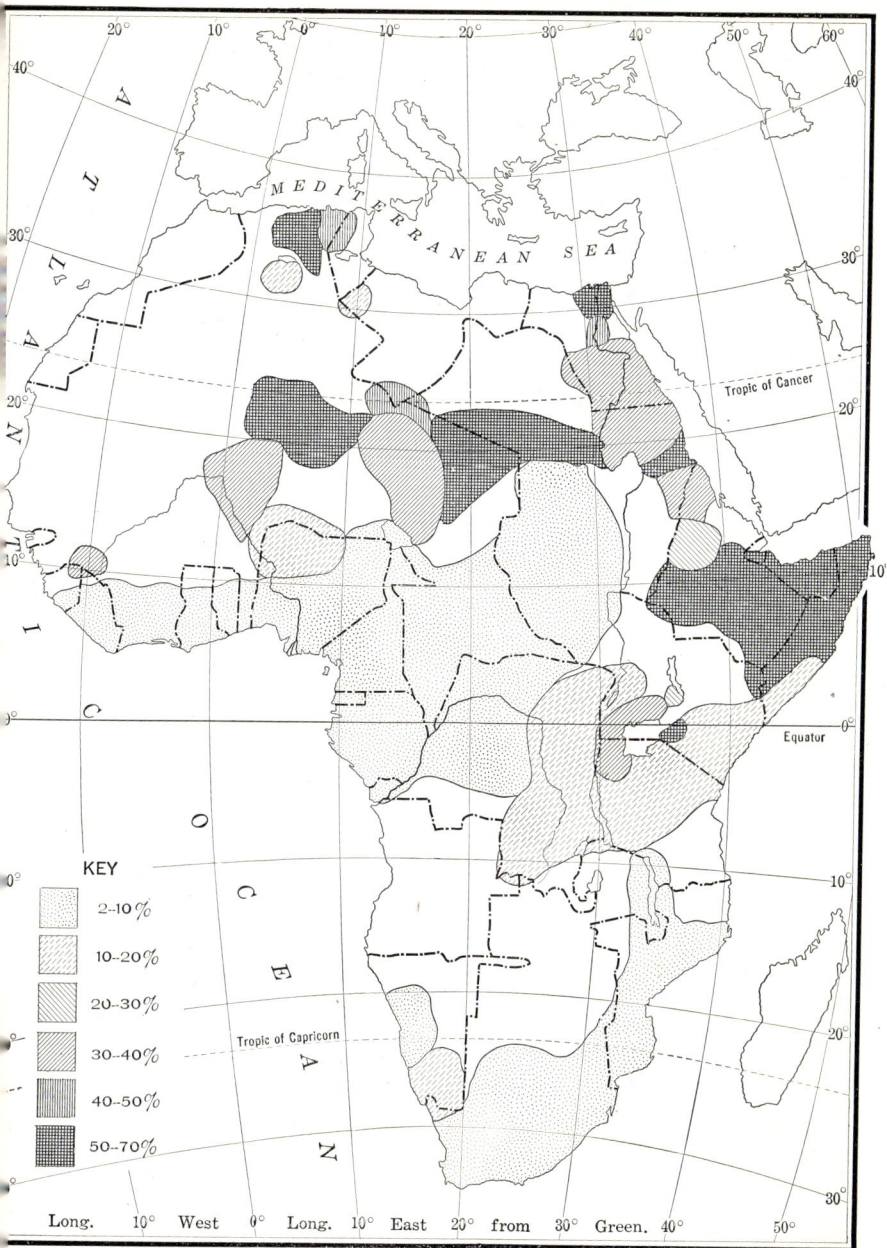

PLATE VIII.  AFRICA.

Percentage distribution of Caspian and Mediterranean Types (slightly generalized).

KEY

2–10%

10–20%

20–30%

30–40%

40–50%

50–70%

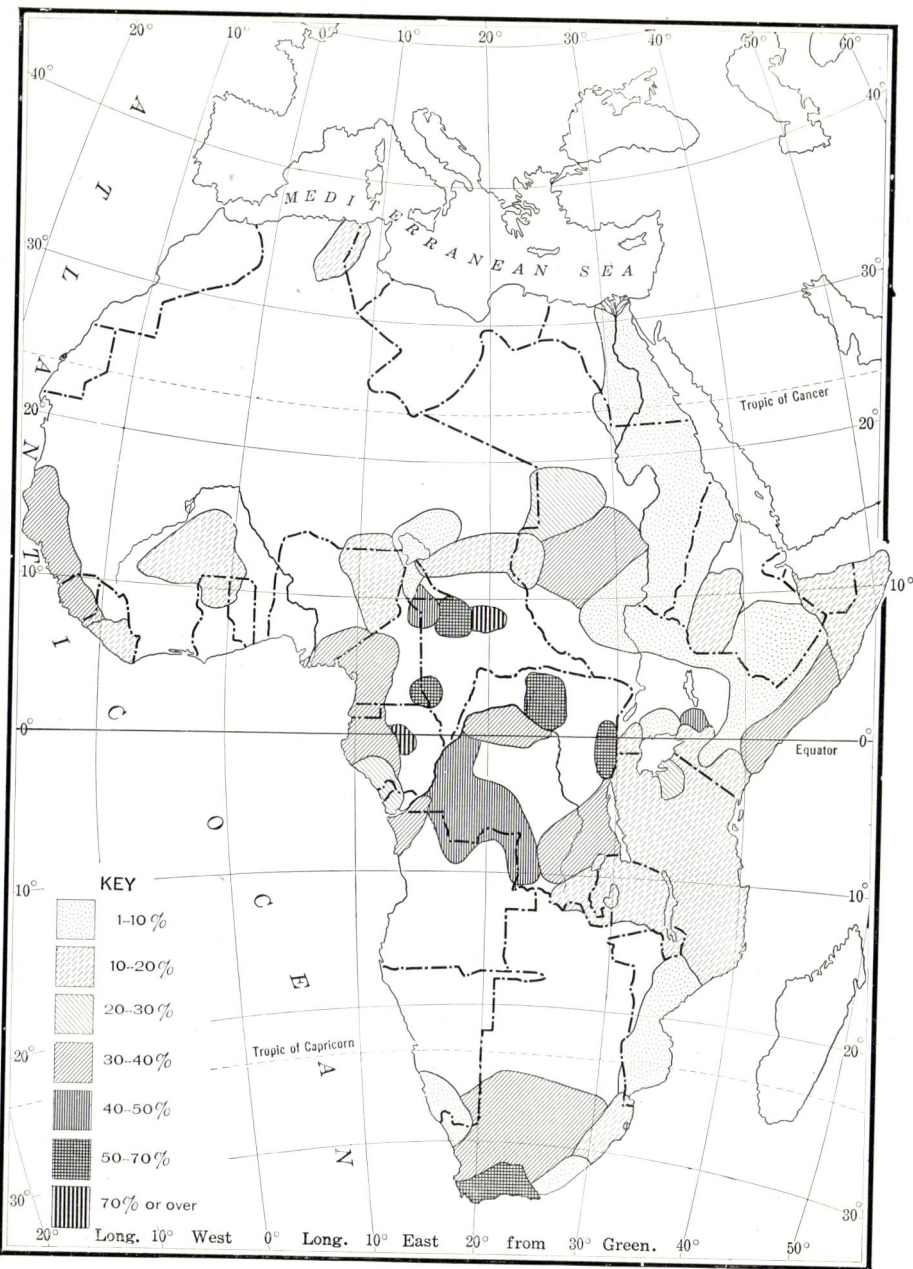

PLATE IX.   AFRICA.

Percentage distribution of Palæ-Alpine and Mongoloid Types (slightly generalized).

KEY

1–10 %

10–20 %

20–30 %

30–40 %

40–50 %

50–70 %

70 % or over

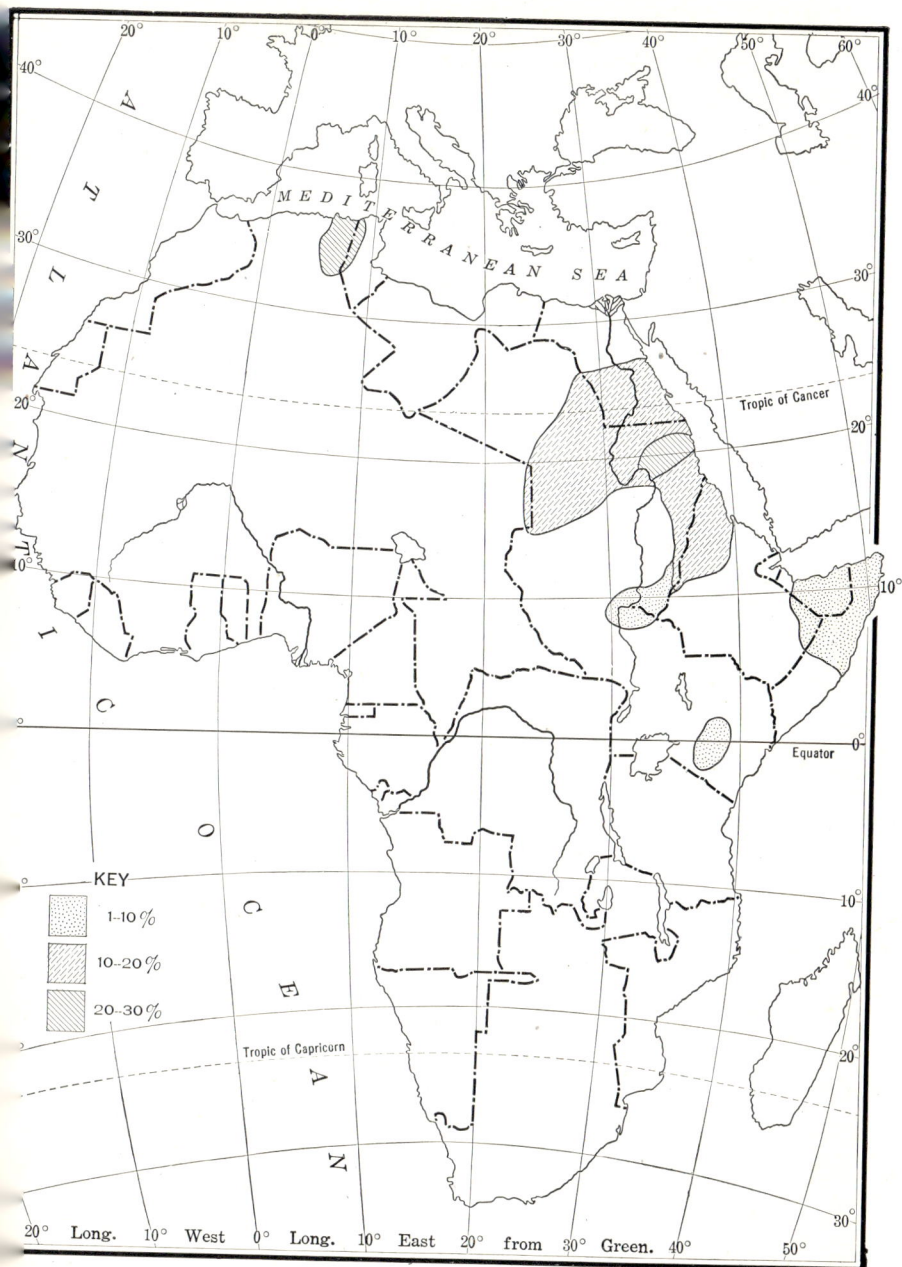

PLATE X.  AFRICA.

Percentage distribution of Alpine and Ural Types (slightly generalized).

by way of Arabia, through the Isthmus of Suez, and from the Yemen shore in the south across to Abyssinia and the "Horn." Pastoral in culture, the newcomers poured into Nubia until they became the main element in the population, in part absorbing, in part displacing, the Negroid blend of Proto-Negroid and Proto-Australoid types to the westward, and passed north, down the valley of the Nile into Upper Egypt, where and in Nubia a generally uniform type of culture, agricultural and pastoral, grew up, being that characteristic in the Pre-Dynastic period. Farther to the north, through Suez, another stream of peoples of Caspian type came into the Nile delta, duplicating there the experiences of their relatives farther south, so that the resulting peoples of Upper and Lower Egypt were essentially similar in the racial elements involved, only that in the north the proportion of Caspian type was larger and was more closely related to the mixed Caspian and Mediterranean peoples, who in northern Arabia were developing into the Semitic folk. In this way the puzzling Semitic features, both in culture and in speech, of the old northern kingdoms of Lower Egypt are, I believe, to be explained.

But the influence of this new immigrant type did not cease with the Nile valley. From Abyssinia and the "Horn of Africa," on the one hand, groups of the newcomers, with their cattle and superior culture, made their way southward and southwestward, following the grasslands of the eastern plateaus, to the region of the great lakes and beyond, blending with the older population and serving as a leaven, which gave the composite group thus derived an advantage over their neighbors. Among them the Bantu languages developed, and spread with them southward and, in earlier times particularly, westward into the Congo basin. Farther north, from Nubia, which seems to have been a great reservoir of these immigrants, they passed west into the Sudan and the region of the Sahara, finding there conditions closely comparable with those of their former Arabian deserts. And so, perhaps as early even as late Neolithic times, some strain of this virile group reached as far as the Atlantic shores, and laid the foundations of the interesting people whose modern descendants are the Fula.

The strong current of this eastern shepherd folk, which set across through Sinai to the Nile delta, continued on westward into Libya, and, reinforcing those who were moving west and northwest from Nubia, pressed west and south the older Negroid population. In the north, along the Mediterranean shores and in the eastern Atlas, the newcomers came to be supreme, forming the foundation of the Libyans and Berbers, among whom as enclaves, the survivors of the older mixed Mongoloid, Proto-Australoid, and Proto-Negroid peoples long remained. In the Sahara proper, however, the latter element was still strong, and here the immigrants blended with the older stock, giving rise to peoples like the modern Tibbu or Teda. Meanwhile the feebler southern stream, following the grasslands of the eastern plateaus, extended its influence far toward the southern tip of the continent, where the older Mongoloid and Proto-Australoid blend, whose descendants formed the Strandloopers, were fusing with the advance guards of the Proto-Negroid type to form the Bushmen and Hottentot.

For centuries, probably for millennia, the leaven worked, and slowly in the favored area of the Nile valley there grew up a higher culture, whose traditions reached back dimly toward Punt and the coast opposite Yemen, along that road by which in the beginning the southern stream of the newcomers had come. The Neolithic period thus was a time in which the older peoples were slowly but surely driven out of most of northern and northeastern Africa, their places being taken by the new immigrants, whose relatives were at the very same time streaming into western Europe and playing there a somewhat similar part.

With the opening of the historic period a new influence again makes itself felt in Africa; another new type appears, at first feebly but then in ever-increasing volume adding its quota to the already existing complex. Whether or not we are justified in ascribing to the Mediterranean type all the credit for the sudden advance in culture which marks the early Dynastic period in

Egypt, it seems to be the fact that this type makes its first appearance in any strength in Egypt in the course of the First Dynasty. From the fact that the burials in the Royal Tombs of the First and Second Dynasties show the Mediterranean type far more strongly than do those of the rest of the people, the conclusion may be advanced that we have in this evidence of a conquering and ruling aristocracy, to whose initiative and ability was due the relatively rapid growth, on the firm foundation already established, of that remarkable civilization whose achievements are still a marvel to this day. Leaving to the final chapter a discussion of the ultimate source of this new racial factor, it will be enough for the present to note that it seems to have entered the Nile valley from the delta, and while at first forming merely the backbone of the ruling caste, as the centuries passed it contributed more and more to the mass of the population, until, by the end of the Middle Kingdom, it had attained to the dominant place among the varied racial elements in the Egyptian portion of the Nile valley, and retained that leadership in Upper Egypt without interruption down at least to Roman times, and in Lower Egypt to the present day.

Other portions of the continent beside the Nile valley, however, felt the stimulus of this "New Race." All along the Mediterranean coasts in Libya and westward to Gibraltar the new type made itself strongly felt, but nowhere else save in Egypt did it lead to the development of any notably higher culture. Nor elsewhere did it penetrate far inland; indeed, it seems to have been in part at least sea-borne, for beyond the Pillars of Hercules it penetrated to the Canary Islands, where, overlaying the older Palæolithic population of Mongoloid and Proto-Australoid origin (which survived most strongly in the outer islands of Hierro and Gomera), it blended with these to form the ancestors of the Guanches, still the occupants of the islands when in the fifteenth century they were discovered by the Portuguese, themselves so largely of this same Mediterranean stock.

Outside of this fringe along the northern border of the continent and along the lower portions of the narrow valley of the

Nile, the influence of the Mediterranean type does not seem to
have extended, until the period first of the conquest, and later
in the eleventh century of the great invasion, of Mohammedan
Arabs took place. A part at least of these new invaders, who
followed thus in the footsteps of their Neolithic predecessors of
Caspian type, were, as will be shown, the result of a fusion of
the old Caspian population of Arabia and Syria with the Mediterranean type, so that in their conquest of most of the Nile
valley and the Mediterranean littoral, and later by their commercial penetration and colonization of much of the Sahara and
the Sudan, they carried far into the heart of the continent an
appreciable factor of the racial elements which the colonial development of modern Africa at the hands of the European powers
has in recent years done so much to expand.

One last racial factor which has played its part, albeit but a
minor one, must not be overlooked, viz.: the Alpine type. When,
shortly after the beginning of the Dynastic period, the Mediterranean peoples made their first appearance in force in Egypt, the
Alpine type, which previously had been absent, or present in
almost negligible proportions, at least in Upper Egypt, increased
nearly twofold. Later it declined again until the period of the
New Empire, when it once more assumed importance and continued to be a factor of significance in Roman times. It is in
Lower Egypt, however, that its influence is most marked, for
here, in the Fourth and Fifth Dynasties, it outweighs even the
Mediterranean itself. If we turn to Nubia, an unexpected state
of affairs is revealed, in that in Pre-Dynastic and early Dynastic
times the influence of the Alpine type is quite evident, and is
stronger than in Upper Egypt. There thus seems to be repeated
in the case of the Alpine type what has already been noted in
connection with the Caspian, i. e., that it appears in this early
period to have been present in greater strength in Nubia and in
the Delta than in the region of Upper Egypt in between. It
was suggested in the former case, that the type probably came
into Africa at two points, Suez and at the southern end of the
Red Sea. It seems to me probable that the same may be said

of the strain of Alpine type, and that this came *in the beginning* associated with the Caspian. Later, when the stream of the latter had dwindled for a time, the Alpine current increased in volume, so that in the period of the Middle Kingdom it nearly doubled its relative importance in Nubia, as it did later in the New Empire, farther down the Nile in Upper Egypt. While in Egypt the type increased still further in Roman times, it did not do so in Nubia, but, after its rise in the Middle Kingdom, returned to the small proportions it showed in the Pre-Dynastic period.

The Egyptian and Nubian data thus suggest that at least as early as the beginning of the metal period a thin stream of Alpine blood had begun to trickle into the Nile valley, making itself felt most in the portions of the valley nearest the Mediterranean Sea. Lack of data for the early period along the littoral farther west makes it difficult to be certain as to the conditions here, but from the evidence it would appear that the Alpine type was present, even as early as late Neolithic times, and became of large importance much later in the Roman period. Whether the thin fringe of Alpine type, which extended and still extends as far west at least as the Gulf of Gabes, is to be regarded as a western extension along the coast from the Nile delta, or explained as sea-borne by pre-Phœnician and Phœnician colonists, is hard to say. The fact, however, that the crania from the Siwah Oasis, lying between Tunis and the Nile delta, which date at least in part from Ptolemaic times, show but slight traces of the Alpine type, together with the fact that this type was at the same early period being carried by sea to Sicily and southern Spain, and probably along the western coasts of France, seem to make it probable that all along the northern coast of Africa the Alpine factor was largely sea-borne.

In the modern population of Africa it plays a small but not wholly insignificant part. In Egypt and in Nubia it is represented to-day in about the same proportions as in Roman times (*i. e.*, 10 to 15 per cent). Among the Hadendoa of the eastern Nubian desert it appears in much greater strength, and suggests a considerable infusion of south Arabian peoples in comparatively recent times, since they have a large element of the Alpine type. The Beni-Amer show a smaller but still considerable factor, which then fades away southward through Abyssinia and Somaliland, until its last traces appear to die out among the Masai, the Swahili, and other coastal tribes of British East Africa, among whom contact with the Arabs of Yemen, the Hadramaut, and Oman has been going on for many centuries. Westward through the Sudan traces are to be found here and there of Alpine blood, but they seem to be, so far as present data go, very slight. Yet in Dahomey the Alpine factor is more pronounced, and further material may show its unexpected strength in parts of the Sudan.

The maps, Plates VII to X, show, so far as the data are available, the distribution among the living population of the various types or their combinations.

Our survey thus seems to show the African continent as, from the earliest times, the battle-ground between the lighter and darker races. Its original thin stratum of Mongoloid and Proto-Australoid types was very early overlaid by Proto-Negroid and Pigmy Palæ-Alpine peoples, who prevailed over the older population and spread virtually over the whole of the continent. But already by the Neolithic period this essentially Negroid population began to give way in the northeast and north before the irresistible advance of the three great lighter-skinned groups, the Caspian, the Mediterranean, and the Alpine types. We can trace the rising of this flood in the Nile valley from Pre-Dynastic down to Roman times, when the population had become dominantly Mediterranean, and has remained essentially unchanged to the present day. West of the long, fertile ribbon of the Nile the same process was repeated. The flood of Caspian peoples swept across the Nile and through the Saharan oases, as well as westward along the coast, where they joined forces with the Mediterraneans, and drove the Negroids from the whole north of the continent. Through the Sudan and south along the grasslands of the eastern plateaus these Caspian peoples penetrated, influencing the mass of the Negroid peoples, who, thus leavened, developed the higher culture of the eastern Bantu and the comparative civilization of the Fula, Mandingo, and Hausa. Thus was the older, more pure and primitive Negro culture confined more and more to the dense forest regions, while the oldest cultures and types of all were slowly becoming extinguished in the Strandloopers of the extreme south and in the outermost of the Canary Islands. Long, long after the first great conquest and leavening of the Dark Continent by this Caspian immigration had occurred, a new invasion and new cultural influences from the old sources came again into Africa. In the military and commercial expansion of the people of Arabia consequent upon the growth of Islam, new factors of the old Caspian type, now mingled with Mediterranean and Alpine elements, poured into the continent by the same old routes, and in the Sudan and all the north of Africa, as also by sea along its eastern shore, further augmented the white as opposed to the Negroid elements. And now again, in our own day, the phenomenon is being repeated, for, coming by sea to the south, where climatic conditions are favorable, the superior civilization of the white peoples is, in South Africa, steadily and for the first time from this direction, pressing the Negroid population back toward the Equatorial Forest, just as the remote ancestors of these Negroids did the true Negroes and Pigmies uncounted thousands of years ago.

# CHAPTER I

## NORTHERN AFRICA

### I. Egypt and Nubia

For no portion of the earth's surface have we as yet such abundant and reliable material for the study of racial history as is comprised within the Nile valley from Nubia to its mouth. The labors of the archæologists have supplied us with a great number of crania, the bulk of which can be quite accurately dated, and it is possible thus (or will be when the gaps in the published data are filled) to trace the racial history of the Nile valley, from the earliest Pre-Dynastic times down to the present, over a period of something like 7,000 years.[1]

The Early Pre-Dynastic occupants of Upper Egypt, among whom as yet little of the distinctive features of Egyptian culture had developed, seem already to have been a mixed people. The major factors were two, the Proto-Australoid and Proto-Negroid, while the Caspian type is present in almost as large a proportion, so that in reality there were three elements, present in nearly equal force. It may be noted that in the females there is in this early period a not inconsiderable element of the Palæ-Alpine type, marked often by rather extreme platyrrhiny. The Later Pre-Dynastic period shows a notable change, in that the proportion of Proto-Negroid type present decreases, whereas that of the Mediterranean (before present only as a trace) rises sharply, so as to be almost equal to the Caspian.

By the beginning of the Dynastic period (somewhere about the middle of the fourth millennium B. C.) we find the Caspian equal in importance with the Proto-Australoid, while the Medi-

---

[1] For ancient Egypt the main material utilized has been Thomson, 1905; and in addition Biasuti, 1905; Fawcett, 1901–02; Fouquet, 1886; Giuffrida-Ruggeri, 1909–10, Oetteking, 1909; P. M. For Nubia the main sources are the *Archæological Survey of Nubia*, especially volume II.

terranean, which at the end of the Pre-Dynastic period for a time assumed significance, now drops back to the inconspicuous place it held at first. In the series of crania from the Royal Tombs of the I and II Dynasties, however, the conditions are different from those found for the common people. For in this case the Mediterranean type drives the Caspian from second place, the Proto-Negroid sinks to relative insignificance, and a new factor, the Alpine type, appears.

The question whether the appearance of a "New Race" marked the beginning of the Dynastic period has long been a matter of discussion. On the basis of the present method of analysis there seems to be no doubt but that the end of the Pre-Dynastic and the beginning of the Dynastic period was marked by the appearance in Upper Egypt of *two* new types of people, of which the more important were the Mediterraneans, the Alpines being in distinctly smaller numbers. There is also for the time being an increase in the Caspian type, and a marked decrease in the Proto-Negroid element. It is difficult, in view of these facts, to avoid the conclusion that the period was one of profound changes in the racial constitution of the people, and one in which, apart from any mass immigration, a ruling dynasty and aristocracy came into power who were of radically different character, and in particular far less Negroid than the mass of the older population. The sources of this Mediterranean factor are not yet by any means clear. Since it was already abundant in the southwest of Europe, it may have crossed from Spain or perhaps from Italy, and journeyed eastward along the northern coast of Africa to the Nile delta, and so on up the river; it may have come from northern Arabia across through Suez, for later, at least, the type was and still is strongly marked among the Bedouin; or, lastly, it may have come in the main by sea from Crete itself (whose earliest population was in very large part, if not wholly, Mediterranean) or from the source whence the Cretans themselves had first come. In view of the indications of some sort of maritime connection between the people of the Nile delta and Crete in the early Dynastic period, the latter explanation is tempting, and seems to me in spite of many obvious difficulties to be the most probable.

That the Mediterranean element must have reached Upper Egypt from the Delta and Lower Egypt is almost certain, from the still greater prevalence of the type in the north. We have no Pre-Dynastic crania as yet from Lower Egypt, and data from the early dynasties are very scarce. Yet what little we have seems to show that not only was there a large Mediterranean element there, but also that the population was very mixed, since the crania of the I–IV Dynasties from the Gizeh Pyramid are primarily dolichocephalic, whereas those of the same period from that of Farashur are brachycephalic and mainly Alpine.[1] The Mediterraneans cannot have come into Upper Egypt from Nubia and the south, for we find no trace of them there, either in Pre-Dynastic or early Dynastic times.

It is difficult to harmonize this evidence of the northern origin of the Mediterranean element and its strength in the crania from the Royal Tombs of the I–II Dynasties with the historical fact that these were in origin southern, and the establishment of the Old Kingdom the result of a conquest of the north by the south. I can only suggest as a possible explanation of the puzzle that the Mediterraneans settling in Lower Egypt mixed there with the older resident Caspian peoples, and toward the end of the Pre-Dynastic period spread southward, bringing with them, as the archæological evidence shows, the use of copper. Later some of these immigrants, who had been for generations in Upper Egypt, may have attained the leadership, and then from the south embarked upon the conquest of the lower valley, and so founded the Old Kingdom.

For the later part of the Old Kingdom our data are unfortunately very scanty for Upper Egypt, although this is to some extent compensated for by fairly abundant data for Lower Egypt. So far as can be seen, however, the Mediterraneans steadily increased to the end of the Old Kingdom in Upper Egypt, as did also the round-headed Alpine and Palæ-Alpine elements, of which

[1] Biasuti, 1905.

in Pre-Dynastic times there was hardly a trace. The source of these brachycephalic types becomes clear when we examine the crania of the IV and V Dynasties from Lower Egypt, for here the racial composition was very different. The Caspian type leads all others, Alpine and Palæ-Alpine types make up nearly a third of the total (in one series almost half), and the Proto-Negroid factors sink into insignificance. The great strength of the brachycephalic types is particularly marked in the female crania, and they may be recognized in some of the sculptured representations of the aristocracy of the period. Whether these factors came into Lower Egypt through Suez, from the Syrian and Palestinian highlands and Asia Minor, or whether they came by sea is not certain. Alpine influences were being water-borne, however, at this period widely throughout the Mediterranean and along the western shores of Europe, and in particular were beginning to reach Cyprus and Crete, so that we may doubtless look to such a source for at least part of these new immigrants. Yet in Upper Egypt we have another direction in which to look, *i. e.*, southward, for in Nubia at this period a considerable Alpine factor was present, having come in probably from southern Arabia. Since in Nubia, in the period of the Old Kingdom, the Caspian type was in the majority, there was an interesting parallel between it and Lower Egypt, since in both the Caspian type was dominant, and in both the Alpine element was large, while the Proto-Negroid was less than in Upper Egypt. That the latter type should be weak in Lower Egypt is not surprising, but that it should also be feebly represented in Nubia, while relatively strong in the region of Upper Egypt lying between the two, is extremely curious.

The early historic period in the Nile valley thus seems to have been one in which, coincident with rapid cultural development, the population received large increments of Mediterranean and Alpine types, the former coming to Lower Egypt first and gradually working up the river; the latter type coming both into Lower Egypt and Nubia and spreading up as well as down the stream.

For the period of the Middle Kingdom in Upper Egypt we have one series of crania dating from the VI to the XII Dynasties, and another from the XII to the XV Dynasties, carrying us thus into the times of the Hyksos conquest.  The first series is remarkable as showing a large increase in the Proto-Negroid element, marked in the male and female crania alike, the Mediterranean factor and the brachycephalic elements remaining about the same as in the latter part of the Old Kingdom.  The second series, which includes the period of renaissance in the XII and XIII Dynasties, shows a remarkable change, since now the Caspian type forges to the front, the Mediterranean increases, and the Proto-Negroid, which had been so prominent during the preceding period of confusion and disunion in Egypt, is relegated to third or fourth place.

Of the Hyksos we have as yet no certain remains, although it is probable that they were, like the later Bedouin of northern Arabia and Syria, mainly of Caspian and Mediterranean types. How far they may have influenced the character of the Egyptian population during the period of their rule we cannot yet say, but with their expulsion and the opening of the New Empire very significant changes had occurred.  The crania of the XVIII Dynasty from Upper Egypt reveal a population in which for the first time the Mediterranean type is dominant, and the importance of this element reaches even as far as Nubia, where it vies with the Caspian and Proto-Australoid types.  For Lower Egypt we have no data, unfortunately, for this or the preceding period of the Middle Kingdom.  The Proto-Negroid type during this period of magnificent renaissance is, in Nubia as well as in upper Egypt, of very slight importance.

For the succeeding periods the data at present available are confined to the XXX Dynasty, the Ptolemaic period, and the time of Roman rule.  In general the characteristics of the population of Upper Egypt seem to have been fixed by the XVIII Dynasty, for the Mediterranean type which then attained first place holds this with only a slight set-back in Ptolemaic times. The Proto-Negroid element relegated to insignificance in the New

Empire makes one last rise in the XXX Dynasty, and then declines again to the relative insignificance from which it has never since emerged. The Alpine and Palæ-Alpine types, however, slowly increase in importance, although never attaining apparently the importance they had in Lower Egypt in the period of the Old Kingdom. At particular sites, however, the Alpine type becomes very prominent, as for example in Nubia, where the graves of the priestly families at Philæ and the Biga cemetery show a very large element of this, for Egypt, foreign type.[1]

The racial history thus of Upper Egypt falls easily into three great periods. During the first, which includes the larger part of the Pre-Dynastic period, the population was primarily a blend of Proto-Australoid and Proto-Negroid types, together with a strong factor of the Caspian, which latter was apparently dominant both in Nubia to the south and in Lower Egypt to the north. The second period, which includes both the Old and Middle Kingdoms, from about 3500 to 1800 B. C., was marked by the striking rise in importance of the Mediterranean type and the decline of the Caspian, which still, however, held its position both in the north and south. In the third period, extending from the beginning of the New Empire down to Roman times, the Mediterraneans become supreme, and the Alpine type, formerly but feebly represented in Upper Egypt, although strong in Nubia and especially in Lower Egypt, becomes a factor of considerable importance.

For the modern population[2] of Egypt, of which an excellent example is given on Plate XI, Fig. 1, we have abundant and excellent material on the living, but unfortunately no published cranial data. It is therefore impossible to determine definitely what changes, if any, have taken place in the period since the beginning of the Christian era. The analysis of the measurements on the living gives, however, the following results. To-day, as in Roman times, the population is primarily dolichocephalic, the brachycephalic elements amounting to only about

[1] *Archæological Survey of Nubia*, vol. II.
[2] Chantre, 1904; Craig, 1911–12; Myers, 1905, 1906–08.

10 to 15 per cent. Significant differences are, however, observable in the types present. Above Assiut the dominant elements among the Moslem population are the platyrrhine, dolichocephalic types (Proto-Negroid and Proto-Australoid), the leptorrhine forms (Mediterranean and Caspian) ranking second, with the Alpine type third. Below Assiut and throughout the Fayum and the Delta (except in the district of Menufia) the importance of the dolichocephalic types is reversed, the Mediterranean-Caspian types being preponderant with the Proto-Negroid and Proto-Australoid secondary, while the third place is held by the Palæ-Alpine. The Copts, who as Christians have intermarried only among themselves for many centuries, are very closely similar to the population of the Fayum. The people of Upper Egypt thus form a transition to the Nubians, of whom an illustration is given on Plate XI, Fig. 2.

## II.  Northern Africa

That portion of the African continent lying west of the Nile valley and north of a line following roughly the 15° of N. Lat. and comprising the whole Sahara region, Morocco, Algeria, Tunis, and Tripoli, may on the whole be treated as a single anthropological unit. In considering the racial history of this immense area, we may most conveniently divide it into two portions, one of which includes the Sahara, the other comprising all the rest.

Beginning with the latter northern and coastal region, it is to be noted that, despite the considerable archæological investigations made in Algeria and Tunis by the French, little data of any value has been published in regard to the crania found. Bertholon and Chantre,[1] in their great monograph, refer to crania of probable Neolithic age, but state only that they are primarily dolichocephalic and belonged to peoples of markedly short stature. From the abundant megalithic remains of this whole region a considerable number of crania have been taken, but no complete measurements have ever been published.[2] All

---

[1] Bertholon and Chantre, 1912–13.

[2] The measurements of the famous crania from the dolmens at Roknia have been reprinted by Randall-Maciver, 1901.

that can be gleaned is that here again dolichocephalic forms are in the majority, both platyrrhine and leptorrhine factors being present, the latter apparently being most numerous, and indicating thus either the Caspian or Mediterranean types. Some crania, however, of Alpine type occur.

The earliest historical period in which we know anything of this region dates from the Phœnician colonization. A very considerable number of crania have been excavated from the ancient cemeteries[1] in the vicinity of Carthage, the majority of which are assigned to the fourth century B. C. We can hardly assume that the large population of this great city was wholly made up of Phœnicians; it must have been a mixed one in which the pureblood Phœnicians were in the minority perhaps. If we may assume that, on the whole, the males would represent this foreign colonial element somewhat more clearly than the females, who would belong in larger measure to the native population, results of some interest appear. Analysis of the data shows that the dominant factor in both sexes is that of the Mediterranean type, but that this is somewhat stronger in the females. The male series shows, further, strong minorities of the Proto-Australoid and Palæ-Alpine types. The females, on the other hand, have a smaller proportion of the former factor, a considerable Proto-Negroid element, and show clearly the presence of a small Mongoloid factor which is entirely absent among the males. If the above assumptions as to the mixed character of the Carthaginian population are correct, these facts would seem to indicate that the Phœnician colonists were largely a blend of Proto-Australoid and Palæ-Alpine types, whereas the native North African population was primarily Mediterranean, with appreciable Proto-Negroid and Mongoloid factors. The presence of this latter type is of much interest in connection with the data presently to be discussed relating to the ancient people of the Canary Islands. One further point may be noted. Chantre[2] has attempted to separate the more ancient from the later crania

[1] Bertholon, 1892; Collignon, 1892; Bertholon and Chantre, 1912–13.
[2] Bertholon and Chantre, *op. cit.*

from the Carthaginian cemeteries, and, although he gives only averages, the figures seem to indicate that the older male crania showed larger proportions of the Proto-Australoid and Proto-Negroid types than the later, whereas the older females comprised a larger element of the Mongoloid.

The dozen or so crania from various sites in Tunis, dating from Roman and early Christian times,[1] are so few that conclusions drawn from them can only be tentative. They seem to indicate, however, the replacement among the males of the Palæ-Alpine by the Alpine, and the presence in the case of the females of an even stronger element of the Mongoloid type than was present in the Carthaginian graves.

For the modern population, although abundant observations have been made,[2] few individual measurements have been published. The people of Algeria and Tunis may be divided into two main groups: (1) the Berber-speaking tribes, who are in large majority, and as a sedentary and largely agricultural population are found in greatest purity in the mountain and higher plateau areas; and (2) the Arabs, in part descendants of the Mohammedan conquerors and immigrants of the twelfth and thirteenth centuries, and in part "Arabized" Berbers, who are seminomadic and most numerous on the southern slopes of the Atlas and the border of the Sahara, although scattered almost everywhere. The Berber tribes represent the dominant population of the whole region, dating back to prehistoric times. In general a people of medium or moderately tall stature, they resemble the Spanish or Italians in skin color, and, like them, are prevailingly brunet in color of hair and eyes. There is, however, a very interesting blond element present, amounting in some places to as much as 10–12 per cent. In head-form there is considerable variation, but the fundamental type seems to be that which is purest in Algeria, a well-marked dolichocephalic, leptorrhine type. A good example of the Berber type is given on Plate XI, Fig. 3. With this are blended minor elements of platyrrhine

---

[1] Bertholon and Chantre, *op. cit.*
[2] Bertholon and Chantre, *op. cit.*; Randall-Maciver, 1901; Lissauer, 1908.

FIG. 1. EGYPTIAN.

FIG. 2. NUBIAN.

FIG. 3. BERBER.

FIG. 4. SOMALI.

PLATE XI.

form, in part at least of Proto-Negroid type. Brachycephalic factors, in the main apparently Alpine, are quite strongly represented, and in the two groups for which individual measurements have been given,[1] the Kabyle and Chauia, amount to something over a fifth of the total. Along the coast itself the proportion is probably still larger, especially in Tunis, where it culminates apparently in the island of Gerba.

Nothing has been said so far in regard to the western or Moroccan area. The data from here are so scanty that it is not possible to reach any conclusions of real value. A few crania from Mogador[2] on the Atlantic coast appear to indicate that the fundamental stratum here is similar to that farther eastward, although most observers are agreed that there is clearly a much larger Negroid element in the population.

The Canary Islands, lying off the coast just beyond the southern limits of Morocco, represent the most isolated and marginal area comprised within the limits of Africa. The people of this group have long attracted scientific interest and speculation. The Guanche, as they are commonly called (although this term strictly should apply only to the inhabitants of Teneriffe), are now extinct, but abundant cranial data in regard to them and the ancient occupants of the other islands in the group exist.[3] Analysis of the material shows that the Mediterranean type was dominant among the Guanche, the most important minor factors present being the Alpine and the Mongoloid types. The contrast between the male and female series is very striking, since in the latter the Mongoloid element is actually in the preponderance, the minority elements being Mediterranean and Proto-Negroid. The facts suggest that the Guanche proper were an immigrant folk closely related to the Berber peoples of North Africa, the people whom they dispossessed and partly absorbed being a remnant of the ancient blend between the very early

---

[1] Randall-Maciver, 1901.  [2] Vernau, 1911.
[3] I have been fortunate in being able to utilize the very large mass of unpublished measurements in the hands of Doctor E. A. Hooton. The large series published by von Behr are useless for comparison, since his nasal measurements do not conform to standard usage.

Mongoloid and the Proto-Negroid.　This suggestion seems to be confirmed by a comparison of the Teneriffe crania with those from the most outlying islands of the group, which theoretically ought to have preserved the largest proportion of the pre-Guanche population.　This proves actually to be the case, for in Hierro and Gomera the Mongoloid type is present in larger proportion than in Teneriffe.　On the other hand, in Grand Canary, which lies nearer the African mainland, the proportion of Proto-Negroid factors is larger.　The fact that in this extreme outlying marginal portion of Africa toward the west there survived, until historic times, a fragment of the ancient Mongoloid stratum, is the feature of greatest interest which the analysis of the data from the Canary Islands reveals.　For we shall see that in no other portion of the continent is there more than a trace of it, except at the extreme southern tip.

The Sahara and Libyan Deserts, comprising an area considerably larger than that of the whole United States, except Alaska, has in general a scanty population.　Anthropologically these people are very little known, and it is usually assumed that they are fundamentally similar to the main mass of Berber peoples farther north, modified especially toward the east by Arab immigration and by a considerable but variable Negroid element derived from Negro slaves.　For the early population the only data we possess consists of a series of crania from Siwah Oasis,[1] on the northern border of the Libyan Desert, most of which, without much question, considerably antedate the Arab conquest.　These show these people to have been primarily of the Mediterranean type, yet with large minorities of the Caspian and Alpine forms.　For the living we have two considerable series of measurements from the eastern and southeastern margin of the region.　One of these, from Charga Oasis,[2] represents the older, sedentary population; the other, from the Kababish,[3] northwest of Khartoum, are examples of the later Arab nomads. The Charga series is virtually identical with that obtained among the modern

---

[1] Puccioni, 1910, but especially a series of eighty-five in P. M.
[2] Hrdlicka, 1912.　　　　　　　　　　[3] Seligmann, 1913.

Egyptians of the Thebaid[1] in being a blend of broad and narrow nosed, long-headed peoples, in whom the chief types represented are probably the Mediterranean, Proto-Negroid, and Proto-Australoid, with some little factor of the Alpine type. The Kababish, on the other hand, show quite a different character. They resemble more the early Siwah people in having a large majority of Mediterranean and Caspian types, but have more Proto-Negroid and less Alpine than these. They are in most ways very closely similar to the Beni-Amer of the Red Sea coast in the vicinity of Suakim, from which direction the ancestors of the Kababish most probably came.

For the whole of the rest of the Sahara area no individual series of measurements have been given, so that only the most general conclusions can be drawn from the averages published. The dominant type is undoubtedly very similar to the Berber, in being largely Mediterranean and Caspian. The Tuareg,[2] who are the dominant people of the western and central Sahara, are the best known representatives of this type, although there is among the lower ranks of the population a considerable amount of Negroid mixture. The Tuareg are further distinguished from the Berber tribes toward the north by their extremely tall stature, approximating in this respect the gigantic Nilotic Negroes and some of the tribes about Lake Chad. In the Fezzan and perhaps in other oases in the central Sahara there appears to be a considerable element of Palæ-Alpine type, which is most likely derived from brachycephalic Negroid slaves brought from the region of Lake Chad. Farther west and north, along the northern borders of the desert, the Negroid element is dolichocephalic, and derived probably from slaves coming from Senegal. This Negroid element seems to increase farther west still in Mauretania. The Tibbu or Teda of the Tibesti[3] range, in the heart of the Sahara, appear to have a large element of this, together with something of the brachycephalic Negroid factor, and may represent a remnant of the ancient Negroid population which has been assumed to have once spread throughout the Saharan region.

[1] Myers, 1905, 1906–08.          [2] Verneau, 1916–17; Zeltner, 1914.
[3] Bouilliez, 1913.

## III. Northeastern Africa

The peoples of northeastern Africa, including the whole area of the "Horn," Abyssinia, and that portion of Nubia lying east of the Nile and north of the Atbara River, have long been grouped together as "Hamitic." The region divides itself topographically into three distinct areas: the steppe-like plateau of Somaliland, lying at an elevation of about 3,000 feet; the sharply defined, much higher and partly forested plateau of Abyssinia, averaging about 7,000 feet and surmounted by mountain ranges and peaks rising to elevations of 14,000 feet; and the lowland of the Nubian Desert. The inhabitants of the whole region may be divided into two groups: (1) an eastern and southern, comprising the Beni-Amer,[1] Somali,[2] Galla,[3] and the Abyssinians of Shoa and Gojam,[4] together with the Masai[5] and Njemps,[5] formerly living north of Lake Rudolph; and (2) a central, including the Abyssinians of Tigre[4] and the region about Lake Tanna.[4] The first group virtually surrounds the second on the north, east, and south, and to it must probably be added the Hadendoa,[1] western neighbors of the Beni-Amer, who are more or less intermediate in racial characteristics between the two groups.

Analysis of the measurements made on the living gives for the first group the following results: All except the Hadendoa show the dominance of leptorrhine, dolichocephalic types, rising in the case of Galla to nearly 70 per cent, and very strong in the Beni-Amer and Somali. From cranial data from the first and last of these tribes we know that the major factor is that of the Caspian type, although in the Somali there is a relatively large element of the Mediterranean present. The secondary factor in all these tribes is of platyrrhine, dolichocephalic types, these being least important among the Somali and Beni-Amer, but increasing among the Abyssinians of Shoa and the Njemps to nearly the strength of the dominant elements. The actual types pres-

---

[1] Seligmann, 1913.

[2] Leys, 1913; Puccioni, 1917; Radlauer, 1914; Paulitschke, 1888.

[3] Virchow, 1889 a, 1891; Sergi, 1891; Verneau, 1909 b.

[4] Verneau, 1909 b; Sergi, S., 1912.     [5] Leys, 1913; Virchow, *loc. cit.*

ent appear to vary, in that in the Somali the Proto-Negroid is more important, in the Galla this and the Proto-Australoid are present in equal proportions, while in the Hadendoa the latter is in slight excess. A characteristic example of the Somali is given on Plate XI, Fig. 4.

The minority factors are of considerable significance. The Hadendoa and Beni-Amer are sharply differentiated from the other peoples in that they have a considerable Alpine factor which the others lack. We may therefore regard these two tribes as having received a considerable south Arabian element. The remaining tribes, on the other hand, have a small platyrrhine, brachycephalic factor, which certainly in the Somali and probably in the Masai and Njemps is of the Palæ-Alpine type. In the Abyssinians of Gojam, however, it is equally clearly Mongoloid. The Palæ-Alpine factor is probably derived from slight mixtures with the Central African Negroids; the Mongoloid element has more far-reaching significance. This type is, as will be seen later, strongly represented among the Bushmen, and it has frequently been claimed that these peculiar people once extended much farther north than they have done in historic times, and traces of them have even been claimed to have been found in early Egypt. It has been shown already that this is indeed true, and that in the Pre-Dynastic crania from the Thebaid this type is unquestionably present, especially in the females, albeit in but very small proportions. Any modern survival of this very ancient type would be looked for in marginal areas of isolation, and the fortress-like plateau of Abyssinia is the one spot in all eastern Africa in which such traces might be expected to be found. It is very significant in this connection that in the series of crania from the Tigre district,[1] dating from the fourth to the sixth century A. D., that this Mongoloid type is present in notable degree. It thus seems probable that in the Abyssinian plateau we have a third region (the other two being the Canary Islands and the extreme southern tip of the continent) in which traces of this type, which goes back to early Palæolithic times, still survive.

[1] Sergi, S., 1912.

The second group into which the population of northeastern
Africa may be divided can be more briefly dismissed.  It includes
the Abyssinians of Tigre and Lake Tanna, and shows a strong
contrast to the first and more numerous group, practically reversing the proportions there found.  In the former series of
tribes the leptorrhine, dolichocephalic types were dominant, the
platyrrhine secondary; here the latter are primary and the former
drop to second place.  In Tigre, the Proto-Australoid type is
most important, as among the neighboring Hadendoa, while the
secondary factor proves to have, in addition to the Caspian, a
considerable element of Mediterranean, as was the case in the
first group among the Galla.  The presence of this type so far
to the south is somewhat unexpected, but some light may be
thrown on the question by the ancient crania from Tigre, above
referred to, in which the Mediterranean type is dominant.
These may, perhaps, represent an immigrant group from north
Arabia or farther north.  In regard to the minor factors in this
northern Abyssinian population, it is clear that there is, as in
the Beni-Amer and Hadendoa, an element of Alpine type and
also a trace of the Palæ-Alpine.

The so-called "Hamitic" peoples of Northeast Africa seem
thus to be primarily of the Caspian type.  In the north, east,
and south this is the majority factor, attaining its greatest
strength in the southeast.  Throughout it is, however, blended
with a considerable Proto-Negroid and Proto-Australoid element, which, in the west and north, along the borders of the
great wedge of Nilotic Negroid peoples occupying the Egyptian
Sudan, equals or even exceeds the underlying original type.  In
the northern half of the area an immigrant Alpine element makes
its appearance, derived probably from the Arabs of southern
Arabia.  The bearing of this modern situation on the problems
of the early population of Nubia and Upper Egypt, now becomes
plain.  The Egyptian and especially the Nubian people of Pre-
Dynastic times comprised a large factor of the Caspian type.
In Nubia it was the dominant element, as it is to-day among the
tribes of the first group into which the people of Northeast Africa

were divided; farther down the Nile in Upper Egypt it was less strongly represented. In both areas it decreased in relative importance from Pre-Dynastic down to Roman times, its importance in the more southerly region of Nubia being throughout this whole period always about three times as great as in the Thebaid. To-day Nubia and the "Horn" of Africa are still the stronghold of this Caspian type. We are justified therefore, I believe, in regarding the Caspian factor in Upper Egypt as having come down the Nile valley from this great reservoir of the type, following along the Red Sea coast of what is now Eritrea, the Land of Punt as it was known to the Egyptians, to Nubia. The source of these Caspian peoples lies across the Red Sea in Arabia. At first sight a serious objection would seem to lie in the way of this statement, in that the population of southern Arabia is primarily Alpine to-day. It will be shown, however, in dealing with the racial history of Arabia, that we have reason to believe that the earliest population here was of the Caspian type, and that this Alpine element has come into southern Arabia relatively late, at any rate after the Neolithic period, which is that when the main body of Caspian peoples came into Northeast Africa. It is, indeed, quite possible that the movement of these people into Africa may have been in part due to pressure by the Alpine peoples who were spreading into Arabia along its southern coast, and some influence from whom was indeed brought into Africa by the Caspian immigrants themselves. The very much larger element of Alpine type found among the modern Hadendoa and Beni-Amer, represents, on the other hand, the effects of a relatively recent, late historic movement from the same south Arabian region, when its population had become pretty strongly Alpine.

# CHAPTER II

## EAST AND SOUTH AFRICA

THE highlands of Abyssinia and the "Horn" of Africa are continued southward along the eastern border of the continent by a broad belt of uplands lying from three to five thousand feet above the sea. Its western edge is roughly marked in the north by the Great Rift Valley, in which lie the remarkable series of lakes, beginning in the north with Albert Nyanza and continuing through Tanganyika to Nyassa. Toward the southern end of Tanganyika the western limit of the uplands trends more and more directly west, and follows more or less closely the divide between the Zambezi and Congo basins to the Atlantic coast. In the northern portion this upland is mainly grassland and open forest, but south of the 20° of S. Lat. the central and western portions are largely dry steppe and desert.

The population of this great area is divisible into three well-marked groups: (1) the eastern and southern Bantu-speaking Negroids, who at the present time occupy all but the southwestern corner of the whole region; (2) the Hottentot, formerly much more widely distributed, but now living mainly in the Orange River Colony and the southern parts of what was formerly German Southwest Africa; and (3) the Bushmen, once spread probably over the larger part of British South Africa as far north as the Zambezi River, but driven north and west into the Kalahari Desert and other unfavorable regions by the advance of the Bantu and Hottentot.

The Bantu-speaking Negroids are divided into a great number of tribal groups, from the Baganda and Wanyamwezi in the north around Lake Victoria, to the Zulu and Kaffir of the south, and so through the Betchuana and Barotse to the Herrero of former German Southwest Africa. Our knowledge of the physical characteristics of these many tribes is very incomplete, and we have cranial data only for a small number.

Beginning with the cranial data,[1] which cover an area extending from the Jagga of Mt. Kilimandjaro on the southern Uganda border, southward to the Kaffir and west to the Herrero, it appears that there are noteworthy differences between the various tribes. For, although all are overwhelmingly dolichocephalic, and show from 75 to 100 per cent of the Proto-Negroid and Proto-Australoid types combined, two groups are easily apparent, one comprising the Jagga, Angoni, Zulu, and Herrero, in whom the former type is in the majority, the other all the rest (*i. e.*, Issansu, Sanduwi, Turu, Burungi, Lake Nyassa tribes, and the Kaffir), in whom the latter type is predominant. The former group is thus more closely related to the true Negroes, whom we shall consider in a later chapter. A further difference is also to be noted in the proportions of the Caspian type present. In the southernmost tribes, the Zulu, Kaffir, and Angoni, this type is present as a mere trace, whereas among the Issansu, Turu, Sanduwi, and Burungi, north of Lake Nyassa, the proportion rises above 10 per cent. It will presently be shown that among the northern Bantu it increases still more, and we have thus a fairly regular increase in the proportion of this type from south to north. The region of Northeast Africa is and has been since the earliest times a reservoir of the Caspian type, and we have thus good reason to believe that it has penetrated southward, its influence diminishing almost in direct proportion to the distance from the source. On the other hand, we find in all of these Bantu tribes a minority factor of the Palæ-Alpine type, which is, on the contrary, present in smaller proportion in the north and increases southward. Since, as we shall see, the Bushmen have a considerable factor of this type, which is probably of the special Pigmy variety, it seems likely that this element was absorbed from the pre-Bantu population in the south by the advancing Bantu tribes, those in the lead of the migratory drift being most influenced.

[1] Widemann, 1899; Shrubsall, 1902; Zeidler, 1914–15.

In stature these southern Bantu tribes are rather above medium, the average ranging from a little below to a little above 170 cm. In skin color there is much more variation, the more southerly tribes being often brown or even light brown, whereas those farther north are generally darker, some being nearly as black as the true Negro. The hair is quite uniformly woolly.

The southern Bantu have been given first consideration because for them cranial data were available; we may now turn to the northern tribes, for whom we have only measurements on the living.[1] Of these northern tribes, the Baganda, Wanyamwezi, and Manyema, in Uganda and the vicinity of Lake Victoria, may be taken as examples. They are a people of medium or slightly over medium stature, the average ranging in general between 165 and 170 cm. In skin color there is here, as farther south, wide variation in individual cases, and it is clearly related to differences in social rank, the ruling aristocracy being often of a deep golden brown, whereas the mass of the common people are quite dark, some individuals being fully as black as the blackest Congo or Nilotic Negro. The hair is invariably black and woolly. A portrait of a member of the Andarobo tribe is given on Plate XII, Fig. 1.

Analysis of the measurements which have been made on these tribes shows that, just as among the southern Bantu, all have a majority of the platyrrhine, dolichocephalic factors; here, however, the proportion of these is in no case as large as in the south. The whole series of tribes may be divided into two groups, according to the relative importance of the leptorrhine, dolichocephalic and the platyrrhine, brachycephalic elements. The Baganda and Kaseri have a much larger proportion of what is almost certainly the Caspian type than the others, who in their turn have more than twice as large a proportion of this factor as any of the southern Bantu. The greatest intensity thus of the Caspian factor lies west and northwest of Lake Victoria, and decreases toward the south and east. If we take into consideration the platyrrhine, brachycephalic factors a new group-

---

[1] Leys, 1913; Johnston, 1902; Virchow, 1893; Roscoe, 1911.

ing appears, in which the Akamba, Sukuma, and Manyema tribes are contrasted with the Baganda, Akikuyu, Kaseri, Wanyamwezi, etc., the former group having a much larger proportion of the round-headed elements than the latter.

The presence of this brachycephalic factor, which is in all probability the Pigmy variety of the Palæ-Alpine, raises some interesting questions. As will be shown later, the northern Bantu peoples seem to have originated from the blending of a southward-moving group of Nilotic Negroes and a westward-moving branch of the strongly Caspian peoples of the northeast of the continent. These latter could hardly have been the bringers of the brachycephalic factors, so that we must either assume a considerable element of this type to have been in the area prior to the arrival of the northern and eastern immigrants, and to have been absorbed by them, or else that the brachycephalic element was brought by the northern Negro group, or has penetrated inland from the coast. So far, however, as our knowledge of the Nilotic Negro goes, he has but a very slight brachycephalic factor, quite inadequate to explain the very considerable proportion (amounting in the Akamba and Manyema to 33 per cent) found among the present northern Bantu folk. The second possibility, however, seems at least a partial solution. Further evidence in favor of a pre-Bantu brachycephalic people in this region is supplied by the actual survival of Pigmy-like tribes in the region about Mt. Elgon, northeast of Lake Victoria, and of several groups of true Pigmy brachycephals, such as the Batwa, north of Lake Tanganyika, and the Bambuto, in the Ituri Forest west of Ruwenzori, along the western borders of the plateau. The probability that a factor of this short-statured, primarily brachycephalic primitive people has been absorbed by the northern Bantu is further indicated, perhaps, by their reduced stature, which is less than that of the tall Galla, Somali, or Masai, from whom the Caspian factor must have come, and much shorter than the gigantic Nilotic Negro.

That some brachycephalic influence may also have worked inland from the coast is evident from the character of the coastal tribes. These all show, in contrast with the majority of the plateau peoples, a higher proportion of brachycephalic factors. Unfortunately, no nasal measurements of these tribes were taken, so that it is impossible to say whether this represents a platyr-rhine or leptorrhine element. Since, however, we know that the whole coast region has had more or less intensive contact with the strongly Alpine Arabs of southern Arabia, at least since the beginning of the Christian era, and particularly since the tenth century, it seems most probable that the greater part of the brachycephalic factors found along the coast are Alpine and derived from the Arabs.

Before passing to the discussion of the Hottentot and Bush-men, it is necessary to speak briefly of a small group of non-Bantu tribes occupying that portion of northern Uganda extend-ing from Lake Rudolph to Albert Nyanza and south around the eastern side of Lake Victoria. These tribes,[1] including the Njemps, Masai, Karamojo, Turkana, Suk, Nandi, and Acholi, are in origin Nilotic Negroes, mixed with more or less of the Caspian type than is the case among the northern Bantu, and speaking Sudanic languages. The Masai and Njemps are tall, with average stature of 170 to 172 cm. of relatively light skin color and with a large proportion of Caspian type, which actu-ally just outweighs the Proto-Negroid and Proto-Australoid fac-tors. They are thus close to the Abyssinians of Gojam. The Masai have been a very virile and powerful people, and from their earlier home on the northern edge of the plateau, east of the White Nile, have raided and conquered southward far be-yond Mt. Kilimandjaro. The other tribes mentioned, speaking languages allied to those of the Nilotic Negroes, appear to repre-sent an older movement of these, who received a much smaller Caspian element than the Masai or Njemps, although equal in proportions with that found among some of the northern Bantu, such as the Baganda and Kaseri, who, it may be remembered, had a much larger factor of this Caspian type than any of the other Bantu tribes. The Turkana most closely resemble the

[1] Leys, 1913.

Nilotic Negroes, such as the Dinka, and among them are often to be found individuals of the extremely tall stature characteristic of the Nilotic tribes. The Nandi and Suk, on the other hand, have almost as large an element of the Caspian type as the Bantu Baganda, and may thus be regarded as racially one with the Bantu peoples, although linguistically allied to the Nilotics. The Suk, moreover, have a large brachycephalic, platyrrhine factor, which would ally them in this respect with the Akamba about Mt. Kenia, and suggests that they belong to an older migration, which had largely absorbed the surviving ancient brachycephalic Pigmy remnants, prior to the period when the Masai came into the country.

Summing up the result of this study of the peoples of the East African plateau region, it may be said that there is evidence that the early population probably comprised a large element of very short-statured, yellowish-red colored, strongly prognathous Palæ-Alpine people, whose purest representatives survive to-day in the Batwa and Bambuto Pigmies, along the western margin of the plateau, and in the other Pigmy groups of the Congo basin. With these there *may* have been a trace of the ancient Mongoloid element, also short, yellow-skinned, but not prognathic. From the lower-lying area of the Egyptian Sudan on the northwest, there then came a great thrust of Nilotic peoples very largely of Proto-Negroid type, while from the east came a drift of peoples comparable with the modern Galla and Somali, with large Caspian elements. The older stratum of brachycephalic peoples was partly exterminated, partly absorbed, and from the blending of these varied groups the Bantu-speaking peoples were, in the course of time, evolved. In comparatively recent times further migrations from these same two sources occurred, giving rise to the Masai and other non-Bantu tribes of Uganda and British East Africa. Along the coastal lowlands, especially since the tenth century, an Alpine element has been introduced by Arabs from Yemen, the Hadramaut, and Oman. Somewhere about the fourteenth or fifteenth century the Bantu peoples about Lake Tanganyika began to press southward

through what is now Rhodesia. Here, and especially south of
the Zambezi, they encountered the Hottentot and Bushman
tribes, whom they in large part evicted from the better lands,
and with whom in some degree the more southern Bantu tribes
mingled, so that a slight factor of the Mongoloid type, derived
from these older peoples, is to be found among the Zulu and
Kaffir of to-day.

For the population of the great island of Madagascar, lying
some 250 miles off the East African coast, available data are
very scanty. Speaking a language allied to those of Indonesia,
the people are apparently divisible into several groups differing
widely from each other in physical characteristics. The Hovas
stand at one extreme of the series, the Sakalavas at the other,
with the so-called Malagasy, the Betsileo and several other tribes
intermediate. The Hova, who occupy mainly the Imerina Plateau
in the interior of the island, seem in the main to be of Palæ-Alpine
type with a small admixture of Proto-Negroid and other elements.
They were immigrants probably within the last eight or nine centuries, and with their short stature, yellowish-coppery skin, and
straight or slightly wavy hair, seem comparable with the older
pre-Malay peoples of Sumatra and Java. The Sakalavas of the
East coast, on the other hand, are of medium or slightly over
medium stature, black-skinned, frizzly-haired, and seem, from
the scanty measurements available, to be primarily of Proto-
Negroid type with some admixture of the Proto-Australoid. In
what way or at what time these apparently older Negroid peoples reached Madagascar is still unknown. The unskilfulness of
the African tribes in navigation makes it unlikely that they could
have reached the island unaided, and there are some grounds
for believing that the Negroid elements may have been brought
by some earlier, pre-Hova Indonesian immigrants, although how
this could have been accomplished is still a mystery.

The questions of the origin and racial relationship of the
Hottentot[1] and the Bushman[2] have long been under discussion,

[1] Fetzer, 1914; Shrubsall, 1897; Deniker, 1889; Macgregor Memorial Museum.
[2] Shrubsall, 1897, 1907, 1911; Virchow, 1886 b; Werner, 1906; Macgregor Memorial Museum.

and many conflicting theories have been proposed. The whole problem is extremely difficult, owing to the uncertainty of the identification of most of the cranial material published. Crania which one investigator regards as Hottentot will be declared to be Bushman by another, and the most conflicting results are naturally secured. A further complication is involved in the question whether or not the so-called Strandloopers, who were a purely coastal group, were really a different people from the Bushmen. They became extinct, apparently, during the earlier colonial period, but some cranial material, supposed to represent them, has been found in caves along the southern coast. Whether or not they were a distinct people, the crania which are called "Strandlooper" certainly present features which differentiate them from those described as Bushman, and I shall accordingly, in attempting to unravel the complexities of racial relationship in the southern portion of the continent, divide the material into the three groups of Hottentot, Bushman, and Strandlooper. The determination of the areas occupied by the Hottentot and Bushmen is by no means an easy task. In general, however, at the period of earliest European contact, the Hottentot occupied the western border regions along the Atlantic coast, whereas the Bushmen were scattered rather sparsely over much of the interior and south, from the Kalahari Desert to the Cape. The Bantu tribes occupied the larger part of the east, although even there remnants of Bushmen still survived in the wilder mountain country.

Data on the living Hottentot and Bushmen, of whom examples are given on Plate XII, Figs. 2 and 3, are somewhat uncertain, since the two groups of people have mixed so much not only with each other but with both Bantu Negroids and Europeans, that the isolation of really pure-blooded individuals is rather difficult. The average stature of the Hottentot probably varies between about 162 and 170 cm., while individuals apparently of pure blood have been noted who were still taller. Their stature is thus essentially comparable to that of the southern Bantu. The Bushmen, on the other hand, are Pigmy-like, the purest groups averaging only about 144 cm. in height, with many individuals falling below 140 cm. They thus approach the Pigmy tribes of the equatorial forest. In skin color the two peoples are much more alike, the Bushmen being of a light-yellowish brown, in which the yellow tint is clearly marked, while the Hottentots are but slightly darker. Both thus stand in the sharpest contrast to the surrounding Bantu Negroids, who are in general extremely dark, if not black. In head-form the Hottentot are apparently quite purely dolichocephalic and platyrrhine, giving evidence of little more brachycephalic mixture than we find among the southern Bantu. Both peoples are finally characterized by the well-known steatopygia of their women, *i. e.*, an abnormal development of fat on the buttocks.

The discussion of the relationship of these peoples to each other and to the surrounding tribes, will be facilitated by presenting the data derived from an analysis of the available material, in the form of a table showing roughly the percentage of the more important types present.

| Type | Strandlooper | | Bush-man | Hottentot | | Kaffir | Zulu | Angoni |
|---|---|---|---|---|---|---|---|---|
| | Fem. | Masc. | Masc. | Fem. | Masc. | Masc. | Masc. | Masc. |
| Palæ-Alpine...... | .... | 12% | 5% | .... | .... | .... | 10% | 6% |
| Mongoloid....... | 50% | 46% | 29% | 32% | 5% | 9% | 5% | 8% |
| Caspian......... | 8% | 4% | .... | .... | 9% | 4% | 5% | 2% |
| Proto-Negroid.... | 17% | 12% | 34% | 41% | 31% | 38% | 57% | 54% |
| Proto-Australoid . | 25% | 25% | 31% | 27% | 49% | 45% | 18% | 29% |

Beginning with the Hottentot, it is clear that the male series reveals them as a prevailingly dolichocephalic people, in whom the Proto-Australoid and Proto-Negroid types comprise the majority of all factors present, the Caspian and Mongoloid appearing as little more than traces. The male Hottentot thus is essentially similar to the Bantu Kaffir, but differs from the Zulu and Angoni in having much less of the Proto-Negroid type and none of the Palæ-Alpine, which both of these possess. The Hottentot females are strikingly different from the males. They have the Proto-Negroid dominant in contrast to the Proto-Australoid

FIG. 1. BANTU. (ANDAROBO.)

FIG. 2. HOTTENTOT.

FIG. 3. BUSHMAN.

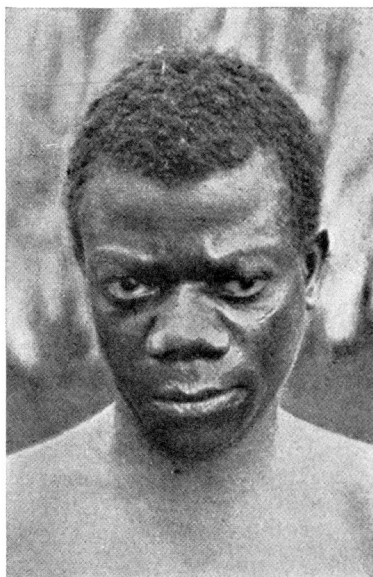

FIG. 4. MBUTE PIGMY.

PLATE XII.

as in the males, and reveal a very strong Mongoloid factor. It is upon this latter which I wish to lay stress, for if, as is rather generally assumed, the women preserve more clearly than the men the older racial characteristics, we have here an indication of the blending of a Negroid population possessing a large Mongoloid factor with one essentially comparable to the Kaffir. If we now compare the male Hottentot crania with the Bushman, it appears that the latter differ mainly in having a larger Mongoloid and a smaller Proto-Australoid element, *i. e.*, the Bushman males differ from the Hottentot males, in the same way that the Hottentot females do. So that we may regard the male Hottentot as essentially a blend between the Bushman, in whom the Proto-Australoid, Proto-Negroid, and Mongoloid types are nearly equally mixed, and a Bantu people comparable to the Kaffir, in whom the latter element is almost absent.

If we now continue the comparison and contrast the Bushman crania with the males of the Strandlooper, it at once appears that precisely the same features which differentiate the Bushman from the Hottentot mark off the Strandlooper from the Bushman, for the Strandlooper has more Mongoloid and less Proto-Negroid than the Bushman, just as the Bushman has as compared with the Hottentot! So that the Bushman may be regarded as a Strandlooper, in whom the Mongoloid has been relatively weakened, by the addition of a considerable Proto-Negroid factor. Lastly, if we look at the female Strandlooper, we find that in them the Mongoloid factor is still further strengthened, and that the Palæ-Alpine element present among the Strandlooper and Bushman males entirely disappears. There is thus a fairly regular sequence, beginning with the southern Bantu Kaffir, and following through the Hottentot and Bushman to the Strandlooper, such that a logical theory of the racial history of the whole of South Africa may be outlined as follows.

The oldest population is represented by the Strandlooper, who at a very early period, perhaps already in Palæolithic times, extended widely over the plateaus of the southern portion of the continent and reached northward, perhaps as far as the region of the Great Lakes. Primarily Mongoloid in type, they were blended with a considerable Proto-Australoid factor and a lesser element of the Proto-Negroid type. Later a southward movement of peoples, mainly of Proto-Negroid and Proto-Australoid types, who had absorbed a small proportion of Pigmy, Palæ-Alpine folk, took place, and, passing through Rhodesia, forced their way into the region of the southern plateaus. Of the older Strandlooper population they absorbed a part, driving the remainder to the coast, where they survived down to the sixteenth century. From the mingling of the immigrants and the Strandloopers the Bushmen developed, and these occupied all of the better lands. Again a new drift, this time of Bantu-like peoples, forced their way over the same route from the northward, and established themselves in the region south of the Zambezi. These folk, who were pastoral, cattle-keeping people, took the better lands, driving the Bushmen into the less favorable localities, and in time absorbed a certain proportion of them, and thus developed the Hottentot, whose language, although possessing several clicks taken over from the Bushmen, nevertheless shows strong Hamitic relationships. Lastly, probably about the fourteenth or fifteenth century, a last thrust of Bantu peoples occurred, bringing into the region the warlike Zulu, Kaffir, etc. Like their predecessors, they drove the earlier occupants from much of the better lands, forcing the Hottentots west and north toward the Atlantic coast, and the Bushmen into the Kalahari and other desert sections. Just as the earlier groups of invaders, these latest Bantu conquerors mingled somewhat with the older peoples, so that when their progress was stopped by European occupation, they had already absorbed a small Mongoloid element, which thus differentiates them from the Bantu tribes farther north. If this suggested theory is correct, the Strandlooper, Bushman, and Hottentot represent three successive stages in the racial history of this part of Africa, the fourth and last stage of which was put an end to by the European colonization. That the Hottentot represented a very old Bushman-Bantu mixture has been often suggested by others; the present theory carries this a step farther, and derives the Bushmen themselves from the still older Strandlooper by a similar process.

Two obstacles may be pointed out in the way of accepting this theory, the presence among the Strandlooper of a small factor of the Caspian type, and the Hamitic rather than Bantu affiliation of Hottentot speech. Were the Caspian factor smaller and also found in the Bushmen, it might be explained as an element brought in by the earliest immigrants from the northward; its absence among the Bushmen, however, and its greater strength among the Hottentot than among any of the southern Bantu is certainly puzzling. The Hamitic relationship of the Hottentot speech would be intelligible if we could assume that the Bantu-like Negroids who, according to the theory here suggested, were the ancestors of the Hottentots, had been Hamiticized in speech before they left their earlier northern home. The larger Caspian element which the Hottentot possesses as compared with the southern Bantu might possibly be held to point in this direction. There are, to be sure, difficulties in the way of this assumed Hamitization, but most writers who have struggled with the Hottentot problem have found no other way to explain the relationship except by bringing the Hottentot, with a Proto-Hamitic speech, from somewhere farther north.

Much light might be thrown on the intricate problems of this portion of the African continent by crania of unquestionably ancient date. Within the last few years two discoveries have been made which, although the exact age of the crania is still uncertain, nevertheless afford evidence of great value and interest. The first of these in point of discovery is the Boskop skull, found in a laterite deposit in the Transvaal in 1914.[1] There is as yet no clew as to the age of the find, and all that can be said with certainty is that the skull is probably very old. The skull is unfortunately fragmentary, and different investigators have reached somewhat different results in estimating its measurements. What seems to be the sounder view is that the skull is mesocephalic and chamæcephalic. The face being entirely missing, it is im-

[1] Haughton, 1917; Broom, 1918.

possible to determine the character of the nose. If this were platyrrhine, the Boskop skull would represent a blend between the Proto-Australoid and Mongoloid types, precisely the form suggested as that of the remote ancestors of the Strandlooper, and still surviving among them at the time when they became extinct. In 1921 the Broken Hill skull,[1] which has aroused so much interest, was found farther to the north, in Rhodesia. This is fortunately much more nearly complete, and, although its age is still undetermined, it is unquestionably of great antiquity. Proto-Australoid in type, it furnishes evidence of the presence in South Africa, at a period perhaps synchronous with Palæolithic man in Europe, of the same type characteristic of the earliest crania there, and that from which, by blending with the Mongoloid, the Boskop skull, like the Gibraltar skull at the opposite end of the continent, may have been derived.

[1] Woodward, 1921.

# CHAPTER III

## CENTRAL AND WEST AFRICA AND THE SUDAN

### I. Central Africa

Central Africa, which is here understood to include, in addition to the Congo basin, the northern portions of Angola and most of the western part of the French Congo, is, except along its northern border, occupied by Bantu-speaking Negroid peoples. Topographically it forms a vast shallow basin, some 1,500 miles in diameter, of which the eastern and southern margins are formed by the eastern and southern plateaus. The western margin, through which the Congo River breaks its way, is formed by a narrow northern extension of the southern plateaus, running parallel to the Atlantic coast and decreasing in altitude as it approaches the bend of the Gulf of Guinea. On the north the limits of the basin are less well-defined, being formed by the low water-parting between the Congo and the streams that flow into Lake Chad or the Nile. In the south and southwest there are considerable grassland areas, but most of the region is covered by the dense equatorial forest.

Anthropologically the peoples of Central Africa are less well-known than those of the eastern uplands. They appear, however, to be divisible into two groups, the first of which includes those tribes in whom the brachycephalic factors are in the majority, confined mainly to the dense forest area within 5° north and south of the equator; the second comprising the tribes in whom the dolichocephalic elements are predominant, who are found chiefly around the periphery of the area, and in places along the main valley of the Congo or those of some of its larger tributaries. The first group includes two very different peoples, the Pigmy tribes being sharply marked off from all the others physically as well as culturally.

The Pigmy peoples[1] are still very imperfectly known. They
live generally as separate tribal groups, surrounded by their taller
neighbors. Of very primitive culture, depending wholly on the
hunt, they are strongly contrasted with the agricultural tribes by
whom they are surrounded, and are to be found here and there
throughout the area within 5° north or south of the equator, from
the Great Rift Valley to the Atlantic. As the term Pigmy implies, they are of very short stature, averaging perhaps 140 cm.
for the full-grown males, with individuals ranging as low as 133
cm., while one Bambuto Pigmy woman had a stature of only
128 cm. (about 4 feet 2 inches). They are further distinguished
from their Negroid neighbors by having a reddish-yellow skin
and a somewhat hairy body. The head hair is, like that of all
Negroid peoples, woolly. Analysis of the measurements of living Pigmies from various parts of the equatorial forest, shows a
predominance, on the whole, of brachycephalic, platyrrhine factors rising as high in some cases as 65 per cent, the only other
element present being the platyrrhine, dolichocephalic types,
which in some cases are dominant. The very few crania which
are with reasonable certainty Pigmy, and whose measurements
have been published in full, indicate that we have to deal only
with two types, the Palæ-Alpine and the Proto-Negroid. To
class the Central African Pigmy as essentially Palæ-Alpine, thus
bringing him into the same group with one of the fundamental
types in Europe, may seem preposterous. There is no question
but that the Pigmy, if in reality belonging in the main to the
Palæ-Alpine type, forms a very special subdivision thereof, distinguished from the main type by several important features.
The problem of the relationship of these Pigmy Negroid peoples
to the Palæ-Alpine type is not confined to Africa, for we shall
meet it again in the Negrito peoples of southeastern Asia and of
the Pacific region. Detailed discussion of the whole question
must be deferred to the final chapter, and for the present we
may only state that the Pigmy group may be in general considered as a very divergent section of the Palæ-Alpine form.

[1] Johnston, 1902; Kuhn, 1914; von Luschan, 1906; Poutrin, 1910; Verneau, 1896.

The dolichocephalic elements usually occurring as a minority among the Pigmies might be attributed to the result of mixture with the surrounding Negroid tribes, yet the wide difference in stature makes the assumption difficult, and it seems probable that the source of this long-headed element is to be found in the remnants of a dolichocephalic Pigmy people, whose existence seems to have been pretty well established by Poutrin and Verneau. Our knowledge of these is extremely limited, and the measurements of only a single skull have been published in full, so far as I am aware, so that determination of the type is as yet impossible. If we might regard these dolichocephalic Pigmies as essentially Proto-Australoid, the shortness of stature would cease to be a disturbing feature, since this type was, in the Palæolithic period and later, often very short. Unfortunately, the single skull known is distinctly Proto-Negroid. This would suggest that, just as in the case of the Palæ-Alpine we have a special Pigmy variety due perhaps to some environmental influences, so there may be a special Pigmy form of the Proto-Negroid. Until, however, more abundant data are available on the whole Pigmy group, further speculation seems useless. All that we can say at present with safety is that the Pigmy peoples appear to be in the main related to the Palæ-Alpine type; that they have among them a remnant of a platyrrhine, dolichocephalic group of unknown relationship; and that, as a whole, they are to be regarded as a very ancient and primitive people, driven back into the dense equatorial forest by the encroaching Negroid groups, who have undoubtedly mingled with them to some extent. An example of the Pigmy type is shown on Plate XII, Fig. 4.

Turning now to the other portion of the population of this whole area among whom brachycephalic factors prevailed,[1] it appears that this includes a number of tribes covering a considable portion of the central and northeastern part of the Congo basin, such as the Baluba, Basongo, and Wangatta, between the Kasai and Lomami Rivers, the Basoko near the mouth of the

[1] Jacques, 1894–95, 1897–98; Virchow, 1886 d; Wolf, 1886; Mense, 1887.

Aruimi, and certain tribes of the lower Welle. All of these, and probably others for whom we have no data, are of moderately tall stature, ranging from 168 cm. in the Basoko to 175 cm. in the Basongo, and are usually of very dark or black skin color, although individuals of lighter shade occur. In head-form all of these tribes are mesocephalic and show on analysis a predominance of brachycephalic factors which rises in some cases as high as 70 per cent. Cranial material[1] shows that the Palæ-Alpine type is in the majority, the Proto-Negroid and Proto-Australoid making up practically all of the remainder. If these tribes be compared with the Bantu of the plateau region toward the east, such as the Baganda or Wanyamwezi, they are found to differ primarily in their large Palæ-Alpine factor, and to have but a trace of the Caspian factor, which was quite strongly marked among the plateau tribes. That is to say, we may regard these Congo tribes as northern Bantu who have been mixed with a large proportion of Palæ-Alpine peoples and are without the Caspian element present in the area east of the Great Rift Valley. A portrait of a man of the Bobai tribe, illustrating the brachycephalic type of Negro is given on Plate XIII, Fig. 1.

Since it seems probable that the Pigmy Palæ-Alpine type was once widely spread throughout the Congo basin, and since many of the Congo tribes have dim traditions of an earlier eastern home, it seems most likely that we may consider them to be early northern Bantus, who have moved westward into the Congo region, where they have appropriated the better agricultural lands, and absorbed much of the older brachycephalic population. Here again, as in the Pigmy question, the difference in stature forms a difficulty, yet nowhere else in all Africa is any other source for this factor discernible than the Pigmy, and we have no evidence that any significant immigration of peoples of Palæ-Alpine type has ever taken place into the continent.

Something of a confirmation of the view that the brachycephalic elements in certain of the Congo tribes are to be explained by absorption of ancient Pigmy Palæ-Alpine peoples, is

---

[1] Bennington, 1911-12.

given by a study of the remaining or dolichocephalic tribes of the whole region.[1] They are distributed both around the periphery of the area on the north, east, and south, and also along the main valley of the Congo River. All these tribes show a large preponderance of dolichocephalic, platyrrhine factors, and a minority of brachycephalic, platyrrhine elements, which is substantially comparable to that found among the northern Bantu on the plateaus. Only, it would seem, in the case of the more easterly tribes of the Congo basin, such as the Manyema and Basonge, and perhaps in some of those along the southern borders, does any Caspian element, strong in some of the northern Bantu, appear. An example of this dolichocephalic Negro type is shown in the portrait of a Tamoa given on Plate XIII, Fig. 2.

The only considerable series of crania from this group comes, unfortunately, from the extreme western margin, from the Gaboon[2] in the French Congo. This shows a rather considerable majority of platyrrhine, dolichocephalic factors, the Proto-Negroid alone amounting to over 40 per cent. Apart from these, the only other type present, except as a trace, is the Palæ-Alpine. If we compare these crania with those for the Bantu of the plateaus on the opposite or eastern margin of the Congo basin, it is evident that the Gaboon tribes differ from their eastern linguistic relatives chiefly in the larger proportion of Palæ-Alpine factors and smaller amount of the Proto-Australoid present. In other words, they differ from the eastern Bantu in just the same way that the other but brachycephalic Congo Negroids do, only the differences are smaller. The Gaboon tribes thus stand intermediate between the Bantu of the plateaus and the predominantly brachycephalic Negroid tribes of the Congo.

The dolichocephalic Negroids of the Central African region would thus be explained as a later wave of Bantu-speaking folk, who, following the earlier, which mingled extensively with the older brachycephalic Pigmy peoples, flowed around the margins of the area, or passed on more directly down the Congo to the

[1] Jacques, 1894–95, 1897–98; Mense, 1887; Virchow, 1886 d; Wolf, 1886.
[2] Bennington, 1911–12.

Atlantic coast. In the Gaboon they found an already mixed population of true Negroes, blended somewhat with the older Pigmy peoples, the remnants of whom still survive as the Babongo, Akoi, and Sangha River Pigmies. With this strongly Negroid group, the Bantu immigrants in time amalgamated, the result of the mixture being the occupants of the Gaboon to-day. Finally, probably about the sixteenth century, a last immigration took place into the region, that of the Fang,[1] a fierce, cannibalistic people, who came in from the east and northeast, and who appear to be true Negroes, with a small element of the Palæ-Alpine type and a trace of the Caspian, resembling thus many of the tribes of the northern portion of the French Congo.

## II. The Sudan and the Guinea Coast

The term Sudan is applied in general to a broad belt of country lying roughly between 7° and 17° N. Lat., and extending east and west across Africa from the Atlantic to the highlands of Abyssinia. Limited on the north by the Sahara and the Nubian deserts, its southern border is formed by the edge of the great equatorial forest. It is in the main an area of grasslands and open forest, and is throughout a relatively featureless plateau, lying at an elevation of 1,000 to 1,500 feet. South of its western portion, and lying between it and the sea, is what may be collectively called the Guinea coast, extending from Portuguese and French Guinea in the west to Nigeria and Cameroon in the east. In the main heavily forested, it is in the north a low plateau, and is bordered along the coast by a narrow lowland and lagoon belt.

Throughout practically the whole of Africa south of about 5° N. Lat. the languages of the various tribes all belong to the great Bantu group. Only along the northern border of Uganda are Hamitic or Negro languages spoken, and in the south the semi-Hamitic Hottentot and the Bushman. In the Sudan and throughout the Guinea coast the languages belong to what is

[1] Pittard, 1908; Schenck, 1905.

now generally called the Sudanic group, characterized by extremely primitive characteristics and quite unrelated to any of the other languages of the continent.

Culturally the population of this whole region falls into two sections, one of which includes the Fula, Hausa, Songhai, Mandingo, and other tribes of the Sudan west of Lake Chad; the other comprising all the rest, who are sometimes known as "true Negroes," in contrast to the Bantu Negroids of much of southern Africa. The first group have been, at least since the twelfth century, notable for their superior culture and ability. In the western Sudan they built up considerable and well-organized states, or else, as in the case of the Fula, made themselves the ruling aristocracy among peoples of lower culture and ability. Mohammedanized in the fourteenth century, or perhaps before, they have been infused with considerable Arabic culture. Curiously enough, these relatively advanced tribes are, from the physical point of view, the least known, very few measurements on the living and practically no cranial data having been published. We are reduced, therefore, to the use of a few averages, from which nothing satisfactory can be derived.

Leaving this least-known group of peoples, however, for the moment, we may turn to the consideration of the second group, which comprises the bulk of the population of the whole region. It is most convenient to begin in the eastern portion of the Sudan, in the region of the upper Nile. Beginning some 300 miles above Khartoum and extending southward well into the great swampy region known as the Bahr-el-Ghazal, are a series of peoples generally grouped together under the term Nilotic Negroes. Of the more important of these, the Dinka,[1] Shilluk,[2] and Nuer,[2] we possess considerable series of measurements. Perhaps the most striking feature of these tribes is their very tall stature, ranging from 172 cm. among the Dinka to 177 cm. among the Shilluk, or even higher, according to some authorities. In skin

---

[1] Seligmann, 1913; Tucker, 1910; Lombroso, 1896; Mochi, 1905 a; Waterston, 1908, Chantre, 1904.

[2] Seligmann, 1913; Chantre, 1904.

color all are very black, and most are markedly prognathic. The measurements show the Shilluk, Nuer, and Dinka (naming them in order from north to south) to be relatively uniform in character. All comprise from 85 to over 90 per cent of platyrrhine, dolichocephalic factors, which, if the few Dinka crania known are a fair indication, are almost wholly of the Proto-Negroid type; indeed, these Dinka crania show a larger proportion of this type than any other African series as yet published. The very small minorities are of platyrrhine, brachycephalic and leptorrhine, dolichocephalic elements, and are in all probability Palæ-Alpine and Caspian. The southern tribes appear to have a slightly larger proportion of these than the northern. The Nilotic Negro may therefore be characterized as a very tall, very black people, with typical Negro hair and marked prognathism, and probably in overwhelming proportions of the Proto-Negroid type. The portrait of a Dinka given on Plate XIII, Fig. 3, may be taken as a good example of the Nilotic Negroes.

West of the true Nilotic Negroes and occupying the major part of central and southern Kordofan, Darfur, Dar-Fertit, and the southwestern portion of the Bahr-el-Ghazal district, are a series of tribes of more mixed character.[1] They fall rather clearly into two groups, one of which, including the Furawi and Bertawi in Darfur and the Bongawi in the Bahr-el-Ghazal, is very similar to the Dinka, Nuer and Shilluk, the chief difference being a considerably shorter stature and a large proportion of brachycephalic, Palæ-Alpine factors, these being more pronounced in the Bongawi in the south than among the Darfur tribes. The other group, which comprises the Nuba, Tagalawi, Kurawi, Fertitawi, and Digawi, is marked by a much larger increase in the Palæ-Alpine element, which reaches proportions of as much as 40 per cent. In the case of the Nuba, there is also an increase in the Caspian factor, with which goes a retention of tall stature, which in the other tribes drops to or even below medium. These facts seem best accounted for by the theory that in the tribes of this group (which penetrates the Nilotic tribes like a wedge from

[1] Seligmann, 1910, 1913; Tucker, 1910.

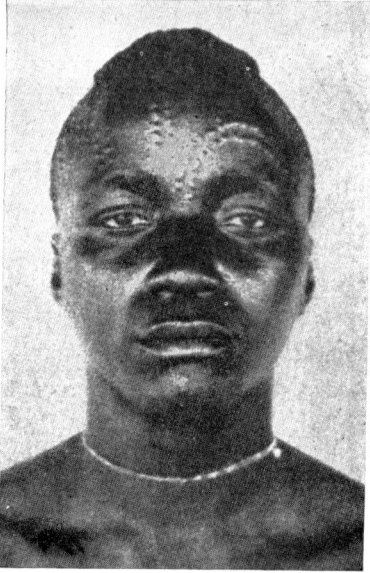

FIG. 1. CONGO NEGRO. (BOBAI.)

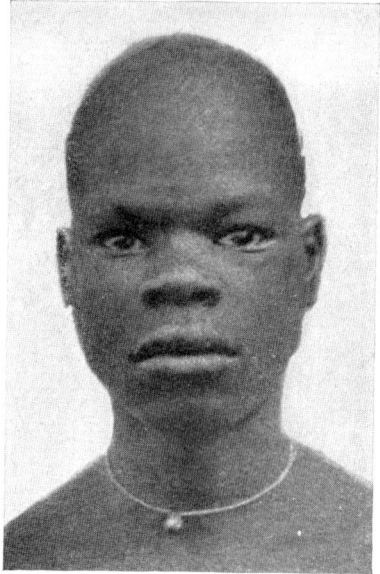

FIG. 2. CONGO NEGRO. (TAMOA.)

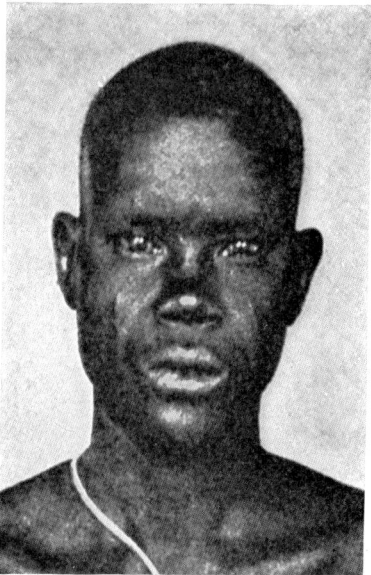

FIG. 3. NILOTIC NEGRO. (DINKA.)

FIG. 4. MANDINGO.

PLATE XIII.

southwest to northeast) we have peoples of mixed Proto-Negroid and pigmy Palæ-Alpine types, which have forced their way northeastward from the region between the Welle River and Lake Chad. In general these tribes resemble in their character the Bantu tribes of Uganda and the eastern plateaus, except that they have much less of the Caspian type in their make-up.

Turning next to the tribes between the Welle River and Lake Chad, with which the group just described seems to be connected, we are faced, at least so far as the Welle drainage is concerned, by an almost complete lack of individual measurements. The most important peoples of this section are undoubtedly the Mangbettu and Azandi (Niam-Niam), who at one time had built up quite a power in the country. According to verbal descriptions and the very meagre metrical data,[1] these tribes vary considerably in color and stature, but seem in general to be somewhat lighter-skinned and shorter than the Nilotic Negroes. The Mangbettus, from descriptions and the two known crania, appear to have a very considerable Palæ-Alpine element. Since they lived in the near vicinity of the Akka, the first of the Pigmy tribes to be clearly described by any European, it is not improbable that we have here one source at least of the brachycephalic factor which the Mangbettus show. The same seems to be true of the Banda and Sango tribes on the Ubangi just above its most northern bend.

For the tribes east and south of Lake Chad our materials are considerably more abundant.[2] Here we may make three groups. The first, which may be called the upper Shari group, comprises the Kumbra, Sara, Wadama, and probably other tribes, extending southwestward as far as the upper Sangha River in Cameroon. They are characterized by a very tall stature, ranging from 174 cm. in the Wadama to 183 cm. in the Kumbra, who thus appear to be the tallest people in the African continent. In all, the brachycephalic factors are predominant, reaching a maximum in the gigantic Kumbras, who are almost purely so, with an aver-

---

[1] Shrubsall, 1901; Chantre, 1904.
[2] Talbot, 1916; Tucker, 1910; Gaillard, 1914.

age cephalic index of over 85. In skin color and hair there appears to be but little difference between the various tribes, all being quite black and with normal Negro hair. The round-headed factor present here in such strong proportions is unmistakably the Palæ-Alpine type, and a peculiar problem is thus presented, for elsewhere, with very few exceptions, the admixture of this element (which throughout the whole of the centre of the continent seems to be derived from the Pigmy peoples) leads to a diminution in stature; here, on the contrary, the Kumbras, who show the largest proportion of this type, are the tallest folk in Africa! In no other portion of the continent have any people as yet been found who are frankly brachycephalic and at the same time above medium stature (165 cm.). Two suggestions offer themselves in explanation of the puzzle. On the one hand, it may be that the Kumbras are not really a brachycephalic people, but one who are normally mesocephalic or dolichocephalic, and who practise some form of artificial cranial deformation which completely modifies the proportions of the head. I have been able to find no indication of this, however, and, if this explanation is ruled out, there seems no other way but to suppose that the same environmental or other causes which have led to the development of tall statures among the almost purely dolichocephalic Nilotic tribes, have been operative here also, and have produced a people of abnormally tall stature from one which elsewhere is markedly undersized; have, in other words, developed a giant Palæ-Alpine type in a region but little removed from that in which the pigmy form of the same type becomes strongly marked! This seems to be so improbable that I cannot but believe that evidences of artificial deformation will be found.

Whatever be the cause of this abnormally tall stature, it is clear that we have in this upper Shari region an area in which the Palæ-Alpine type is very strongly in evidence. Eastward toward the Nuba-Fertitawi-Tagalawi group, just west of the Nilotic Negroes, the proportion of this type falls off quite regularly, and we seem forced to regard this area as the proximate source of the brachycephalic factors, which have penetrated eastward almost to the Nile. Southward along the Ubangi River this brachycephalic element declines rapidly in importance, only to rise again in the Congo region, as described on a previous page. This northern area of round-headedness seems thus to be a portion of a once continuous region, which has been cut off from the main area in the south by the westward movement of dolichocephalic, Negroid tribes who followed down the Ubangi and Congo to the sea, reinforcing thus, as previously pointed out, the long-headed elements among the peoples of the Gaboon.

The second group of peoples in the Lake Chad region may be spoken of as the Chad tribes, and includes the Buduma, of the lake itself, and the Bagirmi, Mundong, Kotoko, Kanuri, Nyasser, Borlawa, etc., to the south and southeast. All of these tribes are again, with one exception, tall, ranging from an average of 170 cm. in the case of the Borlawa to 180 cm. among the Kotoko. The Kanuri are, on the other hand, but just over medium stature. The skin color varies somewhat, but is in general dark to very dark. In head-form, all without exception show a strong majority of the Proto-Negroid type, the Buduma ranking first in this respect. All have a small minority of the Palæ-Alpine and Caspian types, in most cases little more than a trace. The group is thus very similar, apparently, to the Nilotic Negroes, and the Shilluk and Buduma are almost identical. They are also much like the Furawi of Darfur, so that we may almost say that we have a continuous belt of nearly pure Proto-Negroid peoples, normally of tall stature, extending from the Shilluk and Dinka of the Nile westward to Lake Chad, and pressing southward on the eastern and western sides of a wedge of peoples more or less strongly marked by the prevalence of the Palæ-Alpine type, some of which are of tall and others of short stature.

North and northeast of Lake Chad is the third group of tribes, which belongs properly in the Sahara region. Some, such as the Ouled Sliman, are relatively recent immigrants from north of the desert; others, like the Teda or Tibbu, whose centre of distribution lies in the Tibesti Mountains far in the heart of the

Sahara, seem to be very old occupants of the area. On what must be admitted to be very slender evidence, these Tibbus seem to be a mixture of peoples of the Proto-Negroid type, who in all probability in very early times occupied all the habitable portions of the Sahara, and others who were predominantly Caspian. These easterly immigrants were already pouring into Nubia in Neolithic times, and may well have passed through the Tibesti region on their way northwest toward the Atlas and the Algerian plateaus. These Tibbus[1] are tall and, although extremely black, their hair is not woolly like a Negro's, but only wavy or curly. They have, moreover, rather commonly fine faces, with aquiline noses and very little prognathism, and are thus altogether in striking contrast with the Sudanese Negroes.

The portion of the Sudan lying west of Lake Chad to the Atlantic coast is the region in which the Hausa, Songhai, Fula, and other tribes have played so large a part, but the very meagre data which are to be had on them will be more intelligible if we first consider the area to the south, i. e., the Guinea coast. The population of this whole territory, from Cameroon in the east to Senegal in the west, comprises the bulk of the "true Negroes." Extremely black in color in the west, they tend on the whole to become slightly lighter eastward, although the differences would not seem to be great. In stature the Senegalese tribes,[2] such as the Wolof, Toucouleurs, etc., with an average of 172–175 cm., are distinctly tall, and, although eastward the stature drops somewhat, it rises again to about 170 cm. among the tribes of southern Nigeria[3] and the Cameroon coast. The tribes of the central parts both of Cameroon and Nigeria are notably shorter, the Kagoro[4] of Nigeria barely attaining an average of 160 cm.

Without exception all the peoples of this area show a predominance of platyrrhine, dolichocephalic factors, yet everywhere there is a strong minority of the broad-nosed, brachycephalic forms. This latter factor is, in general, somewhat

---

[1] Bouilliez, 1913.                    [2] Deniker, 1890; Verneau, 1896.
[3] Tremearne, 1912.                    [4] Tremearne, op. cit.

larger than among the Chad group of tribes, but is smaller than among the Tagalawi-Nuba-Fertitawi group of the northeastern Sudan. It is to be noted that this relatively considerable element of the Palæ-Alpine type is found in an area forming the long western extension of the equatorial forest, in which in the Congo basin, the Pigmy variety of this type attained its greatest frequency. It is perhaps justifiable, therefore, to conclude that the Pigmy Palæ-Alpine peoples once extended throughout this whole strip of the Guinea coast, but have here ceased to survive as an independent people farther west than Cameroon, although vague reports of Pigmy tribes farther west have been made. In the coastal tribes of Cameroon, such as the Duala,[1] there appears to be very little trace of any Caspian element; farther north, however, in Nigeria, the Kagoro, Kajji, Ekoi,[2] and Munchi[3] have quite a strong dash of it, and it appears again in slighter amount among the Kru and Wei of the Liberian coast.[4] The latter might well be expected to show a leaven of this higher type, since they belong to the Mandingo group of tribes, whose main territory lies inland toward the western Sudan, and who by tradition came into the upper Niger region from farther eastward in the tenth or eleventh century, if not before.

The cranial data which we have from Cameroon[5] bring out clearly the relation of the Palæ-Alpine element to the Pigmy peoples, for the coastal tribes show this in a proportion of about 35 per cent, which increases inland to the Sangha River Pigmies,[6] among whom it reaches nearly 60 per cent. Among the Ashanti[7] of the Gold Coast, however, the proportion drops below 10 per cent, while the Proto-Negroid rises to over 50 per cent. The latter thus seem to be quite comparable to the Chad group in the Sudan and to the southern Bantu, whereas the Cameroon tribes are about midway between the lower Congo peoples and those of the Gaboon.

The neighboring people of Dahomey,[8] on the other hand,

[1] Virchow, 1887.        [2] Keith, 1911.        [3] Malcolm, 1920.
[4] Virchow, 1889 b.      [5] Thorbecke, 1919; Drontschilov, 1913.
[6] Kuhn, 1914.           [7] Shrubsall, 1898.        [8] Elkind, 1912.

seem to show no trace of any Caspian element, but do reveal the presence of a small Alpine factor, which has, I believe, much significance. This seems in all probability to be attributable to the influence of relatively modern Arab mixture, a considerable proportion of these being known to have come from the southern portion of Arabia, where the Alpine element is to-day strongly marked. Nowhere else in Africa, south of the Sahara, does this type appear, except where modern South Arabian influence is probable or proved.

From all the data we may conclude that the early population of the Guinea-coast region was closely comparable to that of the Congo forest, *i. e.*, a Pigmy Palæ-Alpine people, and that these have been overlaid by a strong immigration of typical Negroes, in whom the Proto-Negroid type was in large majority, and associated with a minority of the Proto-Australoid type. This Negro immigration was in part a westerly drift from the Chad-Nile area, and in part a direct southward movement from the western Sudan and the Sahara borders, forced by the expansion in the Sahara region of the Caspian peoples who have poured into northern Africa since very early times.

We come finally to the peoples of the Sudan lying west of Lake Chad. The most important of the tribes here are the Hausa, Mandingo, and Fula. Although they have become rather widely scattered, the first are mainly concentrated toward the east, the second and third in the west. All three have here and there penetrated southward almost if not quite to the seacoast. So far as can be judged by their traditions, the Fula are the oldest residents in the region, having been the dominant power in the western Sudan, at least as early as the tenth century. They expanded eastward, but did not pass the Niger until the early nineteenth century. The Mandingo are probably the next older group, who, coming from the eastward, conquered and gradually displaced the Fula in the eleventh century. They built up the considerable kingdom of Mali and by the thirteenth century had already been converted to Islam. Three hundred years later, however, the Fula again assumed the leadership. While the

Mandingo were building up their power in the west, the Hausa, whose earliest traditional home was in the western part of the Chad basin, had become an important political power in the central western Sudan. More peaceful than either the Mandingo or the Fula, they were agriculturalists rather than herdsmen, as were these, and were, further, great traders, as were, to be sure, the Mandingo. The eastward expansion of the Fula after their conquest of the Mandingo led to the downfall of the Hausa, although this was not fully accomplished until the nineteenth century.

The racial aspects of this brief historical outline are of much interest, for, whereas the Hausa appear to be quite uniform in physical characteristics, the Songhai, Mandingo and Fula show every evidence of considerable mixture. The Hausa[1] are of moderately tall stature, averaging about 168 cm., but, although very black in skin color, their hair is not as typically woolly nor their lips as thick as among the true Negro tribes to the southward. The analysis of Tremearne's measurements shows that the Proto-Negroid and Proto-Australoid types make up over 70 per cent of the total, the most important minority being the Caspian, which amounts to approximately 15 per cent. The Palæ-Alpine factor is very small. In their composition, therefore, they are quite comparable with the Baganda among the northern Bantu of Uganda, although they have slightly less of the Caspian element than these. In comparison with their immediate neighbors of the Chad group, they have, on the other hand, rather more of the Caspian type, and may well have once been a part of this group, who in some way assimilated a larger proportion of the higher cultured Caspian folk. Whether this is to be attributed mainly or in part to an Arab source is an interesting speculation. It was in the eleventh century that the great Arab migration into northern Africa took place, and it was approximately at this time that the Hausa seem first to have attained to political dominance. The Hausa language shows large borrowings from the Arabic, which fact seems to strengthen the

[1] Tremearne, 1911.

above suggestion. On the other hand, it is at least as probable that a very considerable portion of the Caspian element assimilated by the Hausa is derived from a very much earlier immigration, *i. e.*, that which brought great floods of this type into northern Africa far back in Neolithic times, and which apparently was still coming into Nubia and the upper Nile region during much of the period covered by Egyptian history, and passing by way of the Egyptian Sudan into the Sahara and farther north. The rise to political power of the Hausa may indeed have been stimulated by a small, mediæval Arab factor, but the essentials of their racial composition may have been present long before the Arab invasion. The Songhais or Sonrais[1] appear to have a larger Palæ-Alpine element than the Hausa.

The Mandingo[2] tribes seem, in contrast with the Hausa, to be very variable in their characters. This holds true in skin color as well as in the form of their hair, some being fairly light, others very black, while the hair is often long and frizzly rather than short and woolly. A portrait of a Mandingo is given on Plate XIII, Fig. 4. In stature they rank a little above the Hausa, the average ranging between 169 and 171 cm. Except for the Wei[3] or Vei, of the Liberia coast, we have no individual measurements for any Mandingo tribe, and must rely, therefore, as best we may on the mere averages given in French sources. The Mandingo proper, together with the Malinke, Bambara, etc., who form part of the main mass of these tribes in Senegal, are characterized by a very large platyrrhine, dolichocephalic factor, amounting to something like 80–90 per cent, with which is combined a small Palæ-Alpine minority. So far as the data go, there is no trace whatever of any Caspian, leptorrhine element, every one of the sixty or more men measured by Girard being clearly platyrrhine, so that they are closely comparable with the Nilotic Shilluk and Nuer, although lacking their taller stature. The Wei or Vei of Liberia, however, a Mandingo tribe which has pushed southward to the seacoast, are more comparable to the Nuba group in that they have a somewhat

[1] Verneau, 1916–17.      [2] Girard, 1902.      [3] Virchow, 1889 b.

larger Palæ-Alpine element, and also a small minority of the
Caspian type. In stature they are similar to the shorter of the
other Mandingo tribes. The larger proportion of Palæ-Alpine
factors found among the Vei may probably be explained as due
to assimilation from the older brachycephalic underlying population, through which this Mandingo people had to force their way
to the coast.

The Fula,[1] lastly, are very tall, averaging between 174 and
176 cm., and are thus almost on a par with the very tall Negro
tribes of the Chad region and the upper Nile. In skin color
they are generally of a reddish brown, varying to merely olive
tints, and their hair is wavy only and sometimes almost straight.
Thin lips and well-shaped, often aquiline, noses further serve to
differentiate them sharply from all their neighbors. Where, as
in parts of Nigeria, they have intermarried with Negro slaves,
the Fula are quite obviously more Negroid. The extremely
meagre series of measurements of the Fula seem to show unmistakably a relatively large Caspian element, which rises possibly
to nearly 30 per cent in some cases. If in the case of the Hausa
there is much to lead us to suppose that the Caspian element is
of early origin, there is an even greater probability that in the
Fula we must place this amalgamation of Caspian and Negro
peoples in the distant past.[2] Indeed, it seems not impossible that
in this case we are not dealing with a Negro people who have
absorbed a certain element of the eastern immigrants of higher
culture, but rather with a body of these ancient peoples from
Asia who, early penetrating to the western margin of the continent, have, in the long period since, absorbed a large Negro
element from the ancient population of this type, which is believed originally to have held not only the Sudan but most of
the Sahara as well.

[1] Verneau, 1899, 1916–17; Girard, 1902.     [2] But see Verneau, 1916–17.

# BOOK III

## ASIA

# INTRODUCTION

In the present state of our knowledge a sketch of the racial history of the Asiatic continent can be drawn only in very broad outline. We have, it is true, considerable historical information, an aid which is lacking, for instance, in the New World, but we are handicapped by the extreme paucity of any sort of archæological data, so that the prehistoric period can be reconstructed only by inference. It is possible, nevertheless, to draw certain conclusions in regard to the early distribution and movements of the different physical types, which seem to explain the present facts. Before attempting these inferences, however, certain geographical features must be emphasized which have had important bearing on the continent's racial history.

Asia may be divided into three great portions: (1) a northern lowland extending from the Caspian Sea northeastward toward Bering Straits, and from the margin of the interior plateaus northward to the Arctic; (2) a central plateau area, stretching in an irregular crescent from the western end of Asia Minor through Persia, Afghanistan, Tibet, Mongolia, and the dissected uplands of eastern Siberia to the northeastern extremity of the continent; and (3) the southern and eastern borderlands, comprising the great peninsulas of Arabia, India, and Farther India, together with the eastern margin of the continent, thus including the larger part of China, Manchuria, Korea, and Kamchatka, with the Japanese and Kurile archipelagoes.

The northern lowlands are at their southwestern end a region of steppe and desert grasslands, and are continuous with the great plains of Russia, so that peoples have been free to move from one to the other, Asia here having a broad, open gateway into Europe. The northern and eastern portion of these lowlands, however, is forested, and the climate arctic. The plateau belt is divided into two unequal parts by a narrow constriction

in the region of the Pamirs.   The narrower western portion, including Afghanistan, Baluchistan, Persia, Armenia, and Asia
Minor, lies at an elevation of from three to five thousand feet
above the sea, is arid or even desert over large areas, meets
Europe at the Balkan peninsula at its western end, and there
and along the Persian Gulf comes directly down to the sea.   The
eastern and broader portion of the plateau region is more complex in its character, including as it does the high plateaus of
Tibet, ranging in elevation from 10,000 to 17,000 feet; the wide,
much lower uplands of Mongolia, in elevation comparable with
those of the western plateaus; the great basin of Eastern or Chinese Turkestan; and the much dissected upland region which
extends from Mongolia northeastward to Bering Strait.   On
the west the Mongolian plateau opens through the wide corridor
of Dzungaria, onto the steppes of southern Siberia, affording a
broad highway for peoples from the plateau to pass into the
northern lowland and thence on into eastern Europe; the Arctic
termination of the plateaus toward the northeast, on the other
hand, affords a narrow gateway into a similar Arctic land in the
northwest of America.

The peninsulas of the southern borderlands are in striking
contrast with each other.   Arabia, a vast desert plateau, fringed
by deserts excepting for the narrow ribbon of Mesopotamian fertility; India, although desert in the west, mainly a land of low
plateaus and tropical lowlands, rimmed and guarded on the north
by the snowy heights of the Himalayas; and Farther India, a land
of contrasts, of high, cool mountain ranges running northward to
the bleak Tibetan uplands, and low, hot valleys opening on tropical seas, the whole stretching out a long, thin finger into the
archipelago of Indonesia.   The eastern borderlands, too, present
their contrasts: southern China semitropical, hilly, almost rugged; northern China temperate, with the great fertile plain of
the Yellow River and Yangtse deltas; and half-arid Manchuria
joined by the rocky peninsula of Korea to the mountainous and
volcanic archipelago of Japan.

We can hardly attempt as yet to reconstruct the events in

racial history which took place in Asia in Palæolithic times. No authentic find of Palæolithic man has up to the present been made anywhere in the continent, and data even of Neolithic age are all but lacking. Yet the outlines of human distribution at a period roughly synchronous with the Neolithic period in Europe may, I think, be dimly seen. At this time the southern and eastern borderlands, from India around to Kamchatka, seem to have been occupied in the main by a dolichocephalic, dark-skinned, Negroid population which was a blend in varying proportions of the Proto-Australoid and Proto-Negroid types. There is some evidence which leads us to believe that this Negroid population extended farther westward than India, along the shores of the Persian Gulf and the southern coast of Arabia, so being continuous with the great area held by similar peoples in Africa. Whether the Proto-Australoid type definitely preceded the Proto-Negroid throughout this whole region we have as yet no means of knowing, although the distribution of the two types in Oceania seems to show that it did. At any rate, the Proto-Negroid type later came to dominate in the south, at least, and seems to have streamed through the southern borderlands eastward into the Pacific. In the eastern margin of the continent, this type does not seem ever to have become dominant. Nowhere, so far as can be seen, did these ancient Negroid peoples penetrate far into the great plateau region, whose southern and eastern escarpments formed barriers which they rarely crossed.

Although this blend of Proto-Australoid and Proto-Negroid types formed everywhere the fundamental basis of the population of the borderlands, two other types were also present. Probably the earliest of these was the Caspian, which at a very early period had spread throughout most of the northern lowland and had forced its way across the eastern plateaus to Farther India and the eastern coast. Sweeping through Dzungaria and over the upland, they came into China and Manchuria, and passed by way of Korea into Japan, where their presence in Neolithic times has been recently established. Another branch seems to have followed down the great rivers and mountain ranges which spread fan-wise from eastern Tibet, so penetrating into Farther India, from whence they passed on into Indonesia and the Pacific. The effects of this great early thrust of the Caspian peoples toward the east and southeast may still be traced in parts of the borderlands to-day, where individuals of strikingly European features, with light hair and eyes and rosy cheeks, are sometimes found.

The other of these early types present in the borderlands was the Palæ-Alpine, in regard to which, however, several difficult problems arise. At the present day this type exhibits two forms, strikingly different in outward appearance, yet closely similar in skeletal characteristics. One, which forms the large and often preponderant part of the population of southeastern Asia, is short, with a light yellowish skin, straight hair, little progna-thism, and is marked by a variable and sometimes considerable development of the Mongoloid eye; the other, the Negrito, sur-viving to-day in small fragments only in the Andaman Islands and the Malay Peninsula, is shorter in stature, black-skinned, woolly-haired, and rather prognathic. Both groups, in spite of their great outward differences, are round-headed, high-skulled, and broad-nosed, and thus must be classed as belonging to the Palæ-Alpine type. To group together as members of a single type two peoples outwardly so distinct, on the basis merely of their agreement in respect to the three criteria here chosen, seems, to say the least, venturesome. Yet I believe the action is defensible; its justification and the discussion of the problems involved, however, must be deferred to the final chapter, when the similar dilemma in regard to the African Pigmies can also be considered. For the time being I shall simply beg the question, and refer to the short, Negroid, brachycephalic peoples as the Negrito branch of the Palæ-Alpine type. How or when these appeared in the southern borderlands we have as yet no means of knowing, but that they were present already in Neolithic times in Farther India, and perhaps in India itself, seems very probable. How widely, too, they were distributed is very hard to say. The fact that short, Negroid survivals are reported to have been found in the extreme southwest of China, makes it possible that the Negrito once had a wider distribution than was at one time thought.

The great mass of the Palæ-Alpine peoples belonged, however, to the main type, and seem to have come as very early immigrants from the eastern plateaus. Farther north, in Japan, archæological evidence shows that they were mixed with peoples of Caspian type, and, although we have as yet no archæological proof of this in the southeast, the indications afforded by the racial distributions in the Indonesian and Pacific areas strongly suggest the same condition here. As a result of this Palæ-Alpine immigration, the older dolichocephalic population was over great areas dispossessed of the better lands, which were taken by the probably agricultural invaders, and was either forced off the mainland to settle in Indonesia, or driven into the higher uplands and mountain regions, beginning thus the curious horizontal stratification of racial types which is now so marked over considerable parts of the southeast of the continent.

Into India no immigration of Caspian or Palæ-Alpine types seems to have occurred at this earliest period, but farther west the former light-skinned northerners had swarmed across the western plateaus in Persia and so into Arabia and beyond, for we find them in the Nile valley, in Egypt, and in Nubia in Pre-Dynastic times.

Passing over for the moment the area of the plateaus, let us turn to the northern lowland, whence these Caspian peoples seem to have come, and see what may be said of its population in Neolithic times. North of the plateaus the earliest traceable population seems to have been, like that in the southern and eastern borderlands, dolichocephalic, but here made up in the main of different elements. The Aralo-Caspian basin and southwestern Siberia must in Neolithic times have had a somewhat more favorable climate than to-day, and formed the centre of a vast area of grasslands, extending from the borders of central Europe into the heart of Asia, and from the Black Sea and the northern edge of the Iranian plateau to the margin of the northern forests.   Here was the homeland, it would seem, of the Caspian type, horse-loving nomad warriors, fair-skinned and having ingrained in them a tendency toward blondness.   Hence they had streamed eastward across Mongolia to the Pacific; westward through the steppes and the borders of the oak forest of central Russia, to the Baltic lands and western Europe; and southward over the narrow Persian upland to the grazing lands of Arabia.   There is reason to believe that they held not only the grasslands, but extended eastward through the southern forest regions of eastern Siberia far toward Bering Strait.

While the Aralo-Caspian basin was held in the main by the Caspian type, they seem to have shared it in the south with an eastern arm of Mediterranean peoples, whose major distribution lay farther to the west.   Here, in the gradually desiccating region of Turkestan, there grew up among these blended peoples a more sedentary form of life, in which pastoral pursuits were combined with simple agriculture in the irrigable oases; and from this region in later times came fresh waves of migrants, as will be pointed out presently.

The Neolithic population of the plateau region appears to have been strongly contrasted with that both on the north and on the south.   Our existing data leave us no choice but to regard the plateau peoples as everywhere primarily brachycephalic.   Archæological evidence of this there is none, except the scanty material from the northern border region of the Trans-Baikal, where supposedly Neolithic sites have yielded both brachycephalic and dolichocephalic crania.   In Europe the Neolithic period saw a flood of peoples of Palæ-Alpine and Alpine types pressing westward through the Central European Highlands and coasting along the Mediterranean and Atlantic shores, and these could have come, so far as can be seen, only from the western end of the Asiatic plateau belt, i. e., from Asia Minor.   While we are thus led to believe that the Asiatic uplands were at this time, at least, the home of these two brachycephalic types, their localization and the determination of the order of their movements are, as yet, in the total absence of archæological data, practically impossible. Yet it may be suggested that as the Alpine type seems everywhere in eastern Asia to be later than the Palæ-Alpine, that the latter was, at the earliest period to which we can go back even by inference, more widely distributed in the eastern plateaus, in Mongolia and Tibet, than in the west, and that from the eastern plateaus it pushed out on the one hand toward the Pacific, and on the other spread through the Dzungarian gateway westward into Europe, fighting its way through the Caspian peoples, and in a sense thus blazing the trail which was followed some thousands of years later by the Mongol-Tatar hordes.

Yet it must be admitted that, although the Alpine type seems to have been more numerous in the western plateaus, Alpine peoples must have reached Mongolia, China, and the eastern borderlands at an early date. By what routes they came we do not know, but we may perhaps surmise that the basin of Chinese Turkestan had for long harbored a sedentary agricultural branch of these people, who had spread into it across the Pamirs from the western plateaus; while others, remaining more pastoral, followed the Tian-shan range, thus penetrating into northern Mongolia, where they in part amalgamated with and in part drove back farther toward the northeast the ancestors of the later Mongols. In course of time the sedentary agriculturalists may have drifted eastward along the northern base of the Tibetan plateau, and so by way of the Yellow River valley to the eastern borderlands, where some of them ultimately became the ancestors of the original Chinese people. Spreading southward in what is to-day China, they penetrated the areas held by their Palæ-Alpine predecessors, amalgamating with them and passing out into Indonesia as the Malays. Eastward they pressed through Korea into Japan, and northward they swept along the northern borders of the plateau and through the plateau itself, following the route taken thousands of years later by the Turkish Yakut, to the extremity of the continent, and passed in horde after horde across the straits to America. It was perhaps also at this early time that another branch of the

Alpine peoples moved southward from the western plateaus to southern Arabia and eastward across the mouth of the Indus into western India.

In the middle of the second millennium B. C. we get from historical sources evidences of a new period of expansion of the mixed Caspian and Mediterranean peoples of the Aralo-Caspian region. Swarming across the upland of Persia, some settled in the hilly country of Armenia; some known as the Kassites descended upon the weakened kingdom of Babylonia and took it, holding it for several hundred years; others, turning eastward, came as the ancestors of the Hindus into India, where in the northwest they displaced and elsewhere amalgamated with the older Negroid peoples. Possibly also at this time the ancient eastern drift across Mongolia was repeated in much more feeble form, yet bringing to the western borders of China an Indo-European speech, the Tokharian, which persisted there down to the beginning of the Christian era.

Again, however, the pendulum swings, and in the early centuries of our era the Alpine and Palæ-Alpine peoples once more entered upon a period of expansion. Their centre of gravity now seems to be in the east, and from Mongolia wave after wave of Turk and Turko-Mongol peoples poured westward through Dzungaria into the old homeland of the Caspian folk, whose last remnants they thus swept away, and so through Russia into central and western Europe. Northward, too, they spread, both into the Siberian plains and the northern forests, where the Yakut, overrunning the basin of the Lena, have come within a few hundred miles of Bering Strait. Nor was the south neglected, for not only did the brachycephals invade the western plateaus, conquering Asia Minor and passing thence across into Europe, but, turning eastward, descended into India, establishing there the brilliant dynasty of the Moguls. And, although Mongolia was for most of this latest period of expansion the chief focus from which they spread, the eastern margin of the continent also saw their further extension, which in the southward drift of the Shan peoples did not complete itself until the

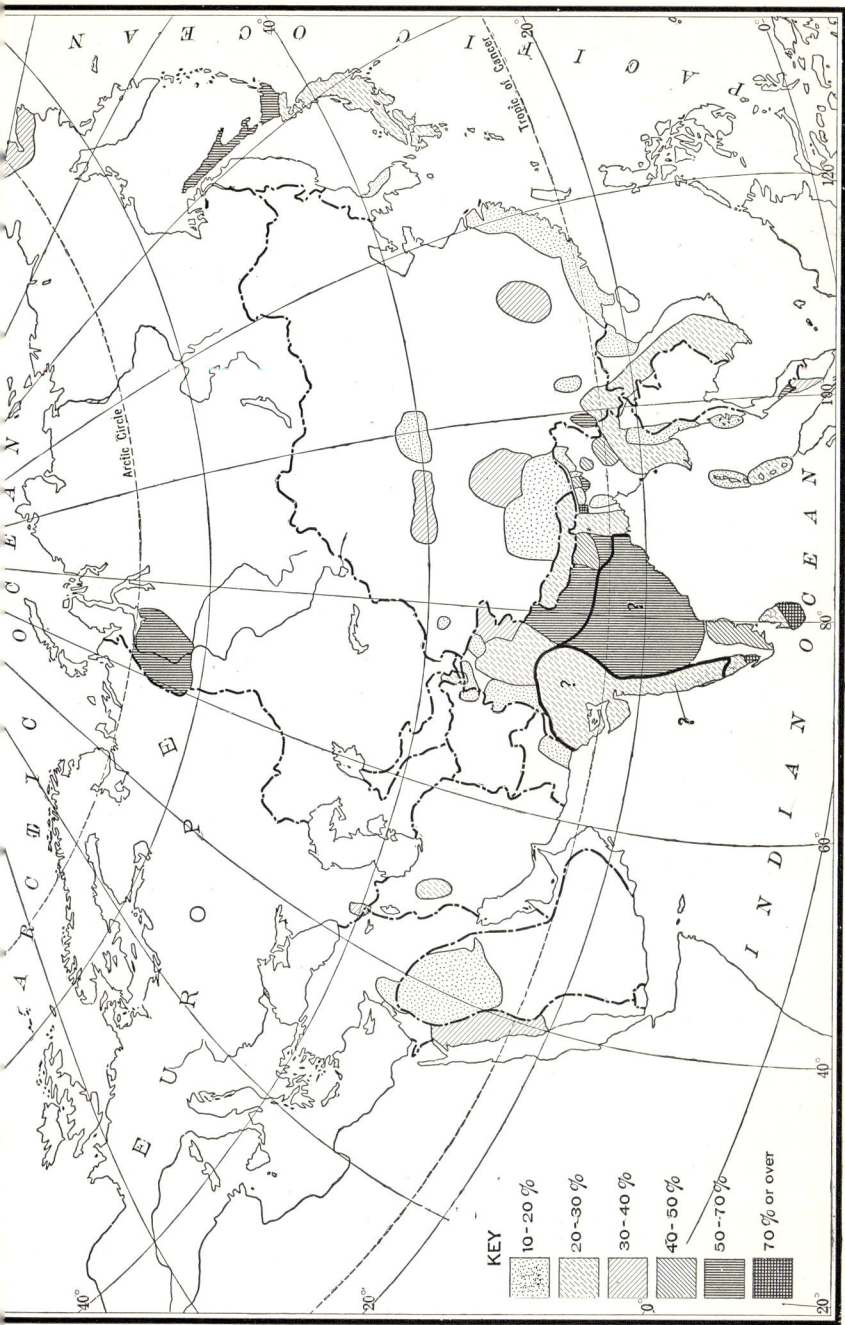

PLATE XIV.  ASIA.  Percentage distribution of Proto-Australoid and Proto-Negroid Types (slightly generalized).

KEY

10-20 %

20-30 %

30-40 %

40-50 %

50-70 %

70% or over

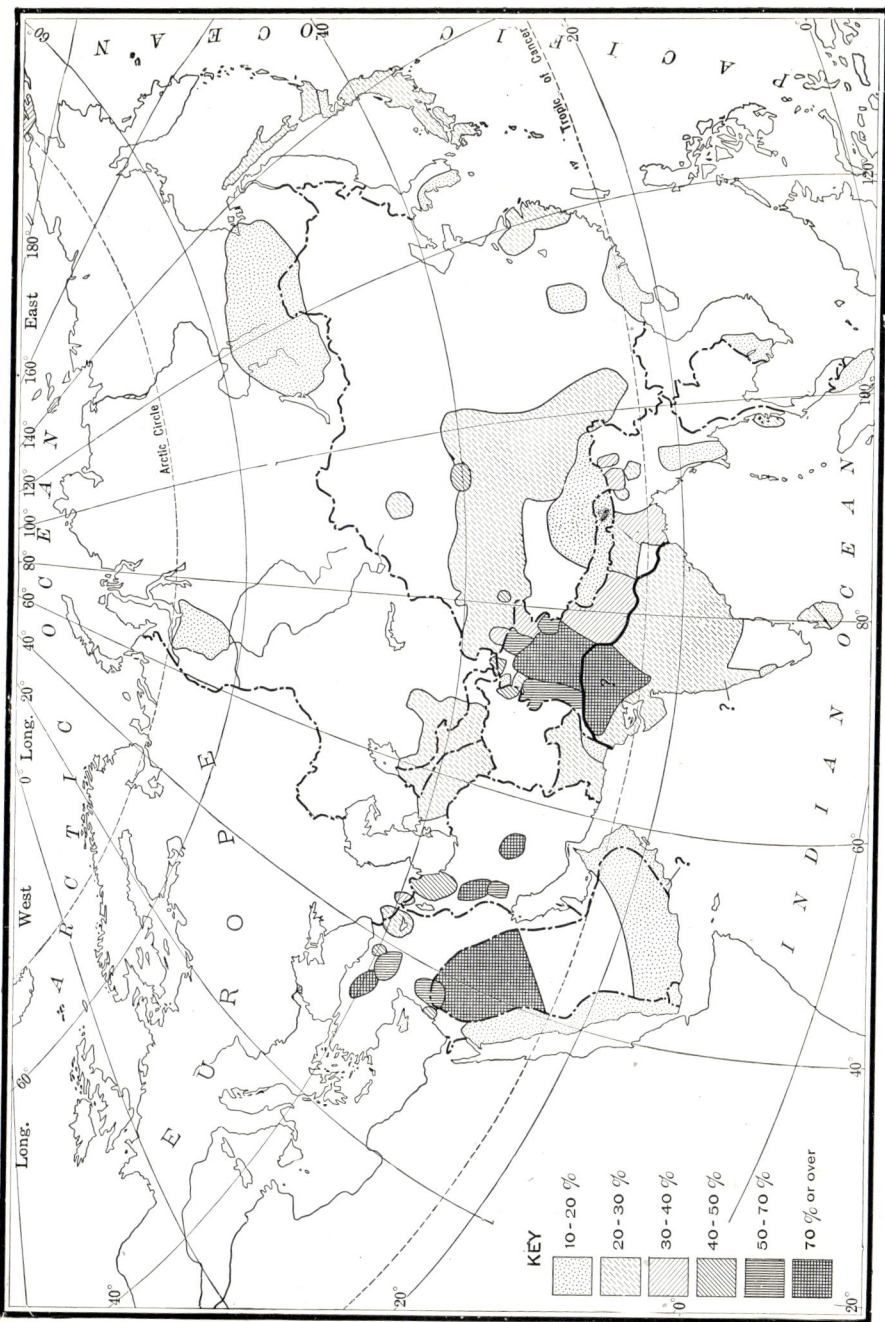

PLATE XV. ASIA. Percentage distribution of Caspian and Mediterranean Types (slightly generalized).

KEY

| | |
|---|---|
| 10 - 20 % | |
| 20 - 30 % | |
| 30 - 40 % | |
| 40 - 50 % | |
| 50 - 70 % | |
| 70 % or over | |

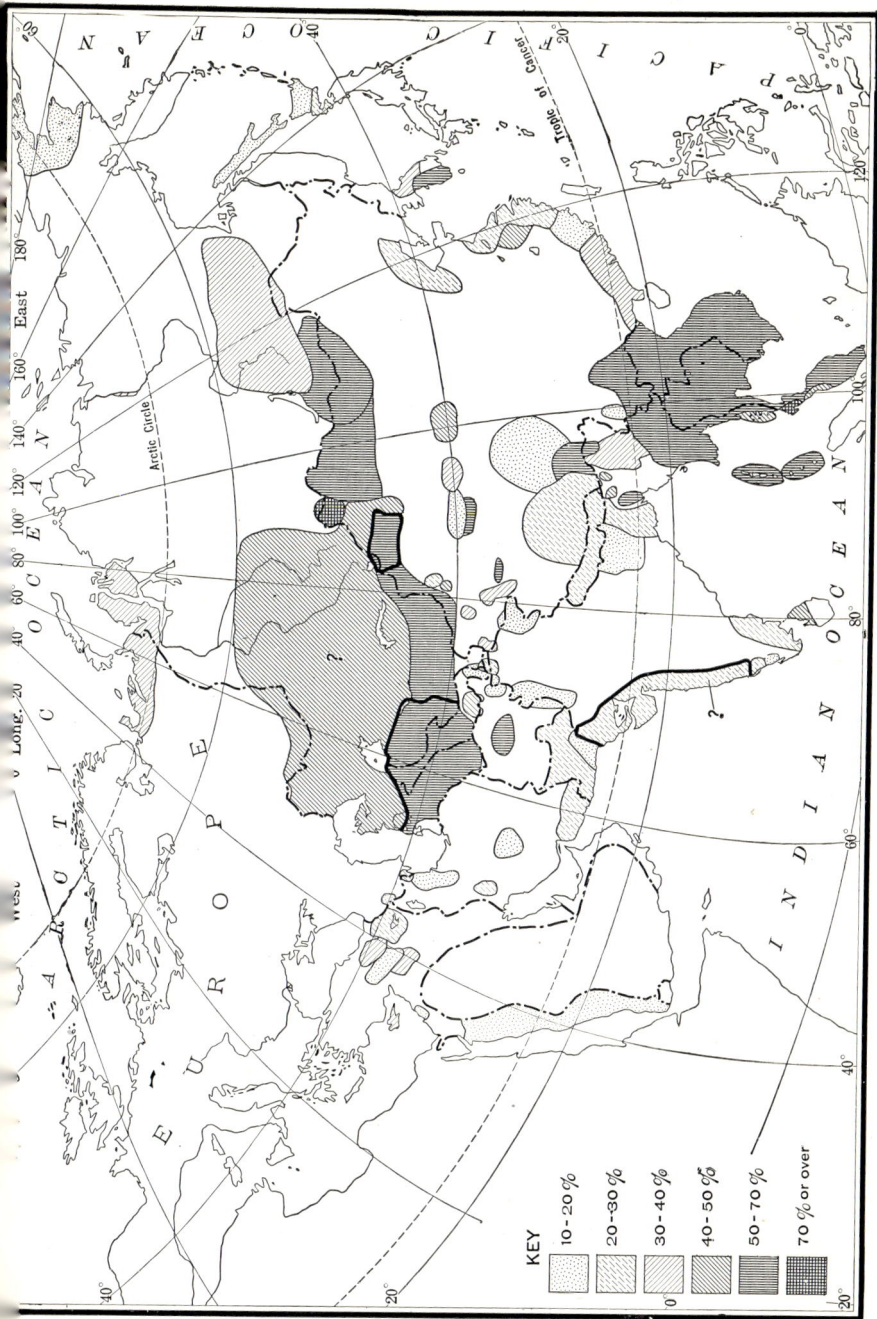

PLATE XVI. ASIA. Percentage distribution of Palæ-Alpine and Mongoloid Types (slightly generalized).

KEY

- 10 - 20 %
- 20 - 30 %
- 30 - 40 %
- 40 - 50 %
- 50 - 70 %
- 70 % or over

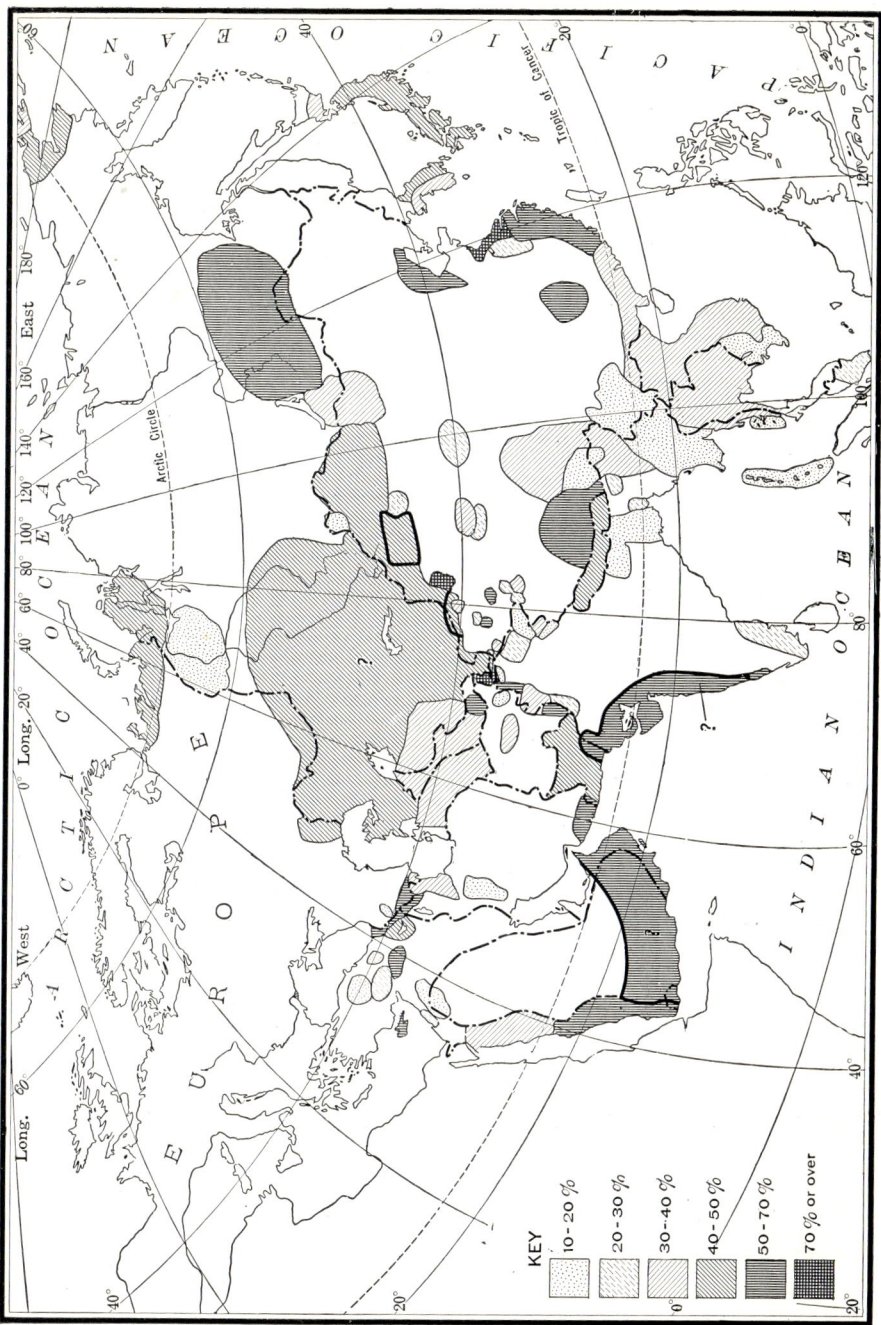

PLATE XVII. ASIA. Percentage distribution of Alpine and Ural Types (slightly generalized).

KEY

| | |
|---|---|
| | 10-20 % |
| | 20-30 % |
| | 30-40 % |
| | 40-50 % |
| | 50-70 % |
| | 70% or over |

conquest of Assam and Siam in the thirteenth and fourteenth centuries.

A few words must lastly be said in regard to the Mongoloid type, whose origin and history are almost wholly unknown. Confined to-day within a narrow area along the northern borders of the Mongolian plateau, their part in the racial history of the continent is very obscure, and until we possess more abundant archæological data must remain so. In Europe and in Africa the type to-day occupies almost everywhere an extreme marginal position, and seems to be a very ancient one. In Asia it survives almost in the very centre of the continent, and we have no record of it back of the mediæval period, when under Khengiz Khan and his successors the Mongols leaped for a brief time into prominence. They spread in company with the last great outpouring of the Alpine peoples, and the type appears in small minority almost everywhere the Turko-Tatar peoples went, but, apart from this, no traces of them seem to be found among the living peoples of the continent.

In Europe we have seen how the early dolichocephalic peoples, step by step, gave way before the brachycephals, until to-day this older population survives only in marginal areas. The maps, Plates XIV to XVII, which give the present distribution of dolichocephalic and brachycephalic types in Asia, show clearly enough that the same holds true also here. Except for northern Arabia, parts of Persia, and most of India the dolichocephalic peoples are nowhere in the majority to-day, except where small fragments still persist, as among the Ostiaks of northwestern Siberia, the vanishing Ainu of northern Japan, the Sakai of the Malay Peninsula, and probably a few of the wilder tribes of the more remote parts of Farther India. Here, as in Europe, they are almost everywhere marginal. The maps show, so far as our data go, the present distribution of the several types among the living population, and tell the story more in detail.

As may be seen, the Proto-Australoid type survives to-day as a factor of importance only among the Ostiaks, in the extreme northwest of Siberia along the Arctic, in the south of India and the Malay Peninsula, and to a less degree among the Ainu of Sakhalin. The Proto-Negroid is confined to India and Farther India; the Caspian to northern India, northern Arabia, and the borders of the Iranian Plateau. Except for the Turkoman and Azerbaidjan Tatars, east and west of the southern end of the Caspian Sea, there is no trace left on the northern side of the plateau crescent of the Caspian type, whose homeland this was apparently in Neolithic times. The Palæ-Alpine type is to-day strongest in Farther India, where it came, as we have seen, in very early times. It plays a considerable part, however, among the modern population of Turkestan and perhaps in Tibet, as well as in the Tamils of southern India and parts of Korea and Japan. Not as marginal, by any means, as the dolichocephalic types, its strongest representation is nevertheless in the extreme southeast, and almost everywhere it seems to have given ground to peoples of Alpine type.

This latter is clearly enough the dominant element in the Asiatic population of the present day. Its centres of greatest strength lie at the western and eastern ends of the great plateau crescent in Asia Minor and the whole eastern part of the continent, but throughout the whole of the rest of the plateau area it is probably one of the most important single types. Four regions only seem to have escaped the overwhelming influence of these Alpine folk—the extreme northwest, Arabia, India, and Farther India. Yet even in the southern borderlands its mark lies on the people, for in Arabia it holds the south; in India it has penetrated along the western coast and somewhat in the north; while the drive of the Siamese down the valley of the Mekong has brought into the heart of Farther India a considerable element of this conquering type, which from the southeast of the continent has passed on into the island world of the Pacific. Lastly, in its movement toward the northeast it has passed by way of Bering Strait into America, supplying thus to the New World the dominating element in its population.

# CHAPTER I

## THE SOUTHERN PENINSULAS

### I. Arabia, Palestine, Syria, and Mesopotamia

THAT portion of the Asiatic continent which lies to the south and west of the western plateaus, and which includes the great peninsula of Arabia, together with Palestine, Syria, and Mesopotamia, has in its geography, its environment, and its racial history a certain unity. Arabia is primarily an arid plateau, rising abruptly from the Red Sea and Indian Ocean and sloping gradually toward the northeast, in the direction of the Persian Gulf, Mesopotamia, and eastern Syria. The elevation of its western margin is continued northward by the narrow belt of upland and mountain country which fringes the eastern end of the Mediterranean, to the ranges of the Taurus on the southern border of the Anatolian plateau. Except for a very narrow belt along its western and southern margin and in occasional oases in the interior, the whole area is arid or desert. From the earliest period down to the present the bulk of the population have been pastoral nomads, except where, adjacent to the southern and western shores, and in the rich irrigated lands of the Tigris-Euphrates valley, it was possible for city-dwelling, agricultural, and trading peoples to thrive.

In Babylonia and the region about the head of the Persian Gulf a great civilization grew up, whose beginnings go back certainly to the early part of the fourth millennium B. C., and which rivalled that of Egypt in character and antiquity. Along the south Arabian coast the old civilization of the Sabæan and Minæan kingdoms goes back at least to the beginning of the first millennium B. C., while in Palestine the arrival of the Hebrews must be placed nearly a thousand years earlier. Yet in spite of the cultural and historical importance of this southwestern corner of the continent, we know next to nothing of the racial character of either its ancient or modern inhabitants.

Of the physical characteristics of the Sumerians, among whom developed the parent civilization of the Tigris-Euphrates region, we know nothing except what can be most precariously deduced from a study of their sculptured likenesses. Neither of them nor of the succeeding Babylonian or Assyrian peoples have we as yet any skeletal remains. Hamy[1] has endeavored to show that on the basis of sculptured heads and bas-reliefs the ancient non-Semitic Sumerians were brachycephalic, whereas the Semitic-speaking peoples, who already at the earliest known historical period were acquiring dominance in Babylonia, were on the contrary dolichocephalic. We have reason to believe that the Sumerians were an immigrant people in Babylonia, having come from the borders, at least, of the Iranian Plateau, where the ancient population was almost certainly brachycephalic; so that Hamy's results accord at least with all that we know or can conjecture of the racial history of this region. That all of the Semitic-speaking folk here were, on the other hand, dolichocephalic, may be doubted, since it is very probable that Alpine or Palæ-Alpine influences had before this made themselves felt in southern Arabia, derived doubtless from the Iranian Plateau, whence the Sumerians themselves somewhat later came.

The most ancient crania[2] from the whole region are four of Seleucidian age found at Babylon, which show that Mediterranean and Caspian types were in the large majority, the Alpine making up the remainder. Of roughly the same age are certain Phœnician crania from Sidon,[3] which in marked contrast are strongly brachycephalic, and probably in the main of Alpine type. From Palmyra in the Syrian desert,[4] we have a half dozen skulls, dating from about the beginning of the Christian era, which, like the earlier ones from Babylon, show the predominance of dolichocephalic, probably Mediterranean factors. This prevalent long-headedness is also stated to be true of the great

[1] Hamy, 1907.
[3] Bertholon, 1892.
[2] Hamy, 1884.
[4] Busk, 1871-72, 1874-75.

series of ancient Hebrew crania excavated by the Palestine Exploration Fund,[1] no study of which, however, has yet been published; it is also true of various small series of crania of considerable although uncertain age, coming from northern Arabia and Palestine.[2]

To draw satisfactory conclusions from such inadequate and scattered data is impossible, but it is perhaps safe to infer that in the latter part of the first millennium B. C. the occupants of this whole territory were predominantly of dolichocephalic types, the Mediterranean and Caspian being in the majority, but that in the south and in the northwest brachycephalic influences had already made themselves more or less strongly felt, being in the main of Alpine type, and derived from the uplands of the Anatolian and Iranian plateaus. For, just as in the earliest period, we have Sumerians coming down from the uplands to the Tigris-Euphrates delta, so in the northwest we have the penetration of Hittites and other brachycephalic peoples from the Anatolian plateau into northern Syria.

The modern population of the whole area is in the main of Semitic speech, and may be conveniently divided into two groups: the sedentary, agricultural peasantry or Fellahin, and the city dwellers; and the nomadic or semi-nomadic Bedouin. The former are concentrated for the most part in the coastal areas, and along the rivers or in the irrigable oases; the latter are widely scattered throughout the more arid interior. In Syria[3] the two groups seem to differ radically, for here the urban population and the agricultural peasantry of the Syrian uplands, together with the Ansarie,[4] Metouali,[5] etc. are predominantly brachycephalic, the Alpine type being dominant, with the Palæ-Alpine as an important minority. On the other hand, the nomad Bedouin are primarily dolichocephalic, although in varying degree.[6] The dominance of the brachycephalic types among the Fellahin, however, seems to disappear toward the south, since

---

[1] Seligman, 1917.          [2] Seligman, *op. cit.*          [3] Huxley, 1905.
[4] Chantre, 1882.                                          [5] Chantre, 1895 b.
[6] A. M. N. H.; Seligman, 1917; von Luschan, 1911.

those of Samaria are strongly dolichocephalic, and the Samaritan crania from Nablus[1] show a large predominance of Caspian and Mediterranean types. Still farther south in Palestine, the Arabic-speaking peasant population also shows similar characteristics.[2] They, as well as the Samaritans, are tall (174 cm.), in skin color comparable to the peoples of southern Europe, and, although not Jews, have a large proportion of what is commonly known as the "Semitic" or "Jewish" nose. A small series of Bedouin crania shows that among them the Mediterranean type is that most strongly represented, the Caspian taking second place; and a comparison with the Samaritan crania brings out the fact that while both have about the same proportion of Caspian factors, the Mediterranean elements are twice as numerous in the Bedouin as among the sedentary peoples of Samaria.

For Arabia we have data only for parts of the Red Sea coast and the southern corners of the peninsula. These data from measurements on the living show that while in the Sinai peninsula the Bedouin are predominantly dolichocephalic,[3] in the Hedjaz[4] these and the brachycephalic factors are evenly balanced, with indications that part, at least, of the dolichocephalic factors are platyrrhine, and derived probably from Negro slaves. Farther toward the south, in Yemen,[5] the balance is turned decisively the other way, and among the Arabs here brachycephalic factors (apparently Alpine in type) are in large majority. And this holds true not only for the sedentary population, but also for the Sheher Bedouin far back of Aden,[6] and is again revealed in the people of Maskat,[6] at the southeast corner of the peninsula. We seem to have, thus, in passing from the northern and western to the southern and eastern portion of the Arabian peninsula, a far-reaching modification of the population, which is predominantly dolichocephalic (Mediterranean and Caspian) in the one and predominantly brachycephalic (Alpine) in the other. The origin of this apparently Alpine factor in southern Arabia is

[1] A. M. N. H.
[2] Weissenberg, 1910.
[3] Giovanozzi, 1904; Chantre, 1904.
[4] Mochi, 1907.
[5] Mochi, 1907; Leys, 1913.
[6] Leys, op. cit.

obscure. We must probably seek its sources in the Iranian Plateau, whence it may have crossed the Persian Gulf to Oman and spread thence along the coasts. As to the period of its coming we know nothing, except that from the African evidence it could hardly have come very early, and the conjecture may be hazarded that the movement of Alpine and Palæ-Alpine peoples into southern Arabia was perhaps in part due to the invasion of the Iranian Plateau in the second millennium B. C. by the Indo-European Kassites (who conquered Babylonia at this period) and the ancestors of the later Hindus. It is also to be noted that there is clearly some Negroid mixture in the population of the southern coastal districts of Arabia. Whether this is to be attributed to the influence of African slaves, either recently or as far back as the period of the Sabæan and Minæan kingdoms, or is evidence of a very ancient stratum of Negroid peoples, connecting those of Africa with those formerly living on the northern shores of the Persian Gulf and still dominant throughout all southern India, it is, in the absence of adequate data, impossible to say.

In stature the modern population of the whole area seems to grade from short in the south to taller in the north. The southern Arabs from Maskat around to Yemen are slightly under medium height, the shortest being the round-headed Sheher Bedouin, who average only about 161 cm. In the Hedjaz and among the Bedouin of Sinai the stature is slightly over medium culminating in the Fellahin of Samaria with an average stature of 174 cm., only to decrease again somewhat among the people of northern Syria. In pigmentation the whole population is everywhere strongly brunet, and it is only in parts of northern Syria that a small proportion of blond types appears. An Arab of the northern or dolichocephalic type is shown on Plate XVIII, Fig. 1.

It will have been noticed, perhaps, that nothing has been said here in regard to the Jewish population. The information which we have on this question will be found presented and discussed in the chapter on the Jews, in the section on Europe.

A word or two may, however, be said here in regard to the island of Cyprus, lying off the coast of northern Syria. The material collected here by Buxton[1] is of great interest, and shows that in the Bronze Age tombs at Lapithos, on the northern coast, the brachycephalic factors slightly outweigh the dolichocephalic, if both sexes are taken together. If the males are considered apart from the females, however, it appears that whereas the latter are brachycephalic, the former are strongly dolichocephalic, and largely, it would seem, of the Caspian type. The females, moreover, seem to show traces of some Mongoloid influence. The few crania of the Iron Age and later appear to be mainly Mediterranean. The abundant data on the living (from which as far as possible all Turks were excluded) indicates that the leptorrhine, brachycephalic forms (probably Alpine) are everywhere in the majority, the platyrrhine, brachycephalic types being secondary and the dolichocephalic element being in the main probably Mediterranean. The two round-headed types, however, differ interestingly in their local distribution. For the Alpine is relatively most important in the east, in the vicinity of Famagusta, while the Palæ-Alpine is most abundant on the northern coast, which is the most isolated portion of the island, and this latter may therefore be considered to be the older element in the population.

## II. India

There are few portions of the Asiatic continent which present more clearly cut natural frontiers than India. The stupendous wall of the Himalayas, swinging in a great arc some 1,500 miles in length, guards the north; to the south lies the sea; on the west the broken ranges forming the escarpment of the Iranian Plateau, limit the featureless arid lowlands of the Indus valley from Peshawur to Karachi; and on the east the mountains along the Burmese frontier serve to mark the edge of India in this direction. The whole area of India may be divided into two portions geo-

[1] Buxton, 1920.

graphically, a northern and a southern. The former comprises the confluent alluvial plains of the Indus, Ganges, and Brahmaputra Rivers; the latter the peninsular plateau of the Deccan. Each of these has played a different part in the racial history of the country.

Of the racial characteristics of the ancient peoples of the Indian area we are still almost totally ignorant. The only crania of any antiquity which have been described are a few from Tinevelly, in the extreme southern part of the peninsula. They seem to indicate the presence of a people dominantly dolichocephalic, platyrrhine, and strongly prognathic, i. e., clearly Negroid, as early perhaps as the first millennium B. C.

In dealing with the living population of India we at once come face to face with a condition peculiar to this area, and one which complicates the problems to be solved, i. e., the caste system. The people of India are divided into two unequal sections, a smaller, comprising the Mohammedans and many small groups of more or less primitive aboriginal folk who are "casteless" in that they are outside the system; and a larger, which is subdivided into a multitude of different castes, each of which has its definite rank and status in the community, holds itself more or less rigidly aloof from all the others, and has, at least theoretically, its own trade or occupation. With the origin of the many castes, whose members may be scattered all over India, we are not for the moment concerned, although later the question of how far the various caste groups show actual racial differences will have to be considered. For the present it is merely necessary to note that the caste group is the dominant Indian unit, and that with few exceptions all existing data have been collected on this basis.

In attempting to analyze the complex population of India into its several racial elements, and to reconstruct tentatively the history of its growth, we may well begin with the people of the northern plains, since from them the great mass of our data is derived.[1] Starting, then, in the west, and basing conclu-

[1] Risley, 1892, 1915; Chanda, 1916; Kitts, 1890–93.

sions in the first place on the measurements of the living (cranial material being very scanty), it appears that the population of the Punjab and the larger part of Rajputana is marked by a considerable homogeneity. Characteristically tall, they attain in some cases, such as that of the Sikhs, a stature averaging 172 cm. In skin color there is a fairly wide variation, although all but the lower castes are quite light-colored, individuals of high caste being comparable with a south Italian, while some may almost be called fair. The hair is usually straight or wavy and dark, as are the eyes. Regardless of caste, the population is dominantly dolichocephalic, with narrow, often aquiline noses. This leptorrhine, dolichocephalic form is in all castes the largest factor, ranging from 45 per cent among the low-caste Chuhra to 75–85 per cent among the Rajputs, Sikhs, and Gujars. The portrait of the Sikh given on Plate XVIII, Fig. 2, may be taken as typical of this group. A platyrrhine, dolichocephalic element is also present, however, being strongest in the lower-caste groups. Brachycephalic factors are in the small minority except among the Pathans of the western border country, where the narrow-nosed, presumably Alpine type is present to the extent of nearly 20 per cent. To the southward, in Sind and Cutch, brachycephalic factors rapidly increase, but here the Alpine is mixed with a considerable proportion of Palæ-Alpine.

As we pass eastward from the Punjab to the Ganges valley, striking changes take place. The stature diminishes, the skin color grows notably darker, and the hair becomes more wavy or even curly. The head-form still remains strongly dolichocephalic, but analysis of the measurements reveals a significant change in the racial types involved. Whereas in the Punjab the leptorrhine forms were in the large majority, and Negroid platyrrhine forms present in small proportion only, in the Ganges valley the latter become, with few exceptions, dominant, the Caspian-Mediterranean types dropping to second place. The relative importance of the platyrrhine forms varies both locally and in the different castes. Thus, in the United Provinces it ranges from 30 per cent to 70 per cent, in Chota Nagpore from 50 per cent to 80 per cent, in Behar from 20 per cent to 60 per cent, and in Bengal from 10 per cent to 80 per cent. Similar wide differences are found in the various castes. Thus, in the Brahmin and Bhuinar castes of the United Provinces it amounts to only about 30 per cent, the Caspian-Mediterranean types being in these two castes in the majority. In the Kayasth and Tharu castes, of lower although still respectable rank, the Negroid types increase to 50 per cent, while in the Chamar and Koiri, of low status, they rise nearly to 70 per cent. In the highlands of Chota Nagpore and the adjacent parts of Bengal, where several groups of "casteless" aboriginal peoples, such as the Munda, Korwa, Malé, Mal Paharia, etc., are found, the proportion of platyrrhine, dolichocephalic factors almost reaches 80 per cent! Generalizing the detailed variations, it may be said that as we pass from west to east down the Ganges valley, the platyrrhine, dolichocephalic forms increase in relative proportion, attaining their maximum among the "casteless" aboriginal and semi-aboriginal tribes of the Chota Nagpore district, and then falls off somewhat farther toward the east.

This striking variation in the relative importance of the Negroid forms, both locally and according to caste, is not the only result of the detailed analysis, for an equally significant change in the factor of secondary strength also becomes apparent. For while in the United Provinces in most castes the Caspian-Mediterranean types were secondary, as we pass eastward the importance of these decreases and they are ultimately replaced by other factors, until in Bengal only three out of eighteen castes for which we have data still show these leptorrhine, dolichocephalic forms in second place. The forms thus replacing the Caspian-Mediterranean are two, the Alpine and Palæ-Alpine. In the Chota Nagpore district it is the latter which assumes the position of secondary importance, and it is this factor which serves to differentiate two of the best-known peoples of this area, the Oraon and the Santal. Both show a strong dominance of the Negroid types (ca. 60 per cent), but whereas the secondary factor in the former is still the Caspian-Mediterranean, in

the latter it is the Palæ-Alpine.   In Behar, while in some cases
the Palæ-Alpine takes second place, in others, such as in the
Dosadh and Kurmi castes, this is held by the Alpine instead.
In Bengal proper the importance of this latter type becomes
more pronounced.   Stated in general terms, the importance of
the Palæ-Alpine type increases eastward along the southern
borders of the Ganges valley, culminating in Chota Nagpore,
whereas the Alpine type becomes more prominent along the
northern border, reaching its greatest strength in northeastern
Bengal, where it actually is dominant in certain castes, such as
the Brahmin and Kayasth.

The explanation of the increasing part played by the Alpine
type is to be found mainly in the character of the population of
the southern slopes of the Himalayas.   In Nepal and Sikkhim
are a series of peoples or tribes, speaking languages allied to the
Tibetan and Burmese and displaying in their physical features
precisely those characteristics whose growth in importance has
been noted among the Indo-European speaking population of the
Ganges valley.   Short in stature (the majority averaging below
160 cm.), slightly yellowish in complexion, with straight black
hair and occasionally showing the Mongoloid eye, the Nepal-
ese, Lepcha, Limbu, Khambu, etc., present a strong contrast
to the people of the Gangetic plain.   All are strongly brachycephalic, and with the single exception of the Gurung have the
Alpine type preponderant.   As secondary factors some, like the
Khambu, Limbu, Bhutani, and the people of Sikkhim, have
the Palæ-Alpine type; the Gurung, on the other hand, have this
latter type dominant, with the Caspian as secondary, a condition
which will be found to be of considerable frequency in Assam
and the Burmese border, to which region we may next turn.

This extreme eastern portion of the northern Indian area includes both the wide Brahmaputra valley and the rugged hill
country lying north, south, and east of this, as far as the Burmese border.   In contrast to the peoples of the Indo-Gangetic
plain, who speak Indo-European languages, the tribes of Assam
and the Burma frontier with but one important exception speak

languages belonging to the Tibeto-Burman stock. The Khasi, living in the hills in the vicinity of Shillong, are linguistically an outlier of the Mon-Khmer stock, whose main area of distribution lies in the southeastern corner of the continent.

From the racial point of view the peoples of this area may be divided into two groups, one of which shows a preponderance of dolichocephalic factors, the other being primarily brachycephalic.[1] The former occupies a continuous area, and includes nearly all the peoples of the Brahmaputra valley, together with most of those in the hill country to the south and the foot-hills of the Himalayas on the north. The more important tribes in this group include the Abor, Miri, Dafla, Kohita, Garo, Sinteng, Manipuri, Kuki, and some of the Naga tribes. In all the platyr-rhine, dolichocephalic types are in the majority, the leptorrhine factors being, except among the Rengma Naga, present merely as a trace. In most instances the Palæ-Alpine is the element of second importance, amounting in some cases to as much as 40 per cent. In stature all are below medium, the figures ranging from an average of 157 cm. for the Khasi to 164 cm. or over among the Angami Naga. The hair is straight or wavy, sometimes curly; the eyes in some cases show the Mongolian fold.

The brachycephalic group, on the other hand, occupies a broken area, and includes the Tipra, Magh, and Chakma in Tipperah in the south, and the Mikir, the Ao and Sema Nagas, and the Ahom of the hill country and Brahmaputra valley. In this group it is the Palæ-Alpine type which is present in greatest strength, rising in the case of the Chakma to over 65 per cent. In the Mikir, Khasi, and Tipra the factor of secondary importance is the platyrrhine, dolichocephalic—the Negroid types so prominent in the Ganges valley further west. In the Ahom, Ao Naga, Magh, and Chakma it is the Alpine type which appears in second place. In stature the brachycephalic group shows a tendency toward shortness compared with the other group.

To the conclusions derived from the measurements of the living may now be added those derived from a study of the all

[1] Waddell, 1900; Hutton, 1921; Dixon, 1922.

too scanty cranial data.[1] This relates almost wholly to the lower castes for obvious reasons. It corroborates in general the results already arrived at, but amplifies and corrects these in two particulars, showing first the presence with the Caspian type of a moderate factor of Mediterranean in the Punjab region and, second, the fact that the bulk of the platyrrhine, dolicho-cephalic forms present are in most cases Proto-Australoid and not Proto-Negroid in type. The latter appears in any impor-tance only, so far as present data go, among the more truly abo-riginal tribes in Chota Nagpore, where it equals the Proto-Aus-traloid. In the north of India thus, the more truly Negroid factor is of relatively small importance. The maps, Plates XIV to XVII, show for northern India all that we know at present on the distribution of types.

For the population of the whole of southern or peninsular India we have but little data which can be directly compared with that from the north.[2] This is the more to be regretted in that the keys to many of the problems of the whole area are to be found probably in the south. So far as the material will enable us to judge, the peoples of this portion of India may be divided into four groups. The first comprises the so-called "jungle tribes," timid folk of primitive culture, living in scattered units in the more inaccessible portions of the western Ghats and the mountainous country of the extreme southwest. The second in-cludes the Toda of the cool uplands of the Nilgiri hills, the Nair, or land-owning aristocracy along the Malabar coast, and per-haps some others. The third group occupies a broad strip along the western coast, from Rajputana south to Canara; while the fourth and last includes all the many Dravidian-speaking peo-ples of the south and east. For central India there are, so far as I am aware, no data whatever.

To the first group belong the Kadir, Kanikar, Kurumba, Pal-liyan, Paniyan, etc., who may be characterized as very short,

[1] Charles, 1892, 1893; Danielli, 1892; Mantegazza, 1883; Turner, 1901; Gupte, 1909.
[2] Holland, 1901; Jagor, 1879; Lapicque, 1905; Risley, 1893, 1915; Schmidt, 1910; Thurston, 1896, 1909; Turner, 1906.

very black-skinned people, with strongly curly or frizzly hair, dominantly dolichocephalic, and having very broad noses and often thick, Negroid lips. All speak languages belonging to the Dravidian stock. In the absence of any individual measurements it is impossible to determine the types present, but it is probably safe to assume that we have a large majority of Proto-Negroid elements, mixed with Proto-Australoid and perhaps a small percentage of the Palæ-Alpine type, not improbably of the Negrito variety. These jungle tribes are generally regarded as the remnants of the oldest stratum of population, who have been crowded back into the unfavorable refuge areas which they now occupy. An example of this aboriginal stratum is given in Plate XVIII, Fig. 3.

Turning next to the fourth group, comprising various Tamil and Telugu speaking folk of the Dravidian stock, we find that they are somewhat under medium stature, with very dark skins, and wavy or strongly curly hair. Unfortunately, the meagre data published on their head-form are rather contradictory. Some caste groups, such as the Palli, Parayan, and Vellalla, appear to be strongly dolichocephalic, with only a small brachycephalic factor; others, such as the Balija, Kapu, and Galla, show brachycephalic elements in much stronger proportions, and in some groups of Tamils these almost preponderate.

The third group, except in the extreme southern portion where Dravidian speech prevails, speak Indo-European languages allied to those of the Indo-Gangetic plain. Still under medium stature, these people are, especially in the north and northwest, of lighter skin-color than the two preceding groups, and in head-form show large brachycephalic factors, which in the north become actually dominant. It seems to be evident from Risley's data that this round-headed element is in the main Alpine in type. We shall not go far wrong, I think, if we assume that the Maratthas and Gujratis, together with the Coorgs and other members of this group, are in the main a blend in varying proportions of Alpine and Palæ-Alpine types, with the Proto-Australoid and Proto-Negroid.

Lastly, we come to the second group, comprising the Toda and the Nair. In striking contrast with all other peoples of southern India, the members of this group are considerably above medium stature, in skin color sometimes as light as the fairest in the Punjab, and have hair which is little more than wavy. In head-form they are prevailingly dolichocephalic and leptorrhine, so that we have here apparently a dominance of the Caspian-Mediterranean types, resembling that found in the western portions of northern India. The minority seems mainly Proto-Australoid.

Before attempting to draw from the foregoing facts a rough outline of the racial history of the whole of India we must glance at the peoples of Ceylon. The existing population is divisible into three distinct sections—the Vedda, the Singhalese, and the Tamils. The first now survive only as a tiny remnant, in the southeastern portion of the island. They are obviously all that remains of the oldest stratum of the population, and have, because of their extremely simple culture, long aroused the interest of anthropologists. The Vedda[1] are in stature short, averaging only about 155 cm.; in skin color they are dark, but usually lighter than the darker groups of the south Indian population. The hair is wavy or curly. In head-form analysis of the data shows a very large majority of dolichocephalic forms, the Proto-Australoid and Proto-Negroid being present in nearly equal proportions, the Caspian type being present as a small minority, while of brachycephalic factors there is hardly a trace. The Vedda thus are comparable with the Tamil population of southern India, with the brachycephalic factors left out, and the Proto-Negroid element much weakened.

The Singhalese[2] are in sharp contrast with the Vedda. Their stature is slightly above the medium, and, with a lighter skin, they have a dominance of brachycephalic factors, which seem to be mainly Palæ-Alpine, the minority being of both platyrrhine and leptorrhine dolichocephalic forms. The Tamils, who form

[1] Sarasin, 1893; Turner, 1901, 1906.
[2] Risley, 1893.

FIG. 1. BEDOUIN ARAB.

FIG. 2. SIKH.

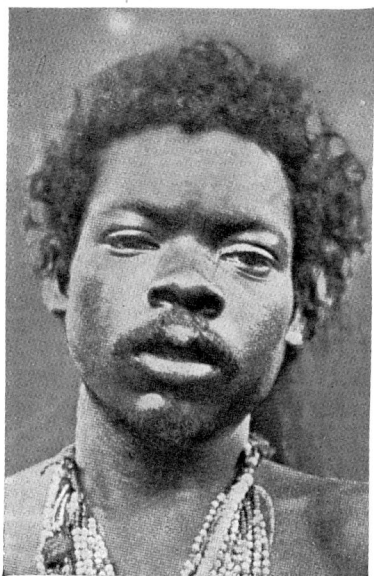

FIG. 3. PALLIYAN. (S. INDIA.)

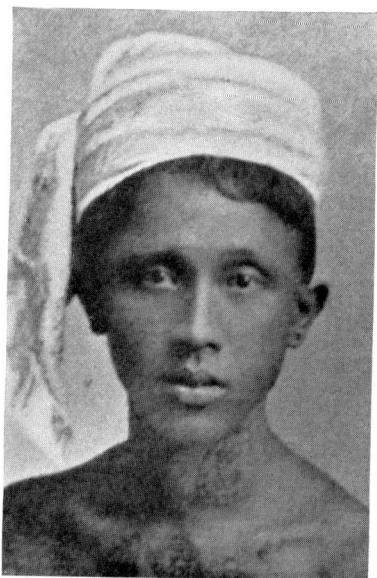

FIG. 4. BURMESE.

PLATE XVIII.

the third group, have already been discussed in speaking of the peoples of southern India.

From all the preceding facts we may suggest as a working hypothesis the following outline of the racial history of the Indian area. The underlying oldest stratum of the whole population is a blend of Proto-Australoid and Proto-Negroid types, the former probably stronger in the north, the latter in the south. This dark-skinned, more or less Negroid population was once in all probability spread over the whole Indian region, but has now largely disappeared in the west and northwest, at least in the castes of higher rank. Farther eastward, in the Ganges valley, it is still the dominant element in the majority of the people, particularly in the case of the remnants of aboriginal tribes. It is in southern India and Ceylon, however, that this oldest stratum is most clearly in evidence. The prognathism often characteristic of the Negroid mixtures in Africa is, as a rule, little developed in India, although showing among some of the jungle tribes and in the ancient crania from Tinevelly.

At a period as yet impossible to fix, but perhaps as early as the second or even the third millennium B. C., this early population became strongly modified by the intrusion of peoples largely of Palæ-Alpine type. The process by which this was accomplished is still wholly a matter of conjecture. That in the south of India and Ceylon it did not precede the Proto-Australoid-Proto-Negroid blend, seems to be shown by its absence from the Vedda and probably, also, the jungle tribes. Similarly, its relative absence in the population of the Ganges valley and the Punjab would appear to render doubtful a direct immigration from the north. As will be seen in discussing the people of Burma and the southeast of Asia, this Palæ-Alpine type is there present in great strength, so that the possibility of an eastern origin at once suggests itself. It has been shown that in Assam and eastern Bengal this type characterizes certain scattered hill tribes, and is strong also among the Khasi, who speak a language strange to India but allied to those of the southeast of the continent. It is therefore tempting to explain the presence of the brachycephalic factor in the Dravidian population of southern India, by an immigration from the eastward, around the head of the Bay of Bengal. This would further help to account for the now recognized remote linguistic relationship between the Munda-speaking tribes of southwestern Bengal and adjacent territory and the Mon-Khmer languages. Until, however, we have much more data, particularly early cranial material, further speculation in this direction is profitless. A word might be said, perhaps, in regard to the possibility of a western source for this brachycephalic factor. It will be shown on a subsequent page that the present population of Baluchistan is predominantly Alpine and Palæ-Alpine. We have seen that a similar factor extends southward along the western coast of India as far as Canara. In the early part of the second millennium B. C. we know that Indo-European peoples were invading the plateau; would it be too precarious to suggest that this may have led to the moving of some of the older brachycephalic peoples into the region of the Indus delta, and so spreading down the west Indian coast? If this explanation be admitted, it would account for the isolated Brahui, speaking a Dravidian language in southern Baluchistan, these being thus the rear-guards of the ancient movement. The brachycephalic immigrants on this hypothesis would have imposed their Dravidian speech[1] upon the older Negroid peoples of the whole of the south, just as the Indo-European immigrants into the northwest did upon the peoples of the Ganges valley.

Whether this theory is substantiated or not, it is at any rate clear that about the middle of the second millennium B. C. there came into northwestern India a considerable body of immigrants, speaking Indo-European languages, coming in from Afghanistan and also probably southward along the Indus valley. The newcomers were tall in stature, fair of skin, and were a blend of Caspian and Mediterranean types, the former being in the considerable majority. They were closely allied probably in physical characteristics as well as in culture with the Proto-

[1] Lapicque, 1905.

Medes and Proto-Persians, who were pressing into the western portion of the Iranian Plateau where it adjoined the Mesopotamian lowlands, and as the Kassites conquered and held Babylon for several centuries. From the Punjab and parts of Rajputana the older stratum of aboriginal Negroid peoples seem to have been largely expelled by these immigrant ancestors of the modern Hindu, although in the lower castes to-day this ancient fundamental stratum still makes itself felt. As the Indo-European Caspian-Mediterranean invasion made its way down the Ganges valley, its impetus and strength gradually waned, and instead of making up the bulk of the population, as it did in the west, it formed only the dominant aristocracy, impressing its language and culture upon the older peoples, and in the course of time mixed extensively with them. So that to-day the lowest castes in the Punjab have more of the blood of the Caspian-Mediterranean immigrants than do the highest castes of Bengal! After a time this immigrant group began to spread southward until they had pushed their conquests to the tip of the peninsula, and invaded and conquered Ceylon. Of this long period of exploration and conquest the echoes are preserved in the great Indian epics. Yet, extensive as were the political and cultural results of these far-reaching activities, the racial influence of the conquerors seems to have been small.

In connection with this penetration of the south by the tall, light-skinned northerners, the problem of the Toda and Nair must be squarely faced. Considered purely from the standpoint of their physical characteristics, as these are defined in the present study, it can hardly be doubted that these two small groups, which differ physically so strongly from all their neighbors, are fragments of this same wave of Indo-European conquerors, which have in some way survived in relative isolation, almost unchanged to the present day. It will be objected at once that the Toda show little trace either in language or culture of such a parentage. This may be admitted without, however, denying the possibility of the assumption. The loss of their language (the Toda is one of the Dravidian languages) is not by any means an insuperable obstacle; and on the cultural side we know that the original immigrants into northwestern India were largely, although by no means exclusively, a pastoral folk. Thus the abnormal development of pastoral life, so characteristic of the Toda, might well occur during some thousands of years of isolation. Space is lacking for the adequate discussion of the whole question, but if the issue be faced it seems that unless some such solution as this be accepted the problem must remain unsolved.

The character and extent of the influences which later movements of peoples have had upon the racial constitution of the Indian population may be dismissed in a few words. Commencing a century or so before the beginning of the Christian era and lasting with intervals for nearly a thousand years, a series of conquerors and invaders entered India through her western gates. With few exceptions, all came directly or indirectly from inner Asia, from that great area of steppe and desert lying north of the belt of high plateaus. All these immigrants and conquerors, Sacæ, Huns, Turks, and Mongols, were mixed peoples; all save possibly the first were, however, primarily brachycephalic, with, on the whole, a dominance of Alpine type. It is doubtful whether the Mogul (Mongol) conquest and the establishment of the Mogul Empire had any very considerable effect upon the racial composition of India. It has been supposed, however, that some of the earlier invasions exerted a greater influence, and Risley derives the brachycephalic elements along the western coast of southern India from the Sacæ and the so-called Indo-Scythian kingdoms, of the period about the beginning of the Christian era. While it must be admitted that the earlier conquests seem to have involved more actual colonization and transference of peoples than the later, yet it may be doubted, I think, whether the final result of the whole Indo-Scythian domination was more than a very thin veneer of Alpine elements laid upon a population already pretty strongly brachycephalic.

A last word may be added on the question of caste. The origin of this institution has long been a matter in dispute, and it has been denied that caste differences rested upon racial differences. The analysis of the data on the lines here followed makes it very clear, it seems to me, that caste groups do differ from each other racially, and that the social status of the caste usually bears a direct relation to the racial composition of its members.

## III. FARTHER INDIA

It is convenient on many grounds to group together all the peoples of southeastern Asia, including within this area Burma, the Shan States, Siam, French Indo-China, and the Malay Peninsula, together with the Andaman and Nicobar Islands in the Bay of Bengal. Topographically the region is very varied, comprising rugged mountain ranges, which rise to very considerable heights in the north; plateaus, like that of Annam; broad alluvial plains like much of Siam, Cambodia, and parts of Tonkin; and deep canyon valleys, as in the upper courses of the great rivers of the area, the Irrawaddy, Salwen, Mekong, and Red. The mountain ranges are practically continuous with the highlands and mountains of eastern Tibet and western China, and the river valleys spread out like the ribs of a fan from this part of the great plateau area, and with the intervening ranges have served to lead and guide migratory movement southward and southeastward from the very earliest times.

The peoples of this whole area are divisible on the basis of language into three main groups. One, including the Burmese, Chin, Kachin, etc., and probably the Karen, are classed with the Tibetans to form the Tibeto-Burman stock; a second, comprising the Shan, Laos, Siamese, etc., belong to the Thai stock; whereas the Palaung, Talaing, Wa, the Mon of Burma, and ancient Khmer of Cambodia, many modern tribes of the same country and the wilder peoples of Annam and Tonkin, known collectively as Moi, together with the Semang and Sakai of the Malay Peninsula, all belong to the Mon-Khmer stock. The Tibeto-Burman and Thai, with the Chinese, form one great group of languages with various important features in common; the

Mon-Khmer stands wholly separate and apart from all of them, and is, on the other hand, related in a similar general fashion to the whole group of Malayo-Polynesian and Melanesian languages which are spread over most of the whole of Oceania. The Andamanese people finally speak a language which is quite independent and unrelated to any other known.

Archæological data relating to the ancient population of Farther India are very few. In Tonkin[1] a few crania, presumably of Neolithic age, have been found in caves. They show the prevalence of dolichocephalic factors, which are apparently a mixture of Caspian and Proto-Negroid types in the males, the females having something of a brachycephalic element. The Cambodian shell-heaps[2] also have yielded a number of crania, of which, however, no detailed measurements have been published. They indicate here again the prevalence of dolichocephalic types. Turner[3] reports on certain crania which are dolichocephalic, and derived from an "ancient cemetery" in upper Burma, but the antiquity of these must be much less than that of the specimens just referred to. From such meagre materials all that can be said is that the early occupants of the region seem everywhere to have been long-headed.

For the living population whose characters are in general sharply in contrast with this older stratum, we have little analyzable data except from Burma[4] and the Malay Peninsula,[5] as nothing but averages are given for the whole of Indo-China. In Burma the population is almost everywhere distinctly below the medium stature, the Burmese themselves being the tallest, with an average of just under 163 cm., while the Kachin, Chin, and Palaung drop almost to 158 cm. In skin color there is wide variation, some of the western and northern tribes, such as the Chin, Kachin, and especially the Wa being quite dark (the latter being described by some observers as almost black !), whereas the Palaung and some of the Karen often have a yellowish-rosy

[1] Verneau, 1909 a.                    [2] Verneau, *ibid.*                    [3] Turner, 1899, 1908.
[4] Turner, *ibid.;* Gupte, 1909; Tildesley, 1921; *Ethnographic Survey of India,* 1906.
[5] Annandale, 1903; Kloss, 1915; Schlaginhaufen, 1907; Martin, 1905; Knocker, 1909; Duckworth, 1902.

complexion. The hair is generally black and straight, although brownish shades are not unknown, and occasionally wavy or even strongly curly hair is to be seen. The eyes are usually dark, but hazel or even grayish eyes are occasionally met with among the wilder tribes of the northeastern frontiers. The occurrence of the Mongoloid eye is more common in the north than in the south.

In spite of these variations and the wide diversity in language and culture, the analysis of the measurements available shows the whole population to be surprisingly uniform so far as the criteria are concerned which we have here adopted. Except for the Kachin, some of the Chin and the so-called "Shan-taloke," all the peoples of the Burmese area show a majority of the platyrrhine, brachycephalic factors, which we know from cranial material is the Palæ-Alpine type. This type is most strongly represented among the Palaung, Talaing, and Karen on the eastern side of the Irrawaddy valley. In all of these brachycephalic peoples, with the exception of the Sgaw Karen, the factor of secondary importance to the Palæ-Alpine is a platyrrhine, dolichocephalic one, comparable to that which is of primary importance among many of the tribes of Assam. In the absence of cranial material except from the Burmese, we cannot determine the type most prevalent, although the Proto-Australoid seems more important than the Proto-Negroid. The cranial material from the Burmese coincides in general in its evidence with the measurements on the living, but indicates a much more considerable proportion of Alpine type, which on the basis of the living population is present only as a small minority. The illustration given on Plate XVIII, Fig. 4, may be taken as typical of the Burmese population.

The Kachin, most of the Chin, and the rather enigmatical Shan-taloke are characterized by a preponderance of dolichocephalic factors which are primarily platyrrhine, while the Palæ-Alpine factors, which in the rest of the population were dominant, are here secondary. The peoples of Burma thus show very significant relationships with those of the area of Assam to the west, in that the larger, brachycephalic section resembles the Khasi, Tipra, and other strongly marked brachycephalic tribes there; whereas the Kachin, Chin, and Shan-taloke are comparable with the dominantly dolichocephalic tribes who occupied the larger portion of the Assamese territory. In other words, what is the dominant and most wide-spread population in Assam is in Burma the minority group, while what is the minority in Assam, in Burma constitutes the main mass of the population. Since, now, the dominantly dolichocephalic group in Assam is apparently the eastern arm of a great mass of more strongly characterized Proto-Australoid and Proto-Negroid peoples in southern and northeastern India, the Kachin, Chin, etc., in Burma may be regarded as a farther extension of the same forms, as far east as the very borders of China. The Palæ-Alpine, brachycephalic group in Burma, on the other hand, may be regarded as the parent mass from which the much feebler representatives of the type in Assam have sprung.

The inhabitants of the Malay Peninsula, the Andaman and Nicobar Islands may conveniently be considered together, since in their history they seem to be more or less closely related. We have in the area an obviously very much mixed population, ranging from the Pigmy-like Andamanese Negritos, through the Semang and Sakai, to the modern Malay. We may best begin by a consideration of the Andamanese,[1] who occupy a remote and isolated area, well fitted for the survival of very early types. Of pigmy stature, averaging only 148–149 cm., with extremely black skin and short woolly hair, they show in their head-form a strong majority of brachycephalic factors, the Palæ-Alpine amounting in the males to about 60 per cent, and in the females to over 80 per cent of the total factors present. The dolichocephalic factors are in the main Proto-Negroid, and both sexes have a small proportion of the Alpine type. The Andamanese thus seem to be in the main true Negrito Palæ-Alpines, with a slight admixture of Proto-Negroid elements. An example of the Andamanese type is given on Plate XIX, Fig. 1.

[1] Flower, 1878–80, 1884–85; Jagor, 1875; Turner, 1901; Sullivan, 1921 b.

If the Andamanese present a relatively simple group, the Semang and Sakai of the Malay Peninsula offer a very puzzling problem. The former, who live in small communities in the more inaccessible parts of Perak, etc., are slightly taller than the Andamanese (averaging about 152 cm.), almost as dark-skinned, and also with short, woolly hair. The data in regard to their head form are, however, very contradictory. The measurements of the living show a predominance of dolichocephalic, platyrrhine factors among the males, with a strong secondary factor amounting to about 40 per cent of brachycephalic, platyrrhine types. In the females the proportions are reversed, the brachycephalic types amounting to over 80 per cent. The cranial data, on the other hand, show both sexes to be dominantly brachycephalic, *i. e.*, Palæ-Alpine. Under the circumstances it is difficult to know which data to accept, yet in view of the fact (1) that the number of crania known is extremely small and (2) that, whereas the certain identification of the crania as Semang leaves something to be desired, the living individuals are more surely identified, it seems safer to accept the measurements on the living as the surest guide, and admit, therefore, a considerable difference between the sexes. On this basis the Semang would represent the result of a mixture between a Negrito Palæ-Alpine people similar to the Andamanese, and a Proto-Australoid-Proto-Negroid group, the females retaining more clearly than the males the original Negrito element. The general similarity of the Semang to the Andamanese is shown by the portrait on Plate XIX, Fig. 2.

The Sakai, who are mainly found in southern Perak and northern Selangor, afford an even more complicated puzzle. On the average a little taller than the Semang (average about 153 cm.) they are, although variable, as a rule much lighter-skinned, and have long, wavy or curly hair, although occasionally individuals with close curly or short frizzly hair are found. A typical example of this group is given on Plate XIX, Fig. 3. The data in regard to head-form derived from the living and from crania are, as in the case of the Semang, in strong contrast. If we rely on the former, the Sakai are predominantly brachycephalic and platyrrhine, *i. e.*, Palæ-Alpine, with a strong secondary factor of the Proto-Australoid or Proto-Negroid types; if we rely on cranial data, they are on the contrary predominantly of these two latter dolichocephalic types, with but a small minority of brachycephalic factors. The situation is rendered still more puzzling by the fact that measurements of the living Sakai of different sections of the country show equally contradictory results, some being dolichocephalic, others brachycephalic! The nomenclature of the various tribes, both Sakai and Semang, is further very much confused, so that it is sometimes uncertain whether we are dealing with Sakai or Semang or mixed groups. Obviously, in the present state of our knowledge, or lack of knowledge, no valid conclusions can be drawn, but I would suggest the following tentative unravelling of the puzzle.

The term Sakai (by some called also Senoi) has been applied to a series of very variable small groups of people, who may be regarded as having originated through the mixture, in varying proportions, of a predominantly brachycephalic people comparable with the modern Burmese or Pwo-Karen and the Semang, who were themselves the result of a blending of a Negroid people with the original Negrito stock. The dominant brachycephalic factor among the Sakai, unlike the case of the Semang, is thus mostly derived from the main, or non-Negroid, Palæ-Alpine type. The Nicobarese[1] would then constitute a rather similar group, differing mainly in having a considerable Alpine element, derived probably from later Malay contacts. It is probable that the Blandas and some of the so-called Jakun of the southern portion of the peninsula also belong to this group, although in the absence of any detailed measurements the question cannot be settled.

Quite another stratum of population is represented by the Malay peoples of the peninsula. Some, such as those of south Perak and the west coast farther north, together probably with the Besisi of the south, represent a relatively old stratum, in con-

[1] Weisbach, 1875.

FIG. 1. ANDAMANESE.

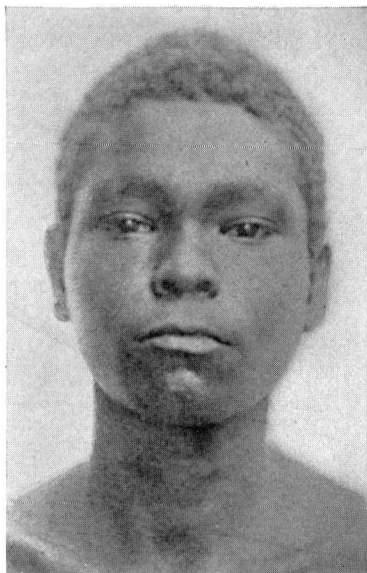

FIG. 2. SEMANG.

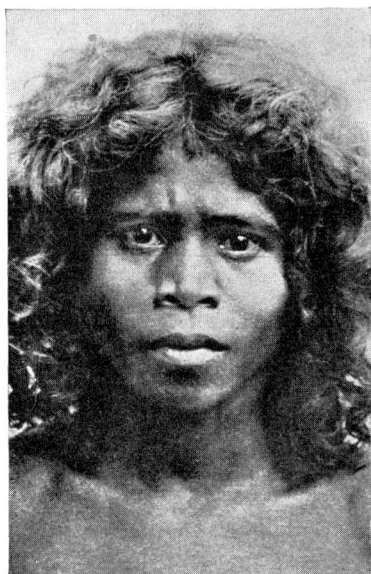

FIG. 3. SAKAI.

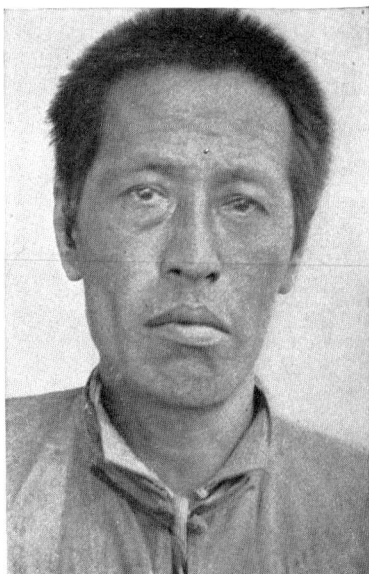

FIG. 4. CHINESE.

PLATE XIX.

trast with the later groups which, coming from Sumatra, overran and conquered the southern part of the peninsula only a
few centuries ago. The older stratum of Malay-speaking folk is
almost exclusively brachycephalic, the Palæ-Alpine type being in
the majority, but combined with a large minority of the Alpine,
which increases in strength as one goes southward, and among
the shore and island folk in comparison with those of the interior.

If the various assumptions herein made are accepted, we may
sum up the racial history of the Malay Peninsula very briefly as
follows: The oldest stratum of population was the Negrito Palæ-
Alpine, which survives to-day in comparative purity only among
the Andamanese. With this was later blended a taller Negroid
people, of mixed Proto-Australoid and Proto-Negroid types, to
form the Semang. This Negroid population is still represented
among some of the hill-folk in Burma, such as the Chin, is more
strongly present in Assam, and dominant in the greater part of
India. Subsequently to the formation of the Semang a strong
immigration came into the peninsula from the north, of the normal Palæ-Alpine type, of which perhaps some of the Karen may
be regarded as the last survivors. From the fusion of these
with the older Semang was derived the Sakai and some, perhaps,
of the Jakun; the later and less modified portions of this wave
forming the older Malay groups of to-day. Finally, in recent
times, came the Menangkabau Malays from Sumatra, who have
overlain the earlier groups throughout the south.

The extreme southeastern corner of the Asiatic continent is
dominated by three great rivers, the Menam, the Mekong, and
the Red. The deltas and lower valleys of these streams are rich
agricultural lands, and have apparently from the earliest times
been contended for by one people after another. The low plateau of eastern Siam and the higher uplands and mountains of
Laos, Annam, and western Tonkin are less desirable, and into
these the older populations have been driven by each succeeding
wave of newcomers, or else quite off the continent into the
archipelago of Indonesia. To the anthropologist this area is of
very great interest, since into it, as into a huge funnel, have

come from the north a variety of peoples, and from it have gone
out some, at least, of the emigrants who have peopled the island
world of the Pacific. It is all the more aggravating, therefore, to
find that we possess little information of real value in regard to
the physical characteristics of any of its present inhabitants.[1]

Linguistically it is a complex region. The Cham and some
of the wilder tribes of the southern Annamese plateau, such as
the Rade, Jarai, etc., speak languages akin, on the one hand, to
the Malayo-Polynesian, and on the other to the Mon-Khmer, to
which stock belongs the speech of the Cambodians and the majority of the hill-tribes, known generically as Moi, Pnong, or Kha.
The Siamese, Laos, Thos, etc., belong, on the contrary, to the
Thai stock, as do the Shans of Burma and southern China. The
Annamese and Tonkinese, finally, speak languages which are
either derived from southern Chinese dialects or have been profoundly influenced by them.

It has already been pointed out that the prehistoric population of this region, as shown by supposedly Neolithic cave remains from Tonkin and from the shell-heaps of the Tonle-Sap
or Great Lake of Cambodia, was prevailingly dolichocephalic.
In the modern population two quite different groups may be distinguished. The first is represented by the Cham and their affiliated tribes, together with a large part of the Mon-Khmer-speaking peoples of the higher plateaus and mountains, i. e., the Pnong,
Moi, Kha, etc. All of these show a large dolichocephalic factor,
and in this respect seem allied to the ancient population. This
more aboriginal long-headed group may be further subdivided
into those who, like the Cham, are tall with straight or wavy
hair, light skins, relatively narrow and sometimes aquiline noses
and non-Mongoloid eyes; and those who, like some of the wilder
Mon-Khmer tribes, are marked by distinctly short stature, dark
skin, curly or even frizzly hair, a broad nose and thick Negroid
lips. While metrical data are almost wholly lacking, it seems
probable that we have in the latter group the much mixed survivors of an early Negroid stratum, of mixed Proto-Australoid

[1] Breton, 1879; Deniker, 1890; Neis, 1882; Girard, 1901.

and Proto-Negroid types (with perhaps some Negrito), whereas in the former we may suspect the presence of a considerable Caspian-Mediterranean element, of which we shall find clear indications farther north in China and in the islands of the Pacific.

The other major division of the population is, in contrast to the first, in majority brachycephalic, and includes the Siamese, Laos, and all the Thai-speaking tribes, together with the Tonkinese and Annamese. All of these are of short stature (averaging under 160 cm.), with light yellowish skin, straight black hair, and eyes which usually show the Mongoloid fold. In all the Palæ-Alpine type is in large, often very large majority, the Alpine being secondary; a small minority of leptorrhine dolichocephalic forms also sometimes appears. The modern Khmer or Cambodians seem to be, on the whole, intermediate between this group and the first.

Now the origin of this brachycephalic, Thai-speaking group can be traced historically with some certainty. In the third century A. D., when we first get any information in regard to this region, the whole area, except perhaps the southern and southeastern coasts, was occupied by Mon-Khmer-speaking peoples, among whom already cultural influences from India had begun to make themselves felt. In the succeeding centuries a considerable civilization grew up among the Khmer, initiated apparently by actual colonies of Dravidian-speaking peoples from the eastern or Coromandel coast of India. By the fifth or sixth century A. D. these states began to be savagely attacked by Thai-speaking tribes pressing southward from China along the Menam and Mekong valleys. In the former their pressure was strongest, and although held in check for a time, in the eleventh and again in the thirteenth and fourteenth centuries they swept away all resistance, and finally conquered the Menam valley to the sea, completely destroying the western Mon-Khmer kingdoms in what is now Siam. Farther eastward the Laos were less successful, and although the Khmer kingdom fell before the attacks of the Thai (Siamese) from the west, and those of the Annamese from the east, their descendants still form the bulk of the population of Cambodia to-day. The modern Siamese, Laos, and other Thai-speaking peoples here are thus the somewhat mixed descendants of the old, non-Chinese population of southern China, who, as will be seen in a later chapter, have been of large historical importance in China since very early times.

What can be said of the Mon-Khmer peoples, who apparently everywhere preceded the Thai peoples in this extreme southeastern corner of Asia? On the basis of our present data, the most reasonable theory would seem to be that they were a mixed people, predominantly of Proto-Negroid, Proto-Australoid, and Caspian types, with a minority of the Palæ-Alpine factor which was dominant in the Thai, and a trace, perhaps, of its Negrito variety. That the early Mon-Khmer had a notable "Negroid" element seems to be corroborated by the Chinese descriptions of them in the third century. In regard to the sources of the Negroid element we have as yet no clear evidence, and can only conjecture that it came in from the westward along the southern border of the Asiatic continent. The Caspian factor, present in this region in minor degree only, seems, however, clearly to have come down from the north along the Mekong valley, from the mountain and plateau region of the Chinese-Tibetan border, where strong remnants of the type are still to be seen. It is tempting to regard the Cham, who appear to have been the earliest historical occupants of the Mekong delta, as a relatively pure advance guard of this Caspian type, which, mingling with the prehistoric Negroid and Negrito aborigines, formed the nucleus of the people who, under the pressure of the Mon-Khmer, emigrated eastward, to form the older or so-called Indonesian stratum of population in the archipelago, and later moved on farther east through Melanesia to the islands of the South Seas. This question, however, we must leave for discussion in the section devoted to the peoples of Oceania.

# CHAPTER II

## THE EASTERN BORDERLANDS

### I. CHINA

THE area included in China proper, the eighteen provinces, comprises three regions of quite different character. In the northeast is the fertile alluvial plain formed in part by the great delta of the Yellow River and extending from the mouth of the Yangtse northward to the Gulf of Pechili and from the sea westward to the base of the escarpment of the Mongolian plateau. In climate this portion of China is essentially temperate. Practically the whole of China south of the Yangtse consists of hilly and mountainous country, the elevation and dissection of which increases westward toward the Tibetan border. The coastal region and parts of the southern interior are distinctly tropical or subtropical in climate, but with the increasing elevation westward, conditions become more temperate, and in parts of Yunnan, Szechuan, and southern Shensi the winters are quite rigorous. The third section is that in the northwest, comprising parts of western Shansi, Shensi, and eastern Kansu. Here what is actually the southeastern portion of the Mongolian plateau forms the great Loess district, with semi-arid environment.

The population of China to-day is far from uniform. Although the Chinese themselves comprise the great majority, there is in addition in the north a not inconsiderable Manchu element, while in the south there are considerable fragments of non-Chinese, aboriginal peoples, called generically by the Chinese "Miaotse" together with peoples of Tibeto-Burman speech, like the Lolo and other tribes of the western marches.

Our knowledge of the physical characteristics of the peoples of China is very limited. A few score crania, mostly of uncertain provenance and age, and a still smaller number of measurements

on the living almost wholly from the single province of Kwangtung, constitute the only data on which to base conclusions in
regard to a population of several hundred millions of people,
scattered over a great and very varied area. Of archæological
material there is as yet nothing whatever, except two skulls, one
from Shantung,[1] the other from Amoy.[2] The first dates probably from about the second century A. D., and shows a mixture
of Alpine and Caspian types; the second, of uncertain but apparently very considerable age, also represents a mixture, in this
case of the Palæ-Alpine and Proto-Negroid. To base conclusions on two crania is obviously impossible; all that can be said
is that they seem to accord in general character with the results
derivable from what other material we possess, as I shall try to
show.

The published data on crania and the measurements on the
living, both published and unpublished,[3] seem to indicate a broad
division of the present population into a northern and a southern
or, more strictly, northeastern and southeastern group. The
northern, which in the main occupies the great alluvial plain, is
in stature tall, averaging slightly over 170 cm. in Shantung and
Chili. In head-form the evidence derived from crania and that
from measurements on the living do not well agree. Both show
a predominance, to be sure, of brachycephalic factors, but this
is very much stronger in the small series of measurements on the
living than in the case of the larger series of crania. In both,
however, the Alpine type is dominant, the secondary factor being
the Palæ-Alpine. The crania indicate a rather considerable minority (ca. 20 per cent) of the Caspian type.

The southeastern group includes the coastal population of
Chekiang, Fukien, and Kwangtung. The stature here is distinctly below the medium (averaging about 162 cm.) and the
head-form is more predominantly brachycephalic than in the
north. Moreover, the more northerly provinces of Chekiang

[1] Virchow, H., 1913.                    [2] Zograf, 1893.
[3] For bibliography, see Haberer, 1902. See also Li, MS., and Gaupp, 1909;
Girard, 1898, 1899; Legendre, 1909, 1911; Mochi, 1908; Talko-Hryncewicz, 1899.

and Fukien show certain significant contrasts with Kwangtung. In the former two provinces the dominant factor is, as in the north, the Alpine, while in the dolichocephalic minority the platyrrhine factors hold first place; in Kwangtung, on the other hand, it is the Palæ-Alpine type which is dominant, and the Caspian factors outweigh the platyrrhine Proto-Negroid.

Before attempting to draw conclusions from these facts we may turn to the very scanty information which we possess in regard to the people in the interior. Legendre's[1] figures for Szechuan indicate a stature still shorter than that found on the southern coast, and a considerably larger proportion of dolicho-cephalic elements. As no individual measurements are given, it is impossible to determine what types are present. In Hunan, if the measurements of a very small number of persons may be taken as indicative, the same conditions would appear to exist, but here the platyrrhine, dolichocephalic factors are of unexpected strength. For Honan and Hupeh, provinces forming the very heart of ancient China, no information whatever is available; and we have no data at all in regard to any of the non-Chinese peoples, with the single exception of the Lolo. Of this vigorous and warlike people of southern Szechuan, still semi-independent and possessing a culture strongly contrasted with that of the Chinese, we have a small series of measurements[2] which are, I believe, of much significance. The Lolo are divided into an aristocracy and a class of common people, and the two groups appear to differ in their physical characteristics. The aristocracy is very similar to the population of Kwangtung, the Palæ-Alpine factors being in the majority, with the Alpine type secondary. The common people, on the other hand, show a still stronger dominance of the Palæ-Alpine type, the Alpine being displaced as a secondary type by the Caspian.

In general the skin color of the population of the whole of China is light, although with a characteristic yellowish tinge, which early won for them the name of the Yellow Race. In the west, however, and particularly among the Lolo and some other

[1] Legendre, op. cit.                         [2] Legendre, op. cit.

border tribes, individuals are not infrequently met with who have a white-rosy complexion, quite like that of a European. In hair and eye color the population is also in general very uniform, dark eyes and straight black hair being the rule. In some areas, however, especially in the west, where European-like complexions occur, we find occasionally among the non-Chinese tribes, and more rarely among the Chinese themselves, brown, wavy, or even curly hair, together with hazel or gray-blue eyes. Reference is made also to small groups of very dark-skinned, curly, or even frizzly-haired folk in this same southwestern borderland,[1] while in the north, in Shantung, there is some indication of occasional red-haired individuals. No adequate data, however, are available on this whole question.

If we attempt to summarize the results so far obtained, it seems that there is a broad distinction between the people of the northeast and those of the south and southwest of China. The former tend toward tall stature and are predominantly of Alpine type; the latter are, on the other hand, distinctly shorter, and are in the majority Palæ-Alpine. Further, although a dolichocephalic minority is present throughout, it is much stronger in the southwest among the non-Chinese population than in the northern or southern coast. The portraits given on Plate XIX, Fig. 4, and Plate XX, Fig. 1, illustrate in the first case a man of mixed Alpine and Caspian type, and in the second the predominating Palæ-Alpine type more characteristic of the south.

The explanation of these contrasts is suggested, I believe, by China's early history. The oldest known home of the Chinese people was in the valley of the Wei River, which flows into the Yellow River from the west, just about at its sharp turn where it emerges from the Mongolian plateau onto the plain. Here, as early perhaps as the third millennium B. C., they lived as a small, sedentary, agricultural people, organized in a series of small city states. On all sides were "barbarians," those to the west and north being the horse-riding, pastoral, nomadic Hiung-nu, in all probability of Turkish speech; to the east were

[1] Farrer, 1921, p. 75.

a crudely agricultural but mainly fishing and hunting people, who held the great alluvial plains; to the south, in what was called "the jungle," were other barbarians, probably of Thai and, toward the coast, of Mon-Khmer speech.  In their expansion the Chinese, who already knew the use of bronze, pushed east and north to the coast, conquering and absorbing, and in part probably driving out the earlier folk, who along the shore and especially in Shantung were maritime traders and pirates. For a thousand years at least and probably more, the Yangtse formed the southern limit of what was China.  Their progress beyond the Yangtse was slow, and began, apparently, along the coast, where they overcame the maritime population long before they penetrated the interior, and it was not until the period of Kublai Khan in the thirteenth century A. D. that the interior provinces in the south became really a part of the empire.

Taking into account these facts of history, the meagre data from China itself, and what we know in regard to the neighboring regions, the following hypothesis in regard to the racial history of China is, with much hesitation, suggested.  The earliest stratum of population traceable in northern China, at least, was dolichocephalic.  The evidence for this is admittedly weak, yet no other conclusion seems equally plausible.  The modern population of the Yellow River delta region contains, as has been shown, a considerable dolichocephalic factor, in part Caspian, in part a blend of Proto-Australoid and Proto-Negroid. These elements are relatively stronger south of the Yangtse, and are known to have been the dominant elements in Tonkin in Neolithic times.[1]  They form the most ancient stratum of population, as will be shown later, in Japan; they survive in considerable strength to this day among the Ainu of Yezo and Sakhalin. We may, I believe, accept an ancient Neolithic population of platyrrhine, dolichocephalic types as having spread northward up the coast.  Next in sequence came the short-statured Palæ-Alpine type, present as a secondary factor throughout northern China to-day, and as the primary type south of the Yangtse.

[1] See ante, p. 270.

Whether it came into China from the north, from eastern Mongolia, where its presence is indicated (?) in Neolithic times, or from the west it is impossible to say. It may have included some Negrito element, or this may have been a still older factor in the south and west, where short, dark-skinned, curly-haired folk have been reported in recent years. Whatever its source, it seems to have become the dominant type throughout China, except on the coasts, where the older platyrrhine, dolichocephalic forms long prevailed. Following (?) this, came a wave of peoples of Caspian type, entering China almost certainly by way of the Yellow River valley, from inner Asia. It spread both in the north and south, and part of the influence of this type now discernible in the southwest of China seems attributable to this early wave. A later proto-historic drift of the same type, terminating only just before the beginning of the Christian era, and coming through western Kansu, the Tsaidam, and eastern Tibet being responsible for the rest. The last of the great movements was that of the people of Alpine type, who, pouring in from the west, flooded first the northern plain and later penetrated southward toward Indo-China. And this drift of Alpine peoples out of inner Asia into China seems to have continued throughout the centuries down to the present, for we find that there is to-day an almost insensible trickle of non-Chinese peoples, primarily of this type, coming into Kansu and Szechuan, where in a generation or two they dissolve into the mass of the population.

To which of the types did the ancient Chinese folk belong? In the total absence of material from the earliest sites of Chinese culture, it is more than hazardous even to guess. In my opinion, however, the little group of town-dwelling, agricultural folk who in the third millennium B. C., in the Wei valley on the verge of the inner-Asiatic steppe and desert, constituted the kernel of what was to be the Chinese people—this little group were, I believe, primarily of the Alpine type, coming from the irrigable oases along the southern border of Chinese Turkestan, but blended with a minority of the Caspian type.

## II. Manchuria and Korea

The peoples of Manchuria and Korea may conveniently be considered together, in spite of the fact that the physical features of the two areas are quite different. The greater part of Manchuria consists of open steppe, drained northward by the Sungari River into the Amur and southward by the Liao River to the Gulf of Pechili. On the west the Great Khingan range emphasizes the edge of the Mongolian plateau; to the north the forested uplands along the Amur mark the beginning of a wholly new environment; in the east the region is again mountainous, and this rugged country extends southward through the peninsula of Korea, which, except on its western and southern sides, contains little good agricultural land. The whole region is in its environment transitional, between the steppe and desert of the plateaus to the west, the heavily forested country to the north, and the agricultural plains of northern China.

Historically, Manchuria has been a reservoir from which successive hordes of Tungusic peoples have swept down upon northern China during the period from the seventh to the seventeenth centuries. Its present population comprises a few Mongols, but in the main is made up of mixed Manchus and Chinese, with, in recent times, many Japanese. Linguistically the region presents some interesting puzzles, for, although the Manchu belongs with the other Tungusic languages spoken in the Amur basin and farther north, the Korean is still uncertain in its affiliations, although relations with Japanese, on the one hand, and the Ural-Altaic languages on the other, have been pointed out.

We possess no data in regard to the ancient peoples of any part of this region, and for the modern Manchus the material is very scanty. Although described by some writers as tall, the Manchus are, according to Torii's measurements,[1] a little under medium stature (average 163 cm.). The skin color is yellowish, the hair black and straight, the eyes dark and usually Mongoloid. In head-form the few measurements show the people to

[1] Torii, 1914.

be purely brachycephalic, the Alpine type being in the large majority. Yet the extremely high indices suggest that cranial deformation may be practised, thus obscuring the real facts. Compared with the other Tunguse tribes farther north, the Manchus seem to be much more purely Alpine.

For Korea we have, fortunately, much more satisfactory materials,[1] although for parts of the peninsula they are very defective, and there are few cranial data. From Kubo's data on army recruits it appears that the Koreans in general are taller than the Japanese, although as a rule slightly shorter than the Manchus. The population of the west coast is slightly shorter than that on the east. In head-form the people show throughout a strong predominance of brachycephalic factors, yet there is a noteworthy difference between the population of the three western and southwestern provinces of Hwang-hai, Chung-ching, and Chöl-la, and that in Pjöng-an in the north and Kjöng-kwi and Kang-wön in the central part of the peninsula. In the former the Palæ-Alpine type is dominant, largely exceeding the Alpine in importance; in the latter the proportions of the two types are reversed. A further difference appears in that in the northern and central provinces the dolichocephalic factors which in the main are platyrrhine, are two or three times more abundant than elsewhere.

From historical sources we know that in the second century B. C. the population of western Korea was closely affiliated, if not identical, with that of southern Manchuria, whereas the southern and eastern coasts were occupied by a different, distinctly maritime people, related in speech to the people of the island of Kiushu in southern Japan, the non-Chinese remnants along the southern coast of China, and the inhabitants of the Philippines. The correlation of this early historical difference in population with the observed two groups among the present people is not yet plain. Perhaps the Palæ-Alpine group in the west may be regarded as the survivors of the ancient population, once continuous with that of Manchuria, whereas the platyr-

[1] Bogdanov, 1878–79 d; Hamy, 1896; Koganei, 1906; Kubo, 1913; Waldeyer, 1899

rhine, dolichocephalic element represents in some way the old maritime coastal population affiliated with that of the Chinese coast, which in very early times seems to have extended northward as far as the opposite shores of Shantung. The Alpine factors, which are strongest in the north, may finally represent a relatively late wave of this type, spreading eastward through northern Manchuria. The dolichocephalic elements are also almost certainly related to the same factors so strongly represented among the Ainu. The entire question is complicated, and no solution can be hoped for until the abundant archæological material in the region is available for study.

### III. JAPAN

The long chain of islands, great and small, stretching from the Riu-kiu group through the Japanese archipelago to Sakhalin and the Kurile Islands, seems to have in its racial history a certain unity. Shaped roughly like a gigantic Y, it touches the Asiatic mainland at three points, *i. e.*, Korea, the mouth of the Amur, and Kamchatka. Throughout the greater part of its extent the islands are rugged and volcanic, and afford relatively little good agricultural land. The Riu-kius are in their environment subtropical, and these conditions fade northward through Japan until in Yezo, Sakhalin, and the Kurile Islands the climate is rigorous. In Japan itself there is much difference in this respect between the eastern and western shores, the latter being much colder than the former.

Of the prehistoric population of Japan we are just beginning to learn, through the investigations carried on by various Japanese archæologists during the last few years.[1] Although the actual measurements of the crania found have not, as a rule, yet been made accessible, it seems that the following conclusions are justified. The earliest remains yet found, regarded as early Neolithic in age, come from the northeastern portion of the main island of Nippon. They show a people short of stature and

[1] Matsumoto, 1921; Suzuki, 1918; Hasebe, 1920.

prevailingly dolichocephalic, who are declared to have resembled quite closely the long-headed element among the modern Ainu. If this is so, then this earliest population of Japan were in the main a blend of Proto-Australoid and Proto-Negroid types, and thus similar to the ancient underlying stratum of the population, southward along the whole coast and throughout Indo-China, and beyond to India itself. Following this earliest stratum there appears in middle Neolithic times, in the region about the Inland Sea, as well as in the extreme northeast, a wholly different people. Shorter, almost dwarfish, they are apparently of the Palæ-Alpine type, and their very short stature raises a question whether some Negrito factor may not be present. From its greater purity in the western portion of the island, it seems probable that these people entered Japan from the southwest, and spread northward. Third in sequence is a much taller people, almost certainly identifiable as Caspian in type. Like its predecessor, it came in from the south and west, and gradually spread northward, driving the earlier groups before it to some extent.

It is unfortunate that no study seems yet to have been made of the crania from the very abundant sites of the so-called Yamato period, attributable to the proto-historic and early historic Japanese. Lacking this, the correlation of the prehistoric data with that derived from the modern population becomes difficult.

The modern population comprises two quite distinct groups of people—the Gilyak and Ainu, aboriginal peoples of Sakhalin, the Kurile Islands, and of parts of the island of Yezo; and the Japanese and occupants of the Riu-kiu Islands. The Gilyak occupy the northern part of Sakhalin and the mainland coast adjoining, from near the mouth of the Amur along the southern shores of the Okhotsk Sea to Ulban Bay. There is some reason to believe that their earlier home was on Sakhalin, and that they have spread thence to the mainland. Linguistically they are quite isolated. From the fragmentary material accessible in regard to their physical characteristics,[1] it seems clear that they

[1] Bogdanov, 1878–79 f; Schrenck, 1881.

FIG. 1. CHINESE. (SOUTHERN TYPE.)

FIG. 2. AINU.

FIG. 3. JAPANESE. (CASPIAN TYPE.)

FIG. 4. KALMUCK.

PLATE XX.

are a considerably mixed people, in whom, however, dolichocephalic factors largely prevail, the Proto-Negroid type being in
the majority. The purer individuals seem to resemble the Ainu
quite closely, lacking, however, the extreme development of hair
characteristic of the latter. They have, on the other hand, much
more hair on the body and face than the neighboring Tunguse
tribes. We may probably regard the Gilyak as a people essentially similar to the Ainu, who have had a considerable infusion
of Alpine types due to contact with the Tunguse peoples.

Although the Ainu to-day are a rapidly disappearing folk, in
the earlier historic and traditional period they were much more
numerous, and extended over a wide area, occupying, besides
parts of Sakhalin, the Kurile Islands, and Yezo, the whole of
the northern half or two-thirds of the island of Nippon. They
speak a language which bears no relation to any of its neighbors,
and as a people have long aroused the interest of anthropologists
because of their striking difference from all the neighboring
groups. Of short stature (averaging from 156–158 cm.), with a
reddish-brown skin, which sometimes is quite dark, they have
long wavy or curly black hair and abundant beards and very
hairy bodies. The eyes are dark and show no trace of the Mongoloid fold. Their whole appearance and expression (apart from
their skin color) suggest European comparisons, especially with
certain Russian peasant types. Some observers have also noted
resemblances to Australian natives. These are apparent in the
portrait given on Plate XX, Fig. 2.

Fortunately the wide-spread interest in the Ainu has resulted
in several careful studies,[1] and these relatively abundant data
yield on analysis results of large significance. The purest Ainu
to-day are those of northern Yezo and southern Sakhalin. They
show a large predominance of dolichocephalic factors, the Proto-
Negroid and Proto-Australoid being of greatest importance, followed by the Caspian. The brachycephalic elements (which increase rapidly southward) are primarily the Palæ-Alpine, the
Alpine being in very small minority except among the more

[1] Koganei, 1893; Tarenetsky, 1890; Török, 1889–99.

southern mixed groups, where the two brachycephalic factors
outnumber the dolichocephalic.  The purer Ainu of the north
are, it is to be noted, quite frequently marked by a considerable
degree of prognathism.  If now we take into consideration the
prehistoric types, whose character and sequence in Japan have
been established, it is clear that in the Ainu we have the descendants of the earliest Neolithic population, mixed with the
later Neolithic Palæ-Alpine, and Caspian types.  The presence
so far to the northward of a strong factor of Proto-Negroid and
Proto-Australoid types is corroborated by the traces of their
ancient presence along the Chinese coastal region and in the
southeast of the continent.  The Ainu thus represent the last
remnants of the ancient population of the whole eastern littoral
of Asia, driven out, absorbed or destroyed elsewhere north of
Indo-China, but surviving here in isolation, much mixed with
the later peoples.

For the Japanese people themselves we have, curiously, much
less satisfactory data.[1]  In the series of crania which have been
published,[2] in spite of the recognized wide differences locally
and between different classes in the community, no attempt has
been made to note the origin of the specimens, nor have even the
sexes been distinguished except by Nakano.  All that can be said
in regard to the older material, is that in a heterogeneous series
of Japanese crania the brachycephalic factors are in the majority; that the Palæ-Alpine is the type of greatest importance;
and that this is followed in order by the Proto-Negroid and
Alpine types.  The Japanese thus, if we may judge by this sample, are in large measure the reverse of the Ainu, i. e., the Palæ-
Alpine, which there was secondary, is here primary; the Proto-
Negroid elements that there were primary are here secondary;
and the Alpine factor, which among the Ainu was slight, here
almost occupies second place.  The Caspian type is represented
but very weakly in this series of Japanese crania, but I believe

---

[1] I am greatly indebted to Doctor Nenozo Utsurikawa, of Keio University,
Tokyo, for references to and translations of Japanese sources.

[2] Baelz, 1881, 1885; Mochi, 1908; Toldt, 1904; Nakano, 1908, 1913.

that if we had material available from the proper areas it would be found to be considerably more abundant. From Nakano's data, although no individual measurements are given, it seems clear that the population of the northwestern coast in the vicinity of Kanazawa shows a rather strong preponderance of dolichocephalic factors, in which the Proto-Negroid and Caspian appear to be of greatest importance. On the northern shores of the Inland Sea, on the other hand, these elements are much weaker.

If no adequate study has been made as yet of Japanese crania, the beginnings of an investigation of the living population afford a little but very welcome light on the geographical distribution of the various types.[1] Although the data have not been published for the individual measurements, except in the older material of Baelz, it is nevertheless apparent that the early Neolithic types are still traceable in the north and northeast, where, as well as in the extreme south, in southern Kiushu and southern Shikoku, the very short Palæ-Alpine type still survives. The Caspian type is widely scattered, but seems especially noticeable in northern Kiushu and on the Shikoku shore of the Inland Sea. It is said to be found also along the northwestern coast of Nippon. A portrait illustrating a man of this type is given on Plate XX, Fig. 3. The Alpine type, finally, seems to be most abundant around the northern shore of the Inland Sea and in the western and southwestern portions of Nippon. On the basis of the data thus far published the various types appear to be distributed in a remarkably regular fashion, such that the more ancient are in general farthest away from the point where the archipelago comes nearest to the mainland in Korea, while the more recent cluster about this spot.

In stature the modern Japanese average slightly below 160 cm. and are thus distinctly short. The skin color is usually fair and slightly yellowish, but there is not a little local variation, and distinctly fair, rosy complexions are sometimes seen, as well as others quite clearly brownish. The hair is in general straight

[1] Baelz, 1885; Matsumara, 1918, 1919 a.

and black, although wavy or even curly forms occasionally occur. The Mongoloid eye is almost always present in some degree.

Any attempt to identify the traditional immigrant groups with these several types must, until adequate archæological material is available, be premature. It may, however, be tentatively suggested that the Izumo group was probably in the main Alpine; the Yamato may be suspected to have had a considerable Caspian element, whereas the invaders under Jimmu Tenno, who came from Kiushu and conquered the southern portion of Nippon, were probably in the main of Palæ-Alpine type, although doubtless with some Caspian and probably Negroid admixture.

The people of the Riu-kiu Islands,[1] which extend from Kiushu southward almost to Formosa, present several features of interest. They have a much larger dolichocephalic element than the population of the adjacent parts of Kiushu. In stature they are shorter than the average Japanese, their skin color is darker, their hair frequently wavy and more abundant on the body than in the case of the Japanese of central Nippon. Unfortunately no data are given in regard to the character of the nose, but tentatively we may regard the characteristics above noted as suggesting that the long-headed elements present are in the main the Proto-Australoid and Proto-Negroid, found strongly represented at the opposite or northern extremity of the island archipelagoes, among the Ainu. Thus the ancient Neolithic stratum in Japan was split by the incoming later peoples who poured in from Korea, the major portion being driven north and surviving as the Ainu, the minor being forced southward and later largely absorbed in the smaller islands of the Riu-kiu.

[1] Baelz, 1911; Matsumara, 1919 b.

# CHAPTER III

## THE EASTERN PLATEAUS

### I. Mongolia

THE eastern wing of the great plateau belt is divisible into three subdivisions, which are distinct not only geographically but in their racial history—Mongolia, Eastern or Chinese Turkestan, and Tibet. The first of these consists of a series of rolling plateaus, ranging from three to nearly five thousand feet in elevation. The northern limits are formed by the Altai, Sayan, and other ranges, and by the higher, now much dissected plateaus of the region about Lake Baikal and the upper Amur River. On the east the plateau falls off in a steep escarpment to the lowlands of Manchuria and northern China, broken only by the gap through which the Yellow River flows, while on the south the great ranges which form the northern border of the high Tibetan plateau, rise like a giant wall. To the west Mongolia has no definite physiographic boundary, for the plateau decreases in elevation and runs out into three arms, divided from each other by the Tian-shan and Altai ranges. The southernmost of these forms the great basin of Eastern Turkestan; north of the Tian-shan and between it and the Altai lies the broad corridor of Dzungaria, opening out onto the steppes of southern Siberia; while north of the Altai and hemmed in on three sides by mountain ranges, is the basin of Kobdo. Except along its mountain borders on the north, west, and south, which are in varying degree forested, Mongolia is throughout an area of steppe and desert, the true desert, however, being of limited extent.

The only data as yet available in regard to the ancient population of Mongolia consist of the two crania reported by Talko-Hryncewicz[1] from the Trans-Baikal region along the northern

[1] Talko-Hryncewicz, 1897.

border. These are apparently of Neolithic age, one being clearly Palæ-Alpine, the other, which is incomplete, is on the border line of dolichocephaly, and shows that at this early period a long-headed element was certainly present in this portion of Mongolia at least.

The modern inhabitants of Mongolia are, with two exceptions, all Mongols. These exceptions are (1) the Chinese colonists along the eastern and southern borders and in the irrigable oases of southern Dzungaria, and (2) the Turkish-speaking Kirgiz and other tribes in parts of the Altai and Tian-shan ranges. The Mongols themselves are divisible into an eastern group, comprising the Kalkas and Mongols of Inner Mongolia, and the Buriats of the region about Lake Baikal; and a western group, formed by the Kalmuck, who are mainly in Dzungaria. In recent years some of the Buriats have forced their way far to the northeast into the basin of the Lena, thus passing outside the limits of Mongolia. All the Mongol peoples speak closely related languages, which are related to the Turko-Tatar, and form a branch of the great Ural-Altaic stock.

The greater part of our data in regard to the physical type of the Mongols comes from the Kalmuck[1] and Buriat,[2] the Kalka Mongols not having been as yet adequately studied. In stature all the Mongol peoples are below the medium, ranging from about 161 cm. in the case of the Kalka to 163 cm. among the Kalmuck and Buriat. The western or Kalmuck group has in general a white-rosy complexion, which in the Kalka and Buriat becomes distinctly yellowish. The hair is, with few exceptions, dark or black and straight, although reddish tones sometimes occur. The eyes are dark, and in the case of the Kalmuck, at least, show the Mongoloid fold only in persons under forty years of age. In the eastern group this feature is much more pronounced. All the Mongol peoples are strongly and preponderantly brachycephalic, but the types present show significant

---

[1] Ivanovsky, 1891, 1896; Kollmann, 1885 a; Talko-Hryncewicz, 1902; Ten Kate, 1882; Reicher, 1913–14; Korolev, 1903; Fridolin, 1901.
[2] Bogdanov, 1878–79 g; Fridolin, op. cit.

variations. In the Kalmuck the Mongoloid type is dominant, followed in order by the Palæ-Alpine, the Ural, and the Alpine. Of dolichocephalic factors there is present but the merest trace, except among those Kalmucks settled on the shores of the Caspian in southern Russia, who have a small long-headed element of uncertain type. The Buriat, on the other hand, show a predominance of the Alpine type, the subsidiary factors being the Mongoloid and Palæ-Alpine. The Ural type, which was quite important among the Kalmuck, here practically disappears. A typical example of the Mongol is given in the Kalmuck portrait on Plate XX, Fig. 4.

The significance of the difference between the Buriat and Kalmuck is not yet clear, in large part because of the lack of information in regard to the other Mongol peoples and the population of the Sayan-Altai border country. Some light appears, however, to be thrown on the problem by the few data accessible in regard to these latter. Much of this mountain border is occupied by Turko-Tatar speaking folk, such as the Soyot,[1] Uriankhai, Telenget,[2] Black Tatars, Teles, etc.[3], most of whom live on the forested northern slopes of the ranges on the upper tributaries of the Yenesei and Obi. Although all speaking related languages, these various tribes are commonly regarded as belonging in two groups, an older stratum by some thought to have been originally Finnic or Samoyede in speech, and a more recent Turko-Tatar stratum, supposed to have overlaid and largely assimilated the older peoples, perhaps as recently as the beginning of the Christian era. We have data only for the Telenget, classed as belonging to the later group. Analysis of the measurements reveals the interesting fact that this people may be said to stand about midway between the western or Kalmuck Mongols and the Buriat as representative of the eastern group. The primary factor among the Telenget is the Palæ-Alpine, followed by the Mongoloid (which was dominant in the Kalmuck) and the Alpine (dominant in the Buriat). Since none of the

[1] Goroshchenko, 1901; Silinich, 1901.      [2] Lutsenko, 1902; Reicher, *op. cit.*
[3] Ivanovski, *op. cit.*

other Turko-Tatar tribes, from which we have material, such as the Kirgiz, Uzbeg, and Russian Tatars (?), comprise any considerable Mongoloid factor, the conclusion seems justified that this element present in the Telenget is derived from admixture with some Mongol group, and is thus primarily a characteristic of the Mongol people.  No data which can be analyzed are available for any other of the border tribes, and it can only be said that the Soyot and Uriankhai of the upper Yenesei region, appear to comprise a considerable element of the Mongoloid type; whereas the Black Tatars have a surprisingly large dolichocephalic factor, which is apparently Caspian.

We are able thus to trace a strong element of the Mongoloid type throughout the border tribes, who are not linguistically affiliated with the Mongols, and who may be regarded either as Mongols, Tatarized both in speech and physical type, or, less probably, as originally Tatar folk, Mongolized to some extent physically.  This suggests an explanation for the strength of the Alpine factor among the Buriat, viz., that they represent a group, originally comparable with the Kalmuck, who have been "Alpinized" either by admixture in recent times with the primarily Alpine Tunguse peoples of the region about Lake Baikal, or much earlier, during the period when most of Mongolia was held by Turko-Tatar rather than by Mongol peoples.  This latter possibility leads us into a brief consideration of the history of Mongolia, which may aid in clearing up the whole problem.

Our earliest knowledge of the Mongolian area is derived from Chinese sources.  From them we learn that at least as far back as the beginning of the first millennium B. C., and perhaps a thousand years earlier, eastern Mongolia at least was occupied by a nomad, pastoral people of warlike character, known to the Chinese as the Hiungnu.  So far as can be determined, they seem to have been of Turko-Tatar speech.  With these "barbarians" the Chinese were in almost constant conflict, and by the third century B. C. had gained considerable knowledge of the whole country, and tell us of tribes of similar type living as far west as Dzungaria and the Altai, and north to the valley of the Selenga. Of any group which can with any certainty be identified as Mongol we hear nothing. A little before the beginning of the Christian era a portion of the Hiungnu were, under the combined attack of the Chinese and certain Tunguse tribes of Manchuria, forced to flee westward, passing through Dzungaria and ultimately appearing in Europe, under their leader Attila, as the Huns. From then on until the latter part of the twelfth century Mongolia continued to be occupied by the remainder of the Hiungnu and other related tribes, which, one after the other, built up powerful Turkish kingdoms, and in a never-ending stream poured westward through Dzungaria into Turkestan and beyond.

We first hear of the Mongols in the seventh century as a small and unimportant tribe living east and southeast of Lake Baikal, holding the fertile meadows and pastures of the mountains along the Mongolian border. Not, however, until the end of the twelfth century did they attain importance, when, under the genius of Khengis Khan, chief of a small Mongol tribe on the Onon River, they began their remarkably rapid and spectacular rise. First conquering the surrounding Turkish-speaking tribes, then welding them together with the Mongols into an invincible horde of horsemen, Khengiz Khan conquered all of Mongolia and Central Asia, and then swept on into Europe. The hordes of the "Mongol" conquests were unquestionably in large part of Turkish speech and origin, although mainly under Mongol leaders, and it seems to have been due in part to the tremendous drain upon this Turkish population to supply the Mongol armies, and in part to wholesale emigration, that the almost complete disappearance of the Turks from the area of Mongolia and their replacement by Mongols was due. Doubtless some of the older population remained, but were completely Mongolized under the Mongol rule.

Of this ancient Turkish population, which for so long held most of Mongolia, we have as yet no crania, although abundant materials could doubtless be secured in the vicinity of their ancient capital at Karakoram. We can only judge of their physical characteristics by the data which we have in regard to their modern descendants. These are, as will be shown in detail in a later section, quite variable, in that some, such as the Uzbeg and Uigur Turks, the Kirgiz of the Tian-shan, and the Turki peoples of the northern oases of Eastern Turkestan, etc., are primarily Palæ-Alpine, with the Alpine type secondary; whereas others, like the Tatars in Russia, the Kirgiz of southern Siberia, etc., are primarily Alpine. The Uigur and Uzbeg are, however, all things considered, the better representatives of the more eastern Turkish tribes, whom we may thus tentatively regard as having been probably more Palæ-Alpine than Alpine in type. All of which finally leads to the conclusion that the Mongoloid type was, in earlier times, probably rather closely restricted to the northern border regions of the Mongolian plateau; that the rest of Mongolia was occupied by a mixed Palæ-Alpine and Alpine people, who were the ancestors of the present Turko-Tatar peoples; and that not until the rise of the Mongols to political supremacy in the twelfth and thirteenth centuries, did the peculiar type which they represent more strongly than any other Asiatic people, become distributed over the great area of Mongolia in which it is found to-day.

## II. Eastern or Chinese Turkestan

Chinese Turkestan is a great oval or rather pear-shaped basin, whose narrower, open end faces the east, and which is surrounded on all other sides by very high ranges of mountains. Its centre is for the most part utterly desert, and lies only about 2,500 feet above the sea. Around this "dead heart of Asia," between the desert and the mountain wall, stretches a string of irrigable oases, widely separated from each other, in which practically the whole population lives. In the mountains are nomadic peoples, like the Kirgiz, Kara-Kirgiz, and a few Mongols. The whole basin is drained by the Tarim River, which at the eastern end dies out in the great, reedy swamps of Lop-Nor, where live a peculiar and very interesting fisher-folk, known as Loplik. Except for the Chinese colonists, the few Mongol nomads in the mountains on the north and south, and the Indo-European-speaking groups in the Pamirs, all the people of Eastern Turkestan speak Turki, a language belonging to the Turko-Tatar branch of the Ural-Altic stock.

We may best trace the racial history of this area by beginning with a consideration of the modern population, most of our knowledge of which we owe to the painstaking investigations of Sir Aurel Stein.[1] The great majority of the population are of medium or slightly under-medium stature, only the Loplik and neighboring Charklik, and the Pamir peoples approaching a stature of 170 cm. In skin color the bulk of the population is described as white-rosy, and all have dark hair and eyes, except among the Pamir tribes, where lighter tones sometimes occur. It is noteworthy, however, that among the Chinese of the extreme southeastern oases nearly 15 per cent of blue eyes are found. The significance of this will be seen later. In character the hair is generally wavy or curly, and really straight only among the Chinese colonists.

In respect to their physical type the peoples of Eastern Turkestan are divisible into three clearly contrasted groups, marked by the predominance of the Alpine, the Palæ-Alpine, and the Caspian types. The first group comprises the Indo-European Wakhi and Sariqoli of the Pamir region, and probably the majority of the inhabitants of the western and southwestern border and oases (Pakhpo, Kökyar, Khotan, Polu, Yarkand (?), Kashgar (?)). In all of these the Alpine type is strongly dominant, and in general seems to increase in importance westward, attaining its maximum (70 per cent) among the Wakhi. In all, also, the Palæ-Alpine type is that secondary in importance, and in all except the Wakhi and people of Kökyar, the Caspian type is present as a strong minority. The second group includes the Kirgiz of the Tian-shan, the occupants of the northern oases (Kelpin, Dolan, Korla, Turfan, Hami) and those of the southern oases east of Khotan (Keriya, Niya, Charklik). Among all these

[1] Stein, 1921. For resumé, see Joyce, 1912.

the Palæ-Alpine type is strongly dominant, the Alpine being secondary; only in Hami and Charklik, the easternmost of the northern and southern oases respectively, does the Caspian factor become important.

The third group includes the Loplik of Lop-Nor and the Chinese of Nanhu and Tunhuang, small settlements two or three hundred miles farther east, near Sachu, on the borders of the province of Kansu. In this group the Caspian type is dominant, the Palæ-Alpine being secondary, and the Alpine being present only as a rather small minority and quite outweighed among the Chinese by platyrrhine, dolichocephalic factors.

The explanation of these facts seems to me best given as follows. The dominance of the Alpine type in the west is due to the influence of the almost purely Alpine population of the Pamir region and parts of Western Turkestan, who have from very early times had very close relations with Kashgar, Yarkand, and Khotan. The fundamental stratum of the population throughout is of the Palæ-Alpine type, and one, therefore, with that characteristic of the Uigur and Uzbeg Turks. The presence of the strong Caspian factor among the Loplik and Chinese of the Kansu border, must be due to the survival there of some early penetration of this type from the west or northwest, since within relatively recent historic times no people of this character is known to have come into Eastern Turkestan.

If we turn to the early history of this area, a probable corroboration of this latter view is found. In the third century B. C. the Chinese refer to a people called by them Yuechi, who were different from the Hiungnu, and who then occupied much of western Kansu. In the second century B. C. these people were attacked by the Hiungnu, and most of them driven west and north to Hami and the Tian-shan region. Later they moved still farther west into Western Turkestan, where on the ruins of the Greco-Bactrian kingdoms they established the new state of Tokharia, which for some time was a great power in this portion of Asia. The recent archæological investigations of Stein have shown that in the southern oases of Eastern Turkestan, between

Keriya and Lop-Nor, there were, in the centuries preceding the Christian era, a people called the Tokhari, who spoke an Indo-European language, related more closely to the Greek and Latin than to Persian and Sanskrit; and that this language continued in use here into the early centuries of our era. There is reason to believe that these Tokhari were related to the Yuechi, and were driven from their homes at the same time, removing with them westward, where the combined people established themselves anew as the Tokharian state. Now Franke[1] suggests that the Tokhari and Yuechi represent a great thrust of Indo-European peoples from the region about the Caspian, which at an early but as yet unknown period penetrated by way of Dzungaria and the Tian-shan region to the southern oases and western Kansu. In discussing the racial history of China it was suggested that probably very much earlier than this there had been another similar great thrust of Caspian peoples, which had penetrated much farther and profoundly influenced the character of the population of the whole of the eastern borderlands. This movement, then, which is supposed to have brought the Indo-European Tokhari and Yuechi, would thus be a repetition on a smaller scale of that ancient drift. If this theory of the source of the Yuechi is true, they would in all probability have brought into western Kansu a strong Caspian factor, and we may therefore ascribe the presence of this element among the Loplik and Chinese of Sachu to-day, as due to the assimilation of the remnants of the Yuechi, who did not flee to the west. That such a remnant did survive we know from Chinese sources, which report them as removing southward into the Tsaidam and northern Tibet for a while, and then returning to their former homes precisely in the region occupied to-day by the Chinese, among whom this strong Caspian factor appears. They even survived there as a recognizable unit under the name of the Little Yuechi, as late as the tenth century.

[1] Franke, 1904.

## III. Tibet

The great girdle of plateaus and mountain uplands which stretches across the continent of Asia from northeast to southwest, culminates in the highlands of Tibet and the mountain area westward to the Pamirs. Lying at an elevation which ranges from ten to seventeen thousand feet, the whole region is, with the exception of some border sections, barren and treeless, yet in spite of the rigorous climate agriculture is possible where irrigation can be obtained up to elevations of as much as 15,000 feet. Guarded on the south by the great chain of the Himalayas, which bars it off from the Indo-Gangetic plain, on the north by the ranges of almost equal height which separate it from the low-lying basin of Eastern Turkestan and the southern Mongolian plateau, and on the west by the high and difficult mountain masses toward the Pamirs, Tibet is in any real sense of the term open only toward the east, where the plateaus, scarred by the tremendous canyons of the upper Salwen, Mekong, and Yangtse rivers, or in the less difficult country about Koko-Nor and the upper Yellow River, break down into the rugged uplands of western China. Except in the border region of Kashmir and the valley of the Indus and its tributaries below the great bend near Gilgit, where Indo-European languages related to those of northern India are spoken, and in the northeast in the Tsaidam and the region about Koko-Nor, where there is a considerable Mongol population, the people of the whole of this area speak Tibetan or related dialects.

Our knowledge of the physical characteristics of the people of the Tibetan region is dependent upon a handful of crania of somewhat uncertain provenance and the measurements of a few score of individuals, for the most part from the borders of the region only. The most extensive data come from the western section in the vicinity of the upper Indus. For the Kashmiris no individual measurements are available, but Ujfalvy's[1] averages seem to make it clear that they are essentially like the pop-

[1] Ujfalvy, 1896.

ulation of the Punjab in northwestern India, *i. e.*, considerably above the medium stature, rather variable in skin color, with wavy hair, and primarily of Caspian and Mediterranean types, with some admixture of Negroid factors. The Dards, who occupy the Indus valley region between Kashmir and Gilgit, are apparently similar, but with an appreciable brachycephalic element, in the main Alpine. The isolated and peculiar little group of the Burusheski[1] just under the Pamirs, is on the whole of much the same character, although the brachycephalic factor here seems more largely Palæ-Alpine. In complexion these latter folk are very light, almost fair, and occasionally have hazel or even gray-blue eyes.

The Baltis[2] and Ladakhis[2] of the upper Indus valley, although Tibetan in speech, present much similarity to these western Himalayan peoples. The Baltis, like the Dards, have a preponderant Caspian-Mediterranean factor, but, curiously, a smaller Alpine element, and are much shorter in stature. The Ladakhis are very evidently more mixed, for, although they have a majority of dolichocephalic factors, these are pretty evenly divided between leptorrhine and platyrrhine forms, the latter being twice as important as in the case of the Baltis, and three times that found in the Dards. Both Baltis and Ladakhis show not infrequently the Mongoloid eye.

Turning lastly to the data for Lahoul[3] and Kulu,[3] which districts lie on the southern side of the main Himalayan divide, toward the plains of northern India, we find that the people of both sections are primarily dolichocephalic, those of Kulu, which is nearer the plains, more so than the Lahoulis. But, while in both the Caspian-Mediterranean factors are the most important, the people of Lahoul have a very small, those of Kulu a very considerable, Proto-Australoid-Proto-Negroid factor, whereas in respect to the Alpine element the conditions are reversed, the Lahoulis having a large, the Kulu people a small proportion.

Before attempting to explain and harmonize these facts, we must present the scanty information we possess in regard to the

---

[1] Dixon, M. S.    [2] Ujfalvy, 1881, 1896.    [3] Holland, 1902.

Tibetans proper.    From the measurements[1] given it appears that the population of the southeastern border region south of Lhassa is somewhat under medium stature, with straight black hair and frequently Mongoloid eyes.    They are primarily brachycephalic, the Alpine type being that most important, although in some sections, such as the Tsanpo valley, the Palæ-Alpine usurps first place.    The Caspian-Mediterranean factors, so strong in the west, here dwindle to small proportions, although apparently in greater strength in the easterly province of Kham than in the Tsanpo valley.    The platyrrhine, dolichocephalic factors seem everywhere more important than the leptorrhine, however.    If these southeastern Tibetans are compared with the people of Bhutan, just to the south, they are found to be very similar, so that there seems to be a substantial unity between the people of southeastern Tibet and those speaking related languages, who occupy the southern slopes of the Himalayas.

For the rest of Tibet we have no metrical data.    From the descriptions, however, it seems clear that both the brachycephalic and dolichocephalic forms are widely scattered and recognizable. The latter is said by Waddell to be most prevalent among the upper or ruling classes.

From the foregoing it seems to be established that in the western portion of the Tibetan plateau area, both in the upper Indus region and on the southern or Indian slope of the Himalayas, the population, irrespective of linguistic affiliations, is primarily dolichocephalic, the most important element being a Caspian-Mediterranean blend, comparable to that forming the mass of the population in northwestern India.    The Proto-Australoid and Proto-Negroid factors become more abundant, both as one ascends the Indus or passes from the plateaus southward toward the Indo-Gangetic plain.    The people of the southeastern portion of the region, on the other hand, are primarily brachycephalic, the Alpine type being generally dominant.    The following tentative explanation of these conditions may be suggested. The earliest stratum of population in the whole area was, like

[1] Risley, 1892; Turner, 1906, 1913; Waddell, 1901.

that of the other sections of the plateau belt, primarily brachy-cephalic, although whether Alpine or Palæ-Alpine it is, in the absence of any archæological data, impossible to say. An inva-sion of the region then took place by a people primarily of Cas-pian-Mediterranean type in the main, by way of the upper Indus valley, spreading thence eastward, a second and weaker stream coming from the northeast by way of the Tsaidam, where at the end of the second millennium B. C. the Chinese report the pres-ence of a non-Tibetan, non-Turkish people. The presence of the platyrrhine, dolichocephalic factors still remains to be accounted for. These seem, from the very few crania available, to be pri-marily Proto-Australoid. Now it has been seen that this and the Proto-Negroid types were both present, apparently in strength, in southern China and Indo-China in Neolithic times, and that isolated groups of Negroid peoples still continue to exist along the Chinese-Tibetan border. Since then these fac-tors among the Tibetan population appear to increase as one goes eastward, it is probable that we may assume that this type came into Tibet from the eastern borderlands.

It is tempting, although certainly premature, to regard the Caspian-Mediterranean influx in the west as a part of, and con-temporaneous with, the great wave of peoples of these types which streamed into northwestern India in the second millen-nium B. C. If, as seems likely, a portion of these immigrants came into India down the Indus valley, we have only to suppose that some, instead of descending the stream from its great bend near Gilgit, ascended it, passing thus into Baltistan and Ladakh and southward across easy passes to the Vale of Kashmir. The cultural and linguistic difficulties in the way of such an assump-tion are by no means insuperable, while on the purely physical side the theory has much to recommend it.

# CHAPTER IV

## THE WESTERN PLATEAUS AND THE CAUCASUS

### I. The Iranian Plateau

WHAT is generally known as the Iranian Plateau forms the eastern and larger portion of the western half of the great series of uplands which reach across the Asiatic continent from Asia Minor to Mongolia and beyond. It extends from the Armenian highlands and the borders of Mesopotamia in the west to the Suleiman and other ranges along the western side of the lower valley of the Indus, and from the desert lowlands of Western Turkestan and the Caspian Sea southward to the Persian Gulf and the Indian Ocean. Politically the area to-day is divided between Persia, Afghanistan, and Baluchistan. Lying for the most part at an elevation of from three to six thousand feet, it comprises in its central and eastern portion large areas of desert or sub-desert land, and much of the remainder is rugged and mountainous. Only in the west do we find any considerable area of desirable land. There are few rivers, and the majority of these, like the Helmund, flow into closed basins or into saline lakes like Urumia. In the southwest, however, some streams like the Karun, rising on the plateau, break through the border ranges into the Tigris-Euphrates valley, affording thus highways leading from the uplands to the rich lowlands, where already, at the dawn of history, a great civilization flourished.

Concerning the ancient population of the Iranian Plateau, we have no data whatever, and can only reconstruct the conditions on the basis of history and what is known of the surrounding peoples. As the present character of the inhabitants cannot easily be understood without something in the way of a working hypothesis in regard to the earlier period, the following brief outline is suggested.

We may probably assume that the earliest traceable population of the region was of brachycephalic type, probably in the main Alpine, and comparable to that which we are also obliged to assume for the Anatolian plateau farther west. In speech these early peoples were probably non-Indo-European. In the south, along the shores of the Persian Gulf, there was a narrow fringe of dark-skinned, frizzly-haired folk of simple culture, blends perhaps of the Proto-Negroid and Proto-Australoid types, comparable with a large part of the population of southern India to-day. At a period still uncertain, but which must go back toward the beginning of the second millennium B. C., the plateau was invaded from the north by an Indo-European-speaking people, probably in the main a blend of Caspian and Mediterranean types. Some of these turned eastward, and in the course of time made their way down from the plateau into northern India, where they formed part of the ancestors of the modern Hindus. The other portion of these invaders (who brought with them the horse from Central Asia) pushed southwestward into the Tigris-Euphrates valley, and under the name of Kassites conquered Babylonia and ruled it for several hundred years. This movement of Indo-European peoples seems to be the first clearly traceable wave of Caspian-Mediterranean type, others of which, from this time on for some 1,500 years, continued at intervals to invade the western Asiatic uplands, both from the region of the Caspian Sea and from Europe across the Bosphorus. We do not know what became of the Kassites, and after their destruction some may have returned to the plateau, where others of their kin may have lingered. We do, however, know that in the first millennium B. C. we find new immigrants of the same type, settling in the better western portions of the plateau as the Medes and the Persians, who established themselves as the ruling aristocracy among the conquered older population.

The results from the racial point of view of these invasions were, I believe, in the main two. First, as a consequence of the pressure of the invading peoples, some of the older brachycephalic folk were forced out southeastward toward the region of the In-

dus delta and so on down the western coast of the Indian peninsula; others perhaps across to Oman, in southern Arabia, where
they contributed a strong brachycephalic factor to the population.   Second, the remainder of the more original, brachycephalic peoples became gradually blended with their Caspian-
Mediterranean conquerors, whose language almost wholly replaced their own.   The Kassites of the second and the Medes
and Persians of the first millennium B. C. were concentrated, so
far as we know, in the western part of the plateau; the Medes
largely in what are the modern Persian provinces of Kurdistan,
Irak, and Luristan, the Persians farther south, in Ispahan, Fars,
and Arabistan.   Here, at least, the immigrant Caspian-Mediterranean type must have exerted its maximum effect.   In one
other portion of the plateau we might expect that the immigrants
would have produced a lasting modification of the population,
i. e., in the valleys along the southern slopes of the Hindu-Kush,
where the Hindu ancestral stream may well have left some remnants on its eastward journey through Afghanistan.

From the period of the Medo-Persian kingdoms for 2,000
years or so, new immigrants from time to time came to add to
the racial complex of the Iranian Plateau.   Hellenic culture was
spread in the Seleucidian period by colonists and traders from
Greece and Macedonia, bringing probably both Mediterranean-
Caspian and Alpine factors; while later, Parthians and other peoples from Turkestan and vicinity, bringing Caspian and Alpine
elements, exerted some influence in Khorassan and western Afghanistan.   After the beginning of the Christian era, however,
the character of the racial elements brought in underwent a
change, since the Ephthalites, Huns, Turks and Mongols, who
followed one another at intervals of a century or so, were all
primarily brachycephalic, and brought probably a goodly factor
of Palæ-Alpine type, together with something of the Mongoloid.
Only the Arab conquest in the seventh century and the Turkoman could have brought any considerable dolichocephalic elements.   The net result apparently of the period since the Arab
conquest has been, in the first place, the reintroduction of a

considerable brachycephalic element, and, in the second, the crowding of the older population, in some measure, into the less fertile and desirable areas. Unlike the Medo-Persians, these later conquerors did not impose their language upon the conquered.

We may now turn to the present population and see how far it reflects this history. The majority of the available data[1] come from the western mountainous border districts, and from those in the east, in Afghanistan and Baluchistan. For the former section individual measurements are not, as a rule, given, and all that can be done is to note the relative importance of long and round headed factors in the population. Among the Kurds,[2] the so-called Azerbaidjan Tatars,[3] and the Mezgliani, near Teheran,[4] dolichocephalic factors pretty clearly prevail; in the case of the Luris of Luristan, these are in very large majority and are apparently in the main Caspian-Mediterranean. That there are other much more brachycephalic groups in the same region, however, is shown by the fact that the Bakhtiari[5] in the district between Ispahan and Kermanshah are probably strongly brachycephalic, although here the practice of cranial deformation must be taken into consideration. Other groups of more or less undefined "Persians" in this region (Hadjemi, Tadjiks, etc.) show a high proportion of brachycephalic factors, greatly exceeding in this respect the Kurds and other mountaineers. In general most of these peoples are over medium stature, and with few exceptions have black or very dark hair and eyes, although lighter shades of both are occasionally met with among the Azerbaidjan Tatars, in Fars and western Kirman. The western Persian area thus seems to have a rather mixed population, whose basis *apparently* is brachycephalic, with a large element of dolichocephalic Caspian-Mediterranean type, particularly noticeable among the mountain and extreme border people—precisely the region in which the Kassite and Medo-Persian influence must have been strongest.

---

[1] Danilov, 1894; Houssay, 1887.   [2] Nasonov, 1890; Chantre, 1882.
[3] Chantre, 1892.   [4] Danilov, *op. cit.*   [5] Chantre, 1895.

In the vicinity of Susa, in the lowland on the borders of the Mesopotamian plain and southward along the coast in Arabistan and Fars, a rather well-marked Negroid factor is observable. These people are said to be shorter than the average Persian, and to have thick lips and broad noses. The only actual measurements in this whole region which we have, are those of Houssay[1] at Disful. These indicate a preponderance of Caspian Mediterranean factors, and only a small Proto-Negroid or Proto-Australoid element.

For the central portion of the plateau we have little satisfactory information. Houssay[1] reports the population here as prevailingly brachycephalic, this character being increasingly apparent as one goes from south to north. One bit of very significant evidence is afforded by the tiny remnant of the old Persian population known as the Guebres or Ghebres, who still retain much of their old pre-Islamic Zoroastrian faith, and are to be found in parts of Yezd and Kirman. All of the few living Guebres measured[2] and all the adult crania are without exception dolichocephalic, a mixture of Caspian and Mediterranean types. In this fragment of the old Persian people, surviving in their own country, we have apparently, thus, confirmation of the evidence as to their original physical type, which thus accords with that found in the Kurds, Luris, and other mountaineers farther west. This statement may seem to be contradicted by the evidence afforded by the Parsees, a group of Persian people who emigrated to Bombay in the seventh century, who have married only within their own group, and who are primarily but not exclusively brachycephalic. I believe the contradiction is only apparent, and that the large brachycephalic factor among the Parsees is to be explained as due to the fact that they represent not a pure but a mixed group of the Persian population, which by the seventh century was probably strongly influenced by the brachycephalic immigrants who had come in in recent times, and by the absorption of the old, underlying brachycephalic population. The Guebres and Parsees, on this supposition, rep-

[1] Houssay, 1887.　　　　[2] Danilov, 1894.

resent respectively a relatively pure and a much mixed group of the ancient population.

For the extreme northeast we have very limited but very significant data. This relates to the remote little group of the Kaffir, living far up in the most inaccessible portion of the Hindu-Kush range, whither they have been apparently forced from a previous habitat farther south upon the plateau. Speaking a very archaic Indo-European language and still preserving their ancient nature-worship in contrast to the fanatically Mohamme-dan Afghans, they show[1] a large majority of dolichocephalic factors, the Caspian-Mediterranean types being strongly predominant. In them we may see, I believe, some of the rear-guard of the great migratory drift which brought the ancestors of the Hindus into India, who have been forced back, little by little, into the mountain fastnesses which they now hold.

On the eastern border of the Iranian Plateau are two peoples who seem to show marked differences. Of the physical type of the Afghans, who occupy that portion of eastern Afghanistan south of the Hindu-Kush and are but one, although the ruling element, in the welter of peoples which are found in the country, we have little or no knowledge, except of one or two of the extreme border tribes. These Pathans,[2] as they are somewhat loosely called, who with the Afghans proper of Kabul and vicinity speak an Indo-European language, are predominantly Alpine in type, with nearly equal minorities of Caspian-Mediterranean and Palæ-Alpine types. Their kinsmen on the Indian side of the border, near Peshawur,[3] have a much larger element of the former types. Of the Afghans proper we know nothing.

For the Baluchistan region in the southeast we possess, fortunately, more abundant data.[4] Here, in addition to the Baloch, who speak an Indo-European language and have given their name to the country, are found the Brahuis, whose Dravidian speech relates them in some way with the peoples of southern India. There are also some groups supposed to be largely of

[1] Stein, 1921.                    [2] Ethnographic Survey of India, 1908, 1909.
[3] Risley, 1892.                   [4] Ethnographic Survey of India, 1909.

Arab descent. So far as the rather abundant data go, all of these people irrespective of language, are fairly uniform in physical type. All are, like the Pathan farther north, primarily brachycephalic, with the Alpine type in large majority; all show a minority of Caspian-Mediterranean type, comparable to that among the Pathan; but, on the other hand, usually have an equally important or more important Proto-Negroid-Proto-Australoid factor, which the Pathan lack. Some, including the Brahui and Baloch proper, have a considerable factor of the Palæ-Alpine type.

These facts find at least a plausible explanation, if we assume that the original Alpine population of the eastern portion of the Iranian Plateau was less intensively affected than that in the west by the dolichocephalic immigration of the second millennium B. C., which in the east passed on into India rather than settle in the rugged and rather unattractive region of the plateau border; and also that this old and only partially submerged population of brachycephalic type received large reinforcements from the people of similar character from inner Asia, who continually poured into and through this region down to the late Middle Ages.

One further word may be said in regard to the Hazara,[1] a Mongol people living mainly between Ghazni and Kandahar, and extending westward toward Herat. These almost purely brachycephalic folk seem to show their Mongol ancestry in the fact that the platyrrhine types are in large majority, which is in accord with what we find among the true Mongols, among whom the Mongoloid and Palæ-Alpine types are strongly dominant.

## II.  THE ANATOLIAN PLATEAU

The western extremity of the Asiatic plateau belt is formed by the Asia Minor or Anatolian Plateau. Separated from the Iranian Plateau farther eastward by the volcanic region of Armenia, the Anatolian upland terminates in a steep escarpment

[1] *Ethnographic Survey of India*, 1909.

on the north and south, to the Black Sea in the former, and the Mediterranean and the lowlands of Mesopotamia in the latter instance. To the westward, where it reaches out toward Europe and the islands of the Ægean, the edge of the plateau is deeply dissected, and fingers out in a series of peninsulas and deep inlets, to which the short streams descend in tremendous gorges. On the south the Euphrates, rising on the plateau, breaks through the border ranges, affording a highway to Mesopotamia; on the north the Halys similarly has cut a great canyon valley down to the Black Sea. Most of the rest of the upland forms a closed basin, occupied here and there by saline lakes. Lying at an elevation of 2,500–4,000 feet, the plateau is for the most part open grassland, more favorable to pastoral than to agricultural life, and forests are found in general only along the borders. The climate, except along the western and southern coasts, is temperate or even rigorous.

The racial history of this great Asiatic finger, outstretched to and touching the European continent at the Bosphorus and the Hellespont, and associated from the earliest times with the older centres of European civilization, has a rather special interest, yet to this day we know surprisingly little of the physical characteristics of either its ancient or modern inhabitants. For the prehistoric and proto-historic period practically the only data are derived from the few crania found in one of the oldest cities on the site of Troy, together with a few others of the Hellenic period from the same vicinity and a single cranium from an ancient tomb in Lycia. The Trojan crania[1] come from the second or Burned City. The oldest settlement on the site was a small Neolithic village of whose inhabitants no remains have been found. The second stratum represents a much higher culture and belonged to a people familiar with the use of bronze, who erected solidly built dwellings and defended their city by a well-constructed wall. This city, after an existence of unknown duration, was sacked and burned by an invading people, probably about the end of the third millennium B. C. The skeletons of

[1] Virchow, 1882 a.

two warriors, and a woman somewhat doubtfully attributed by
Peake[1] to these invaders, were found in this stratum, and two
female crania, one of which is perhaps of slightly earlier date.
These latter, held to represent the resident population, indicate
a blend of the Alpine and Palæ-Alpine types, whereas those regarded as belonging to the invaders are all three dolichocephalic.
They are, however, badly damaged, so that their type cannot be
determined with certainty, but probably represent a mixture of
Mediterranean and Proto-Australoid types.  In any case they
are of a radically different character from that of the assumed
resident population.  The belief that the people of the Asia
Minor region were at the earliest period of which we know brachycephalic, is apparently corroborated by the single skull from
Lycia,[2] which is clearly Alpine.  Indirect evidence is also perhaps afforded by the Bronze Age crania from Cyprus,[3] which
indicate the Alpine type as predominant there.  Upon such
slight actual evidence and the apparently brachycephalic form
of the heads shown on the Hittite sculptures from Cappadocia
in the heart of the plateau, must be based the conclusion that
the oldest traceable population of this whole region was brachycephalic and a mixture of Alpine and Palæ-Alpine types.  As
will be seen presently, there is much in the way of indirect evidence derived from the modern population, which corroborates
this view.

For the whole period of some 4,000 years between the Bronze
Age crania from Troy and the present day almost the only light
thrown on the racial character of the people of Asia Minor comes
from this same region of the Troad,[4] and dates from the period
between the sixth and second centuries B. C.  At Ophrynum a
small series of crania would indicate that the population at that
time was overwhelmingly brachycephalic, and a mixture of Alpine
and Palæ-Alpine types, the only dolichocephalic factor present
being the Proto-Australoid.  At Hanai Tepe, on the other hand,
the conditions are exactly reversed, in that the dolichocephalic

[1] Peake, 1916.                        [2] von Luschan, 1890.
[3] See ante, p. 256.                   [4] Virchow, 1882 a.

forms, which are mainly Caspian and Proto-Australoid, are in the majority in both male and female series. Farther south near Smyrna, a series of crania[1] supposed, however, to be Greek and dating to the third century B. C., also shows the dominance of dolichocephalic forms, here Caspian and Mediterranean. All that this conflicting evidence will enable us to say seems to be that the probably older brachycephalic peoples had been able to hold their own over a period of some 1,500 years, and that they and the invading dolichocephalic peoples still kept more or less to themselves, each people having its own settlements.

While as yet unconfirmed by any direct cranial evidence, we know from historical and archæological sources that settlements of people, probably in the main of Mediterranean and Caspian types, had been formed all along the Ægean and Mediterranean shores of Asia Minor, at least as early as the middle of the second millennium B. C., spreading Minoan and Mycenæan culture and ultimately Greek speech along the narrow coastal strip, although they penetrated but rarely, it would seem, into the upland. About the beginning of the first millennium B. C. the Phrygians, who probably like the Thracians were of mixed Caspian and Alpine types, swarmed across the Hellespont and advanced to the heart of Anatolia, establishing there for a time a considerable power and ruling as an aristocracy over the earlier inhabitants. In the eighth and seventh centuries B. C. the Kimmerians and Scythians invaded the plateau from the opposite or northeastern corner, coming from the region of the Caspian. Although doubtless much mixed in physical characteristics, these nomad, horse-riding warriors almost certainly brought a further considerable Caspian element. Farther eastward toward Armenia, a much earlier invasion, probably of Indo-European-speaking folk related to the Kassites, had established the kingdom of Mitanni, and perhaps contributed further to the northern long-headed factors which were penetrating the upland. No further invasions of anthropological significance seem to have occurred after that of the Scythians, until in the third century A. D. some

---

[1] Zaborowsky, 1881.

Gallic tribes crossed the Hellespont, as the Phrygians had done long before, and established themselves on the plateau. Of far greater importance, however, were the invasions of the Turks in the eleventh and the Mongols in the thirteenth centuries. Of the two, the Turkish invasion was probably of greater significance, although the numbers of the Turks were small relative to the older occupants; and, although they imposed their language on most of the population, their actual influence on the racial character of the people was much smaller than is generally supposed. Unlike the earlier invaders, both Turk and Mongol were primarily brachycephalic, the former of Alpine and Palæ-Alpine type, the latter with a strong element of the Mongoloid. In brief, to sum up the known movements of peoples during a period of some 3,000 years, we find that the earlier immigrants brought into the Anatolian plateau in the main dolichocephalic, Caspian factors, and that these entered both at the northwest and northeast, whereas the later immigrants came in primarily from the east and northeast, and served to reinforce the older, brachycephalic types.

The modern population of the Anatolian Plateau comprises four main groups: (1) The Turkish-speaking, Mohammedan, sedentary and nomadic peoples who make up the bulk of the inhabitants, and occupy the larger part of the plateau; (2) the Christian Armenians, speaking a language mainly of Indo-European origin, and, although now widely scattered and nearly exterminated, formerly occupying the eastern and northeastern region of rugged mountain land which divides the Anatolian from the Iranian Plateau; (3) the Kurds, a turbulent mountain people, Mohammedan in religion, speaking a dialect of Persian, and mainly settled in the southeast, extending across the border into Persia; and (4) the Greeks, living for the most part along the Ægean coast and at some points on the southern shore of the Black Sea.

The first and largest of these groups,[1] although Turkish in

---

[1] Chantre, 1895 a; Eliseev, 1891; von Luschan, 1911; Pittard, 1911; Weisbach, 1873; Hauschild, 1921.

speech, almost certainly includes only a relatively small factor directly attributable to the Turkish immigrants of the eleventh and twelfth centuries. In the main they are the representatives to-day of the ancient population of the upland. They are in general of somewhat more than medium stature, with dark eyes and hair, although in the central parts of the plateau the proportion of light eyes and hair sometimes runs as high as 40 per cent. Since this tendency to blondness seems less marked in the margins and more remote parts of the region, among such groups as the Takhtadjy, Bektash, Aisori,[1] Kizilbash, etc., it seems not unreasonable to ascribe its presence to the influence of the northern invaders and settlers of Caspian type, such as the Phrygians, Kimmerians, and Scythians, although some recent data suggest that the blond element may have been brachycephalic.[2] In head-form this group shows a strong predominance of brachycephalic factors, but in the absence of any individual measurements it is not possible to determine the types present, although indirect evidence would suggest that the Alpine was probably in the ascendant. It should be pointed out here that among the Takhtadjy[3] and other marginal groups the height of the skull is unusually great, and the back of the head commonly greatly flattened, suggesting the practice of artificial deformation. This so-called "Armenoid" form of skull will be discussed more at length in treating of the next group. The small dolichocephalic factor present among the people of this Turkish group is primarily Caspian. Eliseev[4] has presented evidence showing a large increase in the proportion of brachycephalic elements among the urban as compared with the peasant population, and in the latter as compared with the Turkish-speaking nomads. This point is, I believe, of much significance, for it seems justifiable to conclude that it is among these latter more dolichocephalic nomads that we must look for the descendants of the dolichocephalic immigrants, the sedentary agricultural and urban people more truly representing the older population, into which the conquering Turks of the eleventh century have been absorbed.

[1] Arutinov, 1908.   [2] Hauschild, 1921.   [3] von Luschan, 1911.   [4] Eliseev, 1891.

Turning next to the Armenians,[1] a people once widely spread but now all but destroyed, it appears that they exhibit a very striking similarity to the marginal portions of the previous group, which supposedly most truly represent the ancient, pre-Turkish population. Their stature averages, according to different observers, between 166 and 168 cm., and thus accords closely with that of the Turkish-speaking group. Prevailingly brunet in eye and hair color, they show, especially toward the north and northeast, a small percentage of blonds, and in the Trans-Caucasus a rather striking frequency of reddish hair. In head-form they are prevailingly brachycephalic, standing in this respect between the urban and the peasant sections of the Turkish-speaking group. The Alpine type is strongly in the majority. There is, however, a dolichocephalic factor of some strength, nearly evenly divided between the Caspian and Mediterranean types. As in the case of the marginal sections of the Turkish-speaking group, the Armenian skull is extremely high and shows strong occipital flattening. Another feature characteristic of the Armenians which must be noted is the prevalence among them of what is commonly spoken of as the "Jewish" or "Semitic" nose. This is, as previously noted, also found in considerable frequency among the marginal sections of the Turkish-speaking group, although not among the more purely Turkish population itself; its prevalence thus among the pre-Turkish portion of the inhabitants seems clear, and that it was strikingly characteristic of the ancient Hittites is clearly shown by their sculptures. The significance of the fact that this type of nose, remarkable for its "nostrility," is apparently in no way really "Semitic," and the explanation of the way in which it has come to be regarded as characteristic of the Jew has been discussed in the chapter devoted to that people. How far the dolichocephalic factors in the Armenian population may safely be attributed to the influence of the Scythian, Kimmerian, and other early invaders, is hard to say, but it seems almost certain that relatively modern intermixture with the Kurds is partly responsible. A portrait of a typical Armenian is given on Plate XXI, Fig. 1.

[1] Chantre, 1892; Erikson, 1907; Giuffrida-Ruggeri, 1908.

The Greek-speaking population of the coastal region presents an interesting and partially analogous case. In the Kerasunde district[1] on the Black Sea shore, on the basis of measurements on the living, the Greeks appear to be a strikingly pure example of the Alpine type, with less than half the proportion of blonds found among the Armenians, and less than a quarter of that reported for the Turkish-speaking groups in the central part of the plateau. For the Ægean coast[2] the data are primarily derived from modern crania, and indicate the clear preponderance of the Alpine type, although associated with considerable minorities of Palæ-Alpine, Caspian, and Mediterranean types. On the southern coast von Luschan's[3] material from Lycia shows that the relative importance of brachycephalic and dolichocephalic factors varies sharply from place to place; some towns such as Makri, Myra, Adalia, and Levissi being strongly brachycephalic, whereas Limyra, Rhodos, etc., are almost as strongly dolichocephalic. Here, in contrast with the Ægean shore, the latter element is apparently more strongly Mediterranean. From all these facts we may draw the conclusion that the Greek-speaking population of the Asia Minor coast is in the main of the same stratum of mingled Alpine and Palæ-Alpine as the mass of the occupants of the plateau, and represents the old original brachycephalic peoples, Hellenized in speech and more or less in culture. The dolichocephalic factor, on the other hand, is probably attributable in part to very early colonists and invaders, in the south more purely Mediterranean, from the Ægean islands and Crete, in the north more strongly Caspian and derived from the invaders coming across the Hellespont and the Bosphorus; and in part to later Greek immigrants themselves.

The last important group of the modern peoples of the Anatolian Plateau is that formed by the Kurds. This group presents a strong contrast with the previous ones, and raises a number of puzzling problems. We are met at the outset by a certain contradiction in the data. Chantre,[4] who measured over

---

[1] Neophytos, 1890.  
[3] von Luschan, 1890; Petersen, 1889.  
[2] Weisbach, 1882.  
[4] Chantre, 1892, 1895 a.

300 from various parts of Asia Minor and northern Syria, describes them as being prevailingly dark in hair and eye color, stating that there are practically no light eyes, and that only in about a third of the individuals observed was the hair even as light as "dark brown." On the other hand, von Luschan,[1] who studied some 200, describes them as an essentially blond people, with prevailingly fair hair and blue eyes! These two observers (who have furnished the majority of the available data) are furthermore not in accord in regard to the head-form, for, whereas von Luschan declares that the western Kurds are dolichocephalic, Chantre finds that 60 per cent of his subjects had mesocephalic or brachycephalic indices. The only check lies in the small series measured by Nasonov[2] in Erivan, who in general corroborates the results obtained by Chantre.

Such striking disagreement between competent observers can be explained only in one way, i. e., that the name "Kurd" is applied to people of very diverse origin, just as is "Greek" along the coast, and that the Kurds of different sections of the Anatolian area are physically very different. It is possible, also, that the great differences noted may be in part due, so far as regards head-form, to the practice of artificial cranial deformation among some of the Kurds. Unfortunately von Luschan does not give any individual measurements, so that no analysis of his material is possible. Chantre does, however, give individual data for some forty Kurds who showed, in his opinion, no trace of any deformation. If this material be analyzed, it appears that dolichocephalic types are in moderate majority, the brachycephalic elements, however, amounting to nearly 40 per cent. Of the former types the leptorrhine, probably Caspian, factors take first place, while of the latter the Alpine is probably the most important. If Chantre's data be grouped geographically, rather interesting results appear. The Kurds of Armenia and the Trans-Caucasus have, in spite of some slight deformation, a very large proportion of dolichocephalic factors, ranging as high as 80 per cent in some groups. In the vicinity of Kharput on

---

[1] von Luschan, 1911.  [2] Nasonov, 1890.

the plateau in Kurdistan, the figure drops to less than 45 per cent, while the Kurds of northern Syria and Mesopotamia are very strongly brachycephalic, with a dolichocephalic factor of less than 20 per cent. This essentially round-headed character of the southern Kurds is corroborated by the few crania which we possess from here.

It seems that the most probable inference to be drawn from the foregoing facts is that in the Kurds we have a mixed folk who, on the plateau and in Armenia are made up largely of dolichocephalic, in the main Caspian factors, whereas those south of the Taurus range are even more uniformly of brachycephalic, primarily Alpine type. A strong tendency toward blondness appears to characterize the Kurds of the plateau proper, although traces appear both in the north and south. Since the dolichocephalic factors increase rapidly as we pass from south and southwest toward the north and northeast, it would seem justifiable to regard this as an immigrant element, coming from the northeast into an area predominantly brachycephalic. It will be remembered that from historical sources we know of the invasion of the plateau region from just this direction, by the Kimmerian and Scythian nomads in the eighth and seventh centuries B. C., and apparently by others at a still earlier date. It seems, therefore, not altogether impossible that we may regard the Kurds as in considerable measure the descendants of some of these wild, warlike invaders of the first millennium B. C., whose original characteristics have become progressively attenuated through mixture with the older population, the farther they advanced toward the west and south. Peake[1] suggests an even more ancient source for this long-headed element, in the invaders who toward the end of the third millennium B. C. came into Asia Minor across the Hellespont, and whose traces seem to be found, as already noted, in the ruins of the second or Burnt City on the site of Troy. An example of the Kurdish type is given on Plate XXI, Fig. 2.

[1] Peake, 1915.

## III. The Caucasus

The region of the Caucasus may be most conveniently discussed in connection with the western plateaus, of which it forms, as it were, an outlier, and with whose history its own has been closely allied.

The boundary-line between the European continent and Asia is, for the most part, not marked by strong physiographic features, since the Ural Mountains are, throughout their southern portion, a rather insignificant range. In the Caucasus, however, we have a veritable wall, which, running from the Caspian to the Sea of Azov, marks the continental limits with great distinctness. This striking boundary region presents a number of very interesting features in its racial history, and with it is intimately bound up the so-called Trans-Caucasus, the broad trough running almost without interruption from the Caspian to the Black Sea, between the Caucasus and the northern edge of the western plateaus, and formed by the valleys of the Rion and the Kura. The Caucasus itself is, as just stated, a gigantic mountain wall, separating this broad trough from the steppes of southern Russia, and is pierced by only a single pass of low altitude, the famous Pass of Dariel. Except by this narrow gap and by the equally narrow passage around the eastern end of the range where it comes down to the Caspian, there is no easily traversable route between Europe and Asia. The southern border of the Trans-Caucasus is also steep and rugged, and only by way of the valley of the Araxes is there an easy approach to the highlands of Armenia and western Persia.

The earliest data on the physical types of the peoples of the Caucasus region are derived from the Early Iron or Late Bronze Age sites in the valleys of the Koban and Terek, on the northern slopes of the range.[1] Owing to the wide-spread custom of cranial deformation, practised in early as well as modern times, the material is very difficult to interpret with any certainty. It would seem to be shown, however, that on the whole of the north-

---

[1] Bogdanov, 1882; Smirnov, 1877; Virchow, 1890 b.

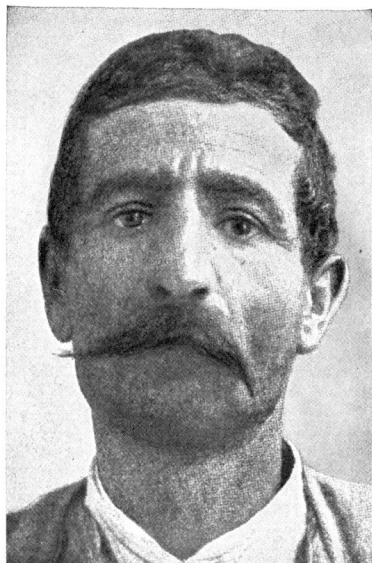

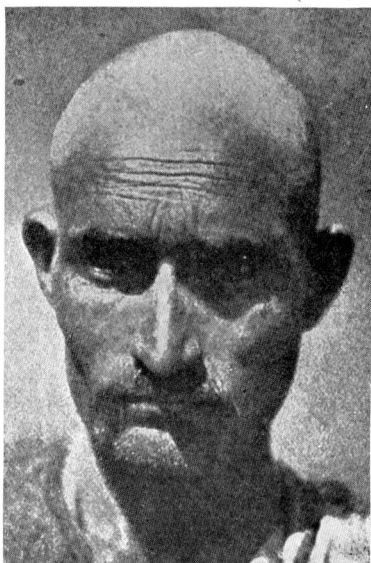

Fig. 1. Armenian.

Fig. 2. Kurd.

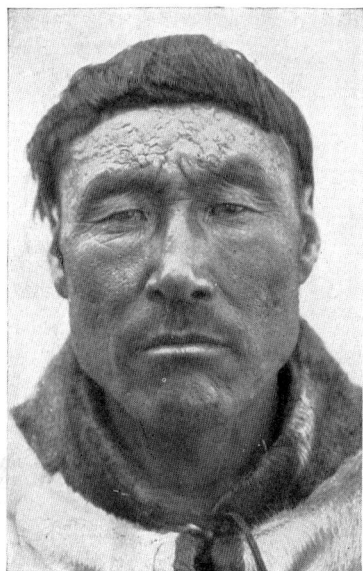

Fig. 3. Koryak.

Fig. 4. Yakut.

PLATE XXI.

ern slope of the Caucasus there was at this period a strong contrast between the male and female population. The former were predominantly tall and dolichocephalic, the Caspian type being in large majority, whereas the latter were short and primarily brachycephalic, the Alpine factors largely outnumbering the Palæ-Alpine.

We may probably interpret these facts as indicating that the early population of the Caucasus was one primarily of Alpine type and thus allied to that of the western plateaus, but that, as early as the beginning of the use of iron, northern peoples, primarily of Caspian type, were pressing against the mountain barrier and already beginning to pass either across it, or around it to the east by the Iron Gates of Derbend, in order to reach (probably by way of the valley of the Araxes) the upland of western Persia.

We have no materials as yet for the long period between these early sites and modern times, and must therefore turn to the living peoples of the region. The modern peoples of the Caucasus region present from the linguistic point of view a striking degree of complexity, for within the limits of this area probably more than two score different languages and dialects are spoken. Apart from this linguistic diversity, the region is noteworthy because, excluding the Turko-Tatar languages spoken by tribes of relatively recent settlement, and that spoken by the Ossetes in the territory adjacent to the Pass of Dariel, the languages of this region stand isolated and unrelated to any other linguistic family. Of the five main groups into which the population is divided on linguistic grounds, three—the Lesghian, Chechen, and Circassian—are found mainly on the northern side of the range; one, the Georgian, is on the southern side and occupies much of the Trans-Caucasian trough, especially its western portion; while the fifth, the Ossetian is found both on the north and the south of the range at either end of the Pass of Dariel. The Turko-Tatar peoples are mainly in the lower Kura valley and along the Caspian.

Although linguistically the people of the Caucasus region are

very diverse, in physical type[1] they show considerable uniformity, but the custom of cranial deformation being widely
spread, all conclusions are more or less uncertain.   The Lesghian[2]
and Chechen groups on the north of the range are very similar.
Both are overwhelmingly brachycephalic, the Alpine type alone
amounting in general to from 80 to 90 per cent.   Among the
Lesghians, for whom we have the more detailed material, some
groups or tribes, such as the Rutuli, Dido, etc., reveal a considerable Palæ-Alpine element, the latter tribe, furthermore, showing a respectable minority of the Caspian type.   The Circas-
sians[3] farther west, are much less uniform, for, although still by a
large majority brachycephalic (Alpine), there is a considerable
Caspian factor present.   The Georgians,[4] also, although prevailingly Alpine, show quite a little variation, the Kachetians and
Georgians of Guria being very strongly brachycephalic, whereas
the Mingrelians along the Black Sea coast show as much as 30
per cent of the Caspian type.   The Ossetes,[5] finally, although
retaining a bare majority of brachycephalic factors, have a Caspian element of over 40 per cent.

The Caucasus area thus, so far as what may be called its
more aboriginal population is concerned, is in general dominated
by the Alpine type.   To this the Ossetes form the clearest exception, since in them the Caspian element is almost as strong
as the Alpine.   Their history and geographical position appear
to explain this divergence.   As already stated, the language of
the Ossetes is not, like that of the other peoples of the Caucasus,
an isolated one, but is Indo-European, its closest relations being
thought to lie with the old Persian and thus also related to the
speech used by at least part of the Scythians, who in the early
part of the first millennium swarmed in the steppe regions of
southern Russia, and in the seventh century B. C. poured across

[1] For general works, see Chantre, 1885–87; Erckert, 1889–90; Pantyukov, 1893.
[2] See, in addition to general works, Arutinov, 1905; Kurdov, 1901.
[3] See, in addition to general works, Malinin, 1905; Virubov, 1890.
[4] See, in addition to general works, Djavakov, 1908; Erikson, 1905; Veniaminov,
1890.
[5] See, in addition to general works, Ivanovski, 1891 b.

Armenia and the Anatolian Plateau. It is probable that a large part of these invaders found their way across the Caucasus by the Pass of Dariel, and the significance of the location of the Ossetes thus becomes apparent, since they are, with one exception, the only one of the peoples of the Caucasus living on both sides of the range, where they are to be found at either end of this pass. On this hypothesis the Ossetes are the modern and much-mixed descendants of some of the Scythian or other northern hordes, who remained in the vicinity of the strategic route across the range. The Caspian element among the Mingrelians along the Black Sea coast is probably (?) to be attributed to early Greek or other maritime colonies along this shore.

The Turko-Tatar speaking peoples of the Caucasus and Trans-Caucasus are in part relatively recent immigrants, dating to the fourteenth century only or even later. On the northern slopes of the range they occupy a small area along the Caspian; on the south they dominate the eastern portion of the Kura valley, especially the swampy region of the lower river and the Araxes, and southward to the Persian frontier. Although all speak closely related languages belonging to the Turko-Tatar branch of the Ural-Altaic stock, they present sharp variations physically. Those on the north[1] resemble the Nogai Tatars and Kirgiz farther north toward the lower Volga. Somewhat over the medium stature, with dark eyes and dark, straight hair, they show a very large majority of brachycephalic factors, primarily Alpine in type, with only a small minority of the Caspian type. Those on the south of the Caucasus are much more variable, but on the whole are quite different. The Azerbaidjan Tatars,[2] as the more southerly groups are called, are taller and more purely brunet than those on the north side of the range, and show a majority of dolichocephalic factors, of which the Caspian is the chief, the Alpine type occupying second place. Essentially they are the same as the group of the same name across the border in Persia, and both these groups of Azerbaidjan Tatars may prob-

[1] See, in addition to general works, Shchukin, 1913.
[2] Kurdov, 1912 b; Chantre, 1892 a.

ably be regarded as remnants of the ancient Indo-European speaking Iranians (Persians and Medes), who have been completely "Tatarized" in speech but only partly in physical type.

Possibly very closely related to these Azerbaidjan Tatars are the Tats or Tadjiks, speaking a Persian dialect, who occupy the Caspian shore of Daghestan on the northern side of the Caucasus, as well as on the south side between the foot-hills and the lower Kura.[1] Although among them the brachycephalic elements (Alpine and Palæ-Alpine) are in the majority, the Caspian type is the largest single factor (45 per cent). Chantre believed them to be Persian immigrants who came to their present habitat about the fourth century, but the parallel which they present to the Ossetes is certainly striking. For, like them, they speak an Indo-European language, and are found on both sides of the range, in this case where the alternative route to that of Dariel leads from Europe into Asia. It is therefore perhaps not impossible that they too may be in large part remnants of one of the early migrations of the northern longheads, who have been somewhat "Tatarized" in their physical characteristics, while preserving, as did the Ossetes, their Iranian speech.

[1] See, in addition to general works, Kurdov, 1908, 1913.

# CHAPTER V

## THE NORTHERN LOWLANDS

### I. Western Turkestan and the Siberian Steppes

The lowland which lies to the northward of the great plateau belt divides itself naturally into two sharply contrasted portions, a western, largely arid and desert but comprising considerable areas of fertile steppe, and a northern and eastern, which is forested; the former has a climate of great extremes, the latter in its northern and eastern portions is typically Arctic.

The first of these subdivisions includes Western Turkestan and the steppes of southwestern Siberia. On the south it is limited by the escarpment of the Iranian Plateau and the high ranges of the Hindu-Kush; on the north by the border of the forest which lies, roughly, along the fifty-fifth parallel; on the east by the Pamirs and the Tian-shan and Altai ranges along the margin of the eastern plateaus. To the west its limits are vague, for, although the Caspian forms a clear boundary in the south and the Ural chain a less well-marked frontier in the north, there is a wide stretch north of the Caspian where the steppes of Asia and those of southeastern Russia merge into one another without a break. While the northern portion of the area may be described as sub-arid, the larger part of Western Turkestan is strongly arid and desert, and only along the courses of its two great rivers, the Amu-Daria and Syr-Daria (the classical Oxus and Jaxartes), especially in their upper courses, is any considerable area of irrigable, agricultural land found.

Of the ancient population of this whole region we have as yet but little knowledge, but that little is significant. The Siberian steppes and the bordering valleys of the Altai contain thousands of kurgans or burial-mounds. Unfortunately the scientific investigation of these has suffered from the fact that the great major-

ity have been rifled in the search for treasure, and but few of the
crania from those which have been carefully investigated have
been adequately described. The age of the mounds varies, some
being of the Bronze period, others (and the majority apparently)
are of the Later Iron Age. Only for a few crania from mounds
along the northern border of our area, from the vicinity of To-
bolsk[1] and Tomsk,[2] have any individual measurements been published. These show that the peoples of these two districts were
in the Iron Age quite different, for, whereas in the first case dolichocephalic factors were in large majority, the Caspian type
occupying first place, in the second the few crania indicate an
overwhelming preponderance of brachycephalic factors, the Mongoloid and Palæ-Alpine types being most important. A large
series of crania from Late Bronze Age sites in the Minusinsk
region of the upper Yenesei, at the extreme southeastern border
of the area under discussion, have been studied by Goroshchenko.[3]
Analysis of his material shows that the male crania comprise
a majority of dolichocephalic factors, in the main of Mediterranean-Caspian types, with the Alpine and Palæ-Alpine secondary. The females, although also primarily of the same dolichocephalic forms, show a much larger proportion of the Alpine
type. It seems clear thus that the dominant elements in this
southeastern margin of the Siberian steppes in the Bronze Age
were of Caspian-Mediterranean types, although the Later Iron
Age crania are apparently, like those from the vicinity of Tomsk,
primarily brachycephalic.

Until more data are available for the whole of the steppe
region only most tentative conclusions may be drawn in regard
to the racial history of this northern portion of the area under
discussion, but, taking into consideration such historical facts as
we possess, the cultural data derived from the investigation of
the Bronze and Iron Age sites, and the character of the adjacent
population, I believe it is safe to assume that the population of
this steppe and mountain border region in the Bronze Age and
earlier was primarily dolichocephalic, the Caspian type being in

[1] Bogdanov, 1878–79 a.      [2] Zaborowski, 1898.      [3] Goroshchenko, 1900.

large majority, followed by a secondary factor of the Alpine. With the Iron Age the region was invaded and gradually overrun by peoples of totally different, almost purely brachycephalic character, the Palæ-Alpine and Mongoloid types being in large majority. These newcomers were nomad, horse-using folk, in all probability Turko-Tatar peoples, allied to the Hiungnu of the Mongolian plateau, and probably invaded the steppes by way of Dzungaria, the first of a series of similar invasions by related groups in later times.

For Western Turkestan the data are much more scanty. Ivanovski[1] has described a few crania dating, it is supposed, from the first or second century B. C., from the region near Issik Kul in the western Tian-shan, which are primarily brachycephalic. The only other material known to me is that obtained in the excavations at Anau,[2] near Merv on the extreme southwestern border. This is, however, so incomplete that no certain conclusions can be derived from it except that it is probable that dolichocephalic factors, if not dominant, were at least equal in importance with brachycephalic. The age of these fragments, which come from the upper layers of the older culture, has been variously estimated, but a conservative computation would place them in the second or perhaps the third millennium B. C. Here again, in the complete absence of adequate archæological material, we are forced to utilize indirect evidence, but, taking everything into consideration, I believe the most probable hypothesis in regard to the ancient population of Turkestan in the late Neolithic or Bronze Age is that it was, like that in the Siberian steppes farther north, primarily dolichocephalic, the Caspian type being in the majority, with a strong element of the Mediterranean. This ancient population was one practising agriculture in the irrigated lands about the border of the desert, yet partly pastoral as well. At some time in the first millennium B. C. this region, as we know, began to be invaded by the first waves of the Turkish-speaking brachycephalic and primarily Palæ-Alpine peoples from the eastern plateaus, who from then on in

[1] Ivanovski, 1890.  [2] Pumpelly, 1905; Sergi, 1907 c.

ever-increasing multitudes poured through Dzungaria and over-whelmed the older population, of which but scant remnants survive to-day. From this region at an earlier period the Kassites, Medes, and Persians had gone forth southwestward into Persia and Mesopotamia and the ancestors of the Hindus southeastward into India, and it is perhaps not impossible that these great emigrations of Caspian-Mediterranean peoples may even have been initiated by the pressure of the Turko-Tatar hordes long antedating their first recorded movements.

The modern population of Western Turkestan and the Siberian steppes may be divided into two groups, one of pastoral nomads, the other of sedentary agricultural folk. Except along the extreme southeastern border where Indo-European speech prevails, all the peoples of this region speak languages belonging to the Turko-Tatar group. To the nomad section belong the Kirgiz[1] or Kirgiz Kazak of the Siberian steppes, the Kara Kirgiz of the Tian-shan, and most of the various "Tatar" fragments of the Altai borderland; the sedentary group includes the Dungans[2] of the vicinity of Kuldja, the Uzbegs and Sarts of Samarcand, Bokhara, Khiva, Ferghana, Tashkent, and other irrigated areas of the lowlands,[3] and the peoples of the upper Oxus region, which includes the Galchas[4] and other Indo-European-speaking fragments on the Pamirs. The Turkoman[5] of the southwestern border fall rather between the two groups, being semi-nomadic.

Except for some of the Kirgiz, whose average stature ranges between 163 and 165 cm., all the people of the region are somewhat above medium height, the two tallest groups being the Sarts (average 169 cm.) and the Tekke Turkomans (average 170 cm.). In skin color they are somewhat variable, ranging from a yellowish or light-brown tint to a white-rosy complexion, hardly distinguishable from that of a European. The straight or wavy hair is usually dark, as are the eyes, although blondish hair and

[1] Ivanovski, 1903; Kharuzin, 1889; Mochi, 1905 b; Topinard, 1887.
[2] Gorbachev, 1886–87; Ujfalvy, 1879.
[3] Blagovieschenski, 1912; Bogdanov, 1886–87 c, 1888.
[4] Bogdanov, 1886–87 d; Ujfalvy, 1896.
[5] Ivanovski, 1891 a; Yavorski, 1897.

blue-gray eyes are quite abundant among the Galchas. In head-form all, with the exception of the Turkomans, show a strong majority of brachycephalic factors, although since cranial deformation is in use to a considerable extent, this statement must be made with reserve. The analysis of the available data seems to show significant differences between the different sections of the population. Thus, in the Galcha and the peoples of Badakshan,[1] on the upper Oxus, the Alpine type is in overwhelming majority, and there is but little trace of any dolichocephalic factors; among the Uzbeg, on the other hand, the Palæ-Alpine is dominant, although there is a strong secondary factor of the Alpine, and a not insignificant minority of dolichocephalic, probably Caspian elements, which increase notably in importance among the Tadjik and the Dungan. The Kirgiz again are in very large majority brachycephalic, with the Alpine apparently dominant, but comprising, in addition to the Palæ-Alpine, a considerable factor of the Ural type, which seems to be totally absent in the south. It may further be noted that the Uzbeg have a small proportion of the Mongoloid type, absent among the upper Oxus peoples, which points, as we might expect from what is known of their historical origin, to the absorption of a small number of Mongols.

To all these groups the Turkomans stand opposed, in that among them dolichocephalic factors are in the majority, the Caspian-Mediterranean types forming nearly 75 per cent of the total. Geographically the position of this dolichocephalic group on the plains at the base of the northern edge of the Iranian plateau is significant, as the Turkomans thus duplicate on the eastern side of the Caspian Sea the dolichocephalic Azerbaidjan Tatars on the west. Like the latter, the Turkomans have a somewhat obscure history, and have always kept more or less apart from their neighbors. They share, moreover, as has been stated, in the type of life of both the sedentary and nomadic peoples. There are thus grounds for believing that in the Turkomans we have (as in the Azerbaidjan Tatars) a partly "Turko-Tatarized"

[1] Stein, 1921.

remnant of the ancient Indo-European-speaking people of Caspian-Mediterranean type, who in very early times occupied the whole of Western Turkestan, and who here have preserved their physical characteristics in large measure intact, but have lost their original language.  Much fainter traces of this ancient dolichocephalic stratum survive among the Tadjik and the Dungan.

The Galcha and other strongly Alpine peoples of the mountain border in the southeast present, I believe, a case which is exactly the reverse, for they are to be regarded as remnants of the ancient Alpine type of people who in Neolithic and early Bronze times occupied the western plateaus, and who at a very early period were "Aryanized" in speech through their close contact with the population of the adjacent lowland, but have preserved their original physical type with but little change.  It seems to me also probable that in the Chitrali[1] and Mastuji,[1] on the southern side of the Hindu-Kush, and in the Indo-European-speaking peoples of the Pamir[1] that we have still other remnants of this ancient Alpine folk.

## II.  THE SIBERIAN FOREST LAND

The immense forested area of northern Asia comprises two very different types of country.  That portion lying west of the Yenesei River toward the Urals, and north of the fifty-fifth parallel to the Arctic coast, is a vast, featureless, swampy plain, where the forest dwindles northward into the Arctic tundra. East of the Yenesei, on the other hand, we have a series of low, much-dissected plateaus, rising in elevation eastward until they merge into the confused, deeply eroded, and higher uplands which form the northeastern termination of the great plateau belt which stretches across the whole continent.  In their climatic features both these areas are much alike, for in both conditions are severe, and throughout the whole northern portion typically Arctic.  Nowhere within this whole region are the conditions favorable for agriculture or for horse-using, pastoral nomads,

[1] Stein, 1921.

and, like the northwestern portions of the American continent, it is primarily adapted for a hunting and fishing population.

Of the ancient population of this whole area we know nothing except along its extreme southern border, where the Bronze Age crania of the upper Yenesei in the vicinity of Minusinsk (already discussed in the previous section[1]) give evidence that at that period the border country at least was occupied by a predominantly dolichocephalic population, who in this favored location were agricultural and skilled workers in copper and bronze. We must, therefore, for the entire area depend upon indirect evidence in attempting to reconstruct the early racial history. Before suggesting an outline of this, however, we may first discuss the modern population.

This may conveniently be divided, primarily on a linguistic basis, into two groups, which have been called the Palæo-Siberian and Neo-Siberian. The first occupies, or in recent historical times did occupy, the northeast corner of the continent, from about the Lena River north of the sixtieth parallel east to Bering Strait, and from the northern shores of the Okhotsk Sea to the Arctic, including the peninsula of Kamchatka. In it are included the various peoples, living or recently extinct, known as the Chuckchi, Koryak, Kamchadal, Yukaghir, Chuvantzy, etc. The Neo-Siberian group comprises all the rest, and is divisible on linguistic grounds again into four sections, (1) the Tunguses, whose habitat lies mainly in the east and southeast, as far as the Amur (and beyond among the Manchus, etc.), but who have extended westward to the Yenesei within traditional times; (2) the Turko-Tatar tribes, of whom the most numerous and important is the Yakut, who in relatively recent times have spread from the southern borders northward and northeastward throughout most of the basin of the Lena and the eastern tributaries of the middle and lower Yenesei; (3) the Finno-Ugrian Ostiaks and Voguls, in the swampy forest region between the lower Obi and Yenesei; and (4) the Samoyedes, who stretch along the Arctic coast from far to the west in northern Russia, eastward to the

[1] See ante, p. 328.

Taimyr Peninsula, beyond the mouth of the Yenesei.   In addition there are several small fragments, now nearly or quite extinct, in the northern Altai region; the so-called Ostiaks of the Yenesei, in regard to whose affiliations there is much uncertainty; and on the Bering Strait coast at East Cape a small group of Eskimo.

The Palæo-Siberian tribes are, as the name given to them implies, generally regarded as the survival of an older fundamental stratum of population once occupying much larger territories, repressed into the northeast corner of the continent by the expansion of the Neo-Siberian peoples farther south and west. From the linguistic point of view, these tribes are sharply differentiated from all the others.   Not only do their languages have no relation with any others in the Asiatic continent, but they show, not in vocabulary but in grammatical structure, many striking similarities to languages in the northwestern portion of America.   This relationship in language is further paralleled by obvious similarities in culture, similarities so striking that the conclusion cannot be escaped that a relationship of some sort exists between these Palæo-Siberian peoples of Asia and the Indian tribes of the northwest coast of America.[1]   To the significance of this we shall revert in the final chapter.   In view of the great importance of this group in the racial history not only of this area but of that of the whole continent and of America as well, it is extremely unfortunate that we as yet have little or no cranial material for any of these people, and that no individual measurements and, indeed, very little in the way of any measurements have yet been published.   The summary of data collected by Jochelson-Brodsky[2] gives us practically all that is known.   From this it appears that the Chuckchi and Asiatic Eskimo are slightly taller (average 162 cm.) than the Koryak, Kamchadal (average below 160 cm.), and Yukaghir, although all are below medium stature.   The latter thus are comparable with the Tunguse, farther south, and also with the Ostiak.   In head-form the Chuckchi, northern Koryak, and Yukaghir all show a

---

[1] Boas, 1905.                        [2] Jochelson–Brodsky, 1906.

predominance of brachycephalic factors, these being stronger among the Chuckchi than among the others. The Kamchadal and southern Koryak, on the other hand, appear (?) to have a predominance of dolichocephalic elements, and in this respect are affiliated with the Tunguse. No nasal measurements being given, it is impossible to determine anything in regard to the types present. The crania collected by Gondatti, and published[1] as Chuckchi, unfortunately give little help in the matter, since the majority are probably Eskimo. The smaller series, however, are probably Chuckchi, but unfortunately are all of such equivocal forms (see p. 18) that identification of types is almost wholly a matter of personal judgment. All that it is safe to say, I believe, is that the brachycephalic factors, which are in large majority, are probably in the main Alpine and Palæ-Alpine, while the dolichocephalic minority is probably of the Caspian type. Further light is thrown on this problem by the measurements of the living, taken by Kroeber.[2] The males show a strong majority of leptorrhine, brachycephalic forms, with the platyrrhine, dolichocephalic factors secondary; the females, on the other hand, have the platyrrhine, brachycephalic forms in the large majority, the platyrrhine, dolichocephalic factors again being secondary. All of which suggests that we seem to have in this northeastern corner of the continent a population which is more purely brachycephalic than that found in the isolation of the Kamchatkan peninsula, as if in the latter had been caught the last remnants of an earlier, more dolichocephalic population, primarily of the Proto-Australoid and Proto-Negroid types, of which considerable traces still exist among the Chuckchi. A portrait showing a Koryak type is given on Plate XXI, Fig. 3.

The Tunguse tribes proper, on the basis of very meagre data,[3] seem to be very variable in their physical characteristics. In the north, in the Gizhiga, Kolyma, and Anadyrsk districts, they are short (average 154–158 cm.), whereas in the plateau region east of Lake Baikal they are considerably taller, although still

---

[1] Fridolin, 1904 b.    [2] Kroeber, 1909.
[3] Bogdanov, 1878–79 h; Mainov, I. I., 1901; Talko-Hryncewicz, 1905.

below medium stature. In head-form a comparable difference exists, the northern Tunguse, although with a predominance of brachycephalic factors, nevertheless have a dolichocephalic element almost as great as that found among the Kamchadal. In the south this almost disappears, and the Alpine type is strongly dominant. The hair and eyes are with few exceptions dark, the hair being straight and the eyes often showing no trace of the Mongoloid fold. Of the other tribes belonging to the Tunguse group, such as the Goldi, Lamut, Orok, Orokon, etc., of the Amur River and Primorsk province, we know little or nothing. The handful of crania show that brachycephalic factors, primarily of Alpine type, are in the majority, and there seems to be a strong similarity with the Manchus, who are the more southern representatives of the stock. The whole Tunguse group, therefore, appears to fall into two parts, a southern, which is below medium stature and prevailingly Alpine, and a northern, which is still shorter, has a rather strong dolichocephalic, Caspian (?) factor in addition to the prevailing Alpine type, and is thus allied apparently to the southern Koryak and Kamchadal.

Of the Turko-Tatar tribes, the Yakut[1] is the chief, and to-day occupies an immense area in the Lena basin and eastward. This wide extension, however, seems to be an affair of recent date, and may have been accomplished mainly during the last three or four centuries. Their earlier habitat lay to the west of Lake Baikal. As a horse-using people they are to-day quite out of their proper environment, over a large part of their range. In stature the Yakut are below the medium, although the local and individual variation is great. Of swarthy skin, they have almost exclusively dark hair and eyes, the hair straight, the eyes commonly Mongoloid. In head-form they are predominantly brachycephalic, but have a small dolichocephalic minority, said to be recognizably of taller stature. In the absence of any sufficient cranial material, the types present cannot be determined, but from their original propinquity to the Buriat, we may expect that in addition to a prevailing Alpine element there is also some-

[1] Bogdanov, 1878–79 c; Mainov, I. I., 1903.

thing of a Mongoloid factor. These resemblances are brought out in the portrait given on Plate XXI, Fig. 4.

The Ugrian-speaking Ostiaks and Voguls of the swampy forest region of northwestern Siberia, and the Samoyedes of the Arctic coast raise a number of interesting and also puzzling questions. The Ostiaks of the Obi (to be carefully distinguished from the small group of the same name on the Yenesei) appear to be a very mixed people. The male crania collected by Sommier[1] show a striking dominance of dolichocephalic factors, in which the Proto-Australoid is in large majority, with the Mediterranean as the element of secondary importance. The small brachycephalic minority is in the main of the Ural type. In the female series, on the other hand, the Mongoloid type is secondary. The crania studied by Ivanovski,[2] however, show a smaller proportion of dolichocephalic types and a considerable Alpine factor. The data on the living collected by the same two observers carry this indication still further, in that brachycephalic factors are predominant, except in one or two districts. In stature the Ostiaks are short (average 156 cm.), and, although prevailingly with dark hair and eyes, yet have a surprisingly large percentage (15 per cent) of blond types.

The Voguls[3] are closely allied to the Ostiaks in speech, but, although at present living on the Asiatic slope of the Urals, in the northern part of the government of Perm, they are relatively recent immigrants, since they are known to have been living west of the mountains in the tenth and eleventh centuries, and only crossed to the eastern side some three hundred years ago. They have a majority of dolichocephalic factors, although not as large as in the case of the Ostiaks. No individual measurements are available, but from the fact that the crania are predominantly low, and give evidence of a considerable platyrrhine element, it seems probable that in the types represented they are essentially comparable with the Ostiaks. The Ostiaks and Voguls thus both seem to have a large dolichocephalic element, primarily

[1] Sommier, 1887. See also Bogdanov, 1878–79 e; Tarenetsky, 1898.
[2] Ivanovski, 1905.                    [3] Maliev, 1901; Silinich, 1904.

of the Proto-Australoid type. With other living peoples of the
north of Asia they show little affiliation; with the Neolithic population of northern and central Russia, however, rather close
analogies exist (see p. 114). I believe, therefore, that we may
regard these peoples as the descendants of the ancient population of northeastern Europe, who were gradually forced west
across the Urals by the expansion of the Slavs, the Ostiaks having come into Asia much earlier than the Voguls, who, as already
stated, were still on the European side of the Urals in the tenth
century.

The Samoyedes,[1] who live along the Arctic coast from the
White Sea to beyond the mouth of the Yenesei River, offer a
sharp contrast in most respects to the last group. Shorter even
than the Ostiaks (average 154 cm.), they are considerably darker-
skinned, have hardly any trace of light eyes or hair, and show the
Mongoloid fold in their eyes much more frequently than the
Ostiaks. In head-form they are overwhelmingly brachycephalic,
the Palæ-Alpine being the type which is most numerous, although the Ural is only little less important. The relation
of the Samoyedes to the other peoples of Europe and Asia is
not as yet clear. Linguistically they stand rather isolated in
the Ural-Altaic family, but are supposed to have some relationship with the almost extinct remnants of the non-Turkish, non-
Mongol peoples who formerly occupied the northern slopes of
the Altai in the vicinity of the upper Yenesei, through the Yenesei Ostiaks, who now live on the eastern bank of the river in its
middle course. Of the physical characteristics of these, however,
little or nothing is known. Rudenko[2] believes that the Samoyedes are practically identical with the Soyots (see p. 295) and
states that the Yenesei Ostiaks are also of the same type. In
the absence of any individual measurements for these two groups,
the question must remain undecided. The large factor of the
Ural type, together with a small Mongoloid element in the Samoyedes, seems to favor some connection with this Altai region.

[1] Bogdanov, 1878–79 b; Sommier, *op. cit.*; Zograf, 1878.
[2] Rudenko, 1914.

There is also some relation, obviously, between the Samoyedes and the Lapps, but this, on the basis of present evidence, seems perhaps more likely to be a modern association and slight mixture rather than an ancient and fundamental one. It is perhaps permissible, in view of all the data, to suggest that the Samoyedes represent a people once resident in the region of the northern Altai, who were driven northward down the Yenesei by the eastern advance of the Caspian peoples from the steppes, and who, on reaching the Arctic coast, moved westward into Europe.

*BOOK IV*

OCEANIA

# INTRODUCTION

UNDER the term Oceania we shall include all those lands lying southeast of the Asiatic continent which stretch far out into the Pacific. These range from the huge continental mass of Australia through the great islands like Borneo, Sumatra, New Guinea, and New Zealand down to the tiniest inhabited islet lost in the immense spaces of the South Seas. This vast insular world may be divided into five sections, (1) Indonesia, extending from Sumatra in the west to the Moluccas and Aru Islands in the east, and from Java in the south to the Philippines and Formosa in the north; (2) Melanesia, including the great island of New Guinea, together with the Bismarck Archipelago, Solomons, Santa Cruz, New Hebrides, New Caledonia, and Fiji, to name only the chief groups—which extend eastward as far as the 180th meridian; (3) Micronesia, stretching from the Pelew Islands and the Marianne group in the west and north, through the Carolines and Marshalls to the Gilbert group in the east and south; (4) Polynesia, including New Zealand and all the islands of the Pacific east of the 180th meridian, and (5) Australia, with the neighboring island of Tasmania.

A few moments' study of a map reveals several points which are of significance in the racial history of the area. In the first place there is from west to east, from the Asiatic continent out into the Pacific, a rough gradation in the size, the character, and the degree of remoteness of these islands from one another. Near Asia we find large islands, mountainous, and with wide diversities of surface, and closely set or joined to one another by chains of smaller islands, so that passage from one to the other eastward as far as New Guinea and Australia and northward as far as Formosa is easy. Beyond New Guinea and the Philippines, to the east, the size of the islands rapidly diminishes, the number of low coral islets and atolls increases and the various groups and individual islands are separated by wider and wider expanses of open sea, until in the Hawaiian group and Easter Island we have either a group or a single island, lying one or two thousand miles from the nearest inhabited land. From west to east, thus, the difficulty of access increases, and only peoples skilled in navigation and supplied with seaworthy vessels could hope to reach the far-off islands in the southern seas. We have thus good grounds for believing that Polynesia could not have been peopled by primitive man, and was probably the last great portion of the habitable world to be occupied.

A second geographical feature to be noted is the location of Australia in relation to the rest of the area, and the peculiar climatic and environmental conditions which made it in most respects the least attractive of all the lands in the region. Pendant, as it were, from New Guinea, the Australian continent lies apart from the main island chains which run from west to east, so that, as we shall see, although reached by the earlier drifts of peoples and colonized by them, the late streams of migrants passed it by. In its environment Australia presents a sharp contrast with all the rest of the Oceanic area, for whereas elsewhere we find luxuriant tropical conditions, here two-thirds of the great continent lies parched and blistered by the sun, one of the greatest and most terrible deserts in the world.

For this whole Oceanic region we have as yet but very few ancient crania and little direct evidence to show the character of its earlier population. The pre-human Pithecanthropus erectus from Java, the Talgai skull from Australia, and a few crania of very doubtful age from New Britain, are all we possess which have or may have a respectable antiquity. History for most of the area reaches no further back than the sixteenth century, for many sections not so far, and for Java, of which we know most, we have little definite information back of the sixth or seventh century. We must, therefore, in attempting to outline the racial history of this immense region, rely almost wholly on the indirect evidence afforded by the present distribution of the several types.

At the earliest period to which we can go back by inference, a

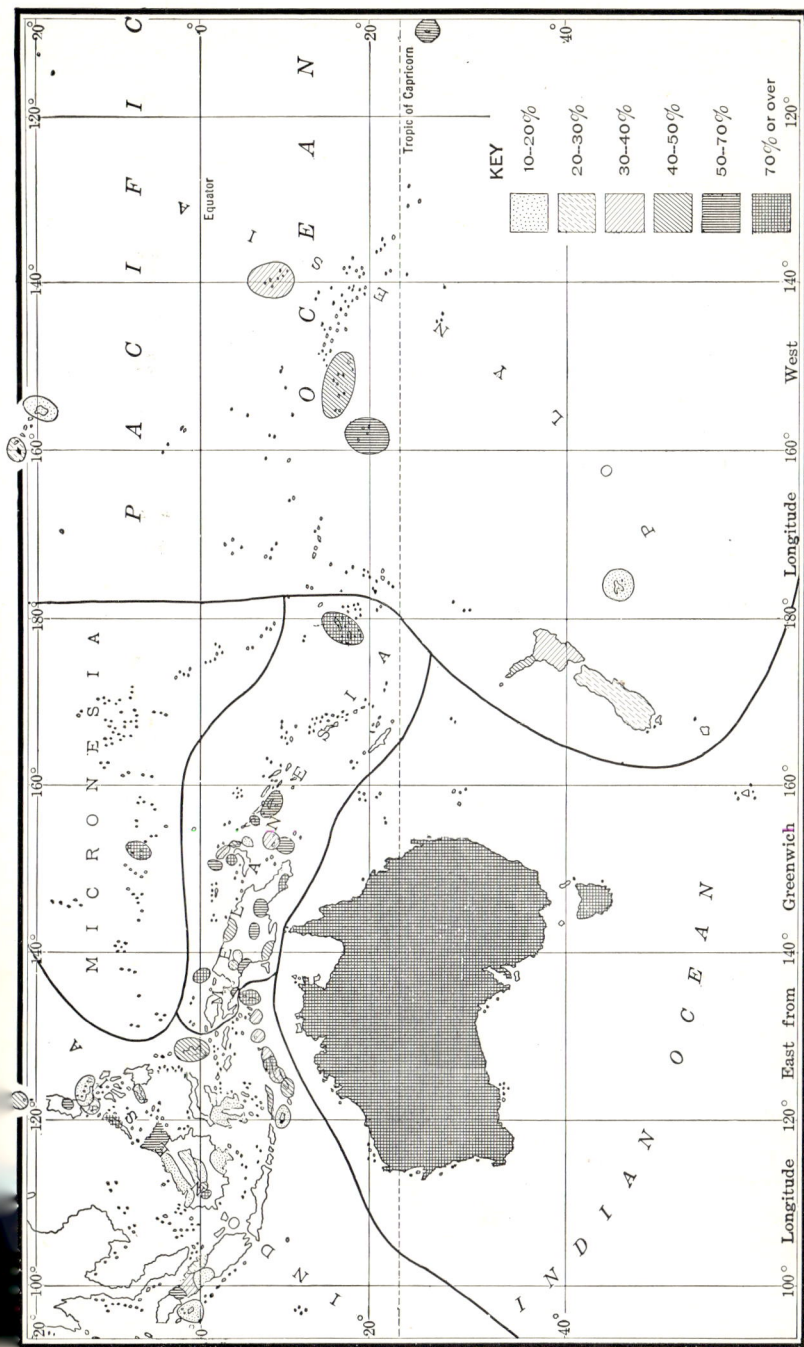

PLATE XXII. OCEANIA.

Percentage distribution of Proto-Australoid and Proto-Negroid Types.

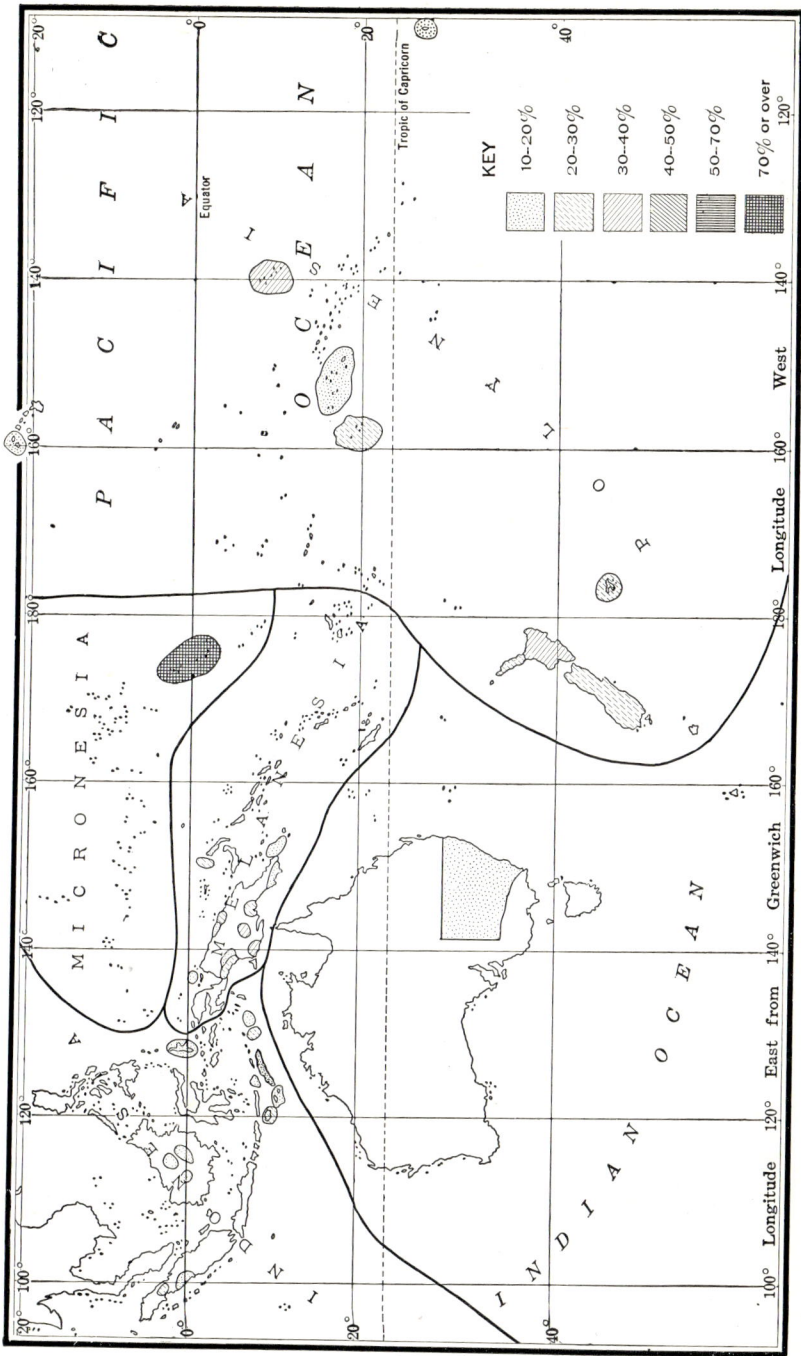

PLATE XXIII. OCEANIA.

Percentage distribution of Caspian and Mediterranean Types.

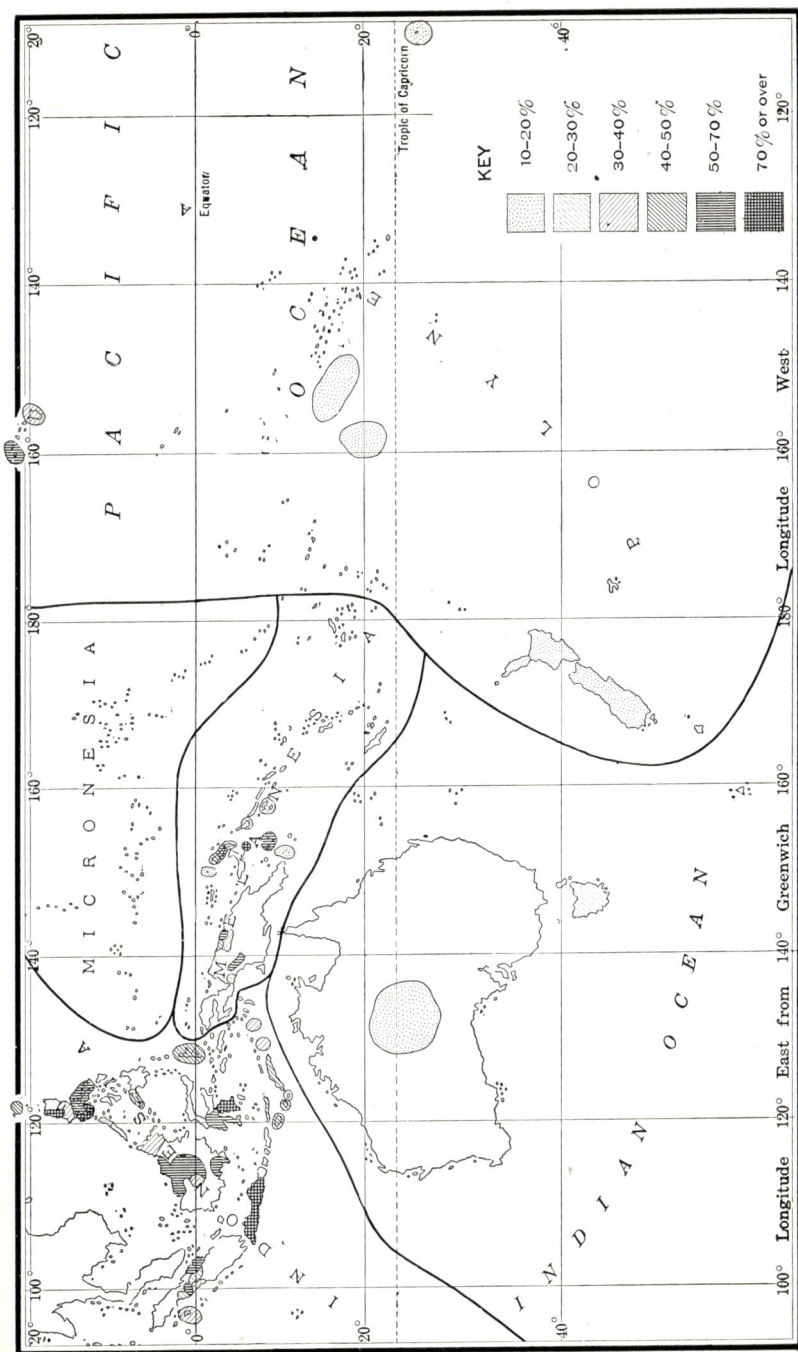

KEY

| | |
|---|---|
| | 10—20% |
| | 20—30% |
| | 30—40% |
| | 40—50% |
| | 50—70% |
| | 70% or over |

PLATE XXIV. OCEANIA.

Percentage distribution of Palæ-Alpine and Mongoloid Types.

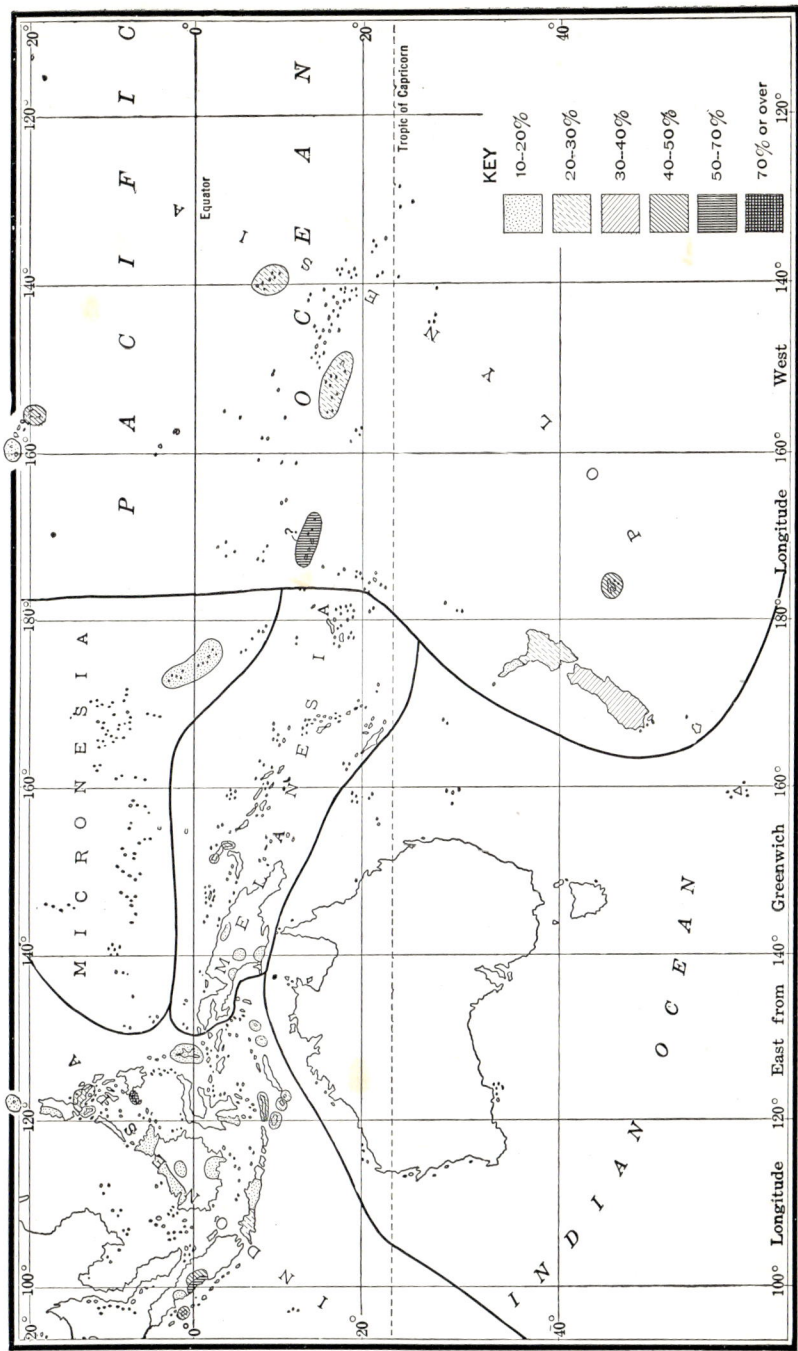

PLATE XXV. OCEANIA.

Percentage distribution of Alpine and Ural Types.

KEY

10–20%
20–30%
30–40%
40–50%
50–70%
70% or over

period which on purely hypothetical grounds may be regarded as contemporaneous with the later or even the middle portion of the Palæolithic period in western Europe, two types of people seem to have occupied Indonesia, the western part, at least, of Melanesia, and Australia. The mass of this earliest population was of the Proto-Australoid type, of medium stature with dark-brown skin and wavy or even straight hair. Associated with it was a minority of Negrito Palæ-Alpine folk, short, dark, and frizzly-haired. Whether these Negrito people preceded the Proto-Australoids or drifted in with them from southeastern Asia we have as yet no means of knowing. How far to the eastward, also, these early immigrants from southern Asia reached, is still far from clear. Of primitive culture, they could hardly have been able to cross very wide stretches of sea. To New Guinea they could surely win, and thence to Australia, for land connection may then still have existed across what is now the shallow Torres Straits. But beyond? To the Bismarck Archipelago almost certainly, and perhaps through the Solomons and the Santa Cruz group to the New Hebrides; but farther than this it is well-nigh certain that they did not and could not go. Thus all Polynesia and Micronesia lay still untouched by man during this earliest period.

After a long period perhaps of quiescence, a new era of migration set in, the echo, perchance, of those great stirrings of peoples in the Asiatic continent in Neolithic times which we can as yet only dimly glimpse. It brought or thrust into Indonesia from the southeastern funnel-like end of the Asiatic continent a flood of peoples, primarily of the Proto-Negroid type, tall, black, and woolly or frizzly haired. Through Indonesia from island to island they swept, and on into New Guinea. The older peoples were absorbed or driven inland from the coasts, which by a people travelling by water were the first areas to be occupied. Southward the newcomers passed on into Australia, following down, in the main, the eastern, more-favored parts of the continent, and forcing westward into the desert the older aborigines. These new peoples were a folk of more advanced

culture and had, or had developed in the course of their drifting
through the islands, vessels of some degree of seaworthiness, and
had acquired some skill in navigation. Thus they were able far
more easily than the pioneers to push their search for new lands
to the eastward. Passing beyond the older limits, they reached
Fiji and thence Samoa and Tonga, the Cook, Society, and Paumotu groups, reached the Marquesas, and by some stupendous
piece of chance won their way to far-off Easter Island, most
remote and lonely of all. Hawaii in the north and New Zealand
in the south they probably never reached; whether or not they
penetrated to Micronesia the dearth of our material from that
area will not permit us to say. Throughout Indonesia, however,
they seem to have spread, and it is possible that a stream of these
Negroid sea-rovers passed northward from Formosa through the
Riu-kiu Islands to Japan.

At this point in the racial history of the Oceanic area a very
puzzling problem arises, which, largely because of the inadequacy
of our data for the whole of southeastern Asia and for the Philippines we cannot as yet satisfactorily solve. For, beginning perhaps feebly almost coincidently with the Proto-Negroid drift,
but coming in greater force some time after its close, a stream
of peoples of very different character came into Oceania. Although doubtless mixed with other elements, they had a core of
tall, fair-skinned, straight or wavy-haired folk, in majority of
Caspian type, with which a strain of shorter, darker Mediterraneans was somehow blended. We can trace them to-day more
or less clearly in southwestern Sumatra, here and there in Borneo, and among one, at least, of the wilder tribes of northern
Luzon in the Philippines. Farther east we find faint traces of
them among the "Alfures" of the Moluccas, in the islands of
the extreme southeast of Indonesia, and even along the southwestern New Guinea coast. Farther into Melanesia or into
Australia they do not seem to have gone, for it was by another
route that they passed far into the heart of the Pacific. We find
them clearly represented thus in the eastern Carolines, and forming the majority of the factors in the population of the Gilbert

group, whence they pressed southward through Samoa and Tonga to New Zealand, and eastward throughout the whole of Central Polynesia. So much seems clear, but whence did they come? We have seen in a previous section (p. 243) how presumably in later Neolithic times peoples of this same type moved eastward through the heart of Asia from their ancient homelands in the Eur-Asiatic steppes, and came into the eastern borderlands of Asia to China and Japan; how, also, they seem to have streamed along the great river valleys leading from the highlands of Tibet southward to Indo-China. From which of these two branches did the stream which passed into Oceania derive? Did it come from Indo-China by way of Sumatra, Java, and Borneo, or, crossing from China to Formosa, did it make its way southward through the Philippines and thence southward into the rest of Indonesia and eastward by way of Micronesia into the Pacific? For the solution of this problem we have only indirect evidence as yet. Our clews are mainly cultural and linguistic, and these point with considerable certainty toward Indo-China rather than to the Asiatic borderlands farther north. Indeed, just as was suggested as a possibility in the case of the Negroid drift, there is much to suggest that a subsidiary stream of these Caspian peoples, with some admixture of Proto-Negroid and other folk, absorbed in their passage through Indonesia, passed northward by way of Formosa to the Chinese coast.

Next in sequence of events in this attempted reconstruction of the racial history of Oceania, came the peoples who to-day form the mass of the population in Indonesia. This folk, primarily of Palæ-Alpine type, short, with brownish-yellowish skin, straight black hair and a strong tendency to have the Mongoloid eye, pressed down into southeastern Asia at an early date (see p. 245), and it is more than probable that this pressure was in large part responsible for the emigration thence of the Caspian peoples. Be this as it may, these brachycephalic migrants swarmed off from the Indo-Chinese shores and made themselves masters of all of Indonesia, in general pressing back into the interior the older population. Later they began to reach out eastward. Coasting along the northern shore of New Guinea, they formed small settlements here and there, in particular on the small islands along the coast, for there the aboriginal "Melanesian," or Negroid, people could more easily be overcome. It seems probable that the largest area which they occupied lay around on the southeastern coast, in British New Guinea, but the lamentable paucity and incompleteness of our data for this region make it impossible to tell whether the lighter-skinned immigrant population of parts of this region are of Palæ-Alpine type and due to this migration, or have a strong Alpine element and so are attributable to the influence of a later wave. Probably some influence of this Palæ-Alpine drift reached as far east as the Solomons, New Hebrides, and New Caledonia, but that it went beyond to Fiji and into western Polynesia we have no evidence whatever. Yet somehow a group of Palæ-Alpine people must have reached Hawaii and been its first inhabitants, although all routes seem closed by which it could have come, and the puzzle of their origin is still unsolved. The problem and the dilemma in which we are landed will be more fully set forth in the chapter on Polynesia.

The last episode in the racial history of Oceania touches almost the edge of history. At a time probably not many centuries before the beginning of the Christian era, there came into Indonesia from some portion of southeastern or eastern Asia—perhaps from Tonkin and Annam or farther north from the southern Chinese coast—a people whom we may call the true Malays. Under medium stature, yellowish-brown in color, with straight black hair and variable development of the Mongoloid eye, the true Malay is primarily of Alpine type, but with a strong secondary factor of the Palæ-Alpine, and bears a striking resemblance, in the proportions of the physical types present, to the modern population of the Chinese coastal provinces of Fukien and Chekiang, opposite the island of Formosa. Who and what the "Malay" is and whence he came is a problem that has long been debated. I believe, however, that the problem finds its solution in regarding them as a group of people derived from the blending, along the southern and central Chinese coast, of the earliest Alpine immigrants (perhaps in the third or fourth millennium B. C.) with the older, primarily Palæ-Alpine and Caspian population of the Yangtse region. Maritime in their culture, it was from these ancient, non-Chinese inhabitants of the coast and Yangtse delta that the Chinese as they extended their control eastward to the sea, learned the art of boat-building and navigation. As the Chinese expanded southward along the shore, they partly absorbed and partly pressed back these older Malay peoples, who were physically more or less akin to themselves, and from time to time groups of these sea-roving folk broke away from the mainland and sought new homes in the islands to the east and south. They settled along the western shores of the Philippines, occupied most of the smaller islands of the central part of the group, the Zamboanga peninsula of Mindanao, and the whole of the Sulu chain; they colonized parts of the lowland shore of Borneo and farther westward, coming to the low east coast of Sumatra, ascended the rivers to the more healthy highlands of the central west coast, where they became the ancestors of the so-called Menangkabau Malays. They spread even farther westward yet, reaching Madagascar, where they contributed a large factor to the population. They spread also eastward, and about the beginning of the Christian era, or perhaps as late as the second or third century A. D., large groups who had possibly been faintly touched by the earliest Indian influences which were beginning to make themselves felt in Java, wandered toward New Guinea and Polynesia.

By what route they went is not as yet wholly clear. They may have coasted along the northern shores of New Guinea and so through eastern Melanesia to Samoa, although if they did they left no traces which our present physical data reveal. Perhaps this black-man's land did not attract them, and they may have gone farther north by way of Micronesia. All that we can be sure of is that they came in considerable numbers to Samoa and Tonga, which groups they came in time to dominate, so that their earlier mixed population of Caspian and Proto-Negroid

elements was largely absorbed.   Bold navigators, they were not
deterred by great stretches of open sea, and so not only pushed
farther east (in the main perhaps by way of the Tokelau and
Union groups to the Marquesas, and in lesser degree through
the Cook group to the Society and Paumotu groups), but their
earlier Samoan generations, having absorbed much of the older
Caspian element, quested south and reached New Zealand.
Farther north, also, they went beyond the bounds which had
hemmed in the earlier peoples and came to Hawaii, finding the
island, however, already occupied by the Palæ-Alpine pioneers,
who had in some unknown fashion reached the group some
centuries before.   To Easter Island, at the extreme eastern
margin of Polynesia, there is no evidence that these latest
migrants ever came.

The racial history of Oceania is thus one in which wave after
wave of immigrant peoples spread, at first timidly and slowly,
later more boldly and with greater skill; each drift, as a rule,
amalgamating with or driving into the interior or toward the
margins of the territory the older folk which it found in occupation, and all alike deriving from the southeastern corner of the
great continent to the west.   Here not westward but eastward
the course of colonization and discovery held its way, until in
Hawaii and Easter Island it reached its limit.   It has been believed by some that this was not the end, that peoples who had
dared to sail thus far could cross the still wider spaces that separate the Polynesian Islands from the New World, and that
America received thus a part, perhaps the larger part, of its population from this source.   He would be rash who would deny
that Polynesian navigators might not once or twice have reached
the American coast, but rasher if he believed that this could have
supplied any appreciable factor in the population.   For such
tiny increments would come too late; America had already been
peopled from the northeast of Asia while yet these lovely islands
lay vacant in their sunny seas.   Some few, perhaps, of the puzzling cultural features which the ethnologist finds the New World
to have in common with the islands of the west may yet be

proved to be the result of the chance drifting to American shores of the few survivors of storm-driven craft; but apart from this we are, I think, right in believing that great as were the abilities and the daring of these rovers of the seas, who sought and from time to time found every habitable islet within their range, Hawaii, the Marquesas, and Easter Island marked the utmost limit of their endeavor.  The maps given on Plates XXII to XXV indicate the distribution in the Oceanic area of the several types and their combinations, and serve to show graphically something of the bases on which the general conclusions just outlined rest.

# CHAPTER I

## INDONESIA

THE term Indonesia will here be understood to include the islands, large and small, which are commonly comprised in the Malay Archipelago, together with Formosa and the Aru and Kei Islands, which lie south and west of the great island of New Guinea. As a group Indonesia forms a rough crescent, which at its ends in Sumatra and Formosa comes almost in contact with the Asiatic continent, and at its centre approaches closely to New Guinea. Several of the islands are of large size, such as Sumatra, Borneo, Java, Celebes, and Mindanao and Luzon in the Philippines, all of which, with their high mountain chains, have a varied surface and environment. The whole archipelago may be described as close pressed, so that from island to island and from group to group only a short sea journey is needed, and one may thus easily pass from one end to the other of Indonesia without going out of sight of land.

From the linguistic point of view the peoples of Indonesia form a unit, since all the languages fall into a single broad group, related on the one hand, to the Melanesian, Micronesian, and Polynesian languages, and, on the other, to the Mon-Khmer stock of southeastern Asia. From no portion of Indonesia do we as yet possess any data in regard to its ancient inhabitants. The famous fragmentary skull of the Pithecanthropus erectus from Java is not a human but a pre-human type; in so far, however, as its evidence is pertinent, it indicates that in late Tertiary times this human precursor possessed a skull which was both long and low, and, since we are probably justified in assuming the nose to have been broad, was thus affiliated with the Proto-Australoid type. The crania from the caves in Samar and the Visayan Islands in the Philippines are probably not of any very great age, and are so much deformed that little evidence of value can be derived from them for our purposes, except that apparently platyrrhine types outnumber the leptorrhine, whereas the reverse is the case among the modern inhabitants.

We may best understand the character of the present population of Indonesia and the evidence which it gives us as to the racial history of the area by considering separately the various larger islands and island groups. Sumatra, which at the Straits of Malacca almost joins the Malay Peninsula, and may have been actually continuous with it even in proto-historic times, is topographically divisible into two very distinct parts. The northeastern half of the island facing the Asiatic coast, is low, swampy, and covered with dense tropical jungle, whereas the southwestern half is, on the contrary, a high, rugged plateau, whose elevation gives to it a much more healthy climate. These differences are reflected in the culture, the occupants of the lower portion of the island being in general rather primitive, while those of the highlands are relatively advanced. On physical grounds, the population is divisible into three groups, characterized respectively by the predominance of the Alpine, the Palæ-Alpine, and the Proto-Negroid types.

The first group comprises the true or so-called Menangkabau Malays,[1] whose habitat is mainly confined to the central highlands of the southwestern side of the island, and who appear to be relatively recent immigrants, reaching their historic homes probably by way of the east-coast rivers from the north. Somewhat below medium in stature (average 161 cm.), they are of a yellowish-brown color, with black, straight hair and variable development of the Mongoloid eye. Predominantly Alpine in type, they have a fairly strong secondary element, which is Palæ-Alpine, together with minorities of Negroid factors, and in the Padang Highlands a surprisingly large strain of the Caspian type. In their general physical characteristics they resemble closely the Chinese of the coastal provinces of Fukien and Chekiang. An example of the Menangkabau Malay is given on Plate XXVI, Fig. 1.

[1] Kleiweg de Zwaan, 1910.

The second group includes probably a large part of the remainder of the population of the island, who represent a much older stratum.   Of these may be mentioned the Battak[1] of the uplands about Toba Lake, probably also the Alas and Gajo, north of them, together with the people of the Lampong and Palembang[2] districts to the south.   The Kubu[3] and other primitive tribes[4] of the eastern lowland seem also to belong to this group.   In stature somewhat shorter than the Malay (average, Kubu 158 cm., Battak 160 cm.); in skin color variable, the Kubu being a reddish brown, the Battak often somewhat lighter; with hair which is often wavy or even curly, they are quite clearly differentiated in appearance from the Malay proper.   In all the Palæ-Alpine type is strongly dominant, and in all probability includes some traces of the Negrito variety.   The Alpine type, so strong among the Malay, is wholly or almost wholly absent, but all have a considerable factor of Proto-Negroid and Proto-Australoid types, and their resemblance to the Sakai of the Malay Peninsula (who have a large element of these types) has been often noted, and may be seen in the portrait shown on Plate XXVI, Fig. 2.

The third group is found, so far as we know yet, only in the Palembang Highlands,[5] at the extreme southern tip of the island, and is contrasted with the other groups in that it is almost purely dolichocephalic.   Unfortunately, the data are old and no nasal measurements are given, so that the determination of the type or types present is not possible, but if these people of the extreme south are not descendants of the Indian immigrants which came into Sumatra in small numbers in the beginning of the Christian era, we may regard them as probably survivors of the oldest or dolichocephalic stratum of the Sumatran population. Still clearer traces of this older stratum are to be found in the islands which lie off the western coast.   In Engano[6] and the Mentawei group,[7] the dominant factor seems on the basis of

[1] Hagen, 1890; Volz, 1900.      [2] Swaving, 1863.      [3] Hagen, 1908; Volz, 1908.
[4] Moskowski, 1908.                                                     [5] Swaving, 1870.
[6] Danielli, 1893; Modigliani, 1894.                    [7] Maas, 1893, 1902.

scanty material to be primarily of the Proto-Negroid and Proto-Australoid types. For Nias[1] the data, although very abundant, are absolutely contradictory, since, while the crania show a strong predominance of these same two dolichocephalic types, with the Palæ-Alpine as next in importance, the measurements on the living indicate a population essentially brachycephalic, and comparable to the Malay! It seems difficult to account for this radical contrast, except on the assumption that the crania represent a relatively old population, and that the character of the people has been wholly changed in recent times by an invasion of Malay peoples. The survival in this distinctly marginal area of the islands off the rugged western coast of Sumatra, of a dominantly Proto-Negroid-Proto-Australoid population, indicates that this is the oldest stratum, which has, on Sumatra itself, been overlaid first by a Palæ-Alpine and later by an Alpine people.

Java, unlike Sumatra, has no extensive lowland, but is throughout a mountainous and volcanic land. The population is usually divided into three sections—the Sundanese in the west, the Javanese proper in the centre, and the Madurese in the east. So far, however, as our data go, there is little difference between them physically.[2] The determination of physical types in Java is difficult, owing to the wide prevalence of the custom of artificial cranial deformation. It seems, however, that throughout the island the Palæ-Alpine type is strongly dominant, with the Alpine secondary, only small minorities of Proto-Negroid and Proto-Australoid being present. The people thus apparently are comparable to the second or main group in Sumatra, who had received a considerable infusion of the Alpine Malay type. That the older, dolichocephalic stratum has not wholly disappeared seems to be shown by the Tenggerese[3] in the mountain country at the eastern end of the island. Although no individual measurements have been published, it seems clear that they have a considerable dolichocephalic, platyrrhine element among them,

---

[1] Kleiweg de Zwaan, 1913–15; Zuckerkandl, 1894.
[2] Garrett, 1912; Hagen, 1890; Swaving, 1861–62; Bleeker, 1851; Arndt, 1854.
[3] Kohlbrugge, 1898.

which is corroborated by the wavy or even curly character of their hair. Whether this represents the ancient, underlying dolichocephalic stratum, or may be due to the influence of colonists from southern India during the period of Indian cultural influence in the middle ages and before, it is not yet possible to say. The probabilities are in favor, however, of this being an ancient, not a relatively modern factor. In stature the population of Java is below the medium, the Sundanese being the shortest, with an average of 159 cm., the Javanese and Madurese being very slightly taller. All have straight or very slightly wavy hair, and a light yellowish-brown skin. We know that strong Indian cultural influences and probably actual colonization on a small scale occurred in central and eastern Java, beginning somewhere about the seventh century A. D. But our present data do not appear to indicate that this contact has affected the present population in any noticeable way.

The island of Borneo is, in contrast to both Sumatra and Java, more massive, and affords thus more "continental" conditions. It is not surprising, therefore, to find in it a more complex population than in the islands just considered.[1] The peoples of Borneo may be divided into two very unequal groups on the basis of their physical types, one characterized by the dominance of the Palæ-Alpine type, the other, apparently of very much smaller size, by that of the Proto-Negroid and Proto-Australoid. The first group may be further subdivided into three different sections, each marked by a different secondary type. The Iban, or Sea Dyaks of the northwestern coast, and the Punan, nomad hunters of the interior, alike show the Alpine type as the secondary factor. The first of these are known to be recent comers to the region. Among the people of the southeastern districts about Bandjermassim, the Kenyahs, most of the Klemantans and some, at least, of the Kayan, the Proto-Negroid and Proto-Australoid types occupy second place, just as among the main mass of the population in Sumatra. The third section

---

[1] Garrett, 1912; Hose & McDougall, 1912; Nieuwenhuis, 1903; Haddon, 1901; Swaving, 1861–62; Turner, 1907; Flower, 1879; Fridolin, 1900.

includes only the Kayan measured by Nieuwenhuis, among whom the Caspian type ranks next to the dominant Palæ-Alpine. While it is possible that this difference is due to variation in methods of measurement, the probability is that it bespeaks a real distinction.

The second and smaller of the two groups into which the population of Borneo may be divided, characterized by the predominance of Proto-Negroid and Proto-Australoid types, includes the Murut, Kalabit, and Dusun of northern Sarawak and British North Borneo, and the Ulu-Ayar of the upper Kapoeas River, and perhaps some of the southwestern Klemantans. Among all of these, except the Ulu-Ayar, the Palæ-Alpine type is secondary, but in their case the Caspian again comes into prominence. The significance of the survival in Borneo of a factor of this type will be apparent later in discussing the population of Micronesia and Polynesia.

The Philippine Islands show very wide variation in the character of their population, and here only in the whole of Indonesia do we find survivors of the Negrito people, who are believed to have once been much more widely spread. With very few exceptions, no adequate data are available for the Philippines,[1] and abundant cranial material is only to be had for the Negrito.[2] We may, on the basis of wofully meagre data, divide the population into four groups. The first of these is that of the Negrito, who are confined in the main to the mountainous country on the eastern and western coasts of Luzon, and to northern Palawan and Mindanao. Of very short, almost pigmy stature (average 145 cm.), the purer groups are dark in color, with frizzly or even woolly hair. Almost purely brachycephalic, they show an overwhelming majority of the Palæ-Alpine type, the only other present, except as a mere trace, being the Alpine. The character and extent of the differentiation between these and other Negroid Palæ-Alpine peoples, such as the Andamanese

---

[1] Barrows, 1910; Bean (all titles); Christie, 1909; Kroeber, 1906; Sullivan, 1918; Virchow, 1870, 1871, 1883; Bauer, F., 1900; Koeze, 1901–04; Reed, 1904.
[2] Baer, 1879; Virchow, 1871; Koeze, *op. cit.*

and the African Pigmies on the one hand, and the non-Negroid peoples of the same type in all parts of the world on the other, together with the problems involved, will be discussed in the final chapter. A typical example of the Negrito is shown on Plate XXVI, Fig. 3.

The second group is characterized by the dominance of the Proto-Negroid and Proto-Australoid types. The available data for this group is, however, very meagre. It comprises what are described as the Tagbanua of Palawan, but which probably are in reality Battak from the same island, and the Igorot of northern Luzon. It is extremely probable that other tribes will be found to belong to this same group, when adequate materials are available. In the Tagbanua (Battak) the Proto-Negroid type is in large majority, followed by the Palæ-Alpine and Proto-Australoid. For the Igorot the material is conflicting, since measurements on the living indicate a predominance of Proto-Negroid and Proto-Australoid types, with the Palæ-Alpine as secondary; whereas the very few crania show a large majority of brachycephalic forms, mainly Palæ-Alpine and Alpine. Owing to the prevalence of head-hunting, it is quite possible that the crania are in reality those of some other tribe, so that we are probably safer in relying on the measurements of the living. The portrait given on Plate XXVI, Fig. 4, may be taken as typical of this group.

To the third group, which is primarily Palæ-Alpine, belong in all probability a considerable part of the population of the islands. The Tagalog and Ilocano certainly, probably the Bisayans and the Mangyan (?), and possibly some of the Mandaya and Manobo are to be regarded as belonging to this group, which here, as in Sumatra, Java, and Borneo, appears to constitute the mass of the living population. The fourth and last group includes the Subanun of western Mindanao and the "Moros" of the same island and the Sulu archipelago. In these the Alpine type is preponderant, with the Palæ-Alpine secondary, just as among the Menangkabau Malays in Sumatra.

Practically all the peoples of the Philippines are below

FIG. 1. MENANGKABAU MALAY.

FIG. 2. BATTAK.

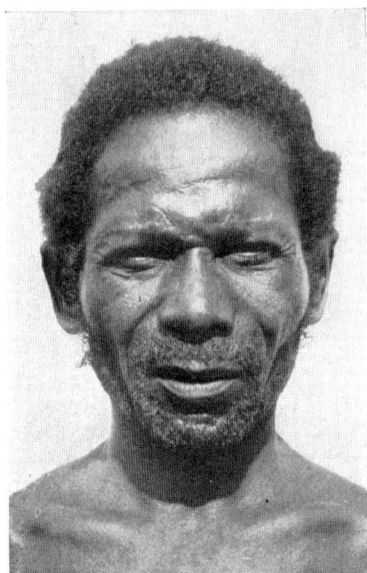

FIG. 3. NEGRITO. (PHILIPPINES.)

FIG. 4. IGOROT. (PHILIPPINES.)

PLATE XXVI.

medium stature. One or two small groups of Tagalogs average just over 165 cm., but the majority of them, together with the Bisayans, Iloko, Manobo, Moros, etc., lie between 160 and 165 cm. The Igorot, Ifugao, Mandaya, Tagbanua, Ilongot, etc., have average statures ranging between 160 and 155 cm., while the Negritos are the shortest of all, averaging between 150 and 145 cm. The hair throughout the Philippines is in general straight or wavy, the latter form being chiefly found among the wilder, interior tribes; only in the case of the Negritos do we get curly and woolly forms. In skin color there is great variation, but few systematic observations are available. The Negrito range from black to dark brown, while the other tribes vary from medium brown to very light shades.

Data on the physical characteristics of the peoples of Formosa[1] are as yet but scanty, although the Japanese have published elaborate accounts of their culture. Torii[2] has, however, made a valuable study of the Yami of the island of Botel Tobago, off the southern end of Formosa, from which it appears that the people here are under medium stature (average 160 cm.), light brown in color, and with prevailingly straight hair. The brachycephalic and dolichocephalic factors are exactly balanced, the Proto-Australoid and Proto-Negroid being, however, slightly more numerous than the Palæ-Alpine. Of the Alpine there is but a small minority. On the whole thus, the people of Botel Tobago resemble the Igorot.

The population of the curiously shaped island of Celebes[3] appears to be divided into two groups. In both the brachycephalic Palæ-Alpine type is in the majority; in one, however, the Proto-Negroid and Proto-Australoid types are secondary, in the other the Alpine. To the first group belong the Toala and Tokea, rather primitive peoples, and perhaps (?) the Bugis and Macassars of much higher culture, all living in the southern peninsula. The first two are short (average 157 cm.), dark-

[1] Eldridge, 1877; Turner, 1907; Davidson, 1903.  [2] Torii, 1912.
[3] Arndt, 1854; Lubbers, 1893; Sarasin, F., 1906; Flower, 1879; Fridolin, 1900; Ten Kate, 1881, 1915 a.

skinned folk with wavy or even curly hair, predominantly Palæ-
Alpine in type with some admixture, perhaps, of the Negrito
variety. The Toala have a strong Proto-Negroid and Proto-
Australoid factor, which is less marked in the Tokea and absent
(?) among the neighboring Tomuna, who are in skin color very
dark. The Bugis and Macassars (who are a rather mixed people,
as we know) are, according to Sarasin, somewhat taller (average
162 cm.) and lighter in color, but, like the Toala, have a considerable Negroid factor. The second group includes, apparently,
all the remainder of the population, except the people of Minahassa in the extreme northeast. Slightly under medium stature,
brown-skinned and straight-haired, they have a considerable secondary factor of the Alpine type. Whether or not the Bugis and
Macassars should be classed with this group rather than with the
first is uncertain, for, whereas Sarasin's measurements would place
them with the Toala and Tokea, Ten Kate's data show them to
have, like the Toradja and the majority of the whole population,
a considerable Alpine element. If culture may be taken as a
guide in the matter, we should certainly accept the latter rather
than the former result. The Minahassa people are the tallest in
the island, with an average of 165 cm. They are very light in
color, have straight black hair and very "Mongoloid" features.
No measurements, however, are available, so that we can only
note that by their own tradition they are relatively recent immigrants to Celebes.

We come finally to the smaller islands east of Java and Celebes, and between them and New Guinea. For the Moluccas[1]
the data are very meagre. Apparently, however, the mass of
the population is primarily of Palæ-Alpine type, although there
are small groups of people among the so-called Alfures in the
mountainous interior of the islands, among whom there is a
large and, in some cases, perhaps a dominant Negroid element.
In all these islands the mixed character of the people is shown
by the wide variation in skin color and in the character of the
hair. For the islands forming a long chain east of Java[2] the facts

[1] Kukenthal, 1897; Virchow 1882 b, 1889 c; Zuckerkandl, 1867.
[2] Ten Kate, 1915 b.

are clearer. In those nearest to Java the brachycephalic factors apparently prevail, whereas in Rotti, Flores, and Timor there are groups among whom the Proto-Negroid and Proto-Australoid types are strongly represented. Farther east, in the Babar Islands,[1] the Tenimber group,[1] and the Kei and Aru[1] Islands, we have fairly good cranial data. In the first the people are evidently very much mixed, but there is a nearly even balance between brachycephalic and dolichocephalic factors, the Palæ-Alpine being in largest proportion, followed by the Caspian and Proto-Negroid. In Tenimber the population is also mixed, with wide differences between the males and females, the former being predominantly Palæ-Alpine and Alpine, whereas the latter are in majority Proto-Negroid. Finally, in the Aru Islands, we have a population primarily dolichocephalic, with the Proto-Negroid strongly dominant, the Palæ-Alpine being secondary, and thus comparable with the Melanesian peoples of New Guinea toward the east. How far these Negroid factors in the more eastern islands are traceable to an aboriginal stratum or how far they are the result of the importation of slaves from New Guinea is not sure; but in most cases where these factors are found they characterize the interior rather than the coastal people, and are most probably, therefore, to be regarded as aboriginal.

If we attempt to reconstruct the racial history of Indonesia as a whole, we may, I believe, assume the oldest stratum of population to have been one made up of the Negrito Palæ-Alpine and the Proto-Australoid types. From the extreme marginal position of the Negrito remnants to-day, it seems probable that in parts at least of Indonesia they were actually the earliest occupants. That the Proto-Australoid was very early in the area, however, seems to be suggested by the existence in Java in tertiary times of the Pithecanthropus erectus, which, in so far as it resembles actual human types, is nearest to the Proto-Australoid.

At a very early period, perhaps contemporary even with the later Palæolithic times in Europe, a stream of peoples primarily

[1] Bickel, 1917.

of Proto-Negroid type, flowed from the southeastern corner of
Asia into Indonesia. The older occupants were in part driven
before them, in part forced into the interior of the islands, in
part amalgamated, with the result that a mixed population, comparable with that of New Guinea to-day, dominated the whole
area. Coincidently perhaps in part with this movement, but in
the main at a somewhat later date, probably toward the end of
Neolithic times, a stream of immigrants of much higher culture
and very different physical type, spread here and there among
the islands. Largely of Caspian type, with a Mediterranean
mixture, they were fair-skinned and straight or wavy-haired,
and, like their Negroid predecessors, seem to have come into
Indonesia from the Indo-Chinese region. Their influence may
have been considerable; until we have more abundant cranial
material we cannot trace its extent, but indications of their presence survive, so far as we know, only in a few places.

The great mass of the peoples of Indonesia to-day are, however, derived from a later wave, this time of brachycephalic
Palæ-Alpine folk, who had come down in great numbers into
Indo-China, as has been shown in a previous section. They
seem to have come on into Indonesia in a veritable flood, and, as
before, the older occupants were dispossessed and absorbed, and
the whole character of the population became radically changed
from one resembling that at present found in New Guinea, to one
essentially like that of to-day. The older stratum, part Proto-
Negroid, part Caspian, with minorities of the now dominant
Palæ-Alpines, fused into what has been called by some the
"Indonesian type," and took refuge in the interior of the larger
islands.

Finally, at a period which may well have been as late as the
middle of the first millennium B. C., a last body of immigrants
appeared—the true Malays. This time the influx came apparently from the north, from the southern Chinese coast, where
a bold, seafaring folk had long occupied the shore and were being
dispossessed by the expansion of the Chinese people. They
sought new homes across the seas, and settled along the western

coasts of the Philippines and Borneo, and, ascending the large rivers of eastern Sumatra, colonized the healthy central high-lands whence, as the so-called Menangkabau Malays, they came traditionally in the twelfth century to the Malay Peninsula, a considerable part of which they conquered and overran. These true Malays also wandered eastward, and added a considerable increment here and there to the coast peoples. Yet in Indonesia as a whole the true Malay forms merely a surface layer, the great bulk of the people being of the older Palæ-Alpine type.

# CHAPTER II

## MELANESIA AND AUSTRALIA

### I. MELANESIA

To the archipelago beginning with the great island of New Guinea and extending eastward to New Caledonia and Fiji, the name of Melanesia is given, because its inhabitants, in comparison with those of the other islands in the Pacific, are much darker skinned. New Guinea, nearly 1,500 miles long and 500 miles wide at its broadest part, is the largest island in the world, and, with its lofty snow-capped mountains rising from the steaming tropical jungle, affords a great variety of environment. The more easterly islands are, as a rule, small, although most are more or less mountainous. On the west Melanesia is in close touch with Indonesia, and on the south with Australia. On the north wide stretches of open sea separate it from Micronesia, but at its eastern extremity, a multitude of small islets connect it with the Ellice, Samoan and Tongan groups of Western Polynesia. Linguistically the inhabitants of Melanesia are divisible into two groups, those on the one hand speaking so-called Melanesian languages, who occupy almost all the smaller islands and considerable portions of the coast of New Guinea, especially in the southeast and north; and, on the other hand, those speaking Papuan languages, who are spread over most of the interior and the rest of the coasts of New Guinea, parts of the Bismarck archipelago, and are found in the interiors of several of the islands in the Solomon group and, perhaps, in parts of the New Hebrides. While the Melanesian languages are related to the Malayan spoken throughout Indonesia, the Micronesian and Polynesian languages, and the Papuan are quite distinct, unless they have some connection with those of Northern Australia, as Schmidt[1] seems to have shown.

[1] Schmidt, W., 1908, 1912–14.

On the basis of their physical type, the people of Melanesia are divisible into two main groups, in one of which the dolicho-cephalic factors are dominant, whereas in the other brachyce-phalic types prevail. The distribution of these two groups is shown on the maps given on Plates XXII to XXV. In discussing these groups more in detail, we may best begin with New Guinea, and then consider the smaller, eastern islands.

The satisfactory determination of the physical types in New Guinea is rendered extremely difficult by the absence of any adequate cranial material, data being available for only a few small areas,[1] and by the absence of any information on the liv-ing except as to the cephalic index, from almost the whole of the region. On the basis of existing materials,[2] however, the primarily dolichocephalic peoples occupy the whole of the west-ern and southern coast from Geelvink Bay around to the Purari delta at the head of the Papuan Gulf. On the north coast, the conditions are more complex, in that while much of the shore is held by them, there are several areas, for example west of the mouth of the Augusta River, about Astrolabe Bay, Huon Gulf, etc., where brachycephalic types prevail. The exact delimita-tion of these areas is not yet possible. Along the southern coast from East Cape to the head of the Gulf of Papua, the popu-lation is clearly very mixed, now one and now the other form prevailing, but we have no data which will enable us to plot the distribution with any accuracy. In the interior of Dutch New Guinea the people are, at least in the south, brachycephalic, and the same holds true for some interior tribes in British New Guinea, such as the Mafulu and among the Kai and other in-terior tribes inland from Huon Gulf. Along the great rivers, however, such as the Fly and the Augusta, dolichocephalic peoples seem to reach far inland.

Further analysis reveals the fact that the dolichocephalic peoples are everywhere primarily of the Proto-Negroid and Proto-

---

[1] Broek, van der, 1915 a; Mantegazza, 1881; Gray, 1901; Dorsey, 1897; Sergi, 1898; Spital, 1906.

[2] Broek, van der, 1915 b, 1918; Chalmers, 1897; Haddon, 1915–16; Koch, 1908; Schlaginhaufen, 1914; Seligmann, 1909.

Australoid types, the brachycephalic groups on the other hand being almost exclusively Palæ-Alpine. As we possess cranial data of any value for so few points only, the problem of working out the distribution of the types is difficult, to say the least, but, so far as one can infer, the situation is somewhat as follows. In the island of Mysore in Geelvink Bay, the Proto-Australoid type is in large majority, as it is in a lesser degree in the Purari delta in the Gulf of Papua, and in the western islands in Torres Straits. On the lower Lorenz River (central southwest coast), however, the Proto-Negroid type is dominant. A further fact of interest is that throughout the coast region of western New Guinea (whence alone we have adequate cranial material) this dolichocephalic population includes a not inconsiderable leptorrhine element, both Caspian and Mediterranean! What is surprising, however, is that these factors appear to increase eastward, and attain their greatest importance in the crania from the Purari delta, where the Caspian type is actually secondary! It is present also among the brachycephalic groups, although generally in smaller proportion, yet in the population of Leitere, about in the centre of the northern coast of the island, it is as prominent as in the Purari delta! An explanation for the presence of this unexpected type will be suggested later, but for the moment a word more must be said in regard to the brachycephalic forms. These are, as stated previously, almost exclusively platyrrhine, the leptorrhine types being present anywhere (so far as our data show) only as a very slight trace. In the three considerable cranial series which we possess (none of which, however, come from a brachycephalic area) the Palæ-Alpine alone is represented. Whether this is the normal or the Negrito form we have as yet no means of knowing, but I believe that in the case of the *interior* peoples, who as we shall see are of strikingly short stature, it is in the main the latter form which is present. On the coast, however, especially in the north, it is much more probably the ordinary form.

In stature, the inhabitants of New Guinea show wide variation. Two groups, the Kai in the interior north of Huon Gulf, and the Tapiro of the high ranges in the interior of southwestern Dutch New Guinea, appear to be true Pigmies, their average stature being less than 145 cm. Most of the peoples of the interior, throughout New Guinea, are also distinctly short, the average stature varying from 151 to 157 cm., and these short statures, furthermore, occupy most of the coast of what was formerly German New Guinea. Those of the southern shore, on the other hand, from Etna Bay in western Dutch New Guinea to East Cape and around approximately to the boundary between what was formerly German New Guinea and the British territories, are taller, with statures over 160 cm., culminating in the Gulf of Papua and the adjacent portion of southeastern Dutch New Guinea, where they reach 167 cm. or over. It may be said therefore that, in a general way, the shorter statures are found among those peoples who are primarily brachycephalic and Palæ-Alpine, whereas the taller types are associated with the dolichocephalic group, culminating where the Caspian factors are strongest.

To attempt to unravel the probably complicated racial history of an area where so little accurate data are available, is certainly hazardous, yet its broader outlines may perhaps be sketched in very tentative fashion. In the absence of all archæological materials, and taking into account the probable history of the adjacent areas, we are led to assume that the oldest stratum of population is represented by the short-statured, Palæ-Alpine folk of the interior. The earliest occupants of New Guinea, on this theory, would have been pigmy Negritos, comparable to those still surviving in the Philippines, and surviving now in New Guinea in any purity only in the more inaccessible portions of the interior, and exemplified in the Tapiro, of whom a portrait is given on Plate XXVII, Fig. 1. Following the occupation by this earliest population, there came from Indonesia a drift of taller folk, predominantly of Proto-Australoid type, who spread along the coasts and up the larger rivers. After a period of unknown length, during which these newcomers became dominant, a new wave, this time primarily of Proto-Negroid peoples,

came from the same direction, spread like its predecessor along
the coasts, and in time acquired almost everywhere the predominant position. An example of a blend between these Proto-
Negroid and Proto-Australoid types is given on Plate XXVII,
Fig. 2. Toward the end of this period a considerable factor of
Caspian type was introduced, either as an element absorbed by
the later groups of migrants while still in Indonesia, or perhaps
as a separate, small stream by itself. I suspect that its influence will be found to have been most intense in British New
Guinea.

The subsequent events are still obscure. We are practically
forced by the conditions which we meet in Polynesia to assume
that the most recent elements in its population are traceable to
a drift of brachycephalic peoples coming from Indonesia. In
part, at least, these eastward-moving migrants, of whom the
earlier were mainly Palæ-Alpine (but not Negrito) and the later
Alpine, must have skirted the shores of New Guinea, and might
be expected to have left traces of their passage. The earlier or
Palæ-Alpine drift must have occurred after that of the Proto-
Negroid. In our search for evidences of its passage we are restricted to the northern coast and the eastern part of the southern, where alone (except for the interior) brachycephalic folk are
found. In the absence of any adequate metrical data we have
to depend on skin color and the character of the hair for clews,
since lighter skins and straighter hair might be expected to be
the result of Palæ-Alpine mixture. Scattered along the northern
coast, areas so characterized are to be found in which either all
the population is lighter and straighter-haired, or individuals
having these characteristics are more common. This is especially true of some of the small islands off the coast, where the
new immigrants could have more easily secured a foothold than
on the mainland. The largest frequency of lighter skins and
straighter hair is found on the southern coast of British New
Guinea, between Cape Possession and Orangerie Bay, but how
far these are due to brachycephalic Palæ-Alpines and how far
to the earlier penetration of Caspian elements, it is, in the ab-

FIG. 1. TAPIRO PIGMY. (NEW GUINEA.)

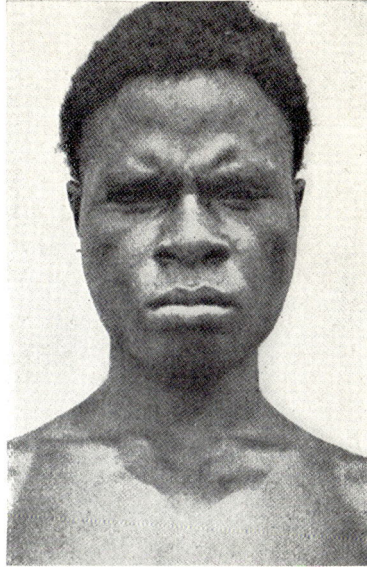

FIG. 2. MELANESIAN. (NEW GUINEA.)

FIG. 3. MELANESIAN. (FIJI.)

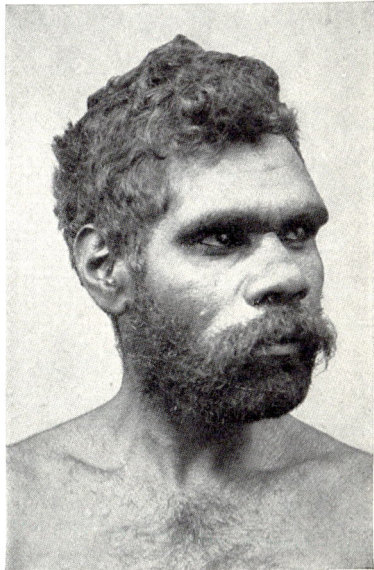

FIG. 4. AUSTRALIAN.

PLATE XXVII.

sence of any cranial material, impossible to say. A further indication of Palæ-Alpine admixture is seen in the not infrequent
occurrence of the Mongoloid eye, which is absent apparently
(?) where the lighter-skinned elements do not show themselves.
On the north coast, so far as our meagre data go, any influence
from brachycephalic, light-skinned folk must be attributed to
the Palæ-Alpine type, since there seems to be no trace of the
Alpine elements.

A puzzling problem, however, arises in regard to the Alpine
type elsewhere. Although not traceable on the north coast, it
does appear as a minority factor in southwest Dutch New Guinea,
both on the coast and in the interior, as among the Tapiro Pigmies, who, on the basis of all our other evidence, we must assume
to be the oldest residents of the region. And although absent
on the northern coast, it turns up among the people of the
Torricelli Mountains inland from the shore! In what way this
Alpine factor, which everywhere throughout the Oceanic area
is evidently of all types the most recent, reached these interior
tribes it is impossible to say and, until we have more adequate
data, it is quite useless to speculate.

The lesser island sof Melanesia present in general the same
problems as New Guinea, and are, for the most part, as imperfectly known. Subject to the same immigrant streams as the
greater western land mass, these smaller islands, owing to their
very smallness, were less able to retain unchanged the older
strata of population. Yet almost everywhere that any study
of the people has been made a difference between the coastal
and interior population has been noted, and in the various islands of a large group, as, for example, the Solomons and New
Hebrides, wide differences in physical type are usually observed.

With a few clear exceptions, the large majority of the people
of the smaller islands are predominantly of the dolichocephalic,
"Melanesian" types (*i. e.*, Proto-Negroid and Proto-Australoid),
as shown by the maps, Plates XXII to XXV. Wherever the
data will permit the determination of the types, the Proto-Negroid is always strongly dominant. This is the case, for example,

in the coastal population of the Gazelle peninsula in New Britain,[1] in the southern portion of New Ireland,[2] and in the island of New Hannover;[3] it is also true in the D'Entrecasteaux archipelago,[4] in the northern Solomons,[5] parts of the New Hebrides, most of New Caledonia,[6] the Loyalty islands,[6] and Fiji.[7] A dominance of brachycephalic forms is clearly proved as yet only among the Baining[8] of the interior of northern New Britain, for the people of central and northern New Ireland,[9] Woodlark Island[4] and (?) the Trobriand group, some of the smaller islands of the central Solomons,[10] and parts of the New Hebrides (especially Espiritu Santo).[11] It is perhaps true also of the southeast coast of New Caledonia. In most cases these brachycephalic peoples are either interior tribes distinct from the coastal peoples (sometimes also in language, speaking Papuan languages rather than Melanesian), or they represent a social class in the community, sometimes the common people, more rarely (?) the aristocracy.

We must now return for a moment to the consideration of the dolichocephalic group, to call attention to one or two points of significance. Although the Proto-Negroid type is in all cases in the strong majority, it is always associated with the Proto-Australoid, which usually holds second place except in New Hannover, where the Caspian takes its place, and in the Telei of Bougainville in the northern Solomons, among whom the Palæ-Alpine is of secondary importance. The latter case may probably be explained on the basis that the Telei, a Papuan-speaking tribe, are in part a purely interior people and have thus preserved a large element of the older Palæ-Alpine type in spite of their mixture with the later Proto-Negroid immigrants who occupied the coast. The strength of the Caspian element among the people of New Hannover is not so easily accounted for. It may have been brought by the Proto-Negroid immigrants, but seems more likely to be due to the influence of the separate drift of Caspian

---

[1] MacCurdy, 1914; Müller-Wismar, 1905.
[2] Friederici, 1912.
[3] Anthropologische Sammlungen Deutschlands.
[4] Sergi, 1895 a.
[5] Frizzi, 1913. [6] Sarasin, 1916–18. [7] Krause, 1881; Flower, 1879.
[8] Bauer, L., 1915; Friederici, *op. cit.* [9] Friederici, *op. cit.*
[10] Guppy, 1885–86; Giuffrida-Ruggeri, 1906 a. [11] Speiser, 1911.

peoples, who, as we have seen, had a considerable influence in parts of New Guinea, and almost certainly passed in large numbers through Micronesia to the north.

In stature the peoples of the smaller islands show, as in New Guinea, much variation. The interior brachycephalic, hypothetically more aboriginal, groups, seem everywhere to be short (Baining 159 cm., Espiritu Santo 152 cm.). The majority of the population ranges from 162 cm. to 168 cm., while in a few restricted areas, such as the southeast coast of New Caledonia and some of the peoples in the New Hebrides, the stature rises to 170 cm. or even more. Skin color is also very variable, ranging from the blue-black of the northern Solomon islands through dark browns to the lighter browns found in parts of the southern Solomons and southwestern New Caledonia. In general, however, dark tones prevail. The hair, lastly, is subject to similar local differences. In general strongly frizzly or even woolly, it is here and there, particularly along the eastern margin of Melanesia, sometimes only curly. A typical example of one of the eastern Melanesians is shown on Plate XXVII, Fig. 3.

We may tentatively reconstruct the history of the smaller islands of Melanesia as follows. The oldest population was a mixed one, the result of the fusion of the Negrito and Proto-Australoid peoples in New Guinea, although in the Bismarck Archipelago the former may have occupied the islands in a fairly pure state in the beginning. There is reason to believe, however, that this ancient Negrito folk were not able to make any lengthy sea voyages, so that, while they might perhaps cross the thirty-mile-wide Dampier Straits from New Guinea to New Britain, they were probably unable to reach the Solomons and more distant eastern and southern groups, although their apparent presence in Espiritu Santo in the New Hebrides raises an interesting question. The predominantly Proto-Australoid peoples who streamed into New Guinea at an early date, however, were better navigators, and with some admixture they spread throughout the eastern islands. Later, when the Proto-Negroid drift began, it swept again through the whole area, occupying the coasts and driving the older population inland, or into certain islands in the group. The part played here by the still later, light-skinned, straight-haired stream of Palæ-Alpine and Alpine peoples, which latter in the main passed on into Polynesia, is, as in New Guinea, still obscure. In the Bismarck Archipelago they must, it would seem, have exerted some effect, and it is probable that the predominantly brachycephalic populations of the central and northern parts of New Ireland owe part of their round-headedness to this influence. In the central Solomons the same may be true, although the lighter skins seem more common in the southern parts of the group, where dolichocephalic types are more in control. In some islands of the New Hebrides and in southeastern New Caledonia, taller stature, lighter skin and the occurrence of curly or wavy hair again bespeak the influence of these later drifts, but the apparent absence of all trace of any leptorrhine element indicates that the very latest or Alpine stream did not appreciably affect Melanesia.

To a slight extent, the taller, lighter-skinned brachycephalic factors along the eastern margin of Melanesia, may be due, as has long been supposed, to a recent "backwash" of Polynesian peoples from Samoa and Tonga; but the fact that these western Polynesian folk are in very large measure Alpine in type, which factor is apparently almost lacking in those parts of Melanesia where their influence is thought to have made itself felt, makes it probable that the number of such recent Polynesian immigrants has been so small as to be from the standpoint of physical type practically negligable, however important it may have proved on the cultural side.

## II. AUSTRALIA AND TASMANIA

The Australian continent together with the adjacent island of Tasmania, contains (or did contain, since the aboriginal peoples in the latter island are extinct) a population of extremely small size, spread over an immense territory. The environment in which this sparse population lived was in sharp contrast with that of all the rest of the Oceanic area, for nearly the whole of the western two-thirds of the continent is desert or subdesert, and only in a relatively narrow strip along the northern and eastern coasts and in Tasmania is there a moderate or plentiful rainfall. At Torres Straits the northern peninsula of Queensland almost comes in contact with New Guinea, so that no skill in navigation would be required for the passage of people from one area to the other. Indeed, at the period when Australia may be expected to have received its first population, it may still have been joined to New Guinea. Elsewhere, only a skilled seafaring folk could be expected to have reached the continent. In general, thus, Australia forms a vast *cul-de-sac* approachable only by a narrow corridor at the north, and from which there was no exit.

Linguistically the inhabitants of Australia and Tasmania seem to be divisible into two main groups, one occupying the northern border of the continent, the other all the rest of the area. The northern group is thought perhaps to have some relations with the Papuan languages of the adjacent parts of New Guinea. Whether or not the Tasmanian languages stood wholly apart from all others, or were very remotely related to those of southeastern Australia, is not yet clear.[1]

The aboriginal population of Australia[2] divides itself naturally into two clearly marked groups, one occupying the north and east (which includes the more favorable parts of the continent) and the other the west and south, which is the desert and arid region. Both groups show an overwhelming majority of dolichocephalic factors, the brachycephalic elements amounting to from 2 to 7 per cent only. The first group is marked by the predominance of the Proto-Negroid type, the second by that of the Proto-Australoid.

Each group, moreover, shows significant variations. In the first, in which are included the tribes of North Australia, Queens-

---

[1] Schmidt, W., 1908, 1912–14.
[2] The main sources of material are: Berry, 1909, 1910; Burston, 1913; Cauvin, 1881; Duckworth, 1893–94, 1894–95; Flower, 1879; Giuffrida-Ruggeri, 1906 a; Houzé, 1884–85 a, 1884–85 b; Krause, W., 1897; Pöch, 1915; Robertson, 1910; Spencer, 1899, 1904; Turner, 1884.

land, and New South Wales, the proportion of the Proto-Negroid
type varies as one passes east and south, in that in Northern Australia it amounts to over 70 per cent, in Queensland to 60 per
cent, and in New South Wales to only just 50 per cent of the
total; and as the importance of this type *decreases*, so that of the
Proto-Australoid *increases*, from 20 per cent in the first instance
to 35 per cent in the latter.  In the second group, which includes
the tribes of West Australia, South Australia, and Victoria the
relative importance of the Proto-Australoid type (which is dominant in all) *increases*, while that of the Proto-Negroid *decreases*
as one approaches the southeastern corner of the continent, so
that while in West Australia the Proto-Australoid factor amounts
to a little ove: 45 per cent, in South Australia and Victoria it
rises to 60 per cent, the Proto-Negroid decreasing from 33 per
cent in West Australia to 25 per cent in Victoria.  The maps
given on Plate XXVIII, Figs. 1 and 2, will help to make these
relations clear.  For central Australia the data are less abundant,
but seem to indicate an even balance between the two types.
The illustration given on Plate XXVII, Fig. 4, shows a representative of the more strongly Proto-Australoid type.

    The Australian population thus appears to be made up almost
entirely of two types, the Proto-Negroid and Proto-Australoid,
of which the former is concentrated in the north and northwest,
the latter in the south and southeast.  This gradual decline in
importance of the Proto-Negroid and increase of the Proto-Australoid is, in a measure, carried a step farther in Tasmania.[1]  The
extremely primitive population of this island became extinct in
the last quarter of the nineteenth century, although a few half-
breeds still survive.  A study of the Tasmanian crania reveals
two points of much significance.  First, that the proportion of
the Proto-Negroid type present is lower (19 per cent) than in
any portion of Australia, and second, that the increase in the
Proto-Australoid type which might perhaps be expected, is replaced by a considerable brachycephalic factor, amounting to
nearly 25 per cent!  In spite of this, however, the Proto-Aus-

[1] Berry, 1909; Duckworth, 1892; Harper, 1897; Turner, 1908.

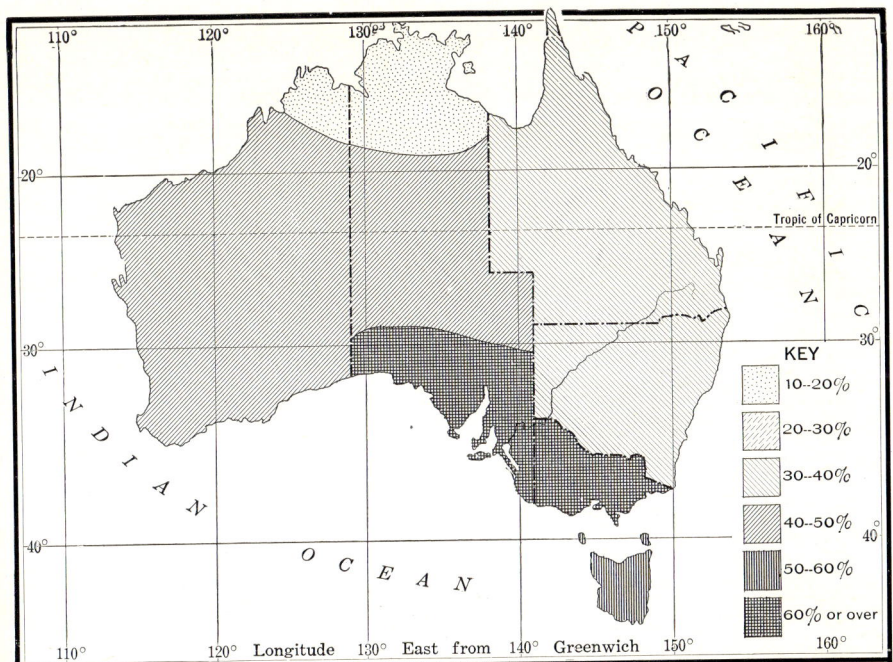

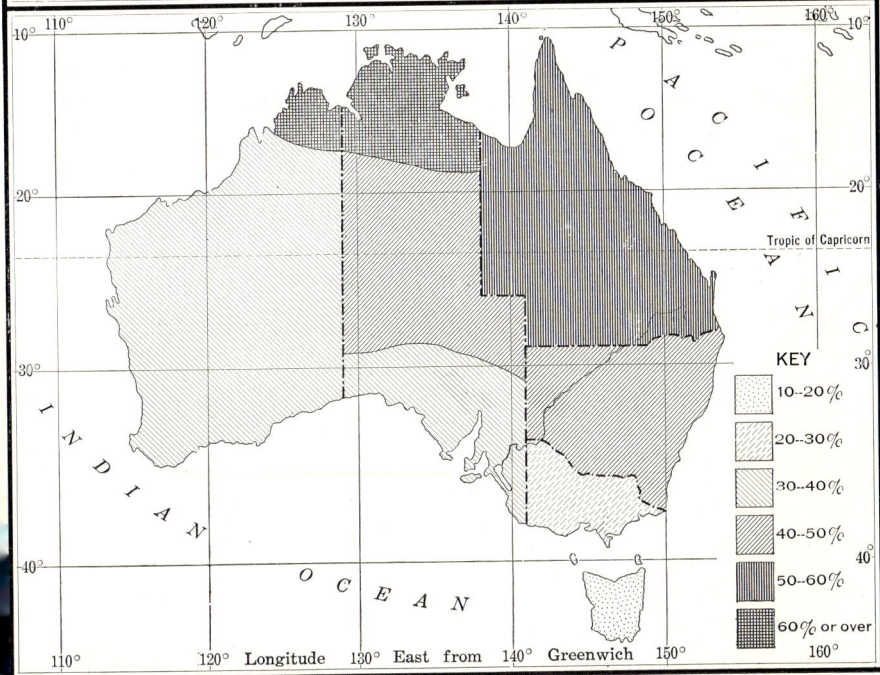

PLATE XXVIII. AUSTRALIA.

Figure 1 (*top*). Percentage distribution of Proto-Australoid Types.
Figure 2. Percentage distribution of Proto-Negroid Types.

traloid type remains, as in the south and southeast of Australia, clearly dominant. The brachycephalic factors are the Palæ-Alpine and the Mongoloid. Of these the former, which is almost certainly the Negrito variety of the type, is found as a trace throughout Australia, but no influence of the Mongoloid seems visible there, so that this type is apparently confined wholly to Tasmania.

In stature, the northern tribes are taller (average 171 cm.) than those in the southern part of the continent and Tasmania (average 165–167 cm.), and approximate the tall folk of the southern part of New Guinea. In skin color the population is everywhere dark, varying from a deep chocolate, which is the most general tone, to darker shades in the north and in Tasmania. The hair is throughout the larger part of the continent wavy or even straight, but in the north individuals with curly and frizzly hair are not uncommon, while in Tasmania the frizzly type prevails.

How are these facts to be interpreted? To my mind the most plausible explanation is this. The oldest stratum of population (one which may date back, I believe, to a time contemporaneous with the Palæolithic period in Europe) was one predominantly of Proto-Australoid type, with minorities, however, of the Negrito variety of the Palæ-Alpine and of the Mongoloid typ s. Coming from the northward through New Guinea this earliest wave of peoples entered the continent by way of the Cape York peninsula, perhaps before the formation of Torres Straits, and spread thinly throughout the eastern more favored portion of the country. The brachycephalic factors were associated mainly with the advance guard of this early drift, the later immigrants being more purely of the Proto-Australoid type. It is perhaps possible that a very early population of comparatively pure Negrito type may have occupied the continent sparsely before the arrival of the Proto-Australoids, but for this there is no clear evidence as yet. The presence of the Proto-Australoid type in Queensland at a very early but as yet uncertain period is, however, indicated by the Talgai skull.[1]

[1] Smith, 1918.

Later, a new wave of immigration, following the route taken by the earlier one but mainly of Proto-Negroid type, came into the continent. Like their predecessors they spread down the eastern side and thence more thinly elsewhere, forcing the older population west and south into the desert sections and Tasmania. Along the northern coast, however, they settled in greatest numbers. To Tasmania the newcomers penetrated but slightly, perhaps owing to the completion of the subsidence which, in recent times, led to the separation of the island from the mainland.

If this interpretation of the racial history of Australia is correct, then in the south of the continent and in Tasmania we have preserved for us, more perfectly perhaps than elsewhere in the world, what are probably the oldest types of the human race. Here in this vast *cul-de-sac*, barred by remoteness, by deserts and by the sea from the great human currents which flowed throughout the rest of the world, these ancient peoples, untouched by any of the later movements, survived as an anachronism. That in Tasmania, the most isolated spot of all, we should find the vanishing traces of the Mongoloid type, is, it seems to me, most significant; for it substantiates the conclusions reached in Africa and in Europe, that this, like the Proto-Australoid, is one of the most ancient of human types, surviving here and there only and chiefly in the uttermost margins of the habitable world.

# CHAPTER III

## POLYNESIA AND MICRONESIA

### I. POLYNESIA

THE island world of the middle Pacific is unique. Composed of small islands, some high and mountainous, others mere low, coral atolls rising only fifteen or twenty feet above the sea; aggregated in groups or scattered singly; separated from one another by hundreds or even thousands of miles of open ocean, it forms in all probability the last portion of the habitable surface of the earth to be occupied by man. For, while men of very primitive culture might spread by means of rafts or clumsy canoes from continental areas to islands visible from the mainland and from each other, and lying at distances of perhaps as much as fifty miles, they could not traverse hundreds of miles of sea, seeking lands unseen and unknown, until they had perfected seaworthy vessels of considerable carrying capacity, and had acquired much skill in navigation. Primitive man could thus have wandered from Asia through Indonesia to New Guinea and Australia, and might even have reached some of the islands of eastern Melanesia; but not until he had the proper vessels and requisite skill, and, further, the courage to quest far beyond the horizon, could he have crossed the wide spaces which for so long had guarded and kept inviolate the paradise-like islands of the South Seas.

If on the map we draw a line from Hawaii to New Zealand, from here to Easter Island, and thence back again to Hawaii, we have formed a nearly equilateral triangle of about 5,000 miles on a side, which includes practically the whole of Polynesia. Clustered roughly in the centre of the triangle and along its western side, lie the great majority of the islands, the Samoan, Tongan, Cook, Society, Tuamotu, and Marquesas groups, whereas Hawaii,

New Zealand, and Easter Island lie isolated at the corners, each separated from the nearest inhabited land by from one to two thousand miles of sea. This "Polynesian triangle" of New Zealand, Hawaii, and Easter Island affords, I believe, the key not only to the problems of the racial but also those of the cultural history of the area as well.

Linguistically the population of the whole of Polynesia forms a unit, since all speak closely related languages, affiliated to the Melanesian and the Malayan or Indonesian, and through them to the Mon-Khmer of southeastern Asia. Culturally and physically the people are, however, far from uniform, for, although it has been the custom to speak of "the" Polynesian type as though there were but one, analysis of the data will show that this is by no means the case.

The occupants of each of the three corners of the "triangle" are marked, as is shown by the maps, Plates XXII to XXV, by the predominance of a different physical type; in Hawaii the Palæ-Alpine; in Easter Island the Proto-Negroid; in New Zealand and the Chatham Islands the Caspian. Let us consider these three groups in some little detail, in the above order. For the people of the Hawaiian group we are fortunate in possessing fairly abundant cranial material,[1] coming in the main from the two extremities of the group, Hawaii in the south and Kauai in the north. The difference between the populations of these two islands is striking, for, although in both brachycephalic factors are in the majority, the types present are not the same. In Kauai, at the northwest or most remote end of the group, the Palæ-Alpine type is in the majority, followed in order by the Proto-Negroid and Caspian; in Hawaii, at the southeastern or nearer end, the Alpine type is dominant, followed by the Palæ-Alpine, Proto-Negroid, and Caspian. That is to say, the population of the island of Hawaii is equivalent to that in the island of Kauai *overlaid* by a stratum of Alpine peoples. It seems probable, therefore, that we may regard the Kauai population as representing an older stratum, once characteristic of the whole

---

[1] P. M.; Otis, 1876; Allen, 1898; Turner, 1884; Flower, 1879.

group, and that there has since entered from the southward an immigration of Alpine peoples who have come to dominate Hawaii, but whose influence has become weaker and weaker toward the farther extremity of the group, until in Kauai the Alpine factor appears only as a very small minority. But, although the Alpines are actually predominant in the south, it is only by a rather narrow margin, and even there the Palæ-Alpine type is very strongly represented. We shall see later that the Alpine element can be very clearly traced to central Polynesia, to the southward, but whence did the Palæ-Alpine factor come? If we search in other parts of Polynesia, it at once becomes apparent that almost *nowhere else in the whole of Polynesia*, so far as our present data go, does this type appear except as a trace. (See map, Plate XXIV.) To account for its presence in the Hawaiian group in such strength, we have apparently two alternatives. We may either assume that it came from some other part of Polynesia, but has there almost wholly disappeared, or that it came from elsewhere. The only other possible region from which it could have come is Micronesia. Unfortunately, our data are especially meagre for this area, and from the Marshall group in particular, the nearest portion to the Hawaiian group, we have nothing at all. Yet, so far as the materials go, Micronesia is as innocent of any traces of Palæ-Alpine peoples as Polynesia outside Hawaii. So that here also, if the people passed through, they must have been mere birds of passage and left no traces behind them. That this Palæ-Alpine factor in Hawaii must be mainly of the normal type and not the Negrito variety, seems clear,[1] for the short stature, dark skin, and frizzly hair of the Negrito seem to find no counterpart in any Hawaiian people that we know. But if it be the normal Palæ-Alpine type, we are faced by a new difficulty, since this is nowhere else in Oceania a very ancient type, yet here it forms the oldest stratum of the population. This difficulty is more apparent than real, however, since the Alpine type which it precedes is the latest of

[1] My previous views on this question have, as a result of increased materials, been changed. See Dixon, 1920.

all, and it has already been pointed out that owing to the remoteness of Hawaii, we need not expect it to have been reached
by any ancient and primitive peoples.  An example showing a
rather mixed Palæ-Alpine type is given on Plate XXIX, Fig. 1.
Let us leave this puzzle, however, for the moment, and turn to
the other parts of the triangle.

The population of Easter Island[1] stands in sharp contrast
to that of the Hawaiian group.  Instead of a large majority of
brachycephalic factors, it shows an overwhelming predominance
of dolichocephalic types, the Proto-Negroid alone amounting to
about 55 per cent, the minority being made up of the Caspian,
Proto-Australoid and Palæ-Alpine in nearly equal proportions.
This predominance of the Proto-Negroid type does not hold
for Easter Island alone, for it is marked, so far as our data go,
for the Society[2] and Cook[2] groups as well.  For the Tuamotu no
data at all are available, but from the fact that the population
is generally described as similar to that of the Society group,
we may tentatively assume the same predominance of the Proto-
Negroid type.  Only in the Marquesas[3] does this not hold, for
here the very much mixed population, although by large majority
dolichocephalic, yet had as its most important single type the
Alpine.  It may, therefore, be emphasized that at the extreme
southeast corner of the triangle and throughout the whole southeastern part of central Polynesia, except for the Marquesas, the
Proto-Negroid type is everywhere the dominant factor, and in
Easter Island, at least, is followed in importance by the Caspian.

The theory has long been expressed that there was a "Melanesian," i. e., a Negroid element, in the peoples of parts of Polynesia, and this has been generally explained as having been
absorbed by the Polynesian ancestors during their passage
through Melanesia.  The alternative theory that a pre-Poly-
nesian stratum of "Melanesian" (i. e., Negroid) characteristics
was widely spread throughout Polynesia has been decried.  The
analysis of the data seems, however, to my mind, to leave no op-

[1] Jablonowski, 1902; Volz, 1894–95.          [2] von Luschan, 1907.
[3] von Luschan, op. cit.

tion but to accept this outlawed view, for it is difficult to see how so large a proportion of "Melanesian" factors (amounting to nearly 70 per cent) could have been brought to far-off Easter Island as the result merely of the "absorption" of these elements in transit.

We may now turn to the third or southwestern corner of the triangle, occupied by New Zealand[1] and the Chatham Islands.[2] Traditionally the Maori, as the people of New Zealand are known, are made up of two groups of people, an older aboriginal stratum and a later, derived from the immigrants who in the thirteenth and fourteenth centuries came to New Zealand from the Society and Cook groups. The Moriori of the Chatham Islands, on the other hand, were emigrants from New Zealand a century or so prior to the period which brought these conquerors and settlers from the east. At the time of the European discovery of New Zealand the descendants of the thirteenth and fourteenth century immigrants formed the great bulk of the population, especially in the North Island, the older aboriginal stock having been almost wholly destroyed or absorbed.

We are fortunate in possessing a considerable body of cranial material from this whole region. Turning our attention first to New Zealand, it appears that, if we take all the crania together in a single series, the Maori are a very much mixed people, with a large majority of dolichocephalic factors. The Caspian type is relatively the most important single type present, followed in order by the Proto-Australoid, Proto-Negroid, and Alpine. The dominant type thus, in this corner of the triangle, differs from that in each of the others. If the material from New Zealand instead of being treated as a whole is divided into three groups made up of the crania coming respectively from the northern peninsula of the North Island, the remainder of the North Island, and the South Island (a division based on certain cultural and historical bases), significant local variations appear. Thus the

[1] Flower, 1879; Mollison, 1908–09; Scott, 1893; Turner, 1884.
[2] Duckworth, 1900 b; Flower, *op. cit.;* Poll, 1902; Scott, *op. cit.;* Thomson, E. J., 1915.

proportion of dolichocephalic factors *decreases* from north to south as follows: northern peninsula 75 per cent, rest of North Island 65 per cent, South Island 55 per cent. The proportion of the Alpine type, on the contrary, *increases;* northern peninsula 6 per cent, rest of North Island 23 per cent, South Island 31 per cent; and whereas, in the whole of the North Island the Caspian is the most important single type present, in the South Island this position is held by the Alpine. Lastly, in the North Island the "Melanesian" elements (*i. e.* Proto-Negroid and Proto-Australoid) are much stronger than in the south. Taking these facts into consideration with the traditional history, it would appear that if we regard the South Island population as more nearly representing the older, aboriginal inhabitants (since it occupies relatively the more remote position), the new factors brought by the fourteenth-century immigrants must have been largely dolichocephalic and, in the main, of Caspian and Proto-Negroid types—precisely those which were actually of greatest importance throughout southeastern Polynesia, whence the invaders came. It would also follow that if the South Island roughly represents the general character of the population prior to the arrival of the immigrants, this older, aboriginal stratum may be presumed to have been primarily brachycephalic, with the Alpine type predominant, and to have had a much smaller representation of the "Melanesian" types.

Now the emigrants from New Zealand who colonized the Chatham Islands traditionally left a century or two prior to the period of the coming of the eastern conquerors; they should, therefore, preserve for us, even better than the population of the South Island of New Zealand, a sample of this ancient aboriginal stratum. If we turn now to the data, we find that our anticipations as to what the character of that older population must have been are amply confirmed. For the Moriori show a slight majority of brachycephalic factors, the Alpine is very definitely the dominant type, and the proportion of the Proto-Negroid and Proto-Australoid types is very materially decreased. Prior to the thirteenth and fourteenth centuries, then, we may regard the population of New Zealand as having been primarily Alpine, the Caspian and associated Mediterranean types being of secondary importance, while the "Melanesian" factors were relatively unimportant. The Marquesan given on Plate XXIX, Fig. 2, shows an example of this Caspian type.

We are now finally in a position to consider the character of the population of western Polynesia, of Samoa, Tonga, and the Ellice groups.[1] Through these and the neighboring small groups and scattered islands which connect Polynesia with Melanesia and Micronesia, we must assume that the great bulk of all the immigrants, who at various times came into Polynesia, passed. These islands stand in the gateway and must have borne the brunt of each succeeding immigrant drift, and therefore the prevailing character of their present population should be an indication of that of the last migration, since this must largely have swept away or absorbed the earlier occupants. Unfortunately, for this very important area we possess next to nothing in the way of cranial material, and, although there have recently been made extensive measurements on the living in Samoa[2] and Tonga,[3] no individual data have been published. The few crania which we possess are, however, very significant, in that brachycephalic factors are in overwhelming majority, the Alpine type alone amounting to 85 per cent. Sullivan's measurements of living Samoans in general bear out these indications, brachycephalic factors amounting to over 75 per cent and leptorrhine elements outnumbering the platyrrhine by 50 per cent. Taking all the information available, therefore, it seems to be clear that the dominant factor in the population of this western gateway of Polynesia is the Alpine type, and that with it go substantial minorities of other types, which cannot, however, be determined. In other words, the peoples of western Polynesia are *in general* comparable with the population which, by elimination, we have inferred was characteristic of New Zealand prior to the thirteenth and fourteenth centuries. An example from Samoa of this western Polynesian type is given on Plate XXIX, Fig. 3.

[1] Flower, *op. cit.*; Krause, R., 1881.　　[2] Sullivan, 1921.　　[3] Sullivan, 1922.

Before attempting a brief sketch of the racial history of the whole of Polynesia, we must first consider some of the other physical characteristics of the population. In stature, all the Polynesian peoples are tall, the average being given as 173 cm., varying for the different groups from 168 cm. in the case of the Maori to 174 cm. in the Marquesas. In general, thus, the Polynesians rank with the tallest peoples in the world. In skin color the prevailing tone is a light brown, although considerable local and individual variations exist, and strikingly light as well as quite dark colored individuals are occasionally reported. Accurate data on this point, however, enabling us to plot the variations, do not exist. The hair is in general wavy, but straight as well as strongly curly and even frizzly forms occur in individuals here and there.

The fundamental facts upon which the explanation of the racial history of Polynesia must rest are: (1) The dominant position held by the Palæ-Alpine type in the Hawaiian group at the northern corner of the triangle; (2) the concentration of the Proto-Negroid type in Easter Island and the whole southeastern portion of the area; and (3) the preponderance of the Alpine type at the present time in western Polynesia and among the population of New Zealand at the southwestern corner of the triangle prior to the fourteenth century. The first people to enter and settle in Polynesia were, I believe, a mixed "Melanesian" folk, primarily dolichocephalic, a blend of the Proto-Negroid and Proto-Australoid, with a dash of the Caspian type. This mixed people had developed in Melanesia. As these dark-skinned, curly or wavy haired people gradually worked their way eastward they had gained, little by little, in skill of navigation and ability to construct seaworthy canoes; the sea distances to be crossed had increased and they had met the need. By the time that they reached Fiji and the small islands on the eastern verge of Melanesia they were already something of a maritime people. Working their way farther, to Samoa and Tonga, they passed by way of the Cook, Society, and Tuamotu groups far to the eastward, and by some lucky chance actually reached Easter

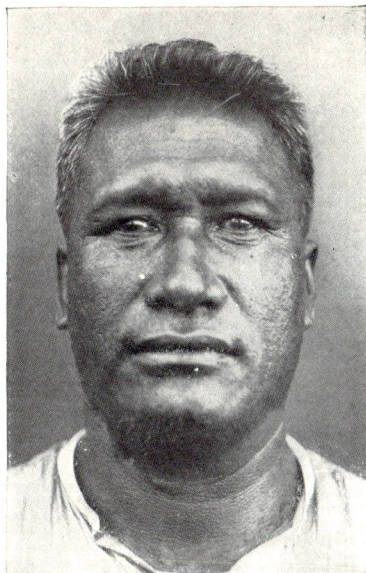

FIG. 1. HAWAIIAN.

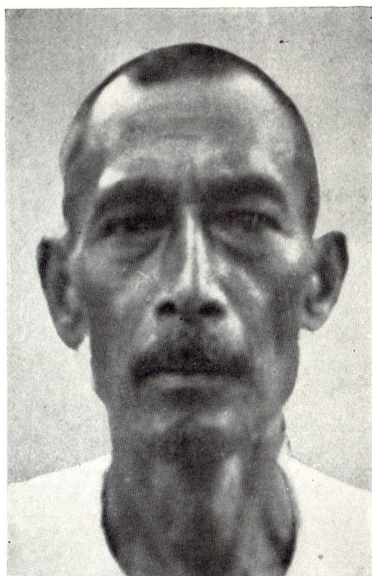

FIG. 2. MARQUESAN.

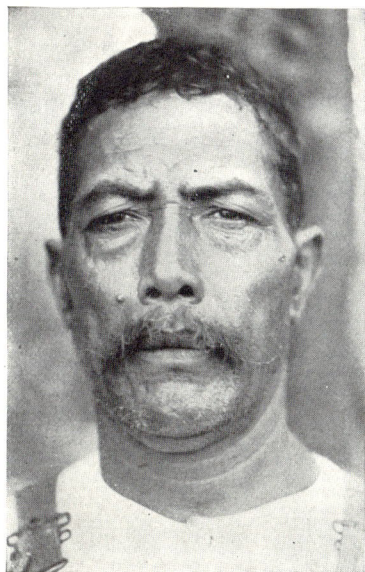

FIG. 3. HAWAIIAN.

FIG. 4. GILBERT ISLANDER.

PLATE XXIX.

Island.  From the Tuamotus they penetrated northward to the
Marquesas, but north of the equator they did not go, and never
reached Hawaii.  Neither, in all probability, did they make the
long southern voyage to New Zealand, so that the first stage of
the discovery and colonization of Polynesia left the northern and
southwestern corners of the triangle still empty.

After these early "Melanesian" wanderers had been in occupation of the lands they had discovered for some time, a new
period of migration set in, bringing to the western margin of
Polynesia a new group of mixed peoples of quite a different character.  These newcomers, who were probably relatively few in
numbers, came down from the north by way of the Ellice and
Gilbert groups rather than from the west by way of Melanesia.
They were, in the main, of Caspian type, but with minorities of
other dolichocephalic forms.  Spreading first to Samoa and Tonga,
they followed the trail of the earlier migrants eastward, one little
group again making its way as far as Easter Island.  Culturally
they were more advanced than their predecessors, and may have
been the bringers of the art of stone construction, the remains
of which in the form of buildings, terraced pyramidal platforms,
and huge monolithic statues we find in many of the islands to
which they came.  Like their predecessors they did not, however, win north to Hawaii or south to New Zealand

The third and last period of migration which played an important part in the peopling of Polynesia, brought again a new
type.  This last movement, which was probably as late as the
early part of the Christian era was in the main Alpine in type,
and came perhaps (?), like the second, by way of Micronesia.
These latest comers were the "ancestors," whose long migrations
are yet dimly remembered by the Polynesian people.  It is current theory that these "Polynesian ancestors" came from Indonesia through Melanesia.  We have seen, however, in the
previous chapter that, so far as our present data go, there is little
certain evidence of their passage, except perhaps in New Ireland
and the central Solomons.  On the other hand, there is not a
little reason to believe that a stream of Alpine peoples came into

and through Micronesia. However that may be, the immigrants
poured into western Polynesia, and thence moved eastward,
largely perhaps by a more northerly route than their predecessors, going by way of the smaller islets (Manihiki, Tongareva,
etc.) to the Marquesas. In the Cook, Society, and Tuamotus,
at any rate, they do not seem to have been numerous enough
to form the dominating element. These latest comers were
more daring and experienced than the earlier, and from Tonga
they quested southward until they reached New Zealand, bringing with them, as a result of fusion with the older western Polynesian population, considerable Caspian and "Melanesian" elements. Thus, New Zealand received its first inhabitants, some
of whom later spread to the Chatham Islands; later, in the thirteenth and fourteenth centuries, this New Zealand population
was profoundly modified by the conquerors who came from the
eastward, bringing primarily dolichocephalic factors.

But not only did these Alpine immigrants into the island
paradise of the South Seas seek for new lands to the southward,
they explored also northward and, by way of the scattered islets
lying north of the Marquesas and central Polynesia, such as
Malden, Christmas, and Fanning Islands (which, although uninhabited when discovered, nevertheless showed evidence of having once been occupied), reached Hawaii. But did they find it
empty? By the theory here suggested none of the earlier peoples
who had penetrated into Polynesia had ever wandered so far to
the north; how, then, could the group have been otherwise than
vacant? It may be remembered, however, that at the beginning
of this chapter, in discussing the character of the population of
the Hawaiian group, we found that the element which was dominant in the more remote northwestern end of the chain, and very
strongly represented even at the southeastern terminus of the
group, was the Palæ-Alpine, a type which is present, except in
Easter Island, as little more than a trace throughout all the rest
of Polynesia. We were, moreover, left in rather a dilemma to
explain its presence. How completely this type is confined to
the Hawaiian group may be realized when it is stated that if

we consider only the crania which are purely of the Palæ-Alpine type, and disregard those in which it appears only as a factor, in the whole series of crania from the rest of Polynesia such skulls number slightly over 1 per cent of the total, whereas in the Hawaiian group they comprise 20 per cent of the series; in the females from Kauai alone they are over 70 per cent! As the distribution of this Palæ-Alpine type in the Hawaiian group, culminating at the remote northwestern extremity, leads to the conclusion that this must have characterized the population prior to the invasion of the Alpines from the south, the problem of accounting for their origin seems for the present practically insoluble. We must await archæological data from the Hawaiian group and also from Micronesia, for I cannot but think that the solution of the mystery may be found there, although our present meagre information gives no intimation of the presence of any people of Palæ-Alpine type in the region to-day.

If this interpretation of the facts as set forth here is correct, we have to recognize in the present Polynesian population not a uniform but a complex people, whose heritage goes back to the older as well as the later strata of Asiatic peoples. Many writers have enlarged upon an elusive "Caucasic" element in the Polynesian area, and this we have found in the Caspian-Mediterranean factor present to-day most strongly probably in the Maori of New Zealand. Just when and by what route this stray branch of Eur-Asiatic blood made its way into the South Seas is not, perhaps, wholly certain. That at a very early date, in all probability in Neolithic times, it had reached the eastern borderlands of Asia has been suggested in a previous section of this book; that later it played some part in the complex racial history of Indonesia we have also seen; its wandering still farther eastward may perhaps come down to what are, in the racial history of the world at large, comparatively modern times.

## II. Micronesia

The island chains of Micronesia, comprising the Pelew, Marianne, Caroline, Marshall, and Gilbert groups have played in all probability a rather important part in the racial history of Oceania, but it is a part which, for lack of data, we can as yet but vaguely understand. Its importance lies in the way in which they link Polynesia with Indonesia, affording as it were a by-pass around the whole Melanesian region, and also link Polynesia through the Marianne and Bonin Islands, with Japan and the central portion of the eastern Asiatic coast.

As the name Micronesia implies, these islands are all small, and, although the western groups (Pelew, Marianne, Caroline) have many more or less rugged and volcanic islands, the Marshall and Gilbert groups in the east and south are wholly composed of low coral atolls. Linguistically, the occupants of all these islands speak related languages, which are affiliated with the Melanesian and Polynesian, and the Malayan or Indonesian languages.

In view of the significance of Micronesia in the history of the Oceanic area, it is disappointing to find that as yet we have little or no data of value regarding the physical characteristics of the people. From the very scanty material,[1] however, some indications of value may be gleaned.

In the first place, leaving out of account the Marshall group for which no material, so far as I know, exists, there appears to be a rather regular and gradual change in the Micronesian region from west to east and south, in that, in the Pelew group and Yap, brachycephalic factors are in very large majority, whereas, passing eastward through the Carolines to Ponapé, the balance swings to a preponderance of dolichocephalic factors, reaching its maximum in the Gilbert group with a proportion of 70 to 75 per cent. Since Krause does not give any nasal measurements, the only indication as to the types present in the Carolines comes from the small series of crania from Ruk given by Virchow. From

[1] Virchow, 1881; Krause, 1881.

these it would appear that the Proto-Negroid type was here in the majority, the Palæ-Alpine being secondary and the Caspian-Mediterranean elements present as a considerable minority. In the Gilbert group Virchow's small series shows that the Caspian type is strongly dominant, the Alpine type occupying second place, while the Negroid or "Melanesian" factors drop to a mere trace. The longer, incomplete series of Krause, indicates a somewhat larger proportion of brachycephalic factors. To the foregoing we may add the fact that in stature the Micronesian population varies in passing from west to east, being of medium stature or slightly under in the extreme west, and growing taller eastward and southward until in the Gilbert group the average reaches that general for Polynesia, i. e., 173 cm. Further, that in skin color and character of the hair there are also great differences, such that while in the Gilberts the skin color is generally comparable to the average in Polynesia, the hair being wavy or straight, in the Caroline group there is great variety, some islands or parts of islands or individuals being very dark-skinned with frizzly hair, while others are light-skinned with wavy or straight hair. The portrait given on Plate XXIX, Fig. 4, shows what is evidently a much mixed type.

Even from this meagre information it seems clear that the Micronesian area contains a very much mixed population, and considerable differences in culture confirm the belief that the racial history of the area has been complex. With our present data it is possible to do little more than speculate as to what this history may have been, but I should like to emphasize three points. First, that the surprising importance of the Caspian-Mediterranean types in the Gilbert group is, although puzzling, extremely significant, as it must indicate the passage through Micronesia of a group of people in whom this type was of great importance. The striking part which these peoples evidently played in Polynesia has already been discussed; but whence can they have come? There would appear to be but two alternatives: either we may suppose them to have come from Indo-China by way of Indonesia, into which, as we have seen, a stream of peoples of this type must have passed; or we might derive them from Japan by way of the Bonin Islands and the Mariannes. The latter is certainly possible, and peoples of this type were present in Japan in late Neolithic times, but, all things considered, it is probably safer at present to regard them as coming from Indonesia.

The second point is that the "Melanesian" or Negroid factors seem to be confined rather sharply to the Caroline group, and may possibly have been derived in relatively recent times by way of Greenwich, Nukuoro, and other islands from Melanesia to the southward. The vague traditions of an influx and conquest of some of the Carolines by savage black men coming from the south, would seem to point in this direction; while the remarkably localized character of the Negroid population, and the fact that it still retains its identity apart from the rest of the people, may be taken to confirm its recent arrival. The greater frequency of the Caspian type among the female portion of the population would also perhaps tend to suggest that this was an older type in the group than the Negroid.

Lastly, the dominance of the Alpine type in the western part of the whole area may perhaps be taken as evidence that a part of the stream of peoples of this type, which came into Polynesia about the beginning of the Christian era, passed through the Micronesian island chain.

*BOOK V*

NORTH AMERICA

# INTRODUCTION

THE racial history of the New World presents some of the most interesting and at the same time most perplexing of problems.  When at the close of the fifteenth and the beginning of the sixteenth centuries America became known to Europeans, it was found to be occupied by peoples in very different stages of culture, ranging from the simplest nomad, hunting and fisher folk to highly cultured, sedentary and agricultural peoples, skilled in architecture, textiles, and metallurgy, and living under elaborately organized governmental systems.  Yet, in spite of the wide variation in cultural status and an amazing diversity in language, the American Indians presented less striking differences in physical type than were to be found among the peoples of the Old World.  In America there were no such differences in skin color, in character and color of the hair or eyes as occurred in Africa, Asia or the islands of the Pacific; so that quite naturally the American Indians came to be considered as an essentially homogeneous people.

With the beginning, however, of the scientific study of racial characters, the fact that there were after all very wide variations in physical type became apparent, and various suggestions in regard to the number of these types and their origin were put forward from time to time.  Yet the older belief in the unity of the Indian held its ground vigorously, and, fortified by a mass of evidence and argument, still remains that held by many of the foremost authorities.  In view of the controversial character of this fundamental question, a brief discussion of the two opposed theories is desirable before we undertake the presentation and interpretation of the facts themselves.

Although at variance in regard to the unity of the population, the adherents of each of the two theories are, to-day, substantially in accord in declaring that the origin of the American Indian is undoubtedly to be sought in Asia; and that the New

World was originally peopled by immigrants who reached the northern continent at its northwestern extremity and spread thence by degrees to the extreme tip of South America. For those who believe in the homogeneity of the Indian, the initial immigration, however prolonged, was the only one; or, if they admit the possibility of more than a single period of movement, they appear to assume that the Asiatic reservoir, from whence the immigrants were derived, retained its racial character quite unchanged. From this point of view the American Indian is essentially Mongoloid, using this term in its ordinary sense, and the divergences from this form, as it is found in northern Asia to-day, are regarded merely as normal variations. The differences between tribe and tribe are considered as, on the whole, of quite random distribution, and as such not particularly significant. The very obvious concentration of dolichocephalic types in the northeast of the northern continent, in parts of Brazil, and in the tip of South America are, to be sure, admitted, but they are explained as the results of local variation in comparative isolation rather than as an indication of the presence of radically different racial types.

Now, in spite of the weight of authority which is ranged on the side of this belief in the unity of the Indian, I believe that it can be shown, by the method of analysis here adopted, that the theory of the homogeneity of the American Indian must be discarded. For not only does it wholly fail to account for certain facts of geographic distribution which have been strangely overlooked, but it breaks down entirely when historical and chronological factors are taken into consideration. When, moreover, the view is extended to the Asiatic continent, from whence the population of the New World must have been derived, further difficulties in the path of the unitary theory become apparent. For we have much evidence which tends to show that, at the period when the ancestors of the American Indian were leaving the Asiatic continent for the New World, the physical types found in that portion whence they must have come were not only quite different from what we find there to-day, but underwent radical changes from time to time, so that, if the migration into America was spread over any considerable period, the immigrants must have been far from uniform.

Can a reasonable and concrete theory of the racial history of North America, built on the assumption that a variety of racial types are present, be devised which shall accord with the facts? I believe that it can, and that if it be kept clearly in mind that the theory is, because of the great incompleteness of the data, necessarily only tentative, it is worth the attempt if it serves to reduce to some sort of order the existing rather chaotic situation.

Before outlining this theory, however, attention must first be called to certain of the main geographical features which have played a large part in the racial history of the North American aborigines. The factor of first importance is the division of the continent into two portions by the great chain which, as the Rocky Mountains, extends almost unbroken from northern Alaska southward to the Mexican line and thence, in the ranges bordering the Gulf of Mexico, onward to the Isthmus of Tehuantepec. The area west of this dividing range falls into two parts, divided roughly by the east and west course of the Columbia River. That to the north is a rugged, mountainous region, in the main forested and rich in fish and game; that to the south is a series of plateaus or closed basins, in part arid and semi-arid, and economically inferior to the country to the north. Along its western border, however, and separated from it by the Cascade and Sierra Nevada ranges, lie the richly favored valleys of western Oregon and California. The eastern portion of the continent likewise falls into two divisions. Limited on the west by the Rocky Mountain range and on the east by Hudson Bay, the Great Lakes, and the Mississippi River, and extending from the Arctic coast southward to the Gulf of Mexico, is a vast, unbroken stretch of plains, in the main unforested, and providing in the buffalo, abundant throughout its whole central portion, an ideal food-supply for a primitive folk. East of this region of the Plains lies the last of the four main divisions, the broad valleys and rolling hills of the eastern woodlands.

Returning now to our problem, we may begin by the assumption (1) that the peopling of the continent began at an early date, a time synchronous perhaps with the end of the Palæolithic period in Europe; (2) that all significant immigration took place from northeastern Asia by way of Bering Strait, and (3) that, as a result of wide movements of peoples in the Eur-Asiatic continent, the primary immigration into North America was followed by other drifts, each of which brought a combination of racial elements different from the preceding, depending upon the factors present at the time in that portion of Asia whence the migratory peoples came.

To the first assumption objection will at once be made by the very active school which stoutly denies the validity of all evidence tending to indicate the early presence of man in America. This is not the place to argue the point, and it will only be submitted that, although no single piece of evidence has yet come to light in proof of early man in America, comparable in certainty with that available for Europe, yet the cumulative value of the sum of our knowledge of man and his culture in the New World is such as almost to force us, even in the absence of absolute proof, to assume the fact. Without this the undisputed data of archæology, culture, and language would be practically inexplicable.

The second assumption, that all significant immigration came into North America by way of Bering Strait, will probably meet with little objection, since the consensus of opinion of all the best students is overwhelmingly in its favor. The last postulate, that we must allow for more than one immigrant wave and that these were of varying racial composition, is one whose probability, I had almost said necessity, it would seem difficult to deny. In every other portion of the world, wave after wave, pulse after pulse of migration has occurred; why alone in the case of the New World should such an event have taken place but once? And if but once, we must either assume that this single wave brought with it examples of every type known throughout the world, as types are understood in the present study, or else that from one single form every known extreme of modification of the cranial criteria adopted has arisen independently and distributed itself geographically in a very systematic and peculiar fashion. The difficulties which must be met, if we accept the assumption of multiple immigrant types, are, it may be frankly admitted, many; but those encountered by denying it seem both greater and more numerous.

Accepting, then, that beginning in very early times a series of immigrant waves of varying racial composition and character came into North America by way of Bering Strait, we may proceed to determine their probable sequence and specific characters.

First, however, we may call attention to certain further geographical factors of great importance in attempting to mark out the probable lines of migration by which any immigrant peoples reaching the American continent from across Bering Strait must have spread. If, as is most likely, the invaders were to land upon American soil at some point on Seward peninsula, they might thereafter either attempt to penetrate into the interior of the country or follow the shore. In the former case, they would, almost of necessity, be led by the topography to follow up the valleys of the Yukon or Tanana. Progress southward from the upper courses of either of these streams lies through difficult mountain country, but eastward there are various large tributaries by which ways across the Rocky Mountains to the Mackenzie basin and the Plains might be found; and, once in the Plains, their spread southward would be easy and rapid. If, on the other hand, the immigrants followed the coast, we again have two alternatives. Southward as far as the Alaska peninsula any attempt to turn inland would still lead to the valley of the Yukon, while once past this point the height and difficulty of the mountains, or their breadth, would tend to confine further advance to the coastal belt. All known or traditional movements here, at least as far as Puget Sound, have been either littoral or from the interior toward the coast. If the immigrant group turned northward from Bering Strait, the Endicott Range would tend to bar penetration from the Arctic coast, but once

the mouth of the Mackenzie was reached, the way to the south-
land and the Plains lay open.

Since, therefore, any direct attempt to penetrate the interior
or any movement northward along the Alaska coast would tend
to lead an immigrant group ultimately into the plains area east
of the Rocky Mountains, while a southward movement along the
coast had for some hundreds of miles at least an even chance of
leading in the end in the same direction, we may regard it as in
a high degree probable that immigrant peoples coming into North
America spread over the continent southward most rapidly, and in
far the largest numbers along the broad highway of the Plains.

Returning now to the questions relating to the physical types
found in North America, it may be noted that for Europe the
determination of the sequence in which the several types appeared in the continent and spread over its surface, rests in the
main upon definite stratigraphic or archæological and historical
evidence. In the New World little evidence of this sort has as
yet been brought to light, so that here we are forced to rely largely
upon what is frankly a less certain indication of relative age,
but one which is, nevertheless, generally accepted as valid in
current studies of the distribution and history of animal species.
This is the principle that in the distribution of species within
any large area, such as that of a whole continent, those which
are marginal are in general to be regarded as the earlier, in comparison with species having a more central habitat. The older
species, whose territory is invaded by another type, gives ground
and is in the end either pushed toward the periphery, or forced
into "refuge areas" where life conditions are less favorable than
in the rest of the region, the better and more favorable lands
being appropriated to themselves by the newcomers.

Assuming, then, that a peripheral distribution tends to indicate a relatively ancient stratum of population, whereas the
more recent immigrants are to be looked for nearer the centre,
we may learn much by observing what is the distribution of the
human types within the North American continent.

Before doing so a last digression must be allowed, to call attention to certain facts of linguistic distribution. The languages spoken by the North American Indians numbered several hundreds. These have been grouped into a series of linguistic stocks, each comprising from one or two to a score of related languages. The number of such stocks is still a matter of some uncertainty, but the generally accepted classification[1] gives approximately eighty wholly distinct stocks for the whole of the northern continent. These stocks are divisible into two clearly contrasted groups, one of which is made up of stocks each of which is geographically extensive, covering scores or hundreds of thousands of square miles; whereas the other group includes stocks which are confined, as a rule, within very narrow limits, covering an area sometimes with a radius of only thirty or forty miles. In the first group we may reckon the Eskimo, Athabascan, Algonkian, Siouan, Uto-Aztecan (i. e., the former Shoshonean, Piman and Nahuan), Iroquoian, Muskogean, and Salishan stocks. In their distribution they cover probably nine-tenths of the whole continent, for the most part in great continuous areas. They appear, however, to a small extent only on the Pacific coast, and mainly at two points—southern California and the region from Puget Sound southward to and slightly beyond the mouth of the Columbia River. The distribution of the small stocks is quite striking, in that the majority are found in a narrow strip along the Pacific shore, while nearly all the remainder are either located in the "refuge area" of the plateau region or along the southern and eastern margins of the continent. This concentration of the small stocks in marginal areas long since led to the suggestion that they may represent an older stratum of population, forced out from the rest of the continent by the expansion of the large stocks, who thus would be regarded as constituting a more recent layer. That this hypothesis fits most strikingly the suggestions here put forward in regard to the racial history of the continent will, I trust, be apparent in what follows. We may now at last turn to the maps, Plates XXX to XXXIII, showing the distribution of the physical types.

[1] Bureau of American Ethnology, 1907, 1911.

The most cursory inspection reveals one fact of great significance, *i. e.*, the dolichocephalic types are concentrated in a very
striking fashion in marginal areas.  Thus, the Caspian and Mediterranean types are found in great strength along the northern
and northeastern coast of the continent and in Greenland, appearing elsewhere, except at one or two spots on or near the Pacific
coast, as factors of minor importance only.  The Proto-Negroid
and Proto-Australoid types are also peripheral, occurring in
largest proportions along or near the Pacific coast and in the
region east of the Great Lakes.  The evidence afforded by
geographic distribution thus indicates that the dolichocephalic
types are, relatively to the brachycephalic, the older occupants
of the area.  Since this result is corroborated by such stratigraphic and archæological evidence as has yet been obtained in North
America, and is furthermore in accord with the evidence which
we possess of the sequence of types in other parts of the world,
it seems safe to accept the conclusion, at least provisionally.

We should next turn to the problems involved in the sequence
of these early dolichocephalic types, but before doing so a few
words of reassurance must be said.  The reader has doubtless
stared with surprise not unmixed with horror at the audacity
of the statement that Mediterranean and Caspian, Proto-Australoid and Proto-Negroid types were to be found among the
American Indians.  That these types were widely distributed
in the Old World, or at least in parts of it, he would be willing to
grant; that they had extended even into the island area of the
Pacific he may somewhat grudgingly admit; but that it should
be suggested that they were to be found in the New World is
an idea so completely at variance with traditional and current
theories that he would be inclined to regard the statement as
utterly absurd!  The suggestion that Mediterranean or Proto-
Negroid types, for example, are to be found in America is indeed
revolutionary, yet not quite so preposterous as it may seem at
first sight, if it be only kept in mind that the statement does *not*
mean that actual Negroes or peoples from the Mediterranean
shores are supposed to have migrated to the New World.  As

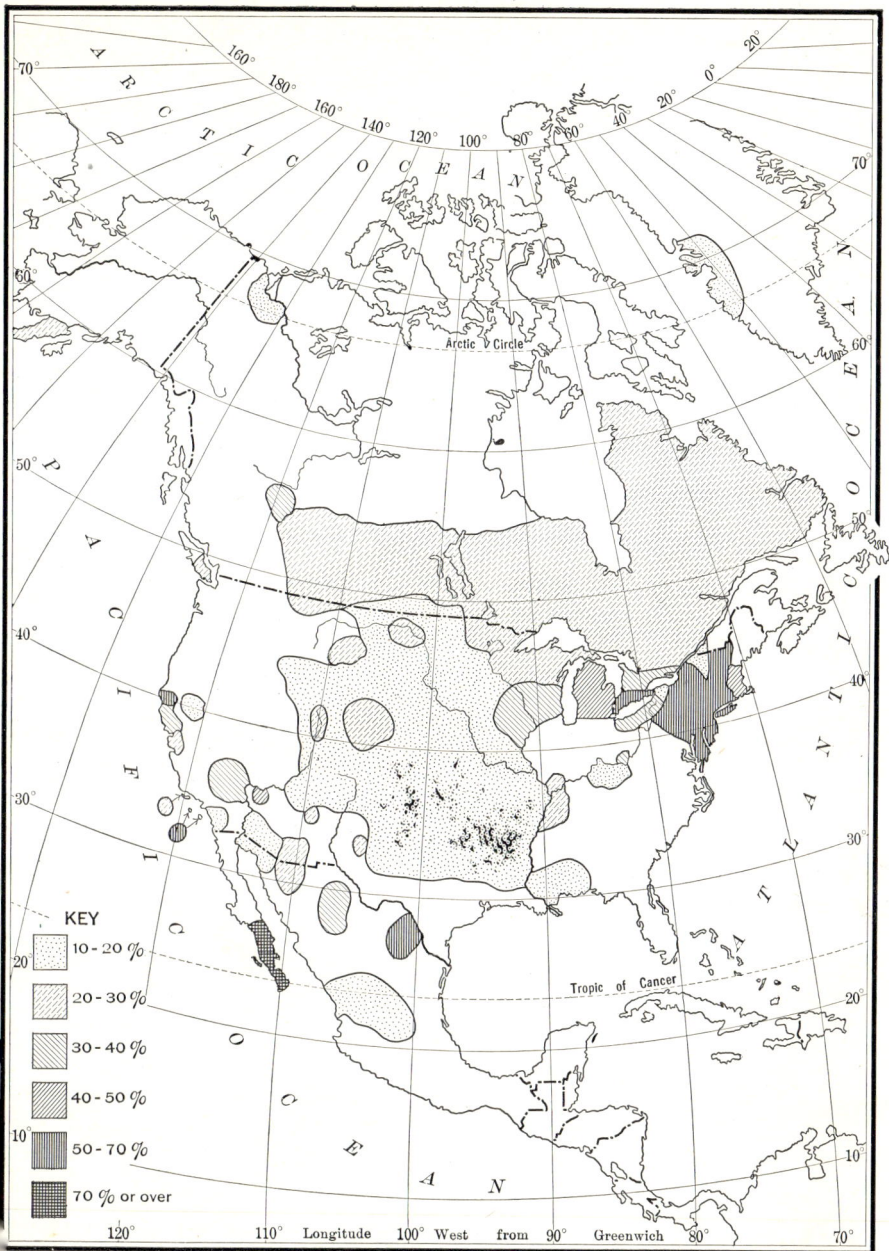

KEY

| | |
|---|---|
| | 10 - 20 % |
| | 20 - 30 % |
| | 30 - 40 % |
| | 40 - 50 % |
| | 50 - 70 % |
| | 70 % or over |

PLATE XXX. NORTH AMERICA.

Percentage distribution of Proto-Australoid and Proto-Negroid Types.

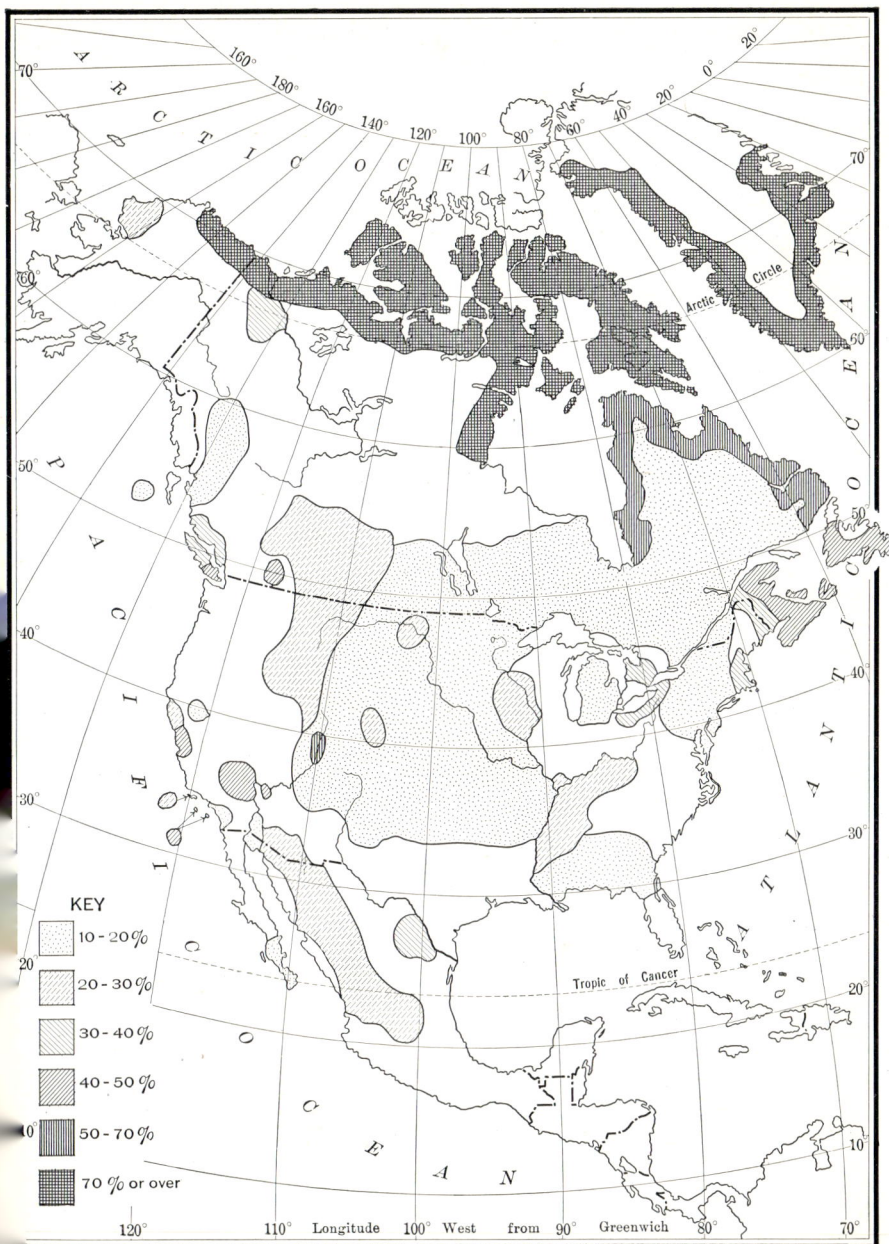

PLATE XXXI.  NORTH AMERICA.
Percentage distribution of Caspian and Mediterranean Types.

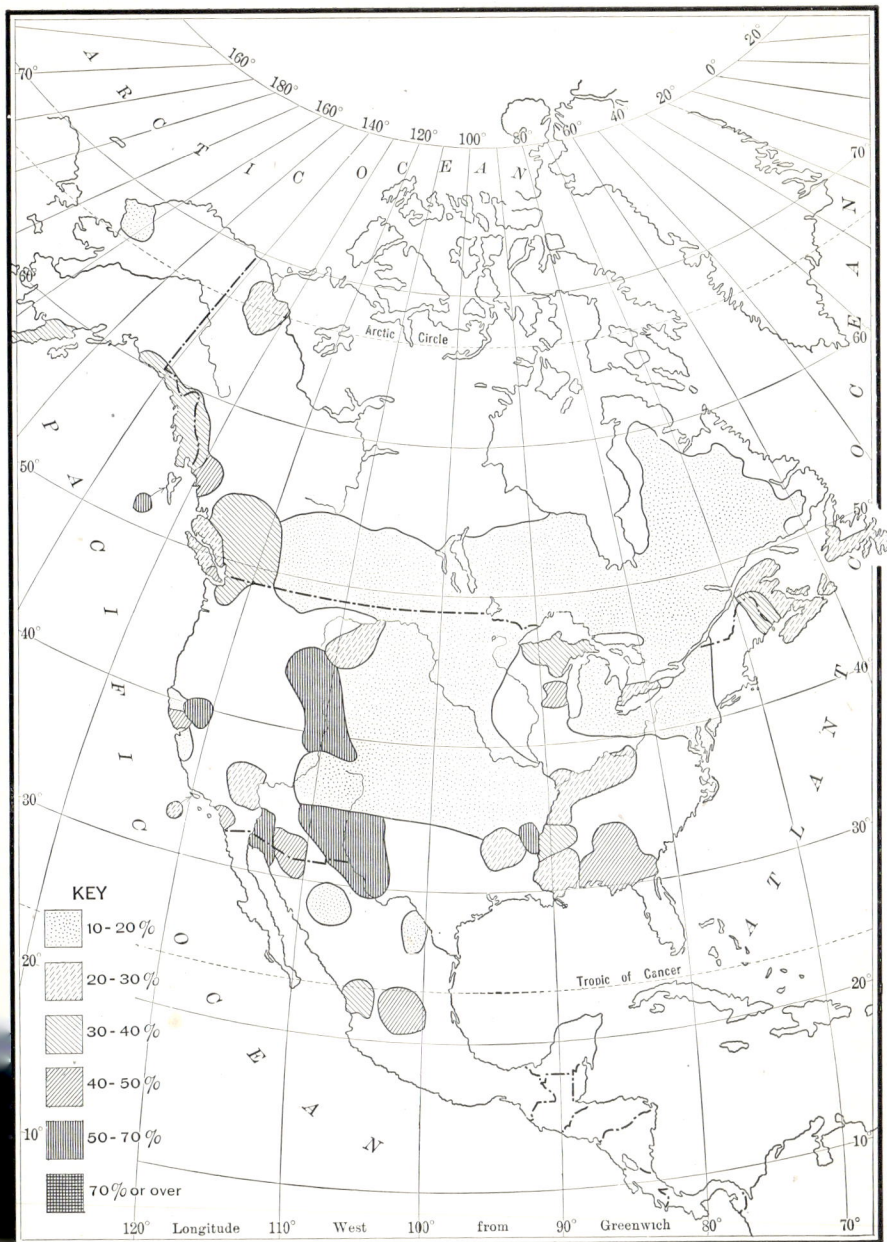

PLATE XXXII. NORTH AMERICA.

Percentage distribution of Palæ-Alpine and Mongoloid Types.

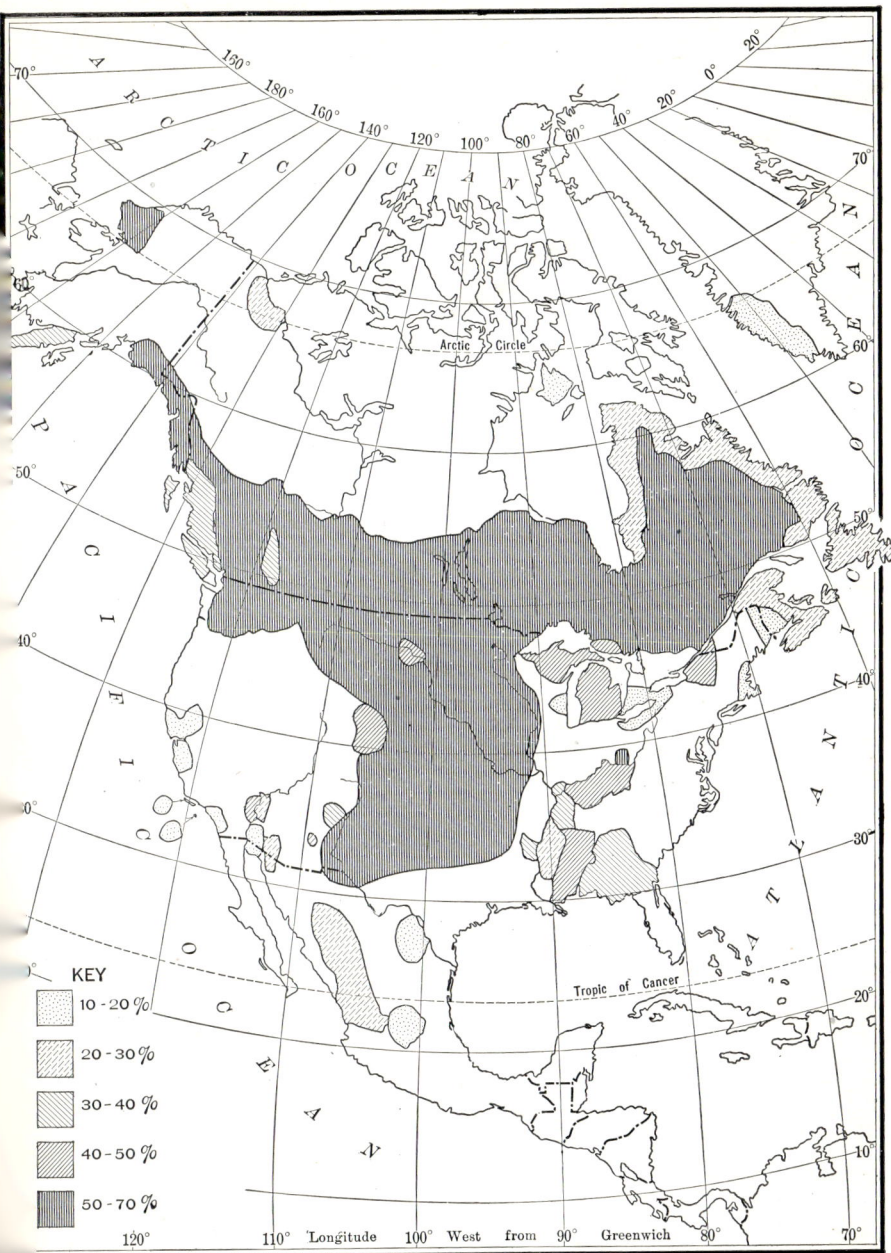

KEY

| | |
|---|---|
| | 10 - 20 % |
| | 20 - 30 % |
| | 30 - 40 % |
| | 40 - 50 % |
| | 50 - 70 % |

PLATE XXXIII. NORTH AMERICA.

Percentage distribution of Alpine and Ural types.

has been pointed out in the introductory chapter, the type to which, for example, the name of Proto-Negroid has been given carries with it no implication in regard to skin color, hair form, or any other superficial or structural features which may be found in the modern Negro. The statement that certain crania from North America are of Proto-Negroid type means nothing more than that, *in so far as the three factors of Cephalic Index, Length-Height Index, and Nasal Index are concerned,* these crania are similar to crania of African, southern Asiatic, or Oceanic Negroid peoples. In how far such similarity *in these particular features* is paralleled by any other similarities, or is in any way indicative of an actual community of origin between the two groups, will be discussed in the final chapter; here and in other sections dealing with the several continental areas we are merely concerned to point out the facts of distribution and apparent historical sequence of our wholly arbitrary types.

If the reader will therefore be lenient for the moment; restrain his indignation at what seems a rank absurdity, suspending judgment in regard to what is after all a novel suggestion; and regard the terms Proto-Negroid, Mediterranean, etc., as merely convenient (although perhaps misleading) names for a series of purely arbitrary types which might just as well be denominated by numbers or the letters of the alphabet, it will be found that the geographical distribution and probable sequence and relations of these types are surprisingly significant and accord in most cases with the known facts of aboriginal history.

After this digression we may return to the problems before us. Although the evidence is still rather contradictory as to the relative priority of the broad-nosed and narrow-nosed long-headed types, it seems on the whole probable that the Proto-Australoid must have been one of the earliest, if not the earliest, type to spread into the North American continent. On the Pacific coast in California and Lower California it appears to constitute the oldest stratum, characterizing as it does the crania from the lower layers of the shell-heaps, from the islands of Santa Catalina and San Clemente off the coast, and from the extinct

Pericue, isolated in the southern tip of the peninsula of Lower California. It is, moreover, prominent among the ancient Basket-makers of northern Arizona, who represent probably one of the earliest peoples in this whole area. In the northeast the type is of importance among the Iroquois and the southern Algonkian tribes, such as the Lenape.

The extreme marginal position of the leptorrhine, dolichocephalic types, particularly the Caspian, make this latter a strong competitor for the honor of being the earliest type in the continent. Concentrated in remarkable strength among the Eskimo east of Point Barrow; occurring in the underlying strata of the Fraser River shell-heaps on the British Columbia coast, and among the undeformed crania from Vancouver Island, but present in the central portions of the continent in but small amount, it must either have been a very early immigrant which has long since been forced to the wall, or have distributed itself at a later period mainly along the shores. In the absence of adequate archæological data the question must be left open, as for North America, at least, evidence of its preceding or succeding the Proto-Australoid type is not clear. South American data, however, would seem to indicate the priority of the Caspian type over all others. If this can be fully substantiated, it would obviously solve the problem for the northern continent as well, since the population of South America must have been derived from the north.

The considerable strength of the Mediterranean type among some of the Eskimo, the Shoshonean tribes in the "refuge area" of Utah and Nevada, and especially in the shell-heaps along the Maine coast, suggest that this type also reached the continent early, for the considerable factor of it among some of the Siouan tribes of the northern plains may be ascribed to their immigration thither from the east. Except in the case of the Eskimo, however, the number of crania on which the evidence of the presence of this type rests is very small, so that here again judgment must be suspended until fuller data are to be had. As a factor in the complex of the whole population, however, it seems probably to have been of very minor importance.

The Proto-Negroid type has a very striking distribution.

Except for its rather unexpected strength among the ancient Basket-makers in Arizona, it nowhere seems to have played an important part in the whole area west of the Rocky Mountains. It is, nevertheless, of considerable importance among the Iroquois and southern Algonkian tribes, and in the early crania from the Turner group mounds in the Ohio valley and the prehistoric cist-grave people of Tennessee. All of which suggests a rather special concentration in the eastern portion of the continent. It is also significant, in connection with the presence of this type in the Basket-makers, that it is the dominant factor in the crania from the burial caves in Coahuila in northern Mexico, since many striking similarities in culture have been pointed out between these two peoples.[1] The complete absence of the Proto-Negroid type in the extreme north and northeast and along the Pacific coast would indicate that it may well have been the last of the dolichocephalic types to make its way into the continent.

If the sequence of the various dolichocephalic types is still more or less obscure, that of the brachycephalic factors which undoubtedly followed is, on the contrary, much more clear. Comparison of the maps giving the distribution of the broad and narrow nosed round-headed types, shows convincingly that the latter form a vast wedge whose base extends entirely across the continent, from British Columbia to the Gulf of St. Lawrence, and stretches southward between the Rocky Mountains and the Great Lakes through the Plains almost to the Gulf of Mexico. The platyrrhine, brachycephalic types, on the other hand, are concentrated among the Shoshonean and Athabascan tribes in the plateau region west of the Rockies and, to a less noticeable degree, in the southeastern portion of the continent among the Muskogean tribes and such isolated southeastern Plains groups as the Tonkawa and the pre-Nahuan Tarascan people of Michoacan in Mexico. The inference is, I think, clear, that here the latter types have been driven back into the less favorable environment of the plateaus and into the southeastern area by a powerful movement from the north of the lep-

[1] Kidder and Guernsey, 1919; Guernsey and Kidder, 1921.

torrhine, brachycephalic peoples, coming southward through the Plains.

While all the previous drifts were probably so ancient as to have left no obvious trace, the very last movements of the most recent type to come into the continent may perhaps be dimly seen in the prehistoric southward migrations of the Navaho and Apache, of whom the former may have come into their historic habitat during the period while the Cliff Dwellings were still occupied; and possibly more faintly yet in the history of the great Siouan stock which will be suggested later in discussing the types present in the region south of the Great Lakes. Actual stratigraphic evidence, moreover, of the supplanting of the older platyrrhine types by the leptorrhine seems to be afforded by the data being secured by the Andover Expedition at Pecos in New Mexico.

Discussion of the relative importance and the historic sequence of the Palæ-Alpine type as compared with the Mongoloid, or of the Alpine as compared with the Ural is, on the basis of our present data, which for much of the region dominated by brachycephaly is confined to measurements on the living, as yet hardly possible. What conclusions we may be entitled to draw in these connections will be pointed out in the later pages, where the several subdivisions of this area are discussed.

In broad lines, then, a hasty survey of the distribution of types in North America leads to the conclusion that, just as in the Old World we can discern, beginning in earliest times, a series of drifts or waves of differing physical types, which have on the whole arranged themselves in such fashion that the dolichocephalic and presumably older peoples are found distributed mainly along the margins of the continent, whereas the brachycephalic, younger peoples occupy in a solid, unbroken mass the whole interior, in North America, just as in Asia, in Europe, and in the Pacific region, the supplanting of the older dolichocephalic peoples by the later brachycephalic ones has gone on relentlessly, and here, as there, the brachycephalization of the continent was by the sixteenth century almost complete.

The peculiar conformation of the North American continent in its connection with South America by a long and narrow isthmus, raises some very special problems. Through this narrowing gateway of Middle America and the Isthmus of Panama the ancestors of the great majority of the peoples of the southern continent must have passed, although a minority may have journeyed from Florida by way of the Antillean chain. Through this restricted passage, therefore, wave after wave of peoples of different types must have forced their way, since, as will be shown in the chapter devoted to South America, the population there was almost as complex as that in the north. Does not the necessity of bringing all these differing types through so constricted a single passage constitute an insuperable obstacle in the way of the present hypothesis and prove its utter absurdity? It might seem so, and the difficulties in the way of the theory are, it must be freely admitted, very great; yet *any* hypothesis which attempts to account for the origin and spread of the South American peoples from the northern continent must meet many of the same obstacles—and no other origin will, I think, be admitted to-day by serious students of American problems.

Further discussion of these questions may be left to the chapter dealing with the South American peoples; they are referred to here in order to emphasize the extreme importance, for any theory, of securing adequate cranial material from the whole Middle American region. That any of the earlier physical types should still survive in such a migration-swept, narrow corridor is surprising, yet the strong dolichocephalic factors present among the Otomi and some of the southern Mayan tribes seem to show that it is not impossible. Far more significant for any hypothesis would be direct archæological or stratigraphic evidence, nothing of which has as yet been reported. Prophecy is a very dangerous pastime, yet I believe it may be confidently predicted that when we obtain, as some day we must, skeletal remains of the people responsible for the so-called Archaic Culture of this region, they will be found to show the presence of a considerable, possibly a dominant, factor of the ancient dolichocephalic types.

At the outset of any attempt to present the facts in regard to the physical characteristics of the aboriginal peoples of North America, and the arguments in favor of the complexity of their origin, it must be pointed out that the published data are still so incomplete that the task appears almost hopeless. For large portions of the continent we possess no adequate materials whatsoever, as, for example, the whole northwestern part of the area with the exception of a few points along the coast, and practically all of the continent south of the United States-Mexican border. For some other sections the data are of the scantiest, so that were it not for the courtesy and generosity which have allowed me to utilize large series of unpublished measurements, both of crania[1] and of living Indians,[2] it would have been impossible to present anything but an extremely incomplete picture of the facts.

If, on the basis of the method of analysis employed in this study, the relative intensity of the dolichocephalic factors present among the various tribes is plotted on a map, the result is that shown on Plate XXXIV. Reference to this map at once reveals the fact that long-headedness is concentrated in two widely separated areas. The largest and most important of these extends over the whole northern and northeastern coastal portions of the continent, including Greenland; the smaller and more broken area lies, on the other hand, in the opposite or extreme southwestern corner. Everywhere between these two marginal regions, brachycephalic factors, so far as known, prevail.

In the presentation and discussion of the data in regard to the aboriginal peoples of North America, it will be most convenient to group the material according to the divisions shown on this map, viz.: (1) A Northeastern Dolichocephalic area; (2) a Southwestern Dolichocephalic area; and (3) a Central Brachycephalic area.

---

[1] U. S. National Museum, Washington; American Museum of Natural History, New York City; Department of Anthropology, University of California, Berkeley, California; Victoria Memorial Museum, Ottawa; Philadelphia Academy of Sciences.

[2] Measurements taken for the Department of Anthropology of the Chicago Exposition, 1893, under the direction of Professor Franz Boas of Columbia University.

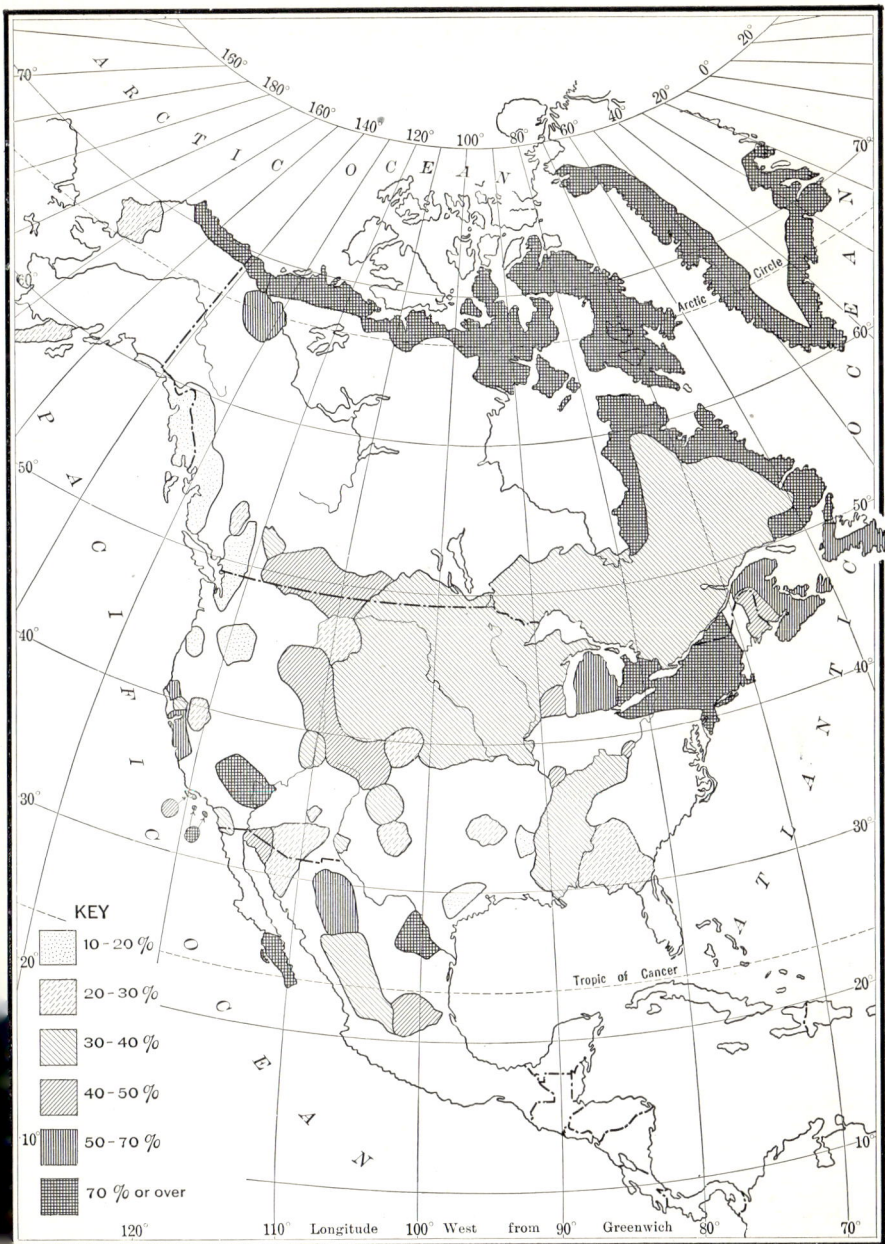

KEY

| | |
|---|---|
| ▫ | 10 - 20 % |
| ▨ | 20 - 30 % |
| ▨ | 30 - 40 % |
| ▨ | 40 - 50 % |
| ▨ | 50 - 70 % |
| ▨ | 70 % or over |

PLATE XXXIV.  NORTH AMERICA.

Percentage of Dolichocephals.

# CHAPTER I

## THE NORTHEASTERN DOLICHOCEPHALS

On the basis of our present knowledge, we may include in this group: (1) all the Eskimo tribes of Greenland and the Arctic archipelago and those of the mainland living east of Point Barrow in Alaska; (2) the eastern Algonkian tribes south of the St. Lawrence to and including the Lenape or Delaware; and (3) the proto-historic and early historic Iroquoian tribes of Ontario and New York.

Although all the peoples of this whole region are similar in showing a larger or smaller majority of dolichocephalic factors, they are divisible into a number of subdivisions, which are rather clearly differentiated in their character.

Although the Eskimo language is spoken along the whole of the main Alaskan coast and throughout the chain of the Aleutian Islands, the physical type of those west and south of Point Barrow is quite different from those to the eastward. These latter show a considerable uniformity in their characteristics. In stature they are for the most part under the medium, those of Greenland[1] and the Arctic archipelago[2] averaging about 162 cm. The Eskimo farther west, in the vicinity of the Mackenzie delta[3] and Point Barrow,[4] are somewhat taller, with an average of 168 cm., whereas those in Labrador[5] are shorter, the average falling somewhat below 160 cm. The skin color is in general lighter than that of the average Indian and the cheeks have not uncommonly a distinct rosy tinge. If the considerable body of cranial data[6] for this whole area be analyzed, it appears that the Caspian type is everywhere in large majority, with the possible exception of the Smith Sound region in northeast Greenland and among

---

[1] Hansen, 1886, 1893.  [2] Tocher, 1902.  [3] Boas, 1901.
[4] Hawkes, 1916.  [5] Pittard, 1901.
[6] Furst, 1915; Bessels, 1875; Duckworth, 1900; Sergi, 1901; Oetteking, 1908; Hrdlicka, 1910.

the people of the Mackenzie delta area, where the Mediterranean type, elsewhere secondary, assumes first place. The two types together everywhere make up from 70 to 90 per cent of the total factors concerned. The only brachycephalic element which appears is the Alpine, present only as a trace except in Southampton Island, in southwest Greenland, and in the small series described by Hrdlicka from Smith Sound. The presence of a considerable minority of the Alpine type in the latter remote group of Eskimo is hard to understand, since the much larger series from the same region, given by Bessels and the Danish collections from the immediately adjacent area to the south, show only the merest trace of this factor. Its presence in southwestern Greenland is probably due to a certain amount of European intermixture, which is known to have occurred here in greater degree than elsewhere. A striking feature of the Eskimo crania is the disharmony between the face and head, the former being exceptionally wide, the latter very narrow; and between the face and the nose, for, in spite of the great width of the former, the nose is almost at the extreme of narrowness. This width of face and narrowness of head have been ascribed to the abnormal development of the chewing muscles, due to special food conditions. In view of the fact, however, that it is less marked in the women than in the men, in spite of the practice by the former of chewing the skins used for making moccasins and clothing, the question of the cause of the phenomenon cannot, perhaps, be regarded as fully settled. An example of the Eskimo type is given on Plate XXXV, Fig. 1.

In the early sixteenth century the Eskimo occupied not only the Labrador coast, but the northern shore of the Gulf of St. Lawrence as far west probably as the island of Anticosti, as well as the northern tip of Newfoundland. The southern shores of the Gulf and the whole area of the Maritime Provinces were occupied by the Algonkian tribes of the Micmac and Malecite. From this region we possess, unfortunately, no cranial data, but measurements on the living[1] (now unquestionably somewhat mixed with

[1] Boas.

French-Canadian blood) show them to be a people of tall stature (average 173 cm.), with a predominance of narrow-nosed, dolichocephalic factors, yet with considerable brachycephalic elements, which are apparently of both Palæ-Alpine and Alpine types, and in part, perhaps, due to the European mixture. A possible source of part of the brachycephalic factors may be found in the absorption by the Micmac of an earlier population. The Beothuk or Red Indians of Newfoundland have in historic times been confined to a portion only of that island. From the two or three crania of this tribe whose measurements have been published,[1] they would appear to have been primarily brachycephalic in type. It is not unreasonable to suppose that they formerly occupied a larger area and were driven into their restricted habitat by the incoming Micmac or other Algonkian tribes, and that their partial absorption by these would account for part at least of the brachycephalic factors found. Owing to the absence of cranial material it is impossible to say whether the dolichocephalic element in the Micmac is the Caspian, which would ally them with the Eskimo, or the Mediterranean, which would affiliate them more closely perhaps with the builders of the shell-heaps along the Maine coast.

In contrast with these more easterly Algonkian tribes, our knowledge of those of New England is wholly derived from crania, since the pure-blood Indian of the greater portion of this area has been long extinct. The larger number of the crania[2] are from sites in central and eastern Massachusetts and Rhode Island, and show on analysis that the dominant element in all this area is, most unexpectedly, the Proto-Negroid! At first thought such a suggestion seems impossible, yet *on the basis of the criteria here adopted* the fact cannot be denied, and, as the crania are with a few exceptions almost certainly pre-European or from the period of the earliest contact, no possibility of historic Negro mixture is admissible. When it is remembered that the same type is found in considerable strength in the Baltic region and northwestern Russia in prehistoric and early historic times, and is a

[1] Busk, 1875–76.                    [2] Knight, 1915; P. M.

strong factor among the present-day Ainu of northern Japan, its presence here in America is perhaps not quite so surprising. We shall return to the problems involved in this case in the final chapter.

The type of secondary importance differentiates the people of the Massachusetts coast from those of the Connecticut valley and Rhode Island, in that whereas in the former this is a Mediterranean factor, in the latter it is of the Proto-Australoid type. The significance of this division becomes immediately apparent when we turn our attention to the adjacent areas. From Maine[1] we have as yet very meagre data, in large part derived from the shell-heaps, some of which are on archæological evidence considerably older than the historic Algonkian tribes of the vicinity, and thus may be taken (?) as representing a more ancient population than that from which the southern New England crania are derived. Be that as it may, the Maine crania show a strong predominance of the Mediterranean type, whose presence in the population of the Massachusetts coast region served to differentiate it from that of the interior and Rhode Island. It would appear, therefore, that there was ground for believing that the Massachusetts tribes of the coast were closely related to the older peoples of the northern New England shores, and that they had been overlaid, in part, by a different people, characterized by strong factors of Proto-Negroid and Proto-Australoid types, who came in from the west and southwest. This gradual modification of the population of the New England area from northeast to southwest, is further brought out by the fact that, whereas in the shell-heaps the male crania are all dolichocephalic, an increasing brachycephalic factor makes itself felt as one goes southward, consisting mainly of the Palæ-Alpine type.

If we turn now to the Lenape or Delaware[2] tribes, also belonging to the Algonkian linguistic group, and occupying a considerable area west of the lower Hudson, south along the coast as far as Delaware and inland toward western Pennsylvania, we

[1] P. M.   [2] Hrdlicka, 1902, 1916.

find that they are virtually identical with the Rhode Island tribes, who thus appear as the extreme northeastern representatives of a group which centres in the Delaware valley.

We are now in a position to consider the complex and interesting problems presented by the various tribes of Iroquoian speech, living in the Ontario peninsula and southward in northern Ohio and Pennsylvania, western New York, and extending in a narrow strip along the St. Lawrence River as far as Quebec. For the Iroquois proper, the Five Nations who formed the original League of the Iroquois, we have both cranial data and measurements on the living; for the Eries of the southern shore of the lake of the same name and for the Canadian tribes, the Neutrals and Hurons, we have only cranial material.

Taking first the Iroquois crania,[1] which are in the main of prehistoric and proto-historic age, we find, on the basis of a combined series from the different single tribes, that these people were at least as similar to both the Connecticut valley and Lenape series as either of these is to the other. In all three the primary factor is the Proto-Negroid, the secondary the Proto-Australoid. With the tribes of central and western Massachusetts the Iroquois have in common a small Mediterranean factor, which is still more strongly represented on the Massachusetts coast and in the shell-heaps of Maine. With the Lenape, the Iroquois agree in having a Caspian factor rather larger than in the case of the New England tribes. To all intents and purposes, thus, the Iroquois, the Lenape, and the southern and western New England tribes formed a single unit.

The Eries,[2] who were the western neighbors of the Iroquois, seem, on the evidence of a small series of crania only, to have resembled the latter, in that the dominant element among them was still the Proto-Negroid, but differed in comprising larger Caspian and Mediterranean factors, which would tend to ally them with the Huron. The Neutrals[3] differ somewhat more, in that they appear to have an unusually large element of the

---

[1] U. S. N. M.; A. N. S. P.; Buffalo Society of Natural History.
[2] P. M.　　　　　　　　　[3] U. S. N. M.; Victoria Memorial Museum, Ottawa.

Proto-Australoid type. Both Eries and Neutrals, moreover, have considerably larger brachycephalic factors (the former Alpine, the latter Palæ-Alpine) than the Iroquois.

The Hurons,[1] finally, carry us one stage farther. As in the case of the Neutrals, the dominant element here is the Proto-Australoid, and the factor of secondary importance is the Caspian, which has risen considerably in strength from its minority position among the Iroquois; the Proto-Negroid, on the other hand, which stood first in the list among the latter, has fallen in the Huron to fifth place, while the Mediterranean on the contrary has doubled in importance. Crania from York and Durham Counties, not certainly Huron and from an area outside their historical limits, are much more like the Iroquois and Eries.

What do all these facts mean? Briefly this, that, whereas the Iroquoian tribes south of the Lakes were physically closely affiliated with the Algonkian peoples of southern New England, the Iroquoian tribes north of the Lakes in Canada, especially the Hurons and Neutrals, stood somewhat apart, and had their relations more with the Eskimo and Algonkian tribes of the Maritime Provinces. This would suggest that the Huron and Neutral tribes represent an older stratum of the Iroquoian group, which, coming into the area while it was still occupied by the Algonkian tribes who later were driven into the Maritime Provinces and northern New England, and still occupied perhaps north of the St. Lawrence by the Eskimo, had amalgamated somewhat with these, before the coming of the later stratum represented by the Iroquois proper.

It will be at once realized that the physical relationships suggested for the Iroquoian tribes have certain interesting consequences. Culturally and linguistically the Iroquoian tribes show unmistakable evidence of southern or southwestern affiliations; culturally with the Muskogean tribes of the Gulf states, linguistically with the Caddoan tribes of the central and southern Plains. From the racial standpoint, however, they have

[1] U. S. N. M.; Victoria Memorial Museum, Ottawa.

FIG. 1. ESKIMO.

FIG. 2. SENECA.

FIG. 3. MAIDU.

FIG. 4. PIMA.

PLATE XXXV.

little or nothing in common with these peoples, who are primarily brachycephalic.  It seems hard, therefore, in spite of numerous difficulties in the way, to avoid the suggestion that we may have here a striking case of acculturation, in which a small but energetic group of immigrants or conquerors, coming from the southwestward and possessed of a higher culture, succeeded in forcing their speech and habits of life upon their predecessors, by whom they were, however, in the end racially absorbed.

We have so far dealt only with the early historic and proto-historic population of the Iroquoian area; there remains to point out briefly the striking contrast afforded by their living descendants.  Data as yet unpublished[1] are at hand only for the Mohawk and Seneca, two of the tribes of the Iroquois group.  The former show a large majority of brachycephalic factors, the narrow-nosed type (presumably Alpine) amounting alone to nearly 50 per cent of the total.  The Seneca series is much smaller, but shows, in contrast to the Mohawk, a slight dominance of dolichocephalic elements, in which the narrow-nosed types are in the majority.  The contrast between the two series is striking, but that between the living and their early historic or proto-historic ancestors is remarkable.  The Mohawk from a strongly dolichocephalic people have changed to a brachycephalic one; and while the Seneca are still by a narrow margin dolichocephalic, they seem to have changed their nasal character from broad to narrow!  The transformation of the Mohawk may perhaps be explained as due to considerable European admixture and to the assimilation of war captives taken from the rather strongly brachycephalic tribes to the south and west, conquered by the Iroquois during the period of the aggressive activity of the League.  The apparent change in the nasal character of the Seneca is not so easy to account for, but may be due to the fact that nasal measurements on the living cannot be exactly correlated with those on the skull.  We shall see that elsewhere in the continent, notably among the Sioux and Ute, even greater

[1] Boas.

discrepancies are to be found between the two kinds of measurements. A Seneca portrait is given on Plate XXXV, Fig. 2.

The results of our study of the northeastern area may be briefly summed up as follows. The whole region is in the first place divisible into two very unequal parts, of which the larger, comprising the great length of coast-line held by the Eskimo, was occupied by an almost purely dolichocephalic population, primarily of Caspian type, but with considerable admixture of the Mediterranean, especially toward the west. No evidence has yet been found that the area occupied by the Eskimo has ever been inhabited by people of any different type. The second and smaller of the two main portions of the northeastern area is less uniform than that occupied by the Eskimo, for it is clearly to be divided into two sections, a northeastern, comprising the St. Lawrence valley and the Maritime Provinces, in which the population, by the presence of large factors of both Caspian and Mediterranean types, shows some relationship to the Eskimo; and a southwestern, the occupants of which belonged primarily to the Proto-Negroid and Proto-Australoid types. The former section was further differentiated from the latter by the presence of a considerable minority of brachycephalic elements.

# CHAPTER II

## THE SOUTHWESTERN DOLICHOCEPHALS

THE other region in which long-headed peoples were formerly or are still in the majority lies mainly in the southwestern part of the continent, extending from the southern part of the British Columbia coast south to the tip of Lower California, and eastward through southern Nevada, northern Arizona and southern Utah, into the states of Sonora and Chihuahua in northern Mexico. In area this region is much smaller than the one just discussed, and the dolichocephalic groups, instead of having a continuous distribution, are, so far as our present knowledge goes, somewhat widely scattered. There has also been more change in the character of the population here since prehistoric times than in the northeast.

The most clearly marginal and outlying dolichocephalic type in the northeastern area was the Caspian, which formed the fundamental stratum in the Eskimo; on the opposite margin of the continent the same element occurs as a dominant or important factor at two points, the shell-heaps of San Francisco Bay and the coastal sites just to the south,[1] and in the lower strata of the shell-heaps of the Fraser River delta in British Columbia[2] and the neighboring parts of Vancouver Island.[3] In the first region the Caspian type is dominant in the graves south of the bay and is strongly represented (although actually secondary to the Palæ-Alpine type) in the upper strata of the shell-heaps, the Proto-Australoid and Proto-Negroid types being more important in the lower layers. Here, therefore, the Caspian type is obviously not the oldest, but was preceded by both broad-nosed dolichocephalic types, and, as will be seen presently, followed by brachycephalic types who were in the majority among the historic popu-

[1] U. C.; Hrdlicka, 1906.    [2] Boas, 1903.    [3] Boas, 1890.

lation. Farther north, in British Columbia, however, the Caspian appears to lie at the bottom of the series. The practice of cranial deformation throughout much of the Washington and Oregon coast region, and the almost total absence of cranial data make it impossible to say whether other traces of the Caspian type exist in this intermediate area. The fact, however, that the Yuki,[1] a small group of Indians speaking an isolated language and living on the coast north of San Francisco, show a large factor of the narrow-nosed dolichocephalic type, suggests that this type was formerly widely spread along this portion of the Pacific coast. In stature, both the prehistoric peoples of Caspian type and the modern Yuki are, like the Eskimo, short.

Associated everywhere with the Caspian type in the northeastern area we found a minority of the Mediterranean, and while the rather meagre character of the data for the area now under discussion makes conclusions less certain, it seems to be clear that the Mediterranean type is strongly represented here, more so indeed than in any other section of the continent except the northeast. It makes up nearly half the total factors in the case of the Ute[2] and Pi-Ute[2] crania from Nevada and Utah; it is overwhelmingly dominant in the ancient crania from the island of San Clemente[2] off the southern California coast, and is a very large factor in the series from the neighboring island of Santa Catalina;[3] and it is of large importance in the male crania from the ancient Basket-maker[4] sites in northern Arizona. Since these latter represent an extremely ancient culture, long antedating probably the Pueblo and Cliff-Dweller peoples, we have convincing evidence that this type, like the Caspian, was a very early one in this whole region, although in historic times it had largely disappeared. On the California coast, in the vicinity of San Francisco at least, it is perhaps significant that this Mediterranean type occurs in combination with the Caspian, as among the Eskimo.

In the northeastern area it was found that the more northerly region was characterized by the predominance of the narrow-

[1] Boas, 1905 a.    [2] U. S. N. M.    [3] P. M.    [4] P. M.; A. M. N. H.

nosed or leptorrhine dolichocephalic types, whereas the region south and west showed a majority of the platyrrhine forms. As a partial parallel to these conditions, we find a strong Proto-Australoid factor present here in the southwestern portion of the continent. It is the dominant type by a large majority in the island of Santa Catalina in both male and female series, and for the females in San Clemente; and it was even more important among the now extinct Pericue[1] of the southern tip of the Lower California peninsula. This latter region and the islands off the California coast are the most isolated and marginal portions of the whole continent here, and the dominance in such large measure of the Proto-Australoid type is, as I shall try to show, of much significance. That the type has been present hereabouts for a long time is shown by the fact that it vies with the Mediterranean type in the Basket-maker crania. It still survives among the Ute and Pi-Ute and also among the Tarahumare[2] and Pima[3] of the Mexican border country.

In the northeastern area the primary factor among the Iroquois, Lenape, and southern New England tribes was the Proto-Negroid. In the present area this type is of relatively slight importance. In the islands off the California coast it is lacking among the males although present as a small minority among the females; it is not found in the Pericue, and occurs only as a trace in the Ute and Pi-Ute. The Basket-maker crania, however, show a contrast to the more modern population, in that the Proto-Negroid type is present in large amount in both sexes. This would appear to indicate that this type was at an early date quite prominent in this portion of the continent; and this belief is corroborated by the crania from the ancient burial caves of Coahuila[4] in northern Mexico, which exhibit this type as clearly dominant! It is interesting in this connection to find that culturally these people of Coahuila were in many respects closely allied to the Basket-makers.[5]

So far little has been said of any brachycephalic factors in

---

[1] Ten Kate, 1884.                                    [2] Ten Kate, 1892; A. M. N. H.
[3] Ten Kate, 1892.        [4] Studley, 1882.        [5] Kidder, 1919; Guernsey, 1921.

this region. It would seem that the northern section was differentiated from the southern by the fact that in the former the brachycephalic elements are primarily Alpine, whereas in the latter it is the Palæ-Alpine which is of greatest importance. This holds true of the crania as well as of the modern tribes,[1] although cranial deformation undoubtedly somewhat obscures the results. The measurements made upon the Utes[2] show the predominance of platyrrhine, brachycephalic factors there, although the crania of supposedly ancient date from the same region show a majority of leptorrhine forms. Ancient crania, however, such as the female series from Basket-maker sites, show, on the other hand, Palæ-Alpine types as forming the main brachycephalic factor. We have thus over considerable portions of this region a modern population which is predominantly brachycephalic, although the ancient prehistoric occupants of the country were dolichocephalic, paralleling thus the situation which we found among the Iroquois. We cannot here invoke the influence of European intermixture since there has been very little miscegenation, particularly among the Utes. Attention must also be called to a fact whose significance will be apparent when we come to discuss the sequence of racial types in the continent as a whole. This is the existence of a moderate factor (ca. 17 per cent) of the Mongoloid type in the series of Ute and Pi-Ute crania, and in smaller measure in the Basket-maker.

The conclusions which we are entitled to draw from this mass of rather tedious detail seem to be these. Judging from its concentration in the extreme marginal portions of the area, the oldest stratum of population was characterized by the predominance of the Proto-Australoid type. Also very early, but evidently of later appearance, were the Mediterranean and Caspian types. The apparent focus of the former was in the interior, in southern Nevada and Utah and northern Arizona, and since its influence was but slightly felt in the tip of Lower California, although strong in the islands off the California coast, it is probable that this factor came in as an intrusion from the north and east. The

---

[1] Boas.  [2] Boas. Ten Kate, 1892.

Caspian type, on the other hand, is concentrated strongly on the coast, being here, as in the northeastern area, quite definitely a littoral type. There is thus reason for thinking that it may represent a coastwise drift from the northward, later overlaid and largely buried by a similar littoral movement of the Alpine type, for which we have, as will be seen, considerable indirect evidence. Lastly, the Proto-Negroid type, in the main absent from the whole coast district (except for the puzzling appearance of it just north of San Francisco Bay), but probably dominant among the Basket-makers and the crania from the Coahuila caves, although historically very early, seems not to have had a wide distribution, and tentatively may be supposed to have penetrated into this region from the east. An interesting but rather confusing light is thrown on this problem by the undeformed crania from the prehistoric strata at the pueblo of Pecos in New Mexico, which I have been most courteously allowed to study.[1] A comparison of the crania from the later prehistoric strata with those of the earlier, appears to show an increase in the proportions of the Proto-Negroid type both in the male and female series; yet, although the males of the still more ancient Basket-makers show a smaller proportion of this type than the oldest group at Pecos, the females have the largest percentage found anywhere or at any time except among the early Iroquois!

In one significant feature there is a similarity between this dolichocephalic region in the southwest of the continent and that in the northeast. It is that, so far as it is possible to infer anything as to the lines of racial drift, in both regions the movements of the Caspian type seem to have been littoral, whereas all other types have exhibited in general a centrifugal tendency, moving from the interior of the continent in the one case northeast and east, in the other southwest and west toward the margins.

[1] Collections of the Pecos Expedition, Department of Archæology, Phillips Andover Academy.

# CHAPTER III

## THE CENTRAL BRACHYCEPHALS

THE two areas which we have now discussed included little more than a fringe along the borders of the continent, and the great mass of the Indian tribes are comprised in the third or central section, in which in general brachycephalic as opposed to dolichocephalic factors prevail. Geographically the whole of this vast area is divisible into three broadly contrasted sections: (1) what may be called the Plateau Area comprising the region lying west of the Rocky Mountains and south of the Columbia River; (2) an Appalachian Area including the whole of the southeast of the continent, and (3) all the remainder, covering the vast plains which extend from the Gulf of Mexico northward to the Arctic Ocean, together with all the rugged mountain country west of the Rocky Mountains and north of the Columbia. In the first, both platyrrhine and leptorrhine brachycephalic types are present, the former being on the whole more important, and each holding itself more or less aloof from the other; in the second both are also present, but so thoroughly intermixed that neither can be said to be in the lead; in the third the leptorrhine forms are overwhelmingly in the majority almost everywhere. In order to bring out the essential facts, we must consider each of these three areas somewhat in detail.

What has been called the Plateau Area covers the greater part of California, Oregon, Nevada, Arizona, New Mexico, Utah, western Colorado, and Wyoming. Much of this region is, anthropologically speaking, one of the most obscure and least known portions of the continent, since except for its borders, we possess very little data on either crania or the living tribes. Furthermore, in much of the west and south, the practice of artificial cranial deformation renders the determination of the real cranial characteristics difficult and uncertain. This much, however, seems clear: the Shoshoni, Bannock, and Ute tribes,[1] who occupy the whole eastern frontier of the area, are characterized by a predominance of brachycephalic, platyrrhine factors, as are probably also the Navaho,[1] Zuni,[1] all the tribes of Yuman[2] stock, the Shoshonean tribes of southern California,[3] together with the Chumash and Salinan peoples of the adjacent coast.[4] No measurements are available from the Nevada tribes, but from the fact that among the Maidu,[5] who were their western neighbors in the Sierra Nevada region of northern California, the brachycephalic, platyrrhine factors strongly prevailed, it seems probable that the Paviotso at least, and perhaps the Pi-Ute, are of the same type. The Papago[6] and Pima[6] may tentatively be added to the list of tribes with these characteristics, although the practice of cranial deformation makes the determination of their type doubtful. The portraits given on Plate XXXV, Figs. 3 and 4, and Plate XXXVI, Fig. 1, may be taken as representative of this group.

Although we have thus strong grounds for believing that the great majority of the modern tribes of this whole area show a predominance of broad-nosed, brachycephalic types, we cannot, because of the absence of adequate cranial material, determine with certainty which of the two such types is mainly represented. From the fact, however, that, in the few Ute and Pi-Ute crania which we have, a rather notable Mongoloid element appears, we may conclude that, although the major factor is undoubtedly the Palæ-Alpine, it is probably accompanied by a minority of the Mongoloid.

For California and Oregon we can, in the absence of adequate material, only hazard the suggestion that dolichocephalic elements are probably strongly in evidence, and that in all probability the Alpine type, which has, as I shall try to show, moved both westward down the Columbia and southward along the coast to and beyond Puget Sound, has made its influence strongly felt as far south as the Sacramento Valley.

[1] Boas.
[4] A. M. N. H.
[2] Boas; Ten Kate, 1892.
[5] Boas, 1905.
[3] Boas, 1896.
[6] Ten Kate, 1892.

The leptorrhine, brachycephalic elements are almost wholly lacking among the bulk of the Shoshonean tribes, but do appear in the Pueblo peoples[1] and the Navaho.[1] Light is thrown on their history by the prehistoric data available from the Basket-makers[2] and the crania from Pecos.[3] In the former and probably most archaic material these factors seem to be entirely absent, although the platyrrhine forms are present in considerable proportions. In the lower strata at Pecos, representing the earliest population at this site, the Alpine type is present, but only in small amount (ca. 15 per cent); in the upper but still prehistoric layers the proportion rises to nearly 40 per cent, and this type becomes dominant. The inference from these facts would seem to be that in very early prehistoric times the Alpine type was unknown in this area; that it had made its way in (presumably from the eastward) by the time the earliest settlement was made at Pecos, and increased in strength there very largely in later times, extending its influence westward in ever decreasing strength as far as the coast. A portrait of an Apache as an example of this mixed Palæ-Alpine and Alpine types is given on Plate XXXVI, Fig. 2.

Summarizing the results of our investigation of this region, it may be said that it appears to constitute an island, as it were, of platyrrhine, brachycephalic peoples, mainly of Palæ-Alpine type, in which are embedded some remnants of the older dolichocephalic types and around which the later-coming Alpine peoples have flowed both on the north and the south, toward the Pacific coast. Or, to put the matter a little differently, we have in this area three successive racial strata, shingling one over the other from northeast to southwest, of which the southwestern dolichocephals are the oldest, the Palæ-Alpines the intermediate, and the Alpine type the latest layers.

A word may be added in regard to stature. All the Shoshonean tribes, together with the Maidu at least of the Californian peoples, *i. e.*, the central core mainly of Palæ-Alpine type, have

---

[1] Boas.                                    [2] P. M.; A. M. N. H.
[3] Collections of the Pecos Expedition, Phillips Andover Academy.

Fig. 1.  Bannock.

Fig. 2.  Apache.

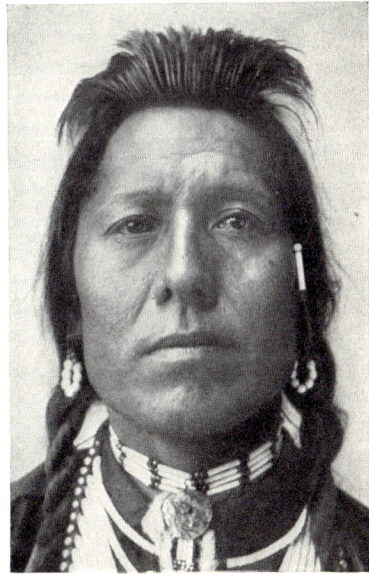

© F. A. Rinehart, Omaha

Fig. 3.  Thompson River.  (Salish).

Fig. 4.  Blackfoot.

PLATE XXXVI.

statures varying in the average between 164 and 168 cm. and are, with the exception of the dolichocephalic Yuki of the northern California coast ranges and the Pueblo peoples, the shortest in the region. To the southwest, the Yuman and Piman tribes are taller, varying from 169 to 172 or over, in average height. To the southeast, the Navaho[1] and Apache[1] also tend toward taller statures, the former averaging nearly 169 cm., while the latter rise above 170 cm. To the north, the Columbia River tribes show a stature in general above the Shoshonean group, and the same holds true even more strikingly toward the eastward among the tribes of the Plains. Thus, we may say that on the whole the taller statures seem to be associated with the later Alpine peoples. The tall stature of the Yuman and Piman tribes, however, appears to rest on some other and as yet uncertain basis.

The third section of the great brachycephalic area, which geographically is contiguous to the one just described, covers an enormous territory. Although for practically the whole of Alaska and the Canadian Northwest, together with the region about Hudson Bay, we as yet possess few or no data of any kind, it seems virtually certain that the peoples of this vast region, the whole of the Plains and the area north of the Great Lakes, are to be regarded as forming essentially one great group, characterized by the predominance of the Alpine type. From the linguistic point of view, it thus included the tribes belonging to the Athabascan, Tlingit, Haida, Tsimshian, Wakashan, Salishan and Shahaptian stocks; all the Plains tribes of the Siouan and Algonkian stocks; the Kiowan and Caddoan stocks; and all the Algonkian tribes north of the Great Lakes and the St. Lawrence.

In dealing with so large an area and with so many tribes, it will be convenient to consider the northern and northwestern portion separately from the rest, since this section presents certain special features of its own. The first point to be noted is that, although throughout the whole of this subsection the narrow-nosed, brachycephalic factors prevail, there is everywhere

[1] Boas.

a considerable, in some cases a large, broad-nosed element also present. It is least marked in the Wakashan[1] tribes, of varying, but generally notable prominence in the Salish[2] group, and most strongly represented in the Tsimshian[3] and Haida[4] of the northwest coast. If we may judge by the very small series of measurements available, it is even dominant in the Haida. I believe that the strength of the platyrrhine, brachycephalic factors here and their relative absence in the Plains is very significant, since this area of British Columbia is the northerly continuation of the region toward the south occupied mainly by Shoshonean tribes, among whom the Palæ-Alpine type was dominant. That is to say, it would seem that we had some reason to believe that the older, underlying population of this British Columbia and Northwest Coast region was of the Palæ-Alpine type as in the country to the south, but that here it has been overlain from the east and north by a dominating stratum of Alpine type. In this connection it may be observed that the hypothetically older Palæ-Alpine type has survived most notably in the Haida in the Queen Charlotte Islands, one of the most isolated marginal spots.

A second group of facts in relation to this region may now be noted, i. e., that, although the Salishan tribes and the Tlingit[5] appear to have no appreciable dolichocephalic factors, the Wakashan and Kootenay[6] on the west and east of the former, and the Haida and Tsimshian lying between the Salish and the Tlingit show noteworthy dolichocephalic elements. For the Kootenay the data are adequate, and indicate that in the Lower Kootenay the leptorrhine, dolichocephalic factors are actually in the majority. For the Wakashan tribes and the area occupied by them, the material is very limited, but the strength of these same factors in the undeformed crania from southern Vancouver Island would seem to confirm the few measurements on the living. In this connection the dominance of the same characters in the crania from the lower strata in the shell-heaps of the Fraser

[1] Boas, 1895.
[2] Boas, 1891, 1895, 1898.
[3] Boas, 1889, 1895, 1898.
[4] Boas, 1891, 1898.
[5] Fridolin, 1899; Tarenetsky, 1900.
[6] Chamberlain, 1892.

River indicate the antiquity of this type in the region. In the case of the Haida and Tsimshian the dolichocephalic factor is not so strong, but it is still of the leptorrhine variety. Since now there is reason to believe that the three northern stocks, the Tlingit, Haida, and Tsimshian, have moved westward from the interior to the coast, and even clearer evidence that the Salishan tribes have done likewise, whereas the Wakashan, who show next to the Kootenay the largest dolichocephalic factor of all, appear to be very ancient residents of the coast, the suggestion may be put forward that the whole of the northwest coast from Puget Sound north to the Copper River in Alaska was formerly occupied by tribes characterized by the predominance of leptorrhine, dolichocephalic types. Later, a series of brachycephalic peoples, at first in majority Palæ-Alpine, later primarily of Alpine type, pressed westward to the coast, largely obliterating the former dolichocephalic population, which survived only as a minority. The actual process seems visible in the Fraser River shell-heaps, where the dolichocephalic type present in the lower strata is not found in the upper, in which only brachycephalic forms appear.[1] An example of the Salish group representing the mixed Palæ-Alpine and Alpine peoples of this region is given on Plate XXXVI, Fig. 3.

If these views are correct, we should then be able to make instructive comparison with the area to the south. In both areas the older dolichocephalic factors are in greatest abundance in the extreme western and southwestern marginal districts, where they have survived more or less recognizably in comparative isolation. In both areas the next succeeding stratum is characterized by brachycephalic, platyrrhine types, but, whereas in the south the relatively unfavorable environment and great width of the arid plateaus saved a large nucleus of these early brachycephalic peoples from being overwhelmed and submerged by the later-coming Alpine peoples who flowed around them on all sides; in the north, where the plateau and mountain region is greatly narrowed, the Alpine stream penetrated much more

[1] Boas, 1903.

readily and completely, and thus came actually to dominate everywhere except in the more remote and isolated islands.

Before turning to the great Plains region brief reference must be made to two other aspects of the problem. The distribution of stature in the area just discussed is in outline as follows. The Tlingit, Haida, and Tsimshian form a group characterized by relatively tall stature, ranging from 173 cm. in the case of the first to 169 cm. in the Tsimshian. The Wakashan tribes are markedly shorter, averaging 164 cm., or slightly under medium stature. Along the extreme northwest border of their range they are even shorter still. The decrease in stature attains its maximum in the Fraser delta and Harrison Lake tribes, the latter having an average of only 158 cm., which with their extreme brachycephaly marks them as a special and peculiarly localized group. The other Salishan tribes increase in stature quite regularly from west to east, reaching an average of 167–168 cm. among the Shuswap and Okanagan. The Athabascan tribes of the interior of British Columbia are, on the other hand, shorter, and are substantially similar in this respect to the Wakashan. While not completely accordant in every locality, still this distribution of statures agrees broadly with the evidence derived from the distribution of cranial types, i. e., that the taller northern tribes represent a westward movement of the tall tribes east of the Rocky Mountains; the diminution in stature of the predominantly Alpine Salish from east to west is due to the progressively increasing mixture with the preceding and shorter Palæ-Alpine peoples; while the short stature of the Wakashan peoples represents in so far the original dolichocephalic stratum. The extreme shortness of the Harrison Lake people is for the moment unexplained, but I might suggest that it may be due to an isolated remnant of the Mongoloid type, which the world over is characterized by extremely short stature. As we possess no cranial material from this group, however, the suggestion cannot be substantiated.

The vast area included in the central or Plains section of the brachycephalic region, was occupied in historic times in the

main by tribes belonging to four great linguistic stocks, the Athabascan, Algonkian, Siouan, and Caddoan. In the southern Plains
the Comanche, an outlier of the Shoshonean stock, the Kiowa,
and the small group of the Tonkawa complete the list. Of the
four great stocks, only the Siouan tribes occupy a continuous
area. Of the northern Athabascan tribes, who held the greater
part of the Canadian Plains and the whole of the interior of
Alaska, our knowledge is extremely meagre, and we may therefore turn first to the rest of the region, in regard to which we
shall be able to draw conclusions of some certainty.[1]

Reference to the map given on Plate XXXIII shows the striking fact that east of the Rocky Mountains and from about 55° N.
Latitude southward to the Great Lakes and the St. Lawrence, and
down through the Plains almost to the Gulf of Mexico, the historic tribes were characterized by the strong and rather even
dominance of brachycephalic, leptorrhine factors everywhere
except in the case of (1) the Mandan and Arikara; (2) the Arapaho
and Cheyenne, and (3) somewhat less certainly in the Sarcee, the
Tunica and the southern Siouan tribes, such as the Kwapa, Kansas and Missouri. So far then as this predominance of brachycephalic, leptorrhine elements is concerned, there is in general
a considerable uniformity among most of the Plains tribes without regard to their linguistic affiliations. If the matter be looked
into more in detail, however, significant differences begin to appear.

If we turn our attention to the factor of secondary importance
present in each case, the whole series of tribes having the brachycephalic, leptorrhine types predominant falls into three well-
marked groups, characterized respectively by the presence of
strong secondary elements of broad-nosed brachycephalic or of
broad or narrow nosed dolichocephalic types. The first group,
that in which the secondary element is a platyrrhine, brachycephalic factor, comprises the Western Ojibwa, the Ponca, and
perhaps also the Omaha, the Kiowa, the Caddo, and the Tonkawa. This underlying secondary element seems to be attrib-

---

[1] For all this region the data on the living are derived from Boas.

utable to three distinct sources: in the Ojibwa and Ponca, to the strength of this factor which, as will be shown presently, formerly characterized the area west of Lake Michigan; in the case of the Caddo and Tonkawa, to the earlier probable dominance of this type in the whole of the southern plains; and for the Kiowa, who have apparently migrated to their historic sites from the mountain region in Wyoming or Montana, to the stratum of Palæ-Alpine character which has been shown to have been formerly strong in that region.  The Ojibwa and Ponca are further linked together by the minority factor of Proto-Australoid or Proto-Negroid type which they possess, factors present in strength, as already pointed out, among the Iroquois and southern New England Algonkian tribes.  The Kiowa, Caddo, and Tonkawa, on the other hand, are in their turn linked together by a minority of Caspian or Mediterranean type (leptorrhine, dolichocephalic), the significance of which will become apparent later.

Since the material on which the foregoing analysis is based is wholly made up of measurements taken on the living, it has been impossible to determine with accuracy the types involved. Cranial data are, however, scanty and are practically confined to the Ojibwa[1] and the Ponca.[1]  In the main the two series corroborate the conclusions based on the measurements of the living, and appear, furthermore, to establish two points of some importance.  These are that the bulk of the platyrrhine, brachycephalic factors, present in these two tribes at least, is due to the Mongoloid type, and that the Ojibwa and Ponca differ from each other in that in the former the dominant brachycephalic element is primarily Alpine, whereas in the latter it is of the Ural type.  Such fragmentary data as are available for the Kiowa,[2] Caddo,[3] and Tonkawa[4] seem to corroborate their forming a group in contrast with the Ojibwa and Ponca, for where these latter have a Mongoloid factor the three former tribes have instead the Palæ-Alpine.  This seems to indicate that the affiliations of the Kiowa, Caddo, and Tonkawa are on the whole with the region toward the south and west, whereas the Ojibwa and

[1] U. S. N. M.    [2] Otis, 1876.    [3] Allen, 1896; P. A. N. S.    [4] Otis, *op. cit.*

Ponca are related more closely to the tribes south and east of the Great Lakes.

The second group which may be distinguished is that in which the factor of secondary importance is a platyrrhine, dolichocephalic one. In extent of area covered it is larger than the first, and includes all the remaining Algonkian tribes of this section (*i. e.*, Montagnais, Ottawa, Missisauga, Eastern Ojibwa, Blackfoot, Arapaho, and Cheyenne); the Mandan and Hidatsa of the Siouan stock, together with the Caddoan Arikara and Pawnee. As in the previous group, if we take into account the factor which is third in importance, the tribes listed fall into two divisions, of which one, comprising the Blackfoot, Arapaho, Cheyenne, and Mandan, has a dolichocephalic, leptorrhine type; the other, including the remaining four Algonkian tribes, the Hidatsa, and the two Caddoan tribes, has on the contrary a brachycephalic, platyrrhine type. If this situation be compared with that in the group just discussed, it will be seen that the brachycephalic, platyrrhine element, which was of *secondary* importance in the first group as a whole, becomes the *tertiary* element in the majority of the tribes of the present group, and that the presence of a dolichocephalic, leptorrhine factor among the Blackfoot, Arapaho, Cheyenne, and Mandan connects them with the Kiowa, Caddo, and Tonkawa. The portrait of a Blackfoot given on Plate XXXVI, Fig. 4, may be taken as an example of this group.

From these facts two conclusions of real significance seem to follow. First, that the three Algonkian tribes of the Plains, *i. e.*, the Blackfoot, Arapaho, and Cheyenne, who are linguistically rather widely divergent from the other members of the stock, are also differentiated from them physically. Second, that the Mandan, who linguistically stand somewhat apart from the other Siouan tribes, are more closely allied physically to the Plains Algonkian tribes than to the neighboring groups of the Siouan stock. Rather brief cranial series are available for the Blackfoot,[1] Cheyenne,[2] and Hidatsa.[1] These show in the case

[1] U. S. N. M.                                    [2] U. S. N. M.; P. M.

of the Cheyenne and Hidatsa close similarity with the measurements on the living; for the Blackfoot, however, the crania indicate not a brachycephalic but a considerable dolichocephalic majority. Leaving the significance of this aside for the moment, the cranial data make it clear that the primary brachycephalic factor is, in all the tribes, the Alpine type; that the most important dolichocephalic element present is the Proto-Australoid; that there is a minority here of the Palæ-Alpine type, in contrast with the Mongoloid, which was that most prominent in the case of the Ojibwa and Ponca; and lastly, that the dolichocephalic element which particularly characterizes the Algonkian tribes of the Plains, i. e., the Blackfoot, Arapaho, and Cheyenne, and probably also the Mandan, is the Mediterranean. From all of which we may conclude that the presence of the Proto-Australoid factor serves in some way to link these tribes with the Iroquois, Lenape, and southern New England Algonkian tribes, among whom it was well represented; and that the Algonkian tribes of the Plains are, by virtue of their considerable Mediterranean factor, more closely related perhaps to the tribes of this stock in the Maritime Provinces and northern New England than to those farther to the south.

The third group may be more briefly dismissed. Characterized by the rise of the dolichocephalic, leptorrhine factors to second place, it includes the Crow and the various tribes of the Dakota or Sioux. In the strength of the brachycephalic, leptorrhine element these tribes exceed the bulk of all the others in this whole area, the Crow in fact surpassing all other tribes for which I have been able to secure data, except the Salish Bilqula, of the British Columbia coast. Cranial material is available only for the Sioux,[1] and shows first that the primary brachycephalic element is the Alpine; second that, as in the case of the Plains Algonkian tribes, the Mediterranean type is a factor of importance; and thirdly that the largest dolichocephalic factor as shown by the *crania* is the Proto-Australoid, and that this is actually dominant, in contrast to the evidence given by the mea-

[1] U. S. N. M.

surements on the living, which showed the Alpine to be in the majority. Now precisely the same conditions prevailed in the case of the Blackfoot, and we may therefore ask whether the phenomenon may not be due in both cases to similar causes. For the Sioux, at least, a reasonable explanation is suggested, if we divide the whole series into a Western and an Eastern group, the former including the Teton Sioux, the latter the Sisseton, Wahpeton, and Yankton Sioux. The two series appear to be quite divergent, the Western showing a predominance of Alpine elements, as in the case of the measurements on the living (who were, indeed, very largely of the Teton group), and according with the Hidatsa, Arikara, Pawnee, Ojibwa, etc.; whereas the Eastern series is characterized by a majority of dolichocephalic factors, mainly Mediterranean and Proto-Australoid, and thus has affiliations with the prehistoric population of the Ohio valley, the Huron, and the extreme northeastern Algonkian tribes. Portraits illustrating the types found among the Crow and Sioux are given on Plate XXXVII, Figs. 1 and 2.

The apparent divergence of the crania thus from the measurements made on the living is not a real one, but is due to the inclusion of the crania of the Eastern Sioux from whom no series of measurements on the living are available. A similar explanation of the divergence in the case of the Blackfoot hardly seems possible. Since, however, the female Blackfoot crania agree with the living series in having a preponderance of Alpine factors, and since the male series is small in numbers and the excess of dolichocephalic elements slight, it seems possible that it is not really significant, and that a larger series would more exactly parallel the results obtained from the living.

From the standpoint of stature, all the Plains tribes are to be classed as tall, the average ranging from 171 to 174 cm. They thus considerably surpass the British Columbia and Northwest Coast peoples, as well as all those of the southwestern dolichocephalic area except the Yuman and Piman tribes.

All that has been said hitherto of the physical types in the Plains area has had reference to the historic tribes. Unfortunately, we are not yet in a position to throw much light on the matter from older materials derived from archæological investigations, since for this whole region satisfactory data of this sort are largely lacking. One or two indications of value, however, may be gathered from the materials at hand. In the first place, it seems to be clear, from the rather random excavations of mounds and burial sites thus far made, that these are attributable to peoples of more than a single type. Some sites, such as the Wallace Mound in Nebraska, have yielded crania exclusively or almost exclusively brachycephalic and in the main of the Palæ-Alpine type; others in the immediate vicinity, such as Ft. Lisa, contain crania which are all dolichocephalic.[1] These differences in physical type are paralleled by differences in culture and we are almost forced to conclude that they represent successive occupations of the same area by peoples of contrasted type. Further examples of this sort are to be found in the crania from mounds in the Red River valley in North Dakota and Manitoba,[2] which show a very large preponderance of dolichocephalic factors, whereas the known historic tribes in the same region all had a majority of brachycephalic forms.

Unfortunately the scientific archæological investigation of the Plains area has not yet progressed far enough to make it possible to arrange the various sites in any kind of chronological sequence, so that we have as a rule no means of knowing which is the older and which the later of the several types. All that it seems possible to say at present is that, wherever in the northern and eastern Plains we do get any indication at all of sequence, the earlier sites usually show the more dolichocephalic forms. The published data are too meagre and imperfect to enable us to determine the actual types. While it would be in the last degree imprudent to attempt to build any valid conclusions upon a single skull, it might be pointed out in this connection that what is probably the most ancient skull yet found in the whole region, the Lansing Skull from Kansas,[3] is clearly long-headed.

---

[1] Poynter, 1915.    [2] Montgomery, 1906, 1908; Russell, F., 1898.
[3] Hrdlicka, 1907.

© *F. A. Rinehart, Omaha*

FIG. 1. CROW.

FIG. 2. SIOUX.

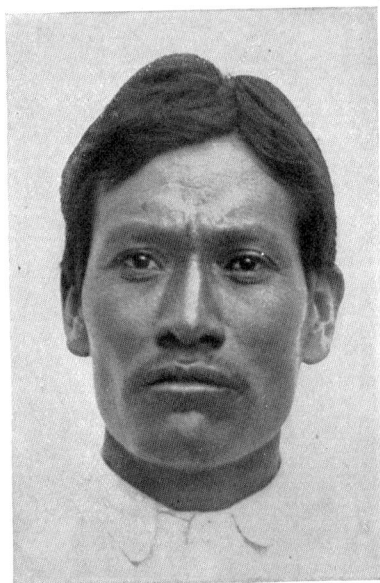

FIG. 3. CHICKASAW.

FIG. 4. AZTEC.

PLATE XXXVII.

For the southern portion of the Plains, the data are meagre and conflicting. The crania from central and southeastern Missouri[1] are unfortunately in such damaged condition that determination of their type is impossible. All that can be said is that dolichocephalic forms seem to prevail. In Arkansas,[2] on the other hand, the few undeformed crania obtained seem to show that, whereas in Arkansas and Jefferson Counties the Alpine type was in the majority, in Union County the Palæ-Alpine alone occurs. In northern Louisiana,[2] in Morehouse, Ouachita, Caldwell, and Franklin Counties, these two types are thoroughly blended so that neither prevails.

With strong emphasis upon the tentative character of the suggestion, it may be said that at least in the vicinity of the Missouri River and in the region east of it the population has apparently changed from one which was predominantly dolichocephalic to one that in historic times has been as predominantly brachycephalic. With this may be coupled the fact already noted in the case of the Sioux, where, in the Teton who have moved from the eastern to the western margin of the Plains, the westward movement was associated with a similar reversal, such that a former majority of dolichocephalic factors is exchanged for one of brachycephalic elements. All of which furthermore suggests that the Plains have in some way been, as it were, a radiant centre for brachycephalic factors, primarily of of the Alpine type, whose influence has spread to the east and southeast among peoples more markedly of dolichocephalic type.

We may now turn to the third and last section of the North American area in which brachycephalic factors were predominant, i. e., the region from the Ohio valley south to the Gulf of Mexico and east of the Mississippi River. The data for this section are very meagre, and its consideration may, therefore, be brief. When first known to Europeans it was occupied by tribes belonging in the main to four stocks, the Algonkian, Siouan, Iroquoian and Muskogean. Of these the first were mainly in the Ohio valley, the Siouan tribes held the middle Alleghanies,

[1] Hrdlicka, 1910.
[2] Hrdlicka, 1908, 1909.

while the southern portion of the range was occupied by the Iroquoian Cherokee. Northern Florida and most of the area of the Gulf States were in the control of Muskogean tribes.

Except for the Muskogean tribes, our knowledge of the physical characters of the inhabitants of this whole southeastern portion of the continent is derived entirely from archæological materials, and these are in large measure of doubtful value owing to the wide prevalence of artifical cranial deformation. Turning our attention to these Muskogean peoples first, it appears that, although the Chickasaw, Choctaw, and Creeks all show a large predominance of brachycephalic factors, these are Alpine in the case of the Choctaw but Palæ-Alpine in the other two tribes. If this difference, as found among the tribes now for many years living in Oklahoma, actually represents the conditions in their former home, it would seem to indicate that there had been an increase in the Alpine factor in a general way from east to west, with a parallel concentration of the Palæ-Alpine type toward the Atlantic coast. The dolichocephalic minority seems to be in the main of the narrow-nosed types, and these are strongest among the Chickasaw who occupy the northwestern portion of the Muskogean territory. A Chickasaw portrait is given on Plate XXXVII, Fig. 3.

The only other living tribe for which data are available is the Shawnee, an Algonkian group who have been great wanderers, but who probably were resident in the region south of the Ohio River in the sixteenth century. Their modern and probably much mixed descendants show a strong predominance of brachycephalic factors, chiefly of the Alpine type, and in general are quite comparable to the Muskogean tribes to the southward.

Neither for the Cherokee nor for any of the Siouan tribes of this area are any data whatever available. For the Ohio valley region our most important materials are derived from the cist burials in western Tennessee, from the cemeteries at Madisonville, and the mounds of the Turner Group. Although the crania from the Tennessee region are for the most part deformed, it

has been possible to obtain a sufficiently large series[1] of undeformed skulls to determine with considerable certainty the characters of the people occupying the area in prehistoric times. Predominantly brachycephalic, the Alpine type is clearly in the majority, the Palæ-Alpine ranking second in importance, as among
the Choctaw of to-day. Unlike the Muskogean tribes, however,
the dolichocephalic minority is in this case primarily Proto-Negroid, which was, it may be remembered, the dominant element
among the Iroquois, the Lenape, and the other Algonkian tribes
of the southern New England region. A small series of crania
from the vicinity of the Cahokia mounds in the extreme southern
portion of Illinois show on the whole similar features to those
from Tennessee. This population thus appears to have been intermediate in its characteristics between the Muskogeans to the
south and the Iroquoian and Lenape tribes farther north and east.

The great richness of the Ohio valley in archæological remains might be thought to have provided us with abundant
data on the former occupants of this area, and the builders of
the many varieties of mounds and earthworks for which the region
is justly famous. Unfortunately, this is not the case. Many
of the more important sites were explored before the era of modern methods, and the skeletal material either irretrievably damaged, lost, or preserved without adequate information. Many
of the crania are strongly deformed, and, as cremation was widely
employed, all opportunities of determining the physical type of
the people were destroyed. For two sites only is reliable cranial
material available, the Madisonville cemetery and the Turner
Group of mounds, both in southern Ohio. Considering the former site first,[2] we find that the people here buried were predominantly brachycephalic, with the Alpine and Palæ-Alpine types
represented in about equal strength, the dolichocephalic minority
factors being primarily the Proto-Australoid and Proto-Negroid
types, which were dominant among the Iroquois and Lenape.
These people were thus in general similar to those whose crania
are found in the cist graves of western Tennessee. The archæo-

[1] P. M.        [2] Hooton, 1920.

logical evidence at Madisonville indicates that the site dates from the period immediately preceding the European contact, and that it continued to be occupied until after the first European influence had made itself felt. It is, therefore, extremely probable that this people of the Madisonville cemetery may be identified with some Algonkian or even some Iroquoian tribe.

The Turner Group of mounds has yielded some of the most remarkable objects ever found in the Ohio valley, and the builders must have belonged to the higher cultural stratum here, sometimes referred to as the Hopewell Culture, from the name of a site where it was particularly well revealed. This culture was, so far as we know, quite extinct in the region at the time of the first European contact, and thus represents an older type than that found at Madisonville. The crania[1] from these mounds are furthermore of two periods, one contemporary with the erection of the mounds, the other later and intrusive. Although the number of crania complete enough for determining the types is small, it seems possible to reach the following conclusions. First, that the builders of the mounds were a people among whom dolichocephalic factors were in large majority; second, that these were mainly of the Proto-Australoid and Proto-Negroid types and thus show affiliation with the Iroquois and southern Algonkian tribes; and third, that the intrusive burials of later date show an even larger proportion of long-headed elements, some of which are, however, leptorrhine, thus differentiating them from the earlier crania among whom the narrow-nosed, long-headed factors were practically absent. Since both earlier and later burials here differ radically from the historic and protohistoric crania from Madisonville, the minority types there being the dominant ones here, we seem to have evidence of two prehistoric occupations of this region prior to the appearance of the people which held the area at the time of the first European contact. Physically these older peoples seem closely allied to the early Iroquois and Lenape, but culturally they were in quite a different category, and historically must have preceded them,

[1] P. M.

since the Iroquois at least were relatively late immigrants into their historic sites in western New York, and were much more nearly contemporaneous with the Madisonville people.

The evidence afforded by such other scattered data as are available may be briefly summarized. In Illinois the mounds have yielded crania of very different types. Those, for example, along the Illinois River[1] closely resemble the older forms from the Turner Group, whereas those from other sites[2] are primarily brachycephalic, with a clear dominance of the Palæ-Alpine type. No indication, however, of the relative age of these mounds is given. Michigan and Wisconsin show a similar situation, if it is fair to judge from very scanty material.[3]

Summing up our information from this whole southeastern area it may be said that the Ohio valley and region north of it toward the Great Lakes was occupied at an early period by a people predominantly dolichocephalic, and allied more closely with the proto-historic and prehistoric Iroquois and Lenape than with any other group in this part of the continent. Apparently (?) the higher or Hopewell Culture of the Ohio valley is to be attributed to peoples of this type. By proto-historic times, this population had been replaced by one of different character, primarily of Alpine and Palæ-Alpine types. Farther to the south in the Gulf States, we have no archæological materials, but the historic Muskogean tribes were predominantly brachycephalic, and in majority of the Palæ-Alpine type.

The problem of disentangling the racial history of the region would be greatly simplified if we had some information as to the types found among the Cherokee, Yuchi, and the Timuquana of southern Florida. If the Cherokee were, as seems not improbable, comparable with the early Iroquois and Lenape, we might suppose this long-headed, broad-nosed group to have extended formerly throughout the Appalachian region and westward down the Ohio valley. From the westward, then, to continue our theoretical reconstruction, came two thrusts bringing brachycephalic peoples from beyond the Mississippi; one moving

[1] Hrdlicka, 1907.  [2] A. N. S. P.  [3] P. M.

eastward up the Ohio and across the Appalachians to the Atlantic coast might then be identified with the Siouan tribes; the other crossing the Mississippi farther down, pressed into the Gulf States as the Muskogi. The more northern or Siouan immigrants brought mainly Alpine factors, whereas the Muskogi in addition brought a considerable Palæ-Alpine element absorbed in the southern plains, which was further increased by the assimilation of the earlier occupants of the Gulf States, who may perhaps also have been largely of this same type. The pressure of the immigrant Muskogean tribes forced some of the Iroquoian tribes toward the north, and perhaps also the Lenape, with the result that the Siouan population of the Ohio valley were driven westward again, leaving those who had settled in the Alleghany region isolated. This western movement of the Siouan tribes would then be that recorded in tradition, and the large dolichocephalic element among the eastern Sioux may perhaps thus be explained as derived from the pre-Siouan long-headed population of the Ohio valley.

We have now passed in review the whole of the area of North America except for the northwestern corner and the extreme southern portion comprised in Mexico and the Central American region. The northwestern portion of the continent is, so far as concrete information goes, almost totally unknown. It was occupied both in Alaska and in the Mackenzie valley by tribes belonging to the Athabascan linguistic stock, except for the narrow coastal strip and the chain of the Aleutian Islands, which were held by Eskimo-speaking peoples. The region west of James's Bay, on the other hand, was occupied by the Algonkian tribe of the Cree. The latter were culturally related to the Ojibwa and we can only infer, somewhat precariously, that in physical type they were also more or less akin.

For the Athabascan tribes we have a few facts, which, taken together, lead to conclusions which are probably approximately true. Thus the Athabascan Nahané and Chilcotin of northern British Columbia are very strongly brachycephalic, with a probable dominance of the Alpine type. The Sarsi, a small tribe long associated with the Algonkian Blackfoot, show also a large factor of the same type. The Loucheux,[1] living west of the lower Mackenzie in close proximity to the Eskimo, although obviously much mixed with these, nevertheless retain large brachycephalic factors. Finally, the very few crania[2] known from this whole Athabascan area are almost exclusively round-headed. It would seem justifiable, therefore, to believe that the whole of this northern Athabascan area was characterized by a strongly prevailing brachycephaly, with the Alpine type predominant. This conclusion seems to be confirmed by what we know of the Alaskan Eskimo.[3] These differ from the more Eastern groups in having a large majority of brachycephalic, Alpine factors.[4] As it seems extremely probable that these Western Alaskan Eskimo owe their differences from the Eastern groups to admixture with the neighboring tribes, these latter must, on this basis, be primarily of Alpine type. For the Aleut the available data are extremely meagre, and cranial deformation greatly obscures the results, yet, making such allowance as is possible for this disturbing feature, it is probable that they are in the majority of the Palæ-Alpine type, with however a dolichocephalic minority, which is stronger in the ancient crania than among the modern tribes. Lastly, although the value of this evidence is probably not great, all the Athabascan tribes in other parts of the continent, for whom we have data, such as the Hupa in California, and the Navaho and Apache in the Southwest, are predominantly brachycephalic. If all these facts are taken into consideration, it seems that it is probably justifiable to regard all of this great area in the northwest of the continent where it most closely approaches Asia, as one primarily brachycephalic and predominantly Alpine in type. In stature these northern Athabascans are probably relatively tall, averaging perhaps 170 cm. or even more, and thus in this respect are affiliated with the taller tribes of the Plains, and of the northern portion of the Northwest Coast, rather than with the undersized

---

[1] Boas, 1901.      [2] Tarenetsky, 1900; Russell, 1898; A. N. S. P.
[3] Tarenetsky, *op. cit.*; Boas, 1901; A. M. N. H.; Bessels, 1875.
[4] In part, probably, the result of artificial deformation.

peoples of the southern portion of that coast and beyond to California.

For the Mexican and Central American areas we have to repeat the old story of utterly inadequate materials. Apart from Hamy's[1] measurements of two or three score of crania from all parts of Mexico, for the most part wholly without clear indication of their cultural affiliations or antiquity, and in majority probably much deformed, Hrdlicka's[2] measurements in the north, and Starr's[3] averages on a series of living tribes in the south, there is no published material of value. Without, therefore, the opportunity of utilizing the unpublished measurements of several large series of crania,[4] it would have been almost impossible to discuss the Mexican area at all.

As far south as the Isthmus of Tehuantepec, Mexico consists primarily of three contrasted regions, the low, tropical coastal plain stretching along the Gulf; the high plateau with its bordering mountain ranges, essentially a southern continuation of the plateau area of the western United States; and the tropical strip along the Pacific coast. At the beginning of the sixteenth century, the larger part of this whole area was occupied by tribes belonging to the Nahuan branch of the now pretty generally recognized Uto-Aztecan stock. Along the Gulf coast and extending inland onto the plateau, from Tampico to Vera Cruz, were tribes belonging to other stocks, such as the Huasteca and Totonac on the coast and the Otomi and Tarascan on the plateau. Of these the Huasteca were an outlying member of the Mayan stock, whose main habitat lay in Yucatan, Honduras, and Guatemala. A second area not occupied by Nahua-speaking tribes, was on the Pacific side, covering the present state of Oaxaca, which was held by the Zapotec.

It has been already pointed out in another connection (p. 417), that the more northerly Uto-Aztecan tribes, such as the Tarahumare and Pima, showed large dolichocephalic factors, in the main very clearly of platyrrhine types, which allied them to that extent with the prehistoric crania from the caves in

[1] Hamy, 1891.        [2] Hrdlicka, 1903.        [3] Starr, 1902.        [4] A. M. N. H.

the Coahuila[1] desert farther east. To the southward, among the Nahuan Cora and Huichol, these dolichocephalic elements become relatively much weaker, these tribes being primarily brachycephalic with a considerable majority of the Palæ-Alpine type. The Tarascans of Michoacan carry the dominance of this type still farther. For the Otomi, who traditionally represented the pre-Nahuan population of much of the plateau, the available data are very meagre, but among them apparently, although the Palæ-Alpine type is dominant, large elements of both Proto-Negroid and Proto-Australoid are present, tending thus to ally them with the prehistoric people of the Coahuila caves. The Huasteca and Totonac on the other hand, to judge from Starr's figures, are overwhelmingly brachycephalic, in spite of the confusing effects of cranial deformation. The modern Aztec or Nahua of the valley of Mexico, as well as the Zapotec,[2] also appear to have a preponderance of brachycephalic factors, these being more marked in the latter than in the Aztec. No certainly identified crania are available. An example of the modern Aztec is given on Plate XXXVII, Fig. 4.

From the foregoing we may perhaps venture to suggest that there was an early stratum of Proto-Negroid and Proto-Australoid types in the Mexican region, driven back into the arid areas of the northeast in prehistoric times, but surviving as a minority still among the Otomi, the Tarahumare, and the Pima. The dominant elements, however, were everywhere a mixture of Palæ-Alpine and Alpine types.

In Yucatan and Chiapas, British Honduras and Guatemala a series of Mayan tribes formed a solid block stretching from the Atlantic to the Pacific shores. Strong artificial deformation obscures the question of the physical characteristics of the Maya proper in Yucatan, although in all probability (?) they were in very large majority brachycephalic. Interest attaches therefore all the more to the fact that in the Zotzil and Tzendal tribes of Chiapas[3] dolichocephalic factors are predominant, probably although not certainly of the broad-nosed varieties, and so com-

[1] Studley, 1882.      [2] Baca, 1897.      [3] Starr, 1902.

parable with the early long-headed stratum whose existence has been postulated farther north.

In stature there seems to be a contrast between the northern Nahuan tribes together with the Tarascans of Michoacan, and all the other peoples for whom we have data, in that the former group are in general somewhat above medium stature, averaging between 165 and 179 cm., whereas the latter are with few exceptions distinctly short, averaging between 155 and 160 cm.

For all the remainder of the Central American area as far as Panama, there are no available data of any value.

# BOOK VI
# SOUTH AMERICA

# INTRODUCTION

For North America and sundry other portions of the world we have had to deplore the lack of data upon which to base a coherent theory of their racial history; for the South American continent the dearth of materials becomes acute, and for no other great area do we know so little in regard to the physical characters of its inhabitants. At least half if not two-thirds of the continent is practically a blank, while the wide prevalence of artificial cranial deformation gives to the data from much of the remaining area a most uncertain value. It is only possible therefore to sketch in the most tentative fashion the broad outlines of the racial problems of South America and trust that the data for filling in the details may be secured before it is too late.

The main features of the geography of South America, so far as they have a bearing on its racial history, may be briefly stated. In the northern continent the dividing range of the Rocky Mountains is located so as to leave perhaps a third of the continent on its western side; in South America the Cordillera of the Andes hugs closely the western continental margin, leaving but a very narrow strip between it and the Pacific. Whereas in North America the whole mountain system beyond the plateau area has a width of from three to five hundred miles, and the plateau area itself in its widest part extends for nearly 800 miles east and west, in the southern continent the Cordillera is rarely more than 200 miles, for the southern third little more than 100 miles in width, while the high plateau area of Peru and Bolivia attains a maximum width only about a third of that of the much lower-lying comparable area in North America. The great mass of the continent lying east of the Andes is divisible into four separate areas, two lowland and two highland. In the first category belong the vast Amazon basin forested and tropical in its climate, and the plains and pampas of the southern portion of the continent, from the Chaco of eastern Bolivia, Argentina, and Paraguay through Patagonia to the Straits of Magellan. In the second group are the highlands of eastern Brazil and those of eastern Venezuela and the Guianas. The great Amazonian forest is in many respects comparable with the Congo forest in Africa, in that it is in a measure a "refuge area" economically less favorable than the surrounding highlands or the great plains of the south. Climatically the greater part of South America is tropical, but, owing to its elevation, the Andean chain carries southward across the equator a temperate climate, so that migrant peoples from the north could, by following the inter-Andine valleys, reach the temperate area of the southern plains without being subjected to unfamiliar conditions.

The peopling of North America must have taken place, as has been shown, by way of Bering Strait, and the topography of the country is such that all immigrants probably tended to spread southward over the continent by way of the Plains, unless they moved along the shores. For the peopling of South America two routes were open, the narrow Isthmus of Panama and the long, curving chain of the Antilles. The topography of the continent gives to each of these two ways a special significance. The Isthmus of Panama lies practically at right angles to the main axis of the Andean system, which in northern Colombia and western Venezuela curves around toward the east, where it forms the rugged northern shore of the continent as far as the delta of the Orinoco. Immigration by way of Panama would thus tend to be diverted either along the Caribbean or Pacific shores, or up the great longitudinal valleys of the Cauca or Magdalena, and so southward along the Cordillera. The route from Florida by way of the Antillean islands, on the other hand, required some seamanship and reached the continent at the delta of the Orinoco, where also two alternatives confront the immigrant; for he may either travel along the coast east or west, or follow up the course of the Orinoco, which would bring him directly into the Amazonian basin. We might logically expect, therefore, that, apart from evidences of littoral drifts, two great streams of immigration might be discerned, one of which, coming by way of Panama, followed southward through the temperate climate of the Cordillera to the southern plains, tending thus to pass around the western edge of the Amazonian forest, while the other, coming from Florida along the Antillean chain, spread up the Orinoco into the tropical region of the Amazon.

Before we turn to the consideration of the physical types, a word must be said in regard to the linguistic characteristics of the South American peoples. As in North America, we find here a great, almost a bewildering diversity in language. More than eighty different linguistic stocks are at present recognized,[1] divisible, as in the north, into the two classes of large and small stocks. The former group may be taken to include the Carib, Arawak, Chibchan, Pano, Ges, Quechua, Araucanian, Puelchean and Tsonekan stocks, which together occupy probably five-sixths of the whole continent, several such as the Carib and Arawak extending over very large areas. The smaller stocks are distributed rather strikingly in a main belt stretching along the eastern base of the Andes and the western edge of the Amazonian basin, and in a less distinct strip fringing the borders of the Brazilian Highlands. It is difficult to avoid the conclusion that these smaller stocks, many of which occupy very restricted areas, represent the survivors of an older stratum of peoples which have been crowded out by the expansion of the larger stocks that have spread through the Andean area and the Amazonian forest.

Turning now to a consideration of the physical types, it will be seen from the maps given on Plates XXXVIII to XLI that the distribution of the dolichocephalic and brachycephalic types in South America, so far as known, strikingly parallels their distribution in the northern continent shown on Plates XXX to XXXIII. Here as there the dolichocephalic forms are concentrated in two main groups, one of which is fairly continuous and fringes the southeastern margin of the continent with extensions onto the Brazilian uplands; the other, consisting of isolated patches, being

[1] Chamberlain, 1913.

scattered along the Andean chain from Venezuela to Chile. The brachycephalic types, as in North America, are in the main spread over the more central portions of the continent. In North America the leptorrhine, dolichocephalic factors were most in evidence in the extreme north and northeast; here they are of greatest importance in the farthest south and southeast. The largest proportions of the platyrrhine dolichocephals are found along the inner margins, as it were, of the leptorrhine forms, in the Brazilian Highlands, paralleling their abundance among the Iroquois and southern Algonkian tribes in the northern continent. There these factors were also present on the Pacific side of the continent where they underlay all other types; here they appear in the ancient crania from the Paltalcalo rock shelters on the Ecuadorian coast, while the dominant character of these types in the Lagoa Santa skulls from the eastern border of the Brazilian Highlands, speaks for their antiquity in that portion of the continent. On the basis of distribution, however, the leptorrhine, Mediterranean-Caspian types are apparently the older, their concentration along the eastern coast and especially their presence in the shell-heaps of the Brazilian shore, together with their dominance among the Ona, Yaghan, and Alikaluf of the extreme southern tip of the continent, being very significant.

In South America as in North, we can be sure that the long-headed groups represent the earlier immigrants, and of these, on the basis of distribution, the narrow-nosed group is probably the older. In view, however, of the vast areas for which we possess as yet no data, it is almost useless to hazard a guess as to the routes by which these types reached and spread over the continent. Possibly the relative strength of the platyrrhine factors in the Brazilian Highlands, in the smaller stocks of the Orinoco area and in the crania from the caves at Ipiiboto in this same region, may point to their arrival by way of the Antillean route. If this be the case, the presence of these factors on the Ecuador coast might be explained as due to a later westward drift across the Andes, for which, on the cultural side, there is some evidence.

For North America cranial data made it possible to deter-

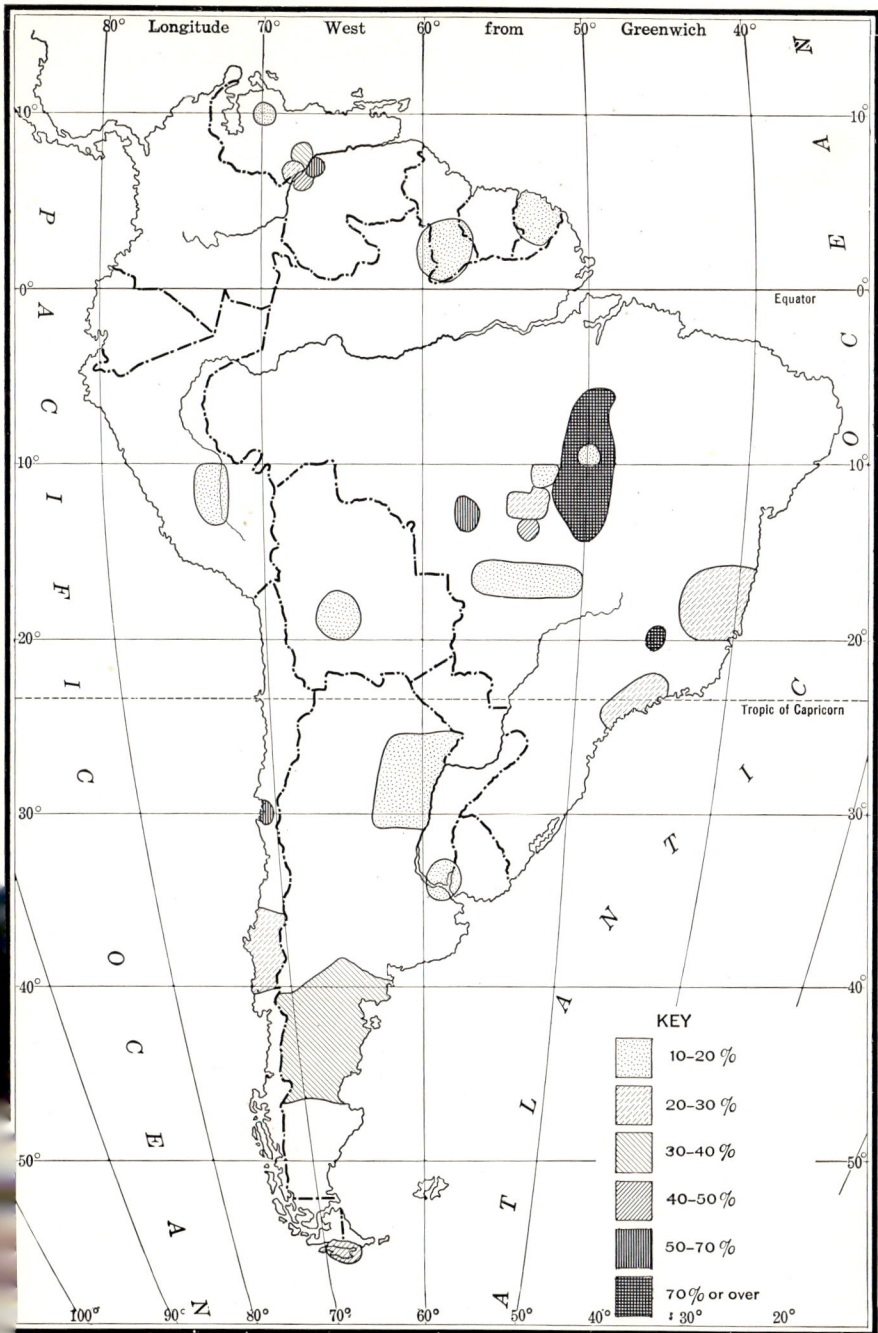

PLATE XXXVIII.  SOUTH AMERICA.
Percentage distribution of Proto-Australoid and Proto-Negroid Types.

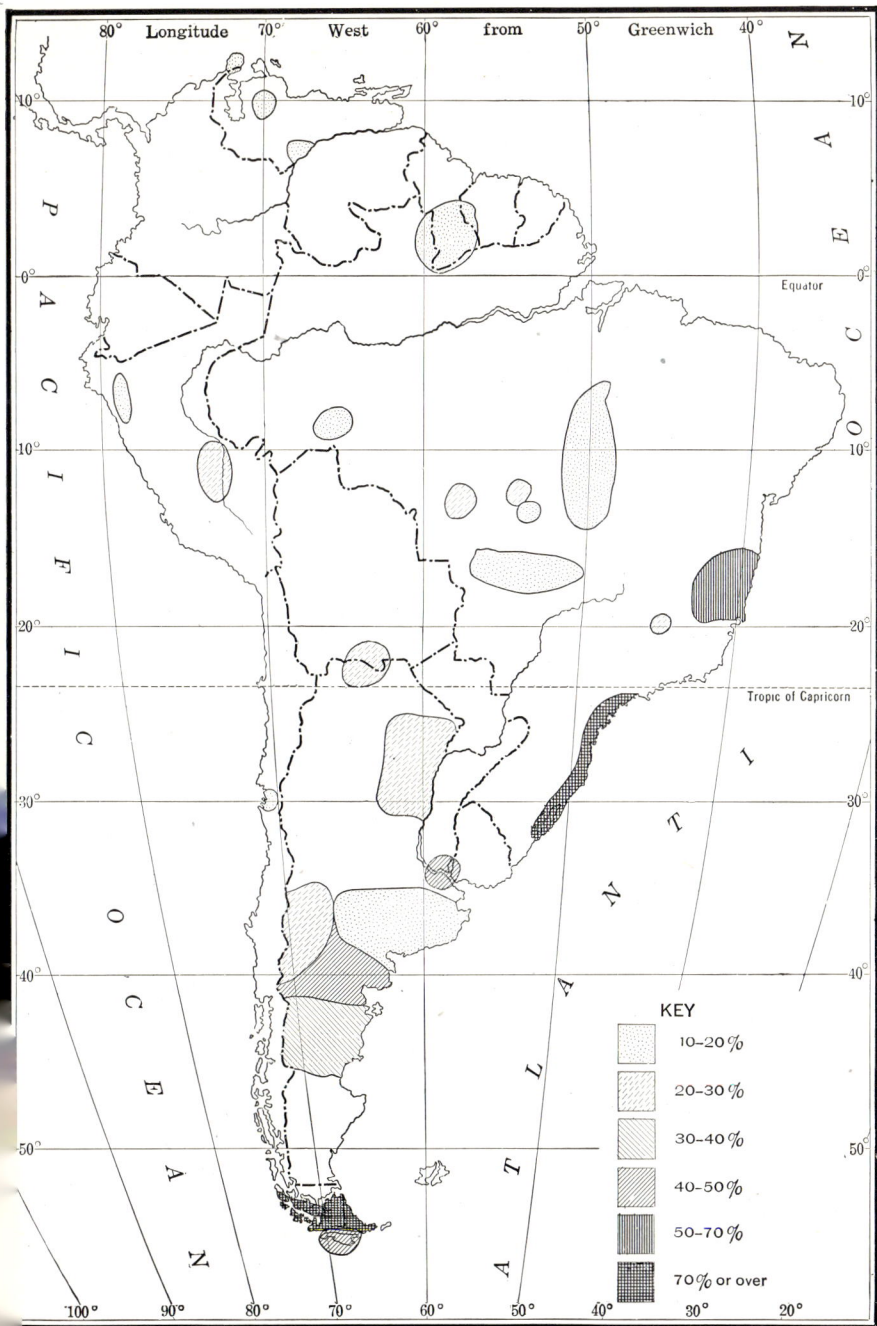

PLATE XXXIX. SOUTH AMERICA.
Percentage distribution of Caspian and Mediterranean Types.

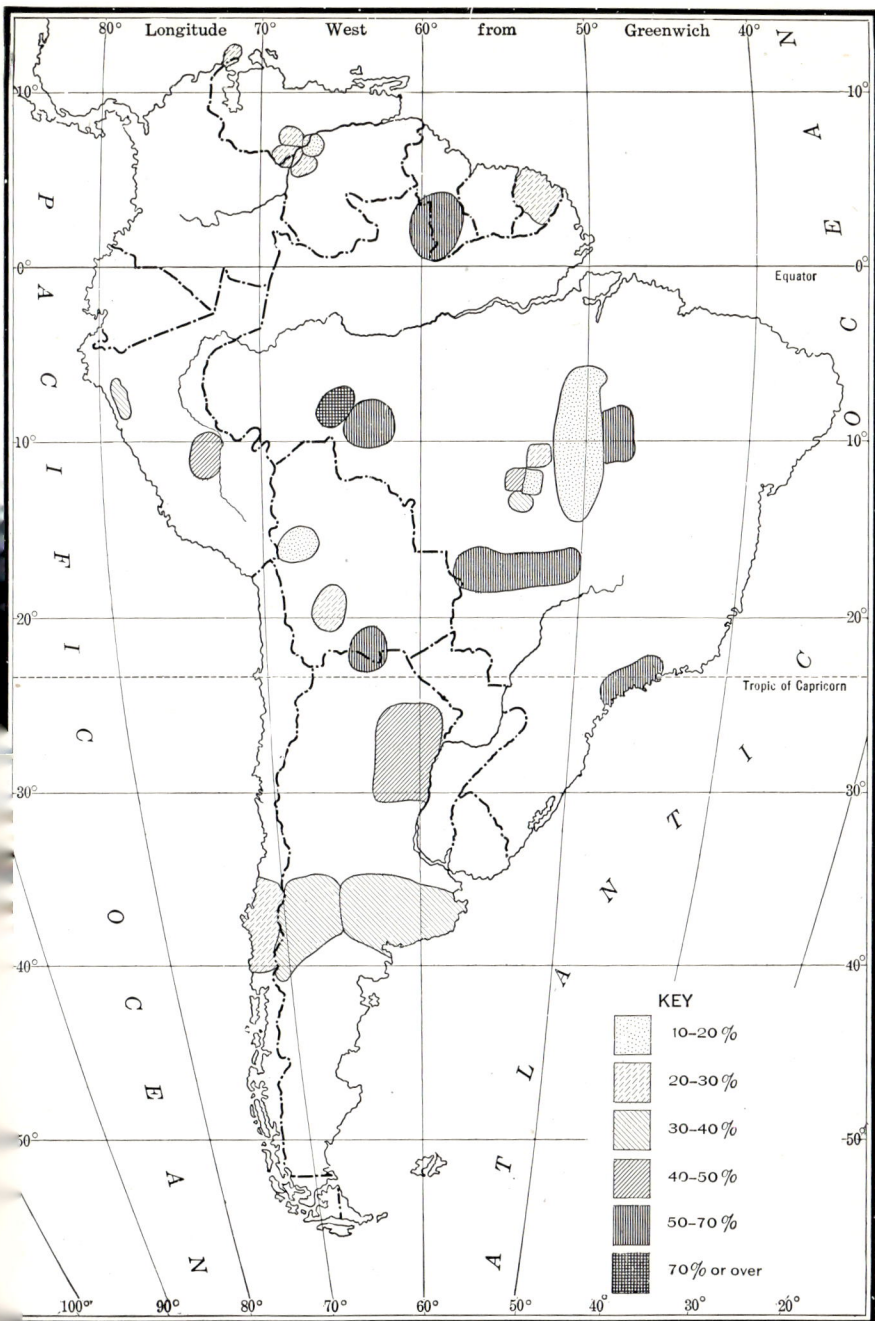

PLATE XL.   SOUTH AMERICA.
Percentage distribution of Palæ-Alpine and Mongoloid Types.

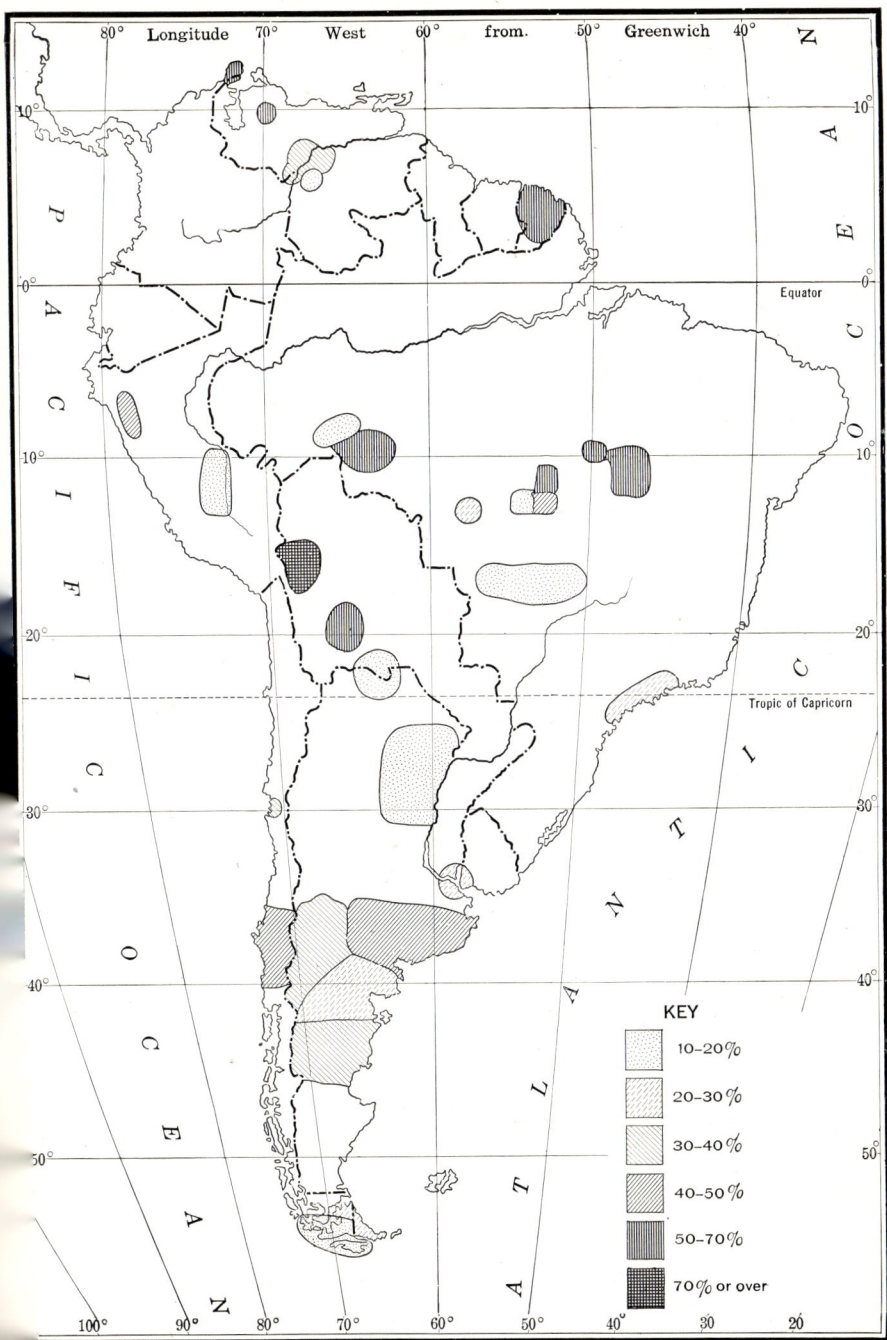

PLATE XLI. SOUTH AMERICA.
Percentage distribution of Alpine and Ural Types.

mine with some degree of certainty the individual types present. In the southern continent this can be done less widely, owing to the absence of cranial material. We can, however, be confident that, as in the north, the Caspian type is far and away the most important one in the leptorrhine group, whereas of the platyrrhine, the Proto-Negroid largely outnumbers the Proto-Australoid, at least in the two most important series, *i. e.*, those from Lagoa Santa in Brazil and Paltalcalo in Ecuador.

Now the presence of a strong Proto-Negroid factor among these prehistoric crania raises a particularly troublesome question. As is well known, the modern population of Brazil, both Indian and white, is known to have had a considerable infusion of Negro blood in the period since the fifteenth century. How are we to tell then in the case of living tribes, such for example as the Caraya of the Brazilian Highlands, when we find evidence of a strong Proto-Negroid factor, whether this element is to be regarded as aboriginal and derived from the ancient stratum of this type, or is to be traced to recent miscegenation with the Negroes introduced by the Portuguese settlers? Unfortunately there is no certain method of distinguishing between these two possibilities, and we can only take probabilities and known historical facts into account in trying to reach a decision. In the case of the Caraya, for example, we may be moderately sure that we have not here to do with any recent mixture. One purely theoretical criterion may be of service in such cases, namely that recent Negroid admixture might be expected to show itself in a deeper skin color, curliness of hair and other features characteristic of the modern Negro, who, as I shall try to show, may be regarded as an extreme development of the ancient Proto-Negroid type, in which these elements were less strongly marked.

Turning now to the brachycephalic types, we found that in North America the indications were quite clear that the platyrrhine forms preceded the leptorrhine. Can any evidence be found in the southern continent which tends to show the priority of one of these over the other? The almost total absence of any sort of data for most of the Amazon basin, and the wide prevalence of artificial cranial deformation along the Pacific coast, renders the problem very difficult, yet I believe that the same sequence is indicated. In the Brazilian Highlands, for example, we have a complex mixture of linguistic and physical types such that all the facts seem best explained by assuming three successive strata of population, the oldest being represented by the Caraya, who show a predominance of the dolichocephalic, platyrrhine forms; the intermediate being represented by the Bororo and perhaps the Carib Bakairi, characterized by platyrrhine, brachycephalic forms; while the most recent, exemplified by the Trumai and the Tupian Aueto show a predominance of the leptorrhine, brachycephalic types. Again, the modern Quechua and Aimara peoples of southern Peru and Bolivia appear to show a concentration of the platyrrhine factors in the more remote, mountainous areas, whereas the leptorrhine elements are more prominent elsewhere. A tentative assumption, however, that the platyrrhine, brachycephalic types in general preceded the leptorrhine, is about as far as it is safe to go on the data at hand. There are indications, to be sure, which suggest the immigration of the former type by way of the Antilles, and its spread from the Orinoco through the core of the continent, and of the entrance of the leptorrhine group, on the other hand, by way of Panama. There are parallels which might be drawn between the Amazon forest as a "refuge area," and the comparable region of the plateaus in the northern continent; there are curious indications of cultural influences which bear out the belief in the southward drift of the leptorrhine type along the Pacific coast. Until, however, the enormous gaps in our material are at least partially filled, no theorizing of this sort can be carried on with profit.

One very significant phenomenon may finally be noted. Although we may have some reason to believe that part at least of the immigration into South America passed through the Antillean region from the northern continent, in historic times this current has been reversed, and South American peoples have been streaming northward toward Florida. The Carib conquest and occupation of the Lesser Antilles were in large measure complete at the end of the fifteenth century, the older Arawak population had been partly destroyed, partly absorbed, and raids had already begun upon the Greater Antillean islands. One cannot help thinking of the South American continent in this connection as a vast reservoir into which for hundreds, probably thousands of years, people had been drifting from the north, by way of the two narrow channels. At last the reservoir was filled, and the pressure of population was such as to reverse the current in one of these channels, with the result that the flood began to pour back toward its source. Whether any such reversal of the older drift had also taken place in the Isthmus of Panama is still uncertain, although there are some indications that it had, and that at any rate along the Caribbean coast a northward movement had actually begun.

In South America as in North the peoples of the higher culture all belonged to the brachycephalic group and, in the main, to the leptorrhine branch, the only exception apparently being the ancient people of the Tiahuanaco region in Bolivia, where the crania of the population responsible at least for the early stages of this remarkable culture were probably (?) strongly long-headed.

In the introductory chapter of the section dealing with North America the question was raised whether the theory of a multiple racial origin for the American Indian did not meet an insuperable obstacle in trying to bring these varied types into the South American continent through two such narrow corridors as the Isthmus of Panama and the Antilles. The difficulties are patent indeed, yet I believe that, great though they are, the peculiar distribution of the physical types within the South American continent can only with greater difficulty be accounted for in any other way. And, if we note the striking parallels between the distribution of the same types in the two continents, the hypothesis of a single racial type with merely local variations becomes a sheer impossibility. Grant, if you will, that the primitive American type, described as "Mongoloid" in the general meaning of that term, has been protean in its ability to vary;

here as long-headed as the purest "Nordic" or Fijian, there as round-headed as a Swiss or Armenian; here as narrow-nosed as an Englishman or an Egyptian, there as broad-nosed as a Papuan or a Tamil—grant all this, and it remains to be explained why the supposed variations have occurred in such a surprisingly regular manner, and have been distributed both in time and space in such a definite sequence! If we regard skeletal characteristics alone, there are just as wide variations in the American continents as are found in Europe, or wider, and if we must regard these in America merely as local and without racial significance, why not also in Europe? Because there, archæology and history make it impossible! We *know* that the Bronze Age Alpine crania in England are not a mere chance local variation of the Neolithic Mediterranean forms; that the long-headed "Nordic" Alemani of northern Switzerland were an immigrant people and not a modification of the Alpine Swiss population. The *facts* are the same in America—why not interpret them in the same way, provided such interpretation does not conflict with other established conclusions? For America we have little that can be called history and have only begun to secure adequate archæological material; yet already this affords us, for example in the Southwest, precisely the same kind of evidence for the succession of racial types as is universally accepted as valid in Europe!

Relying on the old method of utilizing only averages, Wissler can still say, in the latest edition of his very valuable volume on the American Indian, that the different variations in physical type met with in the New World are merely the "natural random fluctuations around the fundamental type," and that these show only an "erratic geographic distribution." The analysis of the data presented in the present volume shows, however, that these variations are neither "random" nor "erratic" in their distribution, but that on the contrary they show a definite sequence both in time and space which accords with the main lines of our knowledge of the spread of the American Indian and the development of his cultures, as derived from other sources. We may, however, defer further discussion of these fundamental problems to the final chapter, and turn to the more detailed consideration of the South American types.

The maps, Plates XXXVIII to XLI, for South America serve to show the geographical distribution of the dolichocephalic and brachycephalic factors. It will be seen that the former are concentrated in three separate areas, one in the south and east, which is in the main littoral; one in the Brazilian Highlands; and one made up of several isolated small areas along the western border of the continent. As in the northern continent, the eastern and western dolichocephalic areas are separated by a great intervening region which is characterized by the predominance of brachycephalic types, which thus occupy the whole of the interior.

# CHAPTER I

## THE SOUTHEASTERN DOLICHOCEPHALS

THE Southeastern Dolichocephalic Area comprises Patagonia, Tierra del Fuego, at least the southern portion of the Chilean archipclago, and the coastal districts of Brazil south of Rio Janeiro, where the ancient but not the historic population were of this type. In this area the leptorrhine, dolichocepahlic forms prevail. Examining the data more in detail, it appears that the tribes of the extreme south, the Alikaluf, Yaghan, and Ona, present a number of puzzling questions.

The extremely meagre and somewhat uncertain material available from the Alikaluf,[1] whose habitat was at the Pacific end of the Straits of Magellan, and from the little known tribes of the Chilean archipelago is rather contradictory. The dozen or so fairly authenticated crania show on analysis a large majority of dolichocephalic factors, the Caspian type alone making up some 70 per cent of the total; yet the still smaller series of measurements on the living indicate on the contrary the predominance of leptorrhine, *brachycephalic* forms! For the Yaghan[2] the situation is, if possible, even more confusing, for if we consider only the dozen or more crania described by Garson, Deniker, Hultkranz, and Ten Kate we find a large majority of dolichocephalic, leptorrhine forms, whereas in the series published by Mantegazza and Regalia, although dolichocephalic factors are slightly in the majority, the proportion of Alpine types is actually greater than any other single form. Finally, if we analyze Deniker's series of measurements on the living, we find, as in the previous instance of the Alikaluf, that a rather strong majority of the brachycephalic, leptorrhine factors is present, and that

[1] Virchow, 1881; Deniker, 1891; Martin, 1892; Hultkranz, 1898; Ten Kate, 1905; Latcham, 1909; Turner, 1884.

[2] Garson, 1885; Mantegazza and Regalia, 1886; Deniker, 1891; Hultkranz, 1900; Ten Kate, 1905.

the dolichocephalic minority is of the broad rather than the narrow nosed type! In the matter of stature, the data are more accordant, and we may have little doubt but that the Alikaluf and Yaghan are both short peoples, the average stature varying between 157 and 160 cm. The contrast between long-headed crania and round-headed living individuals recalls a somewhat similar condition in the Iroquois area in North America, and it is possible although hardly probable that we may here, as there, be dealing on the one hand with relatively old crania, and on the other with modern mixed bloods. On the face of it, the crania are perhaps the safer and probably the older guides, and on their showing we may accept these two tribes as primarily of Caspian and Mediterranean types, with a strong infusion of Alpine factors. A portrait of a Yaghan is given on Plate XLII, Fig. 1.

For the Onas,[1] who occupy the eastern and northern portions of the island of Tierra del Fuego, the data are more meagre yet. On the basis of the half-dozen crania known, the Onas are in very large majority of Caspian and Mediterranean types, and thus in general accord with the Yaghan and Alikaluf so far as cranial characters are concerned. They very strikingly differ from them, however, in stature. For, whereas these tribes are, as we have seen, short, the Onas are notably tall, averaging something over 175 cm. In this feature they agree with the modern Tehuelche or Patagonians, whose still greater stature has long been proverbial, and with whom the Onas are connected by many cultural traits. An example of the Ona type is shown on Plate XLII, Fig. 2.

The Patagonian region, extending northward from the Straits of Magellan to the Rio Negro, was occupied by a series of tribes forming the Tehuelche or Tsonekan linguistic stock. Long famous because of their supposed gigantic stature, these people present again certain contradictory features. The modern Tehuelches are indeed an extremely tall people, their average stature being somewhat over 175 cm., so that they and the Onas slightly exceed in height the tallest tribes of the North American Plains.

[1] Hultkranz, 1900; Rivet, 1908.

Their strongly brachycephalic head-form is due, however, at least in part, to the practice of artificial deformation, and undeformed individuals among them are said to be clearly dolichocephalic. The Tehuelche type is illustrated on Plate XLII, Fig. 3.

The most important data, however, are derived from the large series of proto-historic and prehistoric crania[1] and skeletal remains which have been gathered from the central and northern portions of their habitat. Although a considerable proportion even of the ancient crania show deformation, a large number of quite normal crania are available, and show that dolichocephalic factors are in large majority (ca. 70 per cent), the leptorrhine and platyrrhine types being equally represented, the Caspian type being that which is dominant. The brachycephalic factors are almost wholly of the Alpine type. The female crania present an interesting and perhaps significant difference, in that the platyrrhine elements are noticeably more abundant, in particular the Proto-Australoid, while the Palæ-Alpine displaces the Alpine which was the minority factor among the males. If this greater development of the platyrrhine types is not due to the general tendency of female crania to have somewhat broader noses than in the case of the male, it would suggest the greater relative antiquity of the Proto-Australoid type in relation to the Caspian. In stature these ancient Patagonians were somewhat less tall than the living, and decrease from an average of 173 cm. on the Rio Negro to 169 cm. in the southern province of Santa Cruz.

At various points in the province of Buenos Aires, discoveries of human remains have at various times been made, under conditions suggesting great antiquity. The Pliocene or even Miocene Age of some of these specimens has been vigorously upheld by Ameghino[2] and other South American geologists, who have declared that some of these fragments represented the actual precursors of modern man, and that the development of the human species must therefore be regarded as having taken place in the New World. Recent investigations[3] of the whole problem by other geologists and anthropologists have discredited these ex-

---

[1] Marelli, 1915; Puccioni, 1912; Verneau, 1894, 1903; Virchow, 1874.
[2] Ameghino, 1880, and many later articles.   [3] Hrdlicka, 1912.

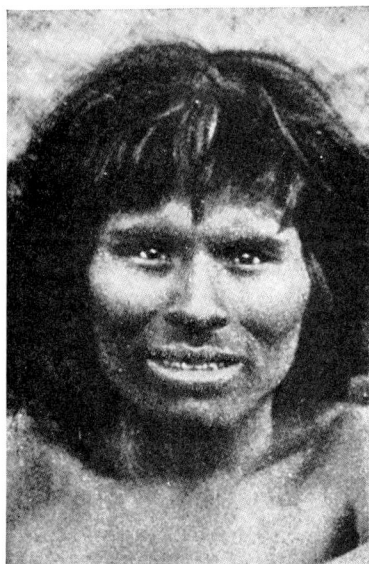

Fig. 1. Yaghan.

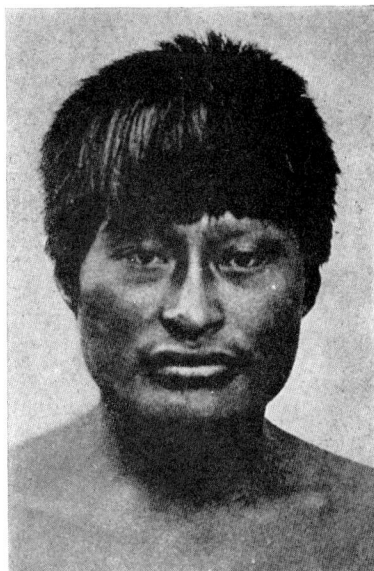

Fig. 2. Ona.

Fig. 3 Tehuelche.

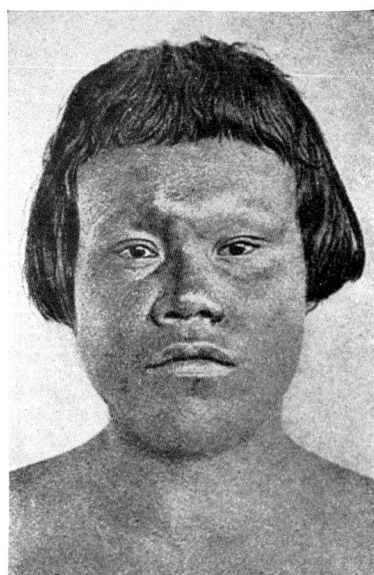

Fig 4. Bororo.

PLATE XLII.

travagant claims, and shown that the remains were unquestionably human and not prehuman, and that the strata in which they were found are certainly Pleistocene, and therefore much more recent than at first stated. The remains found, however, unquestionably represent a population which was living on the eastern shore of the continent several thousand years ago. The more important of the discoveries which include human crania are those of Pontimelo or Fontezuelas, Arrecifes, Miramar, etc. In every case, however, the crania are so incomplete and fragmentary that no nasal measurements are given, so that we can have no certainty as to the types present. It can only be said that the first and last crania are dolichocephalic and high, while the Arrecifes skull is on the lower margin of mesocephaly. These finds indicate, therefore, that the oldest known population along the eastern coast of Argentina was a predominantly long-headed one, according thus with all the other evidence as yet presented.

The historic population of the Brazilian coast region belonged to the Tupi-Guarani linguistic stock, and were probably, as will be seen later, a strongly marked brachycephalic folk. Throughout the whole of the coast region south of Rio Janeiro there are abundant shell-heaps known locally as sambaquis, cosquieros, etc., and in part, at least, attributable to a pre-Tupi people, as shown by the wholly different type of their culture. Of the human skeletal remains from these shell-heaps no adequate study has, so far as I am aware, yet been made, and available data are very few. The published crania[1] indicate a prevailingly dolichocephalic population, in which the Caspian type is in large majority. Yet von Ihering[2] and others declare that a definitely brachycephalic type also occurs, although whether in association with the dolichocephalic or stratigraphically or geographically distinct is not stated. A thoroughgoing investigation of this whole question is obviously urgently demanded. Materials of possible significance in this connection have been obtained by Torres[3] from burial mounds and cemeteries in the region just to the southward in the Parana delta. The simple hunting and

[1] Lacerda, 1885.　　　[2] Von Ihering, 1904.　　　[3] Torres, 1907.

fishing folk whose remains are found here, who in culture show resemblance to the sambaquis builders and who clearly antedated the appearance of Europeans, were an essentially dolichocephalic people, of stature above the average (168 cm.), among whom the Caspian type was strongly dominant.

Somewhat farther to the north, in the basin of the Rio Doce in the coastal portion of the province of Minas Geraes, are the remnants of the once much more numerous people of very primitive culture, known as the Botocudos.[1] Linguistically they belong to the Ges stock, which extended over a large area in the adjacent Brazilian Highlands, and are generally regarded as the underlying stratum of population in this whole region, having preceded and been driven out by the Tupi in prehistoric times. In stature averaging 159 cm., they prove to be an almost purely dolichocephalic people, the Caspian type being in very large majority, but associated with a substantial minority of the Proto-Negroid type. The Botocudos have been generally regarded as closely related to and probably the descendants of the people presently to be discussed, whose remains have been found in the famous Lagoa Santa caves, lying farther westward on the edge of the Brazilian Highlands. In so far as the minority factor of Proto-Negroid type is concerned, this relationship is indeed shown, but their primary affiliation is unmistakably with the ancient builders of the shell-heaps.

Summarizing all of these facts, I believe it may be regarded as pretty definitely established that along the whole eastern coast of South America, from Tierra del Fuego as far at least as the Rio Doce, the underlying and oldest stratum of population was one which was primarily of the Caspian type; that with this was associated a smaller element of the Proto-Negroid and Proto-Australoid types, and that brachycephalic factors, in the main Alpine, were present in general only as a small minority. In culture, all of these peoples were distinctly primitive, and they were in part extinct before the earliest arrival of Europeans.

[1] Ehrenreich, 1887, 1897; Peixotto, 1884; Virchow, 1885.

# CHAPTER II

## THE BRAZILIAN HIGHLANDS AND THE WESTERN DOLICHOCEPHALS

IF we pass inland to the Brazilian Highlands, a striking contrast to the conditions found along the coast at once makes itself manifest. The crania found in the Lagoa Santa caves by Lund,[1] in the middle of the nineteenth century, have long aroused the interest of anthropologists. Associated as they were in the cave with the bones of extinct animal species, they were at one time held to be of very great age. Although these earlier views have been modified in later years, they may still be regarded as probably of very considerable antiquity, long antedating at any rate the whole historic period. The analysis of the measurements of these crania given by Hansen,[2] shows the series to be almost purely dolichocephalic, but overwhelmingly of the platyrrhine types, the Proto-Negroid amounting to approximately 50 per cent, while the Proto-Australoid is secondary with 25 per cent. The Caspian type is only slightly less important. The crania are notably disharmonic, wide faces being associated with narrow skulls, and are all rather notably prognathic. Contrary, thus, to the frequent statement, these Lagoa Santa crania are not of the same type as the modern Botocudo, but point to the presence at an early date of Proto-Negroid-Proto-Australoid peoples, who appear not to have extended to the coast.

Turning to the living population of the Highlands, we find apparent evidence of the presence of the descendants of these early folk in the data collected by Ehrenreich[3] and Ranke.[4] Linguistically the area is one of considerable complexity, since we have here tribes representing on the one hand four of the great stocks, the Ges, Arawak, Carib, and Tupi, all but the first of which

[1] Lund, 1842.
[2] Hansen, 1888.
[3] Ehrenreich, 1897.
[4] Ranke, K. E., 1904.

have their main areas of distribution in other parts of the continent; and also tribes such as the Bororo, Caraya, Trumai, etc., belonging to or by themselves constituting small stocks, confined to this highland area. The distribution among these tribes of the physical types is, I believe, significant. The Caraya and also probably the Cherentes (belonging to the Ges stock), together with the Arawakan Mehinaku and Paressi farther west, are all primarily dolichocephalic, with a strong predominance of the platyrrhine types, allied thus to the Lagoa Santa Proto-Negroids. All the other tribes are on the contrary primarily brachycephalic, the Cayapo, one of the most westerly of the Ges tribes, the Bororo, and the Cariban Bakaïri having a predominance of the platyrrhine elements, the Nahuqua (also Carib), the Tupian Aueto, and the independent Trumai being, on the other hand, more strongly leptorrhine. Portraits of a Bororo and of a Paressi are given on Plate XLII, Fig. 4, and Plate XLIII, Fig. 1.

A logical explanation of these facts which might be suggested is as follows. Although we know practically nothing of the main mass of the Ges tribes lying between the Caraya and the coastal strip of Tupi tribes, we seem to be justified by the little that we do know, in assuming that they were probably in the main characterized by a predominance of the platyrrhine, dolichocephalic factors, and thus with the Caraya allied to the ancient population of the Highlands whose remains were found in the Lagoa Santa caves. The Mehinaku and Paressi may furthermore be regarded as remnants of this same stratum, who have in some way become "Arawakized" in speech, for, although linguistically they are to be grouped with the Arawak farther west and north, their physical characteristics are radically different from all other known tribes of this stock, who are primarily and, as a rule, overwhelmingly brachycephalic. Lest this suggestion of such a complete change of language be thought to be merely an arbitrary and very improbable assumption, it should be noted that similar radical modification and complete change of language has been repeatedly observed and reported by various authorities in other parts of the continent.

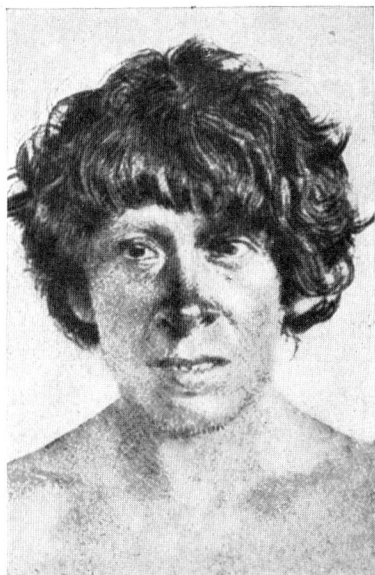

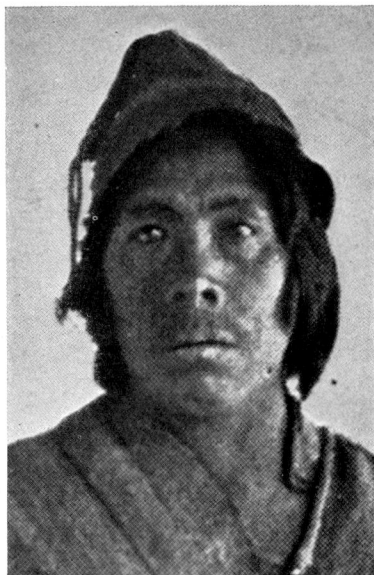

Fig. 1. Paressi.                    Fig. 2. Quechua.

Fig. 3. Huilliche.              Fig. 4. Caduveo. (Guaycuru.)

PLATE XLIII.

The Bororo, Bakaïri, and Cayapo on the other hand, are to be considered as belonging to a later immigrant stratum characterized by a large factor of the brachycephalic, platyrrhine types, of which the Bororo appear to be the present representatives. In the case of the Cayapo we have apparently another instance of linguistic modification, by which the older Ges tribes imposed their speech upon the immigrant group. The position of the Bakaïri is interesting, for the large proportion which they show of dolichocephalic, platyrrhine factors in comparison with either the Bororo or the Cayapo, suggests that they represent the advance guard of the brachycephalic immigrants, who thus mixed to a greater degree with their long-headed predecessors.

The Trumai, Aueto, and Nahuqua, who are in large measure of the leptorrhine, brachycephalic types, may then be thought of as representing a third immigrant stream, penetrating and in part superimposed upon the two older strata. Here again, as in the previous instance, the small independent stock (in this case the Trumai) shows the largest proportion of the new types and these are associated mainly with the immediately preceding platyrrhine forms, whereas the Carib-speaking Nahuqua and Tupi-speaking Aueto represent these same latest immigrants, mixed in the first case with the older Negroid-Australoid types (as also among the Bakaïri), in the second mingled with the still older Caspian-Mediterranean types who were mainly distributed along the coast.

The third and last of the areas in which dolichocephalic types were important differs from the others in being much less continuous. Reference to the maps, Plates XXXVIII and XXXIX, shows that dolichocephalic factors occur in strength in three widely separated spots; the Chilean coast near Coquimbo, the Paltalcalo rock shelters on the Jubones River near the Ecuador-Peru border, and in the vicinity of the Orinoco rapids in Venezuela.

The crania found by Latcham[1] under what are apparently recent marine deposits on raised beaches near Coquimbo, are

[1] Latcham, 1904 b.

obviously of very considerable, although not accurately determined, antiquity. The male crania (four in number) which are in fairly good preservation clearly indicate the dominance of dolichocephalic factors, but determination of the types present is impossible on account of the absence of nasal measurements. If we take into consideration such other fragmentary information as we possess from other parts of Chile, there is some reason to believe that these crania are platyrrhine, and that the Proto-Negroid type is that chiefly represented, but offset by a nearly equal element of the Alpine. Much farther to the south, in Valdivia and among the Pehuenche of the Andes,[1] clear indication of the presence of the Proto-Negroid type is found, often with considerable prognathism. That this is to be attributed to recent Negro mixture seems unlikely. All the rest of the modern population is strongly brachycephalic. If the somewhat uncertain identification of the Proto-Negroid type among these crania from Coquimbo is not correct, then the dolichocephalic factor must be Caspian, which would indicate that on the western as well as on the eastern coast of the southern part of the continent, this type was very early present.

Doctor Rivet has described[2] a large collection of crania taken by him from ancient rock shelters at Paltalcalo on the Jubones River in extreme southwestern Ecuador. The archæological evidence is clear that these represent not merely a pre-European people but one long antedating the historic Cañaris who held this region at the period of the Conquest. Unfortunately, Doctor Rivet has as yet published in full only a small selection of this extremely important series. From the material as given, however, we know that the dolichocephalic factors outnumber the brachycephalic more than two to one, and that among this dolichocephalic majority the Proto-Negroid and Proto-Australoid types are largely, perhaps very largely, represented. In so far then as these two types are here present, we may say that this prehistoric people of rather simple culture, were affiliated with the dolichocephalic substratum in the Brazilian Highlands.

[1] Latcham, 1909; Flores, 1905; Guevara, 1899.            [2] Rivet, 1908,

It may be noted, further, that a significant element of Caspian-Mediterranean types is also present.

In the vicinity of the rapids of the Orinoco, many caves have been discovered, some of which contained large numbers of urn burials. The large series of crania secured by Marcano[1] shows that two quite different types of people must have utilized these caves for burial purposes. In all but one of the sites investigated the undeformed crania show a predominance of brachycephalic factors; at Ipiiboto, however, the reverse was the case, and dolichocephalic elements were present in small majority, the dominant type being apparently the Proto-Australoid, which comprised about half the total factors present. In Marcano's opinion, these Ipiiboto crania were probably those of the early Otomac or Yaruro, two small local stocks. At one other site, that of Cucurital, this same dolichocephalic type was actually the most important single factor, although in the aggregate the brachycephalic elements slightly outweighed the total of the dolichocephalic forms. Doctor Marcano states that some of the Cucurital burials were probably modern Guahiba, another small local stock, but as he does not indicate which burials, and as we know nothing of the character of the Guahiba, the information is of little value. The same author has, however, given the measurements of a small series of crania from the Piaroa,[2] another small stock, living just east of the Orinoco in this same region. These agree most strikingly with the Ipiiboto series and show nearly 60 per cent of the Proto-Australoid type.

We have here again, as in Ecuador and perhaps in northern Chile, dolichocephalic elements which are allied more or less closely with the ancient and some of the modern occupants of the Brazilian Highlands. The fact that the modern tribes showing these characters are, here in Venezuela, members of the series of small, isolated stocks which fringe the eastern slopes of the Andes, and which have been thought to be the remnants of an older stratum of population, is not without significance. Although adequate data are lacking for their certain determina-

---

[1] Marcano, 1893.　　　　　　　　[2] Marcano, 1890 a.

tion, there is reason to believe that dolichocephalic factors survive elsewhere in the Andean region. Thus the Timote,[1] another of these small stocks, on the Venezuelan-Colombian border, seem to show a considerable dolichocephalic, leptorrhine element; undeformed dolichocephalic crania have been found in small numbers in the ancient cemeteries along the Peruvian coast, at Trujillo, Pachacamac and elsewhere;[2] the ancient Aimara of the Bolivian plateau are said by Hrdlicka[3] to have been undoubtedly long-headed, although he has published no data upon them. From the fact, however, that the undeformed (?) ancient crania reported by Flower[4] from the southern portion of the plateau, show a large factor (40 per cent) of the platyrrhine, dolichocephalic types, it seems probable that it was these types which were present in the early Aimara. Here again, then, as in Ecuador and Venezuela, we have links with the ancient people of the Brazilian Highlands.

Summing up the results of the foregoing examination of the regions where dolichocephalic types are or have been in the majority in the South American continent, we may say that, whereas the southeastern leptorrhine group occupies an essentially continuous strip from the middle Brazilian coast to the southern tip of the continent (with a possible outlier on the coast of northern Chile), the platyrrhine group seems to be split into an eastern and a western division, occupying respectively the Brazilian Highlands and a series of scattered areas on the eastern and western flanks of the Andean chain. Between these two extends a great area in which, so far as is known, brachycephalic types prevail.

[1] Marcano, 189:.    [2] Hrdlicka, 1911.    [3] Hrdlicka, op. cit.    [4] Flower, 1879.

# CHAPTER III

## THE BRACHYCEPHALS

THE areas in which we have evidence of the preponderance of brachycephalic factors lie scattered over almost the whole of the continent, but with a strong tendency to mass themselves in the western and central regions. In North America it was possible to show something of a definite geographic grouping of the platyrrhine and leptorrhine forms; here, however, the data are so incomplete that any similar attempt is precarious.

For the whole northern portion of the Andean area in Colombia and Ecuador, occupied chiefly by tribes of the Chibchan stock, data of value are practically absent.[1] The few crania from the mounds and deep well-graves of Ecuador published by Jijon y Caamano [2] suggest, however, that their makers were of somewhat different types, those whose remains are found in the mounds being almost purely brachycephalic (probably in the main Alpine), whereas the burials in the deep graves show that the people, although still in majority brachycephalic, had nevertheless a considerable dolichocephalic factor, which it is tempting to regard as possibly due to the survival of an older type.

Farther southward the almost universal practice of artificial deformation which renders most of the material from the north useless, continues to make the determination of head-form difficult. A small series, however, of undeformed (?) skulls from Cajamarca in northern Peru,[3] shows that brachycephalic elements prevail in very large majority, the Alpine type being that which is clearly in the lead. No adequate study has yet been made of the vast collections of crania from the great cemeteries along the Peruvian coast. That the prevailing types were in great majority brachycephalic, there seems no doubt, and ap-

---

[1] Broca, 1875.  [2] Jijon y Caamano, 1915.  [3] Giachetti, 1905.

parently the leptorrhine forms which prevail toward the north give way to platyrrhine in the south.[1] Undeformed, dolichocephalic skulls are, however, occasionally found, and there is reason to believe that these are more abundant in the very oldest sites, such as those of the shell-heaps.

If we lack good material from the coast, we have a considerable body of data for the highland region. The most important series of crania is that obtained from Macchu Pichu[2] not far from Cuzco. The crania from this great Inca site, which seems probably (?) to be one which had ceased to be occupied for some time before the period of the Conquest, show a small majority of brachycephalic factors, in which the Palæ-Alpine type is the most prominent, and fair-sized minorities of the Mediterranean and Proto-Australoid types. Much the larger number of skulls, however, are those of females, and these show a considerably greater predominance of round-headed forms, due to the presence of an Alpine factor, which was of little importance among the males. The significance of this difference is not yet clear.

For the living population of Quechua and Aimara stocks we possess excellent data in the studies of Ferris[3] and Rouma[4]; Chervin,[5] unfortunately, giving nothing but the cephalic index. From these sources it appears that the pure-blood Quechua of Cuzco and Apurimac is predominantly round-headed, with the broadnosed factors in large majority; the minority element being Caspian-Mediterranean in quite considerable numbers. The Quechua, farther to the southeast in Bolivia, together with the Aimara, are more strongly brachycephalic, and have as the leading type the Alpine. In the dolichocephalic factors present the Quechua and Aimara here differ, the former having the platyrrhine, the latter the leptorrhine types more strongly represented. The southern Quechua thus differ from those about and north of Cuzco, not only in being more strongly round-headed, but in having a different long-headed element present as a minority. We

---

[1] Ranke, J., 1900; Dorsey, 1895; Flower, 1879; Schreiber, 1908–09; Sergi, 1887; Vram, 1900; P. M.; A. N. S. P.; A. M. N. H.

[2] Eaton, 1916.　　　　　　　　[3] Ferris, 1916. *See also* Lorena, 1911.
[4] Rouma, 1913.　　　　　　　　[5] Chervin, 1907.

may, perhaps, regard these southern Quechua as a later group, the result of the historic expansion of the people under Inca leadership, whereas the Cuzco and Apurimac group represent the older, more aboriginal body. Much more investigation is needed, however, before the considerable differences between these upland peoples can be accounted for. An example of the Quechua type is given on Plate XLIII, Fig. 2.

Farther south there is a nearly complete gap in our data until we get beyond Valparaiso, in Chile. A small group of crania from the extreme southwestern portion of Bolivia[1] show a strong predominance of brachycephalic elements, the Palæ-Alpine type being in the large majority.

With the Araucanian tribes of Chile and portions of the western Argentine pampas, we come to more adequate material once more. The Araucanians[2] north of Valdivia are very strongly brachycephalic, the Alpine type being that in the majority, the dolichocephalic minority being mainly of the platyrrhine types. The Araucanians also extended east of the Andes,[3] and there are many reasons for believing that this may have been their earlier home, and that they came west to the Chilean coast not very long before the Inca conquest of the region, a century or two before the coming of the Spaniards. In later, post-Spanish times they again spread over the pampas, as far east even as the province of Buenos Aires. Throughout the area over which they have extended they exhibit a considerable uniformity, being everywhere primarily of the Alpine type. The more easterly groups, however, replace the broad-nosed dolichocephalic minority by a narrow-nosed form, derived probably from the dominant factor of this type among the east-coast peoples. A portrait of a member of the Huilliche tribe of this stock is shown on Plate XLIII, Fig. 3.

Of the physical characteristics of the Calchaqui who occupied parts of the more arid, western margin of the Argentine pampas, and extended well up into the Highlands, where their border

---

[1] Flores, 1895.    [2] Latcham, 1904 a; 1909.
[3] Puccioni, 1912; Ten Kate, 1892; Virchow, 1874.

marched with the higher culture of the Bolivian plateau, little can be said, as practically every skull so far known is strongly deformed. What evidence there is, indicates the predominance here also of the Alpine type.[1]

For the rest of the pampas and for the Chaco region we are in much the same plight. The Guaycuru[2] seem to have a majority of the Palæ-Alpine type, with a strong Caspian-Mediterranean minority. The Matacco[3] farther north are possibly in the majority long-headed. The Tupian Chiriguano,[4] in the Bolivian Chaco, appear to be much like the Guaycuru. Other tribes of the same stock, such as the Guayaki[5] of Paraguay and the Guarani[6] of Sao Paolo in southern Brazil, show these same features, so that we seem to be justified in regarding the whole southern portion of this stock, at any rate, as essentially homogeneous. Since this region is generally regarded as the area from which the stock has spread to the east and north, it would be of much interest to compare some of these migrants with the parent group. Data are, however, lacking except for the Aueto[7] of the Brazilian Highlands area, already referred to on a previous page. They show a dominance of the Alpine element and may be a people originally of different stock; but Tupi-ized in speech. Be that as it may, there was evidently a rather large area in the region between the Amazon forest and the pampas in which the Palæ-Alpine type was the dominant factor. The portraits given on Plate XLIII, Fig. 4, and Plate XLIV, Fig. 1, may be taken as examples of this group.

Our knowledge of virtually the whole of the vast Amazon basin and of the region north of it in Venezuela and the Guianas is very scanty. Only at two or three widely separated points are any data available. The few measurements taken by Ehrenreich[8] of the Yamamadi, Ipurina, and Pammari, Arawak tribes of the Purus River region, show that among them brachycephalic factors largely predominate, the platyrrhine forms prevailing as

[1] Ten Kate, 1896.          [2] Lehmann-Nitsche, 1904.          [3] Otis, 1871.
[4] Ten Kate, 1905.          [5] Ten Kate, 1897.                      [6] Krone, 1906.
[7] Ranke, K. E., 1904.      [8] Ehrenreich, 1897.

a rule. The same holds true of the Wapisiana, Taruma, and other Arawak tribes of the Venezuela-British Guiana border described by Farabee.[1] These, however, exhibit a larger dolichocephalic element, which is mainly also of the broad-nosed types. For the great mass of tribes belonging to the Carib stock I have been able to find data only for the Galibis[2] of the French Guiana shore, who, if it is fair to judge from the half-dozen individuals measured, are primarily of the Alpine type. The Warrau of the Orinoco delta seem, on the averages given by Ten Kate,[3] to be in general similar. Cranial data are extremely scarce. That from the Goajiro,[4] an Arawak-speaking tribe in the peninsula of that name west of the Gulf of Maracaibo, shows a large percentage of Alpine factors, and also a considerable Ural element found here for the first time in South America in any strength. The urn burials in the Aragua[5] district of northwestern Venezuela reveal a somewhat similar situation, except that here the Ural type is present in much smaller proportions, and there is a considerable minority of the Proto-Australoid type. Examples of Arawak types from northwestern Brazil and from Guiana are given on Plate XLIV, Figs. 2 and 3.

The crania obtained by Marcano[6] from the burial caves near the Orinoco rapids supply us with the last of our cranial material. It may be remembered that at one of these sites, known as Ipiiboto, long-headed factors were in the majority, connecting what is an apparently earlier population with the long-headed peoples of the Brazilian Highlands. At the other two sites, Cucurital and Cerro de Luna, brachycephalic factors prevail, in the former slightly, in the latter to a large degree. In this latter the Ural type is in the majority, in the former it is secondary, whereas in the series from Ipiiboto it drops to third place. Furthermore, at Cucurital the broad-nosed, long-headed forms, although not so important as at Ipiiboto, are nevertheless of considerable strength. There seems, thus, to be a rough sort of progression,

[1] Farabee, 1918.
[2] Manouvrier, 1882; Ten Kate, 1887.
[3] Ten Kate, *op. cit.*
[4] Marcano, 1890 b; Virchow, 1886 c.
[5] Marcano, 1893.
[6] Marcano, 1893.

from the Ipiiboto series, through that of Cucurital, to Cerro de Luna, the Aragua sites, and the Goajiro, such that the platyr-rhine, dolichocephalic types decrease in importance regularly; the Palæ-Alpine element remains unchanged; while the Alpine and especially the Ural factors increase regularly to a dominant position. This seems to indicate the flooding of an area formerly characterized by a majority of Proto-Australoid and Proto-Ne-groid types by peoples primarily of Alpine and Ural affiliations. The Goajiro stand out somewhat from the rest by their large proportion of the Palæ-Alpine type, and in this agree with the other tribes of Arawak speech which we know. The Carib, on the other hand, may rather precariously be considered as in the main more Alpine, with probably a goodly element of the Ural type as well, and thus allied physically to what seems, on the whole, to be the later stratum of population in the region. The illustration of a Maku Indian from northwestern Brazil given on Plate XLIV, Fig. 4, may perhaps be taken as an example of the older dolichocephalic types.

Can this hypothesis of a relatively recent flooding of the whole northern border of the South American continent by a people displaying primarily Alpine and Ural types be brought into any reasonable relation with the rest of our knowledge of the region? It seems to me that it probably can. It is now rather generally admitted as a working hypothesis that the Carib tribes have moved from a proximate area of dispersal on the upper Xingu River south of the Amazon, northward across this great river and perhaps by way of the Rio Negro, toward the coast, disrupting an assumed large area of Arawak tribes and peoples belonging to various small, independent linguistic stocks. Reach-ing the sea, the Carib tribes spread in both directions along the shore, and at the period of the discovery had already conquered the Arawak peoples of the Lesser Antilles, and were raiding those of the larger islands nearer the North American shore. They were also engaged in similar raids along the eastern side of Cen-tral America. These Carib tribes are, on admittedly very slen-der grounds, supposed to have been mainly of Alpine and Ural

FIG. 1. GUARANI.

FIG. 2. KARUTANA. (ARAWAK.)

FIG. 3. TARUMA. (ARAWAK.)

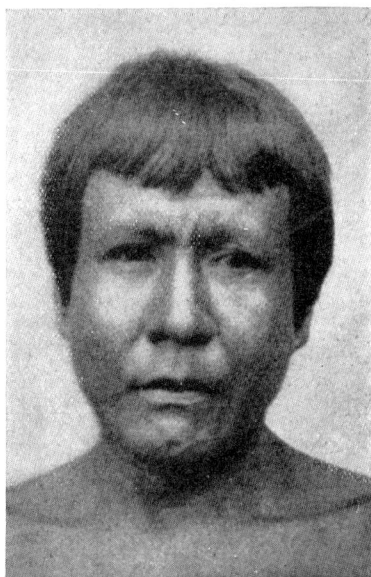

FIG. 4. MAKU.

PLATE XLIV

types, and, if this be true, we might regard their invasion as the cause of the assumed replacement of an earlier population, consisting partly of Palæ-Alpine Arawak and partly of the predominantly dolichocephalic peoples of the smaller stocks, by one of Alpine and Ural type.

The hypothesis of the northward migration of the Carib group rests largely upon the discovery of one or two small Carib-speaking tribes, such as the Bakaïri and Nahuqua, in the upper Xingu region, where the presence of Carib peoples had not previously been known. The speech of the Bakaïri being the most archaic of Carib languages, their habitat was therefore considered to indicate the ancient home of the whole stock, whence the main mass had moved northward to their historic sites. Physically, however, these Bakaïri are far more Palæ-Alpine than Alpine, and moreover show a considerable element of the dolichocephalic factors characteristic of the supposedly oldest stratum of population in the region. Since, then, these supposedly primitive Caribs are quite different in physical type from the recent stratum of population along the northern border of the continent, how can we regard these as essentially Carib speaking immigrants? The key to the puzzle lies, I believe, in the Nahuqua. This other Carib people in the Xingu region are, as stated on a previous page, primarily of Alpine and Ural types, with minorities of the broad-nosed brachycephalic and dolichocephalic factors. If we may suppose that the Bakaïri are a people of the older Palæ-Alpine type, which had blended with the still more primitive dolichocephalic population of the area, and who have been "Caribized" in speech by a prehistoric Carib immigration coming into the region perhaps from the west or southwest, a possible solution of the puzzle is at hand. For then the Nahuqua could be taken as representing the original type of these immigrants who would thus be similar to the Galibis, the only other known Carib tribe for which we have any information. Radical and complete changes in language such as suggested seem to have occurred elsewhere in South America, so that this part of the theory is not as impossible as it might seem at first sight.

The entire hypothesis is, of course, nothing but a guess, which seems to agree nevertheless pretty well with the facts as at present known.

# GENERAL CONCLUSIONS

# GENERAL CONCLUSIONS

In the preceding pages the attempt has been made to analyze the physical characteristics of the peoples of the world on the basis of eight primary types, and to sketch for each continent the broad outlines of its racial history. Before taking up the question of the real nature of these "types," and discussing the various problems whose consideration has been deferred to this final chapter, it will be well briefly to examine these types from the world rather than the continental standpoint, summarizing the results of our previous inquiry.

We may begin with the Proto-Australoid type, which, on the basis of the archæological record revealed to us in western Europe, is the oldest which is certainly identifiable. The probability that some other type or types may well be much older yet must however, in view of the Piltdown skull and other recent discoveries, be kept clearly in view. In its present distribution the Proto-Australoid type is primarily concentrated around the margins of the Indian Ocean. In Africa it is of greatest prominence in the south and along the eastern coast; it forms a large element in the population of the whole of southern India and Ceylon; it is apparently fundamental in much of Melanesia and in Australia, where, especially in the more remote southeastern corner and in Tasmania, it reaches a position of strong dominance. As a minor element we find it all along the eastern border-lands of Asia, and continuing across Bering Strait, in isolated areas along the western littoral of the American continents, everywhere representing an ancient and marginal population. The only exception to this primarily western distribution in the New World lies in its strength among the Iroquois and southern Algonkian tribes southeast of the Great Lakes. In Europe it is nowhere to-day a factor of importance, although archæological data show that it once was, and it has been shown in a previous chapter how we may apparently trace its gradual withdrawal northward and northeastward before the advance of the later immigrant peoples.

For this type an original or earliest ascertainable homeland somewhere on the tropical margins of southeastern Asia, which at this early period included the present islands of Sumatra, Java, Borneo, etc., may with considerable certainty be assumed; the area, in short, in which in late Pliocene times the Pithecanthropus erectus lived. From here the type spread southeast into Australia, where its very early presence is proved by the Talgai skull, and where, isolated and relatively untouched by the later streams of migration, it has survived in relative purity to the present day. Westward the type followed the tropical shorelands through India and the Arabian coasts to Africa, and by way of the Mediterranean passed into western Europe, where it appeared in early Palæolithic times. A third branch drifted slowly northward up the eastern Asiatic littoral, and, crossing into America, spread thinly through the continents, and perhaps mainly along the western shores. We may probably conceive of this type as originally of short stature, with brown skin and straight or slightly wavy hair. In Europe and America, where the peoples of this type lived for thousands or tens of thousands of years in a temperate or even sub-arctic climate, the skin gradually lost much of its pigmentation (as discussed more fully in considering the Proto-Negroid type), whereas in the tropics, to which this type has mainly been confined, and where it has become blended with Proto-Negroid peoples, the color has been intensified, and the hair often become strongly curly or frizzly. Among the purest representatives of the type, however, i. e., in southeastern Australia, the hair is often almost straight.

The belief in the unity of this type wherever found rests upon the similarity observable between series of crania of the type from different parts of the world. In our analysis we have depended only on three indices, and, although in these agreement might exist, in other respects the crania might well differ. To rest the theory of unity of type upon a wider basis, and to show that the separate series agree not only in respect to the three indices selected as criteria but also in absolute measurements and in other respects, tables showing the averages for fourteen absolute measurements and indices of the skull, face, and nose have been prepared, demonstrating the degree of similarity between the different series.

TABLE 1

PROTO–AUSTRALOID TYPE

AVERAGE MEASUREMENTS AND INDICES

| Locality or Tribe | No. | L. | B. | H. | L. B. Ind. | L. H. Ind. | B. H. Ind. | Ns. L. | Ns. B. | Nas. Ind. | Bi-Zy. Diam. | Up. Fc. L. | U. Fac. Ind. | Gnath. Ind. | Cap. |
|---|---|---|---|---|---|---|---|---|---|---|---|---|---|---|---|
| Australia....... | 20 | 190 | 127 | 129 | 66.3 | 67.8 | 101.4 | 47 | 27 | 59.1 | 128 | 65 | 52.2 | 102.9 | 1,283 |
| New Britain.... | 7 | 190 | 135 | 130 | 71.2 | 68.4 | 95.9 | 48 | 27 | 57.5 | 133 | 67 | 50.1 | .... | 1,414 |
| Negro and Bantu....... | 16 | 190 | 133 | 130 | 70.1 | 68.2 | 97.3 | 48 | 27 | 56.8 | 131 | 70 | 51.7 | 99.6 | ..... |
| Egypt......... | 2 | 198 | 131 | 133 | 66.6 | 67.6 | 101.5 | 49 | 28 | 56.5 | 129 | 73 | 56.5 | 94.7 | 1,454 |
| Sardinia and Sicily........ | 4 | 185 | 131 | 125 | 70.7 | 67.5 | 95.3 | 48 | 26 | 55.1 | 127 | 65 | .... | 99.6 | 1,381 |
| England........ | 3 | 191 | 139 | 129 | 72.8 | 67.3 | 92.9 | 49 | 26 | 54.3 | 131 | 67 | 51.5 | 94.2 | 1,445 |
| Germany (Neolithic)........ | 2 | 193 | 138 | 126 | 71.4 | 65.2 | 91.3 | 48 | 23 | 57.9 | 112 | 65 | 55.9 | .... | ..... |
| Ostiak......... | 7 | 185 | 135 | 124 | 72.9 | 66.5 | 91.2 | 49 | 27 | 54.7 | 130 | .. | .... | .... | 1,357 |
| California...... | 6 | 188 | 133 | 124 | 70.6 | 66.2 | 93.7 | 51 | 27 | 53.7 | 136 | 72 | 52.7 | 98.7 | 1,319 |
| Iroquois........ | 4 | 196 | 138 | 135 | 70.5 | 68.1 | 98.1 | .. | .. | 53.6 | (140) | .. | (51.7) | (99.9) | ..... |

The small number of crania available in most areas renders the comparison of very uncertain value, but taking the Australian and Negro series the close similarity is apparent, both in indices and in absolute measurements. With the latter the two American series agree quite closely, indeed more closely than the New Britain series with the near-by Australian. The European data are so meagre that comparison means little, yet, if the Sardinian, Sicilian, and English figures are grouped together, their main difference from the others lies in the absence of the mild prognathism which characterizes the other groups. The extreme platyrrhiny of the Australian is not found elsewhere, although approached by the two Neolithic crania from Germany. If one is willing to admit that, where a type has been exposed to the influence of other types and environments for thousands of years, some modification of the extreme forms of the type itself may occur, then the differences here observed are not too great to admit of the belief that all the series are fundamentally related.

The Proto-Negroid type is, to an even greater extent than the Proto-Australoid, tropical in its present distribution, and mainly confined to areas adjacent to the Indian Ocean. In Africa it is more strongly concentrated, however, in the west. It is a large factor in the population of southern India and the aboriginal remnants in the Malay peninsula; in Indonesia it survives in some importance in marginal areas; it is dominant among part of the population of Melanesia and northern Australia, and has considerable outliers far to the east in Easter Island. It is a minor element among the living, and was a stronger among the ancient peoples of southeast Asia, and in the New World was prominent in the Iroquois and southern Algonkian tribes as well as among the ancient peoples of the region on both sides of the Mexican border, in the Brazilian Highlands, and in Patagonia. In Europe its traces are faint to-day, although here and there individuals exhibiting its characteristic features are to be found. In Neolithic times, however, it was an element of some importance in the Baltic region, and continued to be a clearly discernible factor in the population of western Russia until the Middle Ages. In Palæolithic times its presence has universally been admitted on the northern Mediterranean coasts.

For the earliest assignable homeland or focus of dispersion of the Proto-Negroid type we may probably, although not certainly, look to northern and western Africa. As the Proto-Australoids streamed west along the southern margin of Asia, so it may be supposed the Proto-Negroids, probably at a later date, drifted eastward through India to southeastern Asia and thence through Indonesia and Melanesia to Australia, with a long arm stretched out farther through central Polynesia as far as Easter Island. Like the presumably older Proto-Australoids, they followed northward up the eastern Asiatic borderlands and penetrated to the New World, drifting, or being later driven by other immigrants, southward and toward its eastern shores. From Africa, again, they worked their way northward into western Europe in late Palæolithic times, ultimately reaching the Baltic region perhaps by way of the Black Sea as well as through France.

In stature probably tall, the Proto-Negroids may be supposed to have been dark brown in skin color, with strongly curly or frizzly hair. Among those who remained within the tropical environment the pigmentation was intensified, the hair became increasingly woolly, so that the Negroid peoples to-day may be regarded as much blacker and with hair much woollier than their remote ancestors of thirty or forty thousand years ago. Those branches of the type, however, which passed northward into temperate and for a time perhaps sub-arctic environment may be supposed in the course of millennia to have lost much or all of their original pigmentation and frizzliness of hair. I am quite well aware that such a suggestion of radical change in skin color and particularly of the complete loss of an original frizzly hair is certain to meet with an immediate denial of its possibility. For a change in pigmentation, however, I believe a fair case can be made out; as regards the change in type of hair the question is much more difficult, yet in view of the strong similarities in cranial forms it is difficult to avoid the conclusion that even this seeming impossibility may have occurred.

The causes of pigmentation are not yet wholly clear, yet there is, I think, general agreement to-day that the environment and food of the tropics is an important, although not the only, determining factor. If this be true, I believe it is legitimate to suppose that a people of moderately dark skin living under harsh temperate or sub-arctic conditions for many thousands of years, might well lose their pigmentation in large measure. In Europe, in the region surrounding the Baltic, into which a branch of the early Proto-Negroids are assumed to have come, a powerful if little understood influence toward "bleaching" has made itself felt on every people who have come within its sphere. Here, and here only in all the world, are peoples found who are predominantly blond, and who, although they are alike in this feature, yet belong to sharply contrasted physical types. For the strongly brachycephalic and primarily Alpine Finn is as blond as the fairest dolichocephalic and "Nordic" Swede. Here, therefore, the complete disappearance of the dark pigmentation might be expected; and here it seems actually to occur. It may at once be said in opposition to any such theory of "bleached" Negroid peoples, that we can observe no difference in skin color between the American Negro and his kinsman in Africa; that the one is as black as the other, although the American Negro is no longer living in the tropics. This is of course true, but in fairness it should be noted that the bulk of the Negroes in the United States still live in the Southern States where the environmental conditions are, although not tropical, still by no means harsh or comparable to those found in the Baltic region or the northeast of Asia. It must also be remembered that we know of no groups of Negroid peoples who have been living for any length of time, as time is counted in the development of the human race, in a distinctly northern area. In the history of the race, which grows longer with every discovery, we now have indisputable evidence of man's existence not scores but hundreds of thousands of years ago; there is therefore time for very profound modifications to take place. In a period thus not of five or ten generations, which would include our longest period of observation, but of five or ten thousand, may we not reasonably expect extremely significant changes to have occurred? Add to this the fact that the original Negroid group would have been subject also to blending with other, lighter-skinned types, and the probability, almost the certainty, of the very large loss of pigmentation seems to me clear.

The problem of the hair is much more troublesome. It is, perhaps, conceivable that some climatic factor enters into the question here, as it almost certainly does in the case of pigmentation. Thus as the latter serves a most important need in protecting the skin from the effects of insolation, may not the frizzly, woolly type of hair, by making a natural mat which by its included air-spaces must serve as a most excellent insulator for the brain against the intense heat of the sun, have been slowly developed as an adaptation likewise? It must be confessed that this problem of the hair is a stumbling-block, and a very real one, in the way of the theory of the presence of the Proto-Negroid type among peoples who show no trace even of curly hair. Yet so close is the resemblance in the major measurements and proportions of the skull, that I feel convinced that some explanation may yet be found for the phenomenon.

### TABLE 2
#### PROTO–NEGROID TYPE
##### AVERAGE MEASUREMENTS AND INDICES

| Locality or Tribe | No. | L. | B. | H. | L.B. Ind. | L.H. Ind. | B.H. Ind. | Ns. L. | Ns. B. | Nas. Ind. | Bi. Zy. Dia. | Up. Fc. L. | Up. Fac. Ind. | Gnath. Ind. | Cap. |
|---|---|---|---|---|---|---|---|---|---|---|---|---|---|---|---|
| Cameroon | 5 | 179 | 133 | 137 | 73.8 | 76.6 | 103.7 | 48 | 27 | 57.6 | 133 | 67 | 50.5 | .... | 1,381 |
| Gaboon | 10 | 181 | 133 | 139 | 73.2 | 76.8 | 104.9 | 48 | 26 | 55.4 | 128 | 65 | 51.4 | 98.3 | 1,417 |
| Bantu | 10 | 183 | 133 | 141 | 72.5 | 77.0 | 107.0 | 48 | 29 | 60.0 | 130 | 70 | 54.7 | 100.0 | ..... |
| Pre-Dynastic Egypt | 5 | 181 | 131 | ... | 72.4 | .... | ..... | 48 | 25 | 52.8 | ... | 67 | .... | 100.7 | 1,275 |
| Germany (Neolithic) | 2 | 179 | 132 | 138 | 73.5 | 76.5 | 104.7 | .. | .. | 51.5 | ... | .. | 51.0 | .... | ..... |
| Australia | 8 | 181 | 124 | 139 | 68.1 | 76.5 | 111.9 | 45 | 27 | 60.5 | 130 | 62 | .... | 97.3 | 1,316 |
| New Britain | 9 | 180 | 129 | 135 | 71.8 | 75.8 | 103.8 | 47 | 26 | 56.3 | 134 | 68 | 50.5 | .... | 1,307 |
| East New Guinea* | 20 | 176 | 125 | 135 | 71.5 | 76.7 | 107.3 | 47 | 25 | 55.3 | 126 | 61 | 48.4 | .... | 1,248 |
| New Zealand | 2 | 189 | 138 | 143 | 72.9 | 75.7 | 104.0 | 49 | 25 | 52.1 | 134 | 69 | 51.4 | 97.6 | 1,525 |
| Hawaii | 2 | 179 | 133 | 140 | 74.0 | 78.0 | 105.2 | 47 | 25 | 52.5 | 126 | 61 | 48.2 | .... | 1,327 |
| Easter Island | 6 | 182 | 131 | 142 | 71.7 | 78.0 | 108.2 | 50 | 27 | 53.9 | 128 | 67 | 52.7 | 95.5 | 1,376 |
| Algonkian and Iroquois | 7 | 184 | 135 | 142 | 73.4 | 77.5 | 105.5 | 45 | 24 | 53.9 | ... | 65 | (52.9) | (94.5) | ..... |

* Dawson Straits and Murua (Woodlark).

### TABLE 3
#### PROTO–AUSTRALOID AND PROTO–NEGROID BLEND
##### AVERAGE MEASUREMENTS AND INDICES

| Locality or Tribe | No. | L. | B. | H. | L.B. Ind. | L.H. Ind. | B.H. Ind. | Ns. L. | Ns. B. | Nas. Ind. | Bi- Zy. Dia. | Up. Fc. L. | Up. Fac. Ind. | Gnath. Ind. | Cap. |
|---|---|---|---|---|---|---|---|---|---|---|---|---|---|---|---|
| Cameroon | 9 | 183 | 133 | 134 | 73.3 | 72.5 | 100.0 | 48 | 26 | 55.2 | 133 | 68 | 51.4 | ..... | 1,448 |
| Gaboon | 10 | 184 | 133 | 134 | 72.6 | 73.0 | 100.4 | 48 | 27 | 56.5 | 131 | 65 | 50.4 | 99.4 | 1,391 |
| Bantu | 20 | 186 | 132 | 134 | 71.1 | 72.2 | 101.6 | 47 | 27 | 56.8 | 129 | 68 | 53.7 | 100.8 | ..... |
| Pre-Dynastic Egypt | 20 | 184 | 130 | 132 | 70.7 | 71.7 | 101.3 | 48 | 26 | 55.1 | 122 | 66 | 53.6 | 97.9 | 1,359 |
| Australia | 20 | 182 | 123 | 132 | 67.8 | 72.7 | 106.9 | 46 | 26 | 57.4 | 123 | 65 | 53.1 | 100.3 | 1,234 |
| New Britain | 20 | 183 | 132 | 133 | 72.4 | 72.9 | 100.7 | 48 | 27 | 55.9 | 134 | 67 | 49.9 | ..... | 1,362 |
| Ainu | 5 | 194 | 141 | 140 | 73.2 | 72.3 | 98.9 | 50 | 27 | 54.9 | 139 | 68 | 48.7 | 102.0 | 1,552 |
| Algonkian | 6 | 186 | 134 | 134 | 72.8 | 72.6 | 98.6 | 48 | 27 | 56.7 | 133 | 70 | 52.5 | 100.2 | (1,465) |
| Iroquois | 16 | 190 | 137 | 138 | 72.6 | 72.3 | 100.5 | .. | .. | 54.3 | ... | .. | .... | ..... | ..... |

The demonstration of this close similarity is made difficult, owing to the very small number of Proto-Negroid crania available from non-Negroid peoples. That the number exhibiting the type in pure form should among these peoples be few, is of course expectable, but it is unfortunate that for the Iroquois, who appear to show it so strongly, the data as yet available are

so incomplete. I shall in this case therefore supplement the series
showing the pure Proto-Negroid type by another showing the
blend between this and the Proto-Australoid, and, as this blend
is that which makes up the majority of the actual African as
well as Oceanic Negroids, the resemblance will be equally significant.

In the Proto-Negroid table, the smallness of the numbers in
the series makes the results of only very tentative value, yet
on the face of it the table indicates a very real similarity between
the different groups. The Australian crania are extreme in the
narrowness of their heads, yet all are clearly dolichocephalic,
the higher figure for the small Hawaiian group being probably
due to the strong brachycephalic environment. There is some
variation in the degree of platyrrhiny, but all except the Neolithic German crania, and those from New Zealand and Hawaii,
are clearly and definitely broad, these exceptions being doubtless due to the highly marked leptorrhiny of the mass of the population. The same holds for the upper facial index, which is
for all "mesen," except in the New Guinea and Hawaiian cases,
where the population in general is marked by very broad faces.
The African series, *including* the Pre-Dynastic Egyptian are more
prognathic than the rest. With the exception of having a nose
that is slightly narrower and absolutely smaller, and for being
probably a little less prognathic, the Algonkian and Iroquois series
are as close to the Negroid groups as they are to each other. In
the second table, the figures speak for themselves. I want to
call attention, however, to the extremely close similarity between the Pre-Dynastic Egyptian series and those from the Bantu
and the Gaboon and Cameroon Negroes, as, except for a face
which is absolutely slightly smaller, the Egyptian is almost the
exact duplicate of the Negroids; also to the close correspondence
between the Iroquois series and the Negroids. Unfortunately,
the former series is not complete, but as far as it goes, the paral-
lelism is striking.

The distribution of the Caspian type to-day is a curious one,
since the areas of its concentration are very widely separated.

The largest, and that in which it is present in greatest purity, is, paradoxically enough, that occupied by the Eskimo, the second most important one comprising northern and northeastern Africa. A third area extends along the southeastern coast of South America, while a last includes Scandinavia and Great Britain. As an important minority factor the type is very widely spread, here and there, along the western margin of Europe, around the southern end of the Caspian Sea, in northern India (where in places it is strongly dominant), in Tibet (?), in China, in some of the islands of Micronesia, in New Zealand, and in isolated places along the Pacific shores of America. How is this curious distribution to be accounted for? Archæological and historical evidences come to aid us in some degree, for they show that the type has been present in northern Africa, at least, since early Pre-Dynastic times, coming in apparently from the east and northeast. They show also that the peoples of this type first appeared in western Europe toward the end of the Palæolithic period, here again coming apparently from the eastward, and that during the whole Neolithic period and later they increased greatly, finally concentrating in the region of the Baltic and western Russia, where they fused with other types to form the Baltic or "Nordic" race. The archæological evidence furthermore indicates that in the Bronze Age, and probably long before, the Caspian type was dominant in the population of southern Siberia, having reached China and Japan by the end of Neolithic times. We know, also, that in the middle of the second millennium B.C., or thereabouts, peoples of this type came in large numbers into northern India from the northwest. For the New World we have little or no archæological or historical evidence, and must rely upon that afforded by distribution, which would indicate, from the extreme marginal position in which the type is found, that it was one of the oldest, if not the oldest, in the continent.

These facts seem to lead to the conclusion that the earliest ascertainable homeland for peoples of this type lies in the great Eur-Asiatic steppe region of southeastern Russia and southwestern Siberia, north of the great plateau belt which stretches across

Asia from northeast to southwest. Tall in stature, fair-skinned, probably with brown, slightly wavy hair and hazel eyes, the people of this type had inherent in them a strong tendency toward blondness, which, whenever the conditions favored, became more and more pronounced, reaching its climax in the Baltic region. Although we have as yet no archæological evidence proving the existence of the type here in the Eur-Asiatic steppe earlier than Bronze or possibly Neolithic times, we must probably assume that their occupation of this territory goes back far into Palæolithic times. As early as the Aurignacian period we know that they had come into Europe from the east, and I believe that they very early also moved eastward, keeping along or to the north of the margin of the great plateaus, and so across Bering Strait into America, to which this type may have supplied its first inhabitants. The drift in this direction was, however, later checked, and the expansion turned more and more toward the south. Westward into Europe the current long continued. In Neolithic times a great branch of the type crossed the plateaus eastward into China and Japan, and southward across the Iranian plateau to Arabia and northern Africa. Only much later did they reach India and southeastern Asia, whence a stream of small proportions passed on out into the Pacific.

A so-called "Caucasic" element has long been mooted in parts of Polynesia, and this seems on the basis of the present analysis of the data to be confirmed. But the suggestion put forward that a similar factor came also into America, is far less likely to meet with acceptance and seems at first sight, like the presence of a Proto-Negroid element there, to be not only fanciful but well-nigh impossible. It is true that at various times the suggestion has been put forward that the Eskimo crania showed resemblance to some of the early north European forms, and that the Eskimo might thus be the survivors of Palæolithic man. The theory has, however, been generally rejected, partly because of the difficulty of accounting for the transferrence of the people from Europe to Greenland and Arctic America, partly because of actual differences in the crania, and certain special characteristics of the Eskimo crania on which great stress has been laid. If, however, instead of comparing Eskimo crania in general with a few individual skulls of very early date in Europe, we make our comparison between series of pure types from both areas, the resemblances become much more striking.

TABLE 4

CASPIAN TYPE

Average Measurements and Indices

| Locality or Tribe | No. | L. | B. | H. | L. B. Ind. | L. H. Ind. | B. H. Ind. | Ns. L. | Ns. B. | Nas. Ind. | Bi-Zy. Diam. | Up. Fac. L. | Up. Fac. Ind. | Gnath. Ind. | Cap. |
|---|---|---|---|---|---|---|---|---|---|---|---|---|---|---|---|
| Sardinia........ | 33 | 184 | 134 | 139 | 72.6 | 75.6 | 103.9 | 55 | 24 | 44.2 | 135 | 71 | 52.7 | 93.0 | 1,445 |
| Russia......... | 7 | 186 | 135 | 142 | 72.2 | 76.2 | 105.4 | .. | .. | 44.1 | ... | ... | .... | ..... | ..... |
| Egypt*........ | 20 | 181 | 133 | 139 | 73.2 | 76.6 | 104.6 | 52 | 23 | 44.7 | 126 | 72 | 57.9 | 93.3 | 1,440 |
| Galla and Somali | 5 | 181 | 130 | 138 | 71.7 | 76.2 | 106.0 | .. | .. | 44.1 | ... | .. | .... | .... | 1,366 |
| India.......... | 5 | 179 | 131 | 135 | 73.2 | 75.3 | 103.3 | 50 | 21 | 41.9 | 125 | .. | .... | 94.4 | 1,375 |
| New Zealand... | 3 | 186 | 138 | 141 | 74.3 | 76.1 | 102.6 | 56 | 25 | 44.5 | 141 | 71 | 48.8 | 98.6 | 1,471 |
| Hawaii......... | 2 | 181 | 133 | 139 | 73.5 | 76.5 | 104.5 | 53 | 23 | 44.5 | (130) | (74) | (56.9) | .... | (1,300) |
| Eskimo........ | 20 | 185 | 133 | 140 | 71.6 | 76.5 | 106.7 | 54 | 23 | 42.0 | 139 | 72 | 53.0 | 98.5 | 1,541 |

* Eighteenth Dynasty and earlier.

TABLE 5

CASPIAN AND MEDITERRANEAN BLEND

Average Measurements and Indices

| Locality or Tribe | No. | L. | B. | H. | L. B. Ind. | L. H. Ind. | B. H. Ind. | Ns. L. | Ns. B. | Nas. Ind. | Bi-Zy. Diam. | Up. Fac. L. | Up. Fac. Ind. | Gnath. Ind. | Cap. |
|---|---|---|---|---|---|---|---|---|---|---|---|---|---|---|---|
| England........ | 5 | 191 | 140 | 137 | 73.2 | 71.5 | 97.6 | 53 | 24 | 44.6 | 135 | 72 | 51.8 | 91.7 | 1,486 |
| Sweden*........ | 9 | 190 | 135 | 136 | 71.6 | 71.4 | 99.5 | .. | .. | 44.1 | ... | .. | 53.6 | .... | 1,515 |
| Sicily......... | 12 | 183 | 132 | 133 | 72.3 | 72.6 | 100.3 | 51 | 22 | 42.3 | ... | .. | .... | .... | 1,377 |
| Siwah Oasis.... | 12 | 184 | 133 | 133 | 72.3 | 72.2 | 99.9 | 51 | 22 | 44.2 | ... | .. | .... | .... | .... |
| Egypt.......... | .. | ... | ... | ... | ... | ... | ... | .. | .. | 42.8 | ... | .. | .... | .... | .... |
| Germany....... | 12 | 193 | 141 | 137 | 72.3 | 72.0 | 98.9 | .. | .. | 42.8 | ... | .. | .... | .... | .... |
| Chatham Islands | 10 | 187 | 138 | 136 | 73.6 | 73.1 | 98.8 | 57 | 25 | 44.5 | 136 | 75 | 55.2 | 96.1 | 1,430 |
| Eskimo........ | 10 | 190 | 132 | 136 | 69.6 | 72.5 | 104.3 | 54 | 22 | 41.8 | 138 | 74 | 53.9 | 97.8 | 1,545 |
| Patagonia...... | 10 | 193 | 139 | 139 | 71.9 | 72.4 | 100.7 | 55 | 24 | 44.7 | 141 | 77 | 55.3 | 97.9 | 1,466 |

* Neolithic.

Commenting on these tables it may be noted that in the case of the Caspian type itself, all of the series are closely accordant, almost the only departure from agreement being in the case of the very small Maori group, which has a much wider face and with the Eskimo is somewhat more prognathous. The facial character of the type seems to be clearly lepten, or narrow, and the medium form in the Eskimo may very reasonably be ascribed to the peculiar broadening of the face due to overdevelopment of the chewing muscles, which is universally ascribed to them. The Caspian-Mediterranean blend shows somewhat greater variation, as might be expected, but on the whole corroborates the evidence given by the pure type. I believe that if we only had available a large series of complete individual measurements of Reihengräber crania from Germany, and more satisfactory materials from Russia, that the correspondences would be brought out much more clearly, but even on the basis of the data presented it seems to me that a strong case has been made out for the relationship between the Eskimo and the Old World representatives of the Caspian type. The American branch has been slightly modified in one or two particulars, but remains, nevertheless, substantially identical with the parent stock.

The Mediterranean type, although widely distributed as a minority, is at present found in any considerable strength or purity in a rather limited area, including Arabia and northern Africa, southern Italy, Sicily and Sardinia, the Iberian Peninsula, Great Britain, and the western coast of Norway. It is of less and rather minor importance among the higher castes in north-western India, among some groups of Eskimos, and formerly among some Indian tribes of the Pacific coast. Some evidence in regard to its spread is afforded by archæology. Thus we know that it appeared in western Europe first in the Aurignacian period of later Palæolithic times, coming apparently along the coasts of the Mediterranean. It was strongly represented in the Nile delta in the earliest Dynastic period, but only after the Eighteenth Dynasty became a dominant factor in Upper Egypt. It was the preponderant type in the earlier Minoan periods in Crete, and prominent in the Bronze Age in southern Siberia. In the New World and Oceania it is much less important than the Caspian, and, like it, is found only in marginal areas.

The earliest ascertainable focus of dispersion of the Mediterranean type is less clear than that of the Caspian, but the probabilities seem to favor the region of the eastern Mediterranean and the Black Sea, adjacent on the southwest to the Eur-Asiatic homeland of the Caspian peoples. Shorter in stature than the latter, brunet rather than fair in coloring, the Mediterranean type very early spread through western Europe, possibly in part by sea along the shore. Eastward, it seems to have penetrated far into the heart of the Caspian region, and to have drifted with these peoples as an associated but never dominant element. It has thus come to have tinged the population of many distant areas, but has, outside its own rather narrow sphere, never strongly colored them.

### TABLE 6

MEDITERRANEAN TYPE

AVERAGE MEASUREMENTS AND INDICES

| Locality or Tribe | No. | L. | B. | H. | L.B. Ind. | L.H. Ind. | B.H. Ind. | Ns. L. | Ns. B. | Nas. Ind. | Bi-Zy. Diam. | Up. Fac. L. | Up.Fac. Ind. | Gnath. Ind. | Cap. |
|---|---|---|---|---|---|---|---|---|---|---|---|---|---|---|---|
| Sicily........... | 10 | 187 | 136 | 126 | 72.9 | 67.5 | 92.7 | 50 | 21 | 42.3 | ... | .. | .... | .... | 1,415 |
| Sardinia........ | 12 | 188 | 131 | 129 | 69.4 | 68.1 | 97.7 | 53 | 22 | 43.6 | 126 | 68 | 55.6 | 97.9 | 1,420 |
| Siwah Oasis..... | 6 | 188 | 134 | 127 | 71.1 | 67.6 | 95.2 | 53 | 23 | 43.8 | ... | .. | .... | .... | ..... |
| Egypt*......... | 13 | 187 | 132 | 128 | 70.7 | 68.6 | 97.1 | 53 | 23 | 43.6 | 124 | 71 | 57.3 | 96.5 | 1,362 |
| England........ | 14 | 192 | 139 | 129 | 72.6 | 67.3 | 92.7 | 51 | 21 | 44.3 | 127 | 71 | 55.7 | 94.4 | 1,493 |
| Russia.......... | 6 | 189 | 135 | 129 | 71.8 | 68.2 | 95.4 | .. | .. | 42.2 | ... | .. | .... | .... | ..... |
| India........... | 5 | 184 | 129 | 126 | 69.9 | 68.7 | 98.0 | 52 | 23 | 42.6 | 120 | .. | .... | 91.8 | 1,391 |
| Chatham Islands. | 5 | 195 | 139 | 133 | 71.6 | 68.4 | 95.5 | 57 | 25 | 43.0 | 136 | 73 | 53.9 | 94.7 | 1,410 |
| Eskimo......... | 6 | 194 | 135 | 133 | 69.5 | 68.5 | 98.7 | 56 | 22 | 40.5 | 141 | 76 | 54 1 | 99.8 | 1,563 |
| California....... | 5 | 191 | 137 | 127 | 71.7 | 66.4 | 92.5 | 54 | 24 | 43.9 | 139 | 76 | 55.2 | 96.0 | 1,419 |

* Eighteenth Dynasty and earlier.

The table brings out with sufficient clearness the strong similarities between the various series, the only real discrepancy at all being the somewhat wider faces of the Moriori of the Chatham Islands, and the Eskimo, and this, for the latter at least, is specifically accounted for by the special factors which among this people are supposed to work to that end. It is furthermore to be noted that the Eskimo crania of this series are narrower than those of any other type, and show a somewhat greater prognathism.

Of the brachycephalic types, the Mongoloid is that whose influence seems first apparent in the archæological record, and which, by its extreme marginal distribution in Europe and perhaps in Africa, seems to be a very ancient type. The problem which it presents is, however, one of much difficulty. Although we appear to have evidence of its presence in western Europe and the Balkan peninsula in early Palæolithic times, and of its strong influence in Belgium and probably the north of Switzerland during the Neolithic period, I have been able to find no crania exhibiting the type in purity older than the Middle Ages, from which time down to the present, however, they are to be found in moderate numbers in the Central European Highlands and the surrounding areas, while among the Scandinavian Lapps this type is clearly dominant. It was a minor factor in the area about the Gulf of Gabez in northern Africa in Carthaginian times, and was apparently a strong element in the old pre-Guanche population of the Canary Islands, and, wholly blended with Proto-Australoid and Proto-Negroid types, appears at the extreme southern tip of the African continent among the Bushmen. In Asia it characterizes with great clearness the true Mongols and other peoples who live along the northern borders of the eastern great plateaus from the Altai to Lake Baikal, and faint traces of its presence may even be found in some of the Plains tribes of North America, as well as in Tasmania. Comparative data can, unfortunately, only be presented for the European and Asiatic representatives, since elsewhere the members of this type have been so completely absorbed that no pure examples seem to survive.

### TABLE 7

#### MONGOLOID TYPE

AVERAGE MEASUREMENTS AND INDICES

| Locality or Tribe | No. | L. | B. | H. | L. B. Ind. | L. H. Ind. | B. H. Ind. | Ns. L. | Ns. B. | Nas. Ind. | Bi-Zy. Diam. | Up. Fac. L. | Up. Fac. Ind. | Gnath. Ind. | Cap. |
|---|---|---|---|---|---|---|---|---|---|---|---|---|---|---|---|
| Valais (Switzerl'd) | 8 | 183 | 152 | 125 | 83.2 | 68.5 | 82.3 | 48 | 25 | 53.0 | 136 | 66 | 49.6 | 100.4 | (1,405) |
| Tirol | 10 | 182 | 149 | 124 | 83.5 | 68.4 | 83.1 | .. | .. | 55.2 | ... | .. | .... | .... | ..... |
| Morvan (France) | 9 | ... | ... | ... | 83.6 | 68.4 | 81.8 | .. | .. | 53.0 | ... | .. | 50.4 | 97.6 | ..... |
| Mongols | 5 | 180 | 152 | 124 | 84.8 | 68.0 | 80.6 | 54 | 29 | 53.6 | 142 | .. | 51.7 | .... | 1,438 |
| Lapps | 3 | 173 | 148 | 119 | 85.3 | 68.9 | 80.5 | 49 | 25 | 53.9 | 134 | .. | .... | .... | 1,397 |

Unfortunately the available data are incomplete, yet so far as they go they indicate a rather close correspondence in proportions between the several series, although the Lapp crania, in absolute size, are smaller than the others. The numbers in the series are, however, too small to be satisfactory, but until more abundant material is available we may, I think, tentatively accept the identification as correct. Between the European and Asiatic representatives of the type, on the one hand, and the survivors (or apparent survivors) in Africa, no direct comparisons can be made, since even the blends into which the Mongoloid type has faded in Africa are not comparable with those in other regions, for in Africa the amalgamation has been in the main with the Proto-Australoid type, while in Europe and Asia it has been for the most part with the Palæ-Alpine. When the abundant Bushman cranial material, long stored in the South African Museum, is made available for students, and when we have archæological materials from the homeland of the present Mongols, it may be possible to approach the problem with more hope of definite results. The strong indications that a Mongoloid factor is pronounced in the Bushmen, afforded by the cranial data which we now have, are much fortified by the well-recognized frequency of the Mongoloid eye among them, and by their peculiar yellowish skin color.

From all the materials available, it seems that we may ascribe to the original Mongoloid type a short stature, perhaps very short; a yellowish skin; strong development of the "Mongoloid eye"; and probably (?) wavy hair. The latter feature may then be supposed to have been lost in the present Mongols, as a result of the large admixtures of straight-haired Palæ-Alpine and Alpine elements they have received, whereas, in the case of the Mongoloid factor which made its way into southern Africa, admixture with Proto-Negroid peoples may possibly account for the character of the Bushman hair, although the extremely woolly nature of this seems a serious obstacle to the theory.

What the original focus of distribution of the Mongoloid type (accepting for the moment the identifications here proposed) may have been is, in the absence of archæological materials from the whole of inner Asia, hard to say. Yet the most probable location would seem to be in the northern portion of the eastern plateaus, where the present Mongol peoples have long been at home, and that the entrance of this type into Europe marked the first coming of brachycephals from the Asiatic continent, coincident in time, perhaps, with the westward drift of the Proto-Australoids along the southern border of these uplands.

The Palæ-Alpine type presents us with a problem comparable in many ways to that which we have already met with in the case of the Proto-Negroid type, where a Negroid and a non-Negroid form appear to exist, similar in cranial characteristics, but differing in pigmentation and type of hair. The conditions here are, however, just reversed from those in the Proto-Negroid, for, whereas in that instance the majority of living members of the type are Negroid and the minority non-Negroid, in the Palæ-Alpine the vast majority present no trace of Negroid pigmentation and hair, these being found only among the numerically insignificant Negrito peoples.

The normal or non-Negroid Palæ-Alpine type is very widely spread. It is concentrated, however, very clearly at the present day in the southeast of Asia, Korea, Japan, Mongolia, and Western Turkestan, and in Europe is strongly represented throughout the Central Highlands. In Africa, on the other hand, it is practically absent. In Oceania it is predominant in most portions of Indonesia, and in the New World is found in largest proportion among the tribes west of the Rocky Mountains, in the southeastern United States, and in the Amazon basin. In the following table comparative data have been assembled for the type in Europe, Asia, and Oceania, but unfortunately no materials are accessible from which a series for any portion of America can be obtained.

## TABLE 8

### PALÆ-ALPINE TYPE

#### AVERAGE MEASUREMENTS AND INDICES

| Locality or Tribe | No. | L. | B. | H. | L. B. Ind. | L. H. Ind. | B. H. Ind. | Ns. L. | Ns. B. | Nas. Ind. | Bi-Zy. Dia. | Up. Fac. L. | Up. Fac. Ind. | Gnath. Ind. | Cap. |
|---|---|---|---|---|---|---|---|---|---|---|---|---|---|---|---|
| Valais (Switzerland). | 31 | 175 | 152 | 135 | 86.5 | 77.2 | 89.0 | 48 | 26 | 53.4 | ... | .. | 49.4 | 96.5 | 1,555 |
| Morvan (France).... | 13 | ... | ... | ... | 84.4 | 76.8 | 90.0 | .. | .. | 54.3 | ... | .. | 51.1 | 94.2 | ..... |
| Czechs............. | 14 | 172 | 145 | 133 | 84.3 | 77.0 | 91.4 | 46 | 24 | 54.0 | 129 | .. | 47.0 | .... | 1,446 |
| Mongols........... | 17 | 175 | 151 | 134 | 86.5 | 76.7 | 88.6 | 52 | 28 | 53.9 | 139 | 68 | 51.5 | .... | 1,508 |
| Burmese........... | 17 | 168 | 143 | 136 | 85.3 | 80.5 | 94.9 | 51 | 27 | 55.2 | 132 | 68 | 51.8 | 97.2 | 1,383 |
| Hawaii............. | 8 | 175 | 144 | 140 | 82.5 | 80.3 | 97.3 | 49 | 27 | 55.6 | 133 | .. | 50.7 | .... | 1,455 |
| Tagalog............ | 11 | 174 | 145 | 139 | 83.7 | 79.9 | 96.2 | 49 | 28 | 56.8 | 133 | .. | .... | 99.3 | 1,484 |

TABLE 9

NEGRITO SUBTYPE,

AVERAGE MEASUREMENTS AND INDICES

| Locality or Tribe | No. | L. | B. | H. | L. B. Ind. | L. H. Ind. | B. H. Ind. | Ns. L. | Ns. B. | Nas. Ind. | Bi-Zy. Dia. | Up. Fac. L. | Up. Fac. Ind. | Gnath. Ind. | Cap. |
|---|---|---|---|---|---|---|---|---|---|---|---|---|---|---|---|
| Negrito (Philippines) | 20 | 172 | 145 | 138 | 84.3 | 80.6 | 95.5 | 50 | 27 | 54.5 | 131 | .. | .... | 96.8 | 1,403 |
| Baining* | 10 | 169 | 139 | 134 | 82.0 | 79.7 | 96.6 | 46 | 26 | 56.2 | 130 | 62 | 48.0 | 103.3 | 1,240 |
| Muruaţ | 9 | 174 | 142 | 136 | 82.4 | 78.9 | 95.7 | 48 | 26 | 54.5 | 137 | 63 | 46.0 | ..... | 1,468 |
| Congo | 8 | 171 | 140 | 132 | 81.6 | 77.0 | 94.4 | 45 | 25 | 55.7 | 125 | 61 | 49.2 | 100.2 | 1,299 |
| Cameroon | 10 | 172 | 140 | 135 | 81.4 | 78.2 | 95.6 | 48 | 28 | 58.4 | 132 | 64 | 48.7 | ..... | 1,417 |
| Congo Pigmies | 2 | 166 | 139 | 128 | 84.0 | 77.4 | 92.0 | .. | .. | 58.4 | ... | .. | 46.3 | ..... | 1,352 |
| Andamanese | 7 | 163 | 133 | 128 | 82.8 | 79.7 | 95.4 | 44 | 23 | 52.9 | 123 | 62 | (51.8) | 101.1 | 1,228 |

* New Britain.  † Island east of New Guinea.

An examination of the table will show that the European and Asiatic series are in proportions quite closely comparable, except that the face is proportionately slightly wider in some of the European peoples of this type than in Asia. We are accustomed to think of the Mongol as having a wide face, but the Czech much exceeds the Mongol in this particular in reality. In absolute size, the Asiatic members of the type however exceed the European so far as regards the nose and face. (The possibility of a small amount of artificial deformation in the case of the Burmese, and perhaps the Tagalog crania must not be overlooked.) The Negrito series, comprising the Negritos of the Philippines and the Andamanese, together with the Negroid Palæ-Alpine groups in Melanesia and Africa, are in general somewhat smaller, and in the Congo Pigmies and the Andamanese very much so. The Negrito group as a whole is further distinguished from the other Palæ-Alpines in having on the whole a wider face (although the Czech exceed many of them in this respect) and a greater tendency toward prognathism. There is, however, much variation in this, since the Baining are actually to be classed as prognathous, whereas the Philippine Negritos are almost as orthognathous as the western Swiss. The large absolute dimensions of the crania which have been published as Negrito from the Philippines, are to my mind, however, distinctly suspicious, since if they are as dwarf in stature as the measurements of the living show, it seems most improbable that their skulls should be of larger actual dimensions than those of the Czech and as orthognathous as those of the peoples of Switzerland. Until we possess considerable absolutely authentic check material, no safe conclusions can, I believe, be based on these so-called Negrito crania.

The distribution of the Negrito variety of the Palæ-Alpine type is, in its purer forms, very limited to-day, being confined to the Philippines, the Malay Peninsula, and the Andaman Islands, together with scattered areas in the great Congo forest in Africa. But, although only in these regions do we find the full Pigmy form, what I believe are blends between these very small peoples and the Proto-Australoid and Proto-Negroid types are much more widely spread in Melanesia, where they are particularly clearly marked in portions of New Guinea, and in Central Africa, where they have contributed the brachycephalic factors to much of the modern population.

The Palæ-Alpine type seems first to appear in western Europe at the beginning of the Neolithic period or even just before, and, although it became early of large importance in the region of the Central Highlands, did not spread very widely elsewhere, although toward the west it reached Great Britain in Neolithic times, and extended in minor degree apparently along the coast toward the Baltic. Later, in the Bronze Age, the Palæ-Alpine peoples were in great measure overwhelmed by the Alpine immigrants, with whom they gradually amalgamated. In Asia our only evidences relating to the history of the type come from Japan and the southeast of the continent. On the basis of the single small series of Neolithic crania described from the latter region, the Palæ-Alpine peoples appear to have been absent at this time, although we know that later, as at present, they were factors of much importance. In Japan, on the other hand, it seems to be the oldest type yet found, being present in very early Neolithic times. In the New World we can judge only by the geographic distribution, which seems to indicate that the Palæ-Alpine peoples are here more recent than any of the dolichocephalic types, but older than the Alpine.

We may probably regard the Palæ-Alpine type as originally

short in stature, with brownish skin and straight black hair. The evidence is not wholly clear as to whether we are to consider the Mongoloid eye as characteristic of this type, or not. On the whole I am inclined to believe that, if it was, it was so only in a slight degree, and that this feature, where found, has been derived by intermixture from the Mongoloid type.

Unquestionably of Asiatic origin, the determination of the focus of distribution of the Palæ-Alpine type is made difficult by the total lack of archæological material. On the basis of its geographic distribution and other contributory evidence it seems probable that the earliest assignable home of the type must be placed in the southern and eastern portions of the great plateaus, *i. e.*, in southern Mongolia, Eastern Turkestan and Tibet, and the upper basins at least of the Yangtse and Yellow rivers. Thence they flowed out eastward and southeastward into the borderlands, and westward through the older haunts of the Caspian folk, around the northern side of the Black Sea, and so into central Europe. Toward the north they passed along the plateau to Bering Strait and so into America, where, like others before and after them, they tended to drift southward through the Plains. In the northern part of the Asiatic plateaus they blended with the Mongoloid type to form the historic Mongols. The invasion of the Caspian peoples in late Neolithic times, and still more that of the Alpines, swept the Palæ-Alpines in large part out of the eastern and southern portions of the plateau, and forced them more and more toward the southeast, into Indo-China, whence they moved out into the archipelagoes farther east. Of some of these movements the last phases occurred within historic times.

We must return now to the Negrito, and consider further the questions of their origin and relationships. From the present distribution of the purer groups of Negrito around the fringes of Indo-China, and the reported existence of short, Negroid folk well to the north in the interior of southern China, it seems probable that the Negrito were originally a mainland people, who have been crowded off the continent by the expansion of other folk, especially the Palæ-Alpines. The African Pigmies of Palæ-

Alpine type are now mainly confined to the Congo forest and its borders, but there are reasons for believing that they formerly extended farther eastward onto the East African plateau. If we take this fact in connection (1) with the now clearly recognized existence of a Negroid element among the brachycephalic population of southern Arabia; (2) with the existence as late as Herodotus's day of Negroid peoples along the northern shore of the Persian Gulf, and (3) with the presence of a considerable brachycephalic factor of uncertain origin among the Negroid population of southern India, the hypothesis that the Negrito subtype, as I venture to call it, may have originated in Africa and passed eastward to Indo-China, or in the latter area and migrated west to Africa, leaving traces of its passage along the way—such a hypothesis would seem to meet the facts as known to-day. In view of the similarity which the Negrito, as already shown, possesses with the Palæ-Alpine type, I am inclined to believe that it originated in the Indo-Chinese area.

What finally can be said as to the relations of this Negrito subtype to the Palæ-Alpine? So similar are the cranial characteristics of the two that, were it not for the radical differences in pigmentation and type of hair, I should, from the point of view of one trying to regard the human race as a whole, have little hesitation in believing that the Negrito was a specialized form which had somehow developed from the Palæ-Alpine. For if, as I believe, exposure for thousands of years to tropical environment may result in a very far-reaching modification of pigmentation, a very early branch of Palæ-Alpine peoples wandering southward may have served as the source from which the Negrito was ultimately derived. The difference in type of hair is more serious, and raises the same difficulties as came up in the problem of explaining the Mongoloid elements among the Bushmen. In neither case am I able to offer any suggestion as to how so profound a modification could have been brought about, yet I cannot but feel that the fundamental proportions of the skull are elements of great stability and less likely to suffer modification than the superficial features of the body, and that two groups of men resembling each other as closely in respect to their cranial proportions as the Negrito and the Palæ-Alpine must somehow have had a common origin.

The Alpine type is at the present day unquestionably dominant throughout the larger portion of the world—that is, if we consider the New World as if it were uninfluenced by European settlement, and as if it were still occupied by the aboriginal peoples which were found there in the fifteenth century. In Europe it is in the majority everywhere apparently except along the western and northern borders; in Asia it preponderates except in the extreme south and southeast; in the New World it characterizes the great mass of the aboriginal population; in Oceania it is largely represented in Indonesia and in western and central Polynesia. Only Australia and the greater part of Africa lie outside its range.

That the dominant people of central Europe were immigrants from the Asiatic continent, and retained a considerable similarity with the brachycephalic populations of Asia Minor and the fair-skinned Turkish or Indo-European speaking peoples of Turkestan and the vicinity, has long been recognized,[1] and Reicher[2] has gone so far as to make a very detailed cranial comparison between what are commonly called the Mongoloid peoples of Asia and the Swiss. He found, in spite of the fact that he was comparing what, on the basis of the theory here set forth were really much mixed groups, an unexpectedly close agreement. When, instead of instituting comparisons between composite series, the pure types are placed side by side, the resemblance is still more striking. Although, however, similarities are thus admitted between the Asiatic and European branches of the Alpine race, yet, in spite of the fact that the American Indian is generally regarded as of "Mongolian" origin, the logical extension of the comparison to peoples of the New World has not, curiously, been made; at least so far as I am aware. The theory here proposed claims a large proportion of the American Indians to be primarily of Alpine type, and I should therefore at once

[1] Ripley, 1899; Joyce, 1912.                    [2] Reicher, 1913–14.

proceed, after confirming the resemblances between the Asiatic and European branches, to show that the New World contained peoples equally similar. Unfortunately the reliable data available on American crania are extremely meagre, and it is only with great difficulty that a few undeformed crania of Alpine type can be found. The full demonstration therefore of the identity of the American with the Asiatic and European representatives of the type, must wait until, on the one hand, the thousands of American Indian crania for generations stored in the museums and collections of this country shall have been made accessible to the student, and, on the other, further collections are made in regions in regard to which we as yet know little. The following table is mainly confined to European, Asiatic, and Polynesian series.

### TABLE 10

#### ALPINE TYPE

##### AVERAGE MEASUREMENTS AND INDICES

| Locality or Tribe | No. | L. | B. | H. | L. B. Ind. | L. H. Ind. | B. H. Ind. | Ns. L. | Ns. B. | Nas. Ind. | Bi-Zy. Dia. | Up. Fac. L. | Up. Fac. Ind | Gnath. Ind. | Cap. |
|---|---|---|---|---|---|---|---|---|---|---|---|---|---|---|---|
| Valais (Switzerland) | 50 | 176 | 151 | 137 | 85.5 | 77.4 | 90.4 | 52 | 23 | 43.7 | 135 | 73 | 53.7 | 95.1 | 1,566 |
| Dissentis ( " )... | 11 | 173 | 148 | 133 | 85.8 | 77.1 | 89.7 | 52 | 23 | 44.6 | 133 | .. | 49.8 | .... | 1,463 |
| Morvan (France).. | 16 | ... | ... | ... | 85.6 | 77.9 | 91.5 | .. | .. | 44.1 | ... | .. | 51.1 | 92.3 | ..... |
| Czechs............ | 20 | 172 | 145 | 134 | 84.4 | 77.8 | 92.7 | 51 | 22 | 43.8 | 131 | 69 | 53.1 | .... | 1,420 |
| Turks............. | 5 | 174 | 147 | 138 | 85.7 | 79.2 | 92.4 | 54 | 24 | 44.8 | ... | .. | .. | .... | ..... |
| Armenians......... | 17 | 170 | 144 | 134 | 85.0 | 79.0 | 92.9 | .. | .. | 43.8 | ... | .. | (53.5) | .... | ..... |
| Mongols.......... | 5 | 176 | 149 | 134 | 84.8 | 76.4 | 90.4 | 55 | 24 | 43.8 | 141 | .. | 55.0 | .... | 1,430 |
| Chinese........... | 8 | 173 | 144 | 137 | 83.3 | 76.6 | 95.1 | .. | .. | 44.8 | ... | .. | .... | .... | 1,469 |
| Tagalog........... | 15 | 171 | 144 | 134 | 84.5 | 78.2 | 93.3 | 50 | 22 | 45.0 | ... | .. | .... | 99.7 | 1,525 |
| Hawaii............ | 7 | 175 | 147 | 139 | 83.7 | 79.7 | 94.2 | 53 | 23 | 44.7 | 135 | 69 | 51.1 | 95.6 | 1,422 |
| Burmese.......... | 6 | 171 | 144 | 139 | 86.5 | 80.8 | 94.2 | 57 | 25 | 44.4 | 134 | 77 | 57.7 | 96.8 | 1,391 |
| Araucanians....... | 3 | 175 | 143 | 137 | 81.5 | 78.5 | 94.5 | 55 | 24 | 45.1 | 134 | .. | .... | .... | 1,419 |

Almost the only difference in proportions between these several series is that the Alpine peoples outside of Europe have crania which are slightly higher for their width, *i. e.*, the breadth-height index is a little higher than that in Europe. This in some cases is probably due to slight artificial deformation. The facial index is somewhat variable, but is so in Europe itself, as between such closely related groups as the two from neighboring parts of Switzerland. In absolute dimensions the Armenians, Tagalog, and Burmese have slightly smaller skulls, while the face and nose are slightly larger in the non-European as compared with the European series. As a whole, however, the variation, whether in proportions or in actual dimensions between the series, is no greater than that within the Alpine groups in Europe itself, whose identity of origin has never been questioned.

In stature the Alpine type may, I believe, be regarded as originally above the medium, shown for example in Europe by the tall stature of the Tyrolese and Balkan peoples who are more nearly pure Alpines than the western Swiss. In skin color they were probably fair, the hair being straight and dark, the eyes without the Mongoloid fold. Our oldest archæological record of the Alpine type in western Europe is from the end of the Palæolithic, when so many new types made their first appearance there. Although, however, they seem to have arrived in Europe thus early, they did not begin to be of large importance until the end of Neolithic times and the Bronze Age. Probably early in the Bronze Age peoples of this type reached southern Arabia, and slightly influenced the population of the Nile valley. Perhaps at this same time or possibly later, they passed from the Iranian Plateau along the western coast of India, where they exerted on the population an influence which is still clear. In early Bronze times, also, we may suppose that a strong movement of the type took place eastward, through the eastern Asiatic plateaus to the borderlands in China, as well as northward through the old habitat of the Caspian peoples whose last remnants here they displaced, and then eastward again toward Bering Strait and so on into America, where, following southward through the Plains, they forced aside the older Palæ-Alpine population and made their way along the Cordillera into South America. In China their expansion drove the older mixed Palæ-Alpine and Caspian folk southward, and led in proto-historic times to the movement of mixed groups, largely of Alpine origin, into Indonesia, where they were known as the Malays.

The earliest homeland of the Alpine type seems probably to have been in the western Asiatic plateaus, as that of the Palæ-

Alpine was in the eastern.  All the evidence at our disposal seems to me to favor this view, and we have no indication of any other type having ever preceded them in that area.

The type to which with some hesitation the name of Ural has been given, presents in some ways the greatest uncertainties of all.  With our present data it seems almost hopeless to arrive at any certain conclusions in regard to its place of origin and movements.  Nowhere dominant to-day, it is present as an important minority throughout the Central European Highlands and adjacent territory; on the coasts of the North Sea (where it has already been recognized and by some referred to as the Frisian type); among the Prussians of eastern Germany and among the Finns; and in the Basques, at least those in Spain.  In eastern Europe on the other hand it is, so far as published material goes, largely absent, except among the Turkish-speaking and other non-Indo-European groups toward the Urals, and the Samoyedes of the Arctic coast.  In Asia it is of some importance among the Mongols and Ostiaks, and in the Chuckchi and Siberian Eskimo at Bering Strait.  South and east, however, of a line from the Caspian to the mouth of the Amur, it appears to be wholly absent, as it is in Oceania and Africa, except in the Canary Islands, where it is somewhat doubtfully present in small amount.  Most surprising, however, is the fact of its unmistakable and considerable strength in the New World, among the Siouan and Algonkian tribes in the Plains, and especially, far to the south, in Venezuela, where it actually becomes dominant!  Historically the type may be traced in Europe to the end of the Palæolithic period in southern Germany.  In Neolithic times it appears in Switzerland, France, and Belgium, being of large importance only in the latter region.  Although of little importance in the kurgans or burial mounds of western Russia, dating to the later Iron Age, it is prominent in those of roughly similar age in the eastern portion along the Urals, yet in the limited materials which we possess from the similar kurgans of western Siberia, and in those of the Minusinsk region in the south, there is hardly a trace of it.  In America the distribution of the type makes it probable that it is of late rather than early appearance, coming in probably with the Alpine peoples.  Its total absence from China, Japan, and all southeastern Asia is further evidence of the lateness of its appearance in eastern Asia and of its relatively northern source.

TABLE 11

URAL TYPE

AVERAGE MEASUREMENTS AND INDICES

| Locality or Tribe | No. | L. | B. | H. | L. B. Ind. | L. H. Ind. | B. H. Ind. | Ns. L. | Ns. B. | Nas. Ind. | Bi-Zy. Dia. | Up. Fac. L. | Up. Fac. Ind. | Gnath. Ind. | Cap. |
|---|---|---|---|---|---|---|---|---|---|---|---|---|---|---|---|
| Valais (Switzerland).. | 9 | 185 | 154 | 125 | 83.2 | 67.4 | 81.1 | 51 | 22 | 43.7 | 139 | 70 | 49.7 | 97.9 | 1,563 |
| Tyrol | 18 | 181 | 148 | 124 | 82.7 | 68.3 | 83.5 | .. | .. | 44.8 | ... | .. | .... | .... | ..... |
| Morvan (France) | 12 | .. | .. | .. | 82.6 | 68.0 | 83.1 | .. | .. | 44.3 | ... | .. | 52.2 | 91.8 | ..... |
| North Sea | 7 | 185 | 151 | 125 | 82.8 | 67.7 | 82.4 | .. | .. | 43.2 | ... | .. | .... | .... | 1,451 |
| Basques | 2 | 191 | 155 | 132 | 81.9 | 69.1 | 84.9 | .. | .. | 44.4 | ... | .. | .... | .... | ..... |
| Mongols | 3 | 185 | 153 | 126 | 82.5 | 68.2 | 82.5 | .. | .. | 42.8 | ... | .. | .... | .... | ..... |
| Venezuela | 3 | 181 | 146 | 123 | 80.6 | 67.8 | 83.0 | 55 | 24 | 44.5 | 138 | .. | .... | 95.9 | 1,450 |

The number of crania in most of the series is very small, and the available data incomplete, but, so far as the material goes, it indicates at least as close a resemblance between widely separated groups as between the several European series.

The determination of the most probable focus of distribution of this type is difficult.  From its strength in the region near the Ural Mountains this area has much to recommend it, as has also the North Sea or Frisian region.  On the whole, perhaps the former has the greater probability, and it is possible that in its western movement it represents the so-called Arctic Culture, which seems to have been the earliest to reach the Baltic shores.

Having now completed our survey of the eight primary types and shown that there are good grounds for believing that each forms a definite and well-marked unit, so far as the fourteen measurements and indices employed are concerned, we are at last in a position to determine, from the slightly variant figures for each type, the mean and thus arrive at a generalized statement of the characteristics in these fourteen particulars of each type.

## TABLE 12

### THE EIGHT PRIMARY TYPES

#### AVERAGE MEASUREMENTS AND INDICES*

| Types | L. | B. | H. | L. B. Ind. | L. H. Ind. | B. H. Ind. | Ns. L. | Ns. B. | Nas. Ind. | Bi-Zy. Dia. | Up. Fac. L. | Up. Fac. Ind. | Gnath. Ind. | Cap. |
|---|---|---|---|---|---|---|---|---|---|---|---|---|---|---|
| Proto-Australoid | 190 | 132 | 128 | 69.5 | 67.5 | 93.0 | 48 | 27 | 56.2 | 131 | 67 | 51.7 | 100.6 | 1,363 |
| Proto-Negroid | 181 | 130 | 138 | 72.0 | 76.7 | 106.3 | 47 | 26 | 55.6 | 129 | 65 | 50.4 | 97.7 | 1,337 |
| Mediterranean | 190 | 135 | 129 | 71.1 | 68.0 | 95.6 | 53 | 23 | 43.3 | 130 | 71 | 55.2 | 95.1 | 1,428 |
| Caspian | 183 | 133 | 139 | 72.6 | 76.5 | 105.4 | 53 | 23 | 43.4 | 133 | 71 | 54.7 | 94.0 | 1,450 |
| Mongoloid | 180 | 150 | 123 | 83.5 | 68.2 | 82.3 | 50 | 26 | 53.5 | 136 | 66 | 50.7 | 98.8 | 1,407 |
| Palæ-Alpine | 178 | 146 | 136 | 84.5 | 78.5 | 92.9 | 48 | 26 | 54.6 | 132 | 64 | 49.3 | 97.8 | 1,428 |
| Ural | 183 | 151 | 124 | 82.5 | 68.0 | 82.7 | 52 | 23 | 44.1 | 137 | 70 | 52.7 | 93.9 | 1,491 |
| Alpine | 174 | 148 | 136 | 85.0 | 78.2 | 91.9 | 53 | 24 | 44.0 | 134 | 73 | 53.5 | 95.1 | 1,468 |

* Averages of all data, not averages of averages.

If we make allowances for the fact that the figures for the Ural type are based on too small a number of crania to be really reliable, we may translate the figures into the following descriptive table.

## TABLE 13

### CHARACTERS OF THE EIGHT PRIMARY TYPES

| Types | Head | Face | Nose | Prognathism | Capacity |
|---|---|---|---|---|---|
| Proto-Australoid | Long Low | Medium broad | Broad | Moderate | Small |
| Proto-Negroid | Long High | Medium broad | Broad | Moderate | Small |
| Mediterranean | Long Low | Narrow | Narrow | None | Large |
| Caspian | Long High | Narrow | Narrow | None | Large |
| Mongoloid | Round Low | Broad | Broad | Moderate | Medium |
| Palæ-Alpine | Round High | Broad | Broad | Moderate | Medium |
| Ural | Round Low | Medium | Narrow | None | (Largest) |
| Alpine | Round High | Medium | Narrow | None | Largest |

If the tables are examined it will be seen that the eight types may be grouped into four pairs, in which, so far as regards the size and proportions of the skull, they are alike, but are contrasted in the character of the face, nose, and capacity. Thus the Proto-Australoid and Mediterranean are alike long, low, and with the height standing in a medium relation to the width, but, whereas the former is moderately broad-faced, broad-nosed, with a tendency toward prognathism, and is of small brain size, the latter is narrow-faced, narrow-nosed, is clearly orthognathous and has a large brain. If, however, we arrange the types in relation not to the external dimensions or proportions of the skull itself, but on the basis of capacity (which is thus essentially that of brain size), a much more significant grouping appears, viz.: Proto-Australoid and Proto-Negroid, Mongoloid and Palæ-Alpine, Mediterranean and Caspian, and Ural and Alpine.

To some of the implications which such a grouping leads we shall revert later, but it is now time, after we have finally reached the point where a generalized description of each type has been attained, to answer the question as to what, after all, is the real nature of the types so defined. Are these "types," whose proportions and changes we have been following through-out the world and from the earliest times to the present, really "races"? In approaching the whole problem in the beginning, it was pointed out that physical anthropologists are not by any means yet agreed as to what are the true criteria of race, and that there is considerable doubt as to the real correlation of the various characteristics. For this reason we were led to select rather arbitrarily and by force of circumstances three particular criteria (the length-breadth and length-height indices of the skull and the nasal index), from which were derived what were assumed to be eight fundamental "types." The summary of the data given in the first part of the present chapter has led to the conclusion that, in respect to the criteria selected and the absolute measurements on which these indices are based, the types are on the whole clear-cut units. It has also been shown that with these units are associated further characters of facial form, degree of prognathism, and brain size (capacity); in other words, a real association of several of the most important characteristics has been established, and the conception of the "types" rests not upon three criteria whose relations were only assumed, but upon seven whose association seems to have been proved.

But the tables given in the first portion of this chapter have also proved another thing, *i. e.*, that these "types" are as a rule but scantily represented among the world's peoples, the vast majority of whom present not the characteristics of our pure types but of blends between them. If by the term "race" we mean to describe actually existing groups of people, as I think we should, then our "types" are certainly not "races," since, with few exceptions, there are no groups of men who actually represent them. Are the "types" then mere abstractions—have they no real existence? The answer is, I believe, both yes and no. They are abstractions in that they are theoretical forms, deducible from the existing varieties of men, among whom they are found in pure form as a rule in very small proportions only; but they are abstractions only in the sense that certain parent forms from which different animal species, or different linguistic elements are derived are abstractions; they do not now exist, no person has seen or heard them, but we are led none the less firmly to believe that at one time they must have existed. We may then, I believe, regard these "types" as, so to speak, archetypes, fundamental patterns, more or less perfectly evolved in the process of the development of the human species, and, like other animal varieties and species, having had a definite origin both in time and space. From the complex fusion between these archetypes, or fundamental races, modified by environment especially in outward characters of pigmentation, hair, etc., the existing, actual races which might be described as stable blends, have been derived. Here and there, in remote corners of the world, far removed from the great currents of migration, moderately pure remnants of these older, more original races still survive; as a rule, however, we may trace them only by an analysis of their blended forms, imbedded in which we may find nevertheless a few individuals who represent the ancient type.

We are thus led to the conclusion that the "types" whose distribution and hypothetical migrations we have, in the preceding pages, been attempting to trace, are not races in the ordinary sense of the term, and are not to be confounded with the many more or less clearly differentiated racial groups into which we may divide the peoples of the world to-day. These various living races are each the result of some particular combination of the original "types" or elements, and the difficulty which we find in deciding just how many races there are, is largely due to the fact that the elements have been blended so variously and in such varying proportions. Moreover, from this point of view, a race is not a permanent entity, something static; on the contrary it is dynamic, and is slowly developing and changing as the result of fresh increments of one or another of its original constituents or of some new one. There is not a race in all history that has remained permanently unchanged, although the rate and degree of change have varied. Some races have retained their fundamental characteristics for millennia with but slight modification, whereas others have, as a result of the incorporation of new factors, ceased to exist, because by virtue of such amalgamation they have become something else.

The acceptance of such an hypothesis, of the theory that the existing varieties of man are to be explained not as derived by differentiation from a single ancestral form, but as developed by amalgamation of the descendants of several quite discrete types, places us squarely in the ranks of the long discredited polygenists. But, quite apart from the results of the present inquiry, the whole trend of recent anthropological investigation, together with the archæological discoveries of the last decade, can have, it seems to me, no other outcome than the abandonment of the monogenist position and the frank acceptance of polygenism. For the archæological data have demonstrated that, as far back of the Neanderthaloids of early Palæolithic time as these are back of us, there existed men quite different from the Neanderthal type (or Proto-Australoid, from the point of view of the present theory), not primitive, not more ape-like, but comparable in most respects to the peoples of European type to-day. And, although as yet no actual human remains have been discovered, the presence of stone implements unquestionably of human manufacture, at Foxhall and Cromer in southeastern England, has at last, it seems, definitely proved the existence of

Tertiary man, and has opened up a vista not of scores but of hundreds of thousands of years for man's development and spread. In such vast lengths of time there is place for very far-reaching modifications to have taken place, yet these are, I cannot help thinking, far more likely to have affected the superficial rather than the actual structural portions of the body.

The monogenist may well reply to all this: "I grant you that we now have evidence of the existence in extremely early times of sharply differing varieties of man, but the greatly increased vista of the age of the human race gives ample time for these to have developed by gradual changes from a still older, let us say even a Miocene, ancestor. Why assume that your types ever had any actual existence? They are merely the end result of the differentiations undergone by the original ancestral form; they are ultimate and negligible variants rather than primitive discrete types." Such a statement, however, quite neglects to take into consideration a fact upon which much stress has throughout this book been laid, i. e., the peculiar geographical distribution of these supposed variants. If, as the monogenist would imply, man was distributed over the world in the beginning in a more or less generalized type, and has since gradually been modified in every possible direction, why should not these variants be scattered in a much more haphazard fashion than as a matter of fact they are? The actual present and past distribution of these "types" is intelligible on the basis that they represent the successive drifts of peoples marked by contrasted characteristics; it is, it seems to me, impossible of explanation on the theory of chance local variations. We must, to be sure, postulate an ultimate prototype from which all of the suggested "archetypes" were derived, but to my mind it is more in keeping with the whole trend of modern science to regard these as sharp variations from this prototype, arising in definite areas probably at different times, as in the case of other varieties and species in the animal and plant worlds. Thus we are led to assume that from the phylum which branched off from that of the anthropoid apes, a number of distinct types arose, just as among the anthropoids; and that just as the latter varieties and species spread from their several areas of characterization widely over the world, so did these originally distinct human forms. The degree of divergence in the human phylum was less great than in that of the apes, the separate varieties were fertile *inter se* and have blended and crossed in every imaginable fashion to produce the existing races of man.

In the present study we have been engaged in tracing the distribution and succession of what we have assumed to be certain fundamental types, conceived as originating at a very early date as human varieties, in the same fashion that varieties and species have arisen in other branches of the animal and plant worlds. In picturing their character and dispersion it must be remembered that, in common with varieties and species in the rest of nature, these types are subject to variation, and that only the mean of the oscillations is expressed in the abstract definition of the type. Thus, from the very first, the different groups representative of the several types were not strictly uniform, but consisted of a majority of individuals who completely conformed to the type, with a minority in whom it was expressed in slightly exaggerated or incomplete fashion. In their expansion and consequent contact and more or less complete amalgamation with other types, this lack of uniformity in the group would become more and more pronounced. Yet the increase in medial forms due to fusion of two or more types has in all probability been extremely slow, so that long after contact each group would preserve a core, as it were, of its original type.

We must conceive, therefore, of all the great drifts or migrations of peoples, except perhaps in the very earliest period, as those of actually very complex groups, in which as a rule one type and its closer variants were in large majority. The earlier the period at which such movements took place, the larger we may suppose the proportion of relatively pure types to have been. Yet as late as the proto-historic period of such migrations as that of the Hindu ancestors into India, or the historic expansion of the Slavs in Europe, of the Thai-speaking peoples in southeastern

Asia, of the Kirgiz and Yakut in Siberia, even of the Arabs in northern Africa, it is probable that the majority of the migrants were relatively pure in type. As to the nature of such movements, it is probable that most of them were slow, often almost imperceptible, drifts, rather than sudden and large-scale conquests, although the latter must sometimes have occurred. The possession by the immigrants or conquerors of great superiority in weapons or numbers of course favored a rapid replacement, such as, to take a recent example, the occupation of the New World by Europeans. Similar rapid and wholesale replacements may, however, well have occurred far in the past, for it may be doubted whether the advantage possessed by Europeans in the New World was any greater than that held by the first peoples armed with the bow over those as yet unacquainted with that weapon. So both by rapid conquest as well as by slow, glacier-like advance, or by imperceptible penetration, or as the result of flight before a conqueror, the various types have spread and interpenetrated.

This shifting and drifting of peoples, voluntary or involuntary, blind or purposeful, confined within narrow limits or extending beyond the borders of continents, forms as we look back upon the long history of the human race a very complex picture. Yet in the seeming chaos it seems possible to discern a few general tendencies, a few characteristics of the various types, which stand out in their struggles with one another; a dimly visible drama in which these types assume something, as it were, of personality.

Thus the types for which a tropical origin has been proposed, the Proto-Australoid and Proto-Negroid, have, with few exceptions, never ventured beyond the tropic lands, and when they did were usually forced to yield before other and more able types. In early Palæolithic times both penetrated into Europe, but went to the wall on the appearance of the Mediterranean and Caspian peoples. Some of the remnants, driven northward and absorbed by their conquerors, passed, much modified by their new environment, into the complex of the Baltic peoples, but elsewhere disappeared, leaving hardly a trace behind. In the New World, where their apparent presence is so surprising, with few exceptions the peoples showing the characteristics of these types were of low culture, generally marginal in distribution and largely extinct when Europeans came to the continent. One exception, however, is a paradox, for the Iroquois and southern Algonkian tribes were among the first of those north of Mexico in ability and prowess, and neither in outward appearance nor in culture betrayed what seem to be their actual affiliations. Not only have the Proto-Australoids and Proto-Negroids not been able to reach out and hold any considerable portions of the world outside the tropics, they have had to give ground within their own territory, and half of Africa, the whole of which they seem once to have held, very early passed out of their control. In the great struggle they have, almost from the beginning, been losers.

The Mongoloid and Palæ-Alpine types appear, as we have seen, to have been children of the great central Asiatic plateaus, at a time, perhaps, when these were less arid than they have been in historic times. Larger-brained, and tempered somewhat by a less tropical climate, they were dwellers in the open plains and mountains rather than the dense forest. The Mongoloids were perhaps the first of the plateau dwellers to spread, for we seem to find evidence that they reached western Europe in early Palæolithic times, and may possibly have crossed from Spain into northern Africa, whence some outposts, much mixed with Proto-Australoids, found their way or were driven far into the southern extremity of the continent. The rôlc of the Mongoloid, however, has from the first been a minor one, and they are to-day but an insignificant group. Their supposed African branch passed into oblivion and extinction, except for its survival as one of several factors in the disappearing Bushmen of the cape. The European group were wholly absorbed by the later Palæ-Alpines and Alpines, in the highland regions in which the Mongoloids seem to have taken refuge; only in the Lapps, on the extreme confines of the continent toward the north, can we recognize their survivors. The meteoric rise of the Mongoloids in historic times, led by the genius of Khengiz Khan, himself almost certainly in part of Caspian blood, was but a flash in the pan; the Mongols of history were at least half of Palæ-Alpine and Alpine strain. So far as one can see, the Mongoloid type has contributed little of value either to the sum of human achievements or to the blood of existing races. Quite otherwise, however, with the Palæ-Alpines. Like their probable Mongoloid predecessors, they passed into Europe, although at a much later date. They had there apparently to contend with the Caspian-Mediterranean folk who had come to occupy much of the land, and later with the Alpine peoples who followed from Asia on their heels. Of different mettle from the older Proto-Australoids and Proto-Negroids, they seem to have stubbornly contended for the control of the highland region, outside which their interests did not greatly extend. The increasing flood of Alpines coming from the east ultimately overwhelmed them, but, fusing with these later comers, they have contributed much to the people and the history of Europe. Here, however, the type has been overshadowed by the Alpine; in eastern Asia, and especially in the southeast, the Palæ-Alpines have had a better opportunity to show their character. Dominating after a struggle the older Proto-Australoid and Proto-Negroid peoples, and leavened by some infusion of Caspian and Mediterranean blood, they were capable of long and stubborn resistance to the rising power of the Alpines, the later phases of this struggle being perhaps seen in the conflicts between the early Chinese, as representatives of the latter, and the non-Chinese population south of the Yangtse River. With some addition of Caspian or Alpine factors, they were capable of the development of considerable states (Nan-chao, Cambodia, Siam, Burma, Modjopahit, etc.), or, with still larger Alpine elements, of the display of the considerable abilities of the ancient Turks. Something of these same characteristics and experiences seem to hold also in the New World, for in the region west of the Rocky Mountains, where the Palæ-Alpine type seems to be strongly concentrated, we find peoples of relatively backward culture, whereas in the southeast of the continent, where there is a larger Alpine element, the tribes show notably greater ability. If one were to venture to appraise these two types from the point of view of their value and contributions toward the complex of the whole human race, one would probably rate the Mongoloid low, while the Palæ-Alpine would rank as a type which by itself could claim no great achievements, but which, with some admixture of Caspian, Mediterranean, or Alpine factors, has made its mark in history, and one which has contributed in considerable measure to the developing complex of races.

Whereas the Proto-Australoid and Proto-Negroid types seem to have had their origin in the tropics, and the Mongoloid and Palæ-Alpine upon the great central Asiatic plateaus, the Caspian and Mediterranean types seem to be traceable to the Eur-Asiatic steppes surrounding the Caspian Sea and the regions adjacent to it, north of the plateaus. If the Proto-Australoid and Proto-Negroid types have been, except in the very earliest period, the most stay-at-home of types, the Caspian and Mediterranean, especially the former, have been of all the most adventurous. In late Palæolithic times spreading westward into Europe, and almost as early moving northeastward into America, in Neolithic times they forced their way across the eastern plateaus to the borderlands in China and Japan, and thence southward into Indonesia and far into the Pacific. Southward, also, across the eastern plateaus they made their way early into Arabia and northeastern Africa, driving from the whole northern part of the continent its older Negroid population, and infusing themselves along the East African plateau far to the south. Later yet they moved southward across the Iranian plateau to India. The Palæ-Alpines were on the whole content to be led; the Caspian and Mediterranean peoples were, on the other hand, leaders, the former perhaps, if one may venture so far in attempting an analysis, more in the affairs of the body, the latter in those of the mind. The Caspian was more a conqueror, the Mediterranean a thinker and artist. Each type had in it great latent possibilities, and when the two were blended, a people of great capability was the result. It was thus that, among a Mediterranean folk in whom

was a minority of Caspian, that the striking Minoan civilization
of Crete arose, out of which grew more or less directly and among
a largely kindred people the "glory that was Greece"; that, in
a population where the two elements were perhaps more equally
blended, there were evolved the great systems of Indian philoso-
phy, whose influence has been so profound upon all the Orient;
that among another people, mainly compounded of these same
factors, that most militant of religions, Islam, arose, whose adherents have carried it with fire and sword into Europe, throughout northern Africa, almost the whole of Asia, and far out into
the Pacific; and that in a related group of similar origin in Palestine we have the source of that faith which missionaries have
carried to every land.  Blended also of these two types, but with
considerable elements of the older Proto-Australoid and Proto-
Negroid were the Baltic peoples, that "Nordic" race which
wrecked the power of Rome, as their Caspian-Mediterranean
kindred, the Hyksos, had conquered Egypt, or the Kassites had
plundered Babylon, or the Persians had overthrown Assyria.
Lastly, in modern times, it was largely the adventurous daring,
the genius and the hardihood of these breeds which were responsible for the discovery, conquest, and colonization of America by
Europe, an event which, in the development of the human race
as a whole, was destined to be of great significance.

Singly or together, these types stand pre-eminent in the history of the Old World, yet, strangely enough, in the New they
can boast little in the way of achievement.  In South America
the Caspian type appears in any importance only among the
wretched and fast-dying tribes of the extreme south, while in
the northern continent it apparently forms the dominant element
only in the Eskimo.  It is hard to conceive of a greater contrast
to the forceful, conquering, intellectual peoples of this type in
the Old World, than the timid and simple Eskimo.  Is it not impossible that the one should be of common ancestry with the
other?  Have our criteria and analysis in this instance told the
truth?  It must be confessed that explanation of the failure of
the Caspian peoples in America to live up to the achievements

of their supposed kindred in Asia and Europe is difficult, although for the Eskimo a case can perhaps be made. For if, instead of the strongly favoring environments in which the Old World representatives of the type have lived, we substitute the poverty of that to which the Eskimos have, in historic times at least, been confined, we may have a partial answer. Yet we do not know that the Eskimo have always been held within the Arctic, and for the small groups of people of this type which reached the southern continent no claim of the repressive influence of environment can of course be made. The paradox therefore remains.

The Alpine type, both in the manner of its spread and in its character and history, forms an interesting contrast to all the others. The Caspian and Mediterranean peoples seem to have expanded, in many cases at least, rapidly by invasion and conquest. The Alpines, on the other hand, appear more commonly to have advanced slowly, more insidiously, but yet with the certainty of a glacier, and, latest to reach most portions of the world, they have had to contend against the peoples already in occupation. In Europe they are clearly the last comers, and perhaps this fact may have been one of the reasons why their first spread was apparently by sea along the shores. They came in strength only in Neolithic times, into a Europe held in the Highlands, we may suppose, mainly by Palæ-Alpine folk, elsewhere by Caspian and Mediterraneans. It was a formidable competition, yet, as we note in the archæological record the growing proportions, the wider and wider spread of the Alpine type, we seem to see the evidence that, in face of all resistance, they slowly but surely won. Their success was comparable, however, not so much to the rush of a great flood, sweeping all before it, as to the insidious and irresistible rising of the tide, which, although it may be swept back and held at bay at one point, eventually comes flooding in upon the defenders from behind. By the end of the Bronze or the beginning of the Iron Age the Alpine peoples had probably dominated the Highlands and largely incorporated the older Palæ-Alpines and remnants of the Mongoloids; they had come down into the valley of the Po in northern

Italy, held much of France, and had sent out an arm along the coast to southeastern Britain and the North Sea shores. Then came the great outpouring of the Baltic peoples, bursting through the encircling Alpines southward through France and Spain into Africa; across the Alps into Italy, where the population of Rome was already as fully Alpine as that of France; pouring into southern and eastern Britain. For a time the Alpines were thrown back upon themselves, but not for long. Within a few centuries Bavaria, the Rhine valley in Alsace, the Netherlands, and France were again in majority Alpine, while in the east the pressure of the Slav (whether or not originally akin to the Baltic peoples, now at least strongly Alpine) made itself increasingly felt; while from Asia new floods of Turkish-speaking Alpines and Palæ-Alpines poured into and through the Russian steppes. To-day, although no striking shifts of population have taken place in Europe for centuries, the Alpine type seems to be more or less strongly the dominant one throughout all but the western periphery of the continent.

In attempting to account for the progressive brachycephalization of Europe, in spite of the fact that no large movements of population had occurred there for nearly a thousand years, it was suggested that this change might have been brought about partly as the result of an insensible and unrecognized slow penetration of the dolichocephalic areas by the brachycephalic peoples of the Highlands and eastern Europe. But here and in the world at large, where we have found the process to be very widespread, another still more insidious and imperceptible influence may perhaps be at work. For, although we have as yet no clear evidence that when two distinct types are blended any simple Mendelian laws are in force, there are some indications in the recent work of Frets[1] that, when brachycephalic and dolichocephalic elements are blended, it is the former rather more than the latter which tend to reappear in the offspring. The data are still too incomplete and too limited to establish this even for the single European group; much less have the causes for this ap-

[1] Frets, 1921.

parent greater persistence of brachycephalic types been found. But in view of the evidence already available, we must admit the possibility that the brachycephalic types, and especially the Alpine, have some biological advantage over the dolichocephalic forms, which they thus would tend, in the long run, to dominate.

Just as they were the last to arrive in force in the west, so they were the latest comers in the East. Not much, if any, I believe, before the Bronze Age did they reach out across the plateaus to the eastern borderlands, where then they would appear to have repeated the history of their expansion in Europe. For, although the identification is still in the highest degree tentative, it is not improbable that in the expansion of the Chinese people, beginning so far as we know in the third or perhaps only in the early part of the second millennium B.C., we may see something of the last phase of the penetration of eastern Asia by the Alpines. As in Europe, the expansion was slow but sure, and here more than there associated directly with a definite culture type. The success was more rapid here, perhaps because of the fact that, in the main, the contest was with the Palæ-Alpine peoples, the Caspian and Mediterranean factors here being of course far smaller than in Europe, where they were once largely in the majority.

The great stream of Alpine peoples which found its way into America was again faced by the same fact—the land was occupied. Yet pressing southward through the open Plains the newcomers seem to have won their way, how slowly or rapidly we have as yet no means of knowing; thrusting aside to east and west, absorbing or pushing ahead of them, the less capable Palæ-Alpine folk who stood in their way, and so on through the narrow isthmus and along the Cordillera toward the south. In the New World, as in the Old, the peoples of this type have displayed striking ability, and to them seems to be attributable most of the higher achievements of the aboriginal American peoples. Without their influence the mainly Palæ-Alpine Shoshonean tribes of the basin area exhibit few evidences of cultural advance, but with strong admixture of Alpine elements we have

the development of the great Middle American civilization, and
the less advanced, but still striking cultures of the Cliff-Dwelling
and Pueblo peoples of the Southwest.  In South America again,
it was among peoples primarily of Alpine type that most of the
higher cultural developments of Peru took place, the coastal
tribes as well as the Inca being of this type.

In the eastern Asiatic borderlands we have seen that the
peoples of Alpine type drove southward at a relatively recent
date, and passed on out into the Pacific.  Once again, but at the
very dawn of history, peoples of the same type turned their faces
southward from the plateau and with far-reaching effect.  For
there is reason to think that the Sumerians, who were the founders
of the great civilization of Mesopotamia, belonged to this type,
and came down from the Iranian Plateau into the Tigris-Euphrates valley, whence they, or peoples affiliated with them, penetrated into southern Arabia, and thence in small numbers into
the valley of the Nile, into which at its mouth others of their
kin from Anatolia had come by way of the Syrian uplands in
earliest Dynastic times.  Lastly, we may note that it was possibly another branch of the peoples of Alpine type who, from the
Iranian Plateau, pressed southward along the western coasts of
India, leavening the mass of Proto-Australoids and Proto-Negroids, and leading to the development of the early Dravidian
culture, of whose beginnings and history we know as yet so little.

If, in the history of the race as a whole, the Mediterranean
and Caspian peoples have played a great part, that of the Alpines seems hardly less impressive; and there is not a little reason
to believe that only where these types have met and mingled
have the highest achievements been attained.  Perhaps the idea
is fanciful, certainly many, many other factors are likewise concerned, yet one may point to various cases in history which seem
to bear it out.  Thus Babylonian civilization grew out of the
blending of the supposedly Alpine Sumerian with the Mediterranean-Caspian Semitic peoples who seem long to have been
in occupation of the Mesopotamian plains; in Greece, before the
florescence of Hellenic culture, the earlier Mediterranean popu-

lation was reinforced by the immigration of the probably Alpine Dorians; Rome rose to greatness only after the older Mediterranean-Caspian people of Latium had been half dominated by Alpines coming southward from the valley of the Po and the region where the older Etruscan culture had its centre. In the East Chinese civilization had its rise in an area where strong Caspian elements were absorbed by the incoming Alpine folk; lastly, the marvellous development of modern European civilization has occurred in that region in which Alpine, Mediterranean, and Caspian have been more completely and evenly fused than elsewhere in the world. Is it perhaps more than mere coincidence that the reawakening of culture in Europe after the Dark Ages began at a time when, after a period of centuries during which wide shiftings of peoples had occurred, the new fusion of the elements had been begun? Is it mere chance that it was in the north of Italy, in Tuscany and the valley of the Po, where the influence of the Caspian-Mediterranean immigrants was strongest, that the Renaissance began; that in Germany it was in the south where the Baltic peoples had in large numbers blended with the older Alpine and Palæ-Alpines, rather than in the north where such amalgamation was less clear, that the revival of culture had its start; that many of the forerunners and leaders of the Reformation, such as Huss, Luther, Zwingli, Calvin, all came from regions where the fusion of types must have been vigorously going on? The complexity of the causes underlying all such great movements are, it need hardly be said, very great, yet I cannot but feel that, among the many potent factors which have determined or directed the rise of modern European civilization, this one of the fusion of Alpine with Mediterranean-Caspian elements has an important place. That the contact of two different peoples often produced a stimulating effect upon culture has of course often been noted; the point which I would make here is that this stimulation seems to be at its maximum when the peoples belong to the Alpine and to the Caspian or Mediterranean types. In the years before the war, Teutonic scholars were proving, to their own satisfaction, that most of the great names in the history of the European and Mediterranean world were those of men of Nordic race, and even Christ himself was claimed by some of the more daring as of "Germanic" blood. To no one race or type, however, can the palm be thus arrogantly assigned, rather to the product of the blending of those types which seem of all the most gifted—the Mediterranean-Caspian and the Alpine.

In the history of mankind there have been, from earliest times, many places, many occasions when amalgamations between two or more of the great fundamental types have occurred; and from these blendings, I am tempted to believe, have arisen again and again the cultures or civilizations which mark the progress of the race. From the fusions between types less dowered have come the feebler cultures; from those of types with larger, more richly endowed brains have come greater achievements; from those of the Alpine and Mediterranean types, whose brains in size surpass all the rest, have grown the greatest of them all.

On a previous page I said that the conquest and settlement of the New World by peoples from western Europe was an event of very great significance in the history of mankind. It was momentous from the standpoint of the history of the race, because in America, and later also in Australasia, there was thus opened to the complexly blended, most highly dowered representatives of the three most able types, who in the narrow confines of Europe were rapidly becoming cramped for room, literally a New World in which, but for the negligible opposition of the aboriginal occupants, they might be free, as never before, to achieve the fullest fusion. If we regard from this angle the history of the colonization and occupation of temperate North America, we see that never before have Alpine, Mediterranean, and Caspian folk been mingled upon such a gigantic scale, or with so much of great achievement behind them, with the limitless opportunities and untouched resources of a whole continent to call out their best endeavors. From our retrospect may we not in this see a prospect of a still nobler growth of all that makes for the best in man?

It is feared by some that in this new "melting-pot" the discrete elements are failing to fuse; that segregation rather than assimilation is taking place. Such fears come, I believe, from taking the short instead of the long view of human history; from the failure to realize sufficiently that any such process of assimilation must be slow. If nature counts her time in the making of new varieties and species by thousands and tens of thousands of years, why should we expect a vast fusion of this sort to be accomplished within a few generations? Two thousand years perhaps elapsed, from the time when the Alpine peoples began to blend with the older Mediterranean folk of Italy, before the composite population on the Tiber made the name of Rome feared and respected throughout the Mediterranean world and beyond; and many centuries of fusion were required after the period of the Völkerwanderung before some of its results became apparent in the Renaissance. The process of assimilation is doubtless, for many reasons, more rapid to-day than it was once, yet even so we can hardly hope to observe much progress within the space of a single life.

Two probable dangers there are, however, which we should do well to ponder and strive to avert so far as it is in our power, here in America and in the newer New World of Australasia. The interaction and assimilation of two different types require, it may be assumed, a certain quiet and lack of interference. If after the juxtaposition or interpenetration of the peoples has occurred, new increments of one or the other of the constituents continue on a large scale, the fusion is delayed, the adjustments being made continually upset, the conscious or unconscious rivalries upon which in a measure the results may depend disturbed. After the end of the Bronze Age with its far-reaching mingling of peoples, a long period of relative quiet seems to have ensued, preliminary to the great developments beginning in the Iron Age; since the period of the Völkerwanderung no great movements of population in western Europe have occurred. So in these new worlds into which the Old World has poured unstintingly of its best and bravest, an unrestricted immigration, which should admit year by year enormous numbers of newcomers, must tend, as it were, by the addition of great masses of cold ingredients, to lower in the "melting-pot" the temperature which is necessary to fusion.

The other danger, and undoubtedly the greater, is lest the quality of the alloy to be produced be weakened by the inclusion of other than the best ingredients. That there is a difference between the fundamental human types in quality, in intellectual capacity, in moral fibre, in all that makes or has made any people great, I believe to be true, despite what advocates of the uniformity of man may say. It is no answer to the charge that peoples of certain racial types have never unaided made their mark in history, to say that an unfavorable environment or stress of circumstances has prevented the great achievements of which they are theoretically capable. The mere fact that in all the thousands of years of recorded, and the tens of thousands of unrecorded history they have *not* risen superior to their environment, fought and battled their way out of it and into a better one—this fact alone is proof, to my mind, that they are less dowered with those qualities, the possession of which peoples of other types have proved, by doing again and again what the weaker peoples have failed to do.

In the past the great minglings and fusions of peoples took place largely either involuntarily and suddenly as the result of invasions and conquests, or almost imperceptibly, by a process of slow advance or infiltration. To-day in America or Australasia, wherever immigration on any large scale is taking place, the conditions are quite different, and conscious regulation of the process is possible. Does not the whole racial history of man which we have perhaps too rashly been trying to envisage here, point to the opportunity, I had almost said the duty, of those peoples in whose hands lies the direction of the latest and incomparably the greatest experiment in racial fusion, of seeing that its outcome shall exceed those of all the past? And this can only be done by conscious selection, selection both as to the types themselves and as to the quality of the type. Although, in the light of history, some types and their combinations into races stand out as evidently superior to others, this is not to deny that excellences are present among all. That neither the Proto-Australoid nor Proto-Negroid peoples by themselves have ever attained to greatness does not mean that they have not contributed anything to the progress of the human race. The elements of both, which seem to have been incorporated into the complex of the Baltic peoples, or in larger measure into that of the population of northern India, doubtless brought qualities the value of which has been considerable, if difficult to analyze and appraise. That the Palæ-Alpines by themselves seem never to have reached a plane comparable with that of the Mediterranean or Alpine peoples is not to deny that the strong admixture of the type in the central European population, or that of China, has added elements of very great value to the peoples so derived. Yet to make sure that from this newest, most tremendous fusion, the most perfect product shall result, can it be denied that we should seek to compound it mainly from the best?

And not only the best so far as race is concerned, but best in individual quality within the racial group, for that within the group there is a difference in quality is obvious. In the past, when racial mixture was so often brought about through invasion or conquest, a certain rough selection was exercised in this respect, in that in the arbitrament of war the weaklings were to some extent eliminated; if the fusion were the result of more peaceable migration, it was the bolder and hardier and abler spirits who dared to cross the ranges, the deserts, or the seas in search of new homes. To-day this more or less automatic process of selection exists but little, if at all; the strong and the weak, the healthy and the diseased, the genius and the moron may alike be transported in their thousands from one end of the world to the other. The diseased, the obviously defective can of course be in large measure detected, and may wisely be debarred, but how to the great remainder can something of that selection be applied which dangers and difficulties once afforded? Some tests may doubtless be of value, but it seems doubtful if any man-made substitute can fully compensate for the kind of natural selection which for uncounted ages has controlled in this respect the development of mankind.

Something has been said of late as to the fact that the peoples of "Nordic" race, to whom in quite Teutonic fashion all possible excellences are ascribed, are dwindling and losing in competition with the other peoples of Europe; and also in regard to the peril in which the white races, i. e., the western European peoples of blended Alpine, Mediterranean, and Caspian type, stand in the face of a great rising of the darker folk (derived from Proto-Australoid and Proto-Negroid sources), and the Asiatic Alpines and Palæ-Alpines, against their dominion. So far as regards the danger that the darker peoples may rise to take from the white races the dominion which they hold, I cannot feel any fear. Without the qualities which large admixture of Mediterranean, Caspian, or Alpine factors alone seem able to give, such an attempt could only, it seems to me, end in failure, whether the revolt were on an economic or any other basis. Where the "white" factors are actually in the majority or nearly so the issue might be more in doubt, but of such peoples there are too few seriously to menace the position of those who now stand in the lead. In the case of the "yellow" and "light-brown" peoples, who, if our analysis is correct, are, despite their color, derived from the same great fundamental types as the peoples of Europe, the danger is far greater. In them lie latent many of the qualities and abilities which have made European civilization what it is —not all, however, nor in so full a measure perhaps, yet enough, in the event of their full development, to force upon the peoples now and for so long dominant the most terrible struggle for supremacy they have ever had.

That the "Nordic" race, the result of the long blending in the Baltic lands of the remnants of the older Palæolithic folk with the Caspian and Mediterranean peoples during Neolithic times, is gradually passing from the stage would seem, from the evidence, to be only too true. But their passing is not a recent matter—it has been going on for thousands of years, and was already far advanced before the discovery of America. They have played their part, and it has been a great part, in the world's history. As a "race," as a complex of just these particular factors, in just this combination, it seems doomed in the end to be absorbed in the wider complex which has been forming ever since the Alpine peoples made their appearance in Europe. It is passing, just as the purer Mediterranean peoples are and for long have been passing, in the sense of sinking into the greater racial entity which has been so long in process of growth, and in which the Alpine type seems destined to play perhaps the leading part.

For the long survey of man's racial history which we have been making leads us, if I have read that history aright, to the conclusion that this is one wherein he has passed from an early condition of relative heterogeneity, through a long period of struggle in which gradually the better-dowered forms rose to dominance, to the present, in which the less able peoples have been practically exterminated by those who have risen to the top, and in which the world's population has become more homogeneous through this very elimination and through the long amalgamation of the originally discrete types. In this struggle with its resultant blendings up to the time of the discovery of America, the peoples primarily of Alpine type (though often blended with a considerable Palæ-Alpine factor) seem on the whole to have won. For they dominated already the larger part of Europe, by far the larger portion of Asia and the two Americas, as well as considerable areas in the Pacific. The opening of the New World brought in new complications. It meant much to the peoples of Mediterranean and Caspian type, as from their position on the western margin of Europe the chance came first to them to seize for themselves this great new territory. This they did, wresting it easily from the aboriginal occupants, who, although mainly of Alpine origin, were far less advanced than their remote kinsmen of the Old World. For three centuries or more the colonization and settlement of temperate North America by peoples from the west of Europe went on. And, although the French were in the main of Alpine and Palæ-Alpine type, the growing predominance of English-speaking settlers gave to the Mediterranean-Caspian group a clear majority, which was added to by the large Scandinavian element and slightly by those of German speech. Then rather suddenly, toward the close of the nineteenth century, the conditions changed; the influx of these types dwindled, while Alpine peoples from the east and southeast of Europe began to pour into the continent in an ever-increasing flood. As ages before in Europe, the Mediterranean and Caspian folk were first in the field and the Alpine peoples came late, so here again history seems to repeat itself, and the age-long struggle waged in Europe between these two great contending forces bids fair to be transplanted to a wider stage.

This struggle is not, however, a conscious one—it is masked and hidden under many disguises. For, although in earlier times the contest was more openly between groups of different racial types, to-day it is but occasionally to be glimpsed in the conflicts between those smaller groups in which, united by common traditions, common language, common culture, and common aspirations, individuals of diverse races have been welded together to form nations. While the actual process of amalgamation of types and races now takes place mainly within the nation, the fact that the discrete elements are thus strongly bound together by national ties, enormously complicates and greatly obscures the struggle between the two great opposing groups of the Alpines and Palæ-Alpines and the Mediterranean and Caspian peoples, in which it seems that the process of racial development has culminated not only in Europe but in the world at large. The unconscious opposition of these two groups is, as I say, masked by the facts of nationality, yet in the great conflict from which the world, and Europe in particular, has scarcely emerged the two gigantic adversaries loom dimly behind the scenes, for although, entangled in the net of nationality, peoples of both parties were fighting on each side, it still remains true that the Teutonic allies were preponderantly of the Alpine and Palæ-Alpine types, while against them at the last were arrayed the majority of all the Caspian-Mediterranean peoples of the world.

From the struggle between the two great types of peoples the tropical heart of Africa has been largely immune. The struggles between them have been and probably will be determined elsewhere, and in these, to them forbidden, regions the ancient Negroid peoples must long continue to survive. But for the rest of the world, if the theory here proposed be true, that the racial history of man is in final analysis that of the struggles for dominance among the descendents of differently dowered types, together with their gradual blending into an ever more homogeneous form, the answer to the riddle of the future would seem to be written in the past. The more primitive types and races, those least endowed, must tend to pass from the stage and merge into the complex of their victors, and among these amalgamation and absorption must continue to reduce more and more the remnants of the original types, until in the end, out of many types, through a multitude of races, may come one race, which will be the consummation of them all.

# BIBLIOGRAPHY

# BIBLIOGRAPHY

## ABBREVIATIONS

A. A. A. S.   Proceedings of the American Association for the Advancement of Science.

Aarb. Nord. Oldk. Hist.   Aarboger for Nordisk Oldkyndighed og Historie. Kjöbenhavn.

Abh. und Ber. K. Z. A. E. Mus. Dresden.   Abhandlungen und Berichte des Konigl. Zoologischen und Anthropologisch-Ethnographischen Museums zu Dresden.

Abh. K. Bayr. Akad. Wiss.   Abhandlungen der Königlich Bayerischen Akademie der Wissenschaften. München.

Abh. K. Pr. Akad. Wiss.   Abhandlungen der Königlich Preussischen Akademie der Wissenschaften. Berlin.

Abh. v. d. Senckb. Nat. Ges.   Abhandlungen herausgegeben von der Senckenbergischen Naturforschenden Gesellschaft. Frankfort am Main.

Amer. Anth.   American Anthropologist. (NS—New Series.)

An. Mus. La Plata   Anales del Museo de La Plata.

An. Mus. Nac. Hist. Nat. B. A.   Anales del Museo Nacional de Historia Natural de Buenos Aires.

An. Soc. Esp. Hist. Nat.   Anales de la Sociedad Española de Historia Natural. Madrid.

Anth. Papers A. M. N. H.   Anthropological Papers, American Museum of Natural History. New York.

Arch. p. Ant. e Etn.   Archivio per l'Antropologia e la Etnologia. Firenze.

Arch. f. Anth.   Archiv für Anthropologie. Braunschweig.

Arch. Mus. Nac. R. J.   Archivos do Museu Nacional do Rio de Janeiro.

Atti Accad. Sci. Ven-Tren-Istr.   Atti della Accademia Scientifica Veneto-Trentino-Istriana. Padova.

Atti Soc. Rom. Ant.   Atti della Società Romana di Antropologia.

Atti Soc. Ven-Tren-Istr. Sc. Nat.   Atti della Società Veneto-Trentino-Istriana di Scienze Naturali. Padova.

B. A. A. S.   Reports of the British Association for the Advancement of Science.

Bull. A. M. N. H.   Bulletin, American Museum of Natural History. New York.

Bull. B. A. Ē.   Bulletin, Bureau of American Ethnology. Washington.

Bull. Mem. Soc. Anth. Brux.   Bulletins et Mémoires de la Société d'Anthropologie de Bruxelles.

| | |
|---|---|
| Bull. Mem. Soc. Anth. Paris. | Bulletins et Mémoires de la Société d'Anthropologie de Paris. |
| Bull. Soc. Anth. Brux. | Bulletins de la Société d'Anthropologie de Bruxelles. |
| Bull. Soc. Anth. Lyon. | Bulletins de la Société d'Anthropologie de Lyon. |
| Bull. Soc. Anth. Paris. | Bulletins de la Société d'Anthropologie de Paris. |
| Bull. Soc. Geog. Neuch. | Bulletins de la Société Neuchateloise de Geographie. |
| Field Mus. | Anthropological Series (Field Columbian Museum), Field Museum of Natural History. Chicago. |
| Forh. Videns. Christiania | Forhandlingar Videnskabsselskabets i Christiania. |
| Int. Cong. Amer. | International Congress of Americanists. |
| Int. Cong. Anth. | Congrés internationale d'Anthropologie et d'Archæologie préhistorique. |
| Izv. Imp. Obsh. Liub. Est. | Izviestiya Imperatorskago Obshchestva Liubitelei Estestvoznaniya, Antropologii i Etnografii. Moscow. |
| J. A. I. | Journal of the Royal Anthropological Institute of Great Britain and Ireland. London. |
| Journ. Acad. Nat. Sci. Phila. | Journal of the Academy of Natural Sciences of Philadelphia. |
| Journ. Amer. Eth. Arch. | Journal of American Ethnology and Archæology. Boston. |
| Journ. Anat. and Phys. | Journal of Anatomy and Physiology. London. |
| Journ. Anth. Soc. Bombay. | Journal of the Anthropological Society of Bombay. |
| Journ. As. Soc. Bengal. | Journal of the Asiatic Society of Bengal. Calcutta. |
| Journ. Coll. Sci. Imp. Jap. Univ. | Journal of the College of Science, Imperial Japanese University, Tokyo. |
| K.-Bl. D. Ges. Anth. | Korrespondenz-Blatt der Deutschen Gesellschaft für Anthropologie, Ethnologie und Urgeschichte. Braunschweig. |
| Mat. Ant. Arch. Etn. Akad. Umiej. Krakow. | Materialy antropologiczno-archeologiczne i etnograficzne. Wydawane Staraniem Komisyi Antropologicznej Akademii Umiejetnosci w Krakowie. |
| Medd. Danm. Ant. | Meddelelser om Danmarks Antropologi. Udgivet af den Antropologiske Komite. Kjöbenhavn. |
| Medd. om Grönland. | Meddelelser om Grönland. Kjöbenhavn. |
| Mem. Acad. Sci. St. P. | Mémoires de l'Academie Imperiale des Sciences de St. Petersbourg. |
| Mem. Amer. Anth. Assoc. | Memoirs of the American Anthropological Association. |
| Mem. A. M. N. H. | Memoirs of the American Museum of Natural History. New York. |
| Mem. Bishop Mus. | Memoirs of the Bernice Pauahi Bishop Museum. Honolulu. |
| Mem. Soc. Anth. Paris. | Mémoires de la Société d'Anthropologie de Paris. |

| | |
|---|---|
| Mitt. Anth. Ges. Wien. | Mitteilungen der Anthropologischen Gesellschaft in Wien. |
| Mitt. D. Ges. Nat. Völk. Ostasiens. | Mitteilungen der Deutschen Gesellschaft für Natur- und Völkerkunde Ostasiens. Yokohama. |
| Mitt. Med. Fac. Imp. Jap. Univ. | Mittheilungen aus der medikalische Facultät der Kaiserliche Universität. Tokyo. |
| Mitt. Mus. Völk. Hamburg. | Mitteilungen aus dem Museum für Völkerkunde in Hamburg. |
| Monatsb. K. Pr. Akad. | Monatsbericht der Königlich Preussischen Akademie der Wissenschaften. Berlin. |
| Nat. Tijd. Ned. Ind. | Natuurkundig Tijdschrift voor Nederlandsch Indie. Batavia. |
| Papers P. M. | Papers of the Peabody Museum of American Archæology and Ethnology, Harvard University. Cambridge. |
| Phil. Journ. Sci. | Philippine Journal of Science. Manila. |
| Proc. Amer. Phil. Soc. | Proceedings of the American Philosophical Society. Philadelphia. |
| Proc. Roy. Soc. Edinb. | Proceedings of the Royal Society of Edinburgh. |
| Rep. Arch. Res. Coll. Lit. Imp. Univ. Kyoto. | Reports upon Archæological Researches in the College of Literature, Kyoto Imperial University. |
| Rep. B. A. E. | Reports, Bureau of American Ethnology. Washington. |
| Rep. P. M. | Reports of the Peabody Museum of American Archæology and Ethnology, Harvard University. Cambridge. |
| Rev. Anth. | Revue Anthropologique. Paris. (Continuation after 1911 of Rev. Ec. d'Anth.) |
| Rev. d'Anth. | Revue d'Anthropologie. Paris. |
| Rev. Ec. d'Anth. | Revue de l'École d'Anthropologie de Paris. |
| Rev. Mus. La Plata. | Revista del Museo de La Plata. |
| Riv. di Ant. | Rivista di Antropologia. Rome. (Continuation after 1911 of Atti Soc. Rom. Ant.) |
| Russ. Anth. Journ. | Russkii Antropologicheskii Zhurnal. Izdanie Antropologicheskago Otdiela Imperatorskago Obshchestva Liubitelei Estestvoznaniya, Antropologii i Etnografii sostoyashchago pri Moskovskom Universitetie. Moskow. |
| Sitzb. Anth. Ges. Wien. | Sitzungsberichte der Anthropologische Gesellschaft in Wien. |
| Sitzb. K. Akad. Wiss. | Sitzungsberichte der Kaiserlichen Akademie der Wissenschaften in Wien. |
| Sitzb. K. Pr. Akad. | Sitzungsberichte der Königlich Preussischen Akademie der Wissenschaften. Berlin. |
| Skrifter Videns. Christiania. | Skrifter Videnskabsselskabets i Christiania. |

Trans. B. and G. Arch. Soc.    Transactions of the Bristol and Gloucester Archæological Society. Bristol.

Trans. Roy. Soc. Edinb.    Transactions of the Royal Society of Edinburgh.

Trans. Roy. Soc. Vict.    Transactions of the Royal Society of Victoria. Melbourne.

U. C. Pub. Am. Arch. Eth.    University of California. Publications in American Archæology and Ethnology. Berkeley.

V. B. G.    Verhandlungen der Berliner Gesellschaft für Anthropologie, Ethnologie und Urgeschichte. Berlin.

Verh. K. Akad. Wett. Amst.    Verhandlingen der Koniglijke Akademie van Wettenschappen. Amsterdam.

Veröff. K. Mus. Völk.    Veröffentlichungen aus dem Königlichen Museum für Völkerkunde zu Berlin.

Zeitsch. f. Ethn.    Zeitschrift für Ethnologie. Berlin.

Zeitsch. f. Morph. und Anth.    Zeitschrift für Morphologie und Anthropologie. Stuttgart.

## BIBLIOGRAPHY

1907    ABRAMOV, A. N.    Bashkiri. Russ. Anth. Journ., VII, nos. 3–4, pp. 1–56.

1896    ALLEN, H.    Crania from the Mounds of the St. Johns River, Florida. Journ. Acad. Nat. Sci., Phila. (New Series), X, no. 4, pp. 367–448.

1898    "    A Study of Hawaiian Skulls. Trans. Wagner Free Institute of Science, Philadelphia, vol. V, pp. 11–55.

1880–81    AMEGHINO, F.    La antiguedad del Hombre en La Plata. 2 vols. Paris-Buenos Aires, 1880–1881.

1899    AMMON, O.    Zur Anthropologie der Badener. Jena, 1899.

   A. M. N. H.    American Museum of Natural History, New York. Collection of crania.

1903    ANNANDALE, N., and ROBINSON, H. C. Fasciculi Malayensis. London, 1903.

   A. N. S. P.    Academy of Natural Sciences of Philadelphia. Collection of crania.

   ANTHROPOLOGISCHEN SAMMLUNGEN DEUTSCHLANDS (DIE). Issued as Supplements to the Archiv für Anthropologie. 1877–98.

1889    ARANZADI Y UNAMUNO, T. DE. El Pueblo Euskalduna. Estudio de Antropologia, San Sebastian, 1889.

1914    "    Sur quelques correlations du trou occipital des crânes Basques. Bull. Mem. Soc. Anth., Paris. 6th ser., vol. V, pp. 325–382.

1904    ARBO, C. O. E.    Fortsatte Bidrag til Nordmaendenes Anthropologi. Videnskabsselskabets Skrifter Christiania. Math-Nat. Klasse, 1904, no. 5, pp. 1-112.

ARCHÆOLOGICAL SURVEY OF NUBIA. Survey Department, Ministry of Finance, Cairo. Especially, Report for 1907-08, II, Report on the Human Remains. G. Elliot Smith and F. W. Jones.

1854 ARNDT, J. W. E. Afmetingen van schedels van inboorlingen van Java enz. Nat. Tijd. Ned. Ind., vol. VI, pp. 215-222.

1902 ARUTINOV, A. A. K antropologii Aisorov. Russ. Anth. Journ., vol. III, no. 4, pp. 88-100.

1905 " Udini. Izv. Imp. Obsh. Lyub. Est., vol. CVI, pp. 1-134.

1900 ASMUS, R. Die Schädelform der altwendischen Bevölkerung Mecklenburgs. Arch. f. Anth., vol. XXVII, pp. 1-36.

1897 BACA, F. M. Estudio craneometrico Zapoteca. XIth Int. Cong. Amer. Mexico, 1895, pp. 237-264.

1881-85 BAELZ, E. Die körperlichen Eigenschaften der Japaner. Mitt. D. Ges. Nat. Völk. Ostasiens, vol. III, pt. XXVIII, pp. 330-359; vol. IV, pt. XXXII, pp. 35-110.

1911 " Die Riukiu Insulaner. K.-Bl. D. Ges. Anth., vol. XLII, pp. 187-191.

1879 BAER, G. A. Negritoschädeln von den Philippinen, V. B. G., vol. XI, pp. 331-334.

1914 BARGE, J. A. J. Beiträge zur Kenntniss der niederländischen Anthropologie, Zeit. f. Morph. und Anth., vol. XVI, pp. 329-396; 465-521.

1910 BARROWS, D. P. The Negrito and allied types in the Philippines. Am. Anth. (NS) vol. XII, pp. 358-376.

1904 BARTELS, P. Ueber Schädel der Steinzeit und der früheren Bronzezeit aus der Umgegend von Worms a. R. Zeit. f. Eth., vol. XXXVI, pp. 891-897.

1896 BARTH, J. Norronaskaller. Crania antiqua in parte orientali Norwegiae meridionalis inventa. Christiania, 1896.

1900 BAUER, F. Schädel von den Philippinen. Arch. f. Anth., vol. XXVII, pp. 107-117.

1915 BAUER, L. Beiträge zur Kraniologie der Baining (Neu Pommern). Arch. f. Anth., vol. XLII, pp. 145-203.

1908 BEAN, R. B. The Benguet Igorots. A somatological study of the live folk of Benguet and Lepanto Bontoc. Phil. Journ. Sci., vol. III, pp. 413-473.

1909a " Philippine types. Manila students. Phil. Journ. Sci., vol. IV, pp. 263-297.

1909*b*    BEAN, J. R.    Philippine types found in the Malecon morgue. Phil. Journ. Sci., vol. IV, pp. 297–338.

1909*c*    "    Philippine types. Racial anatomy of Taytay. Phil. Journ. Sci., vol. IV, 359–447.

1910*a*    "    (The same, continued.) Phil. Journ. Sci., vol. V, pp. 1–27.

1910*b*    "    Types of Negritos in the Philippine Islands. Am. Anth. (NS), vol. XII, pp. 220–236.

1910*c*    "    Philippine types. Am. Anth. (NS), vol. XII, pp. 377–391.

1911    "    The men of Cainta. Phil. Journ. Sci., vol. VI, pp. 7–17.

1913    "    Types among the inland tribes of Luzon and Mindanao. Phil. Journ. Sci., vol. VIII, pp. 455–460.

1878–79    BEDDOE, J.    On certain crania disinterred at St. Werburghs Church, Bristol. Trans. B. and G. Arch. Soc., vol. III, pp. 79–82.

1881–82*a*    "    Remarks on some skeletons found at Gloucester. Trans. B. and G. Arch. Soc., vol. VI, pp. 349–352.

1881–82*b*    "    Remarks on a collection of skulls in a vault under the church of Micheldean. Trans. B. and G. Arch. Soc., vol. VI, pp. 353–355.

1908    "    A last contribution to Scottish ethnography. J. A. I., vol. XXXVIII, pp. 212–221.

1910–11    BENNINGTON, R. C.    A study of the Negro skull with special reference to the Congo and Gaboon crania. Biometrika, vol. VIII, pp. 292–340.

1909    BERRY, R. J. A. and ROBERTSON, A. W. D. Dioptrographic tracings in four normæ of fifty-two Tasmanian crania. Trans. Roy. Soc. Vict., vol. V, pt. I, pp. 1–11.

1910    "    A biometrical study of the relative degree of purity of race of the Tasmanian, Australian and Papuan. Trans. Roy. Soc. Edinb., vol. XXXI, pp. 17–40.

1914    "    Dioptrographic tracings in three normæ of ninety Australian aboriginal crania. Trans. Roy. Soc. Vict., vol. VI.

1892    BERTHOLON, L.    Documents anthropologiques sur les Phœniciens. Bull. Soc. Anth. Lyon, vol. XI, pp. 179–224.

1912–13    BERTHOLON, L., and CHANTRE, E.    Recherches anthropologiques dans la Berberie Orientale. Tripolitana, Tunisie, Algerie. 2 vols. Lyons, 1912–1913.

1875    BESSELS, E.    Einige Worte über die Innuit (Eskimo) des Smith-Sundes, nebst Bemerkungen über Innuit-Schädel. Arch. f. Anth., vol. VIII, pp. 107-122.

1905    BIASUTI, R.    Crania Ægyptica. Esame di 42 crani di Egiziani antichi. Arch. p. Ant. e. Eth., vol. XXXV, pp. 322-362.

1917    BICKEL, B.    Einige indonesische Schädel der R. Virchow Sammlung. Zeit. f. Ethn., vol. XLIX, pp. 89-108.

1912    BLAGOVIESHCHENSKII, V. A.    Kratkaya zamietka po antropometrii Ferganskago naseleniya. Russ. Anth. Journ., vol. VIII, no. 4, pp. 76-80.

1851    BLEEKER, P.    Afmetingen van schedels van imboorlingen van Java enz. Nat. Tijd. Ned. Ind., vol. II, pp. 498-520.

   BOAS, F.    Measurements of Indians taken for the World's Columbian Exposition, Chicago, 1892. MS.

1889    "    First General Report on the Indians of British Columbia. Physical characteristics. B. A. A. S., 1889, pp. 807-815.

1890    "    Schädelformen von Vancouver Island. V. B. G., vol. XXII, pp. 29-31.

1891    "    Third Report on the Indians of British Columbia. B. A. A. S., 1891, pp. 424-447.

1895    "    Fifth Report on the Indians of British Columbia. B. A. A. S., 1895, pp. 524-551.

1896    "    Anthropological observations on the Mission Indians of Southern California. A. A. A. S., vol. XLIV, pp. 261-270.

1901    "    A. J. Stone's measurements of natives of the Northwest Territories. Bull. A. M. N. H., vol. XIV, pp. 53-68.

1903    "    [Measurements of crania] In;—Smith, H. I. Shell-heaps of the Lower Fraser River. Mem. A. M. N. H. (Anthropology), III, no. IV, pp. 189-190.

1905a    "    Anthropometry of Central California. Bull. A. M. N. H., vol. XVII, pp. 347-380.

1905b    "    The Jessup North Pacific Expedition XIIIth Int. Cong. Amer., New York, 1905, pp. 91-101.

1898    BOAS, F., and FARRAND, L. Physical characteristics of the tribes of British Columbia. B. A. A. S., 1898, pp. 628-644.

1878-79a    BOGDANOV, A. P.    Kurgannye cherepa Tarskago okruga, Tobolskoi gubernii. Izv. Imp. Obsh. Lyub. Est., vol. XXXI, cols. 263-273.

1878-79*b* BODGANOV, A. P.    Cherepa Samoiedov.  Izv. Imp. Obsh. Lyub.
                             Est., vol. XXXI, cols. 381-387.

1878-79*c*    "            Yakutskie cherepa.  Izv. Imp. Obsh. Lyub. Est.,
                             vol. XXXI, cols. 401-403.

1878-79*d*    "            Cherepa Koreïtsev.  Izv. Imp. Obsh. Lyub. Est.,
                             vol. XXXI, cols. 405-407.

1878-79*e*    "            Ostyatskie cherepa.  Izv. Imp. Obsh. Lyub.
                             Est., vol. XXXI, cols. 408-411.

1878-79*f*    "            Cherepa Gilyaka.  Izv. Imp. Obsh. Lyub. Est.,
                             vol. XXXI, cols. 411-413.

1878-79*g*    "            Cherepa Buryatskie, Cherep Mongolskiĭ, vol.
                             XXXI, cols. 413-417.

1878-79*h*    "            Tunguskie cherepa.  Izv. Imp. Obsh. Lyub.
                             Est., vol. XXXI, cols. 418-420.

1879          "            Zhiteli drevnikh Bolgar po kraniologicheskim
                             priznakam. Izv. Imp. Obsh. Lyub. Est., vol.
                             XXXV, cols. 363-377.

1882          "            O cherep iz Kavkazskikh dolmenov i o cherepakh
                             iz Kavkazskikh kurgannov i mogil. Izv. Imp.
                             Obsh. Lyub. Est., vol. XXXV, cols. 419-434.

1886-87*a*    "            O cherepakh liudeï kamennago vieka naidennykh
                             do sego v Rossii. Izv. Imp. Obsh. Lyub. Est.,
                             vol. XLIX, cols. 102-108.

1886-87*b*    "            O cherepakh iz Krimskikh mogil, Khersonesa i
                             Inkermann i iz kurganov Voiska Donskago.
                             Izv. Imp. Obsh. Lyub. Est., vol. XLIX, cols.
                             123-146.

1886-87*c*    "            Kraniologicheskiya zamietki otnositelno tur-
                             kestanskago narodonaseleniya.  Izv. Imp.
                             Obsh. Lyub. Est., vol. XLIX, cols. 238-287.

1886-87*d*    "            Cherepa plemen Galcha . . . iz Falgor i drevn-
                             yago kladbishcha Zarafshana. Izv. Imp. Obsh.
                             Lyub. Est., vol. XLIX, cols. 507-520.

1888          "            Antropometricheskiya zamietki otnositelno tur-
                             kestanskikh inorodtsev.  Izv. Imp. Obsh.
                             Lyub. Est., vol. XXXIV, pt. V, cols. 1-92.

1908       BOLK, L.        De bevolking van Niederland in hare anthro-
                             pologische sammenstelling.  In:-Galee, Het
                             boerenhuis in Nederland en zijne bewohners.
                             Utrecht, 1908.

1885-86 BONAPARTE, PRINCE R. The Lapps of Finmark.  J. A. I., vol. XV,
                             pp. 210-213.

1913       BOUILLIEZ, M.   Notes sur les populations Goranes.  L'Anth.,
                             vol. XXIV, pp. 399-418.

1879       BRETON          Sur les mensurations du 15 femmes et de 53
                             hommes Tonkinoises.  Bull. Soc. Anth.,
                             Paris. 3d series, vol. II, pp. 592-597.

1912    BREUIL, ABBÉ H.    Les subdivision du palæolithique supérieur et leur signification. Congrés Internationale d'Anthropologie et d'Archæologie préhistorique. Compte Rendu XIV* Session. Geneve, 1912, pp. 165–238.

1875    BROCA, P.    Sur deux series de crânes provenant d'anciens sepultures indiennes dcs environs de Bogota. 1st Int. Cong. Amer. Nancy, 1875, pp. 367–382. (Also in Bull. Soc. Anth., Paris, 2d series, vol. XI, pp. 359–373.)

1913    VAN DEN BROEK, A. J. P.    Ueber Pygmäen in niederländisch Süd Neu Guinea. Zeit. f. Eth., vol. XLV, pp. 23–44.

1915a    "    Untersuchungen an Schädeln aus niederländisch Südwest Neu Guinea. In:-van der Sande, J. A. Nova Guinea: Résultats de l'Expedition scientifique Neerlandaise a la Nouvelle Guince en 1903, vol. VII, pt. II, pp. 163–232.

1915b    "    Zur Anthropologie des Bergstammes Peseschem im Innern von niederländisch Neu Guinea. Ibid., pp. 234–276.

1918    "    Das Skelet eines Peseschem. Ein Beitrag zur Anthropologie der Papuanen von niederländisch Neu Guinea. Ibid., pt. III, pp. 281–353.

1918    BROOM, R.    The evidence afforded by the Boskop Skull of a new species of primitive man. (Homo capensis.) Anth. Papers, A. M. N. H., vol. XXIII, pt. II, pp. 67–79.

1913    BURSTON, R.    Records of the anthropometric measurements of one hundred and two Australian Aboriginals. Bulletin no. 7, of the Northern Territory of Australia. Melbourne, 1913.

1871–72    BUSK, G.    Notes on human remains from Palmyra. J. A. I., vol. I, p. 312.

1874–75    "    Notes of some skulls from Palmyra. J. A. I., vol. IV, pp. 366–367.

1875–76    "    Description of two Beothuc skulls. J. A. I., vol. V, pp. 230–233.

1920    BUXTON, L. H. D.    The Anthropology of Cyprus. J. A. I., vol. L, pp. 183–235.

1909    CANTACUZÈNE, G.    Contribution à la craniologie des Etrusques. L'Anthropologie, vol. XX, pp. 329–352.

1905–08    CARDOSO, F.    O poveiro. Estudo anthropologico dos pescadores da Povoa de Varzim. Portugalia, vol. II, pp. 517–539.

1881    CAUVIN, C. V.    Rapport sur les mensurations et les caracteres morphologiques d'une serie de crânes australiens. Archives des Missions Scientifiques et Litteraries, serie, 3, vol. VII, pp. 91–211. Paris.

1897–98   CHALMERS, J.   Anthropometrical observations on some natives of the Papuan Gulf. J. A. I., vol. XXVII, pp. 335–342.

1892   CHAMBERLAIN, A. F.   Report on the Kootenay Indians of Southeast British Columbia. B. A. A. S., 1892, pp. 549–614.

1913   "   Linguistic stocks of the South American Indians with a distribution map. Amer. Anth. (NS), vol. XV, pp. 236–247.

1916   CHANDA, R.   The Indo-Aryan Race. A study of the origin of Indo-Aryan people and institutions. Rajshahi, 1916.

1882   CHANTRE, E.   Aperçu sur les caracteres ethniques des Ansaries et des Kurdes. Bull. Soc. Anth. Lyon, vol. I, pp. 165–185.

1885–87   "   Recherches anthropologiques dans le Caucase. 4 vols. Paris, 1885–1887.

1892a   "   Recherches anthropologiques sur les Tatars aderbeidjanais de Transcaucasie ou Turkomans iranisés. Bull. Soc. Anth. Lyon, vol. XI, pp. 28–44.

1892b   "   Rapport sur une mission scientifique en Arménie russe. Nouvelles Archives des Missions Scientifiques, vol. III, pp. 1–48. Paris, 1892.

1895a   "   Observations anthropometriques sur les Bakhtiari, les Mamaceni et les Rusteni. Bull. Soc. Anth., Lyon, vol. XIV, pp. 26–29.

1895b   "   Recherches anthropologiques dans l'Asie Occidentale. Missions Scientifiques en Transcaucasie, Asie Mineure et Syrie, 1890–1894. Archives du Museum d'Histoire Naturelle, Lyon, vol. VI, pp. 1–250.

1895c   "   Observations anthropologiques sur les Metouali. Bull. Soc. Anth. Lyon, vol. XIV, pp. 58–61.

1904   "   Recherches anthropologiques en Egypte. Lyon, 1904.

1892   CHARLES, R. H.   Notes on the craniometry of some of the outcast tribes of the Panjab. Journ. Anat. and Phys., vol. XXVI, pp. 1–25.

1893   "   Contributions to the craniology and craniometry of Panjab tribes. Journ. Anat. and Phys., vol. XXVII, pp. 1–20.

1907–08   CHERVIN, A.   Anthropologie Bolivienne. 3 vols. Paris, 1907–1908.

1909 CHRISTIE, E. B. The Subanuns of Sindangan Bay. Ethnological Publications, Bureau of Science, Manila, vol. VI, no. 1.

1892 COLLIGNON, R. Crânes de la nécropole phœnicienne de Mahedia (Tunisie). L'Anthropologie, vol. III, pp. 163–173.

1895 " Anthropologie du sud-ouest de la France. Les Basques. Mem. Soc. Anth., Paris, 3d series, vol. I, pt. IV, pp. 1–64.

1911–12 CRAIG, J. S. Anthropometry of modern Egyptians. Biometrika, vol. VIII, pp. 66–79.

1892 DANIELLI, J. Studio sui crani Bengalesi con appunti d'etnologia Indiana. Arch. p. Ant. e Etn., vol. XXII, pp. 291–341; 371–448.

1893 " Crani et ossa lunghe di abitanti dell'isola d'Engano. Arch. p. Ant. e Etn., vol. XXIII, pp. 401–433.

1894 DANILOV, N. P. K kharakteristikie antropologicheskikh i fiziologicheskikh chert sovremennago naseleniya Persii. Izv. Imp. Obsh. Lyub. Est., vol. LXXXVIII, cols. 1–147.

1903 DAVIDSON, J. W. The Island of Formosa, Past and Present. London, 1903.

1910 DÉCHELETTE, J. Manuel d'archéologie préhistorique, celtique et gallo-romaine, vol. II, Paris, 1910.

1889 DENIKER, J. Les Hottentots au Jardin d'Acclimatation. Rev. d'Anth. 3d series, vol. IV, pp. 1–27.

1891 " Anthropologie, In:–Hyades P. Mission Scientifique du Cap Horn, vol. VII. Paris, 1891.

1890 " and LALOY Les races exotiques. L'Anthropologie, vol. I, pp. 513–546.

1907 " and BONIFACY. Les Annamites et les Cambodgiens. Bull. Mem. Soc. Anth., Paris, 5th series, vol. VIII, pp. 106–115.

DIXON, R. B. Measurements of ninety Burusheski. MS.

1920 " A new theory of Polynesian origins. Proc. Amer. Phil. Soc., vol. LIX, pp. 261–267.

1922 " The Khasi and the racial history of Assam. Man in India, vol. II, pp. 1–13.

1908 DJAVAKOV, A. N. Antropologiya Gruzii. Izv. Imp. Obsh. Lyub. Est., vol. CXVI, cols. 1–306.

1913 " Kaykazskie Evrei. Russ. Anth. Journ., vol. VIII, no. 4, pp. 57–76.

1895 DORSEY, G. A. Crania from the necropolis of Ancon, Peru. A. A. A. S., vol. XLIII, pp. 358–369.

1897 " Observations on a collection of Papuan crania. Field Mus., II, no. 1, pp. 1–39.

1913    DRONTSCHILOV, K.    Metrische Studien an 93 Schädel aus Kamerun. Arch. f. Ant., vol. XL, pp. 161–183.

1893–94    DUCKWORTH, W. L. H.    A critical study of the collection of aboriginal Australian crania in the Cambridge University Museum. J. A. I., vol. XXIII, pp. 284–314.

1894–95    "    Note on skulls from Queensland and South Australia. J. A. I., vol. XXIV, pp. 213–218.

1900a    " and PAIN, B. H.    A contribution to Eskimo craniology. J. A. I., vol. XXX, pp. 125–140.

1900b    "    On a collection of crania with two skeletons of the Moriori or aborigines of the Chatham Islands. J. A. I., vol. XXX, pp. 141–153.

1902a    "    Some anthropological results of the Skeat Expedition to the Malay Peninsula. J. A. I., vol. XXXII, pp. 142–152.

1902b    "    Craniological notes on the aborigines of Tasmania. J. A. I., vol. XXXII, pp. 177–181.

1910–1    "    A study of the craniology of the modern inhabitants of Sardinia. Zeitsch. f. Morph. und Anth., vol. XIII, pp. 439–504.

1916    EATON, G. F.    The collection of osteological material from Machu Picchu. Memoirs Connecticut Academy of Arts and Sciences, vol. V, pp. 1–96.

1887    EHRENREICH, P.    Ueber die Botocudos der brazilianischen Provinz Espiritu Santo und Minas Geraes. Zeitsch. f. Ethn., vol. XIX, pp. 39–61.

1897    "    Anthropologische Studien über die Ureinwohner Brasiliens. Braunschweig, 1897.

1921    VON EICKSTEDT, E.    Rassenelemente der Sikh. Zeitsch. f. Ethn., vol. LII, pp. 318–394.

1877    ELDRIDGE, S.    Notes on the crania of the Botans of Formosa. Transactions of the Asiatic Society of Japan, vol. V, pp. 158–169.

1887    ELISEIEV, A. V.    Antropologicheskiya zamietki o Finnakh. Izv. Imp. Obsh. Lyub. Est., vol. XLIX, cols. 424–469.

1891    "    Antropologicheskiya zamietki ob obitatelyakh Maloi Azii. Izv. Imp. Obsh. Lyub. Est., vol. LXXI, cols. 61–82.

1896    ELKIND, A. D.    Privislyanskie Polyaki. Izv. Imp. Obsh. Lyub. Est., vol. XC, cols. 255–458.

1903    "    Evrei. Izv. Imp. Obsh. Lyub. Est., vol. CIV, cols. 1–458.

1912    "    K antropologii negrov. Russ. Anth. Journ., vol. VIII, nos. 1–2, pp. 20–36.

1889-90 VON ERCKERT, R. Kopfmessungen kaukasischer Völker. Arch. f. Anth., vol. XVIII, pp. 263-337; vol. XIX, pp. 55-85, 211-249, 331-356.

1905 ERIKSON, E. V. K antropologii Gruzin. Russ. Anth. Journ., vol. VI, nos. 3-4, pp. 47-57.

1908 " K antropologii Armyan. Russ. Anth. Journ., vol. VII, no. 2, pp. 168-180.

1906 ETHNOGRAPHIC SURVEY OF INDIA. Anthropometric data from Burma. Calcutta, 1906.

1908 " Anthropometric data from Baluchistan. Calcutta, 1908.

1909 " Anthropometric data from the Northwest Borderland. Calcutta, 1909.

1918 FARABEE, W. C. The Central Arawaks. University of Pennsylvania, Anthropological Publications, vol. IX, pp. 1-288.

1921 FARRER, R. The Rainbow Bridge. London, 1921.

1901-02 FAWCETT, C. D., and LEE, A. A second study of the variation and correlation of the human skull, with special reference to the Naqada crania. Biometrika, vol. I, pp. 408-468.

1916 FERRIS, H. B. The Indians of Cuzco and the Apurimac. Mem. Amer. Anth. Assoc., vol. III, no. 2, pp. 59-148.

1914 FETZER, C. Rassenanatomischer Untersuchungen an 17 Hottentotenköpfen. Zeitsch. f. Morph. und Anth., vol. XVI, pp. 95-156.

1905 FISHBERG, M. Beiträge zur physischen Anthropologie der nordafrikanischen Juden. Zeitschrift für Demographie und Statistik der Juden, vol. I.

1922 FLEMMING, R. M. Sex and growth features in racial analysis. Man, vol. XII, no. 46.

1916 FLEURE, H. J., and JAMES T. C. Geographical distribution of anthropological types in Wales. J. A. I., vol. XLVI, pp. 35-154.

1894 FLORES, L. V. Craneos di indigenas bolivianos. Actes de la Société Scientifique de Chile, vol. IV, pp. 231-250.

1905 " Craneos de paredes gruesos. Revista Chilena de Historia Natural, vol. IX, pp. 172-190.

1878-79 FLOWER, W. H. On the osteology and affinities of the natives of the Andaman Islands. J. A. I., vol. IX, pp. 108-135.

1879 " Catalogue of specimens contained in the Museum of the Royal College of Surgeons of England. Pt. I, Man. London, 1879.

1884–85 FLOWER, W. H.     Additional observations on the osteology of the natives of the Andaman Islands J A. I , vol. XIV, pp. 115–120.

1886     FOUQUET, D.     Observations relevées sur quelques momies royales d'Egypt. Bull. Soc. Anth., Paris, 3d series, vol. IX, pp. 578–590.

1897     FRAIPONT, J.     Les néolithiques de la Meuse. Bull. Soc. Anth., Brux., vol. XVI, pp. 311–391.

1904     FRANKE, O.     Beiträge aus chinesischen Quellen zur Kenntniss der Türkvölker und Skythen Zentral-Asiens. Abh. K. Pr. Akad. Phil.-Hist. Abth., 1904, vol. I, pp. 1–111.

1904     FRASSETTO, F.     Crani moderni di Manfredonia. Atti Soc. Rom. Ant., vol. X, pp. 94–118.

1906     "     Crani rinvenuti in tombe etruschi. Atti Soc. Rom. Ant., vol. XII, pp. 156–182.

1921     FRETS, G. P.     Heredity of head form in Man. Hague, 1921.

1899     FRIDOLIN, J.     Amerikanische Schädel. Arch. f. Anth., vol. XXV, pp. 397–413.

1900     "     Südseeschädel. Arch. f. Anth., vol. XXVI, pp. 691–717.

1901     "     Burjat und Kalmückenschädel. Arch. f. Anth., vol. XXVII, pp. 303–317.

1904a     "     Afrikanische Schädeln. Arch. f. Anth., vol. XXVIII, pp. 339–349.

1904b     "     Tschuktschenschädel. Arch. f. Anth., vol. XXVIII, Supplement, pp. 1–17.

1912     FRIEDERICI, G.     Wissenschaftliche Ergebnisse einer amtlichen Forschungs Reise nach dem Bismarck-Archipel im Jahre 1908. Mitteilungen aus den Deutschen Schutzgebieten, Ergänzungsheft, nr. 5. Berlin, 1912.

1913     FRIZZI, E.     Osteometrischer Befund an Schädeln und Skelett-teilen der sogennanten Telei in Süd Bougainville. Arch. f. Anth., vol. XL, pp. 241–272.

1912     FURST, C. M.     Zur Kraniologie der schwedischen Steinzeit. Handlingar Kungliga Svenska Vetenskapsakademiens. (NS), vol. XLIX, no. 1, pp. 1–77.

1915     "     and HANSEN, F. C. C. Crania Groenlandica. A description of Greenland Eskimo Crania. Copenhagen, 1915.

1920     GADEN. H., and VERNEAU, R. Stations et sépultures néolithiques du territoire militaire du Tchad. L'Anthropologie, vol. XXX, pp. 513–543.

1914     GAILLARD, R., and POUTRIN, L. Étude anthropologique des popu-

# BIBLIOGRAPHY

541

lations des regions du Tchad et du Kanem.
In—Documents Scientifiques de la Mission
Tilho, vol. III, pp. 1-118. Paris, 1914.

1905    GALAI, Y. D.    Antropologicheskiya dannyya o Velikorussakh
Staritskago uiezda, Tverskoi gubernii. Izv.
Imp. Obsh. Lyub. Est., vol. CXI, cols. 1-278.

1912    GARRETT, T. R. H.    The natives of the eastern portion of Borneo
and of Java. J. A. I., vol. XLII, pp. 53-68.

1885-86    GARSON, J. G.    On the inhabitants of Tierra del Fuego. J. A. I.,
vol. XV, pp. 141-157.

1909    GAUPP, H.    Vorlaufige Bericht über anthropologische Untersuchungen an Chinesen und Manchuren
in Peking. Zeitsch. f. Ethn., vol. XLI, pp.
730-734.

1905    GIACHETTI, V.    Studi antropologici sugli antichi Peruviani.
Arch. p. Ant. e Etn., XXXV, pp. 201-298.

1878    GILDERMEISTER, J.    Ein Beitrag zur Kenntniss nordwestdeutscher
Schädelformen. Arch. f. Anth., vol. XI,
pp. 26-63.

1904    GIOVANOZZI, U.    Crani Arabi del Museo antropologico de Firenze. Arch. p. Ant. e Etn., vol. XXXIV,
pp. 343-353.

1898    GIRARD, H.    Notes sur les Chinois de Quangsi. L'Anthropologie, vol. IX, pp. 144-176.

1899    "    Essai sur l'indice céphalique de quelques populations du nord-est de l'Indochine. Associa-
tion Française pour l'Avancement de la
Science, 28th Session, pt. I, p. 287.

1901    "    Contribution à l'étude des proportions du tronc
chez les Jaunes et chez les Noirs. Association
Française pour l'Avancement de la Science,
30th Session, pt. II, pp. 766-789.

1902    "    Notes anthropologiques sur quelques Soudanais
occidentaux. L'Anthropologie, vol. XIII, pp.
41-56, 167-181, 329-347.

1904    GIUFFRIDA-RUGGERI, V.    Ossements du néolithique récemment
trouvés à Vérone. L'Anthropologie, vol. XV,
pp. 37-39.

1905    "    Terzo contributo all'antropologia fisica dei Siculi
eneolitici. Atti Soc. Rom. Ant., vol. XI, pp.
56-104.

1906a    "    Crani dell'Australia, della Nuova Caledonia e
delle isole Salomone. Atti Soc. Rom. Ant.,
vol. XII, pp. 31-35.

1906b    "    Elenco del materiale scheletrico preistorico e
protohistorico del Lazio. Atti Soc. Rom.
Ant., vol. XII, pp. 183-189.

Crani siciliani e crani liguri. Atti Soc. Rom. Ant., vol. XIII, pp. 23-39.

1908 GIUFFRIDA-RUGGERI,V. Contributo all'antropologia fisica delle regioni dinarichi e danubiani e dell'Asia anteriore. Arch. p. Ant. e Etn., vol. XXXVIII, pp. 132-180.

1909-10 " I crani egiziani e arabo-egiziani. Atti Soc. Rom. Ant., vol. XV, pp. 89-148.

1886-87 GORBACHEV, P. Antropologicheskiya nabliudeniya nad Taranchami, Dunganami, Kashgartsami i Kirgizami Djarkenta. Izv. Imp. Obsh. Lyub. Est., vol. XLIX, pt. III, cols. 606-609.

1906 GORJANOVIČ-KRAMBERGER, K. Der diluviale Mensch von Krapina in Kroatien. Wiesbaden, 1906.

1900 GOROSHCHENKO, K. Kurgannye cherepa Minusinskago Okruga. Opisanie Minusinskago Muzeia., pt. II. Minusinsk, 1900.

1901 " Soioty. Russ. Anth. Journ., vol. II, no. 2, pp. 62-74.

1858 GRATTAN, J. Notice on the human remains discovered in the Round Towers of Ulster. Ulster Journal of Archæology, vol. VI, pp. 27-40, 221-246.

1901 GRAY, J. Measurements of Papuan skulls. J. A. I., vol. XXXI, pp. 261-265.

1907 " Memoir on the Pigmentation Survey of Scotland. J. A. I., vol. XXXVII, pp. 375-402.

1921 GUERNSEY, S. J., and KIDDER, A. V. Basket-maker caves of Northeastern Arizona. Papers P. M., vol. VIII, no. 2.

1899 GUEVARA, T. Historia de la civilizacion de Araucania. Annales de la Universidad de Chile, Santiago, 1899.

1885-86 GUPPY, H. B. On the physical characteristics of the Solomon Islanders. J. A. I., vol. XV, pp. 266-285.

1909 GUPTE, B. A. Craniological data from the Indian Museum, Calcutta. Calcutta, 1909.

1912 HABERER, K. A. Schädel und Skelett-theile aus Peking. Jena, 1912.

1919 HABERLANDT, H., and LEBZELTER, V. Zur physische Anthropologie der Albanesen. Arch. f. Anth., vol. XLV, pp. 123-154.

1901 HADDON, A. C. A sketch of the ethnography of Sarawak. Arch. p. Ant. e Etn., vol. XXXI, pp. 341-357.

1915-16 " Note antropologiche sui Papua occidentali della Nuova Guinea Inglese. Riv. di Ant., vol. XX, no. 16, pp. 1-20.

1890   HAGEN, B.    Anthropologische Studien aus Insulinde.   Verh.
K. Akad. Wett. Amst., vol. XXVIII, pp. 1–
149.

1908    "    Die Orang Kubu auf Sumatra.   Veröffentlichungen a. d. Städtische Völker-Museum,
Frankfurt a. M., vol. II, pp. 1–266.

1884   HAMY, E. T.    Documents pour servir a l'anthropologie de la
Babylonie.   Nouvelles Archives du Musée
Sciences Naturelles, 2d series, vol. VII, p. 53.

1884–91    "    Anthropologie du Mexique.   In;—Mission
scientifique en Mexique, Paris, vol. I.

1893    "    Crânes mérovingiens et carlovingiens du Bou-
lonnais.   L'Anthropologie, vol. IV, pp. 513–
534.

1896    "    Documents sur l'anthropologie de la Corée.
Bulletin Musée d'Histoire Naturelle, Paris,
vol. II, no. 4.

1907    "    La figure humaine dans les monuments Chal-
déens, Babyloniens et Assyriens. Bull. Mem.
Soc. Anth., Paris, 5th series, vol. VIII, pp.
116–132.

1888a   HANSEN, S.    Bidrag til Ostgrönlaendernes Anthropologie.
Medd. om Grönland, vol. X, pt. II, pp. 1–43.

1888b    "    Lagoa Santa Racen.   Sammlung af Afhand-
linger e Museo Lundii., vol. I, pp. 1–37, Copenhagen, 1888.

1893    "    Bidrag til Vestgrönlaendernes Anthropologie.
Medd. om Grönland, vol. XVII, pp. 163–248.

1895    "    Bidrag til Eskimoernes Kraniologie.   Medd. om
Grönland, vol. XIX, pp. 347–356.

1914    "    Contributions to the Anthropology of the East
Greenlanders.   Medd. om Grönland, vol.
XXXIX, pp. 149–180.

1907–11a    "    Om Hovedets breddeindex hos de Danske.
Medd. Danm. Anth., vol. I, pp. 221–241.

1907–11b    "    Om Haarets og öjnenes farve i Danmark.
Medd. Danm. Anth., vol. I, pp. 285–319.

1898   HARPER, W. R., and CLARKE, A. H.   Notes on the measurements of
the Tasmanian crania in the Tasmanian
Museum.   Papers and Proceedings of the
Royal Society of Tasmania, 1897, pp. 97–
110.

1920   HASEBE, K.    Study of the human bones found at Ko in the
second excavation.   Rep. Arch. Res. Coll.
Lit. Imp. Univ. Kyoto, vol. IV.

1917   HAUGHTON, S. H.    Preliminary note on the ancient human skull
remains from the Transvaal.   Transactions

## 544      BIBLIOGRAPHY

of the Royal Society of South Africa, vol. VI, pt. I.

1921    HAUSCHILD, M. W.   Die kleinasiatischen Völker und ihrer Beziehungen zu den Juden. Zeitsch. f. Ethn., vols. LII–LIII, pp. 518–526.

1916    HAWKES, E. W.   Skeletal measurements and observations of the Point Barrow Eskimo, with comparisons with other Eskimo groups. Amer. Anth. (NS), vol. XVIII, pp. 203–245

1907    HODGE, F. W.   Handbook of Indians north of Mexico. Bull. B. A. E., no. 30. 2 vols. Washington, 1907.

1884–87   HOLL, M.   Ueber die in Tirol vorkommende Schädelformen. Mitt. Anth. Ges. Wien, vol. XIV, pp. 77–116; vol. XV, pp. 41–76; vol. XVII, pp. 129–152.

1888    "   Ueber die in Vorarlberg vorkommende Schädelformen. Mitt. Anth. Ges. Wien, vol. XVIII, pp. 1–24.

1901    HOLLAND, T. H.   The Coorgs and Yeruvas, an ethnological contrast. Journ. As. Soc., Bengal, vol. LXX, pt. III, no. 2, pp. 59–98.

1902    "   The Kanets of Kulu and Lahaul, Panjab: a study in contact metamorphosis. J. A. I., vol. XXXII, pp. 96–123.

1920    HOOTON, E. A.   Indian village site and cemetery near Madisonville, Ohio. Papers P. M., vol. VIII, no. 1.

   "   Measurements of Canary Island crania. MS.

1896–97   HORTON-SMITH, R. J.   The cranial characteristics of the South Saxons. J. A. I., vol. XXVI, pp. 82–102.

1912    HOSE, C., and MACDOUGALL, W.   The Pagan Tribes of Borneo. 2 vols. London, 1912.

1887    HOUSSAY, F.   Les peuples actuels de la Perse. Bull. Soc. Anth., Lyon, vol. VI, pp. 101–148.

1884–85a   HOUZE, E., and JACQUES, V.   Les Australiens du Musée du Nord. Bull. Soc. Anth., Brux., vol. III, pp. 35–155.

1884–85b   HOUZE, E.   Cranes australiens d'Adelaide. Bull. Soc. Anth., Brux., vol. III, pp. 311–321.

1891    "   Les Francs des cimitières de Belgique. Bull. Soc. Anth., Brux., vol. X, pp. 28–34.

1904a    "   Les Francs de la Nécropole de Coply, Hainault. Bull. Mem. Soc. Anth., Brux., vol. XXIII, pp. 109–135.

1904b    "   Les Néolithiques de la province de Namur. Federation Archæologique et Historique de Belgique. Congrés de Dinant. Comptes-Rendus, vol. I, pp. 304–401. Namur, 1904.

1876    HOVELACQUE, A.    Sur les crânes burgondes. Bull. Soc. Anth., Paris. 2d series, vol. XI, pp. 468–469.

1894      "    and HERVÉ, G. Le Morvan. Mem. Soc. Anth., Paris. 3d series, vol. I, pp. 3–256.

1892    HOYOS SAINZ, L. DE, and ARANZADI Y UNAMUNO, T. DE. Un avance à la antropologia de España. Anal. Soc. Esp. Hist. Nat., vol. XXI (2d series, vol. I), pp. 32–101.

1913    HOYOS SAINZ, L. DE.    Caracteristiques générales des crânes espagnoles. L'Anthropologie, vol. XXIV, pp. 477–494.

1902    HRDLICKA, A.    The crania of Trenton, N. J., and their bearing upon the antiquity of man in that region. Bull. A. M. N. H., vol. XVI, pp. 23–62.

1903      "    The region of the ancient "Chichimecs" with notes on the Tepecanos and the ruins of La Quemada, Mexico. Amer. Anth. (NS), vol. V, pp. 385–440.

1906      "    Contribution to the physical anthropology of California. U. C. Pub. Amer. Arch. Ethn., vol. IV, no. 2, pp. 49–64.

1907      "    Skeletal remains suggesting or attributed to early man in North America. Bull. B. A. E., no. 33. Washington, 1907.

1908      "    Report on a collection of crania from Arkansas. In:—Moore, C. W. Certain Mounds of Arkansas and of Mississippi. Journ. Acad. Nat. Sci., Phila., vol. XIII, pp. 558–563.

1909      "    Report on an additional collection of skeletal remains from Arkansas and Louisiana. Journ. Acad. Nat. Sci., Phila., vol. XIV, pp. 173–249.

1910a      "    Report on skeletal material. In:—Fowke, G. Antiquities of Central and Southeastern Missouri. Bull. B. A. E., no. 37, Washington, 1910.

1910b      "    Contribution to the anthropology of the Central and Smith Sound Eskimos. Anth. Papers A. M. N. H., vol. V, pp. 177–281.

1911      "    Some results of recent anthropological exploration in Peru. Smithsonian Miscellaneous Collections, vol. LVI, no. 16, pp. 1–16.

1912a      "    The Natives of Kharga Oasis, Egypt. Smithsonian Miscellaneous Collections, vol. LIX, no. 1.

1912b      "    Early Man in South America. Bull. B. A. E., no. 52, Washington, 1912.

1916 HRDLICKA, A. Physical anthropology of the Lenape or Delawares, and of the Eastern Indians in general. Bull. B. A. E., no. 62, Washington, 1916.

1898 HULTKRANZ, J. V. Nya bidrag till Sydamerikas fysiska antropologi. Ymer, vol. XVIII, pp. 31-48.

1900 " Zur Osteologie der Ona und Yaghan Indianer des Feuerlandes. In:—Wissenschaftliche Ergebnisse der Schwedischen Expedition nach den Magellanländern, vol. I, pt. II, no. 5, pp. 109-173, Stockholm, 1900.

1921 HUTTON, J. H. The Angami Nagas, with some notes on neighboring tribes. London, 1921.

1905 HUXLEY, H. M. The anthropology of the Samaritans. Jewish Encyclopædia, vol. X, pp. 674-676.

1904 VON IHERING, H. Archæologia comparativa do Brazil. Revista Museo Paulista, vol. VI, pp. 519-583.

1890 IVANOVSKI, A. A. Cherepa iz Oz. Issykkulya. Izv. Imp. Obsh. Lyub. Est., vol. LXVIII, cols. 173-181.

1891a " Turkmeny i Turki po kraniometricheskim izsliedovaniyam. Izv. Imp. Obsh. Lyub. Est., vol. LXXI, cols. 93-110.

1891b " Cherepa iz mogilnikov Osetii. Izv. Imp. Obsh. Lyub. Est., vol. LXXI, cols. 195-246.

1891c " Antropologicheskii ocherk Torgutov, Tarbagataiskoi Oblast, Kitaiskoi Imperii. Izv. Imp. Obsh. Lyub. Est., vol. LXXI, pt. V.

1896 " Zur Anthropologie der Mongolen. Arch. f. Anth., vol. XXIV, pp. 65-90.

1903 " Kirgizy srednei ordy. Russ. Anth. Journ., vol. IV, no. 2, pp. 54-77.

1905 " Surgutskie Ostyaki. Russ. Anth. Journ., vol. VI, nos. 3-4, pp. 167-198.

1907 " Eniseiskie inorodtsy. Russ. Anth. Journ., vol. VII, nos. 1-2, pp. 165-224.

1894-95 JACQUES, V. Les Congolais de l'Exposition Universelle d'Anvers. Bull. Soc. Anth., Brux., vol. XIII, pp. 284-330.

1897-98 " Les Congolais de l'Exposition Universelle d'Anvers. Bull. Soc. Anth., Brux., vol. XVI, pp. 183-243.

1875 JAGOR, F. Maastabelle und Photographien von Andamanesen. V. B. G., vol. VII, pp. 259-268.

1879 " Messungen an lebenden Indiern. Zeitsch. f. Ethn., vol. XI, pp. 1-116.

1915 JIJON Y CAAMANO, J. Contributo al conocimiento de los Aborijenes de la Provincia de Imbabura, en la Republica de Ecuador. Madrid, 1915.

1906 JOCHELSON-BRODSKY, D. L. Zur Topographie des weiblichen Körpers nordostsibirischer Völker. Arch. f. Anth., vol. XXXIII, pp. 1–58.

1902 JOHNSTON, SIR H. H. The Uganda Protectorate. 2 vols. London, 1902.

1903 JOYCE, T. A. On the physical anthropology of the oases of Khotan and Keriya. J. A. I., vol. XXXIII, pp. 304–324.

1912 " Notes on the physical anthropology of Chinese Turkestan. J. A. I., vol. XLII, pp. 450–485.

1911 KEITH, SIR A. On certain physical characters of the Negro of the Congo Free State and Nigeria. J. A. I., vol. XLI, pp. 40–70.

1886 KELSIEV, A. I. Antropologicheskii ocherk Loparei. Izv. Imp. Obsh. Lyub. Est., vol. XLIX, cols. 1–46.

1889 KHARUZIN, A. N. Kirgizy bukeevskoi ordy. Izv. Imp. Obsh. Lyub. Est., vol. LXIII, cols. 1–550.

1890a " Drevniya mogily Gurzufa i Gugusha. Izv. Imp. Obsh. Lyub. Est., vol. LXIV, cols. 1–102.

1890b " Russkie Lopari. Izv. Imp. Obsh. Lyub. Est., vol. LXVI, cols. 1–472.

1919 KIDDER, A. V., and GUERNSEY, S. J. Archæological Explorations in Northeastern Arizona. Bull. B. A. E., no. 65, Washington, 1919.

1890–93 KITTS, E. J. Tables of Caste Measurements. Journ. Anth. Soc., Bombay, vol. II, pp. 367–379, 483–503; vol. III, pp. 61–73, 113–137.

1910 KLEIWEG DE ZWAAN, J. P. Beitrag zur Anthropologie der Minangkabauer. In:—Maas, A. Durch Zentral Sumatra. Berlin, 1910.

1913–15 " Die Insel Nias bei Sumatra. 3 vols. The Hague, 1913–15.

1915 KLOSS, C. B. Measurements of some Sakai of Sungkai and Slim, South Perak. Journal of the Federated Malay States Museum, vol. VI, pp. 71–85.

1915 KNIGHT, M. V. The Craniometry of southern New England Indians. Memoirs of the Connecticut Academy of Arts and Science, vol. IV.

1909 KNOCKER, F. W. Notes on the wild tribes of the Ulu Plus, Perak. J. A. I., vol. XXXIX, pp. 142–155.

1908 KOCH, J. W. R. Bijdrag tot de anthropologie der Inwohners van Zuidwest Nieuw Guinea. In:—Zuidwest Nieuw Guinea, 1904–05. Leiden, 1908.

1908 KOCH-GRÜNEBERG, T. Zwei Jahren unter den Indianern. Berlin, 1908.

1901–04 KOEZE, G. A. Crania Ethnica Philippinica. Veröffentlichungen der niederländischen Reichsmuseum für Völkerkunde. Ser. II, no. 3, Haarlem, 1901–04.

1893–94   KOGANEI, Y.   Beiträge zur physische Anthropologie der Aino. Mitt. Med. Fak. Imp. Jap. Univ., vol. II, pp. 1–404.

1906   "   Ueber Schädel und Skelette der Koreaner. Zeitsch. f. Ethn., vol. XXXVIII, pp. 513–536.

1898   KOHLBRUGGE, I. H. F.   L'Anthropologie des Tenggerois, Indonesiens montagnards de Java. L'Anthropologie, vol. IX, pp. 1–26.

1885a   KOLLMANN, J.   Kalmücken der Klein Doerbeter Horde in Basel. Verhandlungen der Naturforschenden Gesellschaft in Basel, vol. VII, pp. 623–47.

1885b   "   Schädel und Skeletreste aus einem Judenfriedhof des 13 und 14 Jahrhunderts zu Basel. Verhandlungen der Naturforschenden Gesellschaft in Basel, vol. VII, pp. 648–656.

1904   KOLMOGOROV, A. I.   Finny finlyandii. Russ. Anth. Journ., vol. V, nos. 3–4, pp. 12–47.

1897   KONSTANTINOV-SHCHIPUNIN, N. P.   K kraniologii drevnago naseleniya Kostromskoi Gubernii. Izv. Imp. Obsh. Lyub. Est., vol. XC, cols. 528–534.

1903   KOROLEV, S. A.   Astrakhanskie Kalmyki. Russ. Anth. Journ., vol., IV, no. 1, pp. 23–48.

1900   KRASNOV, A. N.   Ob antropologicheskikh izsliedovaniyakh i izmiereniyakh Kharkovskom i Valkovskom uiezdakh. Russ. Anth. Journ., vol. I, no. 2, pp. 12–23.

1881   KRAUSE, R.   Catalog des Ethnologische Anthropologische Abtheilung des Museum Godeffroy. Hamburg, 1881.

1897   KRAUSE, W.   Australische Schädel. V. B. G., vol. XXIX, pp. 508–558.

   KROEBER, A. L.   Measurements of California crania. MS.

1906   "   Measurements of Igorotes. Amer. Anth. (NS), vol. VIII, pp. 194–195.

1909   "   Measurements of Chukchis. Amer. Anth. (NS), vol. XI, pp. 531–533.

1906   KRONE, R.   Die Guarany Indianer des Aldeamento de Rio Itariri im Staate von Sao Paulo in Brazilien. Mitt. Anth. Ges. Wien, vol. XXXVI, pp. 130–146.

1913   KUBO, T.   Beiträge zur physischen Anthropologie der Koreaner. Mitt. Med. Fak. Imp. Jap. Univ., vol. XII.

1914   KUHN, P.   Ueber die Pygmaen am Sanga. Zeitsch. f. Ethn., vol. XLVI, pp. 116–133.

1896    KUKENTHAL, W.    Ueber Alfurenschädel von Halmahera. Abh. v. d. Senckb. Nat. Ges., vol. XXII, pp. 323–334.

1901    KURDOV, K. M.    K antropologii Lezgin. Russ. Anth. Journ., vol. II, nos. 3–4, pp. 165–177.

1905a    "    K antropologii Lezgin. Russ. Anth. Journ., vol. VI, nos. 1–2, pp. 129–135.

1905b    "    Gorskie Evrei Dagestana. Russ. Anth. Journ., vol. VI, nos. 3–4, pp. 57–88.

1908    "    Taty Dagestana. Russ. Anth. Journ., vol. VII, nos. 3–4, pp. 56–67.

1912a    "    Gorskie Evrei Shemakhinskago Uiezda, Bakinskoi Gubernii. Russ. Anth. Journ., vol. VIII, nos. 2–3, pp. 87–100.

1912b    "    Aderbeidjanskie Tatary. Russ. Anth. Journ., vol. VIII, no. 4, pp. 1–38.

1913    "    Taty Shemakhinskago Uiezda, Bakinskoi Gubernii. Russ. Anth. Journ., vol. IX, nos. 1–2, pp. 162–173.

1885    LACERDA, J. B. DE,    O homen dos sambaquis. Contribuçao a archæologia braziliera. Archivio do Museo Nacional de Rio Janeiro, vol. VI, pp. 175–257.

1905    LAPICQUE, L.    Le problem anthropologique des Parias et des castes homologues chez les Dravidiens. Bull. Mem. Soc. Anth., Paris. 5th series, vol. VI, pp. 400–421.

1891    LAPOUGE, G. DE,    Crânes modernes de Montpellier. L'Anthropologie, vol. II, pp. 36–42.

1893    "    Crânes modernes de Karlsruhe. L'Anthropologie, vol. IV, pp. 733–749.

1901a    LARSEN, C. F.    Om Jaedertypen. Forh. Videns. Christiania, 1900, no. 4, pp. 1–19.

1901b    "    Norske Kraniertyper. Skrifter Videns. Christiania, 1901. Math. Nat. Kl., no. 5, pp. 1–53.

1903    "    Trönderkranier og Tröndertyper. Skrifter Videns. Christiania, 1903. Math. Nat. Kl., no. 6, pp. 1–46.

1905    "    Nordlandsbefolkeningen. Skrifter Videns. Christiania, 1905. Math. Nat. Kl., no. 2, pp. 1–32.

1904a    LATCHAM, R. E.    Notes on the physical characteristics of the Araucanians. J. A. I., vol. XXXIV, pp. 170–180.

1904b    "    Notes on some ancient Chilean skulls and other remains. J. A. I., vol. XXXIV, pp. 234–254.

1909    "    Antropologia Chileña. Rev. Mus. La Plata, vol. XVI, pp. 241–318.

## 550 BIBLIOGRAPHY

1922 LEBZELTER, V. Anthropologische Untersuchungen an serbischen Zigeurnern. Mitt. Anth. Ges. Wien., vol. LII, pp. 23–43.

1909 LEGENDRE, A. F. Le Far West Chinois. Races aborigènes. Les Lolos. Etude ethnologique et anthropologique. T'oung Pao. 2d series, vol. X, pp. 340–380, 399–444, 603–665.

1911 " Étude anthropologique sur les Chinois du Setchouan. Anthropometrie. Bull. Mem. Soc. Anth., Paris. 6th series, vol. II, pp. 102–123.

1904 LEHMANN-NITSCHE, R. Études anthropologiques sur les Indiens Takshik (Groupe Guaicuru), du Chaco Argentin. Rev. Mus. La Plata, vol. XI, pp. 263–313.

1913 LEYS, N., and JOYCE, T. A., Notes on a series of physical measurements from East Africa. J. A. I., vol. XLIII, pp. 195–268.

LI, CHI, Measurements of Chinese Students. MS.

1891 LIJIN, N. I. Antropologicheskiya nabliudeniya nad Tavricheskimi Tatarami. Izv. Imp. Obsh. Lyub. Est., vol. LXXI, cols. 6–58.

1908 LISSAUER, A. Archæologische und anthropologische Studien ueber Kabylen. Zeitsch. f. Ethn., vol. XL, pp. 501–529.

1896 LOMBROSO, C., and CARRARA, M. Contributo all'antropologia dei Dinka. Atti Soc. Rom. Anth., vol. IV, pp. 103–126.

1911 LORENA, A. Algunos materiales para la antropologia del Cuzco. 4 Congreso Cientifico (1 Pan-Americano), Santiago, vol. XIV, pt. II, pp. 216–227.

1893 LUBBERS, A. Eene bijdrage tot de anthropologie der Bevolking in de Assistent-Residentie Gorontalo. Geneesk. Tijdschrift van Nederland Indie, vol. XXXII.

1842 LUND, P. W. Blik paa Brasiliens Dyreverden, etc. Skrifter Kgl. Dansk Videnskabernes Selskabs. Nat. Math. Klasse, 4th series, Afh. IX, pp. 195–196.

1890 VON LUSCHAN, F. Die Tashtadschy und andere Ueberreste der alten Bevölkerung Lykiens. Arch. f. Anth., vol. XIX, pp. 31–53.

1906 " Sechs Pygmäen vom Ituri. Zeitsch. f. Ethn., vol. XXXVIII, pp. 716–730.

1907 " Sammlung Baessler, Schädel von polynesischen Inseln. Veröff. K. Mus. Völk., vol. XII, pp. 1–256.

1911 " The early inhabitants of Western Asia. J. A. I., vol. XLI, pp. 221–244.

1913    VON LUSCHAN, F.    Beiträge zur Anthropologie der Kreter. Zeitsch. f. Ethn., vol. XLV, pp. 307–393.

1902    LUTSENKO, E.    K antropologicheskoi karakteristikie Altaiskago plemen Telenget. Russ. Anth. Journ., vol. III, no. 1, pp. 1–29.

1893    MAAS, A.    Ueber seine Reise nach den Mentawei Inseln. V. B. G., vol. XXV, pp. 177–189.

1902    "    Bei liebenswürdigen Wilden. Berlin, 1902.

1914    MACCURDY, G. G.    Human skulls from Gazelle Peninsula. University of Pennsylvania, Anthropological Publications, vol. VI, no. 1, pp. 1–21.

1903    MACDONELL, W. R.    A study of the variation and correlation of the human skull, with special reference to English crania. Biometrika, vol. III, pp. 191–244.

1906–07    "    A second study of the English skull, with special reference to the Moorefields crania. Biometrika, vol. V, pp. 86–105.

MACGREGOR MEMORIAL MUSEUM. Kimberley, South Africa. Measurements of Bushman and Hottentot crania. MS.

1901    MAINOV, I. I.    Dva tipa Tungusov. Russ. Anth. Journ., vol. II, no. 2, pp. 1–17.

1903    "    Yakuty. Russ. Anth. Journ., vol. III, no. 4, pp. 35–62.

1891    MAINOV, V. N.    Materialy po antropologii Mordvy-Erzi Nijegorodskago Uiezda. Izv. Imp. Obsh. Lyub. Est., vol. LXXI, pp. 186–192.

1920    MALCOLM, L. W. G.    Notes on the physical anthropology of certain West African Tribes. Man, vol. XX, no. 60.

1901    MALIEV, N. M.    Voguly. Russ. Anth. Journ., vol. II, no. 1, pp. 73–82.

1905    MALININ, K. N.    K antropologii Kabardintsev. Russ. Anth. Journ., vol. VI, nos. 3–4, pp. 88–106.

1882    MANOUVRIER, L.    Les Galibis du Jardin d'Acclimatation. Bull. Soc. Anth., Paris. 3d series, vol. V, pp. 602–627.

1877    MANTEGAZZA, P.    Studi anthropologici ed etnografici sulla Nuova Guinea. Arch. p. Ant. e Etn., vol. VII, pp. 137–172, 307–348.

1880    " and SOMMIER, S.    Studii antropologici sui Lapponi. Arch. p. Ant. e Etn., vol. X, pp. 173–201.

1881    MANTEGAZZA, P.    Nuovi studi craniologici sulla Nuova Guinea. Arch. p. Ant. e Etn., vol. XI, pp. 149–185.

1883    "    Studi sull'etnologia dell'India. Arch. p. Ant. e Etn., vol. XIII, pp. 177–241.

1886    " and REGALIA, E.    Studio sopra una serie di crani di Fue-

|  |  | gini. Arch. p. Ant. e Etn., vol. XVI, pp. 463–515. |
| 1890a | MARCANO, G. | Ethnographie précolumbienne du Venezuela. Indiens Piaroas et Guahibos. Bull. Soc. Anth., Paris. 4th series, vol. I, pp. 857–865. |
| 1890b | " | Ethnographie précolumbienne du Venezuela. Indiens Goajiros. Bull. Soc. Anth., Paris. 4th series, vol. I, pp. 883–895. |
| 1891 | " | Ethnographie précolumbienne du Venezuela. Note sur les Cuicas et les Timotes. Bull. Soc. Anth., Paris. 4th series, vol. II, pp. 238–247. |
| 1893 | " | Ethnographie précolumbienne de Venezuela. Mem. Soc. Anth., Paris. 2d series, vol. IV, pp. 1–86, 99–218. |
| 1915 | MARELLI, C. A. | Contribucion a la craneologia de las primitivos poblaciones de la Patagonia. Ann. Mus. Nac. Hist. Nat. B. A.. vol. XXVI, pp. 31–91. |
| 1892 | MARTIN, R. | Ein Beitrag zur Osteologie der Alikaluf. Vierteljahrsschrift der Naturforschenden Gesellschaft, in Zurich, vol. XXXVII, pp. 1–12. |
| 1905 | " | Die Inlandstämme der Malayischen Halbinsel. Jena, 1905 |
| 1891 | MATIEGA, H. | Crania Bohemica. I Th. Böhmens Schädel aus dem VI–XII Jahrhundert. Prag, 1891. |
| 1918 | MATSUMARA, A. | The head forms of the Japanese men and their local differences. Tokyo Gakugei Zasshi, vol. XXXV, no. 446. |
| 1919a | " | The head forms of the Japanese women and their local differences. Tokyo Gakugei Zasshi, vol. XXXVI, no. 449. |
| 1919b | " | The head forms of the Riukiu Islanders. Tokyo Gakugei Zasshi, vol. XXVI, no. 457. |
| 1921 | MATSUMOTO, H. | Notes on the Stone Age people of Japan. Amer. Anth. (NS), vol. XXIII, pp. 50–77. |
| 1916–17 | MENDES CORREA, A. A. | Sulla pluralita dei tipi ipsistenocefali, e sopra alcuni crani portughesi. Riv. di Ant., vol. XXI, pp. 241–244. |
| 1887 | MENSE. | Anthropologie der Völker vom mittlerem Congo. V. B. G., vol. XIX, pp. 625–645. |
| 1902 | MEYER, A. B., and JABLONOWSKI, J. | 24 Menschenschädel von der Oster-Insel. Abh. und Ber. K. Z. A. E. Mus., Dresden, vol. IX, no. 4. |
| 1905a | MOCHI, A. | Sull'Anthropologia dei Denca. Arch. p. Ant. e Etn., vol. XXXV, pp. 17–70. |
| 1905b | " | Crani di populazioni Turco-Mongol. Arch. p. Ant. e Etn., vol. XXXV, pp. 71–83. |

1907    MOCHI, A.              Sulla antropologia degli Arabi. Arch. p. Ant.
                              e Etn., vol. XXXVII, pp. 411–428.
1908        "                 Crani Cinesi e Giapponesi. Arch. p. Ant. e
                              Etn., vol. XXXVIII, pp. 299–328.
1894    MODIGLIANI, E.        L'Isola delle Donne. Viaggio ad Engano. Mil-
                              ano, 1894.
1908–09  MOLLISON, T.         Beitrag zur Kraniologie der Maori. Zeitsch. f.
                              Morph. und Anth., vol. XI, pp. 529–596.
1897    MONDIO, G.            Studio sopra 200 teschi messinesi. Arch. p.
                              Ant. e Etn., vol. XXVII, pp. 267–380.
1906    MONTGOMERY, H.        Remains of prehistoric man in North Dakota.
                              Amer. Anth. (NS), vol. VIII, pp. 640–652.
1908        "                 Prehistoric man in Manitoba and Saskatchewan.
                              Amer. Anth. (NS), vol. X, pp. 33–41.
1893    MOSCHEN, L.           Quattro decadi di crani moderni della Sicilia.
                              Atti Soc. Ven-Tren-Istr. Sc. Nat. 2d series,
                              vol. II, pp. 354–403.
1896        "                 Una centuria di crani umbri moderni. Atti
                              Soc. Rom. Ant., vol. IV, pp. 5–35.
1897        "                 Note di craniologia Trentina. Atti Soc. Rom.
                              Ant., vol. V, pp. 5–19.
1898        "                 Crani moderni di Bologna. Atti Soc. Rom.
                              Ant., vol. VI, pp. 38–58.
1908    MOSKOWSKI, M.         Ueber zwei nicht malayische Stämme von Ost-
                              Sumatra. Zeitsch. f. Ethn., vol. XL, pp. 229–
                              239.
1905–06  MOSSO, A.           Crani Etruschi. Memorie della Reale Accade-
                              mia della Scienze di Torino. 2d series, vol.
                              LVI, pp. 263–283.
1906    MÜLLER-WISMAR, W.     Beiträge zur Kraniologie der Neu Britannier.
                              Mitt. Mus. Völk., Hamburg, 1906, pp. 71–187.
1905    MYERS, C. S.          Contributions to Egyptian anthropometry.
                              J. A. I., vol. XXXV, pp. 80–91.
1906–08     "                 Contributions to Egyptian anthropology. J.
                              A. I., vol. XXXVI, pp. 237–261; vol. XXX-
                              VIII, pp. 99–148.
1908    NAKANO, J.            Report on the cranial measurements of the skulls
                              in the Department of Anatomy, Kanazawa
                              Medical College. Juzenkwai Zasshi, June,
                              1908.
1913        "                 Cranial measurements of Japanese skulls. Ju-
                              zenkwai Zasshi, March–April, 1913.
1890    NASONOV, N. V.        Tablitsa izmierenie Kurdov. Izv. Imp. Obsh.
                              Lyub. Est., vol. LXVIII, pp. 400–402.
1882    NEIS, P.              Mensurations de sept crânes de sauvages Mois.
                              Bull. Soc. Anth., Paris. 3d series, vol. V, pp.
                              531–535.

1890     NEOPHYTOS, A. G.     Le district de Kerasunde au point de vue anthropologique. L'Anthropologie, vol. I, pp. 679–711.

1892     NIEDERLE, L.     Die Schädel von Senftenburg. Sitz. Anth. Ges., Wien, vol. XXII, pp. 82–83.

1906     NIELSEN, H. A.     Bidrag til Danmarks forhistoriske Befolkningssaerligt Stenaldersfolkets Antropologi. Aarbog Nord. Oldk. Hist. 2d series, vol. XXI, pp. 237–318.

1911     "     Yderlige Bidrag til Danmarks Stenaldersfolks Anthropologi. Aarbog Nord. Oldk. Hist. 3d series, vol. I, pp. 81–205.

1903     NIEUWENHUIS, A. W.     Anthropometrische Untersuchungen bei den Dajak. Mitteilungen a. d. niederlandischen Reischsmuseum für Völkerkunde. Series 2, no. 5.

1913     NORDENSKIOLD, E.     Indianerleben. Leipzig, 1913.

1893     OBOLENSKY, N.     Les crânes Sundurli-Koba (Grottes de la Crimée) XIth Int. Cong. Anth., vol. II, pp. 71–76.

1908     OETTEKING, B.     Ein Beitrag zur Craniologie der Eskimo. Abh. und Ber. K. Z. A. E. Mus., Dresden, vol. XII, no. 3, pp. 1–58.

1909     "     Kraniologische Studien an Aegyptern. Arch. f. Anth., vol. XXXVI, pp. 1–91.

1903     OLECHNOWICZ, W.     Cmentarzysko w Nowo-silkach. Mat. Ant. Arch. Etn. Akad. Umiej. Krak., vol. VI, pp. 3–12.

1898     ONNIS, E. A.     Contributo all'antropologia della Sardegna. Atti. Soc. Rom. Ant., vol. VI, pp. 209–231.

1876     OTIS, G. A.     Check list of preparations and objects in the section of Human Anatomy, of the U. S. Army Medical Museum. Washington, 1876.

1893     PANTIUKOV, I. I.     Antropologicheskiya nabliudeniya na Kavkaz. Zapiski Kavkaz. Otd. Imp. Russ. Geograficheskiya Obshchestva, vol. XV.

1908     PARSONS, F. G.     Report on the Hythe crania. J. A. I., vol. XXXVIII, pp. 410–450.

1910     "     Report on the Rothwell crania. J. A. I., vol. XL, pp. 483–504.

1919     "     Anthropological observations on German prisoners of war. J. A. I., vol. XLIX, pp. 20–36.

1912     PASHKIN, P. N.     Iz poiezdki k Nogaitsam s antropologicheskoiu tsieliu. Russ. Anth. Journ., vol. VIII, no. 1, pp. 36–43.

1888     PAULITSCHKE, P.     Beiträge zur Ethnographie und Anthropologie der Somali, Galla und Harari. Leipzig, 1888.

1915   PEAKE, H., and HOOTON, E. A.   Saxon graveyard at East Shefford,
Berks. J. A. I., vol. XLV, pp. 92-131.

1916   PEAKE, H.   Racial elements concerned in the first siege of
Troy. J. A. I., vol. XLVI, pp. 154-172.

1884   PEIXOTO, R.   Novos estudos craniologicos sobre os Botocudos.
Arch. Mus. Nac. R. J., vol. VI, pp. 205-256.

1889   PETERSEN, E., and VON LUSCHAN, F.   Reisen in Lykien, Milyas und
Kibyratis, Wien, 1889.

1905   PIONTKOVSKI, A. A.   Bielorussi Gomelskago uiezd, Mogilevskoi gubernii. Russ. Anth. Journ., vol. VI, nos. 3-4,
pp. 152-160.

1901   PITTARD, E.   Contribution à l'étude anthropologique des
Esquimaux du Labrador et de la Baie d'Hud-
son. Bull. Soc. Geog. Neuch., vol. XIII,
pp. 158-176.

1908   "   Note sur deux crânes Fang. Bull. Soc. Geog.
Neuch., vol. XIX, pp. 58-68.

1909   "   Crania Helvetica. Anthropologie de la Suisse.
Geneve, 1909.

1911   "   La taille, l'indice céphalique et l'indice nasale
de 300 Turcs Osmanli de la Peninsule des
Balkans. Rev. Ec. d'Anth., vol. XXI, pp.
488-495.

1920   "   Les Peuples des Balkans. Paris, 1920.

P. M.   Peabody Museum of Harvard University,
Cambridge, Mass. Collection of crania.

1915   PÖCH, R.   Studien an Eingeborenen von N. S. Wales und
an australischen Schädeln. Mitt. Anth. Ges.,
Wien, vol. XLV, pp. 12-95.

1903   POLL, H.   Ueber Schädel und Skelette der Bewohner der
Chatham Inseln. Zeitsch. f. Morph. und
Anth., vol. V, pp. 1-134.

1910   POUTRIN.   Contribution à l'étude des pygmées d'Afrique.
L'Anthrolologie, vol. XXI, pp. 435-504.

1915   POYNTER, C. W. M.   A study of Nebraska crania. Amer. Anth.
(NS), vol. XVII, pp. 509-524.

1903   PROKHOROV, K. G.   K antropologii Velikorussov Elatinskago uiezda,
Tambovskoi gubernii. Russ. Anth. Journ.,
vol. IV, no. 2, pp. 78-82.

1907   "   K antropologii naseleniya Korotoyakskago
uiezda, Voronejskoi gubernii. Russ. Anth.
Journ., vol. VII, nos. 1-2, pp. 128-137.

1892   PRUDENT, H.   Notes sur les crânes provenant de l'ancien cime-
tière de Marcilly d'Azergues (Rhone). Bull.
Soc. Anth., Lyon, vol. XI, pp. 92-103.

1910   PUCCIONI, N.   Crani della necropole di Siuwah. Arch. p. Ant.
e Etn., vol. XL, pp. 131-144.

1912    PUCCIONI, N.    Crani Araucani e Patagoni. Arch. p. Ant. e Etn., vol. XLII, pp. 13–63.

1914    "    Gli eneolitici della Buca-Tana di Maggiano (Lucca), Arch. p. Ant. e Etn., vol. XLIV, pp. 93–142.

1917    "    Studi sui materiali e sui dati antropologici col etnografici racolta dalla Missione Stefanini-Paoli nella Somali Italiana Meridionale. Arch. p. Ant. e Etn., vol. XLVI, pp. 13–165.

1905    PUMPELLY, R.    Explorations in Turkestan. Expedition of 1904. The prehistoric civilizations of Anau. 2 vols. Washington, 1905, vol. II, pp. 445–446.

1914    RADLAUER, C.    Anthropologische Studien an Somali. Arch. f. Anth., vol. XLI, pp. 451–470.

1901    RANDALL-MACIVER, D., and WILKIN, A. Libyan Notes. London, 1901.

1880    RANKE, J.    Die Schädel der altbayrische Landbevölkerung. Beiträge zur Anthropologie und Urgeschichte Bayerns, vol. III, pp. 108–205.

1900    RANKE, K. E.    Ueber altperuanische Schädel von Ancon und Pachacamac. Abh. K. Bayr. Akad. Wiss., Math.-Phys. Kl., vol. XX, pt. III, pp. 629–750.

1907    "    Anthropologische Beobachtungen aus Zentral-Brasilien. Abh. K. Bayr. Wiss., Math.-Phys. Kl., vol. XXIV, pt. I, pp. 1–149.

1908    RECHE, O.    Zur Anthropologie der jüngeren Steinzeit in Schlesien und Böhmen. Arch. f. Anth., vol. XXXV, pp. 220–237.

1904    REED, W. H.    Negritos of Zambales. Ethnological Survey Publications, vol. II, pt. I. Manilla, 1904.

1913–14    REICHER, M.    Untersuchung über die Schädelform der alpenlandischen und mongolischen Brachycephalen. Zeitsch. f. Morph. und Anth., vol. XV, pp. 421–562; vol. XVI, pp. 1–64.

1900    RETZIUS, G.    Crania Suecica Antiqua. Stockholm, 1900.

1902    " and FURST, C. M. Anthropologia Suecica. Stockholm, 1902.

1878    RETZIUS, M. G.    Finska Kranier. Stockholm, 1878.

1911    RIED, A.    Beiträge zur Kraniologie der Bewohner der Vorberge der bayrischen Alpen. Beiträge zur Anthropologie und Urgeschichte Bayerns, vol. XVIII, pp. 1–113.

1899    RIPLEY, W. Z.    The Races of Europe. A sociological study. New York, 1899. With Supplement—A selected bibliography of the Anthropology and Ethnology of Europe.

1892   RISLEY, SIR H. E.   The Tribes and Castes of Bengal. Anthropometric Data. 2 vols. Calcutta, 1892.

1893   "   Measurements of Cingalese Mooremen and Tamils, taken at Ceylon in November, 1892. Journ. As. Soc., Bengal, vol. LXII, pt. III, pp. 43-53.

1915   "   The People of India. London, 1915.

1908   RIVET, P.   La race de Lagoa Santa chez les populations précolombiennes de l'Equateur. Bull. Mem. Soc. Anth., Paris. 5th series, vol. IX, pp. 209-271.

1910   ROBERTSON, A. W. D.   Craniological observations on the length, breadth, and height of a hundred Australian aboriginal crania. Proc. R. Soc., Edinb., vol. XXXI, pp. 1-16.

1912   ROJDESTVENSKI, A. G.   K antropologii Yapontsev. Russ. Anth. Journ., vol. VIII, no. 1, pp. 43-55.

1902   ROJDESTVENSKI, N. N.   K antropologii Bielorussov Slutskago uiezda, Minskoi gubernii. Russ. Anth. Journ., vol. III, no. 1, pp. 49-58.

1911   ROSCOE, J.   The Baganda. London, 1911.

1913   ROUMA, G.   Les Indiens Quitchoua et Aymaras des Hauts Plateaux de la Bolivie. Bull. Mem. Soc. Anth., Brux., vol. XXXII, pp. 281-391.

1914   RUDENKO, S.   Resultats de mensurations anthropologiques sur les peuples du nordouest de la Siberie. Bull. Mem. Soc. Anth., Paris. 6th series, vol. V, pp. 123-142.

1898   RUSSELL, F.   Explorations in the Far North. University of Iowa, 1898.

1903   RUTKOVSKI, L.   Carakteristica antropologiczna ludnosci okolic Plonska i sasiednich powiatow gubernii Plockiej. Mat. Ant. Arch. Etn. Akad. Umiej, Krakow, vol. V, pp. 3-30.

1895   SALMON, P.   Dénombrement et types de crânes néolithiques de la Gaule. Rev. Ec. d'Anth., vol. V, pp. 155-181.

1906   SARASIN, F.   Versuch eines Anthropologie der Insel Celebes. Die Varietäten des Menschen auf Celebes. Wiesbaden, 1906.

1916-18   "   Étude anthropologique sur les Néo Caledoniens et les Loyalties. Archives Suisses d'Anthropologie, vol. II, no. 1, pp. 83-103.

1893   SARASIN, P. and F.   Die Weddas von Ceylan und die sie umgebende Völkerschaften. Ergebnisse naturwissenschaftlicher Forschungen auf Ceylan in 1884-86. 3 vols. Wiesbaden, 1893.

1903    SCHENK, A.    Les sépultures et les populations préhistoriques de Chamblandes. Bulletin de la Société Vaudoise des Sciences, vol. XXXIX, pp. 115–210.

1905a    "    Dix crânes . . . Fang. Bull. Soc. Geog., Neuch., vol. XVI, pp. 296–303.

1905b    "    Ossements et crânes humaines provenant de palafites de l'age de la pierre poli et de l'age du bronze. Rev. Ec. Anth., Paris, vol. XV, pp. 389–407.

1907–09    "    Étude sur l'Anthropologie de la Suisse. Bull. Soc. Geog., Neuch., vol. XVIII, pp. 106–165; vol. XIX, pp. 1–57; vol. XX, pp. 313–367.

1914a    SCHIFF, F.    Beiträge zur Anthropologie von Kreta. Zeitsch. f. Ethn., vol. XLVI, pp. 8–13.

1914b    "    Beiträge zur Anthropologie des südlichen Peloponessus. Zeitsch. f. Ethn., vol. XLVI, pp. 14–40.

1907    SCHLAGINHAUFEN, O.    Ein Beitrag zur Craniologie der Semang. Abh. und Ber. K. Z. A. E. Mus., Dresden, vol. XI, no. 2, pp. 1–50.

1914    "    Anthropologische Untersuchungen an Eingeborenen Deutsch Neu Guinea. Abh. und Ber. K. Z. A. E. Mus., Dresden, vol. XIV, no. 5, pp. 1–82.

1909    SCHLIZ, A.    Die vorgeschichtlichen Schädeltypen der deutschen Länder in ihrer Beziehung zu den einzelnen Kulturkreisen der Urgeschichte. Arch. f. Anth., vol. XXXV, pp. 239–268.

1913a    "    Beiträge zur prähistorische Ethnologie. Praehistorische Zeitschrift, vol. V, pp. 114–148.

1913b    "    Die Schädel aus der Necropol von Nicoloayevka. Praehistorische Zeitschrift, vol. V, pp. 148–157.

1884    SCHMIDT, E.    Die antiken Schädel Pompeiis. Arch. f. Anth., vol. XV, pp. 229–259.

1910    "    Beiträge zur Anthropologie Süd-Indiens. Arch. f. Anth., vol. XXXVII, pp. 90–158.

1912    SCHMIDT, R. R.    Die diluvialer Vorzeit Deutschlands. Stuttgart, 1912.

1908    SCHMIDT, W.    On the classification of Australian languages. Man, vol. VIII, no. 104.

1912–14    "    Die Gliederung der australischen Sprachen. Anthropos, vol. VII, pp. 230–251, 463–497, 1014–1048; vol. VIII, pp. 526–554; vol. IX, pp. 980–1018.

1908–09  SCHREIBER, W.      Beitrag zur Kraniologie der altperuanischen Schädel. Zeitsch. f. Morph. und Anth., vol. XII, pp. 243–261.

1881–91  VON SCHRENCK, L.  Reisen und Forschungen im Amur-lande, etc., vol. III, Anthropologie und Ethnologie. St. Petersburg, 1881–1891.

1905–06  SCHUSTER, E. H. J.  The Long Barrow and Round Barrow skulls in the collection of the Department of Comparative Anatomy, Oxford. Biometrika, vol. IV, pp. 351–362.

1915  SCHWERZ, F.          Die Völkerschaften der Schweiz von der Urzeit bis zur Gegenwart. Stuttgart, 1915.

1916    "                 Untersuchungen der Schädel aus der alämannischen Gräberfeld von Angst. Arch. f. Anth., vol. XLIII, pp. 270–320.

1893  SCOTT, J. H.         Contribution to the osteology of the aborigines of New Zealand and of the Chatham Islands. Transactions of the New Zealand Institute, vol. XXVI, pp. 1–64.

1909  SELIGMANN, C. G.     A classification of the natives of British New Guinea. J. A. I., vol. XXXIX, pp. 246–274.

1910    "                 The physical characters of the Nuba of Kordofan. J. A. I., vol. XL, pp. 505–525.

1913    "                 Some aspects of the Hamitic problem in the Anglo-Egyptian Sudan. J. A. I., vol. XLIII, pp. 593–705.

1917    "                 The physical characters of the Arabs. J. A. I., vol. XLVII, pp. 213–237.

1887  SERGI, G., and MOSCHEN, L.  Crani peruviani antichi del Museo Antropologico nella Università di Roma. Arch. p. Ant. e Etn., vol. XVII, pp. 5–26.

1888    "                 Crani della Papuasia. Arch. p. Ant. e Etn., vol. XVIII, pp. 91–100.

1891  SERGI, G.           Crani Africani e crani Americani. Arch. p. Ant. e Etn., vol. XXI, pp. 215–266.

1895a   "                 Die Menschenvarietäten in Melanesia. Arch. f. Anth., vol. XXI, pp. 339–383.

1895b   "                 Crani Siculi Neolitici. Atti Soc. Rom. Ant., vol. II, pp. 281–288.

1900    "                 Crani prehistorici della Sicilia. Atti Soc. Rom. Ant., vol. VI, pp. 3–13.

1901a   "                 Crani Esquimesi. Atti Soc. Rom. Ant., vol. VII, pp. 93–103.

1901b   "                 Studi di crani antichi. Atti Soc. Rom. Ant., vol. VII, pp. 162–174.

1902    "                 Crani Arabi. Atti Soc. Rom. Ant., vol. VIII, pp. 80–89.

| 1907a | SERGI, G. | Crani antichi della Sardegna. Atti Soc. Rom. Ant., vol. XIII, pp. 13–22. |
|---|---|---|
| 1907b | " | I sepolcreti di Novilara. Atti Soc. Rom. Ant., vol. XIII, pp. 129–142. |
| 1907c | " | Dalle esplorazione del Turkestan. Frammenti scheletrici umani. Atti Soc. Rom. Ant., vol. XIII, pp. 305–321. |
| 1915 | " | Die Etrusker und die alten Schädel des etruskischen Gebietes. Arch. f. Anth., vol. XLI, pp. 309–317. |
| 1912 | SERGI, S. | Crania Habessinica. Contributo al'Antropologia dell'Africa Orientale. Roma, 1912. |
| 1912 | SEVASTIANOV, E. P. | K antropologii Zyrian. Russ. Anth. Journ., vol. VIII, no. 1, pp. 57–69. |
| 1913 | SHCHUKIN, I. S. | Materialy dlya izucheniya Karachaevtsev. Russ. Anth. Journ., vol. IX, nos. 1–2, pp. 29–99. |
| 1897 | SHRUBSALL, F. C. | Crania of African Bush races. J. A. I., vol. XXVII, pp. 263–292. |
| 1898 | " | Notes on Ashanti skulls and crania. J. A. I., vol. XXVIII, pp. 95–103. |
| 1901 | " | Notes on crania from the Nile-Welle watershed. J. A. I., vol. XXXI, pp. 256–260. |
| 1902 | " | A study of a-Bantu skulls and crania. J. A. I., vol. XXXII, pp. 55–94. |
| 1907 | " | Notes on some Bushman crania and bones from the South African Museum. Annals South African Museum, vol. V, pp. 227–270. |
| 1911 | " | A note on the craniology of South African Bushmen. Annals South African Museum, vol. VIII, pp. 202–208. |
| 1901 | SILINICH, I. P. | K kraniologii Soiot. Russ. Anth. Journ., vol. II, no. 2, pp. 74–80. |
| 1904 | " | Voguly. Russ. Anth. Journ., vol. V, nos. 3–4, pp. 94–116. |
| 1887 | SIRET, H. and L. | Les premières ages du metal dans le sudest de l'Espagne. Anvers, 1887. |
| 1877 | SMIRNOV. | Sur les fouilles entreprises dans les régions du Caucase. Bull. Soc. Anth., Paris. 2d series, vol. XII, pp. 541–52. |
| 1918 | SMITH, S. A. | The fossil human skull found at Talgai, Queensland. Philosophical Transactions, London, Series B, vol. CCVIII, pp. 351–387. |
| 1887 | SOMMIER, S. | Sirieni, Ostiacchi e Samoiedi dell'Ob. Arch. p. Ant. e Etn., vol. XVII, pp. 71–222. |
| 1911 | SPEISER, F. | Mittheilungen von den Neuen Hebriden. V. B. G., vol. XLIII, pp. 307–08. |

1899    SPENCER, B., and GILLEN, F. J.   The Native Tribes of Central Australia. London, 1899.

1904      "      The Northern Tribes of Central Australia. London, 1904.

1907    SPIRIDOV, A. A.   Velikorussi Pereyaslavskago uiezda, Vladimirskoi gubernii. Russ. Anth. Journ., vol. VII, nos. 1–2, pp. 137–146.

1906    SPITTAL, R. H.   Observations on fourteen New Guinea skulls. Aberdeen University Anatomical and Anthropological Society. Studies, no. 22, pp. 88–103.

1902    STARR, F.   Physical characters of the Indians of Southern Mexico. Decennial Publications, University of Chicago, Chicago, 1902.

1921    STEIN, SIR M. A.   Serindia. 5 vols. Oxford, 1921, vol. III, pp. 1351–89.

1894    STUDER, T., and BANNWARTH, E.   Crania Helvetica Antiqua. Leipzig, 1894.

1882    STUDLEY, C. A.   Notes upon human remains from caves in Coahuila. 16th Rep. P. M., vol. III, pp. 233–259.

1918    SULLIVAN, L. R.   Racial types in the Philippine Islands. Anth. Papers, A. M. N. H., vol. XXIII, pt. I, pp. 1–60.

1921a      "      A contribution to Samoan Somatology. Mem. Bishop Mus., vol. VIII, no. 2.

1921b      "      A few Andamanese skulls with comparative notes on Negrito craniometry. Anth. Papers, A. M. N. H., vol. XXIII, pt. IV, pp. 175–201.

1922      "      A contribution to Tongan Somatology. Mem. Bishop Mus., vol. VIII, no. 4, pp. 233–260.

1918    SUZUKI, B.   Human skeletons found at Ko, Kanachi and Todoroki, Higo, the Stone Age People of Japan. Rep. Arch. Res. Coll. Lit. Imp. Univ., Kyoto, vol. II.

1861–62    SWAVING.   Eerste bijdrag tot de Kennis der Schedels van Volken in den Indischen Archipels. Nat. Tijd. Ned. Ind., vol. XXIII, pp. 241–289; vol, XXIV, pp. 175–216.

1863      "      Eenige Aanteekeningen over de Sumatrasche Volkstammen. Nat. Tijd. Ned., Ind., vol. XXV, pp. 295–315.

1870      "      Beschrijving van Schedels van Inboorlingen uit de Bovenlanden van Palembang. Nat. Tijd. Ned., Ind., vol. XXXI, pp. 238–279.

1916    TALBOT, P. A.   Notes on the anthropometry of some Central Sudan Tribes. J. A. I., vol. XLVI, pp. 173–184.

1897    TALKO-HRYNCEWICZ, J.    Materialy k palæoetnologii Zabaikalya. Trudy Troitkosavsk-Kiakhta Otdiel, Priamur. Otdiel, Imp. Russ. Geog. Obshchestva, vol. II, pt. III.

1899    "    Zamietki po antropologii sievernoi Kitaitsev. Trudy Troitskosavsk-Kiakhta Otdiel, Priamur. Otdiel, Imp. Russ. Geog. Obshchestva, II, pt. III.

1904    "    K antropologii Tungusov—Iroiskii Khammegani. Trudy Troitskosavsk-Kiakhta Otdiel, Priamur Otdiel, Imp. Russ. Geog. Obshchestva, vol. VII, pt. III, pp. 66–193.

1898–1900    "    Materialy do palæoetnologii mogil Aziyi wschoniej. Mat. Ant. Arch. Etn. Akad. Umiej., Krakow, vol. III, pp. 57–75; vol. IV, pp. 33–35.

1902    "    K antropologii Zabaikalya i Mongolii. Russ. Anth. Journ., vol. III, no. 2, pp. 34–68.

1905    "    Zamietki po antropologii volzhskich inorodtsev, i Kazanskie Tatary. Russ. Anth. Journ., vol. V, nos. 1–2, pp. 160–181.

1890    TARENETSKY, A.    Beiträge zur Craniologie der Ainos auf Sachalin. Mem. Imp. Acad. Sci., St. P., 7th series, vol. XXXVII, no. 13, pp. 1–56.

1893    "    Weitere Beiträge zur Craniologie der Bewohner von Sakhalin, Aino, Gilyaken und Orokken. Mem. Imp. Acad. Sci., St. P., 7th series, vol. XLI, no. 6, pp. 1–45.

1898    "    Ostyatskie cherepa. Trudy Antropolog. Obshchestva, Imp. Voen-Medits. Akademi, vol. III, pp. 12–16.

1900    "    Beiträge zur Skelet und Schädelkunde der Aleuten, Konaegen, Kenai und Koluschen mit vergleichenden anthropologische Bemerkungen. Mem. Imp. Acad. Sci., St. P. Phys.-Math. Sect. 8th series, vol. IX, no. 4, pp. 1–73.

1897    TEDESCHI, E. E.    Studi di Antropologia Veneta. Atti Soc. Rom. Ant., vol. V, pp. 21–59.

1904    "    Contributo alla craniologia dei popoli alpini. Atti Soc. Ven-Tren-Istr. Sci. Nat. New Series, vol. I, pp. 57–69.

1881    TEN KATE, H. C. F.    Sur les crânes malais du Museé de Leyde. Bull. Soc. Anth., Paris. 3d series, vol. IV, pp. 37–46.

1882    "    Zur Craniologie der Mongoloiden. Heidelberg, 1882.

1884    TEN KATE, H. C. F.    Matériaux pour servir a l'anthropologie de la presqu' isle Californienne. Bull. Soc. Anth., Paris. 3d series, vol. VII, pp. 551–569.

1887    "    Observations anthropologiques receuillies dans la Guyane et le Venezuela. Rev. d'Anth., 3d series, vol. II, pp. 44–68.

1892a    "    Somatological observations on Indians of the Southwest. Journ. Amer. Ethn. Arch., vol. III, no. 2, pp. 119–144.

1892b    "    Contribution a la craniologie des Araucans Argentins. Rev. Mus. La Plata, vol. IV, pp. 209–220.

1896    "    Anthropologie des anciens habitants de la region Calchaqui. Ann. Mus. La Plata, vol. I, pp. 1–62.

1905    "    Matériaux pour servir a l'anthropologie des Indiens de l'Argentina. Rev. Mus. La Plata, vol. XII, pp. 33–57.

1913    "    Mélanges Anthropologiques. I. Crânes Indonesiens. L'Anthropologie, vol. XXIV, pp. 651–661.

1915a    "    Mélanges Anthropologiques. II. Insulindiens. L'Anthropologie, vol. XXVI, pp. 235–245.

1915b    "    Mélanges Anthropologiques. III. Indigènes de l'Archipel Timorien. L'Anthropologie, vol. XXVI, pp. 519–564.

1916    "    Mélanges Anthropologiques. IV. Polynésiens. L'Anthropologie, vol. XXVII, pp. 393–406.

1897    " and HITTE, C. DE LA. Notes ethnographiques sur les Indiens Guyaquis et description de leurs charactéres physiques. Ann. Mus. La Plata, vol. II, pp. 25–38.

1911    THOMAS, C., and SWANTON, J. R. Indian languages of Mexico and Central America and their geographical distribution. Bull. B. A. E., no. 44. Washington, 1911.

1905    THOMSON, A., and RANDALL-MACIVER, D. The Ancient Races of the Thebaid. Oxford, 1905.

1915    THOMSON, E. J.    A study of the craniometry of the Moriori. Biometrika, vol. XI, pp. 82–135.

1919    THORBECKE, F.    Im Hochland von Mittel Kamerun. Abhandlungen der Hamburgische Kolonialinstitut, vol. XLI, pt. III.

1896    THURSTON, E.    Anthropology of the Todas and Kotas of the Nilgiri Hills, and of the Brahmans, Hannalas, Pallis and Pariahs of Madras City. Bulletin Madras Government Museum, vol. I, no. 4, pp. 141–236.

1909    THURSTON, E.    Castes and Tribes of Southern India. 7 vols. Madras, 1909.

1921    TILDESLEY, M. L.    A first study of the Burmese skulls. Biometrika, vol. XIII, pp. 176–263.

1902    TOCHER, J. F.    Note on some measurements of Eskimos of Southhampton Island. Man, vol. II, no. 115.

1908–09    "    Pigmentation survey of school children in Scotland. Biometrika, vol. VI, pp. 129–235.

1912    TOLDT, C.    Die Schädelformen in den oesterreichischen Wohngebieten der alt-Slawen, einst und jetzt. Mitt. Anth. Ges., Wien, vol. XLII, pp. 247–280.

1904    TOLDT, C., JR.    Die Japanerschädel der Münchener Anthropologische Institut. Arch. f. Anth., vol. XXVIII, pp. 143–185.

1887    TOPINARD, P.    Description et mensuration d'une série de crânes Kirghis. Rev. d'Anth. 3d series, vol. II, pp. 445–475.

1912    TORII, R.    Études anthropologiques. Les Aborigènes de Formose. Journ. Coll. Sci. Imp. Jap. Univ., vol. XXXII, Art. IV, pp. 1–75.

1914    "    Les Mandchoux. Journ. Coll. Sci. Imp. Jap. Univ., vol. XXXVI, Art. VI, pp. 1–35.

1889–99    VON TÖRÖK, A.    Ueber den Yezoer Ainoschädel aus der ostasiatischen Reise des Herrn Grafen Bela Szechenyi und ueber den sachalinen Ainoschädel des K. Zoologische Anthropologische Ethnologische Museum zu Dresden. Arch. f. Anth., vol. XVIII, pp. 15–101; vol. XXII, pp. 93–94; vol. XXIV, pp. 277–339, 479–575; vol. XXVI, pp. 247–317.

1907    TORRES, L. M.    Arqueologia de la cuenca del Rio Parana. Rev. Mus. La Plata, vol. XIV, pp. 53–120.

1911    TREMEARNE, A. J. N.    Notes on some Nigerian tribal marks. J. A. I., vol. XLI, pp. 162–178.

1912    "    Notes on the Kagoro and other Nigerian headhunters. J. A. I., vol. XLII, pp. 136–199.

1911    TSCHEPOURKOVSKY, E.    Anthropologische Studien. Arch. f. Anth., vol. XXXVIII, pp. 151–186.

1910    TUCKER, W., and MYERS, C. S.    A contribution to the anthropology of the Sudan. J. A. I., vol. XL, pp. 141–165.

1884    TURNER, SIR W.    Report on the Human Crania, etc., etc. Part XXIX in Report on the Scientific Results of the Voyage of H. M. S. Challenger, 1873–1876. Vol. X, pt. IV. London, 1884.

1899    "    Contributions to the craniometry of the people of the Empire of India. I. The Hill Tribes of the Northeast Frontier and the people of Burma. Trans. Roy. Soc., Edinb., vol. XXXIX, pt. III, pp. 703–747.

1901    TURNER, SIR W.    Contributions to the craniometry of the people of the Empire of India. II. The Aborigines of Chuta Nagpur, and of the Central Provinces, the people of Orissa, the Veddahs and Negritos. Trans. Roy. Soc., Edinb., vol. XL, pt. I, no. 6, pp. 59–129.

1903    "    A contribution to the craniology of the People of Scotland. Trans. Roy. Soc., Edinb., vol. XL, pt. III, pp. 547–613.

1906    "    Contributions to the craniometry of the people of the Empire of India. III. Natives of the Madras Presidency, Thugs, Veddahs, Tibetans, and Seistanis. Trans. Roy. Soc., Edinb., vol. XLV, pt. II, pp. 261–309.

1907    "    A contribution to the craniology of the natives of Borneo, the Malays, the natives of Formosa and the Tibetans. Trans. Roy. Soc., Edinb., vol. XLV, pt. III, pp. 781–818.

1908    "    The craniology, racial affinities and descent of the Aborigines of Tasmania. Trans. Roy. Soc., Edinb., vol. XLVI, pt. II, pp. 365–403.

1913    "    Contributions to the craniometry of the people of the Empire of India. IV, Bhils, Frontier Tribes of Burma, Pakokku Tribes, South Shan Tribes, Tibetans. Trans. Roy. Soc., Edinb., vol. XLIX, pt. III, pp. 705–734.

U. C.    University of California. Collection of crania.

U. S. N. M.    United States National Museum. Collection of crania.

1879    UJFALVY VON MEZÖ-KÖVESD, C. E. S. V. Les Kashgariens, Tarantchis et Dounganes. Rev. d'Anth. 2d series, vol. II, pp. 489–495.

1881    "    Sur les Baltis, les Lhassa, les Ladakis. Bull. Soc. Anth., Paris. 3d series, vol. IV, pp. 598–604.

1884    "    Aus dem westlichen Himalaya. Leipzig, 1884.

1896    "    Les Aryens au Nord et au Sud de l'Hindou-Kouch. Paris, 1896.

1912    VELDE, G.    Anthropologische Untersuchungen und Grabungen in einer Höhle der jüngeren Steinzeit auf Levkas. Zeitsch. f. Ethn., vol. XLIV, pp. 845–865.

1890    VENIAMINOV, E. P.    Doklad N. Iu. Zografa ob otchet predstavlennom Dr. E. P. Veniaminovoi v antropologicheskii Otdiel o eya poiezdkie v Ter-skuiu Oblast i Zakavkazskii Krai. Izv. Imp. Obsh. Lyub. Est., vol. LXVIII, cols. 6–8.

1894    VERNEAU, R.    Crânes préhistoriques de Patagonie. L'Anthro-pologie, vol. V, pp. 420–450.

1896a    "    De la pluralité des types ethniques chez les Negrilles. L'Anthropologie, vol. VI, pp. 153–167.

1896b    "    Oulofs, Leybus et Sereres. L'Anthropologie, vol. VI, pp. 510–528.

1898    "    Les sépultures Gallo-Romains et Merovingiennes de Mareuil-sur-Ourcq. L'Anthropologie, vol. IX, pp. 497–530.

1899    "    Les migrations des Ethiopiens. L'Anthropol-ogie, vol. X, pp. 641–662.

1903    "    Les Anciens Patagons. Monaco, 1903.

1909a    "    Les crânes humains du gisement préhistorique de Pho Binh Gia (Tonkin). L'Anthropol-ogie, vol. XX, pp. 545–560.

1909b    "    Anthropologie et ethnographie de l'Ethiopie. In:—Mission en Ethiopie, J. Duchesne Four-net, vol. II, pp. 119–284. Paris, 1909.

1911    "    Les crânes Maroccaines de la Mission de Mme. Camille du Gest. L'Anthropologie, vol. XXII, pp. 667–702.

1916–17    "    Resultats anthropologiques de la Mission de M. de Gironcourt en Afrique occidentale. L'An-thropologie, vol. XXVII, pp. 47–95, 211–242, 407–430, 539–568; vol. XXVIII, pp. 263–283, 403–426, 537–568.

1919    VERWORN, M.    Der diluviale Menschenfund von Obercassel bei Bonn. Wiesbaden, 1919.

1913    VIRCHOW, H.    Aus einem alten Grabe stammenden chinesis-chen Schädel. V. B. G., vol. XLV, pp. 640–644.

1870    VIRCHOW, R.    Ueber die Schädel der alten Bevölkerung der Philippinen. Zeitsch. f. Ethn., vol. II, pp. 151–158.

1871    "    Ueber der Schädelbau der Bewohner der Philip-pinen, insbesonders der Negritos. V. B. G., III, pp. 33–42.

1874    "    Schädel von Araucanen und anderen Süd-Ameri-kanern. V. B. G., vol. VI, pp. 258–263.

1877a    "    Die Bärenhöhle von Aggtelek in Ober-Ungarn. V. B. G., vol. IX, pp. 310–326.

1877b    "    Archaeologische Reise nach Livland. V. B. G., vol. IX, pp. 365–437.

| | | |
|---|---|---|
| 1881 | Virchow, R. | Die Feuerländer. V. B. G., vol. XIII, pp. 375–593. |
| 1882a | " | Ueber mikronesische Schädel. Monatsb. K. Pr. Akad., pp. 1113–1144. |
| 1882b | " | Alttrojanische Gräber und Schädel. Abh. K. Pr. Akad., pp. 1–152. |
| 1882c | " | Alfurenschädel von Ceram und andere Molukken. V. B. G., vol. XIV, pp. 76–93. |
| 1883 | " | Schädel der Igoroten. V. B. G., vol. XV, pp. 390–400. |
| 1885 | " | Schädel und Skelette von Botocuden am Rio Doce. V. B. G., vol. XVII, pp. 248–256. |
| 1886a | " | Gesammtbericht . . . ueber die Farbe der Haut, der Haare und der Augen der Schulkinder in Deutschland. Arch. f. Anth., vol. XVI, pp. 275–475. |
| 1886b | " | Buschmänner. V. B. G., vol. XVIII, pp. 221–239. |
| 1886c | " | Ein Skelet und Schädel von Goajiros. V. B. G., vol. XVIII, pp. 697–705. |
| 1886d | " | Schädel von Baluba und Congo Neger. V. B. G., vol. XVIII, pp. 752–768. |
| 1887 | " | Schädel von Dualla von Kamerun. V. B. G., vol. XIX, pp. 330–331. |
| 1889a | " | Ueber ostafrikanischer Schädel. Sitzb. K. Pr. Akad., 1889, vol. I, pp. 381–391. |
| 1889b | " | Kopfmasse von 40 Wei und 19 Kru Negern. V. B. G., vol. XXI, pp. 85–98. |
| 1889c | " | Schädel von Wetter und Halmaheira. V. B. G., vol. XXI, pp. 669–673. |
| 1890a | " | Excursion nach Langyel (Süd-Ungarn). V. B. G., vol. XXII, pp. 97–118. |
| 1890b | " | Nordkaukasische Alterthümer. V. B. G., vol. XXII, pp. 417–466. |
| 1891 | " | Neuc Untersuchungen ueber ostafrikanischer Schädel. Sitzb. K. Pr. Akad. 1891, vol. I, pp. 123–147. |
| 1893 | " | Kopfmessungen an Ost-Afrikanern, insbesondere der Seengegend. V. B. G., vol. XXV, pp. 484–500. |
| 1893b | " | Ueber griechische Schädel aus alter und neuer Zeit. Sitzb. K. Pr. Akad. 1893, pp. 677–700. |
| 1894 | " | Schädel aus Süd-Amerika insbesondere aus Argentinen und Bolivien. V. B. G., vol. XXVI, pp. 386–408. |
| 1897 | " | Die Bevölkerung der Philippinen. Sitzb. K. Pr. Akad. 1897, vol. I, pp. 284–289. |

## 568 BIBLIOGRAPHY

1894–95  VOLZ, W.  Beiträge zur Anthropologie der Südsee. Arch. f. Anth., vol. XXIII, pp. 97–169.

1900  "  Zur somatischen Anthropologie der Battakker in Nord Sumatra. Arch. f. Anth., vol. XXVI, pt. II, pp. 717–733.

1908  "  Zur Kenntniss der Kubus in Süd-Sumatra. Arch. f. Anth., vol. XXXV, pp. 89–109.

1899  VOROBIEV, V. V.  Materiali k antropologii velikorusskago naseleniya niekatorykh uiezdov Ryazan. gub. Izv. Imp. Obsh. Liub. Est., vol. XCV, pp. 47–85.

1899  VRAM, U. G.  Crani antichi de mediævoli di Aquileia. Atti. Soc. Rom. Anth., vol. VI, pp. 16–37.

1900  "  Contributo all'Antropologia antica dell Peru. Atti Soc. Rom. Anth., vol. VII, pp. 44–93, 67*–80*.

1890  VYRUBOV, N. A.  Otchet o poiezdkie na Kavkaz lietom 1890 goda. Izv. Imp. Obsh. Lyub. Est., vol. LXVIII, cols. 341–350.

1912  WACKER, R.  Zur Anthropologie der Walser des grossen Walserthales in Vorarlberg. Zeitsch. f. Ethn., vol. XLIV, pp. 437–524.

1900  WADDELL, L. A.  The tribes of the Brahmaputra Valley. A contribution on their physical types and affinities. Journ. As. Soc., Bengal, vol. LIX, pt. III, pp. 1–127.

1899  WALDEYER  Koreaner Schädel. V. B. G., vol. XXXI, pp. 748–751.

1908  WATERSTON, D.  Report on the physical character of some of the Nilotic Negroid Tribes. 3d Report Wellcome Research Laboratories, London, 1908, pp. 325–375.

1869  WEISBACH, A.  Die Schädelform der Rumänen. Wien, 1869.

1873  "  Die Schädelform der Türken. Mitt. Anth. Ges., Wien, vol. III, pp. 185–245.

1882  "  Die Schädelform der Griechen. Mitt. Anth. Ges., Wien, vol. XI, pp. 72–97.

1889  "  Die Zigeuner. Mitt. Anth. Ges., Wien, vol. XIX, pp. 107–117.

1897  "  Prähistorische Schädel vom Glasinac (Bosnien). Wissenschaftliche Mitteilungen aus Bosnien und Herzegovina. Vol. V, pp. 562–576.

1892  WEISSENBERG, S.  Ein Beitrag zur Anthropologie der Türkvölker. Zeitsch. f. Ethn., vol. XXIV, pp. 181–235.

1904  "  Karaimy. Russ. Anth. Journ., vol. V, nos. 1–2, pp. 66–75.

| 1909a | WEISSENBERG, S. | Die jemenitischen Juden. V. B. G., vol. XLI, pp. 309–327. |
|---|---|---|
| 1909b | " | Die Spaniolen. Mitt. Anth. Ges., Wien, vol. XXXIX, pp. 225–239. |
| 1909c | " | Die autochthonen Bevölkerung Palästinas in anthropologischer Beziehung. Zeits. f. Demog. und Stat. d. Juden, vol. V, pp. 129–139. |
| 1911 | " | Die syrischen Juden anthropologisch betrachtet. Zeitsch. f. Ethn., vol. XLIII, pp. 80–90. |
| 1912a | " | Zur Anthropologie der nordafrikanische Juden. Mitt. Anth. Ges., Wien, vol. XLII, pp. 85–102. |
| 1912b | " | Kavkazskie Evrei v antropologicheskom otnoshenii. Russ. Anth. Journ., vol. VIII, nos. 2–3, pp. 137–164. |
| 1913 | " | Zur Anthropologie der persischen Juden. Zeitsch. f. Ethn., vol. XLV, pp. 108–119. |
| 1913–14 | " | Die zentralasiatischen Juden in anthropologischer Beziehung. Mitt. Anth. Ges., Wien, vol. XLIII, pp. 257–272. |
| 1906 | WERNER, H. | Anthropologische, ethnologische und ethnographische Beobachtungen ueber die Heikum und Kung-Buschleute. Zeitsch. f. Ethn., vol. XXXVIII, pp. 241–268. |
| 1902–13 | WESTERLUND, F. W. | Studier i Finlands Antropologi. Fennia, vol. XX, no. 2, pp. 1–67; vol. XXI, no. 5, pp. 1–58; vol. XXXIII, no. 5, pp. 1–40. |
| 1899 | WIDENMANN. | Untersuchung von 30 Dschaggaschädel (Kilimandjaro). Arch. f. Anth., vol. XXV, pp. 361–397. |
| 1886 | WOLF, L. | Volksstämme Central-Afrika's. V. B. G., vol. XVIII, pp. 725–753. |
| 1921 | WOODWARD, A. S. | A new cave-man from Rhodesia. Nature, vol. CVIII, pp. 371–372. |
| 1897 | YAVORSKY, I. Z. | Antropologicheskiya otcherk Turkmen. Trudy Antropolog. Obshchestva, Imp. Voen-Medits. Akademi, vol. II, pp. 145–207. |
| 1881 | ZABOROWSKY, S. | Sur seize crânes d'un tombeau Grec d'Asie Mineur. Bull. Soc. Anth., Paris. 3d series, vol. IV, pp. 234–238. |
| 1898 | " | Trois crânes de kourganes des environs de Tomsk. Rev. Ec. d'Anth., vol. VIII, pp. 352–358. |
| 1890 | ZAMPA, R. | Gli scheletri di Remedello e di Fontanello di Casalromano, nelle provincie de Brescia e Mantova. Arch. p. Ant. e. Etn., vol. XX, pp. 345–365. |

1908   ZANOLLI, V.   Studi di Antropologia Bolognese. Atti Acad. Sci. Ven-Tren-Istr., vol. V, pp. 44-79.

1905   ZDROEVSKI, N. L.   Bielorussi Disnenskago uiezda, Vilenskoi gubernii. Russ. Anth. Journ., vol. VI, nos. 3-4, pp. 127-152.

1914-15   ZEIDLER, H. F. B.   Beiträge zur Anthropologie der Herrero. Zeitsch. f. Morph. und Anth., vol. XVII, pp. 185-246.

1914   ZELTNER, F., DE   Étude anthropologique sur les Touareg du Sud. L'Anthropologie, vol. XXV, pp. 459-476.

1878   ZOGRAF, N. Y.   Antropologicheskii otcherk Samoiedov. Izv. Imp. Obsh. Lyub. Est., vol. XXXI, Appendix, cols. 61-87.

1892   "   Antropometricheskiya izsliedovanie muzhkago Velikorusskago Naseleniya Vladimirskoi, Yaroslavskoi i Kostromskoi gubernii. Izv. Imp. Obsh. Lyub. Est., vol. LXXVI, cols. 1-177.

1893   "   Drevnii cherep iz iuzhnago Kitaya dostavlennyi Dr. V. I. Isaevym i ego sravnenie s cherepami Melaneziitsev opisannymi Prof. Sergi. Izv. Imp. Obsh. Lyub. Est., vol. LXXVI, cols. 1-13.

1867   ZUCKERKANDL, E.   Körpermessungen. In:—Reise der österreichischen Fregatte Novara um die Erde in den jahren 1857-59. Anthropologischer Theil, II. Wien, 1867.

1894   "   Zur Craniologie der Nias-Insulaner. Mitt. Anth. Ges., Wien, vol. XXIV, pp. 254-264.

# INDEX